SEXUAL LIFE
IN ANCIENT INDIA

SEXUAL LIFE
IN ANCIENT INDIA

A STUDY IN THE COMPARATIVE
HISTORY OF INDIAN CULTURE

by

JOHANN JAKOB MEYER

DORSET PRESS
New York

Authorized Translation from the German, containing the emendations and additions of the Author. The extra references of one of the Translators are indicated by square brackets.

Originally published in 1930.

This edition published by Dorset Press,
a division of Barnes & Noble, Inc.

1995 Dorset Press

ISBN 1-56619-888-7

Printed and bound in the United States of America

M 9 8 7 6 5 4 3 2 1

EDITOR'S INTRODUCTION

IN the preface to the German edition of this book, Professor Meyer tells us that it is an attempt to give a true and vivid account of the life of woman in ancient India, based upon the immense masses of material imbedded in the two great Epics, the *Mahābhārata* and the *Rāmāyaṇa*. His method has been to make liberal use of the very words of the Epics.

The *Mahābhārata* seems to occupy an unique place in the literature of the world. Parts of it, like the *Bhagavad-gītā*, and the story of Nala and Damayantī, have become familiar to educated readers in almoſt every country of the weſt, but these are only fragments of an enormous work, consiſting of about a hundred thousand couplets, of which Professor Macdonell says [1] :—

> " Its epic kernel, amounting to about one-fifth of the whole work, became so much overgrown with didaſtic matter that it could hardly be regarded as an epic at all, and has rather taken the place of a moral encyclopaedia in Indian literature."

It provides us with moſt valuable sources of information about the relations of the sexes, and the concepts underlying those relations, in India fifteen hundred and more years ago.

Professor Meyer has used the Bombay edition of the *Rāmāyaṇa*, and the second impression of the Bombay *Mahābhārata*. All his references which do not specify a particular title are to this version of the *Mahābhārata*. To some extent, he has consulted what he calls the Kumbakonam version " mainly based on the South Indian texts ". This he refers to as K.

For the present translation, Professor Meyer has completely revised the German work, made various alterations in the text, and considerably enlarged the number of references.

ABBREVIATIONS

SBE.   Sacred Books of the Eaſt (edited by F. Max Müller).
JAOS.   Journal of the American Oriental Society.
JRAS.   Journal of the Royal Asiatic Society.
ZDMG.   Zeitschrift der deutschen morgenländischen Gesellschaft.
WZKM.   Wiener Zeitschrift für die Kunde des Morgenlandes.

[1] *India's Paſt* (p. 88). Oxford, 1927.

CONTENTS
OF VOLUME ONE

vii

Contents

CONTENTS

CONTENTS
OF VOLUME TWO

X.—LOVE

xi

CONTENTS

XI.—WOMAN AS WIFE

XII.—WOMAN AS CHILD-BEARER: THE ORIGIN OF MAN, PHYSIOLOGICALLY AND METAPHYSICALLY

XIII.—WOMAN LYING IN

Contents

Contents

CONTENTS

VOLUME ONE

I

THE MAID

THE Mahābhārata in its present form is a composition from widely separated periods in the history of Old Indian literature, and its elements are derived from various parts of the Old Indian land. It was not written by one man, but it is the work contributed by many hands. It is a growth : one piece from here, another from there ; one from this time, another from that. Like an Indian jungle it spreads out before us in an endless wilderness of trees entwined and tangled with rank creepers, coloured and scented with manifold flowers and blossoms, and the home of every kind of living creature. Bewitching bird-song, the terrifying cries of wild beasts fall on our ears ; the poisonous snake winds its coils beside the mild dove ; the robber dwells therein, free, indeed, from the law, but often the slave of superstitions beyond belief ; and so the self-denying thinker with his eyes set above the earth, and his thoughts reaching into the depths of the world and of his soul. There lie the roots of a glowing, unbounded wealth of life, of a will strong beyond any other power ; and by their side are found the depths of dreaming, the heavy dead sleep of many thousand years, so that we should ourselves sink into it, too, were it not for the swarms of stinging flies. And so we could long go on, setting wonder against wonder, but hardly ever reaching an end to it all ! It is a " great sea ", to sail over which " threefold bronze " is needed, not, indeed, about the breast, but anyhow, about another, not so heroic part of the body.

I

The Rāmāyaṇa, on the other hand, has a closer unity, it being, indeed, very generally attributed by the critics to one poet. But in this case, too, whether or no we put our faith in tradition, it is clear that from the very beginning various parts were brought together and made use of, and that later all kinds of interpolations and changes were made.

Thus in very many points we can look for no inner consistency in either of the two great national Epics of India. In every human being, indeed, we can find a host of contradictions side by side ; how much the more will they be found where so many minds have helped in the building up of one work. Both Epics bear the clearest Indian stamp ; through both, too, runs one view only of the world : the Quietist view. But while this seems fairly natural to the Rāmāyaṇa, to the real stem of the Mahābhārata it is utterly strange, and has been only gradually grafted on to the mighty growth of the wild plant. The Rāmāyaṇa, indeed, is seen from the very beginning to be essentially soft, dreamy, fantastic, and deeply religious— to be a work of the Brahmans. On the other hand, the poetry of the Mahābhārata is often quickened in its older parts by a mighty flame of fire, a manly, undaunted, passionate soul : it was a warrior that sung this heroic song, whoever it may be to whom the "original Mahābhārata" may be referred. Later hands then fixed all kinds of labels on the pieces that had been preserved in greater perfection, utterly re-modelled much, inserted long pieces, and sought, well or ill, to give the whole the tendentious coating of Brahmanism. Out of a rugged epic, in which the proud warrior, boasting his strength and power, was the main, perhaps the only concern, it became the aim to glorify the priest as never before or since in the world's literature, and at an early stage the paragon Arjuna and the wretched canting Yudhishthira were set in the place of Karṇa, the sun's son, and of the mighty Duryodhana, without the result, however, of robbing the old and true heroes of all their splendour, not to speak of raising the utterly worthless favourites of the priests to the same heights.[1] Everywhere the structure of

[1] The fact of this utter reversal of the earlier state of things is beyond any doubt. The explanation of this extraordinary phenomenon will perhaps always be a matter for conjecture. Despite a huge difference,

the Epic itself shows gaping joins and fissures. To this is
added the heavy additional weight of the moſt diverse episodes
and interpolations. In the details, too, of the observations and
wearisome details as to God and the World, as to Man and his
nature and aċtions, we very often find utter contradiċtions;
and this is so whether the ruthless warrior or the softer thinker,
the ardent ascetic or the sly prieſt is speaking, whether individual
peculiarities, or the shades derived from time and place, or
some other influence are to be seen.

When, therefore, there are already so many contradiċtions
found side by side, it is seen at once that, on the subjeċt of
that great bundle of contradiċtions, Woman and all belonging
to her, or to speak more exaċtly, on the subjeċt of the refleċtion
of this objeċt in the brain and heart of Man, the two
great Epics, especially the Mahābhārata, contain very contra-
diċtory utterances, and that often one saying will flatly contradiċt
another. This lies firſt of all in the nature of the Indian. In
other lands, too, the attitude of the feelings and thoughts of
man towards woman very often undergoes changes according
to the ſtate of mind and experience of life, and above all
according to personal experience of the fairer half of mankind,
not to speak of the more or less dominating deeper charaċter
of the individual, or other influences. And thus even in the
cooler Weſt the proverbs, the songs, the tales, and so forth
about women make up the moſt twiſted bundle in the world.
In the soul of the Indian there dwells that twin pair, burning
sensuality and ſtark renunciation of the world and the flesh.
What a delight and torment then muſt woman be to him ! And

Duryodhana reminds me ſtrongly of Saul in the Old Teſtament,
Yudhishṭhira of David. The Pāṇḍava are favourites of the prieſtly
party, and doubtless did not win this place for nothing. These evidently
non-Aryan intruders may have hidden the multitude of their sins, after
the way only too well-known, with the cloak of prieſtly fawning,
as crafty " converts " to Brahmanism. The Kaurava, on the contrary,
as the doughty champions of the warrior nobility, probably aroused
the undying hatred of the Brahmans. Since writing this I have
come upon the excellent remarks of W. Crooke, *The North-Weſtern
Provinces of India* (1897), p. 65, where he describes the spirit of the
two Epics as I have done.

3

since he is wont to express his impressions and views with great violence, has no fear of any deduction and drives everything to its utmost end, we might put together a more than gigantic folio volume on woman from Indian literature, whose various parts would only have this in common : their contradiction of one another.

But I think that there is one thing that can be picked out, from the nature of the Indian we have just been describing, as a specific attribute : among other peoples, or among the Western civilized nations, we find a more delicate colouring, more individuality, a greater variety and richness in the variations on the inexhaustible theme of woman. In India, on the other hand, two personalities, above all, though by no means exclusively, are heard : the voluptuary and the renouncer. This, of course, does not at all necessarily mean that the former will only praise woman and the latter only condemn her, for we know that it is very often those who run after women who despise them most heartily, and any true regard for them must be quite lacking in such men ; and whether we are friendly inclined or otherwise towards the sex, it offers the keen observer so rich and varied a material that in this case a wholly one-sided view or even a feeling of boredom is only possible to a narrow head and heart. The Hindu shows, indeed, a keen observation at all times when he has to do with the way of the world; that is why hardly any other people has so great a proverbial wisdom ; and there has been no want in India of moderate men, standing rather between the extremes.

Thus it is that the Indian in particular, in his views on woman and love, has from very early times shown that capacity for living in earnest, for ethics, for healthy feeling, which with him ever and again in other fields, too, makes itself felt through every kind of dissoluteness : on filth and corruption it will not seldom bring forth to the light of day even sweet flowers of lovely colours. So it is that woman, above all as a loving wife and tender mother—woman, that is, in her most natural and fairest calling—has nowhere else found greater and more heartfelt appreciation ; in most literatures, indeed, there is far less. Let anyone, for instance, set what has been

written in Old India beside what was written in the Middle
Ages, or beside Romance, in particular old and even modern
French literature ; in spite of so many, not always edifying,
though nearly always interesting refinements, there is wafted
to us from the world of the Old Indian books a deeply ethical
spirit, one might even say a wholesomeness, which has a very
pleasing effect in contrast with the so often empty frivolity—
the nauseating filthiness and vulgarity—that meets us out of
those other literatures. To put it otherwise and not to wander
abroad : the Old Indian loose tales, indeed, in spite of the
cautionary thread running all through them, have not been
trimmed and put together by literary tailors working for
girls' schools ; and yet they are like real moral strait-
waistcoats, when compared with a great many of the more or
less highly praised productions of the later and latest German
writers.

It is now well known, and it has been stressed by many with
a special knowledge of India, that these two great Epics
still exert an influence to-day on the mind and the life of the
Hindu people like no other literary work.[1] There is the further
fact that the literature of the " post-Epic " times is often very
greatly dependent on the Epic, or influenced in many places by it.
Owing to these inner relations between the Epic and the Classical
literature, there thus arises, furthermore, a far-reaching indirect
influence. What Indian woman (to speak only of the obvious)
did not know and honour Sītā and Sāvitrī and other heroines
of the Epic poems !

The Epic, however, in many respects only gives us very
fragmentary information about woman and her life and the
value set on her among the Old Indians. But in general it is
only a section of Old Indian life that is opened before us in the
Epic poems. How much, indeed, do we learn as to the great
mass of the people ! The warrior and the Brahman take all

[1] So J. C. Oman, *The Great Indian Epic*, London, 1906, p. 1 ff. ;
Nisikantha Chattopādhyāya in his *Indian Essays* ; Sister Nivedita,
The Web of Indian Life, London, 1906, pp. 95–115 ; Rāmakrishṇa,
Life in an Indian Village, London, 1891, p. 142 ff. ; Basanta Koomar
Roy, *Rabindra Nath Tagore* (New York, 1915), p. 28 ; W. Crooke,
The North-Western Provinces of India (London, 1897), p. 256.

our attention for themselves. I sing arms and the priest !
But happily there' is incidentally a lot more besides in those
huge works, and on our theme, too. Poetry can do without
the husbandman and the burgher, but take away woman and
you cut its very life away.

But however important woman is, her entry into the city of
life is seldom hailed on this earth with hosannas and palm-
strewn roads ; nor is she met with the blare of trumpets that
joyfully greets the warrior-hero.[1] She is neither a world-

---

[1] How unwelcome girls are among the various peoples and tribes has
been, of course, often described. It will be enough to refer to Ploss-
Bartels, *Das Weib in der Natur- und Völkerkunde*[4], i, 247 ff., ii, 473 ;
and Westermarck, *The History of Human Marriage*[3], London, 1901,
p. 311 ff. ; Elsie Clews Parsons, *The Old-Fashioned Woman*, 201 ff.
On India see, for instance, Rāmabai Sarasvati, *The High Caste Hindu
Woman*, and Billington, *Woman in India*, p. 1 ff. ; James Tod,
Rajasthan (that is, *Annals and Antiquities of Rajasthan*, popular ed.,
Calcutta), i, 670 ff. ; S. C. Bose, *The Hindoos as They Are* (1881),
pp. 24, 28, 216 ff. ; Bulloram Mullick, *Home Life in Bengal*, p. 68,
103. The Arabs before Mohammed seem to be the most brutal among
the barbarians, for they simply buried girl-children alive. Hauri,
Der Islam, p. 8 ; Finck, *Primitive Love and Love Stories*, p. 32 ;
Schweiger-Lerchenfeld, *Die Frauen des Orients*, 63 f. ; Hartmann,
Zeitsch. d. Vereins f. Volkskunde, Bd. ii, p. 240 ; Welhausen,
Göttinger Nachrichten, 1893, p. 458 ; and, above all, *Anthropos*,
Bd. iii, p. 62 ff. A sentence in this last may be given here, which could
have been written of far too many other places on the earth : Il
est d'usage parmi les Bedouins que quand un garçon vient au monde,
il est annoncé à la famille et à tous les voisins par des cris de joie qui
se répètent d'une tente à l'autre, mais quand c'est une fille qui vient
augmenter le nombre des membres de la famille on garde le silence
le plus absolu, accompagné de toutes les marques de la tristesse,
qu'on laisse voir à tout le monde (p. 65). When we find here too the
statement that many beat the poor wife that has brought a girl
into the world, we may also refer perhaps to Fr. S. Krauss, *Sitte
und Brauch der Südslaven* (1885), p. 540 f., and also to p. 592 ff.
According to McLennan's theory (*Primitive Marriage*, especially
p. 75 ff.) that once all the peoples of the world were exogamous owing
to girl-killing, all tribes and hordes must then have done away
with their daughters—an unexampled piece of nonsense. As an
opposite example, the Abipones of Paraguay may be named, who

redeemer nor a world-shaker, but Saṃsārahetu, the "source of the world", the cause of the Sansara, in which, as the Indian says, pleasure, and above all the pleasure of love, is but pain. The birth of a daughter is in general not an object of his wishes. Thus xii, 243.20, says : "The eldest brother is the same as the father, wife and son are a man's own body, his servants are the man's shadow, the daughter is the bitterest woe." And i, 159.11 : "The son is his very self, the wife a friend, but the daughter is known for a misfortune." [1] We can thus well understand that among the dreadful omens boding the many deaths in the fight between the Kauravas and the Pāṇḍavas, this one, too, appears : "Many women will bear four and five girls"—and probably at one birth (vi, 3.7). Not to mention anything else, it is only the son who can bring his forbears that offering so absolutely needed for happiness in the other world. With a daughter this can only be done indirectly—through her sons. And that is always an unsure thing. For against wedding with such a maiden advice is given by the Epic (xiii, 44.15), as also by the Smṛiti or law literature. [2] But whatever the event, the important thing is to marry the girl off fittingly. And here there lies a source of sorrow for the parents. Thus in v, 97.15, 16, we hear the wretched father of the marriageable daughter call out "Shame on the coming of a daughter into the house of men of strong character, who are distinguished, praiseworthy, and of kind disposition. The mother's kindred, the father's, and they to whom she is given—three families—are brought to danger by the daughter of

mainly killed the boys, as a wife had to be bought for them, while the girls could be profitably disposed of. Finck, *Primitive Love*, p. 587. Marriage by purchase, not very honourable in itself, has yet been of much effect in enhancing the value of daughters and wife.

[1] Cf. Weber's *Indische Studien*, v, p. 260, 265; Windisch, *Buddhas Geburt*, etc., p. 60 ; Winternitz, *Gesch. d. ind. Liter.*, i, 184; Çukranīti (ed. Oppert), iii, 520–3 ; Otto Stein, *Megasthenes u. Kautilya* (Vienna, 1921), 68, note 3 ; J. J. Meyer, *Kautilya*, 480.3–4; addit. 480.37 ; also Schrader, *Die Indogermanen*, 101 f. ; Feist, *Kultur, Ausbreitung u. Herkunft d. Indogermanen* (1913), p. 108 ; 299 f.

[2] Manu, iii, 11 ; Gautama, xxviii, 20 ; Yājñavalkya, i, 53.

good men." For no one knows how things will go, whether the bride will lead a good life, or bring happiness.[1] What, indeed, shows itself most is the anxiety whether a bridegroom will be found who will do honour through his blood, character, and so forth. This is what we often find in the Mahābhārata, and so, for instance, Rām., vii, 9.10–11 : " To be the father of a daughter is an affliction for him that seeks after honour, and no one knows who will (or shall) take a maiden to his house ; thus it is, O daughter. The mother's kindred, the father's, and they to whom she goes in marriage—three families are brought ever into danger by a daughter." Essentially the same thought is uttered by a harassed father who goes about trying to find a husband for his daughter, in the 12th sarga, çl. 11–12. It is well known that in India often the whole family will ruin itself in the endeavour to find a thoroughly good match for the daughter, and give her a wedding befitting its standing.[2] Having regard to all the evils brought down by a daughter, we very easily understand why the Hindu often hails her without much joy. But the love for children, which is so strong in the Indian, is also felt towards her, and so Bāṇa very finely declares that the parents are saddened at the birth of a girl, as they think of the day when a bridegroom will rob them of the loved one.[3] And little light as the Epic throws on

[1] Cp. Jāt., Nos. 102, 217 (it is not known how the daughter bids to fare in the husband's house). An eloquent description of the sorrows and woes a daughter gives her parents from birth, on account of her marriage, is to be found in Bose, *The Hindoos as They Are* (1881), p. 219 ff. ; Bulloram Mullick, *Home Life in Bengal*, p. 108 ff.

[2] This costs at least 200 dollars in the upper classes (Rāmabai Sarasvatī, p. 12), and even the peasant weddings are dear (cp. Sir B. Fuller, *Studies of Indian Thought and Sentiment*, London, 1910, p. 155 f.). On the Rājput see especially Tod, *Rajasthan*, i, p. 672 ff.

[3] Harshacarita, translated by Cowell and Thomas, p. 122. A beautiful picture is given in MBh., iii, 32.60–63 : King Drupada has his sons taught the prudent way of life by a wise Brahman who lives as a guest in his house. The father sits there, and when his little daughter comes with any message or errand he lifts her up onto his lap, and she listens eagerly to the teacher's words. He then speaks coaxing words to her, and the little girl, to supplement these crumbs she has caught up, gets from her brothers a repetition of the master's

the life of the unwedded girl, yet we may take to be true for
the Epic world what is told us of the happy time spent by the
Indian girl before she goes to her husband's house in, for
instance, Ramabai Sarasvati, *The High Caste Hindu Woman*
(London, 1890), p. 23, and the far too romantic Sister Nivedita,
The Web of Indian Life (London, 1906),p. 35. ` Thus we
read of the merry game which the girls enjoyed in the evening
in the pleasure groves (Rām., ii, 67.17 ; cf. 71.22).   The
ball-game of the grown-up girls, often referred to in the
Classical literature, and described at such length in the
Daçakumāracaritam (p. 290 ff. of my translation), is also found
in the Epic. Çāntā plays ball in iii, 111.16. The small girls,
too, amuse themselves in this way (v, 90.63). The balls used
would seem to have been very finely coloured, at any rate those
of the upper classes (iii, 112.10).[1] Bhīshma declares :
" The son is as one's very self ; the daughter is like the
son. How could it be, so long as she is alive, that any other
should have the property ? " (xiii, 45.11). Then he sets forth

wisdom, doubtless told very solemnly. How greatly the daughter is
loved is described, too, e.g. in Leumann, *Die Nonne, ein Roman aus
d. alten Indien*, strophe 107 ff., 125 ff., 423 ff. ; Kupabai
Satthianadhu, *Kamala* (Leipzig, 1898), p. 120. Of the Rājput
we are told by James Tod, *Rajasthan (Annals and Antiquities of
Rajasthan*, first popular ed., Calcutta), that there are few among even
the lowest of the chiefs whose daughters are not taught to read and
write (i, p. 676). So, too, Shib Chunder Bose, *The Hindoos as They
Are*, p. 226. But see, for instance, Ramabai Sarasvati, p. 57.

[1] How the ball-game befitted the fascination of a young girl, and
how she strengthened her conquest by it is to be gathered, too, from
Bhāgavata-Purāṇa, viii, 12.15 ff. : Rudra or Çiva comes on a visit
to Vishṇu. The latter by his Māyā (magic) calls up a bewitchingly
fair maiden, who plays at ball, and whose garments are carried off
by the wind. Although Çiva's wife is beside him he rushes up to the
charmer and then goes after her as she wrests herself from his grip ;
in the pursuit *semen ejus ejicitur*. It goes, of course, without saying
that in the Epic the girl plays with dolls. But when Hopkins, because
Uttarā still took pleasure in this at the time of her marriage, concludes
she was still in her childhood, he makes a mistake. Cf. Billington,
Woman in India, p. 215 ; Çrīvara's Kathākautukam, Sanskrit and
German by R. Schmidt, vi, 15, 48, 69.

9

that the mother's own portion falls to the lot of the girl ; the property shall be inherited by the daughter's son from the father that has no sons. For he bestows the ancestral food-cakes for his own father and for his mother's father. In law there is no difference between one's own son and the daughter's son. The daughter, too, takes precedence of the son that is born elsewhere, that is, who is not the son of the body ; according to the commentary, she takes three-fifths of the estate. So we find in xiii, 47.25 f. : " That which was given by her father to the wife from the Brahman caste, O Yudhishthira, shall be taken by the daughter. For she is equal to the son." [1]

[1] There is no distinction between son's son and daughter's son (Manu, ix, 130 ; Vishnu, xv, 47). If there are no sons, and also the mother is dead, then the daughter inherits the father's property, and no one else ; for she is sprung from his body just like the son (Nārada, xiii, 50 ; Brihaspati, xxv, 55 ff. ; Yājñavalkya, ii, 135 f. ; Vishnu, xvii, 4 ff.). But cp. Āpastamba, ii, 6, 14, 2–6 ; Gautama, xxviii, 21 ff. ; Vasishtha, xvii, 81 ff. ; Manu, ix, 185 ff. (and Bühler's notes on it, SBE, xxv, p. 365). So the Mahānirvānatantra, xii, 36, states that the daughter of the man without wife or son gets the father's inheritance, even if there is a brother of the father's ; and according to 55 the daughter-in-law or the granddaughter inherits before the dead man's own father. According to Vishnu, xviii, 34 f., the mother and the unmarried daughter get a share of the man's estate according to the son's share (putrabhāgānusārena), that is to say, exactly so much as the sons who are equal to them in the caste have the right to inherit, an arrangement, therefore, which provides for a testator with wives of differing castes, and probably only for one without a son. If the father share out his estate himself, then according to Nārada, xiii, 13, the unwedded daughter receives as much as the sons between the eldest and youngest. But cp. Brihaspati, xxv, 64 ; Manu, ix, 118 ; Yājñav., ii, 124 (the brothers must give the unwedded sisters a fourth part of their own share). According to Yāska's Nirukta, iii, 4, the children inherit equally, regardless of sex (see Bühler's Manu, p. lxi). The woman's estate or mother's own property (stridhana, yautuka) falls to her daughter. Vishnu, xvii, 18 ff. ; Gautama, xxviii, 24 ; Baudhāyana, ii, 2, 3, 43 ; Yājñavalkya, ii, 143–5 ; Agnipurāna, transl. by Manmatha Nath Dutt, p. 925, etc. Cp., too, especially Manu, ix, 130–9 ; J. J. Meyer, *Über das Wesen d. altind. Rechtsschriften u. ihr Verhältnis zu einander u. zu Kauṭilya* (Leipzig, 1927), p. 73 ff.

The sight of pretty and well-dressed girls and being greeted by them with festal honour brings good luck if one is minded to take an important step (vii, 82.22 ; cp. 7.9 ; 112.62 ff. ; xiii, 11.14). Eight girls are named as important objects of good luck on the occasion of the preparations for consecrating Rāma as crown-prince (Rām., ii, 14.36) ; and when at last he comes back from exile and marches to his solemn consecration as king, there go before him, as bringing weal : unhusked corn, gold, cows, young girls, and Brahmans, as also men with sugar-cakes in their hands ; and in his sprinkling or initiation into the rank of prince, maidens also take a part, sixteen in number, as the commentator points out (Rām., vi, 128, çl. 38, 62 ; cp. MBh., v, 140, 14 f.).[1] And like other Indian literature the Mahābhārata shows how a man can get a daughter. According to xiii, 87.10, this is brought about through the ancestral offering on the second day of the dark half of the month. There is other information in xiii, 104.151 ; iii, 83.190. See also xiii, 83.51 ; i, 116.12 (a daughter is longed for). This we shall speak of later.

We find even quite spoiled daughters. Thus i, 76 ff., tells us : "The gods and the Dānavas fight with one another for leadership. Çukra, the sacrificial priest of the Dānavas, knows the charm for bringing back life, and keeps on calling back to life the Dānavas who fall in the fight. The sacrificial priest of the gods, Brihaspati, cannot do this. So the heaven-dwellers are at a great drawback. They induce Kaca, Brihaspati's young son, to go and be a disciple of Çukra, by telling him 'Thou and no other, canst win favour with Devayānī, the beloved daughter of this high-minded one. When once thou hast gladdened Devayānī through a virtuous character, skill, friendliness, right living, and self-control, then thou wilt of a surety win this charm for awakening the dead.'" Çukra takes him. "So as to win the favour of both, the youth would ever

[1] In the body of the wedded and the unwedded woman alike there dwells, too, Çrī, the goddess of happiness and beauty (Vishṇu, xcix, 14), and girls and women also turn aside the "evil eye" (drishṭi-parihāra). Cf. Edgar Thurston, *Omens and Superstitions of Southern India* (1912), pp. 15–17, 23, 118. To see women is lucky according to MBh., ix, 56, 24 f.

gladden Devayānī with singing, dancing, and music. He waited on the maiden, who was in her youth, and rejoiced her with flowers, fruits, and services. Devayānī, too, secretly gave careful heed to this Brahman youth who zealously carried out vows and holy works, as she sang and trifled before him." The Dānavas, however, saw him in the forest as he was herding his teacher's cows, questioned him, and killed and cut him up, and gave him to the wolves to eat, all out of enmity towards Brihaspati, and in order that the magic for bringing back to life, so useful to them, should not become known to the gods. The cows came back in the evening without their herd. Devayānī saw this, and said to her father : " Evidently Kaca has been killed or has died. Without him I do not want to live ; I swear it thee." Çukra made use of his spell for bringing back to life : Kaca broke out of the wolves' bellies, and showed himself hale and whole before the teacher and his daughter. On another day Devayānī sent him into the forest to bring flowers. The Dānavas crushed him, and mixed him up with the sea's waters. And again the teacher called him back to life. But the third time the foes ground him to powder, put it in brandy-wine, and gave the mixture to Çukra to drink. Devayānī spoke and said : " Kaca went forth on my service to bring flowers, and he is no longer to be seen. Clearly he has been slain or is dead. Without Kaca I will not live ; that I swear unto thee." The father put it to her that she need not take so much thought of Kaca, since she had the choice of Brahmans, gods, and demons. The luckless fellow, he said, is indeed always being killed. But she exclaimed : " He is chaste, and greatly ascetic, always ready and skilled in all contrivances. I shall follow Kaca, and hunger myself to death. I love the handsome Kaca." So it came to yielding, and her father began his spell. But now came the quandary : the disciple had to obey, and yet could not ; for he could not come out of the teacher's belly without, at the same time, bringing death on him. This the anguished one brought to the teacher's knowledge in moving words, speaking from the wizard's body, and telling him how he had been drunk down together with the brandy-wine. Devayānī knew no consolation : " Two sorrows burn me like fire : Kaca's death, and the annihilation threatening thee. If Kaca dies then there is no salvation for me ; and if thou art destroyed, then I cannot live." But Çukra found a way out : he initiated the disciple into the magic spell, who broke out of the teacher's belly, and brought back the dead man to life again with all speed. Çukra was now filled with anger against the evil brandy-wine, that had brought about the whole misfortune, and forbade it to the Brahman for all time with great solemnity and under dreadful threats of punishment. Kaca now wished to go back to the gods, and took leave of the teacher. Devayānī went to meet him and besought him earnestly to wed her. But he had no wish to, and came out of it by urging that she as his teacher's daughter, was honourable in his sight, and, moreover, was now his sister, since both of them had now abode in Çukra's body. The loving girl, however, made answer : " If thou dost scorn me for love for virtue, although I have asked thee with tears, then this magic knowledge will be nought in thine hands." He told her that he was unwilling only because he would not offend against the old holy laws, and since she had cursed him so unjustly and unfoundedly, her wish would not be fulfilled : no son of a Rishi would take her with him as wife.[1] So he went back to the gods, taught them the magic, and they were now made happy. They then exhorted Indra to show his valour. He set forth, but saw maidens bathing in the forest and playing in the water. Then he changed himself into a wind, and tossed their clothes about. When they came out of the water, they took the wrong clothes. The bathing girls were Devayānī and Çarmishṭhā, the daughter of the Daitya prince Vrishaparvan, together with the princess's followers. Çarmishṭhā happened to lay hold of the clothes of her friend, Devayānī ; the latter rebuked Çarmishṭhā : "Why art thou, my disciple, taking my clothes ? Wicked girl, it will not go well with thee." Çarmishṭhā answered : " Whether my father is sitting or lying down, thy father as a court singer ever praises him, and stands humbly far below. For thou art the daughter of him that begs, that praises, that takes ; I am the daughter of him that is praised, that grants, that never takes.[2] Burn away, hurt

[1] That is, no man of the Brahman caste.
[2] Cp. Baudhāyana's law book, ii, 2, 4.26 (= ii, 2.79–80).

thyself, be abusive, be angered, thou beggar ! Thou hast nought, thou art weaponless, and art upset over her that is armed, thou eater of alms. Thou shalt find someone who is a match for thee ; thou art nothing to me." [1] Çarmishṭhā, bent on evil, threw Devayānī, who was in a rage of pride,[2] and kept hold of the clothes, into a well, and went back to her town, believing within herself : " She is no more." Without taking any more thought about her, she went into her house filled with mad anger.

Then came thither Yayāti, Nahusha's son, with a wearied team, and wearied horses, hunting after game, and athirst. Nahusha's son saw the waterless well and saw this maiden in it, like a flame of fire. And when he had seen her he asked the maiden, who was like a goddess, he the best among princes asked her, as he reassured her with most sweet and soft words : " Who art thou, fair maid, with the red nails and shining jewels and ear-rings ?[3] Long and over-much hast thou been given up to gloomy thoughts. And wherefore dost thou torture

---

[1] In the MBh. the man of the warrior nobility is always declaring that his kind does not ask and takes nothing ; " grant me," he utters of only one thing : of fighting. Only the Brahmans beg ; begging is, indeed, their faithful mate ; but the Kshattriya owns and enjoys that only which he has won with his own might. See, for instance, i, 92.13 ff. ; iii, 154.10 ; v, 75.23 ; 120.19 ; xii, 199.42, 74, 82, 112. As here, so the warrior, times beyond telling, shows us in the MBh., how removed from the priestly class he feels himself, and how deeply his lordly pride scorns it. For this cp., too, the excellent account of Hopkins, JAOS, xiii, 151–62 ; Fick, *Die soziale Gliederung*, etc., 51 ff., 64. But the nobility is left far and away behind by the mad pretensions of the priestly caste, which has given the poem its present form, and fully indemnifies itself through its one and only weapon— the word, as the MBh. repeatedly points out. Indeed, it has, as is well known, preached the taking of gifts as actually one of its good works, and in xiii, 121.14, we read the pronouncement : " The taker wins the same merit as the giver ; for nothing rolls on one wheel, as the holy seers know." It is only the bestower then, that owes thankfulness ; he is given the chance to win high religious blessing by deeds.

[2] Samucchraya. Cp. vi, 44.6, where, however, " high-billowing fight " would also fit in, and vi, 99.29, where the word = yuddha.

[3] Or, ear-rings of precious stones.

thyself with care ? And how haſt thou fallen into this plant-
and grass-covered well ? And whose daughter art thou ?
Speak the truth, maiden with the lovely waiſt ! " Devayānī
spoke : " I am that Çukra's daughter, he who brings back to life
again the Daityas slain by the gods. He knows of a surety
nothing about me. Here is my right hand with its red-nailed
fingers. Take me, and draw me out. For I know thou art of
noble birth. I can see in thee a man of calm soul, of bravery,
and of renown. Therefore mayeſt thou draw me, who have
fallen in here, out of this well." When the king, Nahusha's
son, had learned she was a Brahman's daughter, he took her by
the right hand and pulled her out of that pit. And when the
prince Yayāti had pulled her quickly out of this well, he took
his leave of the fair-hipped one, and went off to his town.
When Nahusha's son had gone, Devayānī, the spotless one,
spoke, torn with grief, to her handmaid, Ghūrnikā, who had
come from the town : " Ghūrnikā, go quickly and tell my
father : ' I shall not set foot now any more in the town of
Vrishaparvan.' " Ghūrnikā went quickly into the Asura's caſtle,
and when she saw Çukra she spoke to him with a soul filled
with emotion, told the very wise one that Devayānī had been
slain in the foreſt by Çarmishthā, the daughter of Vrishaparvan.
When Çukra heard that his daughter had been slain there in
the foreſt by Çarmishthā, he haſtened out filled with woe,
looking for his child. Then when Çukra had seen his daughter
in the foreſt, he clasped her in his arms and spoke the words :
" Through their own misdeeds (in an earlier being) all men do
compel happiness and unhappiness to themselves.[1] I think
thou haſt done some evil, and the punishment for it has been
thus inflicted." Devayānī spoke : " Never mind about punishment ! Liſten carefully to me : Is it true what Çarmishthā,
daughter of Vrishaparvan, said unto me ? She said thou wert
the singer of the Daityas. That is what I was told by
Çarmishthā, Vrishaparvan's daughter, in sharp, bitter words,
with her eyes deep-reddened by anger : ' Thou art but the

---

[1] Or simply : bring on themselves. Niyacchati=get for oneself,
obtain, is often found in the MBh. (for inſtance, iii, 207.66 ; v,
64.19 ; 72.62 ; 163.41 ; vii, 199.33 ; xii, 290.24 ; 307.40 ; xiii,
48.42 f. ; xiii, 57.21 ; 59.21 ; 143.51 ; xv, 34.8).

daughter of him that praises ; that ever asks and accepts ; but I am the daughter of him that is praised, that bestows and never accepts.' That is what Çarmishṭhā, Vṛishaparvan's daughter, said to me over and over again with anger-reddened eyes and filled with pride. Father, if I am the daughter of him that praises and accepts, then will I beg forgiveness of Çarmishṭhā. That I have said to my friend." Çukra spoke : " Thou art not the daughter of one that praises, that asks, that accepts ; the daughter thou art of one that praises not, of one that is praised, Devayānī. Vṛishaparvan knows that, and Indra and King Yayāti. For the Brahman that is beyond all thinking and has nothing twofold is my kingly power.[1] And whatever there be anywhere in heaven and earth,[2] I am ever proclaimed as its lord by the rejoicing, self-sprung being (Brahma). I make the water to flow for the weal of creatures, I make all plants to grow. This truth I swear unto thee." Thus in friendly wise did the father speak in sweet, gentle words to this girl that had fallen into doubt, that was tortured with indignation : " Let that human being, that bears ever with patience the taunting speech of others, know, O Devayānī, that he has won this All. He that bridles his rising anger, like a steed, that one is called a leader by the good, not he who pulls at the horse's reins. He that drives forth his rising anger by his freedom from anger, know, O Devayānī, that such a one has overcome this All. He that throws off his rising anger by a mild patience, as the snake does its old. skin, such a one is indeed called a man. He that holds his ill-humour in check, he that calmly bears evil report, and he that, when he is tormented, does not torment, such a one is indeed a vessel of profit. If one man, month by month through a hundred years, without wearying, makes sacrifice, and another is not angered by anything (or : against anyone), then of the two he that is not angered is the greater. If boys and girls heedlessly weave enmity, the wise man shall not imitate them ; for they do not know what strength and weakness is." Devayānī spoke :

[1] Or : for the holy knowledge beyond all thought is my lordship and strength (or, warlike power) without rival. Cp. xii, 141.64.

[2] Or, less likely : and that which in heaven and on earth is the everywhere existing something (" the thing-in-itself ").

" Father, though I am but a young girl, yet I know what the difference is on earth between the duties. And as to not being angered, and as to speech, I know what strength is and what weakness is. But that a pupil should bear himself unlike such, that, indeed, none should suffer who would fain be of any worth. Therefore it pleases me not to dwell among such as bring the rightful way into confusion, for the wise man striving after his weal shall not dwell among ill-minded folk that by their behaviour and origin are a stumbling-block unto others. But those that by their behaviour and origin grant him acknowledgment, among good men such as these shall he dwell ; this is called the best abode. The dreadful evil, spoken by Vrishaparvan's daughter in her words, tears my heart, as he that seeks fire tears the kindling-wood. For I deem nothing in the three worlds to be harder than to look, when robbed of fame and happiness, on the fame and happiness of the rival. Death is the best thing for such a one, as those that know acknowledge."

Thereupon Çukra, the best among the race of the Bhrigus, went, ill-pleased, and, without further thought, spoke as follows to Vrishaparvan on his throne : " The evil that has been done does not at once bring forth its fruit, like the earth (gaur iva); slowly rolling along, it gnaws at the roots of the doer. In the sons and grandsons, if he does not feel it in himself, the evil, of a surety, makes itself known, like something heavy which a man has eaten, in the body.[1] Since thou didst kill the Brahman Kaca then, the Angiras who did no evil, who knew virtue, was obedient, and rejoiced in my family, because of the murder of that innocent one and because of the murder of my daughter—hear me, O Vrishaparvan—I leave thee and thy kindred. I cannot dwell together with thee in thy kingdom, O king. Ah ! thou takest me for an empty chatterer, O Daitya, that thou dost not hold back from this sin of thine, but dost look on it calmly." Vrishaparvan spoke : " I know of no evil and no empty words in thee, O son of Bhrigu ; in thee do dwell righteousness and truth. Therefore grant us mercy and forgiveness. If thou leavest us and goest forth, we shall leap into the sea, we have no other refuge." Çukra spoke : " Leap into

[1] Cp. xii, 91.21 ; 95.17–18 ; 139.22 ; Manu, iv, 172–3.

17

the sea, or flee in all directions of the heavens, O ye Asuras ! I can brook no insult to my daughter, for I love her. Soften the heart of Devayānī, in whom my life is wrapped, and I will bring thee welfare and peace, as Bṛihaspati did to Indra." Vṛishaparvan spoke : "All that the princes of the Asuras have on earth to hold, all their elephants, cattle, and horses, of these all thou art the lord, and also of me." Çukra spoke : " If I am lord of whatsoever the Daitya princes own, O great Asura, then let Devayānī be appeased." Thus addressed, Vṛishaparvan spoke : " So let it be ! " The son of Bhṛigu, he the great wise one, went to Devayānī and explained this matter to her. Devayānī spoke : " I will not believe it from thee that thou art lord over the king's possessions, but the king himself muſt say it." Vṛishaparvan spoke : " Whatever thou doſt wish, O bright-smiling one, that will I give thee, even if it be sore hard to get." Devayānī spoke : " I wish for Çarmishṭhā as my slave together with a thousand girls, and she shall follow me wheresoever my father gives me in marriage." Vṛishaparvan spoke : " Arise, go, O nurse, and quickly bring Çarmishṭhā hither. And whatever the bidding of Devayānī, that shall she do." Thereupon the nurse went away and spoke the words to Çarmishṭhā : " Arise, dear Çarmishṭhā, and bring happiness to thine. The Brahman is indeed wont to dismiss his pupils, if Devayānī urges him to it. Whatever Devayānī bids of thee, that thou muſt now do, O kindly one." Çarmishṭhā spoke : " Whatever her bidding, that will I now do, if Çukra so calls on me for the sake of Devayānī. Çukra shall not go forth through my fault, nor shall Devayānī because of me." There-upon in her mildness, at her father's bidding, with a thousand girls about her she haſtily left the fair city. Çarmishṭhā spoke : " I am thy slave with a thousand slave-girls, thy servant. I will follow thee, wheresoever thy father gives thee in marriage." Devayānī spoke : " I am for thee the daughter of him that praises, begs, accepts. How can it be that the daughter of him that is praised becomes the slave ? " Çarmishṭhā spoke : " By whatever the means, well-being muſt be found for the afflicted kindred. Therefore will I follow thee wheresoever thy father gives thee in marriage."

When Vṛishaparvan's daughter had promised to be a slave,

Devayānī spoke to her father the words : " I will go unto
the city, O father ; I am satisfied, O best among the twice-
born. Thy knowledge and the power of thine art is not for
nothing." [1]   Thus addressed by his daughter, the greatest
among the Brahmans, the very famous one, went, rejoiced and
honoured by all the Dānavas, into the city.

Some time later Devayānī of the lovely face went into that
selfsame forest to play.   Together with these thousand slave-
girls and Çarmishthā she cāme there to that selfsame spot
and wandered about to her heart's desire, accompanied by all
these followers, filled with great joy, as all played merrily, [2]
drank sweet heady drinks, ate cakes of many kinds, and partook of
fruits.   And once again there happened to come hunting this
way Nahusha's son, the king, craving for water, and worn
out with weariness.   He saw Devayānī and Çarmishthā and
these fair young girls drinking and sporting, decked with godlike ornaments.   And he saw Devayānī of the bright smile, the
woman above others, of incomparable form, sitting among these
maidens, waited on by Çarmishthā, who was rubbing her feet
and doing other services.   Yayāti spoke : " Two maidens
surrounded by two thousand maidens !   I ask family and
name of both of you, O fair ladies."   Devayānī spoke :
" I will tell thee.   Hearken unto my words, O Prince of
men !   Çukra is the name of the teacher of the Asuras.   Know
then, that I am his daughter.   And she there is my friend and
slave who follows me everywhere—Çarmishthā, the daughter
of the king of the Dānavas, Vrishaparvan."   Yayāti spoke :
" But how comes it that this fair-faced maiden, the daughter of
the Asura king, she with the lovely brows, is thy friend and
slave ?   I am very curious as to this."   Devayānī spoke : " Every
one, O best of men, obeys his fate.   Look on it as the gift of
fate, and do not make divers speeches.   Thy form and garb
are as those of a king, and thou speakest the speech of the
Brahmans (Sanskrit).   Who and whence art thou, and
whose son ?   Tell me."   Yayāti spoke : " As a pupil of the
Brahmans I have heard the whole Veda, I am a king and a

---

[1] Or : Thy worldly knowledge is not for nothing, and thou hast
the power of the holy teaching (or : of magical knowledge).

[2] Perhaps more nearly : as all found their pleasure in play.

king's son, famous under the name of Yayāti." Devayānī spoke : "Why didst thou come this way ? Wouldst thou take something dwelling in the water, or hunt the gazelle ? " Yayāti spoke : "While hunting gazelle, O kindly one, I came hither for water. But now thou hast well questioned me.[1] Give me leave, therefore, to go." Devayānī spoke : "With two thousand girls and my slave Çarmishthā I am at thy bidding. Prithee, be my friend and my husband." Yayāti spoke : "Know thou, O daughter of Uçana, an it please thee, I am not worthy of thee, O lovely one. For thy father cannot be father-in-law to kings." Devayānī spoke : "The warrior nobility is closely bound to the Brahmans, the Brahmans are linked with the warrior nobility. Come now, son of Nahusha, do thou wed me as a Rishi and a Rishi's son." Yayāti spoke : "Although the four castes, O fair woman, come from one body, yet have they varying duties and varying rules for purity ; of them the Brahman is the first." Devayānī spoke : "Such a hand-grasp (as thine) men have not so far practised. Thou didst grasp my hand before, therefore do I ask of thee to be my husband. How should another now touch the hand of me, the proud one, the hand that has been grasped by thee, the son of a Rishi, and a Rishi himself ! " Yayāti spoke : "As more dangerous than an angry, flaming, venomous snake, everywhere darting, must the Brahman be recognized by the understanding man." Devayānī spoke : "Why sayest thou, O prince of men : More dangerous than a flaming, venomous snake, everywhere darting, is the Brahman ? " Yayāti spoke : "The venomous snake kills one man, and with a weapon one man alone is slain ; the Brahman destroys even cities and kingdoms, when he is angered. Therefore do I hold the Brahman as more dangerous, O timid one. And therefore I will not wed thee, unless thy father gives thee to me." Devayānī spoke : "Wed me, then, O king, when my father has given me thee, and I have chosen thee. For him that asks not, and only takes her that is given him, there is no danger." Quickly the nurse then faithfully told Devayānī's father all that Devayānī had entrusted her with for him. And so soon as

[1] Or : But I am very pressed (I have urgent business : bahudhāpy anuyukto 'smi). The expression is found several times in the MBh.

the scion of the Bhṛigu had heard, he appeared before the king. And when Yayāti, the lord of the earth, saw Çukra coming, he showed honour unto the Brahman, the son of Kavi, and ſtood there with folded hands, humbly bowed. Devayānī spoke : " This, O father, is the king, son of Nahusha. When I was in evil plight, he clasped my hand. Honour be to thee. Give me to him. I will choose no other husband in the world." Çukra spoke : " Chosen by this my beloved daughter, take her for thy chief wife; I give her thee, O son of Nahusha." Yayāti spoke : " May this great hurt done to the law that comes from the mingling of the caſtes not be avenged here on me, O scion of the Bhṛigu. On this condition I take thee, O Brahman, as father-in-law." Çukra spoke : " I absolve thee from the hurt to the law. Choose for thyself a favour thou wouldſt have. Do not be despondent on account of this marriage.[1] I will drive the evil away from thee. Take thou the slender Devayānī home as thy wife according to the law and cuſtom, and with her win incomparable joy. And this maiden, too, Vṛishaparvan's daughter, Çarmishthā, shalt thou always honour, O king ; and do not call her onto thy bed." Thus addressed, King Yayāti walked round Çukra to the right, and celebrated the happy wedding in the way laid down by the books of inſtruction. After he had got from Çukra many things and the moſt splendid Devayānī, together with two thousand girls and Çarmishthā, and had been honoured by Çukra and the Daityas, the beſt of princes came into his city, filled with joy, having taken leave of the high-minded one."

The good daughter whom we have juſt seen in Çarmishthā we find also elsewhere. It is now the turn of a Brahman, with whom the five fugitive Pāṇḍava youths are living, to offer himself to an evil Rākshasa. The latter muſt be given every day a cartload of rice to eat, the two oxen drawing it, and the man driving them. After the wife has offered to die for the Brahman, it goes on (i, 159) :—

" When the daughter heard the words of the over-whelmingly saddened parents, she spoke unto them, her body clasped in grief : ' Why do ye weep as bitterly as those beyond

[1] Literally : at this marriage thou shalt not wilt, that is, probably : do thou not be weary, have no fear.

hope, tortured by a mighty sorrow ? Lisen unto my words and then do what is befitting. By all that is right, ye two shall give me up ; of that there is no doubt. By giving me, who do consent, thou shalt save all through me, a single person. This is why offspring are wished for : ' They shall save me.' Since now the time for it has drawn nigh, cross, with me as the vessel, over the misfortune. Here and after death he mus rescue from danger. In every way the son mus sacrifice himself. That is why he is called son by the wise.[1] And the anceors yearn ever for daughter's sons from me. So will I myself save them by shielding my father's life. But if thou goes into that world, then this my small brother will soon perish ; of that there is no doubt. And if my father should have come into heaven, and my younger brother gone to derudtion, then the gift of cakes for the anceors would be cut short ; and that would be a misfortune for them. Robbed thus of my father, and of my mother and brother, I should surely die, falling from one sorrow into a greater, for I am not used to such things as this. But if thou has escaped, safe and sound, then assuredly my mother and brother, the child and the family line, and the offering to the forbears will be preserved and kept. The son is the very self, the wife a friend, but, as all know, the daughter is ever a misfortune (kṛicchra). . . But if I carry out the liberation, then my death will bear fruit, after I have carried through a very heavy task. But if thou goes thither, O bes among Brahmans, and dos leave me behind, then shall I be in raits ; therefore look, too, to me. Save thyself for our sake, and for the sake of religious duty, and for the sake of the offspring, and give up me, who am ready for it. And now let not the time go by for this most necessary deed. Indeed, what greater misfortune could there be than that we, after thy going home, should run round like dogs begging food from rangers ? But if thou and our kinsfolk are set free from this calamity, sound and unhurt, then I shall live in happiness, as one that has not died in the world. As a result the gods will work well-being because of the sacrifices, and, as we have heard, so will the

---

[1] This is how I try to render the etymological word-play that is found countless times : puttra from put + trā.

ancestors for the sake of the water-offering brought by thee." [1]

In the Rāmāyaṇa, in the 17th Sarga of the 7th Book, we read : " Thereupon Rāvaṇa, the strong-armed, wandered over the earth, and when he had come into the wilderness of Himavant, he went about in it. Then he saw a maiden wearing a black antelope-skin and penitent's tresses, taken up with the work of the holy ones (asceticism), and shining like a goddess. When he saw this maiden with the gift of beauty engaged in very heavy mortification, he laughed a little, and with senses blinded by love he asked : " Wherefore dost thou do this work, that is in discord with thy youth ? For it does not befit thee thus to act against this beauty. Thy peerless beauty, O timid one, which arouses mad love among men, is not there to the end that thou shouldst be given up to mortification. That is an evident conclusion. Whom dost thou belong to ? Wherefore this task ? And who is thy husband, thou with the fair face ? Whoever enjoys thee, he is a happy man on earth. Tell me all I ask. Wherefore the weariness ? " Thus addressed by Rāvaṇa the glorious maiden spoke, after she, the penitent, had shown him due and proper hospitality : " Kuçadhvaja was the name of my father, the Brahman Ṛishi of boundless fame, the majestic son of Bṛihaspati, equal in soul to Bṛihaspati. To this high-minded one, ever given up to Veda study, I was born as daughter out of his words, and Vedavatī is the name I bear. Then there came gods and Gandharvas, Yakshas, and Rākshasas, and snake-demons to my father and deigned to woo me. But my father did not give me to them, O Rākshasa prince. I will tell thee why. Hearken, O strong-armed one. My father would fain have Vishṇu, the lord of the three worlds, as son-in-law. Therefore my father would give me to no other. But when the prince of the Daityas, Çambhu his name, heard of this, he was angry with him who boasted his might. This villain did evil to my father in the night, as he slept. Then my excellent mother,

1 I read naḥ instead of na. The text, after the commentator, means : But if thou dost say : "We have heard that the gods and ancestors, when there is such an offering (of the daughter by her own father), do not work well-being," (then I say) " they do assuredly work well-being through the water-offering made by thee."

deep ſtricken, clasped my father's body, and went thus into the fire. With the resolve : " I will make this wish of my father's, directed to Nārāyaṇa, a true thing," I carry this god now in my heart. Now that I have undertaken this vow I am carrying out a mighty penance. With this I have told thee all, O Rākshasa prince. Nārāyaṇa will be my husband, and none but Purushottama. Thus I am giving myself up to dreadful ascetic vows in the yearning for Nārāyaṇa. I know thee, O king. Go, son of Paulaſtya. Through my asceticism I know all that is in the three worlds." Rāvaṇa spoke once more to the maiden in the midſt of her heavy penance, climbing down from his chariot of the gods and ſtricken with the dart of love : " Thou art haughty, O fair-hipped one, to cherish such a resolve. The ſtoring up of virtuous merit is something praiseworthy for old folk, O gazelle-eyed one. But thou, O timid one, that art favoured with every gift, and art the beauty of the three worlds, muſt not speak thus. Thy youthful bloom is fleeting. I am the prince of Laṅkā, dear one, famed under the name of Daçagrīva. Come, be my wife ; take thy fill of pleasures as thy heart may wish. And who is he thou calleſt Vishṇu ? In valour, asceticism, wealth, strength, O dear one, he is not my equal, whom thou, O fair one, yearneſt after." But as he thus spoke, this maiden Vedavatī made answer to the night-spirit : " No, do not speak thus ! Who with any underſtanding but thee, O Rākshasa prince, could wish to scorn Vishṇu, the overlord of the three worlds, held in honour by the whole world ? " Thus addressed by Vedavatī, the night-spirit clutched the maiden by the hair with his fingers. Then Vedavatī, filled with anger, cut off her hair with her hand ; her hand became a sword, and cut the hair away. As though aflame with wrath, as though burning up the night-spirit, having laid a fire, she spoke, filled with haſte to die : " Since shame has been put on me by thee, thou base one, I will not live. O Rakshas, that is why I go before thine eyes into the fire. Since I have had shame put on me by thee, evil-minded one, in the foreſt, therefore will I be born again to thy deſtruction. For a woman cannot slay the man bent on evil. And should I utter my curse on thee, then my mortification would come to nought. But if I have won any merit through deed, gift, and sacrifice, so may I as the fruit of it become the good daughter, not born of mother's womb, of a pious man." As soon as she had spoken thus, she went into the glowing fire, and from the sky there fell around a heavenly rain of flowers. And she was born here as the daughter of King Janaka (as Sītā from the furrow)."

And in other ways, too, it is not always easy for the daughter in the Old India of the Epic. So it is when a Brahman comes as guest ; for this caste demands, especially in the Mahābhārata, the most humble services. In iii, 303 ff., we read :—

" Once to King Kuntibhoja there came a Brahman, strong as glowing fire, and very tall,[1] with a moustache, a staff, and plaits, stately, with faultless limbs, glowing, as it were, with fiery strength, yellow as honey, a sweet speaker, decked with asceticism and holy studies. This very great penitent spoke to King Kuntibhoja : " I wish to enjoy alms in thy house, thou unselfish one. Nothing that is unpleasing to me must be done to me, either by thee, or by thy followers. Under these conditions I will dwell in thy house, thou blameless one, if so it please thee. And I will go and come entirely at my own will, and as to bed and seat none shall be remiss therewith." To him spoke Kuntibhoja these kind and joyful words : " So let it be, and it is right well." And again he spoke to him : " I have a daughter, O wise man, Pṛithā her name ; glorious is the fair one, attended by virtue and a surpassing life, kind and dutiful.[2] She will serve thee with reverence and without disdain, and for her virtuous ways thou wilt be content with her." When he had so spoken unto the Brahman, and had done him honour as it is ordained, he went to the maiden Pṛithā of the great eyes and spoke to her : " My child, this most excellent Brahman wishes to dwell in my house, and I have granted it him with a yea, looking confidently to thee for the contentment of the Brahman. Therefore mayst thou never belie my words. This is a holy penitent, a Brahman who is earnestly set on the study of the Veda. Whatever the most powerful one may ask must be ungrudgingly granted him. For the Brahman is the highest power, the Brahman is the highest

[1] Or : standing up high.
[2] Or : self-controlled.

25

asceticism ; it is through the honouring of Brahmans that the sun shines in the sky. For as the great Asura Vātāpi did not honour those worthy of honour, he was struck down by the Brahman's staff,[1] and Tālajaṅgha likewise. With this a great task is now set thee, my child ; do thou bring content to the Brahman with constant heedfulness. I know, O daughter, thy zealous regard for all Brahmans here and for the dignitaries and kinsfolk, shown by thee from childhood days. So also dost thou show thyself towards all servants, towards friends, marriage-kin, and thy mothers,[2] and towards me in every relation,[3] as is fitting. For there is none here in the city or in the women's house, even among thy servants, whom thou dost not gladden by rightful behaviour, thou maiden with faultless limbs. But I thought I must give thee the reminder, O Prithā, as regards the wrathful-minded Brahman, thinking : " Thou art a child " and " Thou art my daughter ". Born in the family of the Vrishnis, the beloved daughter of Çūra, thou wast given me formerly as a child by thy father himself, bound to me in friendship, O thou sister of Vasudeva, thou the greatest of my children, after he had promised me in the beginning the first-born. Therefore thou art my daughter. Born in such a house, and brought up in such a house, thou hast come from happiness to happiness, as though thou hadst come from out of the sea into the sea.[4] People of bad family, who may somehow have known special favour,[5] do wrong things out of their foolishness, especially women, O sweet one. Prithā, birth in a king's family, and wonderful beauty are thine ; with the one and the

[1] Brahmadaṇḍa. This expression is often found in the Epic, and denotes the might of the Brahman (brahman), resting on the holy word of the Veda (brahman); or, the magical, supernatural, destroying might, at work in the curse. See, for example, i, 2.354; 30.11 ; 54.23,25 (Nīl. is wrong here, in spite of 57.5) ; 57.24 ; ii, 5.122 ; 68.46 ; v, 51.8 ; viii, 34.43 ; xii, 39.10 ; 103.27 ; xvi, 1.9 ; 3.40 (cp. 4.3 ; 8.8,25 ; Rām. vii, 36.20,30 ; i, 56.19.

[2] Or : mother. " Mothers " is, of course, what all the king's wives are called. She had not her real mother at all at Kuntibhoja's court.

[3] Literally : filling everything, penetrating. Cp. v, 107.15.

[4] Hradād dhradam ivāgatā. Cp. i, 195.11 ; v, 90.91,92 ; 134.14.

[5] According to the commentator and Böhtlingk (in the Dict.) : " fall into stubbornness," which does not at all fit in.

other thou haſt been made happy and endowed, O lovely one. If thou shunneſt pride, deceit, and haughtiness, and bringeſt content to the grace-beſtowing Brahman, thou wilt link thyself with happiness, O Pṛithā. Thus, thou good one, thou wilt indeed attain to goodness, O blameless one. And if the beſt of the twice-born is angered, then my whole family will be deſtroyed."

Kuntī spoke : "I will, O king, honourably serve the Brahman with all heed, according to the promise, O lord of kings, and I speak no untruth. And that is my charaċter, that I honour the Brahmans. And I muſt do what is dear to thee, and my greateſt happiness. Whether the holy one comes at evening or in the early morning or in the night or at midnight, he will arouse no anger in me. It is a gain for me, O lord of kings, to bring salvation to myself, O beſt of men, through honouring the Brahmans and faithfully carrying out thy bidding. Thou canſt have a calm truſt, O lord of kings ; the beſt among the twice-born shall suffer nothing unpleasing while he dwells in thy house ; that I swear unto thee. What is pleasing to this Brahman and for thy good, O blameless one, for that will I ſtrive, O king. Let the fever in thy soul leave thee. For the Brahmans, they marked out by deſtiny, can save if they arc honoured ; and if not, then they can deſtroy. Since I know this, I shall rejoice the beſt among Brahmans. Through me, O king, thou wilt suffer no harm from the moſt excellent of Brahmans. In case of a miſtake, O prince of kings, the Brahmans become a deſtruċtion to kings, as did Cyavana formerly to King Çaryāti, because of Sukanyā. With the greateſt zeal will I serve ṭhe Brahman as thou didſt say unto the Brahman." While the king clasped her in his arms and exhorted her, as he repeatedly spoke thus, he told her of all that was to be done in this way and that. The king spoke : "Thus muſt thou do it, without hesitation, dear one, for the sake of my happiness, of thyself, and of the family, O ſtainless one."

But when Kuntibhoja, the greatly famed, had thus spoken, he gave Pṛithā over to this Brahman, he the friend to Brahmans. "This, O Brahman, is my daughter, a child of tender breeding ; if she makes a miſtake in any wise thou muſt not take it to

heart. The Brahmans, they marked out by destiny, never in
general harbour anger against the aged, children and the
sick who may offend against them. Even when the sin is great
the twice-born must show a patient forgiveness. Accept thou
the honour shown to the best of her strength and powers,
O best among Brahmans." The Brahman agreed, and the
king with a glad heart allotted him a house, white as the swan
and the shimmering moon. There he offered him at the place
of the holy fire a shining seat made ready, food, and the like,
and all this just as it should be.[1] But as the king's daughter
threw off weariness and likewise pride, she took the utmost
pains to please the Brahman. Thither to the Brahman Prithā
went, thinking only of purity, and rejoiced him, him worthy of
service, according to precept like a god. So did the maid living
under a strict vow now rejoice with pure soul the Brahman
living under a strict vow. Often the best of Brahmans spoke :
" I shall come in the morning," and then came back at evening
or in the night. And this maid did ever do honour to him at
all hours of the day with hard and soft foods and with comforts,
which both ever more excelled. The care given him with food
and the like, as also that for bed and seat, grew greater, not less,
day by day. And even though the Brahman might scold
Prithā, abuse her, and utter evil words against her, O king,
yet she did nothing then to annoy him. He would come back
again at different times, or often not at all, and of some dish
very hard to get he would say : " Give it me ! " And as she
brought him all this to his liking, so soon as it was made,
bearing herself well, like a scholar, a son, a sister, she aroused
heartfelt approval in the excelling Brahman, she the pearl of
maidens, the stainless one. The best of Brahmans was gladdened
at her virtuous ways ; then she took the very greatest pains [2]
with still greater heed. At morning and evening her father
would ask her : " Is the Brahman pleased with thy service,

[1] Tathaiva " just so, most excellently ". Cp. īdṛica, tādṛiç, tathā-
vidha, tathābhūta " right ; excellent," iii, 221.6,9 ; v, 90.62 ;
ix, 2.62.

[2] I will read bhūyasā instead of bhūyo syāḥ. The text would mean
more or less : Thereupon he took the very greatest pains in the utmost
measure about her.

daughter ? " The glorious one would answer him : " Very much so." At that Kuntibhoja, the high-minded one, felt the greatest joy. When, after a year had gone by, that best of the prayer-mutterers had seen no evil deeds in Prithā, he was delighted at her goodwill. Now when his heart had become filled with joy, the Brahman spoke to her : " I am highly rejoiced at thy services, thou dear and fair one ; choose gifts of grace for thyself, O sweet one, such as are hard here on earth for man to win, that so through them thou mayest outshine all women in splendour." Kuntī spoke : " For me all is fulfilled, since thou, O best among the knowers of the Veda, and my father are sweet-minded towards me. What should I do with gifts of grace, O Brahman ? " The Brahman spoke : " If thou, kind, bright-smiling one, wishest for no gifts of grace from me, then take from me these words of magic for calling up the heaven-dwellers. Whatsoever god thou dost call up by this magic spell, he must be obedient to thee ; whether he will or no, he will come up under the spell of thy command ; tamed by the magic, the god will bow to thee like a servant." The blameless one could not then refuse the best of Brahmans a second time, fearing his curse. Thereupon the twice-born one made the maiden with the faultless limbs take the set of words which stands in the Atharvaçiras. But when he had given it her, he spoke unto Kuntibhoja : " I have dwelt pleasantly, O king, satisfied by the maiden, ever well honoured, while I was lodged in thy house. Now I will set forth." With these words he vanished. When the king now saw the Brahman vanish before his very eyes, he was overcome with astonishment, and did honour to Prithā.

Now when this best of the twice-born had for some reason or other gone away, this maiden pondered on the power or otherwise of the magic spell : " What kind of spell has been given me then by the high-minded one ? I will learn about its strength in a short while. As she was thus thinking, she happened to notice her monthly flow, and filled with shame was the child, who was having the menses in her girlhood (for the first time).[1] Then she saw, who was used to a splendid couch, the

[1] This shame is to be set down greatly to her credit. For the coming of this event is for the Indian girl a source of pride and rejoicing, like

sun's disk rise, resting in the east on the palace roof. The mind and eyes of the slender one clung to it, and as the sun god was only just rising she was not annoyed by the heat of his body. She was granted the divine sight : she saw the god in his divine manifestation, wearing his armour, adorned with two ear-rings. But she was curious as to her magic spell, and so the fair one called on this god. As she then moistened her senses' tools with water, she called on the maker of day ; he came swiftly, honey-yellow, long-armed, muscular-necked, lightly laughing, with rings on his arms, a crown on his head, making the lands of the world, as it were, to blaze up. Splitting his own self by magic into two parts, he came and brightly glowed. Then he spoke to Kuntī, with exceeding kind and friendly words : " I have become of service to thee, bound by thy magic spell, my dear one. What am I to do, as thy vassal, O queen ? Speak ! I will do it." Kuntī spoke : " Go thither, O sublime one, whence thou camest. It was out of curiosity that I called thee. Be merciful to me, O lord." The sun god spoke : " I will go, even as thou hast bidden me, O slender one. But it is not right to call on a god and send him away for a worthless

the sprouting of the moustache for the youth, and in this she is like he, sisters among very many peoples. As almost everywhere on the earth, the girl on the Ganges from her earliest years knows all about every thing, and with her the coming of puberty excites a lively interest, and is even hailed with much rejoicing. That most delightful thing in the world—the maiden blossoming in sweet ignorance, and the half-painful, half-joyful emotional billowing of her soul, wrapped in holy and pure dream secrets—this, indeed, the Hindu does not know. Still this most delicate, ethereal bloom of European culture is by no means so very common amongst us, and, moreover, in our days under sentence of death under the dazzling beams of the sun of " sexual knowledge "—poor, fairy-tale wonder of the moonlight night. Thus no Hindu maiden could give utterance to such a fragrant delicacy of feeling as we find expressed in the fairest puberty poem in the world in *Neidon valitus*, the " Maiden's Lament ", of the Finnish poet Eerikki Ticklén, who died, all too young, in 1827 (cp. J. J. Meyer, *Vom Land der tausend Seen. Eine Abhandlung über die neuere finnische Literatur und eine Auswahl aus modernen finnischen Novellisten* (p. 33). The reader may be here reminded, too, of Peter Hille's wonderful *Brautseele*.

whim. Thy intention is, O lovely one : May I get a son from the sun god, one peerless in heroic ſtrength, clad in armour, decked with ear-rings. Give thyself, then, to me, thou with the elephant's gait ; for a son shall be born thee, such as thou yearneſt after, O woman. I will go then, when I have been joined with thee, O thou with the lovely smile. If thou wilt not do as I say, do what is dear to me,[1] then in my anger I shall curse thee, and the Brahman, and thy father. Because of thee I shall beyond a doubt engulf them all with fire, and thy father, moreover, because he gave no heed to thy wrong behaviour. And on that Brahman I shall deal out a hard chaſtisement for giving thee the magic spell without knowing thy charaćter and ways. For all the gods in heaven there with Indra at their head are witnesses to my having been tricked by thee, and are smiling as it were, O lovely one. Look but at those bands of the gods, for thou haſt that divine sight which I firſt granted thee and whereby thou haſt seen me." Then the king's daughter saw all the thirty-three (gods) at their ſtations in the air, bright as the dazzling, shining, great sun god. When the young maiden, the queen, saw them, she spoke these words, abashed and fearful, to the sun god : " Go, pray, lord of the beams, unto thy heavenly chariot. It was from my maidenly nature that the disaſtrous miſtake arose.[2] Father and mother and any other dignitaries there may be have the power to beſtow this body. I will not do hurt to law and virtue ; in the world the safe keeping of the body is held in honour as the virtuous way of woman's life. It was to try the might of the magic spell that I called thee, O shining one. ' From childish want of underſtanding the child did it,' is what thou mayeſt think,[3] and forgive me for this, O my lord." The sun god spoke : " Since I think that it is a child, I will utter unto thee friendly words ; no other would get such mild words.

---

[1] Literally perhaps : " If thou doſt not make my dear words true," which would remind us of Homeric expressions, or in which " dear " = pleasant, friendly.

[2] Cp. v, 144.22 ; xv, 30.9.

[3] Tat kṛitvā ; oftener, iti kritvā. i, 34.3 ; 7.17 ; iii, 18.9 ; 208.17 ; 302.4 ; 303.22 ; 306.25 ; iv, 20.3 f. ; xiv, 19.78 ; xv, 9.8 ; evaṃ kṛi, iii, 138.25. See also xii, 318.32.

Give thyself to me, Kuntī girl, and thou wilt find peace, O timid one. And it is not fitting for me that I should go forth as one that has been wrongly treated, without having been united with thee, O timid fair one, after being called up by a spell. I shall fall a victim to laughter in the world, O maiden with faultless limbs, and to all the gods, O lovely one, I should be blameworthy. Unite thyself with me ; thou shalt get a son like unto me ; in all the worlds thou wilt assuredly stand forth."

In spite, however, of her many friendly words, this sensible maiden could not soften the thousand-beamed one. When the young girl could not send off the scarer of darkness, she pondered now for a while, filled with fear of his curse : " How shall it be that the curse of this wrathful sun god may not, because of me, light upon my father and likewise the Brahman ? And he that is young and foolish must not through blindness let fiery strength and the power of penitence, which, indeed, have brought much disaster, come near unto him. For how can I, who am now so tortured, how can I myself boldly take in hand and carry out my bestowai on the man, which does not befit me ? " Dreading the curse, with many wavering thoughts in her heart, gripped in her limbs by a swimming weakness, smiling ever and again, and filled with anxiety for her kindred, the curse-afeared one spoke to the god in a voice quivering with shame : " My father is alive, O god, and my mother and my other kinsfolk. So long as they still live let not the holy precept be thus broken. If the unlawful union with thee should come about, O god, then the good name of my family in the world would come to nought because of me. But if thou holdest this to be right and virtuous, O best of the shining ones, without the bestowal by my kindred, then I will fulfil thy wish. But if I have given myself up to thee, O thou so hard to overcome, then I am an unchaste woman. In thee abides the right, the splendour, and the good name of mankind." The sun god spoke : " Neither father, mother, nor dignitaries have any power in this,[1] O thou with the bright smile and fair hips.

[1] Literally : The father has not the disposal of thee, the mother has not the disposal of thee, nor, etc. Or perhaps less well : Not thy father, not thy mother, nor the dignitaries have power (the disposal).

Be pleased to hear my words. Since she covets all, and is from the root " to covet ", O lovely one, therefore (she) is the " maiden ", the fair-hipped, (and she stands) alone, O lovely-faced one.[1] Thou wilt have done no wrong whatever, fair one. How could I in my love for the world choose a wrong deed ! All women and men are without restraint, O lovely-faced one. This is the real nature of mankind, any other is to speak untruly, as the holy tradition teaches. After union with me thou wilt again be a virgin, and thy son will become strong-armed and greatly famed." Kuntī spoke : " If a son shall come to me from thee, thou scatterer of all darkness, who is decked with ear-rings, clad in armour, a hero, strong-armed and very mighty. . . ."[2] The sun god spoke : " He will be strong-armed and decked with ear-rings, and wear divine armour. And both, O kind one, will be made for him from the Immortal."[3] Kuntī spoke : " If that is of the Immortal—the two ear-rings, and the splendid harness of my son, whom thou wouldst beget with me—then let my union with thee, O sublime god, come about, as thou hast said. And may he be endowed with thy hero's strength, thy form, bravery, and power, and with virtue." The sun god spoke : " Aditi, O queen, has given me ear-rings, thou that art as one drunk ; them I will give him, O timid one, and this most excelling armour." Kuntī spoke : " That is well indeed. I will unite myself with thee, if my son shall be as thou sayest, O lord of the beams." " Good," answered the sky-wanderer, Svarbhānu's foe, joined himself with Kuntī, taking on a magic body, and touched her on the navel. Thereupon the maid swooned, as it were, through

K. (308.12) reads more smoothly pradāne te instead of varārohe. Cf. Mārkaṇḍeyapur., cxiii, 14 : In all things one shall listen to the Gurus (dignitaries), but in love they have nothing to say.

[1] Kanyā (maiden, virgin), that is to say, is held to come from kam to covet.

[2] K. has destroyed the beauty of this unfinished sentence by a third çloka line : astu me saṃgamo, deva, anena samayena te.

[3] That is, they are themselves indestructible, and bestow immunity on their wearer ; death, too, has no power over him (iii, 300.17–20). Cp. i, 330.10 ff.; iii, 310.10 ff.; 301.17. As is well known, the world's literature, particularly the Indian, shows very many such magic things.

33

the fiery ſtrength and majeſty of the sun god, and she, the queen, now fell with confused mind on to the couch. The sun god spoke : " I shall bring it about : thou wilt bear a son who is the firſt among all that bear arms, and thou wilt be a virgin." Then spoke the young woman, filled with shame, to the sun god, the many-beamed, as he proceeded : " So let it be." [1] When the daughter of the king of the Kunti thus had spoken, prayerful and ashamed, to the sun god, she fell onto that pure couch, overcome in a swoon, like a broken tendril. He of the sharp beams bewildered her with his fiery ſtrength, united with her through his magic power, and made her his own ; and the sun god did not dishonour her.[2] And then the young woman got back her senses again.

Then the fruit of Pṛithā's body came into being, on the eleventh day of the bright half of the moon, as in heaven did the ruler of the ſtars. For fear of her kinsfolk the young woman kept this child secret, she, the lovely-hipped one,

[1] My translation of sādhayishyāmi and praſthita is quite a possible one, and it was chosen so as to make the tale in some measure consiſtent with itself. But the natural reading would be : " I will now go off, thou wilt, etc. Then spoke the young woman . . . as he went off, etc." In the following there is a change from the çloka into the trishṭubh ; it is evidently a piece from another account which was inserted without the joins being properly filled in—a conſtant pra&tice in the MBh. The çloka and the firſt version is taken up again with : " Then Pṛithā conceived a fruit of her body." Were it not for çl. 125, the two trishṭubh could naturally be easily taken as a concluding summary ; *with* that çloka this is difficult, if we take sādhayishyāmi and praſthita in the usual meaning. There is probably, too, an unskilful join made in the tale in so far as the sun god " touches (the woman) on the navel ", after the way of ascetics who do not want to harm their chaſtity and yet to help in bringing a son into being (e.g. Jātaka, Nos. 497 and 540 ; Windisch, *Buddhas Geburt*, etc., p. 20 ff. ; Reitzenſtein, *Zeitschr. f. Ethnol.*, Bd. 41, p. 648). Of course, divyena vidhinā in 308.13 seems to point to exa&tly such a begetting— which allusion, however, may be secondary—and impregnation through the touch of the hand, is often found in India and elsewhere (e.g. i, 104.51 f.).

[2] Did not deſtroy her maidenhead, or reſtored it again after union. P. 33, line 9, inſtead of " ſtill be a virgin ", perhaps : " be a virgin again."

and folk noticed nothing about her. For no other woman knew of it but her nurse's daughter, a young girl in the city, who well understood how to shield her. Later in due time the lovely-faced one brought forth her child, and as an un-harmed virgin through the favour of that god : like an immortal, wearing armour and shining ear-rings of gold, yellow-eyed, bull-shouldered, just as his father. And so soon as the lovely one had borne this child, she took counsel with the nurse, and laid it in a chest that was well lined all round, waxed over, soft and easy, and well fastened ; and weeping, she set the child forth thus in the river Açva. Though she knew that a maid must bear no fruit of her body, yet she wailed bitterly out of love for her little son. The words spoken in tears then by Kuntī, as she set him forth in the chest in the river's waters—hear them : " Good come to thee from the beings in the air and the earth and in the sky and those in the water, my little son ! Blessed be thy paths ! May the waylayers keep far from thee ! And even so may they that have come hither along the road (āgata) be friendly-hearted towards thee ! May King Varuṇa, the prince of the waters, watch over thee in the water, and in the air the god of the wind, who is in the air, and goeth everywhere. May thy father ward thee everywhere, the shining one and best of the shining ones, who has given me thee, O son, in divine wise. May the Ādityas, Vasus, Rudras, Sādhyas, and the All-gods, the Maruts together with Indra, and the quarters of the world with the wardens thereof watch over thee, may all the gods watch over thee on smooth and on rugged paths ! I shall know thee, too, abroad, for the armour betrays thee. Happy, my son, is thy father, the blazing sun god, who sees thee in the river with his god's eye. Happy the woman who shall take thee for son, O son, and whose breast thou shalt thirstily suck, thou god-begotten one ! What (happiness-bringing) dream she indeed had who makes thee to be her son, thee blazing like the sun, endowed with heavenly armour, decked with heavenly ear-rings, thee that hast long white lotus-eyes, that shinest like a red lotus-leaf,[1] that hast a lovely

[1] Literally : shining like the red leaf of the lotus. We should expect something like padmatāmradalaushṭhakam, " with lips like a

forehead and lovely hair. It is happy folk that will see thee, my son, a little crawler about the earth and, covered in dust, babbling darling words. Happy folk will see thee then, my son, come into the years of youth, like the maned lion born in the Himālaya forest." Pṛithā having thus bitterly lamented in various wise, now set forth the chest on the waters of the Açva river. Weeping, tortured with sorrow for her son, and filled with the yearning to see him, then Pṛithā, the lotus-eyed, in the middle of the night together with her nurse, again came into the king's palace, sick with sorrow, after having had the box sent drifting away through fear lest her father should come to know of the thing. But the chest swam from the Açva river into the river Carmaṇvatī, from the Carmaṇvatī into the Yamunā, and from there into the Gaṅgā. On the Gaṅgā the child in the chest came into the territory of the chariot-driver, to the city of Campā, as the little one was carried along by the waves.[1]

---

red lotus leaf." But the red hue of the new-born is also referred to elsewhere in the MBh.

[1] There he is found by Adhiratha, the chariot-driver of Dhṛitarāshṭra, who takes him to himself as child, and brings him up. The same tale is told earlier, i, 67.129 ff., and shorter i, 111. According to the former, and according to i, 122.35–37, Durvāsas says from the beginning that the purpose of the magic is that Kuntī may get a son from any god she may call up; and we have not to do, as we clearly have in our account, with a begetting without the virginity being destroyed; but we find : " And the god of the brightest splendour gave her back her maidenhead " (i, 111.20). With this xv, 30.16 also agrees. The Brahman of this account was called Durvāsas.

With the motive of the exposed Perseus or Cyrus or of " Moses in the bulrushes " (in his case smeared over with clay and pitch, 2 Moses, ii, verse 3) and of Kuntī, the maiden-mother, compare how in the Shahnameh Darab is exposed by his mother Humāi on the Euphrates in a precious small chest directly after his birth, and is found and adopted by washer-folk; Jātaka, v, p. 429; Chauvin, vii, 97; Hertel, Hemacandra's Pariçishṭaparvan, ii, 238, and his references, p. 228, as also ZDMG (Zeitsch. d. deutsch. morgenl. Ges.), Bd. 65, p. 438 f.; H. Schurtz, Urgeschichte der Kultur (1900), p. 578; " The Wicked Stepmother " in Aino Tales, by Basil Hall Chamberlain, privately printed for the Folk Lore Society, xxii, p. 48; and above all Frobenius,

THE MAID

With this, however, the sorrow that was to light upon the king's daughter from this child Karṇa had only begun. Karṇa becomes, indeed, the friend and faithful comrade of Duryodhana, the fierce foe of her later children, the Pāṇḍavas, and in the desperate fight that breaks out between these and the Kauravas he fights with overwhelming and crushing heroic might against his brothers, especially against his rival Arjuna. When the young Pāṇḍavas have served their full time, their teacher Droṇa makes them show their skill before a splendid feſtal gathering. Arjuna ſtands out before all the others. Then a wonderful hero comes onto the arena, Karṇa, and does

Zeitalter des Sonnengottes, Bd. i, p. 223 ff.; and P. Saintyves, *Les vierges mères et les naissances miraculeuses* (Paris, 1908). The two laſt-named works are, I am sorry to say, not to my hand, and I know them only from reviews. Supernatural fertilization has been very thoroughly treated by E. S. Hartland, *Legend of Perseus*, vol. i, and then in the earlier chapters of his careful and luminous book, *Primitive Paternity* (1909). As is well known, girls at the coming of puberty or of the firſt monthly course muſt among the moſt various peoples and tribes of the earth be carefully looked after, generally even shut up for a shorter or longer time, and especially kept from the sun; and it is quite an aſtonishment when we are told by C. G. and Brenda Z. Seligmann, *The Veddas* (Cambridge, 1911), p. 94, that this people, both on this and remarkably so on many other points (cp. for inſtance, p. 190 f.), has no superſtitions, except where it has loſt some of its primitiveness through contaꞔ with foreigners. The girl is at this very time highly susceptible to magical influences, and easily brings ill-hap on others. It is particularly by the sun or its beams that women in general and above all at the firſt monthly course can be impregnated. See Frazer, *The Golden Bough* (1900), iii, p. 204 ff., especially 219 and 222, and the evidence there; Hartland, *Primitive Paternity*, i, 25 f., 89 ff., 97 ff.; *Anthropos*, Bd. vi, p. 699; Bd. vii, p. 93; Crooke, *Popular Religion and Folk-Lore of Northern India*, new ed., i, 11, 69, and the references there; Reitzenſtein, *Zeitschr. f. Ethnol.*, 1909, p. 658 f.; R. Schmidt, *Liebe u. Ehe in Indien*, p. 477. With Kuntī's swoon, cf. the Maidu Indian tale of Oankoitupeh, the red cloud's son, Hartland, loc. cit., i, 195 f. A Rājput tale often reminding us of the MBh. tale is given by Tod, *Rajaſthan*, i, 251–52; and that the Rājput should thus trace the origin of one of their kings to the sun seems the more natural in that it is their higheſt god (Tod, *Rajaſthan*, i, 596 ff., 250).

all the feats which Arjuna had just been the only one to do ; and when Arjuna flies into a rage, the unwelcome new-comer calmly challenges him to a duel with bow and arrow. The whole gathering, however, is very deeply roused. " The audience split into two, among the women two parties were formed ; but Kuntibhoja's daughter swooned away, when she saw what was happening. As Kuntī thus lay in a swoon, Vidura, the knower of all duties, brought her to herself again through the servant-maids with sandal-water. When her life-spirits had now come back again, and she saw her two sons equipped for the fray, she was utterly bewildered, and knew not what to do." [1] She has then to see how the noble splendid Karṇa is put to shame, first because of the darkness of his origin, then because of his supposed father, Adhiratha, the chariot-driver (i, 136 f.).

Here the party of the Pāṇḍavas wins the victory ; from fear lest Arjuna, their pride, should be overcome by Karṇa, they trick Karṇa shamefully. But afterwards it would be a gift of heaven beyond price for the Pāṇḍavas, if they could win him. Kuntī herself then takes the step that is so painful for her : she goes to Karṇa, just when he is carrying out his worship of the sun god at the river's shore, waits humbly in the burning glow till he is done, and then discloses to him that he is not the chariot-driver's son, but her sun-god-begotten virgin-child, and strives to unite him with his brothers. But the mighty one first remonstrates with her for having treated him before in so unmotherly wise, and having ruthlessly deprived him of the warrior's sacraments and the career laid down for him, while now she was seeking him out for her own ends. He declares both the words of his mother and the voice that comes solemnly from the sun, confirming and supporting what she had said, to be false. Then in a speech showing the inborn nobility of the soul of this the finest hero in all Indian literature he makes known his resolve to stay faithful until death to his lords and friends the Kauravas,

---

[1] Or : she was at a loss (na kiṃcit pratyapadyata). See vi, 119.111,115 ; 120.16. Böhtlingk wrongly has : " kept calm " (but so it probably is in v, 73.20 ; vii, 134.24).

although for him it were better otherwise.[1] But to the
mother, filled with care about her other sons, he gives the
great-hearted promise to spare them all in the fight; only
with Arjuna will he fight a life and death struggle. Thus did
Karna lose her for ever (v, 144 ff.; cp. xii, 1.18 ff.; 6.9 ff.).

Many years after the bloody battles, when the sun's great
son has long been slain through low cunning, Kuntī is still
being irked by the memory of her youthful sin, for which
fate is punishing her so heavily, and to which she had been led,
setting aside a forgivable maiden curiosity, mainly by her
loving thought for her father and the holy Brahman. She
gives a short tale of what happened to her then with the sun
god, and declares : " Although I knew my son, yet in my
blindness I left him unnoticed. This is burning me." The
holy Vyāsa, however, consoles her : " Thou didst do no sin,
and didst become a maid again.[2] And the gods of a truth
have dominion in their hands; men's virtue is not brought to
shame [3] by the virtue of the gods. All for the strong is wholesome, for the strong all is pure, all for the strong is rightful
and virtuous, all belongs to the strong " (xv, 30; cp. Kuntī's
lament for Karna, xv, 16.11 ff.; also xi, 27.6 ff.).

Satyavatī, the mother of the famous Vyāsa, held to be the
compiler of the Vedas and author of the Mahābhārata, offers
less resistance than the maidenly Kuntī. She had come into

[1] Karna knows that the Pāndavas will win, but withal he has already
refused Krishna, who has enlightened him as to his origin and tried to
win him, by the most splendid promises, over to the Pāndavas (v, 140).
The great-souled hero answered him that his foster-father and foster-
mother had done everything for him, that he loved them, and must
bring them the ancestral offering, and so cannot but be true to the
Kauravas (v, 141).

[2] Hardly : " Thou hadst then become a maid," and so hadst a right to
sexual mating. That would indeed agree with the Brahmanic teaching,
that she should have been wedded before, but not at all with the
customs of the Epic. Probably still less : " Thou hadst fallen a victim
to thy maiden nature," didst only act through want of understanding.

[3] Or : " harmed." The maiden's virtue, chastity, has not suffered,
although here the god's righteousness and virtue, his generative hero
nature, not bound by men's laws, came into strife with her. According
to v, 141.3, the sun god bade Kuntī expose Karna.

being in the belly of a fish in an extraordinary way, to be referred to later, and had come out when the creature, really a bewitched Apsaras, had been cut open. She was given by her maker to a fisherman, and was wondrous fair ; only she had a fish-like smell. Her foster-father had a ferry-boat over the Yamunā, and she took over its working for him. Then there came one day the Rishi or holy man Parāçara to be ferried over. He at once fell in love with the lovely-thighed one, and without waiting made her his proposal : " Be joined with me, lovely one ! " She spoke : " See, O holy man, the Rishis are standing on the other shore. How could we unite while they see us ? " Thus addressed by her, the holy and glorious, the mighty one, brought about a mist by which that whole neighbourhood was changed, as it were, into one stretch of darkness. But when she now saw this mist, made by the excelling Rishis, the maiden was greatly astonished and ashamed, poor girl. Satyavatī spoke : " Know, O holy man, that I am a maid, and still subject to my father. Through a union with thee my maidenhead would be lost, O blameless one. And if my maidenhead is harmed, how shall I be able, O Rishi, best of the twice-born, to go home ? I cannot then live, O wise man. Think over this, O glorious one, and then do what lies next to hand." To her thus speaking, said the best of the Rishis, filled with joy and love : " When thou hast done me this favour, then shalt thou become a maid again.[1] And choose thyself, thou fearful one, a favour thou wouldst have, O fair one. For never up to now has my goodwill been without result, thou with the bright smile." Thus spoken to, she chose the loveliest sweet scent in her limbs, and the holy man gave her what she yearned for above all. After she had won the favour, filled with joy, and decked with the greatest gift of woman (a sweet smell), she united herself with the wonder-working Rishi. Hence her name Gandhavatī (the fragrant one) came to be renowned on earth. The scent of her was smelt by men here below a Yojana (" mile ") away. Therefore her other name is Yojanagandhā. Thus was Satyavatī joyful, having received the incomparable favour, and united

[1] Or less likely : " still be wholly a maid " (kanyaiva tvaṃ bhavishyasi).

herself with Paraçara and bore at once the fruit of her body "
(i, 63.67 ff.). Satyavatī herself tells this tale shorter (i, 105.5 ff.)
There she says that the fear, too, of the holy man's curse,
not only this gracious gift, had influenced her, and that the
Ṛishi enjoyed her in the boat, and bade her expose the child
on an island in the river ; and that thereupon she had
become a maid again.

This wondrous keeping or reſtoring of maidenhead is often
found elsewhere in the Mahābhārata. The tale of the princess
Mādhavī reminds us of one of Boccaccio's novels. There
was a pious disciple of Viçvāmitra, by name Gālava, who
after serving long was dismissed by his teacher. He insiſted
on paying the holy man the teacher's fee, so that he (the teacher)
at laſt grew angry, and named him as the price eight-hundred
noble, moon-white ſteeds, each with one black ear. At
length the desperate, vainly-seeking Gālava comes to King
Yayāti. He, indeed, cannot fulfil his requeſt for these rare
beaſts, either, but in fear of the dreadful results of refusing a
suppliant he gives him his young daughter Mādhavī, whom
for her loveliness even gods and spirits desire, and lets him
know that kings would give him as the price of her a whole
kingdom, not to speak of eight hundred such black-eared horses ;
the only condition he would make for himself is that her sons
may make the anceſtral sacrifice for him. Firſt of all Gālava
goes with the fascinating beauty to King Haryaçva, who
sees by the build of her body that she, who is a sight for the
heavenly ones themselves, can give life to many sons, and even
to a world-ruler. But when the love-sick one hears of the
extraordinary price to be paid, he sighs sorrowfully, and
acknowledges he can give only two hundred such horses.
For these Gālava shall let him beget but one son with her.
In this ſtrait Mādhavī now tells him : " I was granted a
grace by a man learned in the Veda : ' After each birth thou
wilt become a maid again.' Give me to the king, so soon
as thou haſt received two hundred peerless ſteeds. By means
of four kings thou wilt thus get my full eight hundred horses,
and I shall get four sons." So then Gālava gives Haryaçva
the maiden for a fourth of the price, that he may live with her
till she has borne him a son. After this happy event has come

about he then goes with Mādhavī, who by the power of her wish has become a maid again, to King Divodāsa, who has already heard of the famous beauty and her story and rejoices greatly. He, too, can only give two hundred such animals, and is allowed to beget one son with her. The next visit of the two is to King Uçīnara ; he gives his two hundred horses and with the glorious one he lives a life of joy in mountain grottoes and by river waterfalls, in gardens, groves, and forests, in lovely palaces and on castle-towers, in windowed imperial abodes and bedchambers, till, after the birth of a son, Gālava comes and demands the woman back again from him. The bird king Garuḍa now tells the owner of the six hundred wonderful steeds that there are no more on this earth, for originally there were only a thousand, and the other four hundred have been carried away by the river Vitastā, as they were trying to get them across. He is to offer the lovely one, he tells him, to his teacher for two hundred such steeds. Thus it is, and Viçvāmitra, who is, indeed, a judge of woman's charms, is at once satisfied, and even exclaims : " Why didst thou not at once give me her here at the beginning ? Then I should have got four sons from her to carry on the line." She bears him a son, and later he withdraws into the forest as an ascetic, giving her up to his disciple Gālava, who brings her back to her father. Her father now wishes to hold a great choosing of a husband, but she takes to a life in the forest and becomes a distinguished penitent (v, 114 ff.).[1]

Draupadī, too, the leading heroine of the Mahābhārata, after union still bears the flower of her maidenhood unplucked. She is wedded to the five Pāṇḍavas one after the other, and we hear : " In this wise the king's five sons, the splendid chariot-fighters, the gloriously-made, continuers of the Kaurava race, then took the splendid woman by the hand, each one on his day. And this miracle surpassing all that is human is proclaimed by the divine Rishi : the lovely one with the glorious waist, the very mighty one, at the end of each day became a maid again "[2] (i, 198.11 ff.). The Rishi is Vyāsa, himself the child of a *semper virgo*, as has already been said.

[1] Cf. Crooke, *Popular Religion and Folk-Lore, etc.*, ii, 204.
[2] Or : was still a maid (babhūva kanyaiva).

Here, however, we must so understand it that Draupadī
gets back (or, keeps) her maidenhead, only four times, that
she may fall into the arms of each of the five brothers as
untouched. For the maidenhead is, as in Old India in general,
set very high in the Epic likewise.[1]   xiii, 36.17, states :

[1] What is, perhaps, very generally known from the novel *Nena Sahib*,
by Sir John Ratcliffe (a Berlin writer whose real name I cannot now
with certainty call to mind) is borne witness to by the *Centuries* of
Hāla for older times, too ; there the ānaṃdavaḍa, " the cloth (garment)
of bliss " is publicly shown with rejoicings on the morning following
the bridal night; though in this case it is not dyed with "the shed
blood of innocence ", for a young rascal goes by it and slily grins to
himself (No. 457). Particularly rich in information here is Kauṭilya.
See my translation (Leipzig, 1926), p. 357.6 ff. ; 35 ff. The little
tricks of the ladies, of which Brantôme can tell us, were, then, already
known in Old India. He tells us that down to his time in Spain after
the *depucellement* of brides their *linge teint de gouttes de sang* was
publicly shown through the window, with loud cries of : Virgen la
tenemos, and that there was a like custom in Viterbo. Then he
entertains us with an account of how those daughters of Eve, who have
already nibbled from the tree of knowledge, supply what is lacking
by art, and with a merry tale of one who quite fruitlessly made use of
the red juice she had so carefully brought with her, and fruitlessly
for the same reason that Iseult White-hand fortifies herself so strongly
to no purpose against the storming of her treasury of love (Heinrich
von Freiberg, *Tristan*, 698 ff.). See Brantôme, *Œuvres compl.* ed. du
Panthéon lit. vol. ii, pp. 242 b, 332 b. Among the Yurakara in South
America, the smock of the bridal night was carried round in triumph
(Mantegazza, *Geschlechtsverhältnisse*, p. 253). The Arabs, too,
publicly show the stained bed-clothes (*Anthropos*, iii, p. 184 f.).
So, too, among the South Slavs, the bed-linen and the bride's smock
are or were searched for the signs of maidenhead, and the happy find
was hailed with joy (Krauss, *Sitte und Brauch der Südslaven*, pp. 225,
461 f.). Quite the same thing happens among the Russians and other
Slavs (*Zeits. d. Ver. f. Volkskunde*, Bd. 15, p. 438 f.), as also among the
Turks in Bulgaria (ibid., Bd. 4, p. 272). Among the Fô in Togo
the man sends the bedding next morning to the mother-in-law, and
if this is not marked as it should be, the parents have to find out the
evil-doer (*Anthropos*, vii, 296). Cf. 5 Moses, xxii, verses 15–17 ;
and further Ploss-Bartels, *Das Weib*[4], i, pp. 365 ff. ; my transl. of
Kauṭilya, 358.27 ff.

" Conceit deftroys the happiness of a man of shallow under-
ftanding, it is by a pregnancy that the maiden is robbed of
honour,[1] and through dwelling and ftaying in the house the
Brahman." And according to vii, 73.17, the man who enjoys
a woman that has already been enjoyed by another belongs to
the abominable whose lot in the world beyond is a dreadful
one. However, what is in mind here, at leaft in the firft
place, is a girl that has loft her maidenhead and is taken to wife.
But all the shame and guilt does not fall withal, as it does in
almoft all lands, on her that has ftrayed, but we are told :
" A third of the murder of a Brahman (that is, of the moft
heinous of all crimes) is what the sinning virgin (kanyā
dushyatī) takes on herself ; but he that brings shame on her
takes two thirds " (xii, 165.42, 34).[2] The heedless giving of

[1] Or : ruined (dushyate).
[2] The law books deal juft as fternly with the maidenhood of the
girl. Only the unsullied one can receive the woman's consecration,
the regular wedding. Manu, viii, 226 ; ix, 176. It is only her son that
takes his father's cafte. Manu, x, 5 ; Āpaftamba, ii, 6, 13.1 ff. A man
is only to wed a maiden that as yet has had nothing to do with a man.
Vasishṭha, viii, 1 ; Gautama, iv, 1, etc. The bride's failings muft,
according to the law writings, be faithfully made known before she is
given away, and, besides certain bodily faults, among these is the loss
of maidenhead. Nārada, xii, 36, etc. Anyone making a false accusation
againft a maid of breaking her chaftity muft pay 100 paṇa. Manu,
viii, 225 ; Yājñavalkya, i, 66 ; Nārada, xii, 34 ; but according to
Vishṇu, v, 47, the higheft possible money atonement (uttama sāhasa).
Cf. my transl. of Kauṭilya, 357.12 ff. ; addit. 357.12–15. Defloration
and intercourse with a girl is heavily punished. In that case the evil-
doer's property shall be confiscated, and he banished ; while the king
muft then see to it that sinful maidens such as these shall be saved
and kept from going wrong. This is the teaching of Āpaftamba, ii, 10,
26.21–24. Manu, viii, 368, lays it down : He that dishonours a
maid shall pay 200 paṇa, if it was done with her will. According to
Nārada, xii, 71–72, that is not an offence ; but the man muft
honourably wed the girl. Yājñavalkya, ii, 288, holds that if the girl
belongs to a lower cafte than the man, then it is not an offence, a view
which others do not share. If a man lie with a maid againft her will,
or with one of a higher cafte, then there are very ftern laws, of which
later. Indeed, union with a maiden is the same as inceft or a wrongful
aft with the teacher's wife, that is it is the moft heinous thing there is.

44

herself to the man by the virtuous maid, which we find so often in the tales of other peoples, especially the Europeans, and later in India likewise, which indeed in many literatures is found as something quite a matter of course, is a thing unknown in the Epic. Devayānī's view in i, 83.1–8 is a monstrosity of Brahman arrogance. True, one might be inclined to apply the words : " My yoke is sweet and my burden is light," to the Gandharva marriage, with which in the Epic even the noble, though untried and innocent Çakuntalā contents himself. But, for the consciousness of the Epic, this form is lawful and blameless and the woman at least treats it as holy and binding, whether the man would like to override it or not.

But in spite of the delightful, shy maids, if not always very hard to win, that are set before us in the Epic, we get the decided impression now and again that here too the woman in love takes the first step, as in general we may hold it to be the mark of Eastern narrative literature.[1] Thus in the Mahābhārata we meet with more than one of these aggressive young women, spiritually akin to the already introduced Devayānī.

When a maiden, threatened by a ravisher, weeping aloud, calls out she wants a husband (iii, 223, 6 ff.), that can be understood. On the other hand, iii, 224.30 ff. does not agree so well with the ordinary rules of womanly reserve ; here we find a reversal, as it were, of the tale of Amphitryon, which is met with in so many variations.

Yājñāv., iii, 231 ; Manu, xi, 58 (milder, 62 ff. ; in 58 perhaps kumārishv antyajāsu to be taken together). The Mahānirvāṇatantra also agrees with this, and says that the sinner must have his member cut off. Agnipurāṇa, 173, strophe 50b–51, lays it down that such a sinner must leave life behind him ; it is on the same level with incest. And so on with other examples. That girls should come to be mothers is a thing that can only happen in the age of Kali. Nārada, i, 31. And the deflowering of maids is one of the horrors that spread around under a bad king. MBh., xii, 90.39.

[1] Manu, viii, 365, lays it down, too, expressly : A maiden that enjoys (bhajantī) a man of high caste goes unpunished : but if she has a love affair (sevamānā) with one of lower caste (jaghanya), she is to be shut up in her house (till she comes to her senses).

The seven Rishis by the might of their spell called down Agni from the sun to their sacrifice, that he might take it to the gods. He saw there the wives of the holy men, all seven like wondrous stars to behold. He fell hotly in love with them, but reproached himself for his own foolish passion, for these faithful, pure women would, indeed, not give him any hearing. So he went into the Gārhapatya, one of the three holy fires, and from there let his eyes have their fill of the beloved ones. Burnt up in the glow of his passion, he resolved, however, in the end to die, and went into the forest. Now Svāhā, the daughter of the god Daksha, and in love with him, had already sought for an opportunity (chidra) to be with him. As he was thus so unhappily in love, she had now an opening offered her : " I who am tortured by love will take on the form of the seven wives of the Rishis, and give my love to the fire god who is blinded by their loveliness. Thus will he get joy, and I shall have my wish fulfilled." She took, therefore, first the shape of Çivā, the wife of Angiras, came to Agni and spoke : " Agni, love me, who am scorched with love. If thou dost not do this, then know that I shall die. I am Çivā, the wife of Angiras, and am come, sent by the others after we have come to a resolve." Agni spoke : " How knowest thou that I am tortured with love, and how do the others know it, all the beloved wives of the Rishis of whom thou hast spoken ? " Çivā spoke : " We have always loved thee, but were afraid of thee. Now that we have come to know thy thoughts from thy gestures, I have been sent to thee and have come hither to lie with thee. Carry out the wish speedily that stands before its fulfilment. The women are waiting for me ; I must be away, O devourer of sacrifices." Thereupon Agni, filled with the joy of love, lay with this Çivā, and the goddess, joined with him in love, caught up the seed with her hand. Thought she : " Whoever sees me here in this shape in the forest will make a false accusation against the Brahmans' wives because of the fire god. Therefore I will prevent that, and change myself into a Garudī.[1] Thus I can leave the forest at my ease." Thereupon she

[1] Garuḍa, mythological huge bird (roc, simurg, griffin, etc. ; cp. Chauvin, vii, 10–14 ; 175) ; also called Suparṇa.

became a Suparṇī, and came out of the great foreſt. She saw the mountain Çveta, which is covered with a cane-thicket, and is watched over by wonderful seven-headed snakes with a poisonous glance, by Rākshasas and Piçācas, and by dread bands of ghoſts, and filled with women Rākshasas, and many foreſt beaſts and birds. Thither hurried the fair one, onto the mountain-top, hardly to be climbed, and threw the seed into a golden vessel (or, a golden fire-pit). Thus she took on, one after the other, the shape of six of the women beloved by Agni, and made love with him. But she could not take on herself [1] the shape of the seventh, of Arundhatī, because of the penitential might and obedience to her husband of this ideal wife. Each time she added the seed to what was already there, and from it there then arose in consequence a six-headed being, the war god Skanda.

A tale, now, which is in many ways remarkable is that of Gaṅgā and her son : Bhīshma's birth, which is told in i, 96 ff. It belongs to the very numerous set of tales of a supernatural being from whom the favoured man or woman muſt not ask or seek to find out ; and the beſt-known of this set of tales is perhaps, besides the Lohengrin saga, the tale of Amor and Psyche, which reaches back to Rigveda times as the myth of Purūravas and Urvaçī.

The king Mahābhisha has won heaven through his piety. One day he is in a gathering of the gods by Brahma. The wind blows up the garment of the river goddess Gaṅgā. The gods quickly caſt down their eyes. But Mahābhisha, without thinking, looks. Brahma takes this very ill of him, and utters the curse againſt him : " Thou wilt be born among the mortals, but then once again come into the world of heaven. This Gaṅgā, who did take thy senses, O fool, will do thee something not to thy liking in the world of men, and when the tide of thy displeasure thereat rises high, thou wilt be set free from thy curse." Now the eight Vasus have just sinned againſt the holy Vasishṭha : The wife of one of them had longed for Vasishṭha's well-known wonder-cow, because she wanted to make a woman-friend she had among mankind

[1] Cf. my translation of Dāmodaragupta's Kuṭṭanīmatam, p. 30, n. 4.

free of sickness and ever young through the milk of this divine beast. Egged on by her husband, the hen-pecked Dyaus, the eight all took a share in carrying off the wonder-cow. Vasishṭha uttered the curse on them all to be conceived in a womb, but changed the curse in such wise that they could be freed from it within a year, excepting only the actual sinner, who had to live long on the earth. Now they do not wish to be born of earthly women, and beg Gaṅgā to become their mother, and throw them directly after birth into the water, so that they may be speedily cleansed of their sin.

Gaṅgā consents, and appears before the king Pratīpa, who is given up to good works in Gaṅgādvāra, in sense-ensnaring loveliness ; she seats herself without more ado on his right thigh. He asked her what he could do for her, and she said : " I want thee ; do thou love me, who love thee. For to repulse women in love is a thing condemned by the good." Pratīpa spoke : " I approach in love no strange woman, nor one that is not of my caste." She made it clear to him that with her he could unite. But he said : " Now thou hast brought on thyself the loss of the boon thou art urging me to grant. And were I to do otherwise, the breaking of the law would bring down destruction on me. Thou hast clasped me by seating thyself on my right thigh. Know thou that this is the seat of children and daughters-in-law. For the left thigh is what the loving woman must make use of, and it thou hast avoided. Therefore will I not make love with thee. Be thou my daughter-in-law, fair-hipped one ; I choose thee for my son." The goddess consented, but made the condition : " Whatever I may do, thy son must never make protest." The king promised her this, and the childless man now together with his wife carried out ascetic practices to get a son. And he, the son, then came, and when he was grown up, Pratīpa gave the kingdom over to him, and went into the forest, having told him that a woman from heaven in love with him would come to him ; he was to live in love with her, but must not ask after her origin, nor ever make question, whatever she should do.

Now Çāntanu, the son, was, as the Old Indian kings so

48

often were, a mighty hunter. "So he would go alone along the strand of the Gaṅgā, the resort of the ghostly bands of the Siddhas and Cāraṇas. There one day he saw a splendid woman, shining with beauty like another Lakshmī, quite without blemish, with lovely teeth, divinely adorned, clad in a thin garment, alone, shining like a lotus-flower cup. When he saw her, the hair on his body bristled, and he marvelled at the perfection of her body. With his eyes the king seemed to drink her in, and yet his thirst was not stilled. And the fair one, too, when she saw the brightly shining king walking there, could not get her fill of gazing at him, gripped by the spell of love. Then the king spoke to her, uttering friendly words to her in a soft voice : " Art thou a goddess or a Dānavī, a wife of the Gandharvas or an Apsaras, a Yaksha woman or a snake fairy, or a woman belonging to the human race, O thou with the lovely waist ? I beseech thee, that art as a child of the gods, become my wife, thou shining one." She consented, but added : "Whatever I may do, be it good or not good, thou must not hinder me, nor utter anything unkind to me. If thou so behave, then will I dwell with thee, O lord of the earth ; but if I am hindered, or anything unkind is uttered to me, then surely shall I leave thee." When he spoke yes unto her, and she had won this best of the lords of earth, she found incomparable joy. And when Çāntanu had won her, he took his joy of her, being obedient to her out of love ; " she must not be questioned," so he thought to himself, and spoke nothing to her. In her virtuous ways and the surpassing nobleness of her form, and her hidden services [1] the ruler of the earth found his joy. For of a heavenly form was this goddess Gaṅgā, the wanderer on the three paths, since she, the lovely-faced one, had taken on a glorious human body. And dutifully obedient to her husband lived the wife of Çāntanu, the lion king, granted his wish by fate, whose

[1] Upacāra, service with an erotic meaning is not seldom found in the MBh. (cp. the waiting-maid's expression : " I must first wait on a gentleman "). See, for instance, i, 98.7, 106.25 ; iii, 295.21 ; xii, 325.35. So, too, Çiçup., v, 27, and elsewhere. Possible, but perhaps less likely, is : In her virtuous ways, and the surprising nobleness of her form.

49

splendour was like that of the king of the gods. With her love-firing skill in the joyous union, and in tender love,[1] which held the senses fettered by amorous wiles and dances, she so delighted the king that he found the utmost delight. So wrapped was the king in the pleasures of love, and so carried away was he by the surpassing gifts of the glorious woman, that he did not mark how many years, seasons, and months were going by. The prince of men, thus partaking with her of the joys of love to his heart's content, begat with her eight god-like sons. And each son she threw after birth into the water, sank him in the Gaṅgā stream, as she spoke : " I give thee joy." Now this the king Çāntanu did not like, but the lord of the earth said nothing to her, for he was afraid lest she should forsake him. Then when the eighth son was born, the king, tortured with sorrow and wishing to save his son, said to her, while she laughed a little : " Do not kill him ! Who art thou and whose daughter ? Why dost thou wrong thy sons ? Thou child-murderess, thou hast laid on thyself a very great and heavily-reprobated sin." The woman spoke : " Thou yearner after offspring, I am not killing thy sons, thou best of them granted sons. But my stay with thee is at an end according to the covenant we made.[2] I am Gaṅgā, Jahnu's daughter, who am served by the bands of the great Ṛishis, and I have dwelt with thee that a thing may be brought about which must be carried through by gods."

She now tells him how it all came about that only he could have been the father of the Vasus, and only she their mother, reveals to him that through this begetting he has won the everlasting world of heaven, and entrusts him with the only son left him. As to this son she tells him of the words of the Muni Vasishtha, that he will be filled with virtue, a knower of all the sciences, and, for love of his father, without any love for woman all his life long. Then she leaves the sorrowing king.[3]

[1] Or : through joyous union, love, and charm.
[2] Or : condition laid down.
[3] Cp. Chauvin, vi, 181–82, and all the cycle, huge beyond words, of the swan maiden tales, whose voluminous literature would take us too far to point out here.

THE MAID

It need not astonish us then, if a young widow, who is moreover a snake fairy, sets about it very earnestly when she is smitten by love's fire. Arjuna has taken on himself a vow of chastity for twelve years, and wanders through various lands. Then he comes to Gaṅgādvāra, and there bathes in the holy stream. Just as he is about to come out he is seized hold of by Ulūpī, the daughter of Kauravya, the king of the snakes, and finds himself set in the magnificent palace of her father under the waters. Laughing, he asks her who she may be, and why she has done this violence. She tells him about herself, and goes on : " At once when I saw thee immersing thyself to bathe in the stream, O tiger among men, I was utterly beside myself with love. Grant me content now, who am devoured with passion for thee, and given up to thee only, by giving thyself to me, O blameless one." Arjuna spoke : " This twelve years' chastity has been laid on me by the king of the law (Yudhishthira) ; I am not my own lord. I would fain do thee the service of love, on the one hand, thou water-wanderer, but on the other, I have never yet uttered an untruth. How may it now be that I shall not be guilty of any untruth, and yet this fortune shall come to thee ? And do thou so act, O snake fairy, that my virtue may not be hurt." Ulūpī said she knew full well that he was pledged to strictest chastity, and why, but then puts it to him : " The distressed must be saved, O great-eyed one. If thou rescuest me, then thy virtue will not be harmed. And if, indeed, in this there be any slight overstepping of duty, yet thou wilt win virtuous merit by giving me life, O Arjuna. Love me, who love, O son of Pṛithā ; of this the good approve. If thou doest not so, then be assured that I shall die ; carry out the greatest of all duties by granting me life.[1] I have come now to thee

[1] Into such straits of conscience the man is very often driven, indeed, by women in love in Indian and other Eastern tales, or those derived from the East ; while in the West it is mostly the man in love who thus presses his lady. The Minnesingers' poetry of the Middle Ages has, indeed, given very strong expression to this reality of love's catechism (see the first part of my book, *Isoldes Gottesurteil*, Berlin, 1914, *passim*). For Arthur Schnitzler, however, the artist of that highly unpleasing world from which is wafted to our nostrils a breath of

for shelter, O best among men. For thou dost ever shelter the needy and shelterless, O son of Kunti. I come to thee for shelter, and lift my voice high in my pain. I am beseeching thee, filled with longing love. Therefore grant me the favour. Thou must fulfil the wish of me, who am in love, by giving thyself to me." Thus addressed by the daughter of the prince of the snake spirits, Kunti's son did all as she said, seeing a reason in virtuous duty. When the loftiness-filled one had spent this night in the palace of the snake-spirit, he rose at sunrise, and came back with her to Gangadvara. Ulupi, the good one, left him, and went into her palace, having given him as a favour the gift of never being overcome anywhere in the water : " All water-spirits will be at thy call ; of that is no doubt " (i, 214).

The teller here speaks minstrelwise of a wonderful deed of one who is praised (adbhuta karman). But what is told us later (vi, 90.6 ff.) would seem to be far more wonderful. Here the fruit of this very remarkable heroic devotion to duty and virtue, a devotion concording, indeed, not only with Heracles's view in *Götter, Helden, und Wieland*, the fruit, a strapping son, presents itself to its father Arjuna. And when the scion has made known his descent, we read : " And the Pandava remembered it all just as it had happened " (çl. 14).

It must be said that the repulse of a fair one aflame with love is not always without its dangers, either elsewhere in the world or in Old India, as is shown both in other Indian works and in the Epic in various places, of which we shall speak later.

decadency and lewdness, often shamelessly frivolous and always-weighed down with world-weariness, for Arthur Schnitzler, it would seem, the following was reserved : In his drama, " Das weite Land," Hofreiter, filled with dread, forsakes, at least for a time, his own wife, because she for the sake of such a phantasy of the brain and unsubstantial shadow, as is a woman's virtue, has refused her lover, whom she also loves, his last wishes, and thereby brought about his death. This Hofreiter is the pattern of a Toda. Among this people of India, according to Rivers, he is looked on as immoral, and must atone heavily in the next world for his crime, who will not give up his wife to another man (Hartland, *Primitive Paternity*, ii, 160).

THE MAID

It is even very solemnly laid down for us in a saying (xiii, 23.75) :
" He that comes in the way of the business of Brahmans,
cows, and maidens, lands himself, of a truth, into hell." It
may be that a humorous smile plays round this expressed
opinion ; while " hell " (niraya, naraka), too, in the Epic
not seldom means, as among ourselves, a great sorrow, a great
mishap, distress, ruin, even wickedness, baseness, vice.[1]

[1] See, for instance, i, 141.37 ; ii, 77.4 ; iii, 96.17 ; 157.23 ;
179.24 ; iv, 19.12 f. ; 18.25 ; v, 25.7 ; 29.45 ; vii, 196.52 ; ix,
59.30 ; xii, 3.17, 18, 21 ; Rām., ii, 36.27.

II

MARRIAGE

MEN in love have always been free and open in laying down rules for maidens, moſtly, of course, only for their own special case, juſt as the sun god did for Kuntī. But we may hold the view which prevails throughout the Epic to be the usual Indian one : The daughter shall live in complete chaſtity and implicit obedience towards her father, mother, and other kinsfolk, and await from them her husband. Mythic examples are, of course, always to be made use of with care, juſt as are, indeed, the manners, cuſtoms, and so forth in the legends handed down from the dim paſt. We have very often to do here not with " survivals " from earlier times, but juſt with freely drawn figures from the eager popular fantasy, impatient of any bars, or even from a brooding meditation.

On the other hand, the father then has the express and holy duty to find a husband for his daughter. Marriage is not only necessary, but it is also the sacramental birth anew of the woman : as the man of the higher caſtes is born a second time by being given the holy cord, so is she through being taken by the hand (Rām., v, 19.10, cp. Manu, ii, 67, and the note in Burnell's translation).[1] In Mahābh., xiii, 24.9, we find : " He that doth not give his own grown-up fair daughter to a worthy wooer, let him be held for a Brahman-murderer." [2]

---

[1] The unmarried woman is asaṃskṛitā kanyā (ix, 52.12), and saṃskṛitā = the wedded woman, e.g. Yājñavalkya, i, 67 ; Vishṇu, xxii, 33 ; asaṃskṛitā the unwedded maiden Vishṇu, xxiv, 41. See, too, Jolly, " Rechtl. Stellung d. Frauen bei d. alten Indern," *Sitzungsber. d. Münchener Akad.*, 1876, p. 427.

[2] Cp. iii, 293.35 f. No less ſtrongly do the law writings ſtress this duty. Each time a (ripe) unwedded maiden has her courses, her parents or guardians are guilty of the heinous crime of slaying the embryo. Vasishṭha, xvii, 71 ; Baudhāyana, iv, 1.12 f. ; Nārada, xii, 25–27 ; Yājñav., i, 64. Cp. Parāçara, vii, 6. Vasishṭha adds the

The kinds of wedlock or marriage are according to the Mahābh. eight all told : the firſt four or the specifically Brahmanic, under which the father hands over his daughter to the bridegroom [1] free and without any price, although in the Ṛishi form it is for two head of cattle, looked on as arhaṇa (honour shown, gift of honour) only ; then there is ᴛhe purchase or demon marriage, the love or Gandharva marriage, the marriage by capture (rākshasa vivāha) and the marriage by ſtealing, as we may perhaps call it, whereby the man gets the woman by some cunning (paiçāca vivāha).[2] These regular methods are found in i, 73.8 ff., and there the marriage by capture, but not marriage by purchase nor the Paiçāca marriage, is allowed to the warrior ; but on the other hand the Vaiçya and the Çūdra may marry by purchase. So, too, the eight kinds are seen in the passage in i, 102, shortly to be dealt with. Many observations, however, are noteworthy enough to be

further condition: "if the girl has wooers," but Baudh. says: even if she has none ; the latter, indeed, like Vasishṭha, xvii, 67, is inclined to grant a three years' grace, but then adds, like Manu's teaching, the threat juſt given. Parāçara, vii, 5, says : If a girl has reached her twelfth year, and has not been given away, then her forefathers in the other world are for ever drinking the blood she sheds every month. He has also the well-known verse wherein a girl of ten years becomes a maid (kaṇyā), and with this a physiologically perfeᴄt woman (vii, 4 ; cp. Jolly's note in SBE [= Sacred Books of the Eaſt], xxxiii, p. 170). Vishṇu, xxiv, 41, lays down : If a maid in her father's house sees her monthly courses without having been dedicated (that is, married), she is to be looked on as a Vrishalī (more or less = Pariah) ; he that takes her for himself without more ado lays no guilt on himself. Cp. Manu, ix, 93. She has thereby loſt the right to marriage, and woe to him that yet takes her. Parāçara, vii, 7. Cp. Vasishṭha, xvii, 69–71 ; my transl. of Kauṭilya, 356.6 ff.

[1] Great is the reward, too, in the other world, for such pious liberality. Cp., for inſtance, MBh., iii, 186.15 ; xiii, 57.25,32. According to Nārada, xii, 41, in the Ṛishi method the father besides the two head of cattle (gomithuna) also gets a garment (vaſtra), anyhow for the bride.

[2] This is, as is well known, the orthodox liſt. Cp. transl. Kauṭilya, 242.20 ff. Āpastamba, ii, 5, 11, 17 ff., and Vasishṭha, i, 28 ff. have, however, only six forms, Prājāpatya or Kāya, and Paiçāca being left ouᴛ.

profitably quoted. So xiii, 44 : Yudhishṭhira spoke : " The root of all duties and virtues, of offspring and family, of the serving of the dead, of gods, and of guests—tell me what it is, O grandfather. For of all ordinances, O lord of the earth, this is held to be the most worthy of mark : To whom should the daughter be given ? " Bhīshma spoke : " The good must give the daughter to a wooer gifted with excellencies, having informed themselves of his character and way of life, his knowledge, his origin, and his business. That is the Brahma form of good Brahmans. Let him that gives her away of his free will [1] win thus as son-in-law a man fitted to wed his daughter. This is the unswerving duty of the learned (that is, of the Brahmans) and of warriors. If a man without regard to his own wish (the father's, etc.) shall have to give the maiden to him whom she loves and who loves her, then the Veda-learned call this the Gandharva kind.[2] If a man buys the maiden for goods in one of the many ways and means, enticing her kinsfolk, then the wise call that the demon form. If a man by force robs the weeping girl from her home, slaying,

---

[1] Āvāhya goes along with āvāha. According to Böhtlingk and Monier-Williams, this word is not found in the meaning of marriage. But it is so found in xiii, 63.33 (wrongly understood by B.) ; and Karṇa says in v, 141, 14 ; āvāhaç ca vivāhaç ca saha sūtair mayā kṛitaḥ. It is the bringing hither, the marrying hither or acquisitive marriage (of the child-in-law), opposed to the marrying away or giving in marriage (of one's own child). Anukūlataḥ might also mean : in fitting wise. The passage is a hard one. I have translated in agreement with the rest of the standpoint of the Smṛiti. By far the smoothest arrangement would be to refer the relative clause to āvāhyam. Then : " With one that in fitting wise (or : of free bent) may give a gift of honour." According to the scholiast, it is true, whom I cannot follow in this, what is referred to is the buying of a bridegroom, and the prājāpatya vivāha is here meant. But elsewhere he is otherwise described.

[2] Here probably " give " = afterwards consent. Bearing in mind çloka 36, one is tempted, indeed, to translate : " Without regard to his own wish, a man shall give his daughter to him who loves her, and whom she loves. This is called the Gandharva form by those learned in the Veda." The wording also would be most naturally so translated, but there are other objections.

and cutting off the heads of the weeping (kindred), that is known as the Rākshasa form. Of five now three are lawful, and two unlawful : the Paiçāca and the demon custom must never be practised. The Brahmanic form, the warrior form, and the Gandharva form are lawful : either separately or mingled they are to be followed, of that is no doubt.[1] Three kinds of wives are for the Brahman, two for the warrior, the Vaiçya shall only wed in his own caste. The children of these (wives from different castes) are on an equality with one another (all take the father's caste). Let the Brahmanic wife be the first (of a Brahman), the Kshattriyā of a Kshattriya. For pleasure a Çūdrā is also allowed. But other people say no. The begetting of offspring with a Çūdrā wife is not a thing praised by the good. But if a Brahman begets with a Çūdrā wife, then he must atone for it.[2] Let the man of

[1] Here we have, in çloka 3–5a, the bestowal form (brāhma), which includes in itself all the first four of the orthodox scheme, which are essentially quite the same as it ; in çl. 5b–6 the Gandharva form ; in çl. 7 the Āsura form (purchase marriage) ; in çl. 8 the Rākshasa form (capture marriage). The Paiçāca form is not described. In çl. 10 kshāttra = rākshasa. The account given by Hopkins, JAOS, xiii, p. 359, I hold to be wrong. Feer, *Le mariage par achat dans l'Inde āryenne*, I do not know. Moreover, Hopkins himself (p. 36) takes rākshasa = kshāttra. And Jolly's remark in *Recht und Sitte*, p. 49, that in our passage the expression is used " in another way " seems to rest on a misunderstanding.

[2] While, for example, Manu, iii, 13 ff., holds that for this crime there is no atonement. According to Mārk.-Pur. (Mārkandeyapurāna), cxiii, 30 ff., the man must first take a wife from his own caste, then there is no objection to his marrying one from a lower caste ; if he brings home first one of a lower caste, then he sinks down into this ; and Agnipurāna, cl, 10–11, states that the children of mixed marriages take in general the mother's caste. There are no restrictions, in what the Vishnu, xvi, 2, lays down, as to the offspring of wives of a lower caste. The law books, indeed, do not speak well of the man's marrying below him. But Manu, ii, 238, allows the pious man an otherwise excellent wife from a lowly house (dushkulā). Vasishtha, xiii, 51–3, gives more particular information. The male offspring of the casteless man is casteless, but not the female offspring. The woman, indeed, when she weds goes out of her father's family into the husband's (this is confirmed by the other law books). A man, therefore, may marry

57

thirty years wed a ten-year-old wife, a nagnikā (one that has not yet menſtruated), or let the man of twenty-one get one seven years old. A man shall never take for himself a woman that has no brother or no father, for she is under the duty whereby her sons muſt be held to be the sons of her father. Three years shall a maiden wait after the firſt coming of her menses, but when the fourth has come, let her get a husband herself.[1] She will then never have loſt offspring and the pleasures of love. But if she do otherwise, then she offends againſt Prajāpati. One that on the mother's side is not akin through the offering to the dead, and not on the father's side through having the same clan (gotra)—such a wife let a man seek ; this is the law Manu proclaimed.

Yudhishthira spoke : " If one man has given the price, and another has said : ' I will give it ,' a third demands her with violence, a fourth shows money, and a fifth has taken hold of her hand, whose wife is she then, O grandfather ? Be thou for us, who would know the truth, the eye." Bhīshma spoke : " Whatever be the deed of a human being, it is seen to serve him in life when it is furnished with holy sayings (mantra), when it is discussed with them. False words, however, are a crime leading to the loss of caſte. Even a wife, a husband,[2] a high prieſt, a maſter, and the scholar's teacher are deserving of punishment, if they utter an untruth."

' No,' other people say. But Manu does not praise a living together with reluctance. What is untrue is without glory and rightness, a harm done to virtue.[3] In no man is only perverse-such a girl, but without a dowry. Cp. Yājñav., iii, 261. See further Jolly, *Recht und Sitte*, p. 61 f.

[1] So, too, Manu, ix, 90 ff. ; Vasishṭha, xvii, 67 f. ; Baudhāyana, iv, 1.14. Others, however, give only three menſtruations as the period. So Gautama, xviii, 20 ; Vishṇu, xxiv, 40. The laſt-named precept is perhaps of later date. Cp. Nārada, xii, 24 ; Yājñav., i, 64.

[2] Or perhaps rather : Even the lord of the wife.

[3] Dharmakopana, cp. Pāli (e.g. Milindapañho, p. 266, bhūtagāma-vikopana ; my Daçak., p. 90, line 4 of the text from the bottom) ; and vidhikopana, v, 29.29 ; prakopayati dharmam, xii, 64.3, here seems = entangle, diſtort ; rājye ſthitim akopayan, xii, 132.5 ; vidhiprakopa, v, 29.29 ; rańgaprakopa (infringement of the laws holding for the ſtage), i, 135.4. Cp. also xii, 135.4.

ness to be found.[1] How should it come to be there, whether
the kinsfolk give the daughter free according to the law, or
whether she is bought?[2] When the kinsfolk have given
their consent, holy words and sacrifices may be used, then these
words have an effect ; but none whatever in the case of a girl
who is not (anyhow afterwards) given. Yet the mutual contract
concluded with holy words by the wife and the husband is
declared to be weightier than that concluded by kinsfolk.[3]
The husband, according to the law's teaching,[4] acquires the
wife given by the gods. So he [5] brings to nought the words of

[1] Nothing is altogether good, and nothing altogether bad, is the
teaching of Jāt., No. 126 ; MBh., xii, 15.50.

[2] The meaning of the whole oracularly dark statement seems to
be somewhat as follows : In marriage all should be agreed on with
openness and friendliness. But just as no one thing in itself represents
the absolutely right, so, too, none of the various kinds of marriage is
utterly to be rejected. Bhīshma probably has in his mind the marriage
by capture, which as a warrior and famous maiden-robber, he commended ; and as he moreover altogether disapproved of purchase
marriage, not to speak at all of marriage by stealing or fraud (paiçāca),
so in the end the better translation is : " In the one (that is, capture
marriage) there is no absolute wrongdoing. How, then, does it rightly
arise (why does one accept it), even when a man robs a woman whom,
however, her kinsfolk offer, and who is bought ? " Perhaps tadaikena
is to be read instead of tadā kena : " There is absolutely no wrong-
doing to be found in this one thing : when the kinsfolk give her away
free according to the law ; through one thing (the other) it (the wrong-
doing) then arises : when she is bought." But then the way of expression
would be a somewhat twisted one. Or lastly yāṃ prayacchanti might
refer to what follows. But then Bhīshma would hardly be answering
Yudhishthira's question. As to the question what is to be done when
a man has taken a girl for himself without her kinsfolk's consent, as in
capture marriage (and Gandharva marriage), we seem to be given an
answer in what follows.

[3] That is to say, the important persons are man and wife ; and what
they agree together under holy forms stands good ; whereby, therefore,
capture and Gandharva marriage are shown as founded on law even
without taking the kinsfolk into account. Cp. Bühler's note to Manu,
iii, 32, in his translation.

[4] Or : at the behest of the law (of the god of justice) ?

[5] Probably the husband, simply by acquiring and holding the woman.

gods and men as untrue." Yudhishṭhira spoke : " If the maiden has already acquired (brought in) the purchase price, and a better wooer now comes, in whom virtue, love, and advantage are found in full strength, can we in that case speak of falsehood ? [1] Here, where from both sides there is the threat of error, he that has to act yet would fain do what is best. . . ." Bhīshma spoke : " The father in no wise accepted it with the thought : ' The price is what decides.' For the good never give their daughter because they are thinking of the price, but, it is from a wooer endowed with other advantages that the kinsfolk demand the price when a man gives her away of his own free choice, decking her out and saying : ' Take her home.' [2] And when he thus gives her away, it is no purchase price, no sale. If he has accepted it, he must then give it (to his daughter), that is a law never to be broken. If a man has earlier thus spoken : ' I will give thee my daughter,' then those are no words (that does not hold) ; if anyone has said this, or if he has said : ' No,' or : ' Of a truth ' (none of that holds). Therefore they woo one another (they woo on both sides) up to the taking by the hand. The wooer of the maiden is bestowed by the Maruts, so we have heard. To none that is not according to her wishes shall a daughter be given. That is demanded by the Ṛishis. That is the root of offspring, which has its root in love. This is what I hold.[3] Pondering

[1] Or : " is a falsehood in that case something blameworthy," the fact, that is, of giving the girl to the second ? Less likely : " Need one in that case be telling a lie," that is, be disowning the earlier agreement ? Perhaps the translation is to be taken according to Nārada, xii, 30 : " Shall a man then declare (the agreement) as invalid (anṛita) or not ? " Is vācyam to be changed to vākyam ?

[2] Hardly perhaps : " saying : ' Take her home, after having decked her out ' " ; where, therefore, the purchase price would consist of ornaments for the bride, or money for these.

[3] In Divyāvadāna, ed. Cowell and Neil, p. 1, we find that three things must combine together that there may be children : mātā-pitarau raktau saṃnipatitau (the loving begetters) ; 2. mātā kalyā ; 3. ṛitumatī gandharvapratyupasthitā. Cp. Windisch, *Buddhas Geburt*, etc., 17 f. ; L. v. Schroeder, *Wurzeln d. Sage vom heil. Gral*, 84 f. On the view that in marriage one must only follow the urge of the heart see my note Daṇḍin's Daçakumāracaritam, p. 301 f., and with it

now, know that in this twofold business [1] there lie many mistakes, for here it is that we have to do with living together. Hear how the purchase price never decided the matter. I brought away two maidens for Vicitravīrya, having therein overcome all the Magadhas, Kāçis and Koçalas. Of one the hand had already been taken, the other had had the purchase price. ' The girl that has been taken (already by the hand) must be at once sent away,' said my father. ' Bring the other girl here.' So spoke the Kuru scion. I asked many others, since I doubted my father's word ; for my father's thirst for virtue and right seemed to me mightily exaggerated.[2] Thereupon, O king, I kept on speaking these words, for I was striving after the right way : ' I would fain come to know the right way to the truth.' When now I had uttered these words, my father Bālhīka spoke as follows : ' If ye believe that it is the purchase price that decides, and not the taking by the hand, tradition (smṛiti) declares : ' He that has received the purchase price, may take steps for another wedding.' [3] For the law-learned do not state that according to tradition a guiding thread is given by the words (the agreement in marriage affairs by word of mouth). Toward those who derive the decision from the price and not from the taking by the hand, the well-known expression, too, which speaks of *giving* the daughter, does not inspire any trust (that is, it makes them out to be wrong).[4] Those who see in the purchase price a sale are not law-learned

Uttararāmacar., v, 17; vi, 12 = Mālatīmādhavam, i, 27; Kirātārj., xiii, 6 (cp. ix, 8) ; my *Hindu Tales*, p. 81, n. 2 ; p. 184, n. 1 ; Jātaka, Nos. 68, 237; vol. v, p. 288, ll. 18 ff.; MBh., xii, 194.27; Divyāvadāna, ed. Cowell and Neil, p. 654 ; Sister Nivedita, *The Web of Indian Life*, p. 187 ; Chavannes, *Actes du XIV. Congrès intern. des orientalistes*, 1905 (vol. 14), *Cinqu. sect.*, p. 140 ; Samayamātṛikā, viii, 23 ; Winternitz, WZKM, xxviii, 20 ; etc.

[1] Pāṇayos, that is, buying and selling of the girl. The word is not found with this meaning in Böhtlingk.

[2] For Bhīshma thought indeed that he had an equal right to the girl that had been taken by the hand, since he had won her by capture and fighting.

[3] Lājāntaram upāsita. Bālhīka is the brother of Bhīshma's father. See e.g. also v, 149.14 ff.

[4] Probably less likely : it is not convincing to them.

men.[1] To such as these a man shall not give his daughter, nor shall anyone bring home such a woman ; for the wife muſt in no wise be bought or sold. Therewith is judgment, too, uttered on the greedy, the evil-minded, that buy and sell a woman as slave (concubine)." [2] On this matter folk asked Satyavant : " The payer of the purchase price for a girl, which latter has had the purchase price, has died, and suppose she had another man taking her hand ; we are then in doubt as to what is right. Decide thou this for us . . ." Satyavant spoke : " If so ye wish, then give her away. In this a man need harbour no hesitation. A man so does, even when (the payer of the purchase price) ſtill lives. If he is dead, then there is no doubt whatever. The maiden may in such a case unite herself to her brother-in-law, or once again, following his guidance only, praſtise mortification in her longing after the taking by the hand (after aſtual marriage). According to some they (the brothers-in-law) lie with her at once, according to others gradually (?). Those that speak thus on this matter know the decision in this present question. The same is true where, before the taking by the hand, an interval goes by, filled with all the happiness-bringing usages and with holy sayings.[3] A fraud, however, is a crime leading to the loss of the caſte. The deciding and culminating point in the holy words of the hand-taking is in the seventh ſtep (at the wedding ceremony). She is the wife of him to whom she is given with water.[4] Thus is (the daughter) to be given away, they declare on this matter ;

[1] Were it a real, legal sale, then it would unconditionally bind.

[2] K. has the less striking reading dāsīvat " like a slave ".

[3] Then, too, nothing definitive has happened. The smoother but rather lame rendering would be : " The time leading up to the taking by the hand is that in which all happiness-bringing usages and holy sayings are put in praſtice."

[4] When beſtowing an objeſt on anyone water is poured on his hands. See, e.g. MBh., iii, 193.36 ; K., iv, 78.37 ; Āpaſt., ii, 4, 9.8 ; Jātaka, ii, p. 371 ; Raghuv., v, 59 ; Vetālap. (ed. Vidyāsāgara), p. 114 (Kathās. Tar., 93) ; Kathās., 113, towards the end. The objeſt is given with the left hand, with the right the water is poured out (Aṅgutt.-Nik., iv, p. 210 ; Chavannes, *Cinq cents contes et apologues*, etc., iii, pp. 367, 383, 388). Hence he that gets the gift is called ārdrapāṇi or klinna-pāṇi.

they know the decision. A pleasing, obedient [1] wife, given away by her brother before the holy fire, her shall the twice-born one wed, walking round the holy fire." [2]

In the next chapter we read among other things : " I do not see that in the following case any ground is given through the law of the daughter's son : the son of daughters sold belongs to his father. But those born of the marriage by purchase are envious, given up to unrighteousness, takers of other men's

[1] Or after the Bomb. text : " equal in birth," which is also very good indeed. K. reads anuvaçām.

[2] The law literature shows very many correspondencies with the teaching here set forth. Yājñavalkya, i, 65, indeed, gives us likewise the well-known maxim : " Once only is the maid given away," but goes on to say that one, however, who has been already given away can be married away once again, if a better wooer than the earlier one comes ; and in Nārada, xii, 30, we find in almoſt literal agreement with MBh., xiii, 44.28 : Kanyāyāṃ dattaçulkāyāṃ jyāyāṃç ced vara āvrajet Dharmārthakāmasaṃyukto, vākyaṃ tatrānṛitaṃ bhavet, " If the price has been given for a maid and a better wooer comes, in whom virtue, advantage, and love are to be found, then in this case the words are to be invalid." And in 28–29 he says that the rule : " Once it is that the maid is given away " is applicable only in the case of the firſt five kinds of marriage, that is, of the Brahma, the Prajāpati, the Ṛishi, the Deva and the Gandharva marriages ; in the case of the other three all depends on the wooers' qualities. That means, then, for moſt cases a nullification of that holy maxim. If a maiden's bridegroom has died before the wedding has been carried out, then according to Manu, ix, 97 (cp. 69, 70) she is to be given to his brother ; according to Vasishṭha, xvii, 74, Baudhāyana, iv, 1.16, even when she has been solemnly given in marriage, she is to be again married. Vasishtha, xvii, 72, says the same. In Mahānirvāṇatantra, xi, 67, it comes as an order of Çiva to marry away such a maiden again. Nārada, xii, 24, lays it down : " If a wooer accepts a maid, and journeys thereupon into another land, then shall she let three menſtruations go by, and then choose another bridegroom." The basic rule, indeed, that is followed is : Woman is the field, man the giver of the seed. Only he that has the seed shall have the field, too (Nārada, xii, 19). But neither the dead, nor the absent man can sow. Cp. my Kauṭilya, 254.3 ff. ; addit. 254.3–17. But cp., for inſtance, Dubois-Beauchamp, *Hindu Manners and Cuſtoms*, 3rd edit., p. 40, on the later cuſtom, wholly opposed to this.

goods, filled with malice, of evil life. Here those with the knowledge of olden times bring up the following verses sung by Yama, they, the wise in the law, they, who are bound to the law books,[1] the bridges of virtue and rightfulness. He that seeks to earn money through selling his own son, or that for the sake of his life gives away his daughter for a price, such a blind one will feed on sweat, wine, and excrement in the dreadful hell called Kāla, the deepest of the seven." Some call the yoke of cattle in the Rishi form a purchase price ; that is quite a mistake. Whether it were small or big there would be a sale therewith. Even if some have had a custom, it is not thereby a law for ever. We can see in the world, indeed, the practices of others too : those that carnally enjoy a maiden who is forced, such doers of evil will lie in thick darkness.[2] Indeed,

[1] Or referring to " verses " : " which are set (written down) in the law books." With the following cp. Manu, iii, 51 ff.

[2] This, of course, does not refer to capture marriage, as the scholiast holds, but to rape. That things must not be done which even gods and holy men have on their reckoning is several times stressed, as elsewhere, in the MBh. So xii, 291.17–18, 294.7. In xii, 262, we are given a splendid exposition : The way of life of the good (of the well-known penitents, etc.) has quite confused the moral ideas ; this " way of life " (ācāra) and the books praising it are rubbish washed up together from everywhere ; a man who has some importance in the world is praised by conscienceless poets greedy for fame, and everything about him is set up as an example, and so on. [N.B.—A washed up chip of wood or whisp of straw of this kind, to use the language of our text, is to be seen, too, in çl. 24 and 25. They must be cast away here ; then we get a sensible and clear text. Çl. 24 is a doublet to çl. 30 ; çl. 25 must be put before 31.] A pretty list of the lewd doings of the gods and holy men is to be found in Daçakumāra-caritam, p. 209 of my translation. Moreover in their case such " devilish tricks " do not bring about any lessening of virtue (ib., pp. 209–10). For the holy man is still unspotted, even when he is in the service of lust and brandy. Mārk.-Pur., xvii, 17 ff. Cp. MBh., xii, 141.67. The poisons of the Saṃsāra are first and foremost wine and women, and can only be driven out by wine and women (that is, the devils by Beelzebub). See Mahānirvāṇatantra, transl. by Arthur Avalon, p. cxvi and chap. viii, 269. But with both passages cp. what follows, as also M. N. Dutt in the introd. to his translation, pp. xxi–xxviii. And this is also a mystical doctrine for the initiated, and has

another human being muſt not be sold, how much less so
one's own children ! From such a possession rooted in wrong
no good can come (or : nothing right can spring). They that
know the times of old bring forward this saying of Prācetasa
(according to Nīl. of Daksha) : If the kinsfolk of a maiden
take nothing for themselves, then it is no sale. This is an
"honouring" (a gift of honour arhaṇa) of a girl, and a thing that
shows very good will. And all of it without leaving anything
over muſt be given up to the girl. Women muſt be honoured
and adorned by father and brother, father-in-law and brother-
in-law, if they wish to have much happiness. True it is that,
if the wife is not pleased, then the husband, too, is not rejoiced
by her ; and if the husband has no joy, then no offspring grows."

In the 47th chapter it is firſt set forth : the Brahman may
take his wives only out of the three higher caſtes ; if from love,
greed, or baseness he weds a Çūdrā, then he muſt make atonement. In sharing an inheritance the son of his Brahmanic
wife firſt gets a tenth of the whole eſtate, that is to say, the moſt
valuable things, such as carts, bulls, etc. The reſt is split up
into ten shares. Of these the son of the Brahman woman gets
four, that of the Kshattriyā three, the son of the Vaiçyā two,
that of the Çūdrā wife one, although under the law nothing
whatever falls to him ; for while the Brahman's sons by the
wives from the three higher caſtes are Brahmans, he is not one.
He is given a little (alpam) or the tenth part because charity
is the higheſt virtue, but only if the father grants it to him.
Three thousand at the moſt is to be given to the wife as her
share in the eſtate, and of this property given her by the husband
she shall have the usufruct, which is meet and fitting. The
share in the inheritance given by the husband is for the usufruct

nothing to do with the sensuality of the many. We often find, too,
the assertion that the Brahman who knows the Veda, and perhaps
also praſtises this or that good work, is pure, even though he were
the moſt dreadful of sinners (e.g. Vasishṭha, xxvi, 19 ; xxvii, 1–9 ;
Manu, xi, 262). By deeds that are in any, even the slighteſt relation
with a particular god, above all Çiva and Vishṇu, even the moſt
shameless offender is wholly cleansed from any ſtain. But this is not
the place to go further into this. Cp. J. J. Meyer, *Isoldes Gottesurteil,*
notes 41 and 43.

of the wives, of this property of the husband nothing shall in any wise be taken from the wife. But whatever property has been given the Brahmanic wife by her father, that her daughter is to have, for she is as the son.[1] Yudhishthira wonders at the property being shared so unequally among the sons of the wives from the three higher castes, for they are yet all Brahmans. Bhīshma enlightens him : " Wife " is uttered in the world with one name only, but within the name thus uttered there is a very great distinction. If a man has first of all made three (not Brahmanic) women his wives, and then gets a Brahman woman, then she is the eldest, she is the honourable one, the head-wife. The bathing and adorning of the husband, the tooth-cleaning, and the anointing, the sacrifices to gods and forbears, and all else that is done in the house on works of the holy law, all this no other may ever care for, so long as *she* is there, but the Brahman woman must attend to it for the Brahman man. Food and drink, wreath, clothing, and ornaments must be handed to the husband by the Brahman woman, for she is the most important. The Kshattriyā shall stand altogether beneath her, the wise man goes on, as the Vaiçyā again under the Kshattriyā ; for the warrior caste, as being the royal one, has a very high and weighty position for the welfare of the world. If a Kshattriya man, although he is really allowed only two kinds of wives, has three, then the sons inherit thus : the son of the Kshattriyā woman gets four-eighths and the father's war booty, the Vaiçyā's

[1] The law literature on this point has already been pointed out. According to this the wife's property (strīdhana) is what was given her by her father, mother, brother, or other kindred, what she received before the wedding-fire, or in the wedding procession, or from her husband, whether out of love or as pain-money on his taking a second wife, or what she has received otherwise since marriage, and then her purchase price (çulka). This last came to be in Old India, as, for example, among the old Germans, a gift to the bride. See Nārada, xiii, 8 ; Vishṇu, xvii, 18 ff. ; Manu, ix, 194 f. ; Yājñavalkya, ii, 143 ff. ; Agnipurāṇa, pp. 742, 925, etc. Cp. espec. Meyer, *Über das Wesen d. altind. Rechtsschr.*, etc., 76–81 ; 186 ; Kauṭilya (transl.), 243.17–245.19 and addits.; Benoy Kumar Sarkar, *Polit. Instit. and Theories of the Hindus*, 28 ff. Worthy of note is Mahānirvāṇatantra, xii, 25, according to which, over and above this, all she has acquired herself is the wife's property (cp. xii, 111).

son three, the Çūdrā's son one, if the father so grants. Of the property of the Vaiçya man the Vaiçyā woman's son receives four-fifths, the Çūdrā woman's one, but again only if the father gives it him. As the Çūdra man can only take a Çūdrā, his sons naturally all inherit quite equally.[1]

This favouring of the higher castes is, of course, easy to understand; and just as easy to understand is it that in the Mahābhārata also, purchase marriage, not to speak at all of marriage by stealing, is treated with such contempt, although not only elsewhere in the world, but in India, too, it is an institution from olden times. The whole catechism of the ordinary Brahman had only the one word : " Give ! " and the Mahābhārata itself shows us in its Brahmanic parts one ever recurring variation on this one tone ; from the soft, wheedling words of the glib, sly rascal (which, however, are those least often heard) up to the shrill, crazy screaming of the dirt-begrimed, howling dervish, with fantastically matted shaggy hair, this all-conquering word of barefaced beggardom runs right through the mighty Epic. How then should the Brahmans not have seen the highest good, and what at least for them was the only dignified course, in those forms of marriage which imply a giving away of the

---

[1] The law books are usually less hard than the Epic against the Çūdrā woman's son. True, Manu, ix, 155, too, lays it down he is to have what the father finds good to give him ; but otherwise, so far as I can see, this restriction is not found. Gautama, xxviii, 39, allows the Çūdra son, even of an otherwise sonless Brahman, only the means of subsistence (vrittimūla); Vasishtha, xvii, 48–50, pays no heed to him at all, and so on. According to Baudhāyana, ii, 2, 3.10 (= ii, 2.10) and Yājñavalkya, ii, 125, of the Brahman's sons that of the Brahman woman inherits four-tenths, that of the Kshattriyā three-tenths, that of the Vaiçyā two-tenths, that of the Çūdrā one-tenth ; the sons of the Kshattriya man get three-sixths or two-sixths or one-sixth, those of the Vaiçya man two-thirds or one-third. So, too, Brihaspati, xxv, 27 ff. and Vishṇu, xviii, 1 ff. ; only Vishṇu says nothing whatever about the sons of the Vaiçya man. Baudhāyana and Manu, ix, 153 ff., deem only a Brahman's sons worthy of a detailed treatment. Brihaspati, xxv, 32, lays down that the Çūdrā woman's son can have one of the ten shares only where land is not in question. Cp. Bühler's note to Manu, ix, 153 ; Kauṭilya (transl.), 259.1–19 and addit. 259.27–28.

bride without, or essentially without, any price being paid ! [1]
The warrior, on the other hand, found his pride in quite another
direction. " Take ! " was his shibboleth—first of all : " Take
for thyself by main force ! Thou art the strong one and to the
strong belongs the earth." But then it gratifies the pride of the
mighty man if he can say to others : " There, take it ! " And
always we are hearing in the Mahābhārata : The Kshattriya
can only bestow, never can he let anything be bestowed on
him ; and often the contempt for the Brahman, ever begging
and accepting, finds expression. In the tale of Devayānī and
Çarmishthā we have already seen an example of this. The
warrior, therefore, praised marriage by capture, and with it
the Gandharva marriage, in which latter, likewise, leave was
asked of no one on earth, but the more or less reluctant maiden
was carried off as booty. Not only Krishṇa, the conscienceless
fellow, who rose to the lofty dignity of highest god from being

---

[1] Cp. MBh., iii, 186.15. Here, too, as is usual in the world, sheer
selfishness, therefore, is the tap-root of progress and of a loftier ethic.
But in saying this we would not deny that there was also a stream
to be found among the Brahmans, rising from nobler depths ; for it
is the strivings of this very priestly caste that India has to thank, in
spite of much that is so unpleasing, for an infinity of good and lovely
things in the domain not only of the intellectual but also of the ethical.
Priestly hands have done dreadful wrongs to the Epic poetry ; but on
the other hand, very many splendid treasures, for instance, of the Indian
mind in narrative literature have been smothered by the pious anointing
oil of the Buddhists and Jains, or at least distorted, and thus, at any
rate, preserved. Hertel in particular has pointed this out. On
the new and the loftier in the world of philosophy, religion, and ethics
the priestly class, however, has never and nowhere on earth looked
with friendly eyes ; and the purer ethic in particular has always at
first a hard fight with the religion in power, the upholder of the old
ways. It is full of meaning to find that the founder both of Buddhism
and of Jainism belonged to the warrior nobility. It would still be left,
then, to show how far the Indian priestly class in its ethical views, too,
followed its own impulse and not the pressure brought to bear on
it by other sections of the population, and probably by isolated Brahmans.
Indeed in the world it is always individuals at first that have risen as
reformers against their times, and it is quite likely that the insurgent
transformers came, too, from the priesthood.

an obscure new-comer, is set before us as a bold woman-snatcher (v, 48.74 ; 158.7 ff. ; cp. iii, 12.31, 115 f.),[1] and not only the Arjuna so wrongly praised to the skies by later revisers of the Kuru saga, but also the truly noble Bhīshma. Among his heroic deeds we often find the abduction of maidens (e.g. in vi, 13.6 ; xii, 46.13), and when he is dead, his mother Gangā sings his praises for this, too (xiii, 168.26, 27). Twice the Mahābhārata tells the tale of how he carried off the daughter of the king of Kāçi for his half-brother Vicitravīrya (i, 102 ; v, 173). In the first and very vivid passage we read : " When now Bhīshma, wisest of the wise, saw that his brother had reached manhood's years, he set his thoughts on finding him a wife. Then Bhīshma heard how the three daughters of the king of Kāçi (like the fairies of heaven they were) were all holding their choice of a husband. Thereupon this best of the chariot-fighters, the overcomer of his foes, the mighty one, with the approval of his mother drove with one chariot to Vārāṇasī. There Bhīshma, Çāntanu's son, now saw gathered together the kings that had come from all sides, and these maidens. But when the names of all the kings were called out, and the surpassingly glorious maidens saw the lonely, old Bhīshma, they all, as though gripped by an unrest, ran away from him, with the thought : ' He is an old man.' ' On what ground has the Bharata steer shamelessly come hither, old, with a surpassingly virtuous soul, wearing wrinkles and white hair ? What will he say, who stands there among the people a breaker of his vow ? For false is the renown on earth of Bhīshma as one thirsting after chastity.' So spoke the low-souled among the princes, and laughed. When now Bhīshma, the mighty one, heard the words of the Kshattriyas, he was fired with anger, himself he made these maidens' choice, and spoke with voice of thunder to the wardens of the earth, as he, Bhīshma, that strikes in all directions, lifted the maidens onto his chariot : ' The bestowal of daughters on valiant men, when these have themselves been summoned, has been handed

---

[1] In the twenty-sixth chap. of the 5th book of the Vishṇupur. and elsewhere the song is sung of how Kṛishṇa carried off Rukminī on the eve of her solemn wedding with Çiçupāla.

down in tradition by the wise. While they deck out their daughters to the best of their power, and even pay money besides, others offer them for a yoke of cattle. Others win consent for a fixed sum of money, and others again through force. Others approach men who are unaware of anything, and others wed on their own terms.[1] Others acquire a wife by following the Rishi way. Then, as the eighth kind, know ye that one chosen out by the poets.[2] The self choice by the maiden (svayaṃvara) again is praised and practised by the nobility. The carrying away by main force of the maiden, however, is declared by the law-learned to be the best thing.[3] These maidens here, ye herders of the earth, I mean to take away hence by force. Make ready with all your strength, whether now it is for victory or for defeat. Here stand I, ye herders of the earth, resolved to fight.' When he of the heroic soul, the Kuru scion had thus spoken to the wardens of the earth and the king of Kāçi, and had lifted all the maidens onto his chariot and taken leave of the gathering, he drove swiftly away with these maidens. Then sprang up in rage all those princes, feeling their arms and biting their lips. Great was the confusion among them, as in tearing haste they took off their ornaments, and girded on their armour. Like the meeting together of stars was this gathering of all the ornaments and the armour from every side,[4] owing to the ornaments being strewn about here and there with the armour.[5]

[1] Wishing to have the maiden in marriage (prārthitā)—in the Prājā-patya form. Cp. Agnipur., 154.10b; Vishṇu's law-book, xxiv, 22.

[2] The Gandharva marriage, anyhow, not, as the comm. has it, the Rākshasa form. It would be possible, of course, to find the Gandharva form already in anumānya, as K. indeed does. Then the meaning would be : " Know now that this is the eighth kind of taking home chosen by the wise." Kavi as a matter of fact in the MBh. quite usually means " the wise man, seer, master ".

[3] Or : " They declare the marriage by capture to be the oldest."

[4] The armour, too, was ornamented with gold and precious stones. When Yudhishṭhira's armour was shot to pieces with arrows in the fight by night, we read : " It fell down in tatters like a swarm of stars from the sky " (vii, 165.39 ; cp. viii, 49.42 f.).

[5] Can go with what follows ; then we should have a kind of loc. absol. : " While the ornaments . . . were being strewed about,

Their brows were drawn with anger and indignation, and their eyes reddened ; thus did these heroes climb into their chariots, made ready by their drivers, shining, harnessed to noble steeds, and now set out, brandishing their weapons, after the Kuru scion as he drove off. Then between them and him, between the one and the many, there was fought a raging, fear-bringing fight. . . . But when the best of all arm-bearers had overcome them in the fight, he went on his way, down to the Bhāratas, the Bhārata he. Bhīshma, Çāntanu's son, was attacked from behind by the Çālva king, the great chariot-fighter, he the man of unfathomed mind, as the warden of the herd, the strongest of the strong, who is after the female, thrusts another elephant in the back with his two tusks.[1] Yearning for the woman, the prince shouted to Bhīshma : " Stop ! Stop ! " he the Çālva king, the strong-armed, goaded by rage. Then this tiger among men, the tormentor of the foemen's armies, roused by his words, blazing up with anger like a smokeless fire, his stretched bow in hand and his forehead in furrows, faithfully followed the warrior custom and turned his chariot round to meet the Çālva, without fear or confusion, he the great chariot-fighter. When all these kings saw he had turned about, they came up as onlookers to the meeting between Bhīshma and the Çālva. The two men endowed with strength and valour rushed on one another like two strong bellowing bulls fighting for the cow. Then the Çālva king, the best of men, overwhelmed Bhīshma, Çāntanu's son, with quick flying arrows in hundreds of thousands. When now these princes saw Bhīshma at first brought into evil plight by Çālva they were astonished and shouted : " Bravo, bravo ! " . . . When now Bhīshma, Çāntanu's son, the taker of foemen's strongholds, heard the words of the Kshattriyas, wrathfully he said : " Stay, stay ! " And grimly he spoke to his charioteer : " Drive to where that

these heroes, whose brows . . . were drawn with anger, and whose eyes were reddened," etc. A like instrum. absol. is repeatedly found in the Epic. Cp. for example vii, 196.12 ; xii, 264.61–63 ; Rām., ii, 111.12.

[1] As we shall learn later, the Çālva king was the secret betrothed of the eldest of the princesses

king is ! I will kill him as the prince of birds kills a snake."
Warding off with arrows the arrows of the Çālva king, Bhīshma,
the Kuru scion, brought down his driver, Bhīshma the tiger
among the rulers of earth. With Indra's arrow magic he slew
his splendid horses. For the maiden's sake, Bhīshma, Çāntanu's
offspring, then let the best of men go off alive. Then Çālva
went to his city, and the prince thereafter ruled his empire with
justice. And the kings that were there to witness the svayaṃvara, they too went back again to their kingdoms, they the
takers of foemen's strongholds. When Bhīshma, the best of
strikers in the fray, had thus won the maidens, he went off to
Hāstinapura, where the king, the Kuru offspring, Vicitravīrya
the just, ruled this earth, like his father, the Kuru offspring
Çāntanu, the best among men. The son of Gaṅgā, in a short
time, went through forests and rivers, mountains and trees of
the most various kinds (the man of boundless valour in the
fray, having worked havoc among the foe, himself unscathed),
and he brought away the daughters of the king of Kāçi, he
the virtuous one, as though they were his daughters-in-law,
as though they were his younger sisters. As though with his
own daughters, the strong-armed one drove into the Kuru
land, and brought them thither, seeking to do his brother's
pleasure. These maidens endowed with every excellence, won
by a hero's prowess, the brother Bhīshma handed over to his
younger brother Vicitravīrya. He, learned in the law, having
thus carried out in harmony with the law a deed beyond human
powers, went on to marry away his brother Vicitravīrya."

In the second account (v, 173 ; cp. 176.44 ff.) given by
Bhīshma himself, he declares that it was because the maidens
were vīryaçulkā (whose price is heroic valour) that he robbed
them (çl. 14) ; and in it he is always calling out : " Bhīshma,
son of Çāntanu, is robbing the maidens." Duryodhana does the
same as Bhīshma. He drives in a gold-decked chariot together
with Karṇa and other heroes into the royal city of the Kaliṅgas,
where the princess is to hold her ceremonial choice of a husband,
and a great and splendid band of kings has come together.
Accompanied by her nurse and by eunuchs,[1] the young beauty

[1] These, of course, show that the tale in at least its present form
is of a late date. It is found, too, in the 12th Book.

walks across the platform, as the kings' names are told her, but passes by Duryodhana. This hurts his angry pride ; he falls on her, lifts her onto his chariot, and drives off with her. The other wooers follow, but in the hot fight they all have to yield before Karṇa's incomparable heroism and strength, and Duryodhana bears off his booty (xii, 4). Bhīshma's rape of the girls had evil results of which we shall hear later, and moreover kindled an undying enmity between him and the family of the abducted maidens. But usually the maidens' kindred put up with the deed. We even are told, indeed, of a famous case where from the very start the girl's brother lends his help.

Arjuna during his time of banishment and " chastity " comes to the Yādavas in Dvārakā, and there lives with Krishṇa in the most intimate friendship. The Vṛishṇis and Andhakas hold a festival in honour of the mountain Raivata, whereat men and women give themselves up to all kinds of frolic and mad enjoyment. Then we read in i, 219.13 ff. : " While this wonderful dazzling festival was being held, Krishṇa and Arjuna walked about together. Wandering round they saw there the glorious daughter of Vasudeva, the bedecked Subhadrā, amidst her girl friends. When Arjuna saw her, at once love woke within him. Krishṇa saw that his thoughts were of her only. The tiger among men spoke, laughing slightly : " Is the heart of the forest-dweller stirred by love ? An it please thee, that is my sister, sprung from the same womb as Sāraṇa, O son of Pṛithā, Subhadrā her name, my father's beloved daughter. If thou hast intentions, I will speak with my father." Arjuna said : " She is Vasudeva's daughter and Krishṇa's sister, and lit up by loveliness ; whom would she not, indeed, ensnare ! All my happiness would undoubtedly be fulfilled, if the Vṛishṇi maiden, this sister of thine, were my wife. But what means is there to get her ? Tell me of it, O Janārdana. Then I am ready to do anything, if it is possible for a man." Krishṇa spoke : " The Svayaṃvara is the way of marriage of the Kshattriyas, O bull among men, but it is bound up with doubt and danger because of the whimfulness of woman's nature. The carrying away by force is also held in honour by the Kshattriyas. Those wise in the laws know it as the marriage way of heroes. Do thou, O Arjuna, take my fair sister by force. For who knows what she will do at the Svayaṃvara ? " Now when Arjuna and Kṛishṇa had made up their minds how the thing was to be done, they sent messengers to let Yudhishṭhira, who was in Indrapraṣṭha, know of everything. And when the long-armed one had learnt, the son of Pāṇḍu allowed it. Being now authorized in the matter of this union, and with Kṛishṇa's leave, Arjuna, the Bharata bull, went forth according to Kṛishṇa's plan, when he knew the maiden to be on the mountain Raivataka. In a chariot whose parts were of gold, which was equipped in full order, harnessed to Çaibya and Sugrīva (horses of Kṛishṇa), wreathed with a multitude of little bells, and fitted with all kinds of weapons, which sounded, too, as the voice of the cloud, was like unto flaming fire, and destroyed the joy of foes—in this chariot the bull among men drove forth under pretext of hunting, armed, clad in armour, wearing his sword, with the leather protector for the left arm, and the bowman's finger-cap. Subhadrā was now coming back to Dvārakā, having offered worship to the mountain prince Raivataka and all the gods, and had the Brahmans to utter wishes for blessings, and having wandered to the right round the mountain. Arjuna rushed down on her, and lifted her into his chariot, he that was tortured by love's arrow thus did unto Subhadrā, lovely in every limb. Then the tiger among men drove with this brightly smiling one on the chariot built of gold to his city. But when the soldiery saw Subhadrā being carried off, they all ran shouting in the direction of the city of Dvāravatī. When they had all come to the assembly hall Sudharmā,[1] they told the warden of the hall of all this heroic deed of Arjuna. So soon as the warden of the hall had heard it from them, he beat the drum that calls to arms, the loud-sounding drum, mounted in gold. Aroused by this din, the Bhojas, Vṛishṇis, and Andhakas, leaving their food and drink, now came rushing up from every side.

A very stormy meeting is now held ; chariots, arms, and equipment are put into order ; Baladeva, the drunken elder

---

[1] Or perhaps better : When they had swiftly reached the assembly hall. Abhitas swift, quick is often found in the MBh., although the dictionaries give this meaning as unsupported (iii, 3.67 ; 175.16 ; 240.1 ; 266.7 ; 276.4 ; vii, 113.66 ; etc.).

brother of Kṛishṇa, in a fury curses the rascally Arjuna, who
thus repays their hospitality, firſt eating the food, and then
breaking the vessel, and threatens by himself alone to make
the earth Kaurava-less. But Kṛishṇa makes a speech " in the
service of virtue and profit " : " It is not contempt that Arjuna
has shown towards our family, there is no doubt as to that. He
holds you Sātvatas never to be greedy for gain ; and the son
of Pāṇḍu believes that one should not venture on the Svayaṃvara. Who would care, too, like a brute to approve the giving
away of a daughter ! [1] And the sale, too, of a child—what
human being on earth would choose to carry it out ! These
miſtakes have been seen by Kuntī's son, thát is what I hold.
That is why the son of Pāṇḍu has carried away the maiden
according to law and wont. On the one hand the union is a
fitting one, on the other this so excelling son of Pṛithā has
aſtually accomplished the rape of the glorious Subhadrā. Who
would not choose, indeed, to have Arjuna, the son of Kuntibhoja's daughter, born in the line of Bharata and the famous
Çāntanu ! And I see none that could overcome the son of
Pṛithā by his might in battle but Çiva. . . . Haſten with the
moſt friendly words to Arjuna, and thus move him to come
back. This is my moſt true opinion. Were Pṛithā's son to
overcome you, and go back by force to his city, then your
renown would come to nought at one blow. But if there is
friendly appeasing, there is no talk of defeat." Thus is Arjuna
brought back and wedded to Subhadrā [2] (cp. also viii, 37.34).

[1] Or : " the giving away like a head of cattle," that is, her being
given away like a head of cattle.

[2] K. after çloka 25 of the Bomb. ed. (which here shows some
difference) has inserted almoſt 150 çlokas, showing a really crazy
diſtortion. On Kṛishṇa's advice Arjuna disguises himself as a Yati,
is honoured by Baladeva and his comrades as a holy man, brought
by Kṛishṇa into the apartments of his siſter Subhadrā, and given into
her care, the cunning fellow spinning a tale to her : " For in olden
times the Yati who were of the calling of begging monks dwelt in the
apartments of the Daçārhas' maidens. The maidens that were in the
harem gave them soft and hard foods, according to the time, and were
untiring in it." Arjuna's excellencies have already been praised before
Subhadrā by Kṛishṇa and others, and she has long quite fallen in love
with the hero through hearsay. Arjuna on his side sighs and groans

In vii, 10.33, 55 also, the carrying off of women is hailed as a great deed of two heroes in Yudhishṭhira's army (cp. çl. 60, and xii, 45.13). The dying Bhīshma praises in vi, 122.17 Karṇa's heroism, when carrying off maidens. When the angry Çiçupāla in ii, 41.22, 23 declares that it was an ill deed of Bhīshma to have carried off Ambā, who already loved another, that means little. Moreover he, the rightly thinking one, let her go again at once, when he came to know of her inclination. So the abduction of women is seen, too, in the comparison : " Suçarman took the king of the Matsyas as

like a true lover that has ever the object of his as yet unfulfilled last wishes before him. At length she grasps the fact that the Yati is Arjuna, and draws him into a jesting talk ; he discloses himself, and they avow their mutual love. From shame Subhadrā now falls quite ill, and after the manner of later literature the love-sickness of the maiden is described. The whole people with her father at their head go off to a thirty-four days' festival on an island. Arjuna makes use of the opportunity (which has been purposely brought about for him by Krishṇa and the kinsfolk), and asks of Subhadrā the Gandharva union. Of it he says that it is brought about from passion and the yearning for sons, and ensures an obedient and fruitful wife ; as opposed to the other four kinds of marriage this fifth one is entered upon by the two lovers without holy ceremony and without friends. Next night he would fain accomplish this marriage with her. But she only weeps. Then Arjuna at a loss calls up through his thoughts his father Indra, and the whole host of the heavenly and the holy ones (indeed even the Yadus come with Vasudeva at their head), and they wed him to the princess. Krishṇa comes, offers him his chariot, urges him to go to Khāṇḍavaprastha, and then discreetly vanishes away likewise to the island. Arjuna bids Subhadrā to have the chariot harnessed under pretext of a holy journey, and to bring it thither. She herself then serves him as a very skilful driver, and finds a great joy when an army opposes her beloved one, and of course is overcome by him. But the leader, who has been told of everything by Krishṇa, jumps from his chariot, embraces Arjuna, and the hero drives away with his blessing and good wishes. Then follows çloka 3, 1 and 2 of the 220th chapter of the Bomb. ed. being omitted : Rathena kāñcanāṅgena, together with 4 and 5 ; then a verse to the effect that Arjuna with an army and Subhadrā goes off in the direction of his city. Verse 9 of the Bomb. ed. comes next, and then the rest essentially the same as this text (i, 239 ff. in K.).

prisoner alive ; lifting him up by force onto his chariot, as the lover does a maid (yuvatī), he drove off with swift steeds " (iv, 33.8–9).[1] However, the carrying off of a bride is often rather an elopement (e.g. MBh., iii, 224.1–4).

But to carry off the wedded wife of a man, which not only often among savages and barbarians,[2] but, as is well known, also, for instance, among our Germanic forefathers, was looked on as a glorious deed, is a thing which is very strongly condemned ; and xii, 35.25 lays down an atonement for this

[1] It is true that marriage by capture is more than once represented as wrong, and according to Vasishṭha, xvii, 73, and Baudh., iv, 1.15, a girl that has been carried off, but not wedded to the accompaniment of the holy song texts, can be given away again as a virgin. But Vasishṭha, i, 34, brings forward this very form as that of the Kshattriyas (kshāttra), and Baudh., i, 11, 20.12 holds that it and purchase marriage correspond with the laws or customs of the warrior nobility ; so also Manu, iii, 24 and 26. Mārk.-Pur. states in cxxxiii, 27 ff. that it is still better for the warrior than the Gandharva marriage, and in cxxii ff. Prince Avīkshita carries off many princesses at their Svayaṃvara, because they do not choose him out ; his heroic mother praises him for it, when he has been taken prisoner in the fight thus brought about, and fires him on to go to war. And there are other such cases. It has often been stated that the very name Rākshasa marriage points to the Aryans having found this form, as also the Āsura or purchase marriage, already among the primitive population, and called it thus after them (e.g. J. Lippert, *Kulturgesch. d. Menschheit*, 1887, Bd. ii, p. 95 ; *Anthropos*, iv, pp. 7 ff., especially 10 ; vii, 102). It would be easy to see how, corresponding to these names, those may have been invented for the other kinds of marriage. But probably the Aryan settlers did not have to be introduced by the aborigines to such ways of marriage ; and I think the terminology arose rather from the " Brahmanic " kind, it being interpreted as " Brahma marriage ". Both marriage by capture and marriage by purchase are, indeed, Indo-Germanic. See e.g. Feist, *Indogermanen*, 305–308.

[2] Of the American Indians, for instance, we often are told that the stronger man simply takes his wife away from the weaker, just as the men do in the knightly age of Europe ; and among the pre-Islamic Arabs it was looked on as highly praiseworthy to take for oneself the wife of the beaten foe (see e.g. *Anthropos*, v, pp.983 ff.; Welhausen, *Götting. Nachr.* 1893, p. 435). To the conqueror, indeed, is the booty. See too 5 Moses, 21.10 ff.

crime. Even from the robber it is expected that he shall keep from stealing women, as also from intercourse with the wives of others (xii, 133.17) ; cp. what the pious robber in 135.13, 14 demands from his men.[1] In the list of Çiçupāla's sins it is also remarked that he has stolen a man's wife, also, however, that he has carried off a girl, though, indeed, not for marriage (ii, 45.10 f.).[2]

The Svayaṃvara, which has been spoken of in the tales we have just given, is one of the splendours of the Indian Epic, not only of older times, but also of later times, and is also often found in the prose tales. It is perhaps generally known from the song of Nala and Damayantī. It was assuredly never a universal custom, but was confined to daughters of Kshattriyas, especially royal princesses. Therefore, at least in the view of the warrior nobility, only this nobility had the right to such wooing.[3]

In Mahābh., i, 122, several kings desire Kuntī, her that is adorned with the highest womanly perfections. Her father holds a Svayaṃvara for her. When she sees the glorious Pāṇḍu among the kings, she is at once fired with love, shyly hangs the garland on his shoulder and the wedding is held

[1] In Anguttaranikāya, iv, p. 339, we read that among the eight qualities that kept a " great " thief or a professional robber on a bigger scale from a speedy fall, and made it possible for him to carry on for a long time, there was this one : " He does not kill a woman, he forces or deflowers no maid."

[2] Bṛihaspati, xxii, 18, enjoins that he who steals a married woman shall be burned on a red-hot gridiron with a straw fire.

[3] Hopkins holds that this splendid knightly Svayaṃvara of the Epic is not a survival from earlier times, but a later growth, and he is probably quite right. He distinguishes, then, two kinds : the older primitive self-choice, and the later splendid form (JAOS, xiii, 168, 169, 357, 360). The fairest Svayaṃvara in the Epic, Sāvitrī's, is on very simple lines, and only at it is the maiden quite free in choosing her husband. As we know, Sāvitrī drives in her chariot through the land and thus makes an inspection, a proceeding that by no means fits into the framework of the usual or court tales of the Svayaṃvara. In the house of King Māndhātar it is, at least according to his words, the custom for the daughters themselves to choose their husband in freedom. Wilson's Vishṇupurāṇa, iii, 270.

without further hindrance. The same thing exactly happens in Damayantī's case, although here there is some slight bantering by the gods.[1] But generally things do not go on so smoothly, a thing of which the literary Epic of later times has likewise made use. So Krishna overcomes the angry rivals, and triumphantly carries off the daughter of the king of the Gandhāras.

From more than one point of view the self-choice by Draupadī is interesting (i, 184 ff.). It belongs to that probably older variety where there is no question of the girl's making a choice, but the decision is reached through a trial of warrior skill.[2]

---

[1] Things would seem to go just as peacefully with Devikā, who chooses Yudhishṭhira, and with Vijayā, who chooses Sahadeva, while Bhīmasena gets Balaṃdharā as vīryaçulkā (i, 95.76 ff.). But here we have only a short account. This comparison is instructive : " As at a Svayaṃvara they (the warriors) rained blows on one another in the turmoil of the fight " (vi, 93.42). Cp. Mārkaṇḍeyapur., cxxii ff. ; cxxxiii, 8 ff.

[2] It is a fight or a contest that often gives the decision between rivals for a girl among primitive peoples (Westermarck, 159–163 ; McLennan, Primitive Marriage, 181). The winning of a bride through skill with the bow, which is often found in India, we find reported also of the American Indians (Finck, Primitive Love, pp. 57–58) as also the widespread bow that can only be stretched by the strongest man (Boas, Chinook Texts, p. 80). On the other hand in the Shahnameh the choosing of a husband by Katajun, who hands Gushtasp a rose-wreath, and so makes him her husband, reminds us strongly of the typical Indian scenes. So, too, for instance, the Buddhistic tale in Schiefner, Bull. d. Petersburger Ak., Bd. xxiii, col. 23 ff., is quite after this style of tale. There we find : " Thereupon the king made proclamation in various lands and cities that his daughter was going to hold a ceremony for choosing a husband, and had that city cleansed of rubbish, stones, and potsherds, sprinkled with sandal-water, and made fragrant with sweet perfumes, awnings, banners, and flags set up, many silken hangings hung with flowers of many kinds, like a grove of the gods, and the joyous proclamation made : ' Hear ye, O honourable city and country-dwellers, and the throngs of people come from various parts ! Forasmuch as the King's daughter is minded to-morrow herself to make her choice of a husband, do ye gather together as is meet and fitting.' Next morning the king's daughter, wearing many

Pāṇḍu's sons, who with their mother have escaped from the burning of the house of resin, and have to wander about the world unknown, go disguised as Brahmans, to witness Draupadī making her choice of a husband. On the way they meet with a great band of Brahmans, and are cheerfully hailed by them : " Come at once with us into the land of the Pañcālas, to Drupada's palace ; a great Svayaṃvara with vaſt pomp is going to be held there. We set out as one united band of travellers, and are going thither. For it will be a wondrous splendid, and very great feſtival there. The daughter of Yajñasena, of the great-souled Drupada, is she who came forth from the midſt of the sacrificial altar, she with the lotus-leaf eyes, worthy to be seen, with faultless limbs, very gentle and underſtanding, the siſter of Dhṛishṭadyumna, the foe of the Droṇas, and shining with power, who was born from the brightly glowing fire, armoured, sword-girt, with bow and arrow, long-armed, like unto fire. His siſter is she, the slender, faultlessly-limbed Draupadī, from whom is wafted a kroça away a scent like that of the blue lotus. We go to behold Yajñasena's daughter, awaiting with longing the Svayaṃvara, and to see this divine high feſtival. There will come thither kings and kings' sons, rich in sacrifices, beſtowing many gifts, zealous in the holy ſtudy, pure and noble-hearted and pious, young and handsome, journeying from various places, and great chariot-fighters and princes skilled in

kinds of ornaments, ringed round by many maidens, came into a grove decked with flowers by the god thereof, surpassing fair through the great gift of happiness, while in the middle of the city many thousand people had gathered together, (she came) into the gathering to choose herself a husband. Kshemaṅkara (the blind son of a king, going about as a beggar) also sat at another place, playing the lute. As men ſtand in reciprocal relation according to their deeds, and through the great power of the cause the power of the effeἀ is aimed at, so the king's daughter, when her mind was touched by the notes of the lute, clung faſt to Kshemaṅkara's lute as he played, and saying : ' This is my man,' she threw the flower wreath over him." The same tale is found in Chavannes, *Cinq cents contes et apologues*, ii, pp. 389 ff., see especially pp. 393 ff. Dozens of tales, indeed, especially Jain, at a later time describe such events. Cp. also Basset, *Contes et Légendes Arabes*, Revue des trad. popul., xiv, p. 118.

arms. These rulers of men will, that they may win the victory, give many presents there, treasures, cows, hard and soft food of every kind. All this we are going to receive, to see the Svayaṃvara, take our share in the festival, and then go off again whither we desire. Mummers, vaitālikas, sūtas, māgadhas,[1] dancers, and strong wrestlers will come there from all the quarters of the world. When ye high-souled ones have thus sated your curiosity,[2] looked on the festival, and received the gifts, then ye can come back again with us. And if Kṛishṇā (that is, Draupadī) sees you all standing there so handsome and with godlike stature, then she may by the working of chance choose one of you as bridegroom. This brother of thine is splendid, worthy to behold, strong-armed ; if he is

[1] All three are bards and singers of princes' praises. The vaitālika calls out the hours of the day, and recites blessings ; the māgadha is, according to the scholiast, a genealogist. In vi, 127.3, indeed, he remarks that the vaitālika is vaṃçāvalīkīrtaka. The most important is the sūta, chariot-driver to the prince, and likewise one that knows and gives a masterly rendering of old songs and traditions, especially of the great deeds of the ruler and his forefathers. It was from this caste, perhaps, that came the makers and carriers of that old song poetry, fragments of which have been strung together in the Epic, especially in the Mahābhārata, but alas ! not without having been often mutilated thereby and distorted. The modern bhāts (and chārans) or bards, among the Rājputs (and Marathas), about whom Devendra Das in his *Sketches of Hindoo Life*, pp. 179 ff., gives a very good account, are undoubtedly their very near kindred, if not their descendants. These bards enjoy among the Rājputs greater consideration than the Brahmans (Tod, *Rajasthan*, i, 30; 217 ; cp. ii, 127 below. D. N. Das, *Sketches of Hindoo Life*, 179). A bhāt was chief representative and army commander of Darjan Sal of Kotah (Tod, ii, 535). Their person is sacred (i, 742 ; ii, 182 ; 674 ff.). Mārkaṇḍeyapur., vi, 23 ff. shows the pride of the sūta, and that to kill him is looked on as Brahman murder. He occupies holy (standing in connection with the Veda ?) or Brahmanic rank (brāhmaṃ padam 30, brāhmaṃ sthānam 32) ; and these expressions would hardly be called " holy place ". Cp. further Crooke, *The North-Western Provinces*, 205, 224, and especially my Kauṭilya, index under sūtas. As to the power the bards held through their knowledge of songs see Tod, i, p. xi ; 672 ; ii, 697.

[2] Or perhaps : taken part in the festivities (kautūhalaṃ kṛitvā) ?

commissioned for the victory he will perhaps get much wealth thereby, and assuredly increase the measure of your joy." Yudhishthira spoke : "We wish to see the most splendid enjoyment and the great festival, all together with you to see the Svayaṃvara of the maiden."

When they had come to Pañcāla-land, the five took lodging with a potter, and begged after Brahman wise. . . . "The king of the Pañcālas had had a stout bow made ready for stringing, and a machine set up in the air. To this machine the prince had ordered the mark to be fastened. Drupada spoke : 'Whoso strings this bow, and, setting the arrows on it, shoots through the mark, shall have my daughter.' With these words the king had the Svayaṃvara proclaimed. At these tidings all the kings gathered together there, as also the high-souled Ṛishis, to witness the Svayaṃvara. Also the Kurus with Duryodhana at their head, accompanied by Karṇa, came thither, and distinguished Brahmans from various lands. Received with honour by Drupada, these bands of kings took their seats on the tribunals, eager to behold the Svayaṃvara; then all the townsfolk, with a din as of the sea. To the north-east the princes strode, and took their seats. North-east of the city, on a smooth clear place shone the enclosure for the gathering, set around with dwellings, having a mound and ditch, adorned with gates and gateways, made fair around with a many-coloured awning, filled with the hundreds of musical instruments, made fragrant with precious aloe-wood, sprinkled with sandal-water, bright with wreaths and garlands, ringed all round by many splendid palaces that were like unto the peak of Kailāsa, and brushed the sky ; and these palaces had pinnacles well updrawn, were wrapped in gold as in a net, adorned with floors of mosaic of precious stones, fitted with easily climbed stairs, and furnished with magnificent seats ; they were covered in wreaths and garlands, and scented with the most precious aloe-wood ; they shone like swans and like the moon's beam, and a yojana away they sent out a fragrant smell ; hundreds of unthronged doors they had, and shone with couches and seats ; their parts were covered with many kinds of metals, and they were like unto the tops of Himālaya. There all the fine-decked princes took up their quarters, in varied palaces, vying with one another . . . . And on moſt exquisite tribunals the folk from the city and the country took their seats all round, that they might catch sight of Kṛishṇā. Together with the Brahmans the sons of Pāṇḍu likewise took their seats, gazing at the incomparable wealth of the king of the Pañcālas. While now the assembly was being held, Draupadī, on a lovely day, the sixteenth, came up onto the platform, having bathed her limbs, and wearing a fair garment, decked with every kind of ornament, and bearing a golden, magnificently made wreath on her head. The house-prieſt of the Somakas, a pure Brahman, learned in mantras, ſtrewed (kuça grass) about, and then offered up clarified butter in the fire after the holy precept. Having appeased the flame god, and bid the Brahmans utter the blessing, he ordered all the musical inſtruments around to ſtop. When now a silence had come on them, Dhṛishṭadyumna, who had a voice like the trumpet of the clouds, took Kṛishṇā by the hand after the precept, went into the middle of the platform, and spoke aloud with a thunder-deep voice these friendly, weighty, and moſt excellent words : ' Here are the bow, the mark, and the arrows. Let all the herders of the earth, here gathered, be pleased to hear me. Shoot with the five sharp arrows, whiſtling through the air, shoot the mark through the hole in the machine. Whoso accomplishes this great task, and is endowed with noble blood, a handsome figure, and ſtrength, the wife of him will this my siſter Kṛishṇā become to-day. I speak no lie.' "

Then he tells his siſter the name and birth of the princes in a long, dry liſt,[1] and concludes : " These and many other kings of the various lands have come here for thy sake, my beloved, Kshattriyas that are famous on earth. These men of heroes' ſtrength will for the sake of thee pierce the wonderful mark. Him that hits this mark, him O fair one, be pleased

[1] This whole chapter (186), whose çlokas are wedged right in among the trishṭubhs, so as to confuse the meaning, is probably a later taſteless intrusion. True, the Old Indians felt the barrenness of such an endless wilderness of names far less than we do, and 185.37, in the text as it is now, points to the following adhyāya. But this, too, is perhaps secondary. Anyhow, the old epic song or ballad poetry, too, naturally harboured good and bad.

to-day to choose for husband." " These highly-adorned youths, decked with ear-rings, the princes among men vying with one another, who believed in their own skill with the bow and their ſtrength, all sprang up, brandishing their weapons. Afire with pride of beauty, heroism, nobility, good repute, wealth, and of youth, like unto Himālaya elephants in rut, and dripping from the fires of rut, looking at one another in the ſtruggle for firſt place, with the fire of love running through their limbs—they spoke : ' Kṛishṇā is mine ! ' and rose swiftly from their princely seats."

Now they climbed like foes (although they were friends) on to the ſtage, with their burning hearts set on Draupadī. Gods, spirits, and Ṛishis came to the speċtacle. " These kings, adorned with crown, necklets, and many bracelets, broad-armed, endowed with ſtrength and ſtout heart, these kings, each in his turn, bellowing with might and heroism, could not even in thought put the ſtring on to this faſt-set bow. These princes, wishful to show their heroic ſtrength, were flung away by the backward-springing ſtark bow, although theirs was praċtice, skill, and method ; they sought to rise from the ground with all their might, and, forsaken by their ſtrength, ſtripped of their crowns and necklets that were fallen down, and panting, they gave up. The ring of princes was now in torturing diſtress, they uttered anguished cries ; owing to this ſtrong bow their necklets and rows of bracelets had slipped off, and their yearning for Kṛishṇā was gone from them. When Karṇa thus saw all the kings, he, beſt among bow-drawers, went there, swiftly snatched up the bow from the ground, raised it and ſtrung it, and set the arrows on it. So soon as the sons of Pāṇḍu, the bow-bearers, saw the Sūta (Karṇa), son of the sun, who had given a passionate promise (to accomplish the task), and excelled Agni, Soma, and the sun god, they deemed the splendid mark to be already pierced through and shot down onto the ground. But when Draupadī saw him, she spoke loud the words : ' I will choose no Sūta.' Looking up towards the sun with an angry laugh, Karṇa let drop the springing bow." [1]

[1] The following verses of this adhyāya, except, perhaps, the laſt one, are again a later forger's crime. K. of course did not let this

MARRIAGE

Then at length Arjuna rose up from amidst the Brahmans to accomplish the feat. To show their applause the Brahmans waved their skin garments, and made a mighty din. Some upbraided such a youth for undertaking what strong men had not been able to do, and feared that shame would thus fall on the whole caste of Brahmans. Others extolled his heroic appearance and bearing, and declared he would do everything he undertook, as indeed there was absolutely·nought that was impossible to Brahmans, in spite of their seeming weakness. After several honorific ceremonies directed to the arrow and some of the high gods, Arjuna grasped the bow, strung it in the twinkling of an eye, took the five arrows, and pierced the mark. It fell onto the ground through the hole in the machine. A storm of applause was heard ; thousands of Brahmans waved their garments, music and bardic praise broke forth. " When Krishnā saw the target hit, she gazed at Prithā's son, him the Indra-like, and went, in her white robe and string of wreaths, with a proud smile to the son of Kuntī. He took her, whom he had won on the stage ; and amidst honours from the Brahmans he left the stage, he the man of unimaginable deeds, accompanied by his wife. But when to him, a Brahman, the prince was about to give his daughter, rage welled up in the herders of the earth, as they looked at one another from near by. ' Putting us on one side and giving us no more heed than to a whisp of straw, he chooses to marry Draupadī, most glorious of women, to a Brahman. First a tree is planted here, then it is felled at the very time it should bear fruit. Let us slay this evil-minded one, who scorns us. . . . Has he then in this meeting of kings, that is like unto a gathering of the gods, seen no fitting prince ? And the Brahmans, indeed, have no prescriptive right to be chosen. The Svayaṃvara is for the Kshattriyas. That is a

opportunity slip, either, to dish up still more of this unappetizing fare, and *in majorem gloriam Arjuni* even describes how also Karṇa in vain tries to draw the bow and is flung away (i, 202.34 ff.). Rādheya, at least, is, of course, also in B. 188.19 (K. 203.23)—a garbling, whether the fault lies with the Epic itself or with revisions, hostile to the Kurus, of the bardic songs. K. is at least quite consistent in leaving out altogether the beautiful passage with Karṇa drawing the bow.

85

holy tradition known to all.[1] Or if this maiden will have none of us, let her throw us into the fire, and let us go back to our kingdoms, ye rulers.'"

They now close in on Drupada, with arms in their hands. But Arjuna and Bhīma turn back and come into the lists on his behalf. Bhīma tears up a tree, and uses it as a club, while Arjuna makes his bow spit out arrows and destruction. The Brahmans wave their garments applaudingly, and their water-jugs, and promise Arjuna to fight by his side. But he only laughs and tells them to look on in comfort ; he will drive back all his foes. Soon a deadly fight with the bow blazes up between Arjuna and Karṇa. The latter, greatly wondering, at last asks his opponent who he may be. He answers : " A Brahman." And the sun's son withdraws. In another part of the forest, meanwhile, Bhīma and Çalya, the king of the Madras, engaged in a raging fight with one another, wrestling and boxing, till Bhīma lifts his adversary up in his arms and flings him to the ground, but with his great soul spares his life. The two hero-brothers get away through the throng, while the band of princes sets out on the way home, and the princess follows the two into the potter's workshop to the mother of the Pāṇḍavas, who is hovering amidst a thousand anxieties as to what has become of her sons.

What is particularly noteworthy here is that the bride goes

---

[1] Hopkins makes this objection : In the beginning the Pāṇḍavas disguised as Brahmans are admitted without any question, and objection is only made when things go in their favour. But his deduction that therefore there is nothing of that warriors' privilege about the " self-choice ", which deduction is based only on this case, is made too quickly, since anyhow the tale in question in its present shape aims at a glowing glorification of the priestly caste. Thus Drupada later on is anxious lest a Vaiçya or even a Çūdra may have won his daughter. But no one will assert that at the Svayaṃvara a man from so low a caste could have really been eligible. Dhṛishṭadyumna's proclamation that he who came from noble blood, was "of family" (kula), might be a wooer, is probably aimed at the Kshattriyas. Our tale, however, assumes that any kind of disguise, even that of a Çūdra as a Brahman, was quite natural at the Svayaṃvara—one of the many bits of nonsense in this patchwork piece of the Epic. Cp. too the singularities brought out in what follows.

off at once with her chosen man (i, 188.28 ; 190.41 ff. ; 191 ;
192 ; 193.4, 6). In the brother's lodging she is then treated
by Kuntī at once as the wife of her sons ; she shares out the
alms they bring home, and sleeps at the foot of the Pāṇḍavas.
The father of the bride meanwhile is trembling with deadly
anxiety ; for he does not know whether even a Vaiçya or a
Çūdra may not have won his daughter, and so he himself
been disgraced for all time. But his son Dhṛishṭadyumna has
followed the two as they secretly went off, overhears them in
the potter's workshop, and listens how they speak only of
battles, arms, chariots, and elephants, and so can bring joyful
news to his waiting sire. The house priest is sent off to the
brothers to learn more particulars, and then a messenger
bidding them to the feast. Outside before the abode of the
Pāṇḍavas the most splendid chariots are waiting. They all
enter, and drive to the royal palace. Kuntī goes with Draupadī
to the womenfolk. Meanwhile the sons of Pāṇḍu are put
to a further trial : tools and implements and things needed
in the various callings have been brought together, but the
heroes go by everything and straight on to the arms.[1] Lastly
Drupada has another conversation with Yudhishṭhira, and
asks him who he is, whether he is a warrior or a Brahman,
a Vaiçya or a Çūdra, and now learns they are really the sons
of Pāṇḍu, as he has so longed for. Draupadī is again lodged
in one house with the five brothers, just as though she were
already given in marriage, and after the difficulty has been
met which is found in the planned polyandric marriage of the
princess, she is then entrusted on each of five days one after
the other to one of the Pāṇḍavas.

Just like this one is the trial in the Rāmāyaṇa (i, 66, 67).
Janaka, the king of Videha, possesses the wonderful bow of
Çiva, and a daughter Sītā, alone in her kind, who came forth at
the ploughing, out of the furrow under the plough ; and this
maiden born from no mother's womb he promises as vīryaçulkā
to the strong man that can lift the huge bow, and string and
draw it. Kings come in throngs and seek Sītā's hand, but none
can fulfil the condition. Filled with anger they besiege

[1] Cp. my note 3, p. xlvii of the Samayamātṛikā and Prabandha-
cintāmani (Tawney), p. 7.

Mithilā, the royal city, but Janaka, who at the end of a year finds himself at the end of his resources, wins the favour of the gods by ascetic deeds ; they give him an army and the kings have to withdraw in shame. Then later the youthful Rāma comes with his brother and the royal Rishi Viçvāmitra to Janaka, and asks him to have the bow brought. A hundred and fifty men drag up an iron chest fitted with eight wheels, wherein the bow, marked out by the people with divine honours, lies. Rāma lifts it out as though in play, strings it, and draws it, whereon the bow breaks in two in the middle, and with such a crash that the earth quakes, and all the people, excepting the king, the two youths, and Viçvāmitra, fall swooning on the ground. Then Sītā is wedded to Rāma.

Even a fight, as a very primitive method, also gives the decision in MBh., vii, 144.9 ff. : " At this very time, at the Svayamvara of the daughter of the great souled Devaka, for which all the Kshattriyas gathered together, at this time of a truth Çini overcame all the princes, and lifted the queen Devakī swiftly onto his chariot for Vasudeva (to whom he then brought her). When the hero, Somadatta, the bull among men, saw Devakī on his chariot, the so mighty one could not bear this with calm. Through half a day the glorious, wonderful fight between the two lasted, a fight with fists was fought between the two strong ones.[1] But Çini flung Somadatta violently on the ground, lifted his sword, grasped him by the hair, and kicked him with his foot in the midst of the thousands of kings watching from every side. But, pitying, he spoke : ' Live ! ' and set him free again." Cp. further iii, 12.31, 115 ; vii, 11.10 f.

In face of the express declaration of the Kshattriyas that the Svayamvara is their peculiar right, it sounds almost like a clumsy pretention of the priestly caste when in v, 35, we find this tale : " Engaged on the Svayamvara was the maiden called Keçinī, incomparable in her loveliness, yearning she was for a right goodly husband. Then the Daitya Virocana came thither, wishing to win her. Then spoke Keçinī there to the Daitya prince : ' Are the Brahmans the better, or the

---

[1] Read : subalinoḥ.

children of Diti ?'" But Virocana spoke scornfully of gods and Brahmans. Yet in the end he had to bring himself to wash a Brahman's feet under the fair one's eyes.

In the so-called self-choice, therefore, the maiden has either no freedom whatever, or else only a reſtricted one. We meet with a less splendid, but much more beautiful form in the Svayaṃvara of Sāvitrī, who wanders about looking and seeking until her heart picks one out. But here likewise it is done at her father's inſtigation. It is with an unusual meaning, therefore, that the word is made use of in Rām., i, 32. The king Kuçanābha has a hundred daughters. "Now in the bloom of youth, with the gift of beauty, fair-decked, they went into the park, like autumn lightning, singing, dancing, and playing musical inſtruments. They, the maidens dight with splendid ornaments, found the greateſt joy. Then the god of the wind saw them, and spoke. ' I love you, do ye all become my wives. Leave the abode and ways of mankind, and ye shall then win long life. For youth is always fleeting, especially in mankind. When ye have reached to a youth beyond harming, ye will become immortal.' But they laughed at him, and cried : ' May the time not come, O fool, when we, scorning our truth-speaking father, make use of self-choice after our own will. He to whom our father gives us shall be our husband.'" Here svayaṃvara = svayaṃgrahaṇa, the independent self-willed union of the maiden with the man. This is one of the dreadful happenings that come about before the end of a world. Thus we read in Mahābh., iii, 190.36 : " No man any longer asks for the daughter, nor is the daughter given away ; they take the man for themselves, when the end of the world (yugānta) is drawn nigh."

Yet this very independence of the girl is of the essence of the Gandharva marriage, which is also part of the orthodox syſtem. It is likewise only a concern of the warrior, as we have already seen (i, 102.16 ; xiii, 44.5 f.). And for him it is even the beſt of the forms, as Dushyanta declares (i, 73.4), who, it is true, is in love, and bent on his purpose—to ensnare the maiden. Indeed, in i, 172.19 it is called the beſt of any forms, although here again it is a man fired with passion that is speaking to his adored one, even if it is not with so great success as

Dushyanta.[1]   This king's Gandharva marriage with Çakuntalā, which is well-known especially through Kālidāsa's drama, is a celebrated example (i, 68 ff.).

That pattern prince Dushyanta, under whom men led a paradise-like life, went forth one day to hunt, "and him in his towering kingly splendour the wives of this hero beheld there, as they stood on the palace battlements, him that won fame for himself, was like the prince of the gods, destroyed his foes and kept off their elephants.   As the band of women gazed on him there, they held him for the wielder of the thunderbolt : 'That is the tiger among men, like unto the Vasus for heroism in the fight.   When the foemen's host comes under his strong arm, then it is all over with them.' With words such as these did the women in their love praise

[1] The Gandharva form is only for the warrior nobility according likewise to Manu, iii, 26 ; Vishṇu, xxiv, 28 (and he that so gives his daughter away, thereby comes into the blessed worlds of the Gandharvas, 37).   On the other hand Baudhāyana, i, 11, 20.13, teaches that the Gandharva marriage is lawful for the Vaiçya and the Çūdra, but according to " others " for all castes, and that because it is based on love. Baudh. himself, however, evidently thinks that maidens who make so free are not of much value after all (see 14 and 15). Nāradastates without hesitation that this kind of marriage belongs to all castes alike (sādhāraṇa), while he roundly rejects capture marriage as also marriage by purchase and by fraud (xii, 44).   Moreover the holy Kaṇva (MBh., i, 73.27) is also in agreement : " The Gandharva form is according to tradition the best for the Kshattriya."   If the current view of the ethnologists and anthropologists were really the right one— that marriage has grown all over the world out of " hetærism " (and it has much to be said for it)—then the Indian views as to the Gandharva home-bringing, that "survival from the time of promiscuity ", might very well be understood from an " inter-ethnic " standpoint, and even a speculative theory built up on the bare names : on this theory the Gandharvas, the owners of the woman before marriage, would be the symbols of the whole clan or tribal community, every male member of which had a right to all the women, and so on.   But such things may be left to others.   Moreover there is still found to-day among very many tribes of the primitive population of India not only an exceedingly loose sexual life, but also marriage according to the free will of the two most concerned.   So the " Gandharva marriage " thus thrust itself on the Aryan settlers.

the overlord of men, and scatter a rain of flowers on his head."

A dreadful slaughter did he deal out among the beasts of the wild, and hungry, thirsty, and weary he came into a forest swept through by a cool wind. It was covered with a right pleasant sward, was far-stretched, and made musical by surpassingly sweet-singing birds, and swarms of cicadas. Trees with mighty boughs and grateful shade filled it ; the leaves [1] quivered under the bees. There was no tree there but bore flowers and fruits, or that bristled with thorns, nor one but was covered with bees. The wind rocked the trees to and fro so that they kept on showering down a many-coloured rain of flowers. Up to the skies rose these forest giants resounding with sweet bird-song, but their boughs bent low under the burden of the flowers. Bough twined lovingly with bough. Spirit beings wandered through the forest, and the cool wind was wafted about it, sweet-smelling, carrying off the pollen from the flowers, and drew nigh the trees, as though minded to sport in love with them. And in the midst of this forest paradise there the king saw an incomparable penitent's grove, like the world of the gods to behold. A splendid, cool, and mighty stream clasped this settlement like a mother, abounding in sandbanks with loving couples of cakravāka, carrying flowers [2] along like foam. Wonderful as this whole forest was this abode of ascetics, throughout which holy men were giving themselves up to good works, and where, as in Indra's heaven, hunger and thirst at once were lifted from the king, while welling joy filled his heart. He wished to visit the holy Kaṇva, the head of the forest brethren, but found him not, but found a young girl in penitent's garb, who came to meet him, on his calling, like the embodied goddess of beauty and happiness. She gave him friendly welcome and showed him the honours of hospitality. On his asking where Kaṇva was, she answered : " My father, the holy man, has gone forth from the hermitage to get fruit. Wait a moment, and thou wilt see him." The king was filled with great wonder at

[1] Is -dalam to be read instead of -talam in 70.6 ? The meaning is essentially the same in either case

[2] Or : flowers and foam.

her beauty, and moral excellence, and spoke : " Who art thou, and whose daughter, thou with the lovely hips ? Wherefore art thou come into the forest ? Whence is thy descent, thou that art gifted with such beauty ? At the sight of thee only, thou hast taken my heart from me. I would fain come to know thee ; therefore tell me, thou shining one." She told him she was Kanva's daughter. But the prince answered : " The holy man is held in honour in the world as a keeper of strictest chastity. Even the god of virtue might fall from good ways, but not this man of the strict vow. How then art thou his daughter ? " Çakuntalā now told him how the gods had sent the Apsaras Menakā to lead that dangerous penitent astray, the king Viçvāmitra, and how she was sprung from this union, had been exposed by her mother, and had been brought up by Kanva as his own daughter. Dushyanta spoke : " Quite clearly thou art a prince's daughter, after what thou sayest, sweet one. Be my wife, thou of the lovely hips. Say, what can I do for thee ? Now will I bring thee a golden wreath, garments, ear-rings, all of gold, gleaming jewels and pearls from various cities, and breast-ornaments and skins too. The whole kingdom shall be thine now. Be my wife, O shining one. Come to me through the Gandharva marriage, O lovely one ; for of marriages that of the Gandharvas is declared to be the best, O maiden with thighs like plantain-stems." Çakuntalā spoke : " My father has left this hermitage to fetch fruit ; wait a moment, O king, then he will give me to thee." Dushyanta spoke : " I wish thee, O lovely-hipped one, thee that art without blemish, to give thyself to me in love. Know thou, it is for thy sake that I am at all, for it is on thee that my mind is bent. Only self is akin to self, and only self is the refuge of self. May thou thyself according to law and justice give me thine own self.[1] Eight

---

[1] As times beyond number in the world's literature, so too in Indian literature, and especially in the MBh. over and over again is heard the partly painful, partly fierily energetic cry : " Each is alone." None belongs to anyone else, we are all but strangers to strangers, utterly cut off even from the dearest and nearest ; none knows the other, the self belongs only to the self. Man is born alone, alone he lives, alone he dies, alone he tastes the fruit of his deeds and his ways ; it is only

forms of marriage, to speak shortly, have been handed down in law and custom : that of Brahman, that of the gods, as his work that bears him company. As night is the mother of things, so too we come out of the darkness and go into the darkness, come forth out of nothingness, and go through a short being into nothingness (cp. Agnipurāṇa, 119.13b, taken from Vishṇu, xx, 48) ; just as little as the tree knows of its flowers and fruits, does man know of whence he comes and whither he goes. Our bodily and spiritual organism is ever changing ; what belongs, then, to us ? Even our body, our sense perceptions, thoughts and feelings are not ours, are only products of the ever-flowing matter. Thus, too, there is really no teacher or leader for anyone, each is his own Guru and must go along the road to happiness alone. Only the self is the friend, only the self is the foe of man ; from others nothing comes to him. Therefore what must be is to honour, to assert the self, to be quite true, never to lie either in word or deed. Self-culture, however, is found in self-discipline. Indeed, he who of his own will renounces all (and only lives in others), he who then really knows and feels that nothing belongs to him, to him everything belongs. But as opposed to this most lofty ethical teaching there is deduced from the saying : " Each is alone, and each is akin only and utterly to himself " the most thoroughgoing egoism or individualism, and the teaching is always being stressed : For the sake of self we must give up everything, even the nearest and dearest, it is only to self that we owe any regard. And : He that wants greatness must be cruel ; moral virtue (dharma) has been put in the way of the strong by the weak. It is perhaps worthy of note that the Buddhists call this " the wisdom of the Kshattriyas " (cp. my Daçakumārac., p. 109). But here the thought of the Indian " Mirrors of Princes " may have played a very great part. See, for instance, i, 140, especially 140.77 (= xii, 140.50); 158.27 ff.; iii, 159.14 ; 215.27, 28 ; v, 33.74; 34.64, 65 ; 37.18 ; vi, 30.5 f. ; x, 1.24 ; xi, 2.6 ; 2.13 (almost = xii, 174.17 and xv, 34.17) ; xii, 139.30 ; 140.5 ; 275.35 ; 288.16 ff. ; 318.104 ; 320.115 ff. ; 321.85, 86 ; 329.32 ff. ; xiii, 111.9 ff. ; xv, 34.17. Cp. my Kauṭilya, p. lx. Many of these thoughts are also often uttered by the Buddhists and the Jains. So Majjh.-Nik., i, 136 ; Mahāvagga, i, 6.38 ff., etc. The Jain monk Amitagati is ready at hand in Subhāshitasaṃdoha, ii, 16, with a Sanskrit model for the celebrated saying of Hans the Stone-breaker in Anzengruber's *Kreuzelschreiber* : Anyajano na kiṃcic chaknoti kartum (" nothing can happen to thee "). Cp. my Daçakumārac., note 1, pp. 110 ; 362, and *Hindu Tales*, p. 153, where indeed the quotations could be multiplied to infinity.

also that of the Ṛishis, that of Prajāpati, and that of the Asuras, that of the Gandharvas and that of the Rākshasas ; that of the Piçācas is according to tradition the eighth. The good among these Manu has explained by turns. Hold it for truth that the four firſt are praiseworthy among the Brahmans, and know, O faultless one, that six in turn are deemed lawful for the Kshattriya man. For kings the Rākshasa marriage, too, is commended, and for the Vaiçya and Çūdra that of the Asuras is traditional. Of five three here are lawful, and two unlawful, according to the tradition. The Piçāca marriage and the Asura marriage muſt never be made. In this way it is that the marriage muſt be carried out, this is the way of the law according to the tradition. Gandharva and Rākshasa marriages are lawful for the Kshattriya man, have no miſtruſt about them ; he may enter upon them, whether they are among others or not, of that is no doubt. Be thou a wife to me, as loving woman to loving man, according to the Gandharva marriage, thou of the lovely face." Çakuntalā spoke : " If this is the path of the law, and I myself have the power to give myself away, O beſt of the Pūru race, then hear my condition, O lord. Promise me the holy truth, juſt as I tell it thee in secret : The son that is born of me muſt be the next after thee, the crown prince, O great king ; this I demand as a sacred thing from thee. If so it shall be, O Dushyanta, then let my union with thee come about." " Thus shall it be," said the king to her, without ſtopping to think, " and I will also take thee into my city, O bright-smiling one, as thou doſt deserve, fair-hipped one, that I swear to thee." After these words the royal Ṛishi, according to the holy precept (vidhivat), took by the hand her of the faultless gait, and lay with her. And when he had consoled her, he went away, and spoke over and over again : " I shall send an army in four parts for thee, and have thee brought by it unto my abode, O bright-smiling one." Having made her this promise, the prince went off, thinking in his mind of Kaṇva : " What will he do, the holy man, endowed with asceticism, when he hears of it ? " With these thoughts only did he come into the city. When he had only been gone a moment Kaṇva came into the penitent's grove. But Çakuntalā from shame did not go to meet her

94

father. Then the great pentitent, endowed with godlike knowledge, knew how it was with her, and the holy one joyfully spoke : " The union, O kindly one, which to-day thou didſt carry out with a man in secret without regard for me, does no harm to law and virtue. For the Gandharva marriage is deemed the beſt for the Kshattriya man, which is made in secret between two lovers without holy words, as the tradition teaches us. Filled with righteousness, and lofty-souled is Dushyanta, beſt among men, to whom thou haſt drawn nigh as to thy husband, the lover, O Çakuntalā.[1] From thee a noble-souled son will be born into the world, who will rule over this whole sea-girdled earth." She now begged the holy man for a blessing for her husband, which, too, was granted her.

The Gandharva marriage was thus a right of lords, a part of the morality of lords, and certainly not seldom found among the nobility. For the Brahmanic outlook it naturally seemed offensive, but the crafty prieſt all over the world, and above all in India, has from shrewdness often kept an eye shut, and the thirſt for syſtematization, as also the pious respeᴄt for all tradition, brought down this part of the marriage theory, too, into late times, where in the narrative literature Gandharva weddings are extraordinarily frequent. But it is not altogether " free love affairs ", as has been thought, that are here to be generally underſtood by this; for however light-heartedly such a union is often entered upon there, it is moſtly held to be binding. True, exceptions are to be found, juſt as here the old holy King Dushyanta looks on his adventure with the penitent-maiden as the foreſt tale of a fleeting hour, and as a result our ſtory develops a long train of effeᴄts.

In spite of all the promises Çakuntalā never heard another word from her husband ; her son came into the world, and from childhood's years ſtood forth as a miracle of ſtrength, courage, and noble fierceness : tigers, elephants, and other dangerous beaſts he bound to trees, when he was six years old, beſtrode them, and rode about on them. Then spoke the holy man : " To dwell long with kinsfolk does not befit women, for it deſtroys the good name, seemly life, and

[1] Read yaṃ inſtead of yas. K. 94.62 has however : abhyāgacchat patir yas tvāṃ bhajamānāṃ.

virtue." [1]   And he sent away his daughter and the boy, accompanied by his disciples, to the king, that his, the king's scion, might be consecrated as crown prince. Çakuntalā presented his son to the ruler, and reminded him of the promise he had given her. But although the prince well remembered all, he said : " I do not remember. To whom then doſt thou belong, thou shameless penitent ?   I know of no union with thee, whether in pious duty, or in love, or in profit.   Go, or ſtay here, as thou wilt ;   whatever thou wisheſt, do it." " Thus addressed, sne of the lovely hips ſtood there as one put to shame, the wretched one, as though senseless for sorrow, like a motionless tree-ſtump. With eyes reddened with emotion and indignation, with quivering lips, scorching him, as it were, with ſtolen glances, she gazed at him sideways. With features drawn, and goaded on by anger, she withheld her fiery powers heaped up through her mortifications. Having pondered a moment, filled with anguish and indignation, she looked at her husband, and angrily spoke the words : ' Why speakeſt thou, O great king, though thou knoweſt it, without scruple like any ordinary man : I do not know about it ? Thine heart knows here of truth and falsehood. Do thou speak what is fitting and good as an impartial witness ; do not scorn thine own self.   He that forces his own self otherwise than it is made, what a crime has he not committed, he the thief robbing his own self ! [2]

> " I am alone," so thy thoughts go
> And thou in thy heart knoweſt not the old Muni,
> Who in it knows the evil doing ;
> Before his face thou workeſt crooked falsehood.

> " None knows me," this is the illusion
> Of the man that has done evil.
> Him the God knows, enthroned above,
> And the Man, too, knows, dwelling in the heart.

[1] Cp. Mārkaṇḍeyapur., lxxvii, 19.
[2] Ātmāpahārin is explained by Nīl. in vii, 73.33 as ātmānam anyathā prakāçayan. Cp. v, 42.37 ; vii, 17.32.

MARRIAGE

The sun and moon, the wind, fire,
Earth, heaven, water, Yama, and his heart also,
Day, night, the two twilights,
The law—they know here man's life.[1]

Yama absolves him from evil done
Who is a joy of the witness to deeds,
Of the mind, to which the field is known,
And which dwells there in our breast.[2]

But the man that is hateful to him,
Because evil-minded he doth evil
And busied is with ill deeds,
Him Yama some day punishes with a burden of torment.

He that himself scorning his own self does
To himself what is not after the heart of the self,
And sees not [3] the ground of action in the self,
To him, too, no gods are kind.

Do not thus scorn me, that am true to my husband, saying that I have come hither on my own impulse. Me thou dost not honour, who am worthy of honour, who am the wife that drew near unto thee thyself. Why dost thou treat me with disdain before the assembly, like a man of low birth ? And I am not calling this out in the wilderness. Why dost thou not hear me ? ' ''

Then from her lips comes a splendid song of praise for family happiness (a rendering of part of which will be given later), and she ends with a lament that her mother had already forsaken her as a child, and now her husband was repudiating her, and she was in the world with no kinsfolk. But the king upbraids her as a bad woman, sneers at her declaration that she is Viçvāmitra's daughter, and jeeringly says that her evil-living mother, Menakā, has picked her up, the evil-living

---

[1] Cp. Garuḍapurāṇasāroddhāra, iii, 16.
[2] Niryātayati dushkṛitam removes, forgives the evil deed, the sin. In the following çloka the literal translation is perhaps : the evil-doer he makes to taste his sins, he punishes in him the evil deed (thus not from dushkṛit).
[3] Or : " In whose self happiness does not lie." So, too, Nīl.

daughter, somewhere else. "All whereof thou speakeſt is unknown to me ; I know thee not ; go thy ways, wherever thou chooseſt." Majeſtically Çakuntalā speaks :

> "The fault of others thou seeſt large,
> That are small as a grain of sesame ;
> Thine own, great as bilva fruits,
> Are not bared to thy seeing eye.

Menakā is with the gods, and the gods are with Menakā. My descent is higher than thine, Dushyanta. Thou wandereſt along on earth, I through the air. So long as the ugly man does not see his own face in the glass, he believes he is handsomer than others. He that has the gift of the higheſt beauty scorns no one. But he that utters a ſtream of immeasurably evil words is an outrage here on earth." Then she opposes, in their nature and ways, the foolish and the bad to the wise and the good, with a telling reference to Dushyanta with his evil and unwise deeds, and winds up with an inspired song, full of fire, on the truth that is so sorely sinned againſt by the man of deceit. "Better than a hundred wells is the tank, better than a hundred tanks the sacrifice, better than a hundred sacrifices the son, better than a hundred sons the truth. If a thousand sacrificial ſteeds and the truth are put on the balance, then the truth outweighs even the thousand sacrificial ſteeds. To ſtudy all the Vedas, to bathe at all the holy bathing-places, and the truth—these things are on an equality with one another, nay, the truth ſtands higher. King, truth is the higheſt "Brahman", truth is the higheſt duty ; do not forsake duty, O king, let truth be thy bosom companion. If thou, however, clingeſt to the lie, if thou doſt not believe from thine own impulse, then I will go of my own self ; with one such as thou there is no friendly relation." Then a voice sounds from the sky, assuring the king that this is his son, and bidding him to take him to himself. Then Dushyanta declares to his miniſters and prieſts that he was not allowed to avow his son otherwise, else would the world have doubted the truth of his descent, and to Çakuntalā he speaks : " Our union took place hidden from the world ; to cleanse thee, O queen, it was that I have so delayed and teſted thee. But what harsh things thou haſt uttered to me in anger over-great, my love, they are forgiven thee by me because of thy tender affeƈtion." He yields her honour now as his head-wife, kisses and clasps his son, and dedicates him as crown prince.[1]

[1] K. has spun the Çakuntalā episode far out, and in part botched it very taſtelessly. How wonderfully did the author of this poetic pearl of the MBh. make the innocent foreſt maid answer the king when he firſt bids her to give herself to him ! Inſtead of this one verse, wholly to the point and almoſt literally repeating the words spoken by her in another conneƈtion, the southern botchwork puts a long speech on the awfulness of the holy ones and the Brahmans into the good child's mouth, as also moral refleƈtions on father, daughter, and wife (çl. 94.6 = Rām., i, 32.22). She is then so cunning, too, in her fear of what the world says, as to demand firſt of all a solemn marriage with all the ceremonies of the law. And the love-goaded king now calls to his Purohita, and has himself married to her by him ! When Kaṇva comes home, Çakuntalā dares not face him, but he gets her to tell what has happened to her, which, of course, is done here *sagadgadam*, and he then magnificently announces that he knew it at once through his " godlike eye ", but consoles her, and says :

> Ṛitavo bahavas te vai
> gatā vyarthāḥ, çucismite ;
> sārthakaṃ sāmprataṃ hy etan,
> na ca pāpmāſti te, 'naghe.

Her son Bharata shows himself even in childhood's years to be a mighty demon-slayer, like unto his father in Kālidāsa. Then Çakuntalā's sorrow when she leaves the hermitage is drawn in very broad and really beautiful lines, but not, it is to be noted, in the tone of the epic poet, but lyrically like Kālidāsa, or even a little ſtronger, although with less flowerlike-delicacy than in the drama ; she wants and does not want to go forth, while the boy urges her and Kaṇva gives her wise inſtructions despite his tears. The penitents who are going with her as escort do not wish to go into the nagaraṃ durjanair vṛitaṃ, particularly since many of the townsmen jeer at them, and go back home from the gates, as Kaṇva has bidden them. Çakuntalā amid the ecſtatic and Indian-like descriptive admiration, called forth in the townsmen by her beauty and Bharata's ſturdy ſtrength, proceeds alone through the city to the palace. Her discussion with the king is also a good deal longer, and not only are a lot of very good sayings added, but also lyric and effeƈtive touches. Thus in describing her origin and how she was exposed Çakuntalā draws a piƈture of how the birds covered the

Beside such romantic love and marriage adventures of the Kshattriyas the marriage by purchase, established from olden times among the mass of the people, could not naturally but seem vulgar and low. So we already saw it described, in agreement with the Smṛiti, and it is often brought up as a dreadful sin. So vii, 43.37 ; 73.42 ; xiii, 93.133 ; 94.31. But it was not at all confined to the *misera plebs*, nor is it still in India to-day.[1] In one case, however, we are expressly

little child with their wings and then had solemnly handed it over to Kaṇva (98.70 ff., cp. 93.20–24), how he had brought her up, and the prince had found the blossoming maid and made her his (98.70 ff.). Instead of the one voice from the sky sarvāṇi bhūtāni and the devās also take a part. Dushyanta, so forgiving and great-souled towards the angry woman, here, showing great reasonableness, goes on to say : " The untrue or unkind words I have spoken, or the but too great evil I have done, my ill words, all these do thou, too, forgive me, thou great-eyed one. Through patience with their husband wives are granted the husband's faithfulness." He leads her ceremoniously into his harem as head-wife, and to his mother Rathantarī.

[1] When the ape in the 219th Jātaka (which I have edited in my *Kāvyasaṃgraha, Metrische Übersetzungen aus indischen und andern Sprachen*) comes back again to his brethren in the forest, he tells them, as characteristic of the topsy-turvy world of men, how wives are bought in it for much money. Many such instances could be quoted. From the law literature, too, it comes out more or less incidentally in many places that marriage by purchase was the general thing. Manu, for instance, is very hard against purchase marriage (iii, 25 ; 51–54 ; ix, 98–100) ; and yet in ix, 93 and viii, 366 the bride-price for the daughter appears as the father's natural right. Other passages are given by Bühler in his translation of this law-book, p. xciii. Baudhāyana, i, 11, 21.1–3 and ii, 2.27 paints the sinfulness of such a proceeding in vivid colours, but grants in i, 11, 20.12 that it is lawful, at least for the Kshattriya. Nārada in xii, 54, even thunders : Only the husband of the unbought woman is a real husband and owner ; if a price has been given for a woman, then the children begotten by another man belong to the wife ; not to the husband, but to the lover. But the earlier quoted passage in xii, 30, shows, however, that the " maiden for whom a bride-price (çulka) has been given " has the same meaning with him also as the " betrothed ". Indeed, Vasishṭha, i, 36, has instead of Āsura simply Mānusha " the way of bringing home with mankind ". Cp. 36 and 37 and Bühler's note on it in *Sacred Books*

told that shame was felt towards it in the upper classes. " Then Bhīshma, Çāntanu's son, he the thinker, bent his mind on a second marriage for the king Pāṇḍu, the glorious. With the old miniſters and with Brahmans, great holy men and an army in four divisions he made his way to the city of the king of the Madras. When the leader of the Vāhīkas heard he had come, the prince went to meet him and brought him into the city. When the ruler of Madra had set before him a splendid seat and water for the feet, as also the honorific gueſt-water and the honey-mixture, he asked about the objeɛt of his coming. To the Madra king spoke Bhīshma, the Kuru offspring : ' Know that I have come to requeſt a maiden, O tamer of foes. It is said thou haſt a surpassing siſter, Mādrī, the glorious one. I would ask for her for Pāṇḍu. For thou art fitting unto us for an alliance, and we to thee. Bearing this in mind, O prince of the Madras, accept us, as is right and seemly.' To Bhīshma, thus speaking, made answer the warden of the Madras : ' For me there is no better wooer than he,[1] that I hold. By my forefathers, the greateſt men in this family, something was introduced ; now whether it be good or bad, I cannot set myself above it. It is known to all and also to thee, of that is no doubt. It is indeed, not becoming to say : Lord, give.[2] That is the wont and cuſtom of our family, and this is our main guiding-thread. Therefore do I speak unto

of the Eaſt, xiv, p. 7. According to Mānavagrihyas., i, 7–8, there are only two kinds of marriage : brāhma and çaulka. As a direɛt contraſt to the Brahmanic view, which in the Mahānirvāṇatantra, xi, 84 even demands that the king shall drive out of the land, as godless and fallen, the man that gives away his daughter for money, let it be mentioned that among our old Germanic forbears the free gift of the bride was invalid, and only the purchase marriage was valid in law (Sohm, *Deutsche Rundschau*, 1878, p. 99 ; Westermarck [3], p. 429 f.).

[1] According to K. : " than thou " (i, 122.8, that is, tvattaḥ inſtead of tvataḥ).

[2] Bhavān dehi. The difficulty would be done away with, if we read yuktas for yuktaṃ (iii, 115.24). But like conſtruɛtions are found elsewhere in the Epic. In the next çloka I read ca for na. If na is kept, then : therefore, it is, that the words I speak unto thee are not without a clause (or reservation).

thee these clear open words, O slayer of foes.' To the Madra king made answer Bhīshma, overlord of men : ' This law is the higheſt, O king, proclaimed by Brahma himself. There lies nothing of evil in it. The forefathers made this rule. And well-known, O Çalya, is this prescription, approved by the good, and laid upon thee.' ¹ After these words the very mighty one gave wrought and unwrought gold, and many kinds of jewels in thousands ; elephants, horses and chariots, apparel and ornaments, precious ſtones, pearls and coral, that shone, did the son of Gaṅgā beſtow. All this did Çalya take with joyous heart, and gave him his siſter for it, having decked her ㄱut. Bhīshma, the son of her that wanders unto the sea, took Mādrī, and went off with her to Hāſtinapura. When then a fitting day and moment was come, approved by the cccellent ones, King Pāṇḍu took hold of Mādrī's hand according to the holy prescript (i, 113, 1 ff.)."

iii, 115.20 ff. is quite the same, a passage with a rather ancient look about it. In Kanyākubja was a great and very mighty prince, famous under the name of Gādhi ; he went off to live in the foreſt. But while he was living in the foreſt a daughter was born to him, like an Apsaras. Ṛicīka, the offspring of Bhṛigu, sought her in marriage. To him, the Brahman of unbending piety, Gādhi then spoke : " In our family a thing is cuſtomary which our forefathers brought in.

---

¹ Bhīshma here speaks as a true Indian : what is traditional, the cuſtom of the fathers, is holy. Ask a Hindu why he follows this cuſtom or that, and he will immediately say that his father taught him to do so and that it was handed down to him from time immemorial. Rāmakrishṇa, *Life in an Indian Village*, London, 1891, p. 27. So, too, Dubois, *Hindu Manners*, etc., ³, p. 100. Whether the buying of a wife is in itself bad or good is left undiscussed withal. In different parⁿ, or even families in India there prevailed in olden times, and ſtill prevail to-day, very varying cuſtoms and laws. Moreover, as is well known, the Indus populations have never fitted themselves to unbending Brahmanism, and were therefore held in ill repute ; and that the Madras, Vāhīkas, etc. under Çalya's rule were held not to be ethically polished is to be seen easily from Karṇa's scornful scandalous chronicle of these, at leaſt so-called, moral barbarians (vii, 40 ff.). But anyhow Bhīshma does not hesitate to take part in this business as the buyer.

A thousand fiery white steeds, each with one black ear [1] is the purchase price. Know this, O best of the Brahmans. And yet I may not say to thee, the holy one : ' Give,' O offspring of Bhṛigu. Yet must I give my daughter to a noble-natured one like thee." Ṛicīka promised him the steeds, and got them from Varuṇa, who made them to come up out of the water. The place where it happened is the famous horse-tīrtha on the Gaṅgā in Kanyākubja. The holy man delivered over the precious race-horses to the father, who gave him his daughter in marriage, and the gods themselves were groomsmen. All this was done dharmeṇa (according to the law).[2] These thousand wonderful horses were then given by Gādhi to the priests, and six hundred of them play a great part in the tale of Gālava and Mādhavī, which also belongs here, and has already been given.

In xiii, 2.18 the ideal king Duryodhana of the race of Manu and Ikshvāku bestows his daughter in marriage on Agni, and demands instead of the purchase price (çulka) the continual presence of the fire god. But it may be that rather we have here a turn of speech.[3] But it does not at all fall naturally under the conception of the çulka, when the fisherman Dāça gives his adopted daughter Satyavatī as wife to the enamoured king Çāntanu only under the condition that her son shall be definitely king (i, 100).

As we have now seen, it does indeed happen that a mythical king may marry a Brahman maiden, even if it is not without preliminary scruples because of his own unworthiness. But the Indian dislike which runs so strongly against dragging down the woman by marriage into a lower caste has here

---

[1] Or : with ears black on one side. So Nīl.

[2] Cp. Bhāgavatapurāṇa, ix, 15 ; Vishṇupurāṇa, iv, 7 (Wilson, vol. 4, pp. 13 ff.).

[3] But it would seem seriously meant in the case of Citrāṅgadā, the daughter of the king in Maṇipūra. The father demands, and Arjuna grants him the only son that is possible of the marriage instead of the purchase price (i, 215.25 ; 217.25). In this family after Çiva's ordinance only one child is ever born, and the present king has a daughter.

borne down almoſt everything before it,[1] and the Kshattriya
wants a Kshattriya maiden, as Dushyanta shows. Cp. also
xii, 320.59. It is true that in xii, 123.21 marriage into a
holy family is prescribed as an atonement (cp. xii, 134.2)
for the king who has done wrong. But whether by the
mahākula a Brahmanic one is meant cannot be said for certain,
but seems here to be necessary. On the other hand, in consonance with the orthodox teaching, Brahmans very often
unite in the Epic with daughters of Kshattriyas. But here also,
as elsewhere in the Mahābh., we meet with the traces of a
more primitive view, and one less flattering to the pride of the
prieſt, among the ruling caſte. To the king Duryodhana,
juſt mentioned, Agni comes firſt in the figure of a Brahman,
and seeks the Kshattriya child in marriage. But, " Poor he is
and not of my caſte," so said the king, and would not give
his daughter to the Brahman. In xiii, 4 we find a variant
of the tale of the thousand wonderful horses. There we learn
that why Gādhi had withdrawn into the foreſt was because he
wished to win offspring by penance. There a daughter was
born to him, the incomparably lovely Satyavatī ; she was
desired by the Brahman Ricīka of the greatly famous family
of the Bhṛigus. But Gādhi, crusher of foes, did not give her
to the high-souled Ricīka ; for he thought within himself :
" He is poor." When the wooer came back again after his
rejeĉtion, the beſt among kings spoke to him : " Give me the
purchase price, then thou wilt obtain (vatsyasi [2]) my daughter."
Ricīka spoke : " What shall I give thee as price for thy
daughter, O prince of kings? ˉSpeak without hesitation.
Let no reluĉtance be there." Then Gādhi demanded the
thousand horses, gleaming like the moonbeam, swift as the

---

[1] It is to be noted, too, that King Yayāti, who is moreover called a
" Rishi " and " Rishi's son ", wins the Brahman's daughter Devayānī
because she has had the curse laid on her that no Brahman shall wed her.
But in the tale there can be heard the clear note of the caſte pride of
the prieſt, often sorely humbled by the nobility. So probably that
curse was purposely invented into the bargain.

[2] Vasati with acc. "to have to look forward to, to fall into something,
to experience, to obtain " is also found elsewhere in the Epic. Cp.
v, 35.30 ; Rām., iv, 20.17.

wind, black in one ear; and the Brahman got them from
Varuṇa, who brought them up from below the Gaṅgā at the
very place the suppliant wished. Gādhi was aſtonished unto
death, for he had naturally by his demand only wanted to be
rid of the unwished for man, but he was afraid of the holy
one's curse, and gave him his daughter for this payment.
" And when she had got such a husband, she was taken with
the greateſt joy."

But it is not only the caſte which muſt be looked to in
marriage, but the younger brother muſt not marry before the
elder, nor the younger siſter before one that is above her in
years, an offence of which, indeed, the law books often speak.
In the case of such an offence all three (the two brothers
and the wife) according to xii, 165.68,69 muſt, since they have
loſt their caſte through this wrongdoing, undertake the
Cāndrāyaṇa or the Kṛicchra mortification to be freed from their
sin. On the other hand, xii, 35.27, 28 lays down an atonement
only for the two brothers, and that only a twelve days' Kṛicchra
vow ; but the younger brother muſt marry a second time
(niveçyaṃ tu punas tena sadā tārayatā pitṛīn), as, according to
xii, 165.70 the " re-marrying man " (parivettar) muſt
respeĉtfully offer the " re-married man " (parivitti) his wife as
daughter-in-law (snushā) [1] ; if then the elder brother has
given him leave, and if his offence has been atoned for, then
he shall take her to himself by gripping her hand.[2] Thus
according to xii, 165.20 the two men and the woman are freed
of their fault. As opposed to this, xii, 35.28 declares : " na
tu striyā bhaved dosho, na tu sā tena lipyate, but in the woman
is no guilt, she is not thereby ſtained," which is in contradiĉtion

[1] According to the comm. as a woman unenjoyed (abhuktā).

[2] In Assam the younger brother cannot marry before the ſtill
unwedded elder one has given leave in writing. But the latter now
cannot marry any longer, and is shunned as one without a caſte
(Starcke, *The Primitive Family in its Origin and Development*, New
York, 1889, pp. 135–36). Among the German people, too, ridicule
and contempt even now fall on such a luckless fellow or lover of
freedom : at the younger brother's wedding " he has to dance in the
swine's trough ", an expression I have heard Heaven knows how many
times.

with the view also represented elsewhere in the Smṛiti ; for according to Manu, iii, 172 ; Baudhāy., ii, 1.1, 39 ; Parāçara, iv, 23, for instance, all three, together with the girl's guardian, and the sacrificial priest who officiated at the ceremony, go to hell. Rām., iv, 17.36 teaches : "The murderer of king or Brahman, the cow-slayer, the thief, he that rejoices in destroying living creatures, the atheist (nihilist), and the re-marrier—they all come into hell." According to xii, 34.4 the following stand on the same level with the Brahman-murderer : the re-marrying man, the re-married man, the younger sister that marries before the elder (agredidhishu), and the husband of an elder sister that marries after the younger sister (didhishūpati) ; another statement is in Manu, iii, 173.[1]

[1] The law books are no less severe. Both the brothers and both the husbands in case of a new marriage must for their defiling offence undertake penances. Āpastamba, ii, 5, 12.22. Brothers stained by re-marriage, the husband of the younger but first-married sister, and the husband of the later-married elder sister must, like the thief, the atheist, the man expelled from his caste, etc., not be invited to a Çrāddha or sacrifice to the dead. Gautama, xv, 16, 18. Cp. xviii, 18, 19. According to Baudhāyana, ii, 1, 1.40 the two brothers, the priest who acted at the wedding, and he that bestowed the bride, must cleanse themselves by a twelve days' Kṛicchra penance ; for the wife a three days' fast is enough. According to iv, 6.5–7 pañcagavya (a mixture of butter, milk, sour milk, dung and urine of the cow) mixed with rice-gruel is a help. All these four men participators fall into a bad offence, like the murder of one that is not a Brahman, or of a cow, like blaspheming the Veda, adultery, etc. Vishṇu, xxxvii, 13 ff. So, too, Yājñav., iii, 234 ff. Cp. Manu, xi, 6. Vishṇu, liv, 16, lays down for the participators just named and the re-married elder sister the Cāndrāyaṇa penance. Parāçara, iv, 24, prescribes for the elder brother, the priest, the bride and her guardian variously graduated mortifications (Kṛicchra, Atikṛicchra, and Cāndrāyaṇa). For the MBh., Vasishṭha, xx, 7–10 is particularly enlightening : The two brothers must undergo certain defined penances (Kṛicchra and Ati-kṛicchra), the younger one hand over his wife to the elder, and the latter take her as his own wife (probably in form, as the expositor says), and then give her back to the other ; then the younger must get married to her again. The man who marries a younger sister before the elder has to carry out twelve days' Kṛicchra, and then wed the elder (probably over and above the other one). The husband

MARRIAGE

In consonance with this rule it comes about that the five sons of Pāṇḍu in the order of their ages take Draupadī to wife on five following days (i, 191.8 ff. ; 198.13).[1] If, on the other hand, the elder brother has been expelled from his caste (patita), or has become an ascetic (pravrajita), then the younger brother is free to wed (xii, 34.27).[2]

of an elder sister married after the younger one must do atonement with Kṛicchra and Atikṛicchra (as in Parāçara the elder brother does with doubled Kṛicchra), and hand over his wife to the husband of the younger one (probably only in form, but see Bühler's note SBE, xiv, p. 103). That the greater shame should lie mostly on the elder brother and the husband of the re-married sister seems understandable. The snushāṃ in MBh. (in itself remarkable) might be therefore a later garbling for an earlier jāyām. In the end, however, it would be better to take Nīlakaṇṭha's snushātvena to be wrong, and to translate : " The re-married man shall offer (in marriage) this daughter-in-law (to the elder brother)." The elder brother, indeed, is like the father.

[1] Winternitz in *Wiener Zschr. f. d. Kunde d. Morgenlandes*, xiv, 65 f. brings forward MBh., i, 191 and Arjuna's speech there as a leading proof of the reality of polyandric marriage, and says : " Arjuna therefore holds it as quite wrong even to think of making Draupadī the wife of him alone. He, Yudhishthira, must, he says, marry her first," etc. But although this reading is in agreement with the marriage of the five, as told in the Epic, and there is also no doubt about the polyandry of the Pāṇḍavas, yet this latter cannot be deduced from that passage. Niviç means simply : to found a household for oneself, and not at all : to wed a certain person. Arjuna says only this : " First Y. must take a wife, then we four brothers come in the order of our ages, and as he is the lord of us all, so he is, too, of Draupadī whom I have won." He might quite well mean here : " If he wishes to marry her for himself only, that is right and good." In any case what is here expressed is only the dread of the sin of " re-marrying ".

[2] According to Parāçara, iv, 25 the younger may marry without regard to the elder, if the latter is hunchbacked, a dwarf, impotent, weak-witted, gadgada (a stutterer ?), blind, deaf, or dumb from birth. Those mentioned here and in our Mahābhārata passage, together with some other afflicted ones, are not entitled either to inherit or to have law dealings. They may, indeed, marry, at least as a general rule, and their offspring can inherit, if this offspring have no defects. See Manu, ix, 201–203, and the parallels given by Bühler in his transl. (according to Vishṇu, xv, 35 ff., the exceptions are the offspring

As is well known the polygamy of the man in Aryan India is as old as the hills and does not form the slightest offence in the Brahmanic system, although since Vedic times, indeed, one wife is seen to be the usual, often the obvious thing. On the other hand, polyandry is utterly repugnant to Indian feelings, and in the Epic only one or two cases of it are found, and these are exclusively cases of a community of wives among brothers.

It is a remarkable fact that the chief heroes of the Mahābh., the five brothers, have one wife or head-wife in common, Draupadī. Yet this is not so wonderful if we bear in mind the origin of the Pāṇḍavas. In very many places the Epic shows with the utmost clearness that the Kauravas are the original heroes of the poem, and, as I hold, not, so to say, only those of " ballads or ballad cycles " which came before the putting together of the actual Epic, but those of a greater poem, of an epic of the Bharatas. No less clearly does the present text also show us what unauthorized stranger intruders of a later date the Pāṇḍavas are. Nothing could be more evident, whatever one's attitude may be to Holtzmann's theory in detail. To all seeming, the Pāṇḍavas were even of non-Aryan stock ; and no one with an open mind can let himself think that they were any cousins of the Kauravas, as the later revision would have us believe. Polyandry must probably be called non-Aryan, in spite of the objection raised by Jolly (*Recht und Sitte*, p. 48), and the five brothers, too, were certainly non-Aryan. They may very well have belonged to one of the many aboriginal peoples or tribes which dwelt and still dwell in India and on its boundaries, and have kept polyandry down to this day.[1] It then

of those deprived of caste, if born after the criminal offence, and that of the child, likewise outside the law, which was begotten of a woman of higher caste. Cp. Gautama, xxviii, 45, and especially Kauṭilya (transl.) 257.3 ff. and addits.) Among the South Slavs also it is held to be " a firm-based principle of customary law "—and this prevails among them as among the Indians, and among all primitive peoples and tribes—" that younger brothers and sisters must not marry before the elder ones." But exceptions are made, when the elder brother has a mental or serious bodily illness, or becomes a priest, or expressly gives his leave. Krauss, *Sitte und Brauch*, etc. 334 f.

[1] A good short account of them in Jolly, *Recht und Sitte*, p. 48. Cp. Hartland, *Primitive Paternity*, ii, 155 ff. The above words, too,

was a task of heavy toil to justify this shocking moral defect of the chief heroes and the pillars of the Brahmanic Mahābhārata. The one explanation is this : When the five brothers, who are going about in Brahman garb, bring Draupadī to their mother, and show her to her, the mother does not notice what this bhikshā (alms) is, that she supposes has been brought home from the begging they ply, and says : " Enjoy it together." The mistake has now been made once for all, and both she and her band of sons now think that the word of a mother is holy and must be held to, absolutely and after the letter. Moreover, they are all aflame with love for the wonderfully fair one, and so Yudhishthira deems that therefore they would rather all possess her together than that, through her, strife should come about among the brothers (i, 191). When now they tell Draupadī's father of their polyandric intentions, who has naturally thought that Arjuna has won her and shall marry her, he along with his kinsfolk is deeply wounded in his moral feelings. He makes the strongest protest against such an unheard of adharma (lawlessness, wrong), conflicting with worldly custom and the Veda. Yudhisthira, however, has his usual Pilate saying ready to hand : " What is Dharma (right, the good) ? No one can find his way in such a ticklish question. We take the path which our forefathers followed one after the other," a way of speech, therefore, like that used of marriage by purchase in royal families, although in our passage it is quite likely that only a general view can be in question. Then a family council is held. Drupada, the father, keeps his ground : " I hold it for an adharma that is opposed to the world and the Veda. For one wife for many—there is no such thing. Neither did the high-souled forefathers have this custom,

were written wholly under the influence of reading the MBh. itself. Afterwards I saw to my satisfaction that other investigators had long ago uttered such views. Thus Winternitz leans towards the view that the Pāṇḍavas were a "non-Aryan mountain tribe" (WZKM, xiv, 71). So Hopkins, *The Great Epic*, pp. 376, 400. On the other hand I do not believe that from the passages brought forward by Winternitz and others polyandry for India can really be deduced. Cp. also Jacobi, *Göttinger Gel. Auzeigen* 1899, p. 885.

nor muſt we in any wise be guilty of this offence againſt custom and law." His son Dhrishtadyumna gives his opinion : " How could an elder brother of virtuous ways draw nigh unto the wife of his younger brother ? " Yudhishthira keeps to it that the higheſt authority on earth is the mother. In olden times, too, he says, Jatilā of Gotama's race had seven Rishis as husbands, so, too, did the Muni's daughter Vārkshī have regular intercourse with the ten ascetically cleansed Pracetas brothers.[1] Kuntī agrees with him : " So it is. And I have a dreadful fear of lying." The holy patriarch of the family, Vyāsa, is present and announces : " It is the holy and eternal law even as Yudhishthira has spoken." Then he rises, takes the king by the hand, with him leaves the gathering, and now tells him of the cause :

Once the gods made a great sacrifice ; Yama was the slaying prieſt ; he now utterly neglecſted his office as god of death ; creatures no longer died, and their numbers brought anxiety. There was no longer any diſtincſtion between mortals and immortals. Then went the gods to Brahma to complain to him of this diſtress. He consoled them by telling them that Yama would split up his personality, and they were now to fill this second half with their power, and thus it would bring death to beings. In content the gods went to the sacrifice. Then they saw on the Gaṅgā a lotus-flower. The hero among them, Indra, was sent off to find out whence it came. He saw a glorious woman weeping at the source of the Gaṅgā, and her tears as they dropped became golden lotus-flowers. He asked her the reason of her sorrow. She led him on to the mountain top. There he saw a handsome youth playing dice together with a young lady ; as the youth, however, in his eagerness to play gave him no heed whatever, the king of the gods grew angered, and boaſted of being lord of the world. The youth laughed at him, and looked at him. At this Indra became as ſtiff as a tree-ſtump. Çiva (this was the dicing hero) bade the woman that shed tears of golden lotuses to

[1] How this " daughter of a tree " came wonderfully into being from the trees, and her marriage with the ten Pracetases is told in the Purāṇas, e.g. Vishṇu, i, 15 ; Agni, xviii, 22 ff. ; Bhāgavata, iv, 30.47 ff. Her name was Marishā.

take the haughty one into a cave in the mountain.[1]   There
he saw four shining figures sitting, like him down to the laſt
hair.   At the sight of them he was gripped by sorrow : " Shall
I perhaps become like these ? "   Angrily Çiva told him that
these were four earlier Indras that had been as haughty, too,
as he.   For this they had all had to come into human life,
and would bring about great deeds in it.   The four Indras
begged : " May the gods of right and of the wind, Indra
and the two Açvins, beget us."   Indra promised to give them
a fifth as fellow, sprung from his seed.   Now this is Arjuna,
and his four brothers are the four former Indras.   In kindness
of heart Çiva also granted them the boon that that weeping
woman, the goddess Lakshmī, should be their wife in mankind.
She was then born in wondrous wise to Drupada out of the
ground (mahītalāt).   Vyāsa through his ascetic powers then
endowed the king Drupada with the eye of a god ; so Drupada
saw the five brothers and Draupadī in their heavenly forms,
and was now fully contented.

Then quite needlessly Vyāsa told him the same tale he had
told (i, 169) the five brothers before their wooing of Draupadī,
and in more or less the same words ; the trishṭubh metre
goes over into the çloka at the beginning of this piece : There
was once the daughter of a Ṛishi, who because of her deeds
in an earlier exiſtence found no husband in spite of her beauty.
Then she gave herself up to hard penance, and when the rejoiced
Çiva asked her what she would have, in her fierce yearning she
uttered five times : " Give me a proper man."   " Good ;
five shalt thou have, since thou haſt said it five times."   And
her remonſtrance that she only wanted one was of no help
(i, 191 ff.).[2]

The ſtate of things brought about by this marriage now gave
rise to some difficulty.   The divine Ṛishi Nārada, the
wandering journaliſt of the Indian heaven comes up and begs

[1] The world as the dice-game of a god, and Çiva and his wife as
players, are often-recurring Indian thoughts.
[2] The two laſt legends are clearly marked as being very late,
childish inventions. See, too, Winternitz, JRAS, 1897, pp. 733 ff.
An explanation that is partly more sensible, but partly nonsense is
given in Mārkaṇḍeyapur., v.

the brothers in heartrending words not to quarrel among themselves because of the woman, as the over-fierce Daitya brothers
Sunda and Upasunda once had done ; and as a warning example
he tells them the tale of these demon giants, who held all three
worlds in the ban of their rule of terror until the Apsaras
Tilottamā through her peerless loveliness so strongly fired
them both that they slew one another (i, 209–212). Then
the Pāṇḍavas settle it between themselves : if one of us comes
to another while the latter is with Draupadī, then he must
live in chastity twelve years in the forest.[1] Now one day
a Brahman comes who has just had his cows stolen, and sets
up a truly priestlike outcry before the rulers forgetful of their
duty, the Pāṇḍavas. Arjuna is at once ready to punish, and
only wants to fetch his arms quickly. But alas ! these are in
a room where, at this very moment, Yudhishṭhira is with

---

[1] The first half of the çloka (212.29) is = Draupadyā sahāsīnam
anyam no 'nyo 'bhidarçayet. Böhtlingk's rendering : " to betray "
is quite a mistaken one. Cp. 213.19, 27, 31, 32. It can be seen how
foreign to the Aryan Indians polyandric relations are. Where polyandry prevails the matter is mostly very easily arranged. Either each
sharer in the marriage then takes his turn on his fixed days, or a sign
before the entrance to the woman warns the others. Such a *cave
canem* before the gate to the common love-paradise was among the
Massagetae the quiver, of the man who was with her, hanging to the
wife's waggon ; among the Nasamones in Libya the happy man left
his staff at the door ; so, too, in Arabia Felix and among the Sabæans.
Hartland, *Primitive Paternity*, ii, 130 ; Ed. Meyer, *Geschichte des
Altertums*, i, 1³, pp. 25, 30; Lippert, *Kulturgesch.*, ii, 11–12. The staff,
arrow, or shoe among the old Arabs had to be shown to keep away
him that was not called. Welhausen, *Gött. Nachr.* 1893, p. 462.
Cp. 464. The Tiyan in Malabar make use of a knife in the door-
frame as a warning sign, the Izhuva or Taudan in South Malabar
make use of a vessel with water before the entrance. Hartland, l.c.,
ii, pp. 165 f. As is well known it is not only poverty that is the cause of
polyandry, as has been asserted. Rather the wife of many is just as
proud of her wealth in husbands as the polygamist is of his crowd of
wives ; and the Tibetan woman, for instance, pities her poor European
sister who has to be satisfied with only one representative of manhood.
No : the more husbands, the greater happiness. Hartland, ii, 161 ff.
Cp. 182.

Draupadī. He has also the holy duty to take leave of his eldeſt brother. After long wreſtling with his conscience Arjuna decides for the higher duty; he goes in and fetches the weapons. After he has run the robbers to earth, he comes home again to the sound of rejoicings, and makes ready for his long exile in chaſtity. Yudhishṭhira is utterly overwhelmed, declares he bears him no anger whatever, and that all is well. " For if the younger goes in to the elder (while the latter is with the woman) then that is no harm or wrong (upaghāta); but if the elder goes in to the younger, then that is a breach of the holy ordinance." But Arjuna in his true boyish way rises proudly up, and shouts : " How should I swerve from the truth ! " For Draupadī this parade of virtue muſt have been the more unpleasing in that she did not fully share in the disintereſtedness of the brothers ; she is accused of having preferred Arjuna, and has to atone for it at the great departure for heaven (xiv, 87.10 ; xvii, 2.3 ff.).

It is in harmony with Yudhishṭhira's words that even Dhṛishṭadyumna only proteſts againſt one thing, that the younger brother Arjuna, to whom Draupadī really belongs, has to share her with the elder. But that the younger brothers have access to the wife of the elder one seems to appear to him not at all unnatural or unlawful (i, 196.10). This exaċtly corresponds with the well-known arrangement in group-marriage, or better, fellowship marriage of brothers, and is refleċted, too, in a mythical tale in the Mahābh. " Now there was once a famous wise Ṛishi, called Utathya. Mamatā was the name of his much-prized wife. But Utathya's younger brother, the sacrificial prieſt of the heaven-dwellers, Bṛihaspati the majeſtic, forced himself on Mamatā. But Mamatā said to her brother-in-law, beſt among speakers : ' But I am with child by thine elder brother. Desiſt. And this offspring of Utathya within my body has already ſtudied the Veda with its six auxiliary sciences. But thou art a man of irresiſtibly powerful seed. Two cannot find room here. But as things are so, do thou therefore now withdraw.' Though thus addressed by her aright, yet the noble-minded Bṛihaspati could not hold back his soul filled with love's urge. Then, with love's longing full, he united himself with her,

113

who had none of love's longing. But as he ejaculated the seed, he that was in the womb said to him : ' Listen, father dear, do not give way to love's heat, there is no room here for two, the space is small.[1] And I came here first. And withal, thy seed, O holy one, is not barren ; I pray thee not crowd me.' But Brihaspati listened not to these words of the child in the womb, but only forced his way into the lovely-eyed Mamatā to beget. When he that rested in the womb marked the spurting seed, with his feet he barred the way against Brihaspati's seed. Then the seed fell swiftly onto the earth, driven back without reaching its place. At this Brihaspati was angered ; when he saw the seed fall down, filled with rage he cursed Utathya's son that was in the womb, he the holy seer, did abuse him : ' Since thou hast spoken such words to me at a time like this, which all beings yearn after, thou shalt go into a long darkness (dīrghatamas).' " The Rishi was of a truth born under the name of Dīrghatamas, blind from his birth owing to the curse of the high-famed Brihaspati, equal to Brihaspati in strength and power (i, 104.9 ff.).[2]

It is, indeed, a strange thing to find a usage, which aroused the moral feelings of the Indian, unhesitatingly ascribed to this priest of the gods, Brihaspati, and to his brother, as also to other Rishis and holy women ; and one feels tempted to look on such things as echoes from a time when, among even the Aryans also, group-marriage may have been a recognized institution. But such a conclusion would seem to be at least a highly uncertain one ; for what stories are not told among the different peoples of gods and holy men ! The Indian has often declared, in the Epic, too, that such divine figures as these are not tied down to the laws of earth, that mankind indeed must follow a loftier ethic than they. True, enlightened views such as these belong to a later time, of noble spiritual and emotional culture, and can hardly be assumed in the age

[1] Less likely : " for two, with the narrow space, there is no being begotten " (literally : there is no being begotten in a small space).
[2] The same ancient legend, which of course has been devised as an explanation of the name of the seer and singer Dīrghatamas, is found again, told shortly, in the xiith book, chap. 341, çl. 49 ff. Cp. also Winternitz, WZKM, xx, 31 ff.

when such myths were being shaped, or in the days before it. And if for that earlier period, too, the same lofty charaɗter of at leaſt some minds were to be assumed, such as shows itself already in the oldeſt Upanishad, that would prove nothing for or againſt the conditions that might be aɗtually exiſting. Thus there is left always a certain doubt. But it is quite clear that, as it was, Draupadī's marriage was reluɗtantly taken ; and the words of Karṇa, the bitter foe, indeed, of the princess of Pañcāla, may not have ſtood so isolated in a more primitive form of the Epic : " One husband is appointed unto the wife by the gods. But this one yields herself into the power of more men than one, and therefore this is certain : She is an evil woman " (ii, 68.35).[1]

Like these legendary traditions of polyandric marriages is the evidence in the Epic as to earlier or ſtill exiſting conditions of hetærism.[2] The gospel of unreſtriɗted free love, from the

[1] In the Daçakumārac. (p. 209 of my translation), among the "devilish wiles " of the gods and holy men (which, however, ·" because of the power of the knowledge of their virtue," were not " detrimental "), it is also alleged that Bṛihaspati used to visit the wife of Utathi. With this cp., too, for inſtance, Samayamātṛikā, iv, 20–35.

[2] Such mythical tales of earlier times often ſeem to me to be altogether too bold to be used as wholly credible grounds of proof. Like other peoples, the Indians too—and especially often and gloomily—speak of an earlier " time without a ruler and filled with terror " : there was at that time utter lawlessness, they ate one another, all crimes were daily events, until men met together, and chose themselves a king (from the Epic cp. for inſtance MBh., xii, 67 ; Rām., vii, 76.33 ff. under the text as çlokāḥ prakshiptāḥ). To say nothing of the faɗt that this piɗture does not correspond with more primitive conditions, the Indians who told such tales had at any rate no longer any memory of such miſty far-off days. A pet theory set the powers of imagination at work. The 'Aino, who are well known to be monogamic, relate in their tales that men were allowed in olden days to have more wives than one (Chamberlain, Aino Folk Tales, p. 48). Here it is a quite natural sophiſtication of the underſtanding that is speaking, or the knowledge that such a thing is cuſtomary among other peoples. Polyandry is nowhere found in the Veda, but probably, as already pointed out, it was to be found among the primitive population in and about India. The conditions among them have, anyhow, been the leading cause of such suggeſtions. But then, mainly under their influence, polyandry

lips of the sun god—in this case, indeed, not unprejudiced—has already been listened to by us. The Indians tell many tales of the Uttarakurus dwelling in the north, an ideal people in an ideal land that is a real Utopia. There, we are told, the women follow their own inclinations (kāmacarā bhavanti), and neither man nor woman knows jealousy (īrshyā nāsti narīnarāṇām, xiii, 102.26 ; cp. xiii, 2.13 ff.).[1] In the thirty-first chapter of Book ii there is a description of how Sahadeva, Yudhishthira's brother, when on his world-conquering expedition (digvijaya), reaches the farthest south. Before Māhishmatī, the city of the king there, Nīla,[2] he finds himself in very great distress, for the god of fire is standing by Nīla, and everything

may have been found in isolated cases among the Aryan Indians also. The Aino just mentioned believe that, in the far past, girls enjoyed full freedom in sexual intercourse (*Anthropos*, Bd. v, p. 770). Among them it is not so, but it is so among a vast number of peoples and tribes of older times and of to-day, and in the most different lands. The Kanakas have a tradition that originally a man had always but one wife (*Anthropos*, ii, p. 385), a shrewd blow against current " proofs " of the development of marriage, by way of promiscuity and other horrors, into monogamy. Those who play about with survivals often seem quite to have forgotten that man, and above all, more primitive man and the child, has not only his actual experience and his memory (which is, however, exceedingly weak) of it, but still more a heart filled with yearnings, an inquisitive understanding, and unchecked powers of imagination. And in the name of Heaven what would be the good of poor mortal man making himself gods, legendary heroes, and saints, if they could not do things which the everyday child cannot allow himself to do !

Horace Man reports a remarkable case of polyandry in the Nicobars. The woman had no children by her first husband ; she therefore married a second, and could then prove the truth of her suspicion as to number one ; both the husbands lived peacefully together, but everyone laughed at the family (*Transactions of the 9th Internat. Congr. of Orientalists*, vol. ii, p. 891).

[1] There, indeed, the " beauteous maidens grow on trees ", and all live only for the pleasures of love, as the Epic, too, relates (see, for instance, Rām., ii, 91.19 ; iv, 43.37 ff.). [From Melanesia for plants turning into women cp. G. C. Wheeler, *Mono-Alu Folklore* (London, 1926), pp. 25–6 (Translator).]

[2] " Blue-black."

in Sahadeva's army, man and beast, goes up in flames. " For it is learned that the uplifter of sacrifices (Agni) that dwells in Mīhishmatī had once been found out as an adulterer.[1] The daughter of King Nīla was fair beyond everything. She always came to kindle the burnt sacrifice. But the fire would not blaze up, even when fanned with fans, until it was set alight with wind coming from the lovely rounded lips. Then the holy Agni fell in love with this maiden, who was sweet to look on, for King Nīla and all, and she took him to her.[2] But once when he happened to be sporting in love (with her) in the form of a Brahman, the just king chastised him according to the precept. Then the glorious uplifter of sacrifices blazed up in wrath. When the king saw him he was filled with wonder, and bent his head to the ground. Then, in time, the prince, with head bent likewise,[3] gave this maiden as wife to the fire god with the Brahman form. Then when the shining one had accepted this lovely-browed daughter of King Nīla, he bestowed his favour on the king. The most excelling fulfiller of wishes offered the prince a favour, and the lord of

---

[1] Pāradārika, therefore, here used of wrongful behaviour with a woman who is not (here even : not yet) wedded to a man. As to the position of Māhishmatī, " sacred to Agni," see Pargiter, Mārkandeya Purāṇa (Calcutta, 1904), p. 333, note ‡.

[2] Hardly : "while Nīla, yet, was the king of all." We might perhaps read : Nīlasyājñasya sarveshām, or better still : Nīlasyājñāte sarveshām " without Nīla (and) all knowing anything of it, she took him to her ". The genitive too in -sya is sometimes, however, used as an ablat. in the MBh. (i, 228.17 ; ii, 81.37 ; xii, 198.6, 11 ; 218.28 ; xiv, 24.11 ; espec. too x, 2.6, where daivasya = without favourable fate). See further x, 10.14 ; xii, 216.8. If taken so, the traditional text, " without Nīla (and) all," would come to the same thing. That is to say, therefore : " without N. or anyone else having known of it." Fire, moreover, must not be blown up by the mouth. Mārk.-Pur., xxxiv, 112 ; Manu, iv, 53 ; Gautama, ix, 32 ; Āpast., ii, 5, 15.20 ; Vasishṭha, xii, 27. Nor must the feet be warmed at fire, nor put over or under it, nor must one jump over it. Vishṇu, lxxi, 37 ; Yājñav., i, 137 ; Manu, iv, 53 f. Of course, it must not be touched with the foot (MBh., vii, 73.30 ; K., xiv, 108.13 ff. ; Yājñav., i, 155).

[3] Or perhaps: as it should be, in the right way (tathaiva).

earth chose invulnerableness in his army. From that time all that through want of understanding (or : knowledge) try to take this city are forcibly burned by the fire god. And in this city of Māhishmatī, as is well known, the women, too, were then freed from interference as to their wishes.[1] Thus Agni granted women the favour that they are not to be held back ; for there the women are wholly free, and go the way that pleases them."

In the Mahābh., i, 122 King Pāṇḍu makes the following speech to his wife, "harmonizing with law and virtue." "Now will I make known to thee the true essence of dharma (law, custom, virtue), listen unto me, the ancient dharma perceived by the lofty-minded knowers of it. In former times, as is well known, women were left unhindered,[2] O thou of the lovely face, going the way of their desires, in freedom, O sweet-smiling one. When they, from the years of maiden-hood on, did trick their husbands,[3] that was nothing wrong, O lovely-hipped one, but rather that was the right thing in former times. And the same moral law of early times is followed still to-day, free from love and anger, by the beings that linger in an animal-birth. This is the moral order laid down by

---

[1] Babhūvur anatigrāhyā yoshitaç chandataḥ kila. More exactly, that is to say : freed from encroachments. I take the word as = avini-grāhya. "Not to be outdone in their sexual longing" (according to a meaning given by Pāṇini) would not go well here.

[2] Anāvṛita unhindered, not forbidden, accessible to all, not restrained, unbridled, free. This word is often found in the MBh., particularly as applied to woman, and always with this meaning. As a commentary take only i, 229.9, 13 : anāvṛita = apratishiddhabhoga ; vii, 40.36 compared with 44.13 = asaṃyata. It has also the meaning : unclad, naked, and so Jacobi takes it here. Context, use of words, and çl. 14 forbid this rendering, important as this further statement would be.

[3] A maiden, who does not keep her chastity, sins against her future husband. While this view is rooted in the rough conception that the man's right of property has even a retrospective force, yet in a noble and beautiful meaning it is true ; only it must likewise be applied, too, to the man's behaviour before marriage. Agni is perhaps accordingly accused of adultery for lying with a maiden.

118

the rule of conduct [1]; it was honoured by the great Rishi through observance, and to-day is still honoured among the Uttarakurus, O thou with the banana-like thighs. For this is the eternal law that shows favour to women. By whom, however, and on what grounds, a short while ago the barrier of to-day was set up in our world—learn this now at full length, O brightly-smiling one, from me. There was once a great Rishi, Uddālaka by name, thus we have heard. Çvetaketu was his famous son, the Muni. This Çvetaketu set up this barrier of the moral law, and from anger, O thou with lotus-leaf eyes. Hear from me why. Once, then, a Brahman took Çvetaketu's mother by the hand, before his father's eyes, and said : ' Let us go.' Driven by displeasure, the Rishi's son gave himself up to wrath, when he saw his mother thus led away as though by force. To the angry Çvetaketu his father spoke, when he saw him thus : ' Do not yield thyself up to wrath, O dear one. This is the eternal law. For the female beings of all kinds are unhindered (anāvrita). As the cows stand before our eyes, dear one, so are all creatures in their various kinds.' [2] But the Rishi's son would not bear

[1] Pramāṇa. This word is rendered by Nīl. in an earlier passage by veda. Na cirāt, in the following, might perhaps mean : after a short time (instead of : a short while ago).

[2] The Old Indians have indeed here too, fully anticipated the theories of modern science : In the beginning all the men of the clan, the horde, or the tribe had the right to enjoy all the women of the community ; then came marriage, whether polyandric, polygamic, or monogamic, " simple or mixed," but at first always with the very actual consciousness still (and one that was often obeyed) that, in spite of it, access to a woman was not barred to the other men. In perfect harmony with our tale, for example, is the custom among the polygamous Nasamones and the monogamic Massagetae, among whom even after marriage the wife could be freely visited by all the men. Withal, in all probability, father-right prevailed in the original Indo-Germanic people, not, as has been held, mother-right. Yet among many Indo-Germanic peoples in later times there is evidence even of a community of wives, not to speak of other loose customs. See Ed. Meyer, *Gesch. d. Altertums*, i, 1, pp. 26 f. And the patriarchate is in itself consistent with the greatest unconcern as to the woman's chasteness, and even after marriage. Cp. for this chapter, among the moderns, Hartland, *Primitive Paternity*, especially the second volume, and in

with this law, and he laid down the following moral order for woman and man, among human beings only, O excellent one, but not among other creatures ; and since that time this moral rule has been in existence, and so we have heard : ' If a woman is unfaithful to her husband, then, from to-day onwards, that is a crime leading to loss of caste, like the killing of a child in the womb, gruesome and bringing down evil. And in like wise it is a crime leading to loss of caste, if a man is unfaithful to his wife, that has walked in maidenly chastity and keeps faith with her husband. A wife lays the same burden on herself, if she be charged by her husband for the sake of a son,[1] and does

this especially 101–248 ; H. Schurtz, *Urgesch. d. Kultur* (1900), pp. 105 ff.; Ed. Meyer, loc. cit., pp. 15–30. I name these three excellent works, too, because they are written from differing standpoints. Schurtz, indeed, believes that he finds the " way out of the dilemma " in the highly important theory arising out of his studies on " age-classes and men's associations " (1902, see espec. pp. 54–56), namely, that the " general course of development was this, that the younger men had the utmost freedom of sexual intercourse with all the girls of the tribe, but the older men married " (*Urgesch. d. Kultur*, espec. 123 f.). In which case therefore only the cripples of love, so to say, would have agreed to marriage—just as it happens so often among us. Eduard Meyer, who here often finds himself with Schurtz, even makes the monstrous assertion that " the free union of the sexes, and there-fore promiscuous likewise, exists without exception among all peoples and in every community, whether it be that intercourse is left fully free, or whether it is put under fixed regulations, and, for instance, is only allowed between members of certain groups, or whether it is allowed to the girls before marriage, or, as with the widespread religious prostitution, is directly enjoined. . . . Among Christian peoples, in direct contrast to this, free sexual intercourse . . . is officially forbidden, but is not thereby the less zealously practised " (*Gesch. d. Altertums*, i, 1. 3, pp. 17 f.). Things, indeed, are bad enough on this point, but such words give an untrue and distorted picture ; in olden and in modern times there are plenty of peoples who give much heed to the girl's chastity, to say nothing of the married woman ; and in civilized Christian mankind there are, in spite of everything, very many chaste wives, and unspotted maids. Here we are not speaking of the men.

[1] To let offspring be begotten of herself by another man. Niyukta and niyoga (charged, ordering) is the technical term for begetting

it not.' With these words, O timid one, did Çvetaketu, the son of Uddālaka, set up by force the barrier of the moral law . . . At the time of the Ṛitu,[1] O king's daughter, thou so faithful to thy husband, the wife shall not go afield from her husband ; these are the words of the law recognized by the law-learned. At all other times the woman has free independence (svātantryaṃ strī kilārhati) for herself. It is such a law that good men call the old one."[2]

in another's ſtead, especially when the brother-in-law or some other kinsman raises up, with the widow, children for the dead man. On this see below.

[1] The days immediately following the menses, which are proper for conception. The husband, therefore, shall not then be injured in his title to beget children. Cp. Kauṭilya (transl.) addit. 252.26 ; MBh. K., xiii, 58–59.

[2] The teaching here set forth is anyhow more acceptable than the aĉtual cuſtom of the Hassanieh Arabs, of whom J. Petherick (*Egypt, the Soudan and Central Africa*, p. 151) reports that the wives in this tribe are only bound to be faithful to their husbands for three or four days out of the seven in the week and that the latter feel themselves highly flattered if their fairer halves have a great many love adventures during the marriage holiday ; for they would look on this as a proof that their wives were attraĉtive (Finck, *Primitive Love Stories*, p. 92 ; Henne am Rhyn, *Die Frau in der Kulturgesch.*, Berlin, 1892, p. 20 ; Hartland, ii, 222). The Bahuana in the Congo area demand faithfulness of their wives only during pregnancy : they believe that at this time other sexual intercourse harms the child. Not only is the husband, among not a few peoples, left cold if his wife beſtows her favours on others, but often it is even the greateſt honour for the wife if she is embraced by a great many ; her owner then basks, like the Hassanieh juſt mentioned, in the consciousness of calling such a treasure his own. So the Brame in Africa is proud when his wife has many lovers ; the Kamchadale women plume themselves on the number of their lovers ; among the Gindans the fair, like the "lady in the cheſt", who is especially known from the Arabian ſtory-book, used to wear, as a token of each man conquered and embraced by them, a leathern anklet ; among the Bullam, Bago, and Timmaney in Weſt Africa the married woman who should repel a man she had kindled would be held as extremely uncivil and badly brought up ; and among the inhabitants of the island of Augila, and the Nasamones, the more men lay with a newly-wedded wife on the wedding night, the greater the

brilliance in which she shone. Hartland, ii, 119, 183, 131, 118; Ed. Meyer, loc. cit., p. 24; Lippert, *Kulturgesch.*, ii, 14; cp. J. J. Meyer, *Isoldes Gottesurteil*, p. 15 and note 9, and on this Hartland, ii, 174; Müller-Lyer, *Phasen d. Liebe* (München, 1913), pp. 7 ff.

The woman is only a chattel; her good points or her defects have their meaning and being only with reference to the man : to his sexual pleasure, his feeling of power, his vanity, and so forth. The virginity of girls is very generally, among the ruder peoples and tribes, not in the slightest an object of desire. Prostitution as a matter of course for the as yet unmarried woman is what may be really called the rule among them. Of course there are many exceptions. Indeed, what is there for the man in such a comfortless " fiction of the brain ", as Brantôme calls the maidenhead ! Maidenly purity, indeed, often is looked on as a shame, even a crime, plenty of intercourse as an honour for the girl—anyhow a more consistent view for all that than that found among us, which one-sidedly so appraises only the man. See, e.g. Daçakumāracaritam (in my transl.), p. 45, n. 2; Ploss-Bartels[4], pp. 172, 349, 429, 459; ii, 429; Finck, *Prim. Love*, 44; 543 ff.; Engels, *Ursprung d. Familie*, etc. (1894), pp. 35 f.; Westermarck, *Human Marriage*[3], p. 81; Starcke, *Prim. Family*, 121 ff.; Hartland, i, 31; ii, 102 ff. (the whole of the 6th chapter with numberless examples), 254 ff., and elsewhere in the 7th chapter; Schurtz, *Urgesch. d. Kultur*, ch. ii, espec. p. 123 ff.; *Altersklassen u. Männerbünde*, 91–93; Reitzenstein, *Zeitschr. f. Ethnolog.*, Bd. 41, p. 676; *Anthropos*, vi, 372; vii, 100; Yule's *Marco Polo*[3], ii, 44 (in Tebet [Tibet] every girl got a ring from each man that had enjoyed her, and unless she could show at least twenty she did not find a husband; cp. the further examples there p. 48). And so on *ad infinitum*. This may then not seldom lead to such incidents as the Finnish peasant writer Alkio describes in *Puukojunkarit* ("Knife Heroes"), his great picture of life in Österbotten in the sixties of last century : here too, many girls at least find a pride in letting as many young men as possible have a share in their bed. If a new love candidate then comes while one is already lying in the fair one's arms, then there is a proper fight, in which the knife, too, is often used, till one of them is beaten and thrown down the stairs. Then while the loser is picking up his bones down below as well as he can, the one favoured by the god of battle refreshes himself upstairs in the bosom of the large-hearted country girl. The same thing is also often found elsewhere among the peasantry. Cp. for instance Jeremias Gotthelf's great novel *Anne Bäbi Jowäger*, espec. i, ch. 13–15. That retrospective proprietary feeling of the man is either not yet to be found there, or it is satisfied by the vanity of the

MARRIAGE

owner of a wife that formerly was so run after, feeling itself highly gratified ; he it is that has carried off such a pearl and cut the others out ! How, then, should this vanity not be juſt as delightfully puffed up, when she that is already married has a ſtrong attraction for others ! If we read this sentence (already, indeed, anticipated by Rousseau) in Engels, *Der Ursprung d. Familie*, etc. (1894), p. 17 : " If anything is sure, it is this, that jealousy is a feeling developed relatively late," then at firſt we call such a thing monſtrous beyond words. And yet, Finck above all (pp. 82 ff. ; 438 ff. and elsewhere, as also Hartland, *Primitive Paternity*, especially ch. vi) has brought together overwhelming evidence that real jealousy is hardly to be met with among more primitive peoples ; among the men we can only speak, at moſt, of anger at the infringement of their rights of property, among the women, of envy for her that is favoured by the husband with better treatment. Here and there outward circumſtances may have contributed towards men and women manifeſting an indifference like this—lower than among the beaſts—in things of love. Thus among the Eskimos there is the ſtress of life (Dr. H. C. Stratz, *Die Frauenkleidung in ihrer natürl. Entwickl.*[3], p. 18). Especially when the chief, prince, or prieſt drinks from the same cup as ordinary mortals, the men thus favoured feel the moſt devout, nay, proudeſt joy, and that not only among the Kalmucks (Weſtermarck, p. 79 ; Finck, 44–45). *Tout comme chez nous* is what even the civilized European muſt acknowledge, who is familiar with hiſtory and the present day.

The " cattle-girl " in Johannes Schlaf and her sly mate *in spe* is often far outdone. So, for inſtance, by many tribes in Algiers. There the father sends the daughter who is ripe out into the world, that she may gather as much together by her charms as possible. Then the girls get married, and those get a husband the quickeſt who can show by plenty of jingling money how greatly the treasures of their love have been sought after. This is reported particularly of the Uled Nail, and indeed the father, so it is said, there takes the money brought home (Robert, *XIV. Internat. Orientaliſtenkongress*, 3rd Sect., pp. 572 ff. ; Schweiger-Lerchenfeld, *Die Frauen d. Orients*, p. 296). In the same way the fathers in Nicaragua used to send their daughters through the land, for them to get themselves a dowry by way of proſtitution (Finck, 565, note ; 610). And in old Grecian times on the island of Cyprus the girls earned their wedding-portion by going to the shore and giving themselves to seafarers and travellers (Brantôme, vol. ii, 375a). Cp. Lippert, *Kulturgesch.*, ii, 13–19 ; Ploss-Bartels, i, 413–15 ; ii, 17. Of very many peoples it is reported that the men make a full use of their wives as a source of income by giving them up to others. There is a particularly rich collection

Another account of the origin of to-day's conditions is given in i, 104.22 ff. The blind seer, Dīrghatamas, who had already been disturbed in the womb by the unbridled passion of his uncle, and possibly was thereby already disposed this way—one of the Vedic singers—finds a young and lovely Brahmanic wife, by name Pradveshī, and begets several sons by her. " The Muni, filled with righteousness and virtue, noble-minded, and who had reached the further shore of the Veda and Vedāṅga, learned fully from Saurabheya (the son of the divine cow of wishes) the " custom of the cattle ",[1] and he set about practising it, full of yearning [2] and without fear. As the excellent Munis now looked on him as one that was following a wrong ordinance, they were all angered, who dwelt there in the hermitage, and overcome by a foolish blindness, speaking thus of the Muni

again in Finck, passim, and in the 6th chapter of Hartland's *Primitive Paternity*. The old king Pāṇḍu was therefore on the right track.

But it is another question whether we can regard as proof his and the other statements in the MBh. as to promiscuity in the Aryan pre-history of India. The theory of hetærism or promiscuity as the primary stage of mankind is, indeed, now given up by the most competent investigators, and since the Indo-Europeans evidently already had a well-ordered family life before their dispersal, and the Veda, too, knows nothing of any hetærism, we cannot put our trust in such legends for taking so break-neck a leap into the greyest dawn of time. The Greeks and probably other peoples, too, spin tales in the same way, of certain men having introduced marriage, the women having been up till then in common.

[1] According to Nīl. this is public copulation. But why should D. have to " fully learn " such a usage ? One would be inclined to think of the joyous heat, painted by Boccaccio, of the stallions and mares on the Thessalian plains, which the woman described to us by him (and before that by Apuleius in the *Golden Ass*) imitates with her lover, as she stands by the great vat in which her good, scouring husband is toiling away. The amorous enjoyment paçuvat is of course looked on as orthodox. There were also probably other special " refinements " in this case. Of course, D. likewise did the thing publicly, as we must conclude. On the public sexual act cp. Müller-Lyer, *Phasen d. Liebe*, 16 f.; 65; Schrader, *Die Indogermanen*, 76.

[2] This would seem to be the translation. Otherwise çraddhāvant usually means " he that is filled with belief ".

Dīrghatamas [1] : "Alas! this man hath broken the moral rule, and therefore must not live in the hermitage. Therefore will we all shun this evil-minded one." And since his wife had won sons, she was then not at his call and bidding. And to the hating wife the husband said : "Wherefore dost thou hate me?" Pradveshī spoke : "Because the husband gives food to the wife, therefore, after the tradition, is he called husband ; and because he offers her shelter, he is called her lord.[2] I that have not power to maintain thee will not be ever drudging and keeping thee, blind from birth, together with thy children, O great penitent." When the Rishi had heard her words, he spoke, filled with wrath, to Pradveshī and her sons : "Lead me into the house of a Kshattriya, and wealth of possessions will be our lot." Pradveshī spoke : "Possessions given by thee, O Brahman, I would not have ; they bring sorrow. Do as thou wilt, O prince among the Brahmans ; I shall not keep thee as hitherto." Dīrghatamas spoke : "From this day on the course of law in the world is laid down by me. One husband is for the woman the first thing and the last (parāyaṇa) so long as she lives. Whether he be dead or alive, she shall have no other man. But if a wife goes to another man, then unfailingly she sinks out of her caste. And for unwedded women, too, it is from to-day a crime leading to loss of caste.[3] But if copulation does come about, then all men must give money ; the women withal are not to have any profit from the pleasure, but it shall ever be dishonour and shame for

---

[1] The accus. with *verbis dicendi* in the meaning : of, about is often found in the MBh. (e.g. i, 48.20 ; 123.14 ; 124.17 ; 127.5 ; 165.6 ; 167.47, 48 ; 192.11 ; 193.12 ; iii, 61.17 ; 105.20 ; 191.50 ; 294.20 ; vi, 120.13, 15 ; vii, 72.23 f. ; 155.41 ; viii, 40.38 ; ix, 59.20 ; x, 9.26 ; xi, 24.21 ; xii, 156.3 ; 249.29). Cp. evaṃ taṃ vadati, so he speaks of thee, Jāt., iii, p. 150, l. 14.

[2] The well-known, often-found, etymology : bhāryāyā bharaṇād bhartā pālanāc ca patiḥ smṛitaḥ, that is, from keeping her that must be kept (that is, the wife) he is called the keeper (that is, the husband), and from sheltering, the lord (or husband, given as also = shelterer).

[3] That is, if they copulate, and thereby sin against their future husband.

125

them." [1] His wife is now overcome with anger, and in obedience to her bidding, the sons bind the blind man onto a raft, and leave him to be carried away by the Gaṅgā. Thus at laſt he comes into the land of King Bali, who rescues him, and, having heard his ſtory, makes use of him in a way corresponding with the peculiar ſtrength of the holy man and of which we shall hear later. We thus learn, too, from this episode who it is that has proſtitution for money—that pillar of shame among mankind—on his conscience.

We are often told that the Madras in north-weſtern India, the Sindhusauvīrakas, dwelling on the Indus, and the Panjāb peoples had an evil reputation among the Brahmans of the poſt-Vedic age. Even if, indeed, both these views, and Karṇa's words in the Mahābh., which among other things mock at the women and the promiscuity prevailing in these places, are to be perhaps taken with caution, yet it is not impossible that they were not altogether without foundation. "Father and son, mother and mother-in-law, father-in-law and maternal uncle, son-in-law, daughter, brother, nephew, and other kindred, friends, gueſts, and others, slave-men and slave-women—all pair, one with the other. With the men the women mingle, known or unknown, juſt as the longing comes on them. How should there be virtue among the befouled [2] Madras, a byword for their unlovely deeds, among these untutored eaters of groats and fish, who drink heady drink in their houses, and with it eat cow's flesh, and then shout and laugh, sing unrhymed rubbish, follow their luſts, and chatter such things at one another as they choose ? How should the Madra man speak of virtue, the son of women that throw off their clothes, and so dance, clouded by heady drink, that pair without heed of any barrier, and live as their luſts lead them [3] ; that make water ſtanding, like the camel and the ass, have loſt seemliness and virtue, and in all things are without shame—the son of such as these, thou wouldſt speak here of virtue ! If the Madra

---

[1] The double conditional particle (yadi and ced) also in ix, 27.25, cp. xii, 34.32 ; 152.6 ; xiii, 115.3 ; xiv, 48.2.

[2] Avalipta, probably not " haughty " : cp. viii, 44.15.

[3] So, if we read—caräç. According to the text with—varäç: " who woo (themselves) according to their luſts."

woman is asked for sour rice gruel, she shakes her buttocks, and utters—she, infatuated with giving [1]—these dreadful words : ' Let none ask me for my beloved sour rice gruel. My son I would give, my husband I would give, but I would not give sour rice gruel.' Pale-faced (gauryas), big, shameless are the Madra women, clad in woollen wraps, greedy, and usually without cleanliness or neatness. Thus do we hear " (viii, 40).[2] In the forty-fourth canto Karṇa, among many other bitter draughts, knows how to pour out the following for Çalya, the king of those parts (a Brahman brought in by Karṇa speaks) : " The people dwelling between the five streams and the Indus as sixth, these that are outside the law, and also the unclean Bāhīkas, let men shun... When the women have taken heady drink of corn and molasses and taken cows' flesh with garlic—they, who eat cakes, flesh, and roasted barley, and know not the ways of goodness, sing and dance, drunk and unclothed, on the earth-walls of the city and of the houses, without wreaths and unanointed, and amidst drunken, lewd songs (avagīta) of various kinds, which sound like the noise of asses and camels. They know no bridle [3] in their pairing, and in all things they follow their lust. They utter fine sayings against one another, they, who hold forth maddened by the drink : ' Ho there, ye outcasts ! Ho, ye outcasts ! Cast off by your husband, cast off by your lord !' Screaming, this refuse of women dance at the festivals, putting no restraint upon themselves. A husband of these foul, evil women of the Bāhīkas, one that dwelt in Kurujāṅgala, sang with but little rejoicing soul : ' She the tall one, the fair (gaurī) one, clad in a thin wool wrap, lies, I know, and thinks of me, the Bāhīka in Kurujāṅgala. When I have crossed the Çatadru and the delightful Irāvatī, and come into my home, then shall I see

[1] Ready to give.
[2] But how can one look for anything better of them ? " They are non-Aryans (barbarians) born in a bad land, who know nothing of the holy laws." The allusion to such people being like the Mlecchas, that is, belonging to the aboriginal population is worthy, however, of notice. Cp. for instance, Pargiter, Mārkaṇḍeya Purāṇa, p. 311, and what is there said.
[3] Anāvṛita.

the great-shelled,[1] splendid women, the outward corners of whose eyes [2] shine with red-lead, the light-skinned women anointed [3] with ointment from the mountain of Trikakud, wrapped in woollen cloaks and skins, screaming, fair to look on.'" Then we are further told how the Bāhīkas strengthen themselves with cakes, groats, and butter-milk, and then mishandle and rob the wayfarers, and how their great, light-skinned women devour flesh, and soak themselves with heady drink.[4] In the forty-fifth canto, çl. 11 ff., we are told why the women of the Gāndhāras, Madras, and Bāhīkas are so evil. These tribes or peoples robbed and outraged a good and chaste woman, and she uttered the curse that for this their women would be loose, and they would not be able to be freed from this dreadful evil. Therefore, too, among them it is not the sons,

[1] Çaṅkha is here an expression for vulva, though the dictionaries do not show anything of this kind. In the "gallant" time of German literature also," Muschel " (shell) was used for the woman's pudenda.

[2] Or : forehead marks (apāṅga) ?

[3] Cp. Caland, *Die altind. Toten- u. Beſtattungsgebräuche*, pp. 123 f. So far as I know this ointment does not seem to be particularly valuable otherwise, and if we take our passage in the Mahābhārata, it was looked on, indeed, as something vulgar. The Hindu, indeed, has often declared that "what mankind eats its gods eat". And yet we know that often only the worthless is dedicated to gods and spirits and their service ; they are cheated. Thus, to keep to the dead, these in Old India get fringes of garments to clothe themselves, and have to nourish themselves with only the hot steam of the cakes (Caland, *Altind. Ahnenkult*, 9 ; 64 ; 180 ; the same, *Totenverehrung*, 6). If now what is worse was, in an earlier culture, looked on as altogether excellent, to the supernatural powers it is, as something old, doubly pleasing (cp. Schurtz, *Urgesch. d. Kultur*, 306). When the Indian Aryans learned how to prepare a better drink, the soma was therefore left for the gods. So this ointment which is so highly prized in the ritual of the dead in " pre-Epic " times may also have seemed a thing of excellence to the ritually pure Aryans. K. for trikakudañjanāḥ has the easier reading : gauryas tāḥ kākukūjitaḥ "these mournfully cooing".

[4] Their beloved rice gruel is naturally one such heady drink. Sir Bampfylde Fuller writes that the mountain-tribes make a gruel from a dwarf-rice, that quickly changes to an alcoholic state ; even that which has only been boiled a short time before it, he says, a mild intoxicant (*Studies of Indian Life and Sentiment*, p. 152).

MARRIAGE

but the sisters' sons who inherit.[1] Çalya, who is thus mocked at, asserts, on the other hand, that in the land of Aṅga which is under the rule of Karṇa, they sell their children and wife (xiii, 45.40) ; and in the Rām. (ii, 30.8 ; 83.15) we are told that the çailūshas (actors) hand their wife over for others' use, as Manu, viii, 362, also tells us. Neither of these, however, is really a case of hetærism, but they show the man, indeed, as the lord, free and none too tender, of the wife.[2]

[1] Traces of the matriarchate cannot be proved from the Epic. ix, 4.9 gives the list of the dearest kindred : son, brother, sister's son, and uncle on the mother's side; ix, 9.46, likewise : son, brother, grandfather, maternal uncle, sister's son, friend. Cp. vi, 46.2 f. In ix, 5.12 Krishṇa's great grief for the dead son of his sister is referred to. But he is also the son of his dearest friend. The relation between mother's brother and sister's son is looked on as naturally a very close one in viii, 7.9 f.; ix, 7.20, 39 too : Çalya has even left his bhāgineya, and is fighting for the Kurus. But the mātula is also often missing where a list of dearest kinsfolk is given. So, for instance, in x, 8.98, 121 ; xi, 12.7 ; 16.19, 55 ; 27.2 f. And that the particularly near relation to the mother's brother does not in itself give any proof of mother-right is stressed by Ed. Meyer, loc. cit., p. 29. According to Hopkins, *Journ. Americ. Orient. Soc.*, xiii, note, pp. 141 f., the importance of the mātula in the MBh. would even be a later phenomenon. See too *Journ. Roy. Asiatic Soc.*, xiii, 139, note, and Jacobi, *Gött. Gel. Anzeig.*, 1899, pp. 882 ff. WZKM, xxiii, 165 ; Schrader, *D. Indogermanen*, 75, 107. On the other hand the matriarchate is often found among the primitive population of India. Thus according to Dalton among the Pani-Koch the property belongs to the wife, her daughters inherit it, the husband lives with his mother-in-law and must obey her and his wife ; if he commits adultery he pays 60 rupees, or is sold as a slave (*Zschr. f. Ethnol.*, vol. v, p. 336). Among the Khasi in the mountains of Assam the matriarchate is found remarkably developed. See Fuller, *Indian Life and Sentiment*, 171–174, and *Anthropos*, iv, 892 f.

[2] The law books make, of actors and singers, the same statements as something which is a matter of course and known to all, and therefore in the case of their wives there is neither the strict prohibition against a man speaking to another's wife or having connection with her, nor does the general principle hold that the husband is not responsible for his wife's debts. For these wives have intercourse elsewhere with the knowledge and will of their lords ; these are hidden near by,

SEXUAL LIFE IN ANCIENT INDIA

In spite of the ill-report, probably not altogether unfounded, as to the loose morals of certain districts, and in spite of occasional passages where utter freedom in things of sex is described as the primitive and as the ideal,[1] there is likewise to be seen in the Epic that earnest and strait view of wedlock which is so often manifested by the Indian ; and in spite of the somewhat curious Indian garb we get a quite modern feeling of pleasure when Yudhishthira in xiii, 19 ff. is wrestling with dark doubts : what is marriage, then, really ? Is it a holy and divine thing,

and then naturally come forward to claim the rent of love : they live on their wives. Baudhāyana, ii, 2, 4.3 ; Manu, viii, 362 ; Yājñavalkya, ii, 48. Cp. Kauṭilya (transl.), 252.12 ff. ; 196.7 ff. They are thus like the men of so many peoples, who are overjoyed when a man flirts with their wives, and they can thereby get something out of him. Many examples, for instance, in Finck, passim, and Hartland, especially ii, 120, 127, 129, 203, 205, 208, 215 ff. Cp. *Anthropos*, i, p. 935 ; iv, 619.

[1] It is this very fact, that promiscuity is set before us so persistently as the primitive state, which must be puzzling to the reader. Here we have the sensual and the thinking Hindu : how then could it be but that his glowing passionate love, his boundless, eager fantasy, and his piercing understanding should have led to such thoughts ? Thus, too, the sexual freedom among the more primitive peoples, dwelling around the Indian Aryans and among them, may well have led to the conception that these were indeed the more primitive conditions ; and what is old, is also, to the Hindu, that which is perfection. It should also be borne in mind that among the Uttarakurus, dwelling far to the north, and the people of King " Blue-Black ", dwelling in the farthest south, a love paradise of this kind is to be found. And it is the women that have pleasure and profit from these loose sexual ways, they who compared with men have so little freedom, and according to the Indian view are yet by nature so infinitely more sensual. Here the philosopher has the word. Here and there, anyhow, there may have been in " Epic times ", too, great immorality and hetæristic abominations, it may be, not without the influence of the non-Aryan tribes. The people and culture of India is, indeed, from earliest times, a mixture, ever growing in complexity, of what is Aryan and what is due to the aboriginal population. But this is the exact opposite of " survivals " and memory, of the far past of the Aryans. It is truly Indian to find Bṛihaspati, ii, 28 ff. saying that, in the East, the women practised promiscuity, and that there this was, as the custom of the land, right.

130

or has it only the practical purpose of begetting, or does it only serve the ends of the lowest sensuality, does it spring from evil powers ? So he comes to Bhīshma and asks : " But what is called married duty,[1] O bull of the Bharatas, which first arises at the time of taking the hand of women, how is it with this according to tradition ? Does that, which the great seers have called the rule of duty in common, spring from the holy Rishis (the compilers of the divine word, of the Veda), or from the god of procreation, or from the demons ? Here, so methinks, lurks a great and conflicting doubt. And whatever wedded duty is here on earth, what becomes of it after death ? For the dead in heaven,[2] is there still wedded duty ? But when one (of the husband and wife) dies first, where stays then the other, tell me, since mankind, the many, partake of divers fruits of their toil, are set to divers work (karman), are going towards divers hells as their destination ?[3] ' Women are untrue,' is the verdict of the compilers of the Sūtras.[4] If, now, women are untrue, why does the tradition speak of the duty in common ?[5] ' Women are untrue,' so we read, too, in the Veda. Is dharma (duty, order) now here a first (real) term ? A metaphorical expression ? A rule for a determined case [6] ? This seems to me dark and confused, as I ponder on

[1] Sahadharma, the common duty, ordering of life, virtue.

[2] Read svarge for svargo.

[3] All men, especially kings, save those wholly without sin, must go to hell ; either they first enjoy in heaven the fruits of their good works, and then in hell those of their evil works, or the other way about. MBh., xviii, 3.12 ff. ; Agnipurāṇa, 369.15–18.

[4] According to a saying, which is very often found, giving the list of women's defects and beginning with anritam. Translated in Kressler, *Stimmen indischer Lebensklugheit*, p. 31 ; Böhtlingk, *Ind. Sprüche* [2], 328 ; cp. my *Hindu Tales*, 256, note.

[5] Because of the falseness of womenfolk one could not even be sure with them of one's own begotten children ; as Kshemendra, Darpadalana, i, 15 very well reminds us, no one must be proud of his origin, for none knows indeed who his father is. How then could women take any share in the higher, religious things ?

[6] I do not know whether this translation is the right one. K. (50.7) has : dharmo yaḥ pūrviko drishṭa, etc. I would therefore translate : " Is then the dharma (order, system) that one which is looked on as

it ever. Therefore, do thou, O grandfather, thou so deeply wise, unfold this all to me, set beyond doubt according to revelation, and in its wholeness, when, of what kind,[1] and how it was introduced." Bhīshma's answer to these truly hard and intricate queſtions is, in more ways than one, truly Indian. He tells him as follows : The mighty one in penance, Ashṭavakra, wishes to wed, and woos Suprabhā, without compare on earth for loveliness, the daughter of the Ṛishi Vadānya, diſtinguished, too, on account of her excellent charaſter and pure life, one who ravishes Ashṭavakra's heart at the firſt sight like a flower-ſtrewn foreſt in spring. The Ṛishi says the wooer muſt go up to the holy north, where Çiva and Umā with their servants do dwell and take their delight, where the periods of the world's ending and the seasons of the year, the periods of men and of the gods, in bodily shape, bring the god their worship ; he will at laſt come into a dark-leaved, glorious foreſt, and meet with a splendid old woman ; then he is to come back home and wed. Ashṭavakra now wanders ever towards the north, reaching, in the Himālaya, Kubera's abode, where he is entertained moſt splendidly, so that, to the sound of godlike music, he there spends a whole year of the gods.[2] Then he goes on his way and reaches that foreſt country, which is glorious with

firſt (that is, procreation) ? (Or) eroticism (upacāra) ? (Or) the carrying out of the aſtion of divine service ? Then Yudhishṭhira would seem to come back to his firſt thought : Is it (duty) founded by the Ṛishis, that is, for the fellowship in religious and holy life ? Or by Prajāpati, that is, for begetting ? Or by the demons, that is, for satisfying sensuality ? But there is nothing said here of three ways of solemnizing marriage, which have been supposed.

[1] Yādṛiçam " how conſtituted ".

[2] That is, 128,600 human years (see Manu, i, 65 ff.; Mārk.-Pur., xlvi ; Vishṇupur., i, 3, etc.). Naturally with the heavenly sounds he did not notice the time going by, any more than, in Pauli's *Schimpf und Ernſt*, the Monk of Heiſterbach (so well known especially through Wolfgang Müller's poem) amid the sweet notes of the small bird—a motive which has a vaſt number of parallels. Thus the king Raivata with his daughter liſtens to the song of the Gandharvas in praise of Brahma ; an endless time goes by in this, but seems to him like an inſtant, and when he gets back he finds everything on earth changed. Wilson's Vishṇupurāṇa, vol. iii, pp. 249 ff.

fruits and filled with birds at all times of the year, and a wonderful penitential grove there. Then he sees a magnificent dwelling, surpassing even Kubera's, great mountains of jewels and gold, all kinds of precious ſtones, flowers from one of the trees of the gods, and other splendours. Seven ravishing maidens, differing in form, welcome the gueſt, and whichever of them he beholds, each delights him, and he can make no choice of one ; but he bids his heart be ſtill. They lead him up to an old woman who is lying on a couch, decked in magnificent ornaments. He says that they are all to go away, and only the moſt underſtanding and passionless one is to ſtay behind to wait on him. The seven take their leave, and only the old woman ſtays. But in the night she comes up into his bed, pretending that she is so cold. When she then clasps the Ṛishi, he lies like a log. "This she saw with sorrow, and said : ' Brahman, otherwise than through love, to women there can come no reſt and content from the man.[1] I am crazed with love. Love me, her that loves. Be roused, Ṛishi of the Brahmans, unite with me. Take me in thine arms ; I am sore tried with love for thee. For thereby it is, thou that art ſteeped in virtue, that the fruits of thy work of mortification come into their own ; and the bare sight of them gives a longing.[2] Thou art the lord over

[1] K. reads: Brahmann, akāmakaro 'ſti, for which read—karāſti : "Brahman, ſtaunchness of mind (as towards sensuality) arouses displeasure in women," or : "ſtaunchness of mind in the man is of no use to women."

[2] The enjoyment of women is, countless times in Indian literature, praised as the moſt glorious thing in heaven and on earth, as the one meaning and end of living, or anyhow of the years of youth. The ascetic, too, often sees the love of many and lovely women, shining before him as the goal and reward in the world beyond, or in a future incarnation. Even in grave, deeply ethical writings the like view breaks through. So, for inſtance, Uvāsagadasāo, § 246 with comment., praises bliss with women as the one happiness, the goal of asceticism ; redemption (mokkho) without it is but a threefold captivity and only it is the Real in the empty world. Indeed, he that is melted together with his beloved in the spell of delight has come into Brahma, into Nirvana (cp. Kuṭṭananimatam, 558, and my Daçakumārac., pp. 3 and 356, where many further parallels could be given). Copulation, this

all this wealth here, and over me myself. In the entrancing foreſt we will dally in love together, all divine and human delights we will try. For to the woman there is never anything higher than sexual union with the man ; that is her higheſt reward. Driven on by love, women live after their own appetites. And so they are not burned, though they walk on hot-glowing sand.' Ashṭavakra spoke : ' To ſtranger women I never go. By those learned in the text-books of the law the touching of ſtrange women has been declared to be evil. Know, my dear one, that I will wed, I swear it on the truth ; I know nought of the pleasures of the senses ; offspring is here for the sake of the holy dispensation. So I wish through sons to come into the heavenly worlds. My dear one, acknowledge the moral good, and cease.' The woman spoke : ' Neither the god of wind, nor he of fire, nor Varuṇa, nor the other thirty-three gods are so dear to women as the god of love ; for to women the pleasure of love is all. Among thousands of women, nay, among hundreds of thousands, there is to be found only one that is faithful to her husband, if, indeed, one at all. They know not father, family, mother, brothers, husband, or brothers-in-law ; given up to their pleasure, they deſtroy families, as great rivers deſtroy their banks.' Once more repelled by the Ṛishi, she exhorted him to ſtay ; then would his work be done. She bathed[1] and anointed him, and gave him hospitality in the moſt splendid wise ; thus the night and the next day went by without his noticing it. In the following night she again slipped into bed to him, but he said : ' My dear, my mind does not lean to ſtrange women. Rise, if it please thee, and desist of thine own will.' She answered : ' I am without ties. Thou doſt, then, not deal wrongly with righteousness and virtue.'[2] Ashṭavakra spoke : ' There is no being without ties for women, for the fair are tied. The teaching of Prajāpati is this : " Woman is not fit for independence." ' The woman spoke :

higheſt of the five things (paramatattva) leading to perfeƈtion, or being as the gods (siddhi), according to the Tantra writings even brings about siddhi and the knowledge of Brahman.

[1] For arriving heroes, gueſts, etc., to be bathed by women is quite epic in India, too. Cp. Rām., vi, 121.1 ff.

[2] Na dharmacchalam aſti te.

MARRIAGE

'I have an urge to pair, an urge that is pain, O Brahman, and do thou consider my sacrificing love. Thou dost sin against rightness and virtue in that thou scornest me.' Ashtavakra spoke : 'The divers kinds of vices carry that man away with them, that has given himself up to his lusts. I am ever lord of my soul by my staunchness.[1] Go into thine own bed, my dear one.' The woman spoke : 'With my head I bow, O Brahman ; mayest thou bestow favour on me, be thou the refuge of her that is sinking onto the ground. But if thou seest something forbidden in stranger women, then I give myself to thee ; take thou my hand. No guilt will fall on thee, that I assure thee on oath. Know that I am free. If there is any wrong withal, then it shall fall onto me. I have set my heart on thee, and am my own lord ; enjoy me.' Ashtavakra spoke : 'How shouldest thou be free ? Tell me wherefore. In the three worlds is no woman capable of freedom. The father wards them in childhood, the husband in youth, the son in their old age ; for woman there is no freedom.' The woman spoke : 'I have kept maidenly chastity ; I am still a maid ; of that there is no doubt ; make me thy wife ; do not repel my yearning.' Ashtavakra spoke : 'It is with thee as with me, it is with me as with thee (that is, we both are in love, but not with one another).' Must this not of a truth be a test, a hindrance set by that Rishi ?[2] For that is a wonder beyond measure (what I now suddenly see before me). What is best for me ? For it is as a maid in heavenly comeliness that she (the former old woman) has now come to me. But how has she now the most splendid of forms ? And how was it that her shape seemed aged ? And whence now a maiden's form like this ? What else will happen there ? Yet will I call up all my strength to keep myself from sexual infidelity. For such infidelity pleases me not. By truth will I win her (the beloved)." He now asked the woman, what all this might mean, and she made acknowledgment : " To strengthen thee did I make this trial. Through thy faithfulness in love (avyutthāna) thou

[1] Or : I am ever lord of my staunchness, it is ever in my grasp.
[2] Less likely : " I would fain know whether it is a (testing) hindrance, and one to be overcome, set by the Rishi, and not the truth."

135

haſt won these worlds, thou truly ſtout and ſtrong one (satya-parākrama). Know thou that I am the proteƈting goddess of the northern quarter of the heavens. Thou haſt now seen the fickleness of woman. Even old women are plagued by the feverish longing for man.[1] Brahma is now content with thee,[2] as also the gods and Indra. And as to the business on which thou, O holy one, didſt come hither, sent by the Brahman the father of the maiden, to give thee inſtruƈtion—that has all been carried through by me. Thou wilt come happily back home, no weariness will come on thee, thou wilt get the maiden, and she will bear a son." [3] Then Ashṭavakra went back home again, related, when queſtioned by the holy man, what he had gone through, and he (the holy man) said : "Take my daughter, for thou art moſt highly worthy." He wedded the maiden, and lived with her, full of joy and without sorrow.

This may seem to some extent a curious "education for marriage " ; at leaſt, such a thing would hardly be likely to arouse very great pleasure in a wooer, and this answer to a puzzling and tangled queſtion is shadowy enough, indeed. Yet out of this ſtory, by no means friendly towards women, there looks forth a spirit of deep and earneſt morality, and a beautiful meaning. It sounds cynical, but it is ſteeped in the light of an infinitely higher and purer idealism than the seemingly myſtical ecſtatic lifting of the eyes of the typical knight of weſtern lands, dreaming of his " madonna ". In unsullied chaſtity and truth, and ſteadfaſt in both—thus shall the man enter into wedlock with the beloved maiden, urged by religion, not by the lower luſt of the senses, and fully aware with himself that the woman is a wavering reed. Thus he will not make too great demands on her, but rather on himself. This may then, too, have an ennobling and ſtrengthening effeƈt on his mate, who as a woman is so susceptible, and the husband may experience untroubled joy with her, as did Ashṭavakra. Marriage,

---

[1] So Brantôme in his *Dames galantes* has a lengthy dissertation on the theme : Woman never grows old below the girdle.

[2] Holtzmann gives a small seƈtion on the relation of Brahma to wedlock, as it is found in the MBh. (ZDMG, 38, p. 184).

[3] Or : " sons ". For the whole adventure with the old woman cp. the 61ſt Jātaka.

therefore, comes from the inspired seers, it is divine, even if men fall behind it—a great and fine thought and of deep truth.[1]

[1] With this ordeal of chastity imposed on the man before marriage cp. Hartland, *Prim. Paternity*, ii, 80–82 ; 90–91 (the last case, however, reminds us rather of the Finnish custom, where the youth and maid lie together by night without consummating the sexual union, which is well known as a feat of Christian and other saints and of medieval love). The law literature in marriage demands from the man not only the like love and faithfulness as from the wife, but also unsulliedness before the wedding. Since the various books of rules for the behaviour of the Indian make complete sexual continence a holy duty of the scholar, and he must enter into wedlock at once after this period of life is over, this insistence on chastity is to be really found in them all. But Yājñavalkya, i, 52 ff. also lays it down expressly that : Without ever having spotted his chastity, thus shall he that is discharged by his teacher take home as wife a young woman *beloved* by him, and that has as yet belonged to no man, is healthy, and so on. And Baudhāy., iv, 1.11 gives this guiding thread : Let a man betroth his daughter as nagnikā to one that has not broken his vow of chastity. For the Brahma marriage particularly, he demands such an unspotted wooer in i, 11, 20.2. Cp. Manu, iii, 2. It is true that a good deal can happen between the consummation of the marriage and a marriage of this kind with a child-bride, as prescribed by some at least of the legal writings. Cp. too R. Schmidt, *Ind. Erotik*[1], pp. 632 ff.—Besides the tale from the MBh. there is Mārkaṇḍeyapur., lxi, 5 ff. : A young Brahman obtains a magic salve for the feet by whose help he covers 1,000 yojanas in one day. In the far-off Himālaya the melting snow washes it off him, he cannot get home again, and an Apsaras falls in love with him. He repels her advances in spite of the loveliness of the heavenly fay : " Dear to me is the hearth, and my beloved wife is my divinity dwelling about me (ramyaṃ mamāgniçaraṇam, devī vistaraṇī priyā 65). He calls on Agni, who sets him home again in an instant of time. And happiness comes, too, for the poor loving woman : a Gandharva named Kali has long been in love with her, but has never been listened to by her. As she now sits there in her disconsolate abandonment, he takes on the shape of the Brahman and dwells long with her in a thousand joys ; for she suspects nothing of the trick. During union, however, she has always, at the Gandharva's bidding, to shut her eyes ; for at such times and in his sleep he that is magically changed must appear in his true shape, as indeed is seen from the tale of Amor and Psyche (the mark of an Indian origin ?). Cp. Mahāvagga, i, 63 ;

also *Wide Awake Stories*, p. 193 ; Benfey, *Pantschatantra*, i, p. 254. Perhaps with this there is a connection also of the motive so widely found in the fairy tales of various lands, and in particular so finely treated by William Morris, *The Earthly Paradise*, ii, pp. 164 ff. ("The Lady of the Land ")—the motive, namely, that the bewitched human being or spirit gets back his true shape by being kissed or clasped in love. An Indian form, for instance, Mārk.–Pur., lxvi, 13 ff. (a goddess turned into a gazelle is so restored).

III

The Wedding

A LOFTY view of marriage meets us, too, in connection with the wedding ceremony in very many places in the Old Indian marriage ritual. In the Gṛihyasūtras or precepts for the religious side of domestic life there are found, besides much old-inherited superstition, as an ardently sought-for goal, two things particularly : first, the blessing of children,[1] especially a wealth of stout sons ; secondly, cordial relations between husband and wife, rooted in mutual love. Starting with the choice of a bride, that girl, according to a fine verse, often cited, but perhaps seldom followed—stifled, too, among other rules—she shall be chosen towards whom the man's soul feels drawn in joyful inclination, and beside this nothing else must weigh. At the wedding itself there is a whole array of ceremonies and formulas for bringing about a true bond between the hearts ; and Kāma, the god of love, is called upon in the wedding ritual, too. With children and grandchildren playing round them, and with these filled with gladness, the couple hopes to live a hundred autumns in a tender union of souls. This is the ideal handed down from Vedic times, only that in actual life, and also through later growths, it is often darkened.[2] Here let mention only be made

---

[1] "The Hindu only marries to have children, and the more he has the happier he feels. . . . No Hindu would ever dream of complaining that his family was too large, however poor he might be, or however numerous his children." Dubois-Beauchamp, *Hindu Manners*, etc.[3], p. 94, cp. 593.

[2] "The keen observer of the inner life of Hindu society will have no difficulty in discerning . . . that the poorest Indian villager loves his wife as tenderly and affectionately as the most refined mortal on earth." Rāmakrishna, *Life in an Indian Village*, p. 100. And so many another Indian. On the other hand another picture is given by S. C. Bose (*The Hindoos as They Are*), who is prejudiced the other way.

of those exquisite verses of the Ṛigveda (x, 85.24), with which
the bride is addressed : " I loose thee from the shackles of
Varuṇa (the warden of the moral law in the world) by which
the kindly Savitar has held thee bound (up to now to thy father's
family). Into the womb of the Ṛita,[1] into the world of good
works, I set thee, together with thy husband." Descriptions
of the wedding as such an important event in the life of the
heroic couple are often given, too, in the literary epic poetry,
moſt beautifully perhaps in Kālidāsa's Raghuvaṃça, canto 7.
The references, however, in the popular Epic are somewhat
scanty.

It is already well known from the Song of Nala and the
inserted tale of Sāvitrī that, as on every important undertaking
in India, at the wedding, too, a lucky day and prosperous
hour was carefully looked for. When Rāma has won Sītā
and called his father by messengers, and also the family regiſter
has been brought forward by both sides, Janaka, the bride's
father, says to Daçaratha that he wishes to give another
daughter, Urmilā, to Lakshmaṇa, and goes on to say : " Now
the moon ſtands in Maghā (the tenth house of the moon).
On the third day (from to-day), at the time of the moon's
house Uttaraphalgunī, hold thou the wedding ceremony.
Let the anceſtral sacrifice be made, the godāna ceremony [2]
be done over Rāma and over Lakshmaṇa, and happiness-
bringing gifts be made on their behalf." Viçvāmitra then
seeks the two daughters of Janaka's brother in marriage for
Bharata and Çatrughna, the younger brothers of Rāma, and it
is agreed that the four couples shall be wedded on one day.
Daçaratha goes home with the prince, has the Çrāddha or
cuſtoms of the dead and the godāna rite carried out, gives

---

[1] The natural and moral law, governing the whole world, and,
according to the Indian belief, having its origin and moſt important
centre of life and activity in the family.

[2] Godāna is a sacramental proceeding carried out on the youth's
hair in the 16th or 18th year, and described in the Gṛihyasūtras—
"giving the family cut to the hair " (Hopkins, JAOS, xiii, p. 109).
Çrāddha (this kind is called ābhyudayika) are prescribed for all happy
family events. See, e.g. Caland, *Ahnenkult*, p. 100, and especially
" Totenverehrung " (among some Indo-European peoples), 36–39.

the Brahmans on behalf of each son 100,000 cows—golden-horned, splendid, blessed with calves, yielding a brass pailful of milk ; 400,000 of the cows, and many other treasures he gives the Brahmans on the occasion of the godāna. On the same day Bharata's uncle on the mother's side comes, having in vain sought for his sister's son in Ayodhyā, and takes part in the festival. Next morning the princes, in full decoration, with the wedding string [1] in hand, then go together with the Rishis to the place of sacrifice. Janaka says his daughters are standing in full wedding apparel at the foot of the altar, and so let all be carried out forthwith. " Vasishtha set up the altar in a shed (prapāmadhye), took sweet-smelling flowers, golden cooking-pots (suvarṇapālikā), and coloured pitchers, which were all furnished with shoots of trees, as also earthen platters (çarāva) decked with shoots, incense-pans with perfumes, shell-shaped vessels,[2] and great and small sacrificial spoons, and vessels holding the water for guests ; further, dishes filled with roasted corn, and unhusked corn laid out ; and he decked the altar round with these things. Vasishtha, having strewn darbha-grass about according to the precept, and to the recitation of holy words, lighted the flame on the altar and made sacrifice in the fire. Then Janaka led up Sītā adorned with every kind of ornament, set her before the fire, facing Rāma, and now spoke to Kauçalyā's son : ' This is Sītā, my daughter, thy wife. Take her, I beg ; take her hand with thy hand. As faithful wife she, the one favoured of happiness, follows thee evermore as thy shadow.' After these words the king poured the water, consecrated with holy sentences, on Rāma's hand. The same holy rites were then repeated with the other pair. All walked to the right thrice

[1] It is of wool (Raghuvaṃça, xvi, 87) and red (Mālatīmādhavam, v, 18).

[2] Thus according to the dictionaries. But perhaps : vessels with shells. Shells, like water-filled pitchers, shoots, gold, etc., bring luck. See my note Samayamātṛikā, ii, 7 (p. 12) ; Kuṭṭanīmatam, p. 12, n. 1 ; Toru Dutt, *Ballads and Legends of Hindusthan*, pp. 55, 56 ; Edgar Thurston, *Omens and Superstitions of Southern India* (London, 1912), p. 111 ; Rajendralala Mitra, *Indo-Aryans*, i, p. 288 ; Caland, *Altind. Toten- u. Bestattungsgebr.*, 151.

round the fire, the king, and the Rishis. Next morning Janaka gave his daughters their dowries (kanyādhana) : many hundreds of thousands of cows, magnificent cloths, linen garments and 10,000,000 dresses, elephants, horses, chariots, and foot soldiery, all of heaven-like stature and well equipped, also a hundred girls, fine men and women slaves, worked and unworked gold, pearls, and coral. Then all went home " (Rām., i, 70 ff.). In Mahābh., iv, 72 the wedding of Abhi-manyu, Arjuna's son, with Uttarā, the daughter of the king Virāṭa is celebrated with great pomp. Shells, trumpets, drums blare out,[1] all kinds of beasts are slaughtered in hundreds, divers kinds of heady drinks are plentifully drunk ; singers and tale-tellers, dancers and praise-utterers take their share in giving glory to the festival, bands of lovely, splendidly decked women take part and engirdle the shining bride. Her father bestows on the Pāṇḍava, probably for his son, seven thousand steeds swift as the wind, two hundred thoroughbred elephants, and many things besides ; and Krishṇa likewise a great number of precious things, such as women, jewels, dresses. Yudhishṭhira naturally shows himself on this occasion, too, as a true god of blessings for the Brahmans.

i, 198 f. is more important. Vyāsa exhorts Yudhishṭhira : " To-day the moon goes into the house of Pushya ; to-day be thou the first to take Krishṇā's hand." Her father has her brought up, she having been bathed and decked with many jewels. Full of joy the prince's friends come, the state counsellors, the Brahmans, and the leading burghers, to witness the wedding. The palace shines with people and precious stones. The court is decked with strewn lotus-flowers. The five youths draw nigh in festal attire, with rings in their ears, clad in fine garments, sprinkled with sandal-water, bathed, consecrated by happiness-bringing ceremonies. Together with their sacrificial priest they come in. The priest makes the fire, sacrifices amid holy hymns (mantra), and unites Yudhishṭhira with Krishṇā. To the right he has the two led round, who have taken one

---

[1] Din and music are well known to be held by the Indians, indeed, to be very powerful in scaring away demons and bringing good luck. Cp. too Winternitz, *Das altind. Hochzeitsrituell*, 30.

another by the hands. In the same way the four other brothers, too, are then joined in wedlock with Draupadī. After the wedding the bride's father beſtows enormously rich gifts.[1] And the linen-clad Krishṇā, with the wedding-ſtring faſtened to her, was greeted by her mother-in-law ; and with bowed body, her hands folded before her forehead, she ſtood there. To Draupadī, her daughter-in-law, gifted with loveliness and happiness-yielding bodily features, endowed with virtuous ways, to her spoke Prithā in tender love the words : " As Indrāṇī towards the god with the yellow ſteeds (Indra), as Svāhā towards the brightly-shining one (Agni), as Rohiṇī towards the god of the moon, as Damayantī towards Nala, as Bhadrā towards Kubera, as Arundhatī towards Vasishṭha, as Lakshmī towards Vishṇu—so be thou towards thy husbands, a bearer of ſtout, long-lived children, a bearer of heroes, endowed thou with much good fortune, beloved by thy husband, fully gladdened with delights, disposing of sacrifices, and faithful to thy husband. May ever the years find thee, as they go by, honouring, as is seemly, gueſts and new-comers, the good and those that thou shouldſt heed, old and young. In the kingdoms, firſt among which is Kurujāṅgala, and in the cities be thou dedicated to the king as 'wealth of virtue' (as queen to Yudhishṭhira). The whole earth, conquered by thy ſtout husbands with valiant heroes' ſtrength, do thou make over to the Brahmans at the horse sacrifice, the great offering. Whatever surpassing jewels there be on earth, O thou that art gifted with excellences, win them for thine, O lovely one, and be happy through a hundred autumns. And as I greet thee linen-clad to-day, O daughter-in-law, so will I with far greater joy greet thee, O thou gifted with excellences, when thou haſt borne a son."

Likewise when Arjuna wedded Krishṇa's siſter, Krishṇa made magnificent gifts. " To them (the Pāṇḍavas) Krishṇa, he in high renown, gave very great wealth because of the

---

[1] A hundred slave-girls in the firſt bloom of youth are among the treasures beſtowed by Drupada on each of the five Pāṇḍavas. Cp. also v, 192.31 ; i, 199.13 f. As Kshattriyas are here concerned, the Rājput cuſtom may also be compared, by which at the wedding the bridegroom's every wish, whatever it is, muſt be fulfilled by the girl's father. Tod, Rajaſthan, i, 526.

kinship through marriage,[1] the marriage-portion (haraṇa) of Subhadrā, the gift to the kinsfolk. A thousand chariots with golden fittings, wreathed in numberless bells, four-horsed, with skilled and tried drivers, did the glorious Kṛishṇa give, and a myriad of cows from the neighbourhood of Madhurā, rich in milk, shining fair. And a thousand thoroughbred[2] mares, that shone there like the moon's (white) beam, and were decked with gold, Janārdana gave out of love, as also, to each, five hundred[3] well-trained, wind-swift, black-maned white she-mules.[4] A thousand women the lotus-eyed one gave (them)— light-skinned,[5] clad in fair raiment, shining splendidly, decked with hundreds of gold ornaments on their necks, free of body-hair, well cared for, and skilled to serve, skilful at the bath, at the drinking, and at feſtivals, and endowed with youth. And a hundred thousand saddle-horses from Bāhḷi did Janārdana give (Subhadrā), as an all-surpassing morning-gift (kanyādhana), and of the beſt worked and unworked gold, gleaming like fire,

---

[1] Janyārthe. I do not know whether janya can altogether have this meaning, not given in the dictionaries. The translation might also be : for the newly wedded wife (janyā). According to Nīl. the meaning is : he gave to them for those made kin by marriage, as to these kin by marriage.

[2] Or : faultless.

[3] That is, 500 for each of the brothers. Literally : " five and five hundred." Is it then rather : a thousand (in all) ?

[4] As the ass, indeed in the Eaſt is often a big, fine, nimble beaſt, so in the Indian Epic, too, he is usually looked on as swift and valuable (i, 144.7, 18 ; ii, 51.19, 20, 25 ; xiii, 27.9 ; Rām., ii, 70.23). The mule, especially the she-mule is seen as being ſtill swifter and more highly prized (i, 221.48 ; iii, 192.51 ; v, 86.12 ; viii, 38.5 ff. ; xiii, 66.3 ; 93.31 ; 103.10 ; 118.13 ff.). A chariot harnessed to especially swift she-mules travels fourteen yojanas a day (v, 86.12). The " Epic " yojana, therefore, cannot be either 9 or 10 or 7½ English miles, but probably only about 2 to 3 (hardly 4 or 5). Cp. note 5 in my *Twice Told Tales* (Chicago, 1903).

[5] Or : splendid (gaurī) ? According to the schol. = that have not yet menſtruated, and so also he explains aroma " in whom the line of hair (so highly praised by the poets) above the navel has not yet sprouted ". On this charm of the woman see my translation of Dāmodaragupta's Kuṭṭanīmatam, p. 10.

loads for ten men. But Rāma, the plough-bearer (Kṛishṇa's elder brother Baladeva), the lover of pert, bold deeds, joyfully gave Arjuna as wedding-gift (pāṇigrahaṇika), to honour the union, a thousand rutting elephants, streaming three-fold rutting-sap,[1] like unto mountain-tops, and fleeing not in the battle, harnessed, hung with loud-ringing bells, splendid, wreathed with gold, furnished with drivers " (i, 221.44 ff.).[2] According to the commentary, Rām., 39.2 and 66.4 alludes to a custom not without its charm : at the wedding of Sītā with Rāma her father takes a jewel out of (or, from ?) the hand of her mother and hands it to the father of her bridegroom for the latter to fasten it on her as a head-ornament.

[1] At the sides of the head, the roots of the ears, and the genitals. Cp. i, 151.4 ; vi, 64.58 ; 116.56. But saptadhā sravan in vi, 95.33, as repeatedly in the literature elsewhere.

[2] So we see, that when the girl flies out of the father's nest, then plenty of golden birds fly out at the same time from the purse (or, to speak as the Old Indians, out of the money-knot) of her father. So it is among the Turks (Osmani Bey, *Die Frauen i. d. Türkei*, Berlin, 1886, pp. 49–50, 54, 70). It is well known that to marry off daughters in India often means to ruin the family, and even down to the children and children's children.

IV

Life in Marriage

WHEN now the woman is married, how does her life in marriage go on ? What is expected of her ? What is granted her ? The first purpose of woman is the bearing of offspring. In a quite wholesome, if often exaggerated stressing of this great task in life of the woman, the Epic agrees with the rest of the literature.[1] In addition to the well-known reasons more or less active almost all over the world, which set such extraordinary importance on offspring, and that usually male offspring, there are especially in India religious ones, too : the son must make the sacrifices for the dead to his fathers which are absolutely necessary for their welfare in the other world. He saves them from an existence in hell or among ghosts, and leads them to heaven. Thus marriage is necessary for both sexes.[2]

[1] This view, indeed, is the more or less prevailing one throughout the world. For the woman, cursed already through her very sex, the son is atonement and reconciliation. To give one example only, and that from a Christian people : among the Armenians the young wife must not even speak, except with her husband, until she has borne a son (Lucy M. J. Garnett, *The Women of Turkey and Their Folk Lore*, London, 1893, i, p. 241 ; Schweiger-Lerchenfeld, *Die Frauen d. Orients*, 440). From the Indian law literature only Nārada, xii, 19 ; Manu, ix, 96 will be mentioned.

[2] We can read, for instance, in Westermarck [3], 136 ff. and Ploss-Bartels [4], ii, 285 ff. how absolutely necessary marriage is looked on by the various peoples and tribes. Here we give only one further example : ' " When a servant (of God)," said the Prophet, " marries, verily he perfects half of his religion." He once asked a man, "Art thou married ? " The man answered, " No." " And art thou," said he, " sound and healthy ? " The answer was, " Yes." " Then," said Mohammed, " thou art one of the brothers of the devils ; for the most wicked among you are the unmarried, and the most vile among your dead are the unmarried ; moreover, the married are those who

An impressive legend meant to show this is told more than once in the Mahābhārata. The great penitent Jaratkāru goes throughout the world, living by the wind, dried up, bathing at holy places. Then one day he sees hunger-racked, emaciated, woeful beings hanging head down in a cave, clinging to a bunch of the *Andropogon muricatus* plant, which itself holds on only by a thread, which is furthermore being greedily gnawed at by a mouse. All the other roots have been already bitten through by it. Moved by pity, he asks the wretched creatures : " Who are ye ? When the mouse has gnawed through this one root, then ye will fall headlong down. What can I do for you unhappy ones? I will give you a fourth, a third, or the half of what I have earned by penance, or even the whole of it, to save you." " Thou art old, and livest in chastity, but our sore plight cannot be altered by asceticism. We ourselves have penitential fruits. It is through the lack of offspring that we are falling into the unclean hell. For to beget offspring is the highest duty and virtue, so Brahma has said. While we hang here thus, there is no glimmer of consciousness in us ; therefore we know thee not, whose manly prowess is famous in the world. We are the race of the Yāyāvaras, Rishis of strict piety, sunk down hither from a pure and holy world through the lack of offspring. Our mighty asceticism is lost, for we have no thread of family left. One man there is, indeed, for us unhappy ones, but he is as good as wanting ; for this fatal one does but give himself up to asceticism ; Jaratkāru is the name of the famous knower of the Vedas and the Vedāṅgas. By him we have been set in this awful plight because of his greed for strength by penance. He has neither wife nor child, nor any kinsman. Therefore do we hang in the cave, robbed of consciousness. The mouse is time, which now having gnawed through all our other family threads, is fastening its teeth, too, into the last : into that simple, mad Jaratkāru, who yearns only after asceticism. Look how we have come down to the depths

are acquitted of filthy conversation ; and by Him in whose hand is my soul, the devil hath not a weapon more effective against the virtuous, both men and women, than the neglect of marriage." ' Lane, *Arabian Society in the Middle Ages*, London, 1883, p. 221 ; Garnett, *Women of Turkey*, ii, 480.

like evil-doers; and when we have fallen down together with all our kindred, then he, too, will go unto hell. Penitence, or sacrifice, or whatever other mighty means of purification there is, all these are not to be set by the side of continuing the family. If thou seest him, tell him what thou haſt seen, that he may take a wife and beget sons. But who then art thou to pity [1] our race, the race of his kindred, like thine own race and as if a kinsman ? " In a voice choked with tears, Jaratkāru spoke : " Ye are my forbears : fathers and grandfathers. *I* am Jaratkāru, your sinful son. Punish me, an evil-doer without nobility of soul ! " " What a happiness that thou shouldſt have chanced to come into this neighbourhood, O son ! And wherefore haſt thou taken no wife ? " " In my heart was ever this one purpose, to bring my body in full chaſtity into that other world. But since that I have seen you hanging like birds, my mind has now turned away from fleshly continence. I will do what ye so ſtrongly wish, and settle down to domeſtic life, if I find a maiden having the same name with me, who is offered me of her own accord as a gift, and whom I have not to support. But not otherwise. The child that is born to us shall save you. Eternal and knowing no decay shall my forefathers remain."

But no one would give his daughter to the old man. Filled with despair, thrice he then cried out in the wilderness : " I ask for a maiden. All beings that here dwell shall hear me. My forbears are in dreadful torment, and drive me on to marriage." Then he made known his conditions. The servants of the snake spirit Vāsuki told their lord of the matter, who brought him his siſter, who bore the same name as the penitent, and the prince of snakes furthermore promised that he himself would support and proteƈt them ; and the laſt condition—that nothing unpleasing was to be done to the difficult ascetic, otherwise he would leave his wife—was agreed to ; and so he dwelt with his young wife in great splendour in the palace of Vāsuki, the prince of the snakes, and begot a son.[2]

Of Jaratkāru this tale is told twice : in i, 45 f., and in a version somewhat shorter, in part agreeing literally, in i, 13.10 ff.

[1] Read : bandhur iva, as in 13.21.

[2] Why the prince of the snakes is so complaisant is shown especially in i, 38, 39.

LIFE IN MARRIAGE

On the other hand the celebrated holy man Agaſtya appears as the hero in the condensed account in iii, 96.14 ff. When this Ṛishi then wishes to wed, he sees no woman worthy of him. Therefore from various creatures he takes the fineſt parts, and forms, correspondingly, an incomparable female being, whom he gives as a daughter to the king of Vidarbha, who is leading an ascetic life to obtain offspring. Lopamudrā is her name. At the prince's court she grows up to unheard of loveliness, and when she has come to marriageable age, she is surrounded by a hundred fair-decked maidens, and a hundred slave-girls ; but through fear none dares to sue for her. Through her form, that outshines even the Apsarases, and her virtuous ways she rejoices her father (that is, her foſter-father) and her kinsfolk. But gloomy thoughts come on the king, as he asks himself to whom he shall marry her. Then Agaſtya comes, and desires her. The prince cannot refuse him, but neither has he any wish whatsoever to marry her to him. At a loss he complains to his wife that if the Ṛishi is angered by anyone, he will burn him with the fire of his curse. Then the daughter comes to her troubled parents and speaks : " Give me to him and save thyself through me." And so it comes about.[1]

Pāṇḍu in i, 120.15 ff. bewails his sorrow to the holy men : " For him that has no offspring no door to heaven is known or is named ; this torments me. I am not free of my debt towards my forbears. When my life is at an end, then it is the end of my fathers. Men are born on earth with four kinds of duty : towards the forefathers, the gods, the Ṛishis, and mankind, and to them the debt muſt be paid according to the holy law. But for those that do not look to this debt at the fitting time, for them are no worlds of heaven ; thus have those learned in the law laid it down. It is through sacrifices that the gods are appeased, the Munis through the ſtudy of the

[1] Cp. with this legend Bhandarkar, *Ninth Internat. Congress of Orientaliſts*, vol. i, p. 426 ; and the tale how his forefathers appear to the ascetic Ruci, who has never taken a wife, upbraid him, and remind him of his duty to beget a son ; and how through their power he gets Mālinī, the daughter of an Apsaras, as wife. Mārk.-Pur., xcv f. ; Garuḍapur., 88–90.

Vedas (composed by the Rishis) and through asceticism, the fathers through sons, through gifts to forbears, and mankind through benevolent charity." And in v, 118.7 f. Gālava speaks to King Uçīnara : " Thou art childless ; beget two sons. In the boat of ' son ', ferry thy forefathers and thee thyself over to the other shore. For he that partakes of the fruit of sons is not caſt down from heaven, nor does he go to the dreadful hell like the sonless." So vii, 173.53, 54 teaches : " For men yearn for sons to this end : Who shall save us from sorrow ? For their own good do fathers yearn after sons, who with friendly hearts bring them salvation from out of this world in that beyond." Sadly speaks Pāṇḍu to Kuntī (i, 120.28–30) : " Offspring, indeed, is the abiding-place in the worlds that concords with the law. I have sacrificed, given alms, praćtised asceticism, thoroughly carried out vows of mortification, but all this, it is declared, does not purge the childless man of sin. I, a childless man, shall not reach the pure, fair worlds." Here belongs ii, 41.27, 28 : " To make offerings to the gods, to give alms, to ſtudy the holy writings, and to sacrifice with abundant sacrificial gifts, all this is not worth a sixteenth part so much as offspring. Whatever he brings about with many vows and much faſting, all is fruitless for the childless man." So in i, 100.67–69 : " The sacrifice in fire, the three Vedas, and the propagation of the family are everlaſting. All of them (that is, of the other things) are not worth a sixteenth part of offspring.[1] So it is among mankind, and juſt so among creatures. Thus it is. What is called offspring, *that* it is which is the threefold Veda of the ancients, and of the godheads that

---

[1] According to the comment., however, as also according to the printed text : " The fire-sacrifice and the propagation of the three-fold wisdom (of the threefold Veda), which indeed are everlaſting, all these," etc. Cp. i, 74.64. The three things named in the text are the " threefold debt " which is very often found in the Veda and then later ; that is, everyone owes sacrifices to the gods, gifts for the dead to the forefathers, Veda ſtudy to the Rishis. MBh., xii, 28.55 ; 63.20 ; 234.7 ; 269.16 ; Manu, ii, 36 ; Vishṇu, xxvii, 15–17 ; Yājñav., i, 14 ; Baudhāyana, ii, 9, 16.4–7 ; Vasishṭha, xi, 48, and Bühler's note to it SBE, xiv, p. 56.

which lasteth for ever." [1]—" Three are the lights which man has on earth : children, deeds, knowledge " (ii, 72.5 ; and K., i, 107.73) ; and as a rule of life we find in xiii, 68.34 : " Let a man wed and beget sons, for in them there is a profit greater than any other profit." The sonless man was born to no end (iii, 200.4 f.), and he that does not propagate himself is godless (adharmika) ; for to carry on the blood is the highest duty and virtue (xii, 34.14).[2] As is well known, therefore, for the Indians the birth of a son is looked on as the greatest happiness on earth. From the Epic we will take only one saying about this, and it we take because of the nobility of soul shown there : " The gift of a kingdom, the birth of a son, and the saving of a foe from a danger—these three are one and the same thing " (iii, 243.13 ; v, 33.67). The son is the very self of his begetter in many meanings of that word, born anew from his wife, as we so often read in Indian literature, and also, for instance, in iii, 313.71 ; xiv, 81.20 ; 90.63.

Therefore, and quite logically, of the four stages of the Indian earthly pilgrimage, the condition of father of the family is over and over again declared as the best and highest—a rank for which it undoubtedly has mainly to thank the fact that with this condition the priestly caste, depending on charity, stands and falls. And the Epic, naturally, often is found in agreement with this. So, for example, xii, 295.39 ; xiv, 44.17 ; 45.13 ; xii, 234.6 ; 12.6 ; i, 2.390. Cp. xii, 64.6 ; 66.15, etc.

Nay, just as in the old Upanishad, life itself with its pains and sorrows is called tapas (asceticism), so the Mahābh. proclaims the condition of father of the family, family life, to be tapas [3]

---

[1] According to the Grihyasūtras the father thus solemnly speaks to his scion : " Thou art named the Veda, (thou art named) son ; O live a hundred autumns ! "

[2] And so the man that has died childless becomes an evil, harmful ghost. Garuḍapur., Pretakalpa (ed. Çrīveṅkaṭeçvara-Press, Bombay, 1906) 9.56–62 ; 11.4–10 ; 20.4–47 ; 21.1 ff. ; Crooke, *Popular Relig. and Folk-Lore of Northern India.* New ed. ii, 77, cp. what follows ; Schmidt, *Liebe u. Ehe in Indien,* 475.

[3] Life itself or its sorrow appears as tapas also in xiv, 35.32, and cleansing through suffering in vii, 78.30 ; for there Subhadrā bewailing her fallen son names in a long formula of blessing the

(xii, 66.23 ; 269.7 ; and especially 11) : "Here they tell this old tale, the words of Indra with the penitents. . . . Some Brahmans left their house and went into the forest ; before their moustache had grown, the foolish ones, who sprang from good families, became ascetics. This is the 'good' (dharma), they thought, who were rich and practised chastity, and left brother and father. On them Indra took pity. The sublime one spoke to them, having changed himself into a golden bird : ' Hard unto men is that which is done by the devourers of the remains of food. It is a holy deed, and a praiseworthy life. They have reached their goal, having come onto the most excellent path, they, given up to virtue.' The Rishis spoke : ' Listen now ! This bird is praising the devourers of the remains of food. He is, of a surety, praising us ; we too are devourers of the remains of food.' The bird spoke : ' It is not ye, the fools that devour dirt-coated, dusty [1] refuse that I praise ; of a truth the devourers of the remains of food are others.' The Rishis spoke : ' This is the highest good (çreyas), so we think, and give ourselves up to it. Speak, O bird, what is the "good ", we have great trust in thee.' The bird spoke : ' If ye do not split yourselves up into yourselves, and put doubt into me, I will speak to you according to the truth, wholesome words.' The Rishis spoke : ' We hearken to thy words, the paths are known unto thee. And we will cling to thy precept, thou that art informed by virtue ; teach us.' The bird spoke :

çokāgnidagdhās, too, as among the noblest and holiest men to whose world the dead man shall go. A parallel to this is to be found in the *Wigalois* of Wirnt von Grafenberg : the Mohammedan woman Jafite from grief for her husband has died by his body. The poet prays God to show her his grace for : " Her baptism was the sorrow she suffered for her love." But, probably, that Wolfram so greatly admired by Wirnt, together with *Parzifal*, i, 824 ff., was here the pattern. Cp. too my note to Dāmodaragupta's Kuṭṭanīmatam, 297 (p. 44). Tapas is also the work in life (iii, 33.72 ; cp. 313.88 ; the Bhagavadgītā ; Manu, xi, 236), and according to MBh., xii, 263.27 it is the service of God (yajña, sacrifice)—both of which are thoughts which Luther, as before him Berthold von Regensburg, preached so magnificently. That marriage is self-denial, purgatory, etc., is also an utterance of the people in various places.

[1] Or : filled with passion ?

' It is among the four-footed that the cow is best, among the metals (loha) gold, among the sounds the holy saying (mantra), among the two-footed the Brahman. The holy saying is for the Brahman, so long as he lives, according to the time, a precept from the holy customs, directly after birth unto the end on the field of the dead.[1] The Vedic deeds are for him the unsurpassable path to heaven. Hence they (the holy men of early ages) have so contrived that all deeds have their perfection and effect in the mantras. He that holds his own stoutly—it is thus that success is won on earth, so it is assumed.[2] The months and half-months, the seasons of the year, sun, moon, and stars—all beings strive after what is known as action (karma). This is the holy field where success grows, this is the great occupation in life (açrama). Therefore does a debt of sin rest on the blinded, aimless men who dispraise action, and walk on an evil path. The deluded ones live betraying the various divisions of the gods, of the forefathers, and of the Brahmans, these the ever enduring ; therefore do they go along a path that belongs not to the holy revelation.[3] Let that be the fitting tapas for you, which says : I give ; that the seers have straitly enjoined. Therefore is endurance in this very thing called the asceticism (tapas) of the rich in asceticism. The dividing oneself among the bands of the gods, the bands of the Brahmans, and the bands of the fore-fathers, the ever enduring, and the service of the gurus [4] (that we should let each one of these have his share)—this, of a truth,

---

[1] Read nidhanād abhi ? K. here also smooths things and has nidhanāntakaḥ. Abhi with the ablat. = " hither from " is found in xii, 8.23 (adhi with ablat. = " from ", v, 55.47). Since now ā with ablat. means " from " and " until ", my proposed emendation perhaps has a good deal to be said for it.

[2] Or : striven after. I read : atha te instead of katham me. K. offers the unattractive : atha sarvāṇi karmāṇi mantrasiddhāni cakshate Amnāyadṛidhavādīni, tathā siddhir iheshyate. Ātmānaṃ dṛidhavādin, liter. : he that stoutly addresses the self, or, that declares the self as firm.

[3] Or : they go (after death) the path of forgetfulness, that is, they are born again as low beings ; or : their name and memory fades out.

[4] Guru is father, mother, husband, teacher, etc.

is called the heavy task. The gods have performed this heavy task, and so have reached the highest place of power ; therefore I declare unto you that it is a hard thing to live for the condition of father of the family. For this root of beings is the highest tapas, of that is no doubt. For everything has its existence in it through this family order. This tapas was known to the unenvying Brahmans, set above all dissension ; therefore the midway duty of life (that standing between the Brahmans and the hermit's duty) is called tapas among men. And those that eat the remains come to places in heaven hard to win, having at morning and evening shared out, as is seemly, food among their dependants. Devourers of the remains of food are called those that eat what is left, after having given to the guests, the gods, the forbears, and their own folk. Therefore, if they fulfil their duty, are pious, and speak the truth, they become gurus of the world, and without stain. These unselfish men, that do hard deeds, come into the paradise of Indra, and dwell years everlasting in the world of heaven ' "—This the brothers then took to their hearts, went back home and took wives.[1]

---

[1] With this tale compare Jātaka No. 393. The demand that the wife and servants shall eat first is often made in the MBh., too, but is well known to be in sharp contrast with the Indian custom. Also the law literature lays down : First the master of the house must feed pregnant women, maidens, women under his protection, children, old men, servants, etc., and then last of all may he (or : he and his wife) eat. See Baudhāyana, ii, 7.19 ; Gautama, v, 25 ; Āpast., ii, 2, 4.11–13 ; ii, 4, 9.10 ; Yājñav., i, 105 ; Vasishtha, xi, 5 ff. ; Manu, iii, 114–116. Moreover, Manu, iii, 114 = Vishṇu, lxvii, 39 declares that the master of the house must feed, even before his guests, an unwedded or newly-betrothed maiden, a sick and a pregnant woman. Cp. Kauṭilya (transl.), 3.13, and above all J. J. Meyer, *Altind. Rechtsschriften*, 271 f. Mahānirvāṇatantra, viii, 33 lays it down very strongly that, even if he were at the last gasp, he must not eat before he has satisfied mother, father, son, wife, guest or brother. On the other hand, Vasishtha, xii, 31 (this being according to Çatapathabrāhmana, x, 5, 2.9) gives the warning that if a man eats together with his wife, his sons will be without manly power. In the same way Gaut., ix, 32 ; Manu, iv, 43 ; Yājñav., i, 131 ; Vishṇu, lxviii, 46, forbid eating in the company or the presence of the wife. Baudhāyana, i, 1, 2.1 ff. describes it as a usual, and therefore there, but there only, a good custom in

How utterly needful for woman marriage is, we have already been told ; and ix, 52 makes a parallel to the tale of the forefathers hanging in the cave. The Ṛishi Kuṇivarga, mighty through penance, begot from his mind a daughter, and then went into heaven. Though he wanted to give away the fairbrowed, lotus-eyed one in marriage, she would not. She saw no men that were worthy of her as a husband. " With ſtrenuous asceticism she racked her own body, found her delight in the lonely foreſt in worshipping her forefathers and the gods, and believed as she ſtrove, that she had done all that was her duty. When, worn out by age and asceticism, she could not walk another ſtep by herself, she resolved to go unto the other world. But when (the heavenly Ṛishi) Nārada saw that she wished to caſt off her body, he spoke : ' How should the worlds of heaven be open to thee, the sacramentally unconsecrated (that is, unwedded) maiden ! Thus have I heard in the world of the gods. Thou haſt won the higheſt penitential merit, but not the worlds of heaven.'" Now she promised the half of the fruits of her asceticism to him who should take her hand. The Ṛishi Prākçriṅgavant took her to wife ; and she changed for a night into a wonderful and glorious young girl, and lay with him. Next morning she left the wrapping of the body, and went into heaven. Deeply the Ṛishi sorrowed over his short happiness with the enchanting one, but he had, indeed, the half of her penitential merit at his free disposal ; so he followed her into heaven, drawn by her loveliness. The end and reward of woman is this indeed : the pleasures of love and children (she is ratiputraphalā, ii, 5.112 ; v, 39.67) and the barren wife is worthless (xii, 78.41). Nay, what a childless woman (aputrikā) looks on, that the gods and forbears will not accept at the sacrifice, for it is ſtained (xiii, 127, 13,14) ;

the south for the man to eat with his wife. And Nārada enjoins that he shall quickly drive out of the house a woman that eats before her husband, as also the woman who is always doing evil to him, or being unfriendly to him (xii, 93). The reason of the prohibition will be found in J. J. Meyer, *Altind.Rechtsschr.*, 12 ; 369, note: Apaſtamba, ii, 4, 9.11 says : The father of the family may ſtint himself and his in food, but not the slave that works for him.

and the gifts that are made by a woman without husband and children, rob the receiver of his life-powers (xii, 36.27).[1]

From the Song of Nala we know already that barren marriages were to be found in Old India, too, and " in the best families ", indeed, oftenest of all in them ; and that this mishap was very sorely felt. And the Epic, too, has a whole set of tales of how in a particular case the evil was at last overcome. As the universal remedy, in this case likewise, asceticism, of course, is efficacious. " Sons, that bring much happiness, are won by fathers through tapas, the practise of chastity, truth, and patience. Mothers win a fruit of their body through fasting, sacrifice, vows, holding festivals, and luck-bringing things, and carry it ten months in the womb ; and then these poor ones think to themselves : Will they be safely born, or keep alive, or, when they have been brought up and are strong, bring us joy in this world and the other (xii, 7.13 ff.). Cp. iii, 205.18 ff. ; xii, 150.14. Among the most efficacious things, too, handed down from of old is magic of every kind ; and, indeed, in India there is no essential difference between worship of the gods and witchcraft. It is significant that mantra can denote a song filled with characteristic depth of thought, or a nobility of heart truly raised above this earth, and also a magic spell, of an evil that out-devils the Devil. Spells against barrenness are to be found, for instance, in Weber's *Ind. Studien*, v, 23 f. ; and a witches' ceremony in Pāraskara-Gṛihyasūtra, i, 13. Schmidt, *Erotik*, 891.

The Epic likewise naturally knows of magic for this end, or at least what is bound up with magic. The well-known fruit of the tree [2] is found in ii, 17.18 ff. Bṛihadratha, the king

[1] In the belief of to-day the Yamunā (Jumna) is not wedded, and therefore many will not drink its unclean water. Crooke, *Popul. Relig.*, etc., i, 36 f. And among the Nambutiri the marriage ceremony must be done over the body of an unwedded girl. Dubois-Beauchamp [3], pp. 16–17.

[2] Cp. Chauvin, vi, 84 ; vii, 84 ; Hartland, *Prim. Pat.*, i, 4 ff. ; Fr. v. d. Leyen in *Herrigs Archiv*, Bd. 114, p. 14 ; Bd. 115, p. 12, and the quotations there ; Crooke, *Pop. Relig.*, etc., i, 225 ff., and the evidence there ; further Tod, *Rājasthan*, i, 612 ; Reitzenstein, *Zeitschr. f. Ethnol.*, Bd. 41 (1909), p. 665 ; Chavannes, *Cinq cents contes*, i, 305 ; etc.

of Magadha, wedded the two lovely twin-daughters of the prince of Kāçi. "While he lay sunk in sensual enjoyment, his youth [1] went by him, and no son, no upholder of the line was born to him. With luck-bringing things (maṅgala), many fiery sacrifices, and smaller offerings aimed at a son, the best of the herdsmen of men yet got no son to carry on the family." Then in despair he went off with his wives into the penitential forest.[2] One day he there heard that the great ascetic Caṇḍakauçika had happened to come thither, and was sitting by a tree. Together with his wives he waited on him [3] with most earnest feelings. The rejoiced penitent told him to choose a favour for himself." Then Bṛihadratha bowed low and spoke unto him, his voice choked with tears, for he despaired of seeing a son : "O glorious and holy man, I have forsaken a kingdom, and have come into the penitential forest. What could I, an unhappy man do with a favour, what should I, a childless man, do with a kingdom ! " Moved to sorrow by these words, the holy man took his seat under a mango-tree. Then there fell onto his lap a juicy mango-fruit that no parrot had pecked at.[4] This he wrapped with mantras, speaking

[1] Read : atyagāt.

[2] This sentence after K., where the episode is also further spun out.

[3] Read : sarvayatnais.

[4] All that is broken, torn, or harmed is in Brahmanic belief uncanny and calamitous. The Jātaka, which often mocks at superstition, has a pretty tale of a man, one of whose garments the mice gnawed, and who then looked on this as an embodied curse and evil boding of dreadful things. His son had to take it with all speed on a stick to the place of dead bodies (No. 87). Cp. Rhys Davids, *Buddhist Suttas*, p. 171 ; J. v. Negelein, *Traumschlüssel des Jagaddeva*, p. 209; MBh., xiii, 104.49, 59, 66 ; xvi, 2.5 ; J. J. Meyer, *Altind. Rechtsschr.*, espec. p. 440, addit. to p. 360. Moreover in the German Middle Ages also, it was believed that anyone who had his clothing gnawed by mice would have a mishap. *Ztschr. d. Ver. f. Volksk.*, Bd. 11, p. 278. The fruit that birds have pecked must not be eaten, otherwise atonement must be made by strict mortification. Vasishṭha, xiv, 33 ; Vishṇu, xxiii, 49 ; li, 17 ; Manu, iv, 208 ; Gautama, xvii, 10. It is otherwise in Vishṇu, xxiii, 49 ; Vasishṭha, xxviii, 8 ; Baudhāyana, i, 5, 9.2 ; according to which the bird that throws down a fruit by pecking at it does not make it unclean.

in his heart, gave it, without compare and bestowing sons, to the prince, and spoke : " Go home again ; thy wish is fulfilled." The king gave it to both wives so as not to hurt one of them ; they divided the wonderful gift and ate it. But then, alas, each of them bore half a little human being ! [1] They had these lumps of flesh exposed outside the city by their nurses. But a Rakshasi found the misbirths, put the two halves together, and a strong boy came out of them, which she had handed over to the king.

Also trees in themselves are bestowers of children. To the already-mentioned Brahman Ricika there comes, after his marriage with the king's daughter Satyavati, his father Bhrigu, and leaves it to his daughter-in-law to choose a favour.[2] She chooses a son for herself, and one for her mother. He says they shall clasp a tree ritau,[3] the daughter an udumbara-tree, the mother an açvattha-tree,[4] and each eat a sacrificial dish (caru) consecrated by a mantra. But the mother gets her daughter to exchange the food in the pot, and the tree, with her, and so things go wrong here, too. For the object of the arrangement was this : the Brahman's wife was to bring forth a

[1] [From Melanesia for conception through eating nuts cp. G. C. Wheeler in *Archiv f. Religionswiss.*, vol. xv, p. 355 (Translator).]
[2] So according to iii, 115.31 ff.
[3] In the favourable time for conception, from the fourth day onwards after the first coming of the monthly purification.
[4] As to the endless theme of the tree and woman's sexual life— on which a note will also be found (No. 212) in my book *Isoldes Gottesurteil*, p. 285—reference will here only be made to Chavannes, *Cinq cents contes et apologues extraits du Tripitaka chinois*, ii, p. 14 ; Storfer, *Marias jungfräuliche Mutterschaft*, p. 165 ; Crooke, *Pop. Rel.*, ii, 99, 102, 122 ; *Cultus Arborum, A Descriptive Account of Phallic Tree Worship*, 1890, pp. 7, 35, 38, 93 f. ; Reitzenstein, *Zeitschr. f. Ethnol.*, Bd. 41, pp. 648–671 ; W. Mannhardt, *Baumkultus d. Germanen* (1876), *passim*. And for the clasping of the tree cp. besides Hartland, i, 127 f., Agnipurāņa, 198.4b ff., where, however, kaṇṭha-sūtra probably means "necklace". If mankind comes from trees (see also Albrecht Dietrich, " Mutter Erde," *Archiv f. Religionswiss.*, viii, pp. 16 ff.; Hartland, i, 13 ff.), then it is no wonder that the human race at first lived, too, in trees, as we are told in the good Darwin way in Mārkaņḍeyapurāņa, xlix, 26 ff., 52 ff.

pattern Brahman, and her mother, the king's wife, an outstanding warrior ; and now things would have been just the opposite, but that through the grace of a second miracle the warlike nature of the Brahman's child came to be put off at least to the grandchild, the celebrated Paraçurāma ; while the queen bears the Viçvāmitra who afterwards became a Brahman. This tale is told at greater length in xiii, 4.21 ff. ; and in this account it is Ṛicīka himself who grants the favour, gives the directions, and appears throughout. A third form is found in xii, 48. There only the two sacrificial dishes appear, and not the trees.[1]

The main constituent of the caru is rice. A rice-dish also acts as putrīya (son-granting) in Rām., i, 16 ; only this account has a far more modern and artificial character. King Daçaratha is childless, and makes the horse-sacrifice to overcome this misfortune. When the putrīyā ishti is sacrificed, there floats out of the fire in mighty form Vishṇu, who has once already been besought by the gods to become man, and he offers the prince in a mighty dish heavenly milky-rice (pāyasa) prepared by the gods, and says that the queens are to eat this food, and will then bear sons. Thus are born Rāma and his brothers.[2] A magical sacrifice where the queen is to eat of the sacrificial food, to get twins, is also held by King Drupada (MBh., i, 167). Tīrthas, or holy bathing-places that bestow children, are mentioned, for instance in iii, 83.58 ; 84.98 (= 87.9). If anyone in the right condition of soul makes a pilgrimage to the tīrtha Kanyāçrama, and there fasts three days, he wins a divine hundred of daughters, and heaven (iii, 83.190). This second reward will be found a very fitting one.

But it is well-known that pious devices do not always help in this matter ; a good friend must then play his part.[3] And

---

[1] Cp. Vishṇupur., iv, 7 ; Bhāgavatapur., ix, 15. Here also Ṛicīka is the bestower, and only the caru-dish is used as a means.

[2] Cp. Agnipur., v, 4–5.

[3] In India, at least according to many accounts, the spiritual gentry are ever ready to act as such charitable brethren. Some temples have a great renown, because in them " barren " wives become pregnant ; while the Brahmans in their humble piety leave the honour to the god (Vishṇu). As their wages, however, they demand the handsomest

this helpful neighbour, among the Hindus, has not always
found opposition from the husband's side, if he himself was
unfitted for the task ; rather the husband has even invited or
exhorted him, as the Epic and the other literature tells us. In
the Mahābh. the begetter by proxy has a very important place.
We have already heard of the blind-born Dīrghatamas, his
unpleasing ways in love, and his repulsion by wife and children.
Fastened by the latter onto a raft, he drifted down the Gaṅgā,
and in the end came into the kingdom of King Bali. And the
virtuous-souled Bali, the truly brave one, took him and chose
him out for the business of sons, having learned who he was :
" For the carrying on of my line, do thou beget, with my wives,
sons skilled in religious and worldly things." Thus addressed,
the very mighty Ṛishi answered : " Yes." Then the king
sent him his wife Sudeshṇā. But the queen knowing that
he was old and blind, did not go, but sent the old man her
nurse's daughter. With this Çūdrā he begat eleven sons (i,
104.41 ff.). In the 56th çloka Bhīshma thus ends his account :
In this way there were begotten on earth by Brahmans other
Kshattriyas also, great in bowmanship, with most excellent
knowledge of virtue, brave, and with mighty strength.

Pāṇḍu, himself prevented from the use of his manly powers,
bewails in i, 120 his being condemned to unhappiness in this
world and the next, because he has no son ; he exhorts his wife
Kuntī to see to it that this be made otherwise, and goes on
to say : " Therefore do I now send thee, being myself deprived
of begetting. Do thou win offspring from one that is equal to
me, or better than I. Hearken, O Kuntī, to this tale of
Çāradaṇḍāyinī. This heroic wife was charged (niyukta) by
her husband to get a son. She now went, having had her
period, with pure and holy mind, having bathed (on the fourth
day) ; she went in the night to a cross-road, and picked out a
Brahman that had come to perfection (dvijaṃ siddham), after
she had made sacrifice to the fire god to get a son. And when

women as " wives for the god ". Dubois-Beauchamp, *Hindu Manners,*
etc. [3], pp. 593, 601 f. Cp. Thurston, *Omens and Superstitions,* etc.,
pp. 147 f. Moreover, it is enough in itself for a woman to kiss the
member of an ascetic to get a child. Schmidt, *Liebe u. Ehe in Indien,*
481. Cp. further Hartland, i, 62 ff., 69, 76, 116 ff., 121 ff.

this work was done, she lived with him, and there gave life to three sons : Durjaya, and the two others, great chariot-fighters. Do thou, O lovely one, be swiftly stirring about my business (manniyogāt) so that thou raise up offspring for thyself from a Brahman of outstanding asceticism " (i, 120.35 ff.). So, too, in 122.30, 31 he makes the beseeching request that she shall obtain for herself sons of excelling gifts, from a Brahman distinguished for tapas. In like wise the Brahman Vasishṭha calls a son into being for the king Kalmāshapada (who is here, be it said, divyena vidhinā), and at this prince's own request. Here, too, a curse is at work, i, 177.32 ff. ; cp. 182.26. The same old holy man does this service in i, 122.21 f. : " By the son of Uddālaka, Çvetaketu Sandāsa, the pious Madayantī (his wife) was charged (niyukta), and went to the Rishi Vasishṭha, so we have been told. From him the fair one got a son, Açmaka by name. And this she did to show a favour to her husband."

And indeed the whole caste of warriors now living owes its origin to the Brahmans ; for when Paraçurāma had blotted out all Kshattriyas on the earth, " then Brahmans wise in the Veda united with all the Kshattriya women, and begat offspring. ' The son belongs to him that has married the woman,' [1] so it is laid down in the Vedas. Setting their minds steadfastly on righteousness and virtue (dharmaṃ manasi saṃsthāpya), they went to the Brahmans. Among ourselves, too, has been seen the same revival of Kshattriyas brought about " (i, 104.1 ff.). i, 64.4–26 paints in glowing colours what a strong, virtuous, blissful race sprung from this union.

When King Vicitravīrya has died childless, his half-brother Bhīshma, who carries on the government, says : " I will also name the means (hetu) that is necessary for the propagation and increase of the Bharata blood. Hearken thou unto it from my lips : Some Brahman gifted with excellences must be invited for money to raise up children on Vicitravīrya's field for him " (i, 105.1–2).

In these last two cases the husband of the women is at any rate dead ; but both of them belong rather to our case than to the real niyoga or levirate ; and it is to be particularly noted that in

[1] Pāṇigrahasya tanayaḥ; pater est quem nuptiae demonstrant; l'enfant conçu pendant le mariage a pour père le mari (Code Napoléon).

the place laſt mentioned the begetter by proxy has to be paid. It is in the light, too, of this that Pāṇḍu's words juſt given, about him " that is better " than he (i, 120.37), are undoubtedly to be underſtood ; and no less so his utterance : " Men in their misfortune yearn after a son from a more excellent subſtitute in begetting.[1] (So) men acquire offspring that beſtows the fruits of pious order, and is more excellent than even that from their own seed—so has Manu, the son of him that sprang from himself, spoken " (i, 120.35–36). Here uttama devara certainly points also to a Brahman ; from him a better progeny naturally springs than from the seed of the nobility. No less are Pāṇḍu's words in i, 120.22–23 probably aimed at the Brahman's aſting as the love-proxies for others : " Here on earth, therefore, the beſt of men (narottamāḥ) are born for the sake of offspring (that is, to get it for others). How can offspring arise on a field, as I arose on my father's field through the great Ṛishi (Vyāsa) ? "

It is significant that even the disciple is found as the marriage representative of his teacher, while otherwise one of the moſt awful sins is in this very thing of the disciple lying (gurutalpin) with his teacher's wife. Thus in xii, 34.22 we read : " For the mounting of the teacher's marriage-bed, when this is done on his behalf, does not smirch the man ; Uddālaka had Çvetaketu begotten for him by his disciple."

The gods themselves, who, indeed, in the sagas of the moſt different peoples take in hand the begetting of famous heroes, ſtep in with their help in the moſt famous case in the Epic of the love proxyship contrived by the husband : the birth of the

---

[1] This ſtock expression āpadi " in the time of misfortune " is thus explained, for inſtance, by the commentary on Manu, ix, 56 : " When there is no male offspring."—" More excellent " than the husband himself. Or : " From one that is moſt excellent." Less likely : "A son is yearned for from a more excellent man as proxy in begetting." Devara " proxy in begetting " would seem to be made sure by our passage alone, but is also found in the MBh. In Yājñav., i, 68, and Nārada, xii, 80, the word perhaps has this meaning likewise, if we take in the firſt passage vā—vā = " either—or ", which would be quite possible, and in Nārada, xii, 85 tathā as " also, likewise " (Jolly translates by " or "), and not " in this wise ".

chief heroes of the Mahābh., the five Pāṇḍavas (i, 120 ff.).
King Pāṇḍu has drawn down on himself the curse that he shall
at once die, if he do copulate. Therefore from then on he
refrains. But he needs sons. Therefore does he urge his
wife Kuntī to get from another what he cannot give her.[1]
But she makes answer : " Thou muſt not speak thus to me,
who am a virtuous wife, and find my delight by thee, O lotus-
eyed one. But thou, O hero, wilt beget with me, in lawful
wise, children endowed with heroes' ſtrength. I will go into
heaven together with thee. Come thou to me that there may
be offspring. I myself, indeed, could draw nigh unto no other
man in my thoughts but thee. And what man on earth were
more excellent than thou ? " Then she relates to him the old
legend of the loving wife who even got children from her dead
husband ; and winds up by saying he shall beſtow offspring
on her in purely spiritual wise, through the yoga powers he
has won by ſtern asceticism. But now he tells her of the
primitive hetæriſtic conditions that were done away with by
Çvetaketu, and of the charge which Çvetaketu himself then
laid later on his wife Madayantī ; he teaches her that wives
are ſtill sexually free except at the time after their period, and,
that they muſt be wholly obedient to their husband, whether
he demand right or wrong of them ; and he ends by beseeching
her not to deprive him of the well-being in the beyond which
belongs to those endowed with sons. Then she consents, tells
of the magic given her by Durvāsas, and asks which god she shall
now call up.[2]   He names Dharma, the god of right and

---

[1] K., i, 135.24 ff. makes the penitents in the foreſt there say that
they it was who had shown Pāṇḍu that he muſt not yet go of his own
will into heaven, but muſt firſt win the worlds of bliss through
offspring ; therefore he muſt win over Dharma, Vāyu, Indra, and the
Açvins to beget him sons. This is, of course, a late interpolation.
Cp. B, i, 120.23 ff.

[2] According to K. (i, 129.1 ff.) Kuntī leaves him a second choice
open : " Or let me have a Brahman, if thou so please, perfeéted in
all excellences, rejoicing in the weal of all beings. Whatever thou
sayeſt, god or Brahman—as thou biddeſt, so will I do. From a god
the fruit of a son comes forthwith, from a Brahman after a time."
This, too, of course is a tendentious insertion.

virtue, for then of a surety, he thinks, no stain will lie on the matter, and a pious son will be his. She offered up the bali gift, and murmured her cabbalistic prayer. Then came the god in a heavenly chariot shining as the sun, and laughingly spoke : " Kuntī, what shall I give thee ? " She answered, though he laughed at her : " Give me a son." He united with her in a shape formed by his magic powers, and so she received that Yudhishthira, the friend to all beings. When he had been born, Pāṇḍu spoke : " It is said that what is greatest in the Kshattriya is strength, therefore do thou choose for thyself a son marked out by his strength." So she called the god of the wind. And to his question she answered with a shame-faced laugh : " Grant me a son, a strong, a great one, a shatterer of the pride of all ! " So came the warrior-giant, the man of might, Bhīma or Bhīmasena to life, who directly after birth fell from his mother's lap onto a rock, and crushed it with his limbs. Indra was to beget her the third son, that he might become an all-powerful hero and overcomer of foes, like the king of the gods himself ; and so her husband taught her a strict way of mortification, which she had to carry out for a whole year, and he, too, gave himself up, for the same end, to most fervent devotion and asceticism, standing on one leg. And this yielded fruit. Indra appeared to Pāṇḍu and promised to fulfil his wish ; Kuntī now brought up the prince of heaven by magic, and he begat Arjuna with her. The happy father, for whom others, immortals too, themselves so willingly brought the finest boys into the world, was now really caught up in a wave of enthusiasm and in a stronger yearning after sons ; so he wanted still more of Kuntī. But she repulsed him angrily : " More than three sons are not granted even in misfortune. If there were another the wife would become one that is unbridled (svairiṇī), and with a fifth she would be a worthless woman (bandhakī). How canst thou, a wise man, who hast learned this law, now go beyond it and ask me for offspring ? " Then came Pāṇḍu's second wife, Mādrī, and said to him : " I am not sorrowed that thou art not a proper man, nor that I am ever set behind her that is worthy of thy favour (Kuntī). But this is my great sorrow, that I, though we are equal (both thy wives) have no son." As she herself cannot ask her rival, through her angry pride towards her, Pāṇḍu, she says, muſt beg her to get offspring for her (Mādrī), too. He then exhorted Kuntī to do this, and she said to her fellow-wife [1] : " Think only once of the divinity. He will grant thee the gift of fitting offspring." Mādrī called up the two Açvins, and so got the twins Nakula and Sahadeva. Of the father thus blessed the pious and noble Vidura (i, 127.4) then said that he was not to be pitied, but to be praised.

The niyoga in the narrower meaning, the levirate, on the other hand is represented by the well-known begetting of Pāṇḍu himself, and of Dhṛitarāshṭra (i, 103 ff.). After King Vicitravīrya has died childless, his mother Satyavatī comes to her husband's son, to Bhīshma, and says that, as the only shield of his family and its earthly and heavenly welfare, and as one that knows and carefully follows the law and the truth, he muſt in agreement with these both, and at their beheſt (niyoga) beget offspring for his dead brother with the two young and beautiful wives of the dead man. Bhīshma now sees that this is dharma, but he reminds her that for her sake, so that his father might marry her, he has sworn never to touch a woman ; and the sun can lose its light, and the host of the elements their properties, but he cannot be faithless to the truth and his word. He tells her now how the whole Kshattriya caſte was after its utter deſtruétion called back again to life through the union of the Kshattriya women with the Brahmans, how Bṛihaspati, Utathya's brother, lay with his siſter-in-law, and how the fruit of her body, Dīrghatamas, born blind through the holy man's curse, had been appointed royal purveyor of children to the court in the house of Bali ; and he puts it to her that in this case, too, a Brahman should be hired. But she then tells him, in laughing confusion and halting words, of her youthful adventure with the penitent Parāçara, and the result of this affair, the famous Vyāsa. So soon as she thinks of him, he will come, she says. He it is that, appointed by her (niyukta), shall see to the matter. Bhīshma is satisfied with this ; she tells the Yogi, who at once appears, as follows : " To the father

---

[1] Read uktā (çl. 15). Inſtead of " once only " perhaps better : once for all, conſtantly, fixedly (sakṛit) ? But Kuntī only grants her rival one son, at leaſt at firſt. So that " once " might be very deliberate.

and the mother children are born as common property. Just as the father is lord over them, so is the mother. As thou by the hand of fate art my first son,[1] so Vicitravīrya was my child born after thee. As Bhīshma on the father's side, thou art Vicitravīrya's brother on the mother's side." Bhīshma, she says, cannot undertake the business after his oath, so Vyāsa, out of regard for his brother, and to carry on the line shall raise up children by the young and lovely wives at Bhīshma's spoken word, and at her bidding ; and he has the power to do it. The penitent consents, but makes it a condition that the two widows must first for a year keep a vow of mortification to be drawn up by him,[2] so as to be cleansed, for otherwise a woman may not draw nigh to him ; also they must take his personal qualities as part of the bargain. Splendidly decked, and having bathed on the fourth day after the monthly cleansing, the eldest first awaits the appointed—but to her wrapped in mystery—father of her future child. Now the smell of holiness is not to everyone's liking, particularly in Old India, where penitents look on dirt and piety as inseparable ; moreover Vyāsa after the Rishi kind has red hair, and with it flaming eyes and a red-brown moustache, and other ugly qualities. So she shuts her eyes at the sight of him. As a result her son shall, according to the inspired man's words, be born blind. The mother Satyavatī wails : " A blind man cannot rule ; beget another." He agrees. But the second wife becomes quite wan (pāṇḍu) when the visitor appears by night. So she bears a pale son, Pāṇḍu. Satyavatī now wants a third grandson, and therefore once more charges Vyāsa and the eldest daughter-in-law. The latter, however, thinks of the evil smell and the ugliness of the Rishi, and sends in her own stead a splendidly adorned slave-girl. With this latter the ascetic then helps to bring Vidura into being. Cp. v, 147.17–47.

The bringing in of this son of an unmarried girl, who never lived in the family of his mother's husband, does not seem after all to have been in such a very near correspondence with

[1] Read sa tvaṃ instead of satyam.
[2] It is the vow to keep always quite faithful to the truth—a spitefulness which is not only very ungallant, but is only at all possible for a woman-hater.

the laws of the levirate, although as a Brahman he muſt have been moreover especially well fitted for his part. For King Çiçupāla makes the reproach to Bhīshma : " Why didſt thou, an it please thee, ſteal the maiden named Ambā, that loved another, and knew the law ? In that thy brother Vicitravīrya would not have this maiden that had been robbed by thee, he walked the way of the good. And with his two wives children have been begotten by another, through a proceeding which good men do not follow, and thou, smug in thy wisdom, doſt calmly look on." He then goes on to suggeſt that this love service should have fallen to Bhīshma's lot. These words, it is true, are found in the bitter speech, so heartening and refreshing in itself, againſt the worthless and profligate upſtart Krishna, and Bhīshma, who has sung such burning praises of Krishna, has to come in for his share here. There may be, however, a finger-poſt to be read by us here (ii, 41.24 ff.).[1] Moreover

[1] The tale in its form to-day has been naturally much changed. At firſt Bhīshma evidently really did fulſil his brotherly duty, and became the father of Pāṇḍu and Dhṛitarāshṭra. See xi, 23.24. That has already been shown by Ludwig, and Holtzmann after him (*Das Mahābh. u. seine Teile*, i, 154 ff. ; ii, 172 ; iv, 193). Then Vyāsa was brought in, perhaps not only through Brahmanic pride, but because, too, the tale of Bhīshma's vow of chaſtity now ſtood in the way ; for the reverse relation of the ages for the two tales is less likely. But it is only to his Brahmanhood that Vyāsa owed this honour, not to his threadbare-thin authorization as a kinsman. This can clearly be seen from Pāṇḍu's own words in i, 120.22, 23, and juſt as clearly from his speech to Kuntī, if we compare 122.23, 24 with 122.21, 22 and 121.35–41. So, too, our tale itself shows that it is as a Brahman that Vyāsa is to come in. According to i, 2.101 it was also a varadāna. But in the end offence was perhaps taken to this " singing the praises " of the " gods of the earth ", and " gods of the gods ", remarkable as that might seem, if the alteration here sprang from a Brahmanic source. Arjuna, nearly always so correct from the prieſtly ſtandpoint, indeed calls out very angrily : " What grounds had King Kalmāshapāda, then, in his thoughts for assigning (saṃniyojita) his wife to his teacher, the beſt of the Brahma-knowers ? Why did the high-minded Vasishṭha, who yet knows the higheſt holy law, the great Ṛishi, thus lie with her that for him was not for lying with ? It is unlawful what Vasishṭha did in former days " (i, 182.1 ff.). Then recourse was had to the levirate

the levirate is at least well enough known to the heroes of the Mahābh. for them to use it in comparisons. So in xiii, 8.22 : " As the woman when her husband dies makes the brother-in-law [1] her husband, so the earth makes the Kshattriya her

of the Smṛiti, and now a " brother-in-law ", of course, had to be brought in (Gautama, xxviii, 23 ; cp. Manu, ix, 144).

[1] Or : a proxy in begetting (devara) ? From the kurute patim it is hardly to be concluded that a real marriage is referred to. I myself can just as little get this for Bhīshma out of dārāṃç ca kuru dharmeṇa (i, 103.11). True, it seems as though xiii, 44.52–53 at least in the first place allots the widow, too, to the brother-in-law (the brothers-in-law ?) as the regular wife. Note too, the angry words of Sītā later on aimed at Lakshmaṇa. According to Yule's *Marco Polo*, ii, 376, all Indians even have had the custom of marrying the brother's widow ! In many parts of India it is moreover still a very usual custom to-day for the younger brother to take the widow of his brother to wife. Crooke, *The North-Western Provinces*, p. 229. Bṛihaspati refers to it as a usage of the people of Khaça that the brother marries his brother's widow (ii, 31), and in this passage he finds this quite in order there ; on the other hand in xxvii, 20 he calls it a very reprehensible practice of " other lands " that the brother lives with the brother's widow. It is open to question whether he is here speaking of the Indian area ; and the Khaças were held at least for degenerated, which, it is true, means little for us. As is well known, the law writings only deal with the narrower niyoga, that is to say, the brother or some other near kinsman, usually sapiṇḍa or sagotra (in Gautama, xvii, 5, even piṇḍagotrarishisambandhās or yonimātra) of the dead man and the widow are solemnly entrusted with the begetting of offspring for the dead man, one or even two sons, but not more ; and two are allowed only by Manu and Gautama. Apart from the relations needful for this the two must be to one another as father-in-law and daughter-in-law. Even during the embrace all passion must be most strictly kept away. This is very strongly stressed by several law-givers. According to Vasishtha the widow must first lead a life of mortification for half a year, then come in her ṛitu to him appointed for begetting (this last detail is also given by others) ; but according to Baudhāyana a whole year (but he mentions the half, too, as Maudgalya's opinion). Such a son is then called kshetraja ; and for the most part the word is used only in this narrower meaning. On the other hand the expression is in Parāçara, iv, 22, probably like datta and kṛitrima a collective concept, and then denotes any fruit that has grown up on the husband's " field ", that is, also the kānīna,

husband, when she does not get the Brahman." Cp. xii, 72.12.

Our attention is aroused by the fact that it is almost only the Brahmans in these tales that are used as stud-bulls, and then as those of the warriors. It is just this that casts suspicion on the matter so soon as we ask how much ground, indeed, there may have been for such statements in reality, even if it is only in more ancient times. This, indeed, is true : in later times in India, too, as so often in many other places, the priest is found as the lawful third in the alliance, and Old Indian literature often bears witness to the belief that especially the son begotten by an ascetic grows to excel others in capacity ; thus it is that in the pious legends also of the non-Brahmanic sects the monks and holy men often get into straits through

sahodha, gūdhaja (and paunarbhava). Manu first allows and describes the niyoga, and then absolutely forbids it. Brihaspati finds the explanation in its not being fitting in this present evil age. Cp. Bühler's Manu, p. xciv, and Brihaspati, xxiv, 14. On the levirate son begotten in the prescribed way there rests no stain, but such a stain there is if the matter has not been rightly carried out. Gautama in xxviii, 23 declares that where the widow has still a brother-in-law, her son called into life by another man cannot inherit. Nārada, xii, 48, indeed, applies to the woman who is given by her kinsfolk to a sapinda, there being no brother-in-law, the abusive term " married again ". The main passages dealing with the niyoga, especially of the widow, are : Manu, ix, 58 ff. ; 143 ff. ; Baudh., ii, 2, 4.7 ff. (= ii, 2.60 ff.) ; Gautama, xviii, 4 ff. ; Yājñav., i, 68 f. ; Brihaspati, xxiv, 12 ; Vas., xvii, 55 ff. ; Nārada, xii, 80 ff. (cp. 48, 50). The two last-named law teachers, especially Nārada, are very detailed and characteristic. Yājñav., i, 68 f., probably has reference to the niyoga of the widow as the commentators understand it. If we take the words, it is true that the husband might be still alive, and even be what is meant by guru. Moreover, the same law teacher says that the kshetraja has been begotten with a sagotra (a kinsman bearing the same family-name) or " another man " (ii, 128). The addition of " man " would probably be more natural than the " kinsman " of the commentators. On the other hand Yājñav. condemns him that goes to the brother's wife without an injunction as strongly as the other law-givers. Cp. especially Kautilya (transl.), Index under " Vikariatszeugung ". [From Melanesia for indirect reference to the Levirate idea cp. G. C. Wheeler, *Mono-Alu Folklore*, p. 41 (Translator).]

women wishful to be made fruitful.[1] Then the begetting by proxy with the husband's authorization is to be found for Old India in general in the other narrative literature also,[2] it has

[1] See e.g. Āyāraṅgasutta, ii, 1, § 12.
[2] I have referred in my Daçakum., p. 54, to a very drastic case from the Jātaka. According to Manu, ix, 59 the " commissioning " can or must take place wherever there is no offspring, that is, probably, even if the husband is still alive. But only the kinsman is there named as one qualified. The rest of the law and Purāṇa literature also contains highly instructive statements on begetting by proxy in the husband's life-time. According to Āpast., ii, 10, 27.2 ff., the custom of giving up the wife to a man of the clan (gentilis) to get a son, not to speak of another man, is forbidden in this age of Kali ; a union with the clan-fellow is now looked on as adultery, both husband and wife alike then go to hell ; there is a better reward given in the world beyond for keeping the law than for offspring so begotten. This passage is enough to show that in such cases of need, at least at first and in many places, the help of a clansman or member of the family was asked, as is indeed quite natural. " For they say that the bride is given to the family," that is, the whole family has a right to hope that from her an upholder of the line will come ; and if the husband is unsuccessful then he calls for the help of those so nearly concerned. But why should the express charge be needful at all, if the wife anyhow were at the disposal of all the members of the family ? There is therefore here no trace of such a handing over of the bride to the whole family or, indeed, to the gens ; just as there is nothing of the kind to be deduced for India from Bṛihaspati's statement that in " other lands " there is found the highly reprehensible custom of marrying the girl to the whole family. Indeed, Bṛishaspati himself directly afterwards names the Persians as evil sinners, who unite even with their mother (xxviii, 20–21). Gautama, xviii, 11 ff., gives rules as to whom the child belongs to, if the husband himself has given his wife over to another man to raise up children. So Baudhāyana, ii, 2, 3.17 ff. speaks of the son of a man who cannot beget or of an incurably sick man, that had been ordered from another. Yājñavalkya, ii, 127 says : " If a sonless man through niyoga (commissioning) begets a son on another's field, this son is the heir and giver of the forefathers' cake to both men." Parāçara, xii, 58 ff. lays it down that : " If by leave of the owner of the field (the husband) seed is sown in his field, then the offspring is looked on as the property of both, the seed-giver and the owner of the field. . . . But the offspring does not belong to the man that unites in another man's house with a woman ; this is looked on by the learned as adultery

always been in existence in various lands, and, be it noted, in princely families, and even to-day it has not yet died out.[1] But the Mahābh. in its present shape is so deeply concerned with the craziest glorification of the Brahman, that we shall hardly go wrong, if in the legends in the Epic of this priestly activity as proxies we see little else but partisan suggestion.[2] Furthermore, by the Brahmanic mind, as it is reflected in Smṛiti and other later literature, begetting by proxy, whether in the life-time or after the death of the husband, was looked on generally as wrongful. The teaching there is ever : Quod licet jovi non licet bovi ; what the gods and the holy men of the pure early times have done is right for them, but for us ordinary mortals of another age, namely, the evil age of Kali, it is forbidden ; indeed, as has been already mentioned, neither in the Mahābh. nor elsewhere is blame wanting for those only so-called models of virtue.

except when the wife herself has come into the house (of the strange man)." From this it will be seen that : if the child is to be looked on as the husband's child, then it must be begotten in the husband's house ; but if the outsider begets it in his own house, then he has his own, natural, absolute, right to the fruit of the union—a view very easily understood. Cf. Kauṭilya (transl.), 260.1–18, and especially the addition to it.

[1] See, for instance, Kauṭilya (transl.), 43.4 ff. ; Brantôme, Œuvr. compl. ed. du Panthéon lit., ii, 243b. In his view the wives, however, must not reckon on such politeness in their husbands as is shown by many, who themselves invite gallants to their wives, and charge the lovers to treat the beloved one well (p. 250 f.), but those fair ones who are burdened with an ugly, stupid, pitiful husband must have children made for themselves by dapper, proper serviteurs—pour l'amour de leur lignée (262 ff.). Cp., too, Henne am Rhyn, Die Frau in der Kulturgesch., p. 113 (among the Spartiatae the lover could even demand of the husband to share in the wife).

[2] In German : Tendenzfiktion (tendentious fiction). Further, Vishṇu, xv, 3 also says that the kshetraja is begotten by a sapiṇḍa or a Brahman (uttamavarṇa) (it is not said whether the husband is still alive). That a ripe (but not yet married) maiden should without hesitation let children be begotten to her by an excelling Brahman (or : by a Brahman as being the most excellent of men) Devayānī finds quite in order (i, 83.1–8). She is a Brahman woman, and the girl in question a Kshattriyā. Cp. Malory's Morte d'Arthur, iii, 3.

171

In itself, it is true, such a service of love found no hindrance from the law, even when the husband was alive, if the husband authorized or invited his wife. The view that is always stressed in Indian literature is this : The wife is the husband's field (kshetra) ; that which grows on his field belongs to him, no matter who has sown it (cp. for instance Manu, ix, 32–55). And the owner can himself till his ground, or have it tilled by another ; the fruit is always his.[1]

[1] Perhaps few so true and fruitful sentences—always presuming that our modern scientific method is justified—are to be found in the literature of the subject as this one in Starcke, *Primitive Family* (1889), p. 241 : " We must therefore regard marriage as a legal institution, and the sexual intercourse between husband and wife as only one of the matters with which this institution has to do ; it is by no means its central point and *raison d'être.*" Cp. p. 255 f., where, however, the view that the man is afraid of losing his wife, if she have intercourse with another man without his consent, is a very extraordinary one. The words on p. 260 there are just as excellently said : " Marriage is sharply distinguished from the mere relations of passion . . . His (the husband's) ownership (of the children) does not depend on the fact they were begotten by him, but upon the fact that he owns and supports their mother" (cp. p. 106). As a matter of fact " supports " should here be deleted ; for among savages it is so often far rather the duty of the wife to support the man ; indeed, the main reason for his marrying is this, that he wants a beast of burden. Jealousy in our meaning primitive man does not know, or only very seldom indeed, or, anyhow, not where his mate is concerned. It is only the unauthorized use of his property that angers him. Not any Tom, Dick, and Harry may use his tools without more ado, ride his horse, and so on. But to the owner belongs whatever his field—the wife—brings forth, as, for instance, the Australians, celebrated though they are as a mother-right people, also hold (Finck, 175, after Cunow, *Die Verwandtschaftsverhältn. d. Australneger*; cp. Henne am Rhyn, pp. 16–17 ; Starcke, 284 (Amerinds) ; Osman Bey, *Die Frau in der Türkei*, p. 7 (Mohammed)). It is true we have reports from by no means few mother-right peoples and tribes that among them the husband has nothing whatever to say about the children. But such exceptions, even if they be very many, cannot upset the general rule. A matriarchate because of the fatherhood being uncertain is an utterly ungrounded hypothesis (except perhaps for certain very clearly determined cases). How

little heed was given even by our forefathers, who stood so high in sexual matters, the Old Germans, to the question whether they were actually the father to their children, is shown in detail by Dargun, *Mutterrecht u. Raubehe*, in the third chapter; and on p. 45 he gives a valuable passage (which, indeed, sounds rather like a witticism) from the Westphalian peasant laws, according to which the man who was not able to satisfy his amorous wedded wife had to take her himself to another one. Cf. Grimm, *Deutsche Rechtsalter-tümer*, ed. by Heusler and Hübner, 1899, vol. i, p. 613 ff. " Of the Arabs we are told there is a form of marriage according to which a man says to his wife when menstruation is over, Send a message to such an one, and beg him to have intercourse with you.' And he himself refrains from intercourse with her until it is manifest that she is with child by the man in question. The husband acts this way in order that his offspring may be noble." Starcke, *Prim. Fam.*, pp. 123–124. Also the Chukchi in Siberia get their wives to be made pregnant by others; and it is reported of certain Koryaks that they were wont to get the Russian postman as a stud-bull (Hartland, ii, 181). Childless Bantu bring their brother to their wife; and among the Wakamba in Africa rich men who have no offspring give one of their wives to a friend, that there may be offspring (Hartland, ii, 214, 196). The best-known case is Sparta, where a law ordered the elderly owner of a young wife to mate a young and lusty likely father with her (Hartland, i, 322; ii, 134). On this and on begetting by proxy among the Greeks in general, and among others of the older peoples, cp. Engels, *Ursprung d. Familie*, 49; Henne am Rhyn, *Die Frau in der Kulturgesch.*, 193 ff.; Starcke, loc. cit., 124; O. Schrader, *Die Indogermanen*, p. 93; Ed. Meyer, *Gesch. d. Altertums*, i, 1³, pp. 28–30, and what is there said. It is on very good grounds that Hartland can say that the examples are " innumerable " where the husband, to get children, brings in another man in his stead (ii, 247).—Now proper men above all others are the priest, the chief, the ruler. Above and beyond this, as already said, he confers an honour on the commonalty thereby. So among the Eskimos a man and his wife look on themselves as lucky when a shaman takes pity in this way on the family. They believe that the son of a holy man with such power over the spirits will outstrip other mortals in excellence and good fortune. The Greenlanders even paid the Angekoks for such services (Starcke, 123; Westermarck ³, 80; Hartland, ii, 141; Elsie Clews Parsons, *The Old-Fashioned Woman*, p. 87; Müller-Lyer, *Phasen der Liebe*, p. 22 f.). And from the woman, who is almost everywhere in the world unclean and a bringer of destruction, and her husband, set into danger by her, spirits and evil

It is to this view that a good proportion of the twelve kinds of sons enumerated in the law books owes its being. They are also named in the Mahābh., i, 120.32–34, and the account given here, too, has a singularly mild tone towards the " pretty sins " of the woman, and differs considerably from the account in the law writings. As bandhudāyada, that is, as sons who are kinsmen (belong to the family) and are entitled to inherit, are named : 1st, svayaṃjāta (one begotten by the husband himself, aurasa) ; 2nd, praṇīta (brought by the wife to the husband, and, as the commentary declares in agreement with çl. 35–36, begotten by the free grace of a better man) ; 3rd, parikrīta (bought, according to Nīl. begotten with the wife by another, who has been paid for the seed ; which in view of 1, 105.2 is certainly right) ; 4th, paunarbhava (the son of a re-married woman) [1] ; 5th, kānīna (unmarried woman's child) ; 6th,

---

influences are warded off by the priest as a partner in the bed or fellow in wedlock. In this, therefore, the Brahmans do but stand in a row with others of their stamp. Holtzmann quotes (*Mahābh. u. seine Teile*, i, 155) the testimony of Graul that even " to-day " the women in Malayala, all and each, are accessible to the pleasure of the unmarried Brahmans, and that this does not in any way degrade them, but rather it is looked on as an honour. In Dubois-Beauchamp [3], p. 117, we can read that when the Gurus or spiritual fathers of the Çivaites come to a place, the people vie with one another to see who shall lodge them. Those who are thus sought after decide on a house—and as a matter of fact it is said of them that in this they make their choice according to the youthfulness and good looks of the women living there—then all the men leave the field open and keep away so long as their reverences are pleased to tarry amid this delightful band. So, too, the leaders of the Vishṇuite Vallabhācāryas claim absolute power over the female part of their flock (Crooke, *The North-Western Provinces of India*, p. 250). On niyoga and the begetting of Dhṛitarāshṭra and Pāṇḍu, see further Winternitz, JRAS, 1897, p. 716 ff.

[1] Paunarbhava is the son of a punarbhū (re-married woman). According to Baudh., ii, 2, 3.27 punarbhū is a woman that has left an impotent husband and taken another ; according to Vasishṭha, xvii, 19 f. she is one whose former husband is impotent, expelled from his caste, mad, or dead, and who has married another man, or else one that has left the husband of her youth, linked herself with another, and then has come back again into her husband's house. According to

svairinyāṃ yaç ca jāyate (conceived by the woman in adultery, that is = kuṇḍa, gūḍhotpanna, gūḍhaja). The six sons that can inherit but do not belong to the family are called ; 1st, datta ("given away by father and mother," as Nīl. says, but here also probably as a small child, that is, *adoptatio*) ; 2nd, krīta (bought from the parents) ; 3rd, kṛitrima, "and (therefore) he that himself goes thither," that is, the svayaṃdatta, while kṛitrima or kṛita is otherwise the son that is taken over as a grown up ; 4th, sahoḍha (with whom the mother was at the wedding already pregnant by another man) ; 5th, jñātiretas ("seed of kinsman," that is, begotten in the levirate) ; 6th, hīnayonidhṛita (begotten of a woman from a low caste, that is, especially the "Çūdra son ".[1]

A list that partly differs is given in xiii, 49. Yudhishṭhira says : "We hear of many disputes that arise out of the question of the sons. Do thou solve the doubt for us, who are bewildered." Bhīshma now first of all sets forth nine kinds of sons : 1st, ātman (the one begotten by himself, and therefore the son belonging to the begetter himself) ; 2nd, anantaraja (begotten by the next of kin to the husband, that is, in the

Vishṇu, xv, 7 ff. she is one that has been married for the second time as a virgin, or that has lived with another man before her marriage at law ; according to Manu, ix, 175 she is one whose husband has left her, or is dead, and who has married again. Yājñavalkya, i, 67 says : one that is, or is not harmed in her maidenhead, and that lets herself be "dedicated" for the second time (cp. Manu, ix, 176). According to Nārada, xii, 45 ff., there are three kinds of punarbhū, of which each is worse than the one following : (1) the girl that has not, indeed, lost her maidenhead, but has lost her honour through an earlier taking by the hand ; (2) a woman that has run off from the husband of her youth, and gone to another, but has afterwards come back to the first husband ; (3) a woman that is given to a sapiṇḍa of the same caste, because there are no brothers-in-law. Elsewhere there are also other interpretations of the term.

[1] Practically this is the most natural interpretation. It also agrees with the comment. Philologically more exact would be : 3rd, kṛitrima (the son taken over as a grown up) ; 4th, he that comes of his own accord ; 5th, he with whom a kinsman had already impregnated the mother before the wedding.

levirate) [1] ; 3rd, niruktaja (begotten by one expressly named, that is, by one that has been asked to fertilize, and that probably by the husband) ; 4th, prasṛitaja (" begotten by one that has come ", that is, according to Nīl., by another man from sexual appetite, who has not been asked to do it, that is, the gūḍhaja) ; 5th, the son, begotten with the man's own wife, of one that has been expelled from his caſte (?) [2] ; 6th, datta ; 7th, kṛita ; 8th, adhyūḍha (added by marriage = sahoḍha or acquired by marriage) ; 9th, kānīna. After this come the twelve other kinds of sons which are found as the result of a quite different principle, namely : the six apadhvaṃsaja (three sons of the Brahman with Kshattriyā, Vaiçyā, and Çūdrā ; two sons of the Kshattriya with Vaiçyā and Çūdrā ; one son of the Vaiçya with Çūdrā), and the six apasada (three sons of Çūdra with a Brahman woman, Kshattriyā, Vaiçyā, that is, the cāṇḍāla, vrātya, vaidya ; two sons of the Vaiçya from a Brahman woman and a Kshattriyā, that is, the māgadha and the vāmaka ; and one son of the Kshattriya from a Brahman woman, namely the sūta). Then Yudhishṭhira asks : " Some say that a son is the produ&ct of the field, others that he is the produ&ct of the seed. The same is true of both : that they are sons. But whose ? Tell me that." Bhīshma spoke : " He that is begotten of the (husband's own) seed is his son, and he that has

[1] According to Nīl. " dire&ctly begotten," for he paraphrases by aurasa " bodily ", that is, takes ātmā in another meaning. We should then have only eight kinds.

[2] Patitasya tu bhāryāyā bhartrā susamavetayā. In this barbaric conſtru&ction we muſt probably firſt change bhāryāyā to bhāryayā. But the wife of a patita is not bhartrā susamavetā. I would therefore put bhāryayābhartrā : " The son of a man expelled from his caſte (being) by his wife, who had equipped herself probably with another man not her husband." But since bhartar here, like pati and dārās in the above-quoted verses, perhaps simply means a proxy-husband, one would get with bhartrā, too, essentially the same meaning : " who had probably provided herself with a (proxy-)husband." The patita is an outlaw, a dead man ; and juſt as the younger brother of such a one may marry before him without fear, so the wife of the expelled man may unite sexually with another man, and the child is then looked on as her a&ctual husband's (probably if he is then rehabilitated ; cp. K, xiii, 84.6).

grown up on his field, if he has been given up (by his real begetter), he that is 'added by marriage', if the contract is broken (samayaṃ bhittvā)." He then explains this thus : " If a man begets a son from himself, and then on some ground gives him up, then the seed has nothing to say here, but he belongs to the lord of the field. If a man weds a maiden in his yearning for a son, for the sake of a son, then it is the growing up from his own field that decides, and he is not the son of his begetter. Moreover the son that has grown up on the field (anyatra lakshyate) betrays himself, for the self (of the begetter) (which shows itself again in the child) cannot be destroyed ; we come to it (come on its tracks) through the pattern (that is, we look at the father, and know by the likeness that he has again produced his self in a certain child)." [1] According to this it would therefore seem that the husband need only to recognize this child of his wife, already pregnant at marriage, if he knew of her being pregnant, and approved of it, or, indeed, actually chose the girl for that reason.[2] Anyatra generally

---

[1] Of this the Liburni were evidently fully convinced. They had a community of wives, and the children were brought up in common until they were five years old. Then they were called together by beating the drum, examined, and assigned to their fathers according to likeness (Starcke, p. 126, after Bachofen, *Mutterrecht*, p. 20). The same is reported from other ancient peoples. Hartland, ii, 131 ; Ed. Meyer, 24 ; Welhausen, *Gött. Nachr.* (1893), 462 f. And that woman, of whom we are told in Kirchhof's *Wendunmut* (ed. Oesterley, Stuttg. Lit. Ver.), i, p. 397 (No. 338), seems to have firmly believed this. She had much to do with the clergy, and once when she was lying in child-bed, a woman caller exclaimed : " The son looks exactly like his father." The pious dove started up in fright : " Oh ! has he got a bald patch, too ? " On how strong the Indian belief is in the inheritance of character see J. J. Meyer, *Altind. Rechtsschr.*, 263–265.

[2] " So among the hill tribes of Northern Aracan sexual intercourse before marriage is unrestricted, 'and it is considered rather a good thing,' we are told, ' to marry a girl in the family-way, even though by another man.' " Hartland, i, 312. So also among the Wakamba (Hartland, ii, 196). Thus it is natural that it is the very girl who has already given birth who among several peoples is more sought after in the marriage market than her sister, who has not been blessed with

means "in the other case" (and Böhtl. does not once give "moreover"). Taking all into account we muſt so translate here too ; and the çloka that begins with it would then all the more clearly leave the husband the right to assign to the begetter as revealed by nature the fruit of his wife's body, of which he had no knowledge at the wedding, and which he does not want. The kṛitaka or kṛitrima is then thus draſtically defined : He that is put out on the ſtreet by his parents, and then is taken to himself by a man (yas taṃ prakalpayet), and whose parents are not known, this is the kṛitrima.[1] His sonship is derived only from the taking over (saṃgraha) by the adoptive parents, not from the "seed" nor from the "field". This man who was once maſterless belongs to his present maſter, comes into the caſte of him that rears him, muſt be equipped by him like his own son with the sacraments of his caſte and kindred, and may be chosen for kinship by marriage.[2] Further on we find it said : "The son of an unmarried woman, and he that is added by marriage are to be looked on as sprung from sin (kilbisha), but the sacraments are to be carried out on them also, as on the sons of the body."

A third passage where a liſt of the various sons is found is i, 74.99. Here according to the commentary—and the learned men of Europe follow it—five classes are named. But, so far as I can see, this view is hardly a possible one. The moſt obvious translation would be : "Manu has made known the five sons born from a man's own wife, (then) the acquired, the bought, the reared, the 'made' (kṛita) sons, that is, the (four) that have come into being in other women." The labdha could then include in himself the datta and the svayaṃdatta of Manu, whereby naturally I do not mean to say that we are to give weight to the conſtant appeal to the famous law-giver. The "reared" one might then perhaps be the apaviddha. Also the five by the man's own wife offer a difficulty. But as

a proof of her fruitfulness, and that in many places, and in German-speaking diſtriĉts, too, the young man will hardly take a girl to his home who has not first become with child by him.

[1] The man here described is, as is well known, in the law books called apaviddha.

[2] Cp. in the MBh., the example of Karṇa.

the son of the " re-married woman " in the second list of the
Mahābh. has been eliminated, so here he may also have dropped
out, and thus we should have the other five, as taught by Manu.
Yet this rendering, which in itself is the most natural one, is
not without an element of strain ; therefore the çloka is
perhaps better understood thus : " Those that came into
being from a man's own wife (and) the five (kinds of) sons
that have been acquired (that is, given), bought, reared, ' made,'
and born of other women." That would then give twelve
kinds, if Manu and Mahābh., xiv, 49 are brought in to explain,
but fourteen if MBh., i, 120.32–34 is so brought in. K. has
instead (i, 99.25–26) : " Those sprung from a man's own
wife, those acquired, made, brought up under an agreement
(samayavardhita), bought, and sprung from maidens—these
Manu has declared to be sons. These are the six who are
kinsmen and heirs (and) the six who are kinsmen, but not
heirs." [1]

[1] There is not complete agreement in the various law writings
either as to the order of rank of the twelve kinds of sons, or as to the
two divisions : (1) sons who belong to the family and have also the
right to inherit ; (2) sons who only belong to the family, but have not
the right to inherit. The category, " capable of inheriting, but not
belonging to the family," moreover, is found only in the MBh.
Here we give only one or two details which are perhaps of special
importance for the subject of this book. All the law books put the
kshetraja (the son begotten by a proxy) next after the son of the body ;
only Yājñavalkya names before him and as fully equal to the
aurasa the son of the inheriting daughter (putrikā). While the son of
the inheriting daughter according to the general view is the heir of
his sonless grandfather, and also of his father, if this latter has no other
son, but in return also takes over in both families the duty of the
sacrificing to the forefathers, Gautama, xxviii, 32 throws him into the
last place but two in the second group. The gūdhotpanna or he that is
begotten in adultery is reckoned by all to group I, the sahodha (he
that marriage brought in the bride's body) only in Nārada (xiii, 45),
while otherwise he generally takes the second place in category II,
in Vasishṭha, xvii, 26 and Vishṇu, xv, 15 the first place, in Yājñav., ii,
131 the last place but one. The kānīna or unmarried woman's son is among
the first and privileged set of six in all except Manu, ix, 161, as also
Gautama, xxviii, 33 and Baudhāyana, ii, 2, 3.32 ; but these two
agree here exactly with Manu, only that Baudh. brackets the

putrikāputtra with the datta of Manu, and so gets thirteen classes, and Gautama handles the son of the heiress-daughter like a very cruel father in the way already mentioned. In these three the kānīna is found at the head of group II. The paunarbhava is taken by Vasishṭha, xvii, 13 ff., Yājñav., ii, 128 ff., Vishṇu, xv, 1 ff., into I, while in Nārada he ſtands in the firſt place in II, in Manu and his followers in the laſt place but two. Yājñavalkya and Vishṇu, it is true, do not expressly mention the two categories. All lay it down that if there are no sons really entitled to inherit, then the others muſt come into the inheritance according to their rank. The greater number, that is, Vas., Nār., Yājñ., and Vishṇu in their six firſt classes have only actual children of the mother, no matter who the father may be. Vas., xvii, 22, 23, and Yājñ., ii, 129 (= Agnipur., 256.16) assert that the unmarried woman's son belongs to the girl's father, which sounds the more remarkable in that these two law teachers reckon the kānīna among the very members of the husband's family who are entitled to inherit. Whether this prescription is only to hold when the mother does not marry is very much open to queſtion. The meaning is rather as follows : If the father has no sons, then that son of his daughter, whom she has borne in his own house, is his natural heir. Cp. Nārada, xii, 60 ; Meyer, Kauṭilya, p. 765 at foot. The usual doctrine is that the kānīna like the sahoḍha belongs to him that takes the mother to his house. So, for inſtance, Manu, ix, 172 f. ; Vishṇu, xv, 12, 17. In fact the great queſtion in dispute is found running, too, through the law books : What is it that decides, field or seed ? Manu, ix, 31 ff. and x, 70, declares that " the seed is more important ", and proves it without hesitation. But then it is shown, if possible ſtill more clearly, that the field is all in all (ix, 42 ff.). Vasishṭha, xvii, 6 ff., does no more than give the for and againſt ; Āpaſt., ii, 6, 13.6 f. and Baudhāyana, ii, 2, 3.33 decide that the seed is the decisive thing (the son belongs to the begetter). Nārada, xiii, 17, and Parāçara, iv, 20 f. hold the opposite opinion ; for according to Parāçara not only the kuṇḍa (son of the adulteress) but also the golaka (widow's bastard) belongs to the husband, and Nārada also names the kānīna, sahoḍha, and gūḍhaja as son and heir of the husband. So also MBh. K, xiii, 84.9–12. Moreover Parāçara in iv, 22 gives only four classes of sons : aurasa, kshetraja, datta, kṛitrima. But all twelve can be brought under these. The Mahānirvāṇatantra teaches as to the kānīna, golaka, and kuṇḍa that they are like the atipātakin, cannot inherit, and do not bring uncleanness by their death, that they are therefore utter outsiders (xii, 82). Cp. Bṛihaspati, xxv, 41 ; Yājñav., i, 222 ff. It is a ſtatement often found that he that is sprung of a begetting by proxy muſt—naturally in an emergency—bring the offering to

If thus the many kinds of sons whom the wife has gathered elsewhere have their fixed place, recognized by law, in the husband's family, it is probably due in the first place to the Indian passion for systematizing and their worship of tradition, and respect for the usage of different districts. That which once had been stated as a principle was dragged on faithfully down through the centuries, nay through thousands of years. But on the other hand the life to-day of our civilized mankind also, for instance, would really offer without a doubt quite as much, if not, indeed, far more, foundation for suchlike codifying of the fruits of women's freedom in love. To speak only of one thing, it is no wonder that, in a land where sons—whether begotten by a man himself or not—meant so much, a man was often inclined just to enjoy such fruits without letting himself be worried over the question of whence the life-bringing pollen might have been wafted for them. We are not to draw from this the conclusion of a remarkable lack of morals, not even for earlier times. The Epic, anyhow, gives no sure foundation whatever for such an assumption. It is true that in many regards the ethical feeling was still raw and undeveloped; for it the woman, indeed, was usually only a chattel ; but of this we shall speak by and by. But is it truly any better among ourselves who have progressed so wonderfully ?

Now there were, indeed, in the India of the Epic, too, people who did not wish for any children, and in the Mahābh. (xii, 331.16, cp. 20) astonishment finds expression at the strange way of the world, that they who wished not for children should get them, while to others who yearned for them with all their heart they were denied.[1] But married folk undoubtedly

the forefathers for both men, his begetter and the husband of his mother, and is heir to them both. Cp. also Caland, *Ahnenkult*, 28, 193 (how the son born out of wedlock takes the ancestral gift away from his real father and bestows it on his father by law). See especially also J. J. Meyer, Kauṭilya, pp. 765–767 ; *Altind. Rechtsschr.*, 224 f. ; 315 ; 343.

[1] The passage is noteworthy in many ways. The poet wonders at the remarkable course of the world, whose tangled riddles are insoluble from the empirical standpoint, but can perhaps be explained by metaphysics. The sinner and the fool grow old in pleasure and

thriving, for the good man and the capable things go badly, and so on. " To the one man, who sits still and does not stir, happiness comes, the other runs along after toil, and does not reach that which is utterly beyond his grasp. Make it known unto me from man's own (empirical) nature wherein he makes his mistake. [Probably what is meant is : explain to me from his personality or nature, as determined by the karman ; cp. xii, 290.13 ; 301.24.] The seed that came into being at one place (in the man) goes over to another (into the woman). If it has been set into the womb, then a fruit of the body comes into being, or none ; we become aware that we vanish like the mango-blossom [liter., whose disappearance, that is like the mango-blossom, is perceived ; the blossom is lost and leaves a fruit behind it, or does not ; even so is it with the seed of man. Thus, if we read nivrittir instead of the nirvrittir often confused with it. If this latter is kept to, then the meaning is the same : " whose growth is perceived as like unto that of the mango-blossom "]. For some persons that yearn for the continuation of the line, and strive to bring this about, no ovum comes into being, and to others who start back from pregnancy as from an angry snake a lusty boy is born. How then has he come into being, as though out of death ? Poor fools that yearn for sons make sacrifices to the gods, undertake penances, and then shameful slurs for their family are born unto them, carried for ten months in the womb. Others are born into money and corn, and all kinds of things of delight gathered together by their fathers, have fallen to the share (of their parents) through these very happiness-bringing things (cp. iii, 209.11 ff.). The two having drawn nigh unto one another, a fruit of the body comes into the womb, like an intruding misfortune, at the union in the pleasure of love [perhaps : in just as inexplicable wise. I read yonim, which is confirmed by K. But possibly the somewhat unusual yoni is older : " a bodily fruit of the womb comes into being "]. Dost thou see through what pains the fruit of the body lives, deposited by pure chance as an unconscious drop of seed in the womb, (the fruit) which (as a soul again embodied), separated (from its earlier abode) with other bodies, cut off from its earlier source with the bearer of a body (that is, with a new being), stirring in flesh and slime at (that is, after) the ending of its (earlier) life, is bound up with a (new) living person, after being burnt, indeed, in one body with another moving or unmoving body, and perishes when this (body) perishes in the end, like a little ship that is fastened to another one (cp. Meyer, Kautilya, addit. 56.47) ? [I read with K. çirnam instead of çighra·. on purely stylistic grounds, and take çaririṇam, prāṇinam, and paradeham as accusatives depending on ahitam ; of course çaririṇam and prāṇinam could also be referred

were at least only very seldom in the first set. And if married men and women were granted offspring, then they proved thankful, too, especially, of course, if it was male offspring. Just as the Old Indian literature in general stands out through its pictures of the tenderest family life, so the Epic gives us, too, beautiful glimpses into this delightful world. We have a very sweet song on the happiness of family and children from the lips of a woman in the words of Çakuntalā (i, 74). She first paints a glowing picture for King Dushyanta of the true wife and the blessing she brings; then she goes on (çl. 53 ff.): "When the son runs up to his father, covered with the earth's dust (in which he has been playing), and clasps his limbs, what could there be more glorious than that! . . . Not the touching of garments nor of beautiful women nor of water is to compare, is so pleasing as the touching of the son who is being clasped. The Brahman is best among the two-footed, the cow excels most among the four-footed, the best among the revered is the teacher, the son is the fairest of all that men touch. . . . Yes, men, when they have gone into another village, (at their home-coming) joyfully welcome their children, taking them, lovingly onto their lap and smelling their heads.[1] And the

to the accus. garbham, but there is very much to be said against this]. Why, in that very belly where food and drink, and the solid dishes that have been eaten are dissolved by the digestion, is not the fruit of the body dissolved just like the nourishment taken ? [Cp. xii, 253.11 ; Märk.-Pur., x, 5 ; Chavannes, *Cinq cents contes*, etc., iii, p. 124] The course of the urine and fæces in the body has been laid down by our very nature ; none here is a free agent, whether he wishes to withhold or to discharge. Sometimes also the fruits of the body come out of the belly before their time, being so born, and other times likewise they fall to destruction when they have to come into the world [or agame na written separately : " others on the contrary do not thus fall to destruction at their coming into the world," that is, are happily born] ". All connected with the origin of life is therefore a secret, throned in the darkness of nature. None has the power here to arrange things as he might wish them.

[1] In the Epic, too, this Eastern, and especially Indian, sign of tenderness is mentioned over and over again. In Rām., vii, 71.12 we read : " I will smell thee on the head ; that is the greatest sign of tender love " (snehasya parā gatih). Cp. Meyer, Kautilya, 11.26 ff.

twice-born utter this set of sayings, which are in the Veda, at the birth ceremony for sons, and this is known to thee :

Thou art begotten limb from limb,
Thou art born from the heart,
Thou art the self, that son is called ;
Live thou a hundred autumns !

My life hangs from thine,
On thee hangs the everlasting span of the race ;
Therefore, mayest thou, my son, in happiness high
Live a hundred autumns long ! [1]

From thy limbs this one (my son) came into being, from the man another man ; see, as in a clear lake, thy second self in the son. As the sacrificial fire (āhavanīya) is fetched from the fire of the master of the house (gārhapatya), so did this one arise out of thee ; thou, that wast one, art become twofold." [2]

The already mentioned Brahman who is to bring the cartload of rice as tribute to the evil Rākshasa, and then be eaten together with the steers by the monster, bewails his wife and children (i, 157.26 ff.) : " Thou knowest, O Brahman woman, once I did strive to go away elsewhere, where there is peace and plenty, but thou didst not hearken unto me. ' Here I was born and grew up, and my father likewise.' So didst thou speak in thy foolishness, when more than once I besought thee. Thy old father has gone into heaven, and thy mother, too, long ago ; thy kinsfolk have been and are gone ; what joy hast

[1] See the Grihyasūtras : Hiraṇy., ii, 1, 3.2 ; Gobhila, ii, 7, 21. Āçval., i, 15, 3.9. Pārask., i, 16, 18 ; 18, 2 ; Baudhāyana's law book, ii, 2, 3.14.

[2] The Christian Fathers of the Church of the first centuries disputed among themselves whether the soul had existed from all time (Pre-existants), or whether God made it at the begetting (Creationists), or whether it came from the father, as one light is lit at another (Traducianists). Among the Indians neither the second nor the third of these doctrines was able to emerge. And yet they often show this very Traducianist comparison. Thus Kālidāsa says in Raghuv., v, 37 : " It was the same mighty form (Aja's as his father Raghu's), the same natural majesty ; the boy differed not from his cause, like a light that has been lit at the light." Of course that only refers to the origin of the body. Cp. MBh., xii, 210.26.

thou then in dwelling here ? Filled with loving yearning for thy family thou waſt, and since thou didſt not hearken to my words, thy family now perishes, which brings great sorrow on me, or I now lose my life. For I cannot yield up any of mine, remaining myself alive like one without pity. Thou haſt carried out the holy duties with me, thou art kind, always to me as a mother, thou art the friend whom the gods have appointed unto me, always my sureſt refuge, robbed of father and mother,[1] ever busied with household cares. Thee I did woo in prescribed fashion, and thee I then led round the fire with holy prayers. Thou comeſt of good family, art endowed with virtuous ways, and haſt borne me children. Thee, my good wife, who never doſt hurt me, and art ever obedient to me, I could not yield up to save my own life.—How could I myself give up my daughter, a child, who has not yet come to the flower of youth, and whose form does not yet bear the marks of sex, who has been entruſted me by the high-souled Maker, like a pledge for her future husband. How could I forsake her, from whom I together with my forefathers hope for the worlds made ready by the daughters' sons, her whom I myself begot ? Many there are who hold that the father's love for the son is the greater, others the love for the daughter ; for me both are alike.[2] Even though I give myself up, I shall suffer torment in the other world too, for left behind by me, these (my family) it is evident, cannot live here. To

[1] I read vihīnāṃ inſtead of vihitāṃ, which perhaps may have come from the preceding line of verse. It muſt be said, however, that K. also has vihitāṃ, and this is likewise clear, though not very good : Prepared, brought up, deſtined by father and mother (to be combined with what follows).

[2] According to Rām., i, 61.19 the father loves the eldeſt, the mother the youngeſt son, which agrees with Jāt., v, p. 327 ff. Of the great love of the Hindus for their children we have very plentiful evidence. Here we give one or two cases only : A. W. Stratton, *Letters from India*, Lond., 1908, p. 99, to be compared with Çrīvara's Kathākautukam ed. R. Schmidt, iv, 86 ; Fuller, *Studies of Indian Life*, etc., 162 ; Dubois-Beauchamp, 307 f. (but according to the laſt passage only a foolish fondness, which is very ill requited by the children, which ſtatement, if made universally, seems wholly groundless).

yield up one of them is cruel and reprobated by the wise ones ; and if I give myself up, then without me they will die." See especially also xiv, 90.24 ff.

Rāma cries out (Rām., ii, 111.9–10) : "The way the father and mother deal conſtantly by the child, what the father and mother do to it, it is very hard to requite them for [1] ; they give it whatever they can, they lull it to sleep, they rub its body with oil, they speak ever loving words to it, and rear it." Cp. MBh., xiii, 14.112 ff. ; above all 132 f.

Bitter, therefore, was the sorrow when death took a child with it. Such piċtures are often drawn in Indian literature, but generally, it is true, with an emphatic ſtressing of the foolishness of such grief in a world where all is fleeting and mortal. Here the inconsolable mother, Kisagotamī has won renown. An edifying legend, which was perhaps only later touched up to glorify Çiva, but is very beautiful, makes up the content of xii, 153 :

The son of a Brahman, who had been gotten after much trouble, had died while ſtill a child with great eyes, seized by a demon of children's sickness. Filled with sorrow, his own took him, and bore him, that was all to his family, weeping and overcome by woe, out to the field of the dead. And as now with the dead darling on their arm they went along sobbing, they kept on telling one another everything he had said while he was ſtill alive (cp. iii, 298.8). Outside in the place of the dead they laid him down on the earth, but could not part themselves from him. Then a vulture heard them weeping, and came up and spoke : " Thousands of men, and thousands of womeii, have brought their kindred hither, and then gone back home. See how the whole world is ruled by pleasure and pain ! Union and separation fall to men in the wheel of change. Those who come here, indeed, with the dead, but go back without them,[2] they themselves go hence with the faſtsetmeasure of the length of their lives. No one was ever awakened again to life, when once he had fallen before the law of time, beloved

[1] Cp. Manu, ii, 227.
[2] After ye na add gṛihītvā. K. reads more smoothly : ye 'nuyānti (152.10). Kālena in çl. 8 probably means : in the course of time. It might also = (brought hither) by fate, etc.

or hated—this is the lot of the living. The world ſtops from its daily task, the sun goes home, do ye, too, go back to your abode and let be your love for the child." When now the kindred, wailing in despair, for the child was indeed dead, were about to go forth, there came a jackal, black as a raven's wing, out of his cave and spoke to them : " Mankind knows no compassion. The sun is ſtill in the heavens. The fleeting inſtant can bring much ; perhaps the child will come back to life again. You have no love for the child, whose words once gladdened your hearts. But see what love the beaſts and birds cherish for their young, and yet they have nothing to gain from having them. They, who are filled with loving attachment, and see their pleasure in their young, have not, as the Munis and they who carry out the business of sacrifice,[1] when they go over into the other world any advantage either here on earth or in the life beyond, and yet they love and cherish their offspring. Look on him long with love. How could you go and leave him, that had such lively, great lotus-eyes, and whom you bathed like a newly wedded man, and decked out with every ornament ? " Then they all went back to the dead child. The vulture once again began : " Why do you bewail the dead child, who feels no longer, and why not yourselves ? Leave sorrow and the dead one, and do good with all your ſtrength. What a man does, be it pure or dreadful, that he does enjoy ; what have kinsfolk to do there ? " The jackal answered : " By manly deeds and untiringness men reach the goal and happiness. Whither then will ye go, and leave behind in the foreſt here him that came into being [2] through your own flesh, the body which is the half of your body, him that carries on the line for the forefathers ? " The vulture spoke : " I have now been living over a thousand years, and I have never yet seen one dead brought back to life. They die in the mother's womb, they die at once after birth, they die when they walk about,[3]

[1] Muniyajñakriyām inſtead of muniyajñakriyāṇām, with the genitive ending for consonantal ſtems, in the Vedic way.

[2] Literally : " Came up here," at the begetting, of course. Boehtlingk's reading is wrong.

[3] Of course : when they can walk (cankramantas). Cp. çl. 45 ; vi, 10.7.

187

and others in the bloom of youth. Whether it be a moving or
an unmoving being, its span of life is already laid down at the
beginning. Torn away from the much-loved wife, filled with
grief for the child, burning with sorrow, people are ever going
from here (from the place of the dead) home. This love is
useless, this wearing oneself out is fruitless. This one there sees
not with his eyes, hears not with his ears ; he has become as a
block of wood. The pain is doubled, if we dwell on the doings
of the dead one, and call them up into memory." The jackal
ran up and said : " There is no ending [1] for love, nor for wailing
and weeping. If ye leave this dead one, sorrow is sure for you.
As before now dead persons have come to life again, so too
may a holy man, wise in magic, or a godhead take pity on you."
At these words they came back to the dead body, laid its head
on their lap, and wept bitterly. But the vulture reminded
them : " He is all wet with your tears, and is tormented by the
touch of your hand,[2] and yet through the working of the god

[1] Literally : no abolishing.

[2] Jul. von Negelein, " Die Reise d. Seele ins Jenseits," *Ztschr. d.
Ver. f. Volksk.*, Bd. 11, p. 16 ff., 149 ff., 263 ff. shows the widespread
belief : (1) that the soul stands in relation with the body even after
death ; (2) that it stays on at first in the neighbourhood of the body,
but for a very variously estimated time ; (3) that in the body, so long
as it has not decayed, there abides a potential life. As to the last
point mention might also be made of India : " So long as even only a
bone is there, the dead man enjoys glory in the world of heaven."
Cp. Caland, *Toten- u. Bestattungsgebräuche*, 107, 109. That it was
thought in certain cases at least that the soul was still in the dead man's
body is well seen, too, from the custom of splitting the skull with a
coco-nut, that the spirit of life might escape. But it is not true to say
with Negelein : " According to the teaching of the Vedic ritual
books the soul of the dead man stays along with the body for a time "
(pp. 22–23), and to bring forward so confidently as proof Hillebrandt,
Rituallit. 90 and (seemingly taken from Hillebrandt) Oldenberg,
Rel. d. Veda, 555, and Caland, *Ahnenkult*, 22. The last-named citation
is moreover some mistake in Hillebrandt. But Caland, *Toten- u.
Bestattungsgebräuche*, 166, perhaps means to say that at the time when
the body was buried the dead man's earthly wrapping was still looked
on as the abode of his soul. Our passage in the Epic is particularly
worthy of note on this point, and so also Mārkaṇḍeyapur., x, 70 f. :

of Juſtice has been sunk into the long sleep. All of us muſt die. Shun all that is evil, and do all that is good. He that sees

" When the body (of the dead man) is burned, he feels a ſtrong glow, and when it is beaten, torment, and when it is cut up, very awful torment. When (the body) is moiſtened, the (dead) person suffers very long-laſting pain through the ripening of his deeds, although he has gone into another body." Still more remarkable, perhaps, is the tale of the king's young son whose soul and its life is ſtill so fully ſtirring in the buried body. Chavannes, *Cinq cents contes*, etc., iii, p. 218. That the man whose soul is gone feels what is done to his body is indeed a view which is found in various places, and in agreement with the passages juſt named the dead man, according to Mohammedan belief suffers under the wailing of his kindred. Negelein, p. 24. The soul is looked on, indeed, by the Moslem as united with the body before the burial, and also for the firſt night in the grave. Garnett, *The Women of Turkey*, etc., ii, 492 ; 495 f. ; Lane, *Arabian Society*, etc., 263 ; M. Horten, *Die relig. Gedankenwelt d. Volkes im heut. Islam*, pp. 280, 284 f. We are even told of them : " For a whole year the bond laſts between the spirit and the body laid in the grave." Negelein, p. 25. (Though I have not been able to look up his authority. But see M. Horten, loc. cit., 296–300.) This reminds us of the Indian doɛtrine that the dead man only reaches Yama's city after a full year has gone by. A very general idea is that the dead man goes on ſtaying a shorter or a longer time in his former house, or near to it ; indeed, even those who have been taken among the " fathers "—to say nothing of the Pretas—are well known in India to approach the offerings to the forefathers ; and in particular " one day in the year is free for the dead ", in the middle of the rainy season ; then Yama lets all his subjeɛts go off to the world of men. Caland, *Totenverehrung*, 43–46. See also Dubois-Beauchamp [3], p. 488 ; Vasishṭha, xi, 39 f. ; Vishṇu, lxxviii, 51–53 ; Mārk.-Pur., x, 75 ; Garuḍapurāṇasārod., i, 55. According to the two laſt the dead man is allowed to ſtay twelve days longer near his former abode, and take his nourishment from the pious gifts ; then he is led away to Yama's city ; Dubois speaks of ten. The difference is probably to be explained by the varying length of the " uncleanness " of the kindred, depends, that is, first of all on the caſte. See Caland, *Toten- und Bestattungsgebräuche*, 81–84, also in Dubois ; Crooke, *Anthropos*, v, p. 461 (five days among the Baidyas in south Kanara, cp. 463). Further matter in Negelein ; then Sartori, *Ztschr. d. Ver.f. Volksk.*, Bd. 18, p. 375 ; Sartori, ibid., Bd. 4, p. 424 ; Krauss, ibid., Bd. 2, p. 180 at bottom ; Krauss, *Slav. Volkforschungen*, p. 111 ; Freiligrath's *Gesicht des Reisenden*, etc.

not (does not heed, neglects) father and mother, kindred, and friends, who are still alive, he has broken the moral law.[1] He that no longer sees with his eyes, nor stirs at all, that has reached his goal and end—what will you do for him by weeping ? " When the two beasts had been disputing with one another and harrowing the poor people a little longer, Çiva came, urged on by his wife, and gave them the choice of a boon. They spoke : " Give back life again to this only son, and thereby to us, too." And the god fulfilled their prayer, and granted him that had risen again to live hundreds of years. Thus was the sorrow of the wailers turned to joy, and hastening they came back into the city with the child.

Like them, the old blind king Dhṛitarāshṭra, wringing his hands, and sighing so deeply that a mist, as it were, rises from him, bewails the death of his sons, fallen on the battle-field (ix, 2) : " When I think of their youth and of their childish play, of all the slain sons, then my heart is bursting. Since with my want of eyes I have not seen their form, that love springing from tenderness towards children was kept ever for them. When I heard how they were coming beyond childhood's years, were entering on the bloom of youth, were reaching the middle years of life, I was filled with joy. When now I learn that they are cut down, robbed of their lordship and of their strength, I find rest nowhere, overwhelmed by my soul's anguish for my sons. Come, come, my son, to me who am shelterless ! How shall it be for me without thee ! Thou that wast the refuge of thy kindred and friends, whither wilt thou go, leaving me behind, an old, blind man ? Who will now say : ' Father dear ' to me, when I have risen ? Put thine arms around my neck once more with eyes dimmed with love, and speak those good words to me : ' Bid me ! ' "

So, too, calls out Bharadvāja from his tortured soul when his only son is slain : " Happy indeed are the men to whom no son is born, who go their way at their pleasure, without knowing the sorrow for a child " (iii, 137.16). This, however, is but one note from that song which wails and triumphs through the

[1] Or: For them that see not mother and father, kindred, and friends, who are still alive (that is, for the dead) the moral law has come to an end (disappeared, towards them there is no need, therefore, to observe it)?

LIFE IN MARRIAGE

whole post-Vedic literature : " He only is happy that calls
nought his own." [1]

And the parent's heart in Old India often quavered for the
child still living, especially if it was the only one. On this
an excellent tale was told (iii, 127 f.) : " There was a pious
king, Somaka by name. He had a hundred wives of his own
rank. But in spite of every most strenuous endeavour the prince
had no son by them even after a long time. One day among
his hundred wives there was then born to the old man, who
used every care and endeavour, a son named Jantu. When he
had seen the light of day, all his mothers constantly circled
round him, and turned their backs on all wishes and pleasures.
An ant now once bit Jantu on the buttocks, and at the bite
the child called out loudly with pain. Then all his mothers
screamed in violent distress, standing quickly in a ring round
Jantu ; there was a great uproar. These cries of distress were
suddenly heard by the ruler of the earth, as he sat in the midst
of the council of his ministers with his sacrificial priest. The
lord of the earth sent and asked : ' What is that ? ' The door-
keeper told him what had happened to his son. Quickly
Somaka, the queller of his foes, rose up with his councillors,
went off to the women's apartments, and soothed his son.
When the prince had soothed his son, he left the women's
apartments, and seated himself together with his sacrificial
priest and his ministers of state. Somaka spoke : ' Grievous

[1] When all his sons are snatched away from the holy man Vasishṭha,
he becomes a kind of Old Indian Ahasuerus : he resolves to die, and throws
himself from the cliff, but falls as though onto a heap of cotton. He
goes into the blazing fire, and to him the flame is cool. He hangs a
stone on his neck and leaps into the sea, but the waves cast him ashore
(i, 176.41 ff., cp. 177, espec. 177.16 ; 178.2). As an instructive
counterpart an American Indian Ahasuerus may be given here : A son
is beaten by his father, and goes into the forest. After he has wandered
a long time he comes to a place where a lot of wood has piled itself up.
He wants to die, and leaps from the pile into the water, but comes
up to the surface again safe and sound. Then he comes to a steep
cliff. He climbs up and throws himself down, but is still quite unharmed
(Boas, *Ztschr. f. Ethnol.*, " Abhandl. d. anthrop. Gesellsch.," Bd. 24,
p. 406).

191

it is, when a man has but one son on earth ! It were better to have no son. Since beings are always shadowed by suffering, it is a sorrow to have only one son.[1] When I had carefully picked myself out these hundred wives of equal birth with me, I took them home that I might have sons. And now they have no children ! One son has come into being with trouble and care, this my Jantu, by the exertion of all. What sorrow could now be greater ! The vigorous age has now departed from me and my wives. Their life and mine rests on this one little son of mine. Is there now a work that were such as to give me a hundred sons, whether through a great, or a small deed, or one hard to carry out ? ' The sacrificial priest spoke : ' There is such a work whereby thou wouldst have a hundred sons. If thou canst do it, then I will speak, Somaka.' Somaka spoke : ' Be it possible or impossible, that by which I get a hundred sons, it is already done. Know that, O glorious one ; tell it unto me ! ' The sacrificial priest spoke : ' Sacrifice Jantu, O king, in a sacrifice carried out by me, then thou wilt speedily have a hundred splendid sons for thine own. If his retina is offered up in the fire, and his mothers smell the smoke, they will bear sons mighty and strong as heroes. But their son will come into being again in his own (bodily) mother. And on his left side he will bear a golden birthmark.' Somaka spoke : ' Brahman, even as this must be carried out, so indeed do thou carry it out. In my longing for sons I will obey all thy words.' Then for Somaka he sacrificed this Jantu. But his mothers tore him away [2] by force, filled with pity, wailing in their burning sorrow : ' Woe, we are death's,' weeping bitterly and seizing him by the right hand. But the sacrificial priest seized him by the left hand, and so dragged and tore the child away from them, who wailed like she-eagles of the sea. And having cut him up according to the precept, he offered up the retina of his eye in the fire. When the retina was offered up in the fire, and the mothers smelt the smoke, they fell in

---

[1] One son and one eye is something and is nothing ; both can so easily get lost. K i, 107.69.

[2] K. again touches it up, and has pratyakarshan. Apākarshuḥ is anyhow from kṛish.

tortures suddenly onto the ground, and all these exquisite women there received a fruit of the body. Ten months afterwards the gift of a full hundred sons was made by these wives together to Somaka. Jantu was born first, and from his own mother [1] ; he was the much beloved for them all, not so their own children ; and that golden birthmark was on his right side, and among these hundred sons he was the first too in qualities. Then that Guru (teacher, high priest) of Somaka went into the other world. And in the course of time Somaka, too, went into the other world. There he saw him scorching in the dreadful hell. He asked him : ' Wherefore dost thou scorch in hell, O Brahman ? ' Then his Guru, who was being sore tortured by the fire, spoke unto him : ' I have made sacrifice for thee, O king, this is the fruit of that work.' When the royal Rishi had heard this, he spoke to the king of justice (to Yama, the lord of the dead and of hell) : ' I will go in there. Set thou my sacrificial priest free ! For it is for my sake that the excellent one is being burned by hell fire.' Yama spoke : ' None other but the doer ever enjoys the fruit of the work. Here (in heaven) the fruits of *thy* deeds are seen, O best of those that speak.' Somaka spoke : ' I crave not for the holy and heavenly worlds without the knower of the Veda, only with him will I dwell in the abode of the gods or in hell, O king of justice ; for I am the same as he is in the work. Let the fruit of the good or of the evil work be alike then for us both.' Yama spoke : ' If thou so wishest, O king, then enjoy together with him the fruit of the work which he reaps, and for the same length of time. After that thou wilt come unto the place of the good.' Then did the lotus-eyed king do this all, and when his sin was blotted out, he was set free from there with his Guru. He came together with this Guru into that pure heavenly joy which he had won for himself through his deeds, he who loved his Guru." [2]

[1] That the dead child appears again in the one born next is a wide-spread belief. Here we will only refer to Hartland, *Primitive Paternity*, i, 209 f. ; 218 ; 221 ; 226 ff. ; 230 ff. ; 242 ff.

[2] For the sacrificing of the one child so as to get many, cp. Hopkins, *The Fountain of Youth*, JAOS, 26, p. 6 ; Chavannes, *Cinq cents contes*, etc., i, 127 ; ii, 171.

In the same way as this sonless man, so, too, his fellow-king in Old India, Çāntanu, the father of Bhīshma, declares : " To have one son is to have none " (i, 100.67 ; cp. " one son is no son, the wise say " v, 147. 18). More moderate than these fathers, carried away, manlike, by their feelings, is Lopamudrā, the princess and wife of a beggar : her husband, Agastya, mighty in penance and digestive powers, leaves her the choice of having a thousand or a hundred or ten sons, or only one, who shall be equal in worth to thousands. She shares the view already known from the Hitopadeça, and chooses the one son (iii, 99.20 ff.).

And the children repay, too, this tenderness of their parents : no land and no people shows a more beautiful attitude of children to parents, and few can show one to be compared at all to that in India. Witness is borne to this in the Epic, too, and innumerable times. Here only a few examples are given.

The youthful penitent mortally wounded by Daçaratha through a mistake, bewails really only his old blind father and mother, whom up till now he has supported and cared for, and who without him are lost,[1] and then comes transfigured out of Indra's heaven, into which he, the son of the Vaiçya man and Çūdrā woman, has gone owing to his good deeds towards his parents, to the broken couple, and consoles them by telling them that they are soon to join him (Rām., ii, 63–64). One of the most pleasing figures in the Mahābh. is the dharma-vyādha, the pious butcher, to whom father and mother are the divinity, Brahman, Veda, and sacrifice, who lovingly honours and cares for them, and through his bearing towards them reaches the loftiest perfection. Although only a Çūdra, he brings a proud Brahman penitent, who has run away from his parents, back to his duty towards them, to that greatest form of piety (iii, 207 ff., especially 214 and 215).[2]

One day, King Çāntanu is going along in the forest. There he smells an incomparably sweet scent. He follows it up, and finds a fisherman's daughter, the Satyavatī already known to us, who looks after her foster-father's ferry-boat, and thus

[1] Cp. Jāt., vi, p. 76 ff.
[2] Cp. Çukasaptati, the main tale.

has had the adventure leading to the birth of Vyāsa, and at the same time to her fragrant smell. By her divine beauty, her sweet charm, and her indescribable fragrance a burning love is kindled in him, and he asks her of her foster-father, the fisherman. But this latter will only give his consent if the king promises him on oath that the son of the pair shall be king without any rival. Now as Çāntanu has already a splendid scion, the Bhīshma born of Gaṅgā, and has already consecrated him as heir to the throne, he will not do so. " Burning with hot love, his mind darkened with passion, thinking only of the fisherman's daughter, he went back to Hāstinapura." Then Bhīshma once saw him thus grieving and asked him why he was always thus pining in sorrow, why he was pale and haggard and always deep in thought; he would know, he said, his sorrow, and help him. " But Çāntanu, the father, could not disclose to the son this unavowable love of his for the fisherman's daughter." [1] He said : " Thou art the only son in a warrior race, and ever busied with warlike things ; therefore wilt thou fall in the fight. And, indeed, all things in the world are thus fleeting. I do not wish for myself to marry a second time, but I wish to do so that the line may not die out." Then Bhīshma went to the old minister of his father, and asked him. From his lips he learned the details.[2] At once the noble son with old Kshattriyas sought out that fisherman, and asked on his father's behalf for Satyavatī's hand. Her foster-father granted that this was a highly honourable match, and that King Çāntanu had already been named to him by the maiden's real father as a worthy husband, and so the divine Rishi Asita, who was violently in love and was seeking her hand, had had to withdraw rebuffed. But as a father he had to point out, he said, that the son of these two would not be able to stand up against so mighty a rival as Bhīshma. Bhīshma then before all the witnesses solemnly renounced his father's throne. But the fisherman, like a prudent adviser, then reminded them that even then Bhīshma's offspring would make a claim. Now did the good son make the awful vow : " From to-day onwards

[1] This sentence according to K. (107.63). It is not absolutely needed.
[2] In K. (107.76 ff.) he learns everything through a long conversation with his father's Sūta.

I shall live in utter chastity, and the imperishable worlds in heaven will fall to the sonless one's lot." In great joy the fisherman now gave his consent. At once Bhīshma made request : " Come up into my chariot, mother ; we will drive home." He brought his father the bride, and the father for his hard deed granted him the boon of only having to die when he wished it himself (i, 100.45 ff. ; cp. v, 172.17–19 ; 173.5 ; vi, 14.2 ; 120.14).[1]

But the most famous example of a child's love is probably Rāma. Everything is ready for his being consecrated as heir to the throne, when his step-mother, Kaikeyī, who at first with a joyous love for him has approved of all, but has then been goaded on by the hunchbacked, spiteful serving-woman, makes a stubborn protest, and wants to see her own son consecrated as the king's successor ; Rāma for safety is to go off for fourteen years into the forest of banishment. Since the old king Daçaratha on the one hand is passionately devoted to her, but on the other is also bound by his earlier solemn promise of favour, he does not, indeed, agree, and even bitterly remonstrates with her, but he cannot meet her with the needful resolute negative. When Rāma learns what is happening, he is at once ready, and his only sadness is that his father does not speak to him. Among other things he says : " I should not wish to live a moment, if I were not gladdening the great king, if I were not obeying my father's words, if the prince were angered with me. How should a man act wrongly against him in whom he sees the root of his own life, and who is the visible godhead ? (Rām., ii, 18.15–16). At the king's bidding I would leap into the fire or the sea, and I would eat strong poison (ii, 18.29–30). There is no practice of virtue which were greater than obedience to the father (ii, 19.22). What is the good of our seeking by every means the favour of fortune, which lies not in our hands, and neglecting what we have in our hands : father and mother and teacher ! " (ii, 30.33). Lakshmaṇa, who is devoted with a most heartfelt love to his injured brother, uses, indeed, in his anger words other than these, and

---

[1] There is something very much the same from the history of the Rajputs in Tod, Rajasthan, i, 295 ff. ; 415–416 ; ii, 144.

very unusual with Indian sons. He chides the tottering old
fool, blinded by love of women, wants to bind and if needs be
even kill his father, to ſtir up a rising againſt him, and so on.
But Rāma calms him, speaks kind words to Kaikeyī and of her ;
he says that she who did after all so love him cannot be guilty,
but that fate is driving her on againſt her will ; he even spurs
on Lakshmaṇa to ſtop without any delay all preparations for
the consecration, that her suspicious, painful anxiety about her
own son's happiness may at once be set at reſt. But now he
finds himself in a conflict of duties, which, however, does not
unduly diſturb him : his mother Kauçalyā declares she will
on no account give him leave to go off into the foreſt, and she
puts it to him thus : " Obedient to his mother, with chaſtened
soul, dwelling at home, Kāçyapa won the higheſt ascetic merit,
and came into heaven. Juſt as the king, so muſt I, too, be
honoured by thee with deep respect. Parted from thee, life
and fortune is nothing to me ; by thy side, to eat grass only
is the greateſt weal. If thou leave me behind overcome with
sorrow, and go into the foreſt, then I shall ſtarve myself to
death ; in such wise as that I cannot go on living." But Rāma
makes it clear to her by the examples of the old Ṛishis that the
father's bidding muſt always be unconditionally fulfilled. She
is as one dead in her sorrow, and insiſts : " As thy father, so
also am I a Guru for thee because of my right and my love.[1]
What can life mean to me without thee, what can the world
mean, or the food of the dead or of the gods ! An inſtant near
thee is more to me than even the whole world of the living."
When Rāma heard the woeful plaint of his mother, he burned
once more in torture like a mighty elephant that is scared by
men with fire-brands, and hurls itself once more into the

---

[1] So too, for inſtance, Nārada, xii, 59 declares : " The fruit of
the field cannot be born without the field, nor without seed, therefore
in law the child belongs to the father and the mother " ; and according
to Parāçara, vii, 6 the giving away of the daughter is the right of the
following three : the mother, the father, the eldeſt brother. This is in
harmony with the well-known Vetāla tale of the three wooers and the
maiden that was killed by a snake's bite, but called back to life again
by magic. Cp. Meyer, *Altind. Rechtsschr.*, 227 f.

darkness." [1] But in spite of all he wavered not ; he showed her that Daçaratha it was who was in authority over them both, and that he would come back himself, and gladden her heart (Rām., ii, 21).

[1] The elephant scared with fire-brands is very often found as a comparison in the Epic. So, iv, 48.12 ; vii, 22.14 ; 109.12 ; viii, 50.42 ; 80.26 ; ix, 17.4 ; xi, 18.25 ; Rām., ii, 27.54 ; vi, 13.19 ; 24.38.

V

WOMAN AS MOTHER

AT the centre point in this intimate family life is the mother, covered with much glory by Indian literature ; and, as has been already pointed out, to the Hindu it is just this side of a woman's life that is the beginning and the end. Woman as a mother takes up in the Epic, too, an important place. In Mahābh., i, 196.16 we find : "Of all guru the mother is the highest guru " ; in xii, 342.18 : "There is no higher virtue (or : no higher law) than the truth, no guru to equal the mother, a greater thing for weal than the Brahmans is found neither here nor there " (cp. xiii, 63.92) ; in xiii, 105.14 : "Above ten fathers or even the whole earth in worth (gaurava) stands the mother ; there is no guru like the mother " [1] (cp. 106.65). Cp. iii, 313.60 ; xii, 301.44. For all curses there are means of averting and destroying (pratighāta, moksha), but for the mother's, and hers only, there are none (i, 37.3–5).[2] Indeed,

[1] The spiritual master (ācārya) stands above ten private teachers (upādhyāya) in worth and dignity, the father above a hundred spiritual masters, but the mother above a thousand fathers. Manu, ii, 145 ; Vasishtha, xiii, 48. Cp. MBh., xii, 108.16 f. ; K, xiv, 110.60. Also according to Yājñav., i, 35 and Gautama, ii, 51, the mother stands at the head of the venerable ones (guru), and above priests and religious teachers. To the " golden rules which the teacher gives the disciple to take with him on life's way " belong the following in the old sacred Upanishad : "Honour thy mother like a god. Honour thy father like a god. Honour thy teacher like a god. Honour the guest like a god." (Taitt.-Up., i, 9.1, 2 ; Deussen, *Sechzig Upanishad d. Veda*, p. 222.) The mother comes first here also, as, indeed, in the Sanskrit compound it is always ; " mother and father ", and never " father and mother ". If the two are united by " and " then, on the other hand, it is oftener the other way. The mother is more venerable than the father because she has carried the child, and had to suffer pain. K., vol. i, p. 212, line 1.

[2] So also Mārkaṇḍeyapur., cvi, 28. Though according to lxxvii, 31 there has never yet been such a thing as a mother forgetting her love and cursing her own child. Cp. cvi, 32.

xii, 161.9 states : " There is no pious exercise either in the world or in the ascetics' forest that can stand above the mother (nāti mātaram āçramaḥ)." Yudhishthira in xii, 108 asks Bhīshma : " What is the highest of all duties (virtues, law precepts, dharma) ? " ; and he gets the answer : " The honouring of mother, father, and teacher (guru) I set high ; whoso is diligent about these enjoys the worlds of heaven, and high renown.[1] And the task that these bestow, be it the law, or opposed to the law, that must be done.[2] What they allow is what is right ; they are the three worlds, they are the three spheres of duties in life (āçrama), they are the three Vedas, they are the three holy fires. The father is held to be the gārhapatya fire, the mother the southern fire, the teacher the āhavanīya. This fire trinity is the most important. If thou givest the proper heed to these three, then thou shalt win the three worlds ; of this world thou wilt unfailingly be master through the rightful behaviour towards thy father, of the world beyond through that towards thy mother, of the Brahma world through that towards thy teacher. Whoso cares for these three has won all three worlds ; but whoso cares not for them, his holy deeds are all barren. Whoso does not at all times hold these three venerable ones in high esteem, for him there is no salvation in this world or the other.[3] The mother stands above ten fathers, or even the whole world, in worth (gurutva), there is no guru to equal the mother." [4]

---

[1] Father, mother, and the guru who brings a man into the knowledge of Brahman are the mahāguru or Very Venerable, the First Masters. Anyone speaking evil words of them or to them must fast five days. Mahānirvāṇat., xi, 145. Atiguru (" Values above all ") these three are called in Vishṇusmṛiti, xxxi, 1.

[2] Opposed to this in the Epic is also an often-recurring saying, that a bad guru, walking along evil paths, must be punished (i, 140.54 ; xii, 55.15 f. ; 57.7 ; 140.48 ; Rām., ii, 21.13). Cp. MBh.,iv, 51.15, and the words, following later, of Bhīshma addressed to Paraçurāma. —With K. read : dharmam dharmaviruddham vā.

[3] The same teaching in Manu, ii, 228–234 ; Vishṇu, xxxi ; and often elsewhere.

[4] In what follows, it is true, all is nicely touched up again, and the spiritual teacher (ācārya) set high above the mother and father ;

WOMAN AS MOTHER

Cp. xiii, 104.45. It is even asserted that the mother's origin casts no slur (matridosho na vidyate, K., i, 99.6). On the other hand we are also told that the father stands above the mother. According to xii, 297.2 the father is the highest godhead for men, and is above the mother. " The mother is the wallet (for the father's seed), to the father belongs the son ; he is his by whom he has been begotten " (i, 74.110).[1] But we have already seen that the mother is the field, and thus the important thing, the seed can be thrown in by anyone ; and while the man might wed a woman from a lower caste, it was most strictly forbidden for a woman to lower herself.

How Rāma in a case where his duty towards his father comes into conflict with that towards his mother bears himself as the pattern hero of the Rāmāyaṇa, almost always faithfully Brahmanic, we have already seen. Another example is that Paraçurāma, destroyer of the Kshattriyas, who is so highly glorified by the priestly caste, but who in reality is most repugnant. In the Mahābh. also is related shortly his resolute act towards his mother (iii, 116). Jamadagni, the holy son of that Ṛicīka already mentioned, followed his father's example and wedded a royal princess named Reṇukā. She bore him five sons, of whom the youngest was Rāma with the axe. One day, the sons being away to get fruit, the pious mother went to bathe. There she saw King Citraratha wreathed in lotuses playing in the water with his wives, and her heart was gripped by a longing for him. As a result of this unfaithfulness of hers she came back from the water to the hermitary all wet, with troubled mind, and filled with fear.[2] The penitent saw she had lost her determination, and had been robbed of her holy splendour, that she had sinned, and one after the other be bade his four

these latter are the instrument for the earthly body, while the ācārya brings about the heavenly birth (cp. Manu, ii, 144 ff. ; Vishṇu, xxx, 44). And from what has been said before, through him the world of Brahma is won, a doctrine often found in Smṛiti.

[1] Cp. for instance Wilson's Vishnupur. (ed. Hall), vol. iv, p. 133 and note ; Bhāgavatapur., ix, 20 f. ; Kauṭilya (transl.), 260.3.

[2] K. adds : " having fallen from the air into the Narmadā," which suggests a remarkable variant of this tale.

eldest sons, as they came home in turn, to kill the mother. Overcome with confusion,[1] stunned, they answered not a word. Therefore did the angry man curse them, and at once they were bereft of reason, like unto dull beasts. When Rāma appeared, he called on him to slay the sinful woman. Rāma hewed her head off at once with his axe. Then of a sudden the old man's rage passed away, and he left it to his son to wish anything he wanted for himself. The son asked first that his mother should wake again to life without remembering what had happened, and that his brothers should be roused to live once more like reasoning men; and this came about.[2]

Less resolute was the behaviour of another in a like case (xii, 266). Gautama, of the family of the Aṅgirases, had a son who pondered everything slowly, set about it slowly, carried it out slowly, wherefore he was called Slow Doer (Cirakāri, Cirakārin, Cirakārika), and short-sighted people who were brisk and sharp called him a blockhead. When his mother one day had been guilty of unfaithfulness to her husband,[3] the holy man went over the heads of his other sons and angrily bid Cirakāri : "Slay thy mother !" After these words the most excellent Gautama, best among the prayer-mutterers, went off without further thought into the forest. Slow Doer said, true to his nature, only after a long while : "Yes," and being a slow doer, he pondered and reflected long : "How shall I contrive to carry out my father's bidding and yet not kill my mother ? How shall I not sink down like an evil man in this shifting turmoil of duties ?[4] The father's bidding is the highest law, my own (the natural) law is to shield my mother ;

---

[1] Probably saṃmohāḥ is the reading, as in K.

[2] Cp. Zachariae, " Goethes Parialegende," *Zschr. d. Ver. f. Volksk.*, xi, 186 ff. ; xii, 44 ff. ; Thurston, *Omens and Superstitions*, etc. (1912), p. 148 f. (interesting variants).

[3] Her name was Ahalyā. Of her love adventure with Indra more will be said later.

[4] Dharmacchala, lit., deceit of duties, deceit of virtue, seeming virtue, juggling with virtue. The word is often found in the MBh., and generally means a deceitful injuring of virtue, especially under the cover of virtue. So ix, 60.26 ; xii, 270.12 ; xiii, 20.13.

and to be a son is to be subject. But what is there then that will not torment me later ? Who could ever be happy, if he has killed a woman, and moreover his own mother ! And who could ever win calm and peace who has not heeded his father ? Not to disregard the father is right and fitting, and it is a firm principle to shield one's mother. Both duties are right and salutary. How can I act, that the matter may not get beyond me ? For the father sets his own self in the mother at the begetting, we are told, to keep virtue, good ways, race, and family in being. I here have been made a son by my mother and father ; how should I not have the knowledge ! Of both I know that they are my origin. That which my father said at the birth ceremony and at the by-ceremony—its confirmation is made complete in the firm resolve to honour my father.[1] The first guru who has nourished and taught a man is the highest law ; what a father says is the moral rule set down as fixed even in the Vedas. For the father the son is but a joy, but for the son the father is all ; he alone gives as an offering his body and all else there is to give. Therefore a man shall act according to his father's words, and never take thought upon it ; mortal sins (pātaka) even are washed away from him who follows his father's bidding. In matters of eating and of other things that are for use, in the instruction and in the whole view of life, at the union with a lord (or with the husband), and at the holy custom of parting the hair the father is the law, the father is heaven, the father is the loftiest asceticism. If the father is made to rejoice, then all the gods rejoice. Those words of blessing are fulfilled for a man which

[1] At the birth ceremony the father says to the son :—

> Be thou a stone, be thou an axe,
> Be thou gold that is beyond valuing !
> Thou art the Veda called " son ".
> Live a hundred autumns long !

If the father comes home from a journey, he must say to the boy : Thou art born limb from limb, etc., as already given (Āçval., i, 15.9 f.; Pārask., i, 18 ; Gobh., ii, 8.21 ; Hiraṇy., ii, 1, 4.16 ff. ; Āpast., 15, 12 ff. ; Khād., ii, 3, 13 ff.). This according to Nīl. is the by-ceremony, and he says that this precept holds good till the boy is brought to the teacher.

the father utters. It is absolution from all sins when the father finds his joy in him. The bloom loosens itself from the ſtalk, the fruit from the tree—if the father has to suffer sorrow and pain (through his son), yet because of his tender love for the child he does not loosen himself from the son.[1] Thus then have I pondered the reverence the son owes his father[2]; the father is no small thing. Now will I consider the mother. The cause of this body here with me in the mortal world, and made up of the five elements, is my mother, as that of fire is the rubbing-ſtick. The mother is the rubbing-ſtick of the body for mankind, the comfort of all that suffer. If one has a mother, one is sheltered, but unsheltered if one has her not. He does not grieve, age does not weigh on him, even though fortune betray him, who comes back home to his house and can say ' Mother !' And let a man be surrounded by sons and grandsons, and ſtand at the end of his hundredth year, yet if he takes refuge with his mother, he acts like a child of two years.[3] Whether he is capable or incapable, unimportant or important, the mother protects the son ; no other career has been appointed by fate. He is old, he is unhappy, the world is an empty desert for him, if he is parted from his mother. There is no shadow like the mother,[4] there is no refuge like the mother, there is no shelter like the mother, there is no beloved like the mother. Since she has carried him in her body, she is, according to the tradition, the carrier (dhātrī), since she has borne him she is the bearer (jananī), since she has nourished his limbs to greatness, she is his little mother (ambā), since she has borne a man, she is the bearer of men, since the child humbly liſtens to her, she is the kinswoman (çuçrū) ; the mother is his own body.[5] Could a man who is in his senses and whose head is

[1] So according to K., where sutasnehaiḥ ſtands inſtead of sutaṃ snehaiḥ (272).

[2] Nature of a guru, that is, dignity, or else, worth, importance (for the son).

[3] Or : If he goes to his mother, he is wont to act like a child of two years.

[4] So cooling and so faithful.

[5] Liter. : the identical, unparted body.

not hollow [1] kill *her* !   The purpose which the married pair cherish when they unite their life powers is also cherished by the mother and father, so it is said ; actually the case is so only with the mother.[2]   The mother knows to what paternal family (gotra) he belongs, the mother knows whose he is.   The mother by the mere carrying (of the fruit of her body) feels a joyful love and tenderness ; for the father the children are offspring (pituḥ prajāḥ).   If men at first (at the wedding) themselves carry out the entwining of hands, and enter on the state of common duty, and then go off to others, women do not deserve any blame.[3]   For from supporting the wife the man is called her spouse (bhartar), and from protecting the wife her husband (or lord, pati) ; but where this attribute is gone, there there is no longer spouse, and no longer husband.[4]   Therefore the woman does not sin, only the man sins ; and if he goes astray into the great crime of

[1] K. (272.33) reads more smoothly : cetanāvān sa ko hanyād.

[2] The man in sexual union really seeks only his pleasure, but the woman seeks the child, which rule will always be true.

[3] Should they break faith, too, with the faithless men.   I read vācyatām instead of yācyatāṃ.   The Bomb. text would mean : then women are not fit for wooing, that is, if they are asked, then they cannot say no.   K. has yāpyatāṃ, which is translated under the text by tyājyatāṃ.   According to Böhtlingk Bühler for yāpya gives the rendering : to whom a rebuke is to be given.   This would agree with my amendment, but I should not be able to justify it.   Essentially the meaning is always the same, and we should here have a confirmation of my reading of xiii, 19 ff. : Women are what men make them, which, indeed, Forel, for example, also rightly stresses in his *Sexuelle Frage.* —With yāsyati I follow the interpretation of the schol., which fits in well with the exposition that follows.   It is true that there is only there : " if men (had to) go," and Deussen in his *Vier philosoph. Texten des MBh.* gives the rendering " run away ".   This, indeed, fits in with the general position : Gautama has evidently neglected his wife from the beginning, and after her offence also he at once runs off again into the forest (cp. also çl. 62).   But with such sermons we must not insist unbendingly on such strict logic.

[4] According to the context, this saying, which we found already in i, 104.30, means : The husband has as his duty, by his own example especially, to give in the ethical sense strength, stay, and protection to the wife, not only to feed her, and cherish and care for her.

205

adultery, it is only the man who sins in this.[1] The greatest thing of all for the woman, according to the tradition, is the husband, he is her highest godhead. But now she has given him her own self, that stands equal to his self, as the highest thing.[2] On women no sin is laid, only the man sins ; since in all cases it is women who have to let themselves be the object of sin, so women do not sin. And since from the woman's side no invitation [3] has gone to him to satisfy the desire for love, the wrongdoing is undoubtedly his, who clearly gave the call to it. But even the unreasoning beasts would thence know that a woman, and moreover the mother that is in highest honour, must not be killed. In the father is seen the whole assemblage of the divinities united in one person ; but in the mother, because of her love, we come to the whole assemblage of mortals and gods." [4] While in this wise he, pondered deeply because of his slow doing, a long time went by him. Then his father came up, the very wise Medhātithi, that Gautama living an ascetic life, having during this time weighed the offence against the established order done by his wife. In great torment he spoke, shedding tears in his pain, filled with remorse by the helping grace of his holy knowledge, and firmness of character : " Into my hermitage came Indra, the ruler of the world, the shatterer of strongholds, giving himself out as a guest, and taking a Brahman's shape. Friendly words I spoke to him, and honoured him with a joyful welcome ; guest water and water for the feet I brought him, as is seemly. And if he is told, ' I am at thy bidding,' he will then start love-making.[5] If then something evil happened, it is not

---

[1] According to Manu, viii, 317 ; Vasishtha, xix, 44, the adulteress casts off her sin onto the husband ; he should have kept her from it.

[2] The very expression ātmānam dadau does not seem at all to allow of a reference to the son she has borne him.

[3] Liter.: suggestion, reference, hint. On this conception cp. Freidank's *Bescheidenheit* ed. Bezzenberger, p. 158 : Swâ wîp, etc.

[4] Probably not so well : the whole assemblage, etc., comes into the mother.

[5] Or : If a man is told : " I am at thy bidding," then he (in the world, anyhow) will show his inclination. This version is after all

the woman that has done wrong. So neither the woman, nor myself, nor the wanderer (the guest) Indra can be accused of sinning against the law.[1] But it is my want of thought that sinned. Therefore do the holy men that are wholly chaste say that from jealousy comes woe. Carried away now by jealousy, I have sunk into the sea of evil-doing. Who will bring me safely to the shore, who have slain a good woman and a wife, and one brought to lechery through evil fate,[2] and, as I should have cherished and cared for her, my 'foster-ward' (my wife, bhāryā)? If Slow Doer, he with the noble soul, to whom in a weak moment I gave the order, were to-day indeed a slow doer, then he would keep me from a mortal sin (pātaka). Slow Doer, hail to thee! Hail to thee, Slow Doer! If thou to-day art a slow doer, then thou art indeed a slow doer. Save me and thy mother and the penitential merit I have acquired, and thyself from mortal sin; to-day be a slow doer. Long wast thou yearned for by thy mother, long borne in the womb; to-day let thy slow doing yield fruit, thou Slow Doer."[3] As Gautama, the great Rishi, thus was grieving himself, he saw his son Cirakāri standing near. But so soon as Cirakāri had seen his father, he threw the knife away, filled with deepest sorrow, and set about winning his

to be preferred, and because, too, Indra's guilt thus stands out all the sharper.

[1] I did in accordance with law, custom (and reason) when I welcomed the guest so unreservedly, and Indra was only following his own law (his nature, dharma) when he as a woman-hunter paid her court.

[2] Indra came in Gautama's shape to her, at least according to the usual version. But here it is not clear whether this is the leading motive here, indeed, Gautama's words in particular about the guest in Brahman's shape rather speak against it, so that after all "through evil passion" might be better. Of course, for this meaning of the word I can only bring forward from the MBh., xii, 290.20: avya-sanitā, passionlessness. Cp. too the later note on the fact that Ahalyā knew Indra very well.

[3] K. reads Cirakārika. But the nom. too can be read ("as Slow Doer"). The following çloka to me seems to be an insertion, although K. too has it (272.58).

favour with his head. When Gautama then saw him with head sunk towards the ground, and saw his wife all mazed,[1] he was filled with the greatest joy. He clasped his son long in his arms, and in a lengthy speech praised him for his blessed procrastination ; for : "Slowly let the friend be knit to one, and slowly let go again the friend that has been won ; for the friend slowly won can be long kept. Where passion, pride, arrogance, hurtfulness, evil-doing, and anything unfriendly that is to be done (to another) are in question, then is the slow doer praised. Where the question is of trespasses not cleared up of kindred and friends, servants and wives the slow doer is praised."

In the eyes of the law, of course, and also in practice, so far as the rule was not weakened or altogether annulled through more than ordinary strength in the woman or for some other reason, the patriarchal system prevailed in India then as now, and, to the aforesaid high position of the mother, was opposed her, in many respects, lower valuation as a woman. But the Epic gives us glimpses enough to show us that in those times the woman held in general a more important position than she did later.[2] We shall speak of that below. And again, in the narrative parts themselves are to be found plenty of indications not only of that loving and pious attitude towards the two parents, but also of the attitude towards the mother in particular. When his house-priest or Purohita has given Yudhishthira a long lecture on the proper behaviour which the brothers must observe as servants to the prince, he that is thus preached to says: "Now we are instructed, and I beg leave to say, that none can set this forth but our mother Kuntī and the high-souled Vidura " (iv, 4.52). Together with his brothers he shows over and over again throughout the long narrative the same attitude of mind towards his mother ; and Bhīma, the man of deep feelings, by far the most human and attractive of the Pāṇḍavas,

---

[1] Lit. : without (fair, dignified) appearance ; cp. " to lose countenance ", and " like a whipped dog ". Cp. xii, 333.18 ; vii, 72.10.

[2] Or perhaps rather : that in the world of the MBh., which at least grew up out of an original Kshattriya poetry, the woman was in far higher esteem than she was when controlled by more priestly notions and conditions (or in other social classes).

ſtands out, too, through a tender regard towards Kuntī. The visit paid by the Pāṇḍavas to their old mother in the hermitage, their farewell of the aged woman, and their sorrow at learning that she has been burned in the foreſt, are likewise affeċtingly drawn for us (xv, 21 ff. ; 36.27, 28, 35 ff. ; 37.18 ff.). We hear, too, the note of the heart's true feeling in Yudhishṭhira's words about Kuntī's womanly virtues, motherly tenderness, and bitter lot (v, 83.37 ff.). For her is the firſt and far the moſt urgent greeting sent by him through Vidura to Hāstinapura. And so for other cases.

And towards the other wives of the father the sons show in the Epic a pious spirit like that we have already met with in Rāma. Along with other heroes Yudhishṭhira should here again be mentioned, who begs Nakula off from death and not his own brothers, when the Yaksha in the pond lets him have only one of the four dead, and who gives as the reason : " Both the wives of my father are dear alike to me ; both Mādrī and Kuntī shall have a son " (iii, 313.13).[1]

But not only the Pāṇḍavas, who are painted as Indian patterns of virtue, but even Duryodhana, set before us in the colours of the arch-villain, liſtens rather to his mother than to his father and his other kinsfolk. Kṛishṇa goes as the messenger of the five brothers to the court of Dhṛitarāshṭra to negotiate a peace. In a solemn ſtate gathering all ſtrive to talk Duryodhana into giving way and coming to terms with the sons of Pāṇḍu. But in vain. Then Kṛishṇa, who has it in his heart only to offend Duryodhana and light the fires of war, addresses biting words to the ſtubborn man, and at laſt the latter together with his followers leaves the hall, blazing with anger. Now no other means can be thought of : his mother Gāndhārī, the " far-seeing one ", is sent for, and she begins by reading her husband a fitting lesson before all the illuſtrious lords, and then she orders Duryodhana to be at once called. And though he is spitting

---

[1] For the tale itself cp. e.g. Jāt. No. 6 (this one is weak and secondary, patched up late from various fragments; for Yaksha's queſtions, Jāt. No. 377); Franke in WZKM, xx, 324 ff.; Hertel, Kathāratnākara, i, 58 ff. ; Daçāvatāracaritam, viii, 533–540; Holtzmann, Das Mahābhārata, etc., ii, p. 82, 96, 246 ; my transl. of the Daçakumārac., p. 297 ; Crooke, Popular Relig., etc., ii, 128.

with rage like a snake, he obediently comes there, " filled with longing for his mother's words." In a long speech she shows him how wrong he is, and points out to him that the kingdom really belongs to the Pāṇḍavas, and that he muſt be satisfied with the half of it, otherwise he will yet lose all through his wilfulness and blindness, and bring disaſter on all. But, on the one hand, her words are not very motherly and loving in tone, on the other the self-willed, angry man is not now disposed to liſten to such things ; so he ſtorms out again indignantly without speaking a word, away to his comrades.[1]

The mother of Old India, like her daughter to-day, shows herself fully worthy of this childish love. The Epic, too, offers both in the inwoven tales and in the main narrative many heart-gladdening pictures of the tender love of the mother, self-forgetting and only thinking of the child's welfare. Here only one or two features in the life of the leading heroines may be given. Kuntī, whose youthful adventure with the sun god was to bring her so much sorrow throughout her life, had also to go through much anxiety, care, and suffering for the sake of her other sons.[2] In their childhood days they, indeed, already gave her many an anxious moment. Bhīma was a very

---

[1] Yudhishṭhira, indeed, once also speaks harshly to his mother. But one muſt say she had really acted then to all appearance with unwarrantable thoughtlessness (i, 162.5–11). Then we hear from Vidura's wise lips : " These six always despise him who earlier has done good by them : disciples despise the teacher, when their instruction is ended ; the sons the mother, when they have married ; the lover the woman, when his love is dead ; they whose business has been carried through, him that does it ; he that has crossed the waſte of the sea (niſtīrṇakāntāra, cp. e.g. ' pilot of the waſte ' in the 2nd Jātaka), the ship ; and the healed sick, the leech " (v, 33.87 f.). Of the lover the rule holds all over the world ; Ward especially in his *View of the Hindus* has tried to show how thankless in general the Hindus are, but partly without sufficient warrant ; and Bose, *The Hindoos as They Are*, p. 223 note, has something to say of the married son's contempt towards his mother. But it is certain that the son's love for the mother cannot be denied of the Indian, and really unique evidence of it is given in Samayamātṛikā, iv, 44–65 (pp. 44–46 in my translation).

[2] " It is decreed of mothers that their birth pangs shall not cease until they die." John Galsworthy, *The Country House*, p. 236.

high-spirited lad, and as he had the strength of a giant, not only did he surpass his cousins and play-fellows in all trials of strength and skill, but he picked them out to be the victims, too, of the wildest pranks. " By the hair did the strong one catch hold of them, pulled them headlong down, and dragged them screaming along the ground, barking their knees, heads, and shoulders. When playing in the water he clasped ten boys (at once), took a long dive with them under the water, and only let them go when they were half-dead. When they climbed trees to look for fruit, Bhīma would make the trees quiver by kicking them. Then the trees would shake to and fro under the wild force of his blows, and the frightened boys would soon fall down, together with the fruit " (i, 128.19 ff.). In this wise he found he had no friends at all, and Duryodhana especially pursued him with a bitter hatred. This cousin now one day had splendid " houses of cloths and rugs " made by the Ganges, and furnished with choicest food and heady drinks. There the princes then made merry, and threw cakes into one another's mouths. Duryodhana kept this game up with Bhīma a long time with great spirit, for Bhīma, the " wolf's belly " (Vṛikodara), was a mighty eater. But he put poison withal into the cakes, and while Bhīma lay fast asleep, wearied with many athletic exercises, and overcome with drunkenness, Duryodhana had him bound and thrown into the Ganges without his brothers knowing anything about it. When they wanted to go home, they could not find him, and the good mother was now in mortal anguish, when they came back without him ; for she knew his cousin's hatred and cruelty (i, 118 f.).—But they all grew up to be strong and skilful youths, and at the festal exhibition, where the accomplished sons of Pāṇḍu and of Dhṛitarāshṭra gave a show of their skill, Kuntī sat glad and proud among the women onlookers. When now Arjuna so greatly distinguished himself and was greeted with a storm of shouts by the onlookers, then did Kuntī's bosom grow wet with the flood of her tears of joy (i, 135.13).[1] But short was the time her delight lasted, as we

[1] Her milk also flows from her, as it so often does from the Indian mother, even the elderly one, at the sight of her child (e.g. i, 105.26 ; 135.13 ; iii, 226.24 ; vii, 78.16 ; ix, 44.12. In K, i, 310.13 even from a woman that has never brought forth).

have seen : Karṇa came onto the stage, the son of her maiden-
hood, and the embittered opponent of Arjuna, and challenged
him to fight. Swooning, the mother of them both sank to the
ground (i, 136.27 ff.). Together with her sons she was to be
burned in the house of resin but escaped with them, and now
shared their wanderings filled with danger and hardship [1] ;
her splendid children, from whom she had hoped so much, were
fugitives and beggars, and with them she lived on alms.
Arjuna's skill with the bow now won the princess Draupadī,
and in spite of the strong opposition of the disillusioned rivals
they brought home this fair prize of victory. The mother knew
nothing of all this, and hovered in the darkness of anguish lest
the hostile men or evil spirits had slain the sons who did not
come back in the evening at the proper time (i, 190.43 ff.).
The evil game of dice followed, and the thirteen years'
banishment of her children. Filled with the sorrow of despair,
she bade them farewell, and showed herself especially anxious
on behalf of Sahadeva, the son of her fellow-wife Mādrī—
a complement to the love which the sons in the Epic are wont
to give the fellow-wives of their mother.[2] But not one word of
reproach against Yudh., who has brought about all the wretchedness, escapes from her lips here ; it is only her own, her deserved
fate that she makes responsible — a true Indian mother (ii,
79.10 ff.). In the end the great fight blazed up which brought
her the long wished for triumph of her reviled sons, but along
with it sorrow abounding beyond words, and so finally, as an
old woman with her blind brother-in-law and his wife, she
went off into the penitential forest—a much-tried, much-
loving mother, but no weak or faint-hearted one, as we shall
yet see. Characteristic, too, is Draupadī's behaviour (ii,
71.26 ff.). She has been gambled away by Yudhishthira, and has
fallen into slavery and shameful ill-treatment, and Dhṛitarāshṭra

[1] The episode of the burning of the house of resin is imitated,
altered, and further elaborated in the Jain tale in my *Hindu Tales*,
p. 21 ff.
[2] Passages which there show how attached she is to Sahadeva,
and he to her, are : ii, 79.8, 28 ; 19.32 ff. ; v, 90.35–42 (here including
Nakula, Mādrī's other son) ; xv, 16.10 ; 26.9 ff. ; xv, 24. espec. 8 ff. ;
36.36 ; 39.18.

now offers her a favour. She says : " Yudhishṭhira muſt be free, that my son may not be called a slave's son." [1] The unmotherly disposition shown by Gāndhārī towards her son, which comes out especially in her sermon to Dhṛitarāshṭra, ii, 75, ſtands alone, and has been put in her mouth by a calculated partisan diſtortion.

[1] The Indian mother liſtens with greedy ears to the prediſtions uttered of her little son by the wise Brahmans, and hopes for their fulfilment later, even when he seems to show no promise whatever (v, 134.8, 9). And even of Kuntī we read at that teſt of her sons in doſtrine : " But since K. in the maſter of the Aṅgas (in Karṇa) had recognized her son, betrayed by his divine marks, a secret joy glowed in her " (i, 137.23). A woman has truly lived when she with her husband has praſtised the duties of religion, has enjoyed companionship with him, and has had children from him (i, 158.33). Parents and daughter are saddened beyond measure in this tale, because the father muſt be the food of the Rākshasa. Then the little son runs up to all these as they weep, tries to comfort them, takes a hay-ſtraw, and shouts : " I will kill the monſter with it ! " And joy shines into the darkness of their souls (i, 159.20 f.).

VI

Woman in her Sexual Relations

WHILE woman in the Indian view is above all destined for motherhood, yet this cannot be brought about without man, and woman in her sexual relations, therefore, makes up an important chapter. Furthermore, there is the fact that love and the life of love presents in itself a subject which is ever new, ever inexhaustible, ever filled with enchantment ; and poetry, moreover, has in more senses than one its vital nerve therein. The Epic, too, yields many contributions to this theme : tales, sayings, details. But in agreement with the stricter, relatively pure and moral outlook governing the Epic poetry, we are not to seek here any variegated collection of love and even lecherous adventures, allusions, and so forth. Dramas and short plays of adultery, or merry cuckold tales are not found in the fare here set before us ; and the loose relations, too, between maidens and men, which are in many other lands so much a matter of course, and not a rare thing in the later Indian literature, are quite foreign to the Epic, for all that even Vyāsa, the so-called author of the Mahābh., and playing no unimportant a part in it, and the hero Karṇa, unsurpassed in Indian literature, are sons of unmarried women. We saw, indeed, how they owed their life only to the whim of their fathers, and not to the loving choice of their mothers. True indeed that also the Epic has in it very many tales and references that in the Western world would be branded as improper. But in this a great injustice is done them. Such things are almost always brought forward in all scientific seriousness, and quite simply as a matter of fact, as though we were in an anatomical lecture-room. The Indian, the old Italian novelist, a French poet of Troubadour times, and, for instance, a Brantôme can apparently tell us something more or less of the same kind, but *si duo faciunt, idem non est idem.* Brantôme grunts in his slush like five hundred erotomaniac swine ; the fabliau poet

214

treats us, indeed, to the nastiest filth, sometimes with finesse, but often to our taste unspeakably gross ; from the Italian's face there not seldom looks out what is rather a very naughty, but almost innocent child of nature—one might almost say urchin—and this along with even a fully ripened mind and style. How the Old Indian, however, describes such things, at least usually, is seen, we hope, clearly enough in this book. Love tales of the usual, and above all European kind are, therefore, not to be found in the Epic. Love and wedlock here cannot be separated.[1] The Trojan War came about through a flighty wife choosing to let herself be seduced—the struggle between the Pāṇḍavas and the Kauravas, the subject of the Mahābh. proper, breaks forth, as we are assured several times in the poem, because the slight cannot be forgotten which has been cast on a noble lady, though this can only be looked on as " the straw that breaks the camel's back ", and in the Rāmāyaṇa all that is really dealt with is the chastising of the insolent robber of the chaste Sītā, and the setting free of this great lady. The world's literature has no more lovely songs of the faithful wife's love for her husband than the poem of Damayantī and that of Sāvitrī. Both are found in the Mahābh., and they are not the only ones to treat of this subject. The heroine, moreover, of the Rāmāyaṇa has for thousands of years in India been shining forth as a picture of most spotless womanhood.

" When women become ripe for love "—this for the Indian is no romance, but a practical chapter in the physiology of sex.

[1] Love for one's wife is impossible ; this is what the basic principle, as we well know, of the old French polite world tells us ; and to-day love between husband and wife is still almost always scorned, particularly by works of romance, as a subject for treatment. But times out of count on the other hand we find in Old Indian books, just as in the Epic : It is on the wife that the attainment of the three great goals of life depends—religious merit, worldly gain, and kāma (enjoyment, love) : and Mārkaṇḍeyapur., xxi, 74 lays down the principle : " Without a wife no love." The man of the world in India—and often enough he has his say in Hindu literature—will, it is true, add in brackets as an explanation not only : itarasya, the other man's, that is to say, the wife or the future wife, as with us, but besides this the main object of Indian eroticism—the harlot.

This, the moft important part of the woman's life, makes its appearance with the ṛitu ; with the ṛitu love begins, with it it ends, in it it has always its central point. Ṛitu denotes the monthly cleansing, and then in particular those days after the period, from the fourth day onwards,[1] which in the Indian view are proper for conception. In what follows I shall use the Sanskrit word only in the second and narrower meaning. The setting in of the menses brings with it not only the capacity for the full sexual life, and the right thereto, but firft and foremoft the divine call to it, the unavoidable duty. A menftruating girl in a father's house is a heavy sin for him ; the daughter is now dedicated to the divinities of married ftate. The legal provision, therefore, already touched upon often makes its appearance, namely that the father shall marry his daughter off before the beginning of this time, and then, so soon as she is sexually ripe, the husband fetches her home.[2] As already

---

[1] The firft twelve, or according to other ftatements, the firft sixteen nights after menftruation begins, excluding the three (or four) firft nights. Also the eleventh (and the thirteenth) and certain moon-days are often put under a ban. Cp. Manu, iii, 45–50 ; iv, 128 ; Jolly, " Medizin " (in Bühler's *Grundriss*), p. 50 ; Winternitz, *Die Frau i. d. ind. Religionen*, p. 32 [6]. See further below.

[2] Pradānaṃ prāg ṛitoh " the girl muft be married before the coming of menftruation ". Gautama, xviii, 21 ; so also Vishṇu, xxiv, 41 ; and in 23 Gaut. gives as the opinion of others : " before she wears clothes." This view is also in Vasishṭha, xvii, 70 ; Baudh., iv, 1.11. Cp. Manu, ix, 88 f. The point ftressed by the law books is the fear left otherwise the ṛitu of the young woman be left unused. As a matter of faĉt child marriage is really based not so much on religious grounds, as on economic : on the heavy competition in the marriage market. The father muft find his daughter a good husband, and dare not wait long. This Risley has penetratingly and underftandingly shown in *Cafte in Relation to Marriage* (quoted in Billington, *Woman in India*, p. 59 ff.). Love comes, too, according to him, in marriage. Indeed, it comes perhaps the more surely juft because a very early marriage may keep the girl from falling in love elsewhere, and perhaps very foolishly. Anyhow the thing is one that commends itself because of this fear too, to those in authority over the girl. Cp. Daçakumāracar., p. 285, line 27 ff. of my translation. Indeed, the fear that the daughter may one day bring shame on the family

mentioned, child marriage has no place in the narrative parts of the Epic.[1] The heroines of the main story and of the inserted episodes are already grown up on their marriage, just like the love heroines of the ordinary Indian narrative literature (cp. Leumann, *Die Nonne*, strophe 122 ff. ; Meyer, Kautilya, addit., 246.14). But the Epic also stresses the point that that time, the ritu, must not slip by without being made use of. For the woman is there that she may bring forth, and her calling must not be barred to her or made harder. Therefore, during each ritu not only has she the urge to coition, but for her this is then also a holy right and command.

It is often emphatically laid down that the husband during the ritu must visit (ritugamana) the wife, and it is a sin for him not to fulfil his married duty then. In Rām., ii, 75 in a long imprecatory formula, a very great number of the worst sins and atrocities is set forth, and in çl. 52 is mentioned the evil-minded man (dushtātman) who does not let his wife have her rights, when she has bathed after the monthly cleansing. In MBh., vii, 17.28–36 we likewise find a list of especially horrible

through love entanglements is even given as a main reason for the killing of girls among the old Arabs (*Anthropos*, iii, p. 62 ff. Perhaps a misunderstanding ? Cp. Welhausen, *Gött. Nachr.* (1893), p. 458). Dubois ed. Beauchamp[3], p. 207, even states that Indian maidens could not be entrusted with their own honour up to their marriageable years, since they would not be able to resist temptation. "Therefore measures cannot be taken too early to place them intact in their husband's hands." On the other hand he himself declares on p. 314 that " Hindu women are naturally chaste " ; and on p. 354 he remarks that they are chaster than the women of many lands possessing a higher culture.

[1] Bhandarkar in ZDMG, Bd. 47, " History of Child Marriage," has very skilfully defended the statement that " in the time of Āçvalāyana and many other authors of Grihyasūtras marriages after puberty were a matter of course " (p. 153). Mahānirvāṇatantra, viii, 107, seems to be opposed to the marrying of the daughter before she has reached ripeness of understanding ; and Nārada, who in matters of women otherwise shows a remarkably open mind, says she must be given away when the monthly flow has shown itself (pravritte rajasi) ; but what goes before teaches that then this is to be at once (xii, 24–27).

sins, punished with torments in the other world, and among them we find the neglect to approach the wife at the ritu times.[1] On the contrary, it is highly virtuous to practise love on those days with the wife. Subhadrā in vii, 78 bewails her son fallen in the tender bloom of youth, Abhimanyu, and for him wishes in a long drawn out prayer of blessing that he may in the world beyond enjoy the happiness to be won through the noblest, best, and most pious human deeds and thoughts. And here she brings this in, too : " Thine be the lot of those that are obedient to father and mother, and of those that only find their delight with their own wife ; and mayest thou hasten towards the lot of the wise men who at the time of the ritu go to their wife and keep from strange women " (çl. 31, 32). In the same way in xii, 110.9 : " They who do as is fitting with their own wife at each ritu, and faithfully carry out the sacrifice by fire, overcome disasters." Cohabitation in the ritu is one of the virtues leading to heaven (xiii, 144.13–14), and also one of the things whereby a Çūdra obtains the being born again as a Brahman (although not without intermediate stages, xiii, 143.29 ff.). But on the other hand it is then found to be an ethical command that the husband keep not only from all other women, but from his own wife, too, outside the ritu or ritukāla (time of the ritu). He that obeys this law practises chastity, is equal in virtue to him that wholly abstains. So, for instance, in xiii, 162.41,42. Cp. iii, 208.15 ; 207.33 ; xiii, 157.9 ff. ; xii, 193.11. Chastity has two forms : monasticism, and copulation in the ritu only (Rām., i, 9.5, and comment.). " How does one become a brahmacārin (sexual ascetic) ? " Yudhishthira asks Bhīshma, and the answer is : " Let a man go to his own wife during the ritu " (xii, 221.11). In xii, 243, the holy duties of the father of the family are enumerated, and there in çl. 7 we find : " Let him call his wife only at the time of the ritu (nānritau)." In xiii, 93.124, copulation outside the ritu is set beside killing a cow and relieving the body into water, and in 94.27 it stands along with the denial of the divine

[1] Whoso does not know his wife carnally during the ritu must suffer the pains of hell. Mārk.-Pur., xiv, 1 ff. ; Garuḍapurāṇasārod., iv, 40 ; Parāçara, iv, 12 f. (the wife that forgets her duty goes to hell, the husband who does so becomes an embryo-slayer), etc.

revelation of the Veda. The ethical standpoint is given, for instance, by the fine saying in xii, 110.23 : " He who eats only to maintain life, who copulates only to beget offspring, who speaks only to utter the truth—he escapes vexations." [1]

Sexual union not from the fire of love, but only during the ṛitu is the old and holy rule for all the four castes, too, which prevailed in the golden age ; and great was the blessing. Thus, i, 64.4 ff. tells us : When Paraçurāma had destroyed all the Kshattriyas in the world, the Kshattriya women to get children approached the Brahmans. With them the pious Brahmans united at every ṛitu, but not from greed of love, nor at any other time. The Kshattriya women now bore offspring strong and long-lived beyond the ordinary, and all creatures ever kept to the pious rule of rightful copulation, even the beasts. So, then, they went to their wives during the ṛitu only, then they throve through their virtuous ways and lived a hundred thousand years. From all pain, of mind and body, mankind was freed ; none died in childhood ; none that had not reached the bloom of youth knew woman (na ca striyaṃ prajānāti kaçcid aprāptayauvanaḥ, çl. 17). They practised all that was fair, good, and pious ; the kings ruled with justice ; and so it rained at the right time and in the right place, and everywhere prevailed nothing but happiness, and strength and peace—it was the golden age. Such glory as this was naturally in the first place due to the most excelling begetters of this race, the Brahmans, but then, too, to their way of begetting virtuous, strong, and beautiful offspring. At this time the woman is not only well fitted and with the right and duty to procreate, but also she is clean. Otherwise uncleanness dwells in her, and every kind of magical harm,[2] and in the peculiarly mysterious menstrual blood are concentrated all these dread powers, but in it, too, they are discharged. Therefore, the Epic declares, too : " This according to the law is an incomparable means of cleansing the woman, O Dushyanta ; for month after month the menstrual

---

[1] For the sake of offspring was the coitus made. K. i, 107.21.

[2] This belief, spread over the whole earth, has its place, too, in the Old Indian marriage-songs, and in the wedding ritual (Çaṅkhy.-Grihy., i, 16, 2 ff. ; 18, 2 ff. ; Pārask., i, 11 ; Hiraṇy., i, 6, 20.2 ; 7, 24).

blood takes all the evil in them away " (duritāni in the magical and in the moral meaning, K., i, 100.5). Indeed, even if the man suspects his wife of unfaithfulness, he must confidently lie with her again after she has had her courses, since she is thereby cleansed again, like a vessel by ashes (xii, 35.30).[1] So, therefore, the woman can for this reason, too, demand her natural and religious rights during the ritu.

And she wills to have them : " As the fire at the time of the sacrifice by fire awaits its time (the time when the offering shall be brought it), so the woman awaits in the time of the ritu the ritu embrace " (xiii, 162.41). Ritum dehi, the menstruating woman says to the husband, " give me the ritu right, the ritu embrace, make that my ritu may not be in vain." So it is in the following tale. As we have seen, the energetic daughter of a Brahman, Devayānī, made the king Yayāti her husband. Her father straitly enjoined on him not to touch her friend and slave-girl, the king's daughter Çarmishthā. Çarmishthā saw that the time of her ripeness was come, and she thought of her period. " The time of the ritu is come, and I have chosen no husband. What is fitting now, what is to be done now ? What am I to do that the matter may be truly done ? Devayānī has borne, but I am become ripe to no end. As she chose her husband, so will I choose him. The king must grant me the fruit of a son ; that is my fast resolve. And now at this very time perhaps he of the just heart will secretly come before my eyes." And about this time the king happened to go forth, and tarried near the açoka-wood (where the fair one was dwelling), and gazed at Çarmishthā. When the sweet-smiling Çarmishthā secretly saw him thus alone, she went up to him, folded her hands before her forehead, and spoke the words unto the king : " Who can visit a woman in the house of Soma, Indra, Vishnu, Yama, and Varuna, or in thine, O son of Nahusha ? Thou knowest that I am ever gifted with beauty, nobility, and good character. I pray thee, as I ask thy favour of thee : Give me the ritu, O highest herdsman of men ! " Yayāti spoke : " I know thee to be perfected in good character,

---

[1] The parallels will be given later. We even encounter a belief that intercourse with the adulteress is magically dangerous to her husband. Hartland, *Prim. Patern.*, ii, 122.

thou faultless daughter of the Daitya. And in thy form I cannot see a needle's point of anything that were to blame. But Uçanas, the Kāvya, said, when I brought Devayānī home : ' This daughter of Vrishaparvan shalt thou not call onto thy bed.' " Çarmishthā spoke : " An untrue word spoken in jeft, or among women, or at a wedding, or when in danger of life, or where all a man's belongings are to be taken from him, does no hurt. These five lies, it is said, are not grave sins (pātakāni)." Yayāti spoke : " The king is the law of life for beings ; he falls to deftruction, when he utters untruth ; even though earthly ill [1] befall me, I cannot aft falsely." Çarmishthā spoke : "These two are held to be identical : one's own husband, and the husband of the woman friend. Marriage, it is said, is the same for both (one and the same, common, sama). Thee, as the husband of my friend, I have chosen." Yayāti spoke : " To him that asks muft be given, this rule of life I have taken for mine.[2] And thou art asking me for the fulfilment of a wish. Speak, what can I do for thee ? " Çarmishthā spoke : " Keep me from a wrong, O king, and let me share in the law [3] ; granted offspring by thee, let me praftise in the world the higheft holy law. Three there are, O king, that cannot own anything : the wife, the slave, and the child ; that which they acquire is the property of him who owns them.[4] I am the slave of Devayānī, and she is in thy power : I and she belong to thee for thy pleasure ; enjoy me, O king." Thus addressed, the king acknowledged this, and said : " True it is " ; he honoured Çarmishthā, and let her share in the holy law. She then bore him a lotus-eyed boy like a child of the gods, and then two more besides. But Devayānī found out these deeds of pious devotion,[5] and at firft bitterly reproached Çarmishthā. But

[1] Arthakricchra. [2] As a Kshattriya.
[3] Or : set me on the path of the law (the fulfilment of the law, virtue). In K. (76.30 ff.) she furthermore explains that he who gives clothing, money, cows, land, etc., gives something external ; it is a serious thing to give oneself, one's body, that is, to beget a child for a woman.
[4] Cp. e.g. Manu, viii, 416 ; Nārada, v, 41.
[5] Devayānī once went for a ftroll with the king. Then she saw the three little boys playing, and said in aftonishment : " Whose children

221

she made answer : " I have acted in accordance with law and virtue, and therefore I fear thee not. When thou didst choose thy husband, I, too, chose him. For the husband, according to the law, becomes the friend's husband. Thou art for me worthy of honour and respect, thou art the first wife and the Brahman lady, but for me still worthier of honour is the kingly Rishi ; how dost thou not know that ? " With weeping eyes and angry soul Devayānī now hastened off to her father, and complained to him that right had been overcome by wrong, for Çarmishthā had outdone her and humiliated her : with Çarmishthā Yayāti had begotten three sons, and with her herself only two.[1] The king, who had hastily followed her, made excuses : " Because she asked me for the ritu, O holy man, and from no other reason did I do this rightful service to the daughter of the Dānava prince. If a woman asks for the ritu, and a man does not give her the ritu, then by them that know the holy writings he is declared to be an embryo-slayer. And he who, having been secretly asked, does not approach a woman that is seized with desire and is meet for union, is, in the laws, called by the wise a slayer of the fruit of the body. These considerations I had before me, and, moved by fear of doing a wrong, I went to Çarmishthā." But with the angry father, deeply devoted to his daughter, these considerations availed not (i, 82, 83).

At such times the woman will even lure an unhappy disciple into the awful crime of adultery with the teacher's wife. The prose tale in i, 3.42 ff. tells us as follows : The Rishi Dhaumya had to be away from home for a long time, and entrusted his

are those ? They look so like thee." She asked the boys themselves, and they pointed with their fingers to Yayāti as their father, and said Çarmishthā was their mother. They all ran up to their begetter ; but he " did not in the presence of his wife welcome them at all joyfully ", but was " as it were filled with shame ", and the poor repulsed little boys ran screaming to their mother.

[1] This outdoing in child-bearing, and the sorrow and rage of the woman thus injured reminds us of Kuntī and Mādrī and of 1 Moses, chap. 30, v, 1–23 (that here the children of the concubine or of the secondary wife are looked on as the children of the lawful wife has not only Indian but also other Eastern parallels).

disciple Uttanka with the care of the house ; he was to see to it that no harm came. While he was dwelling there, all the wives of the teacher together called him and spoke : "The teacher's wife has the ṛitu, and the teacher is away. Do thou so aċt that her ṛitu be not fruitless ; she is in despair." Thus addressed, he made answer : "I muśt not at the urging of women do this monśtrous deed. For the teacher did not enjoin on me : 'Even a monśtrous deed shalt thou do.'" When the teacher then came home again, and learned from him what had happened, he rewarded him mośt magnificently, but the woman took her revenge by and by, when she found the opportunity.

King Uparicara was more thoughtful and kindlier to women than this holy man and his disciple, for he sent off the longed for fluid to his beloved wife at this critical time by bird pośt. At the bidding of his forefathers, he had to go off to hunt, juśt when his wife was ready for impregnation (ṛitusnātā).[1] Now he was roving the foreśt, obedient to the call of his forefathers, but his thoughts were away at home with Girikā, his young beloved one, who was surpassingly lovely, like unto another Lakshmī. Spring had made its entry, and the trees were glorious with the splendour of their flowers and their weight of fruit ; the kokilas sang their sweeteśt, and, all around, the honey-drunken

[1] The reason would be the same as in Mārk.-Pur., cxx, 6 : King Khanīnetra, who has no son, goes hunting to get flesh to offer his forefathers, and through this sacrifice a son. Cp. Caland, *Ahnenkult*, p..172. The flesh of various kinds of game and tame beaśts is used for an offering to the dead, and nourishes them for far longer than many other foods, as is carefully reckoned up for each kind of flesh in the Smṛiti and in the Purāṇas, and elsewhere, I think; and as, according to a widespread belief, children are only the dead appearing again, especially kindred and forbears, or else the shades send or beśtow the children, we cannot but hold the Indian belief to be quite natural, that the Çrāddha give their help towards getting offspring. See, for example, Albrecht Dietrich, " Mutter Erde," *Arch. f. Religionswiss.*, vii, 19 ff., 39–43 ; Hartland, *Prim. Pat.*, i, 199 ff. ; Crooke, *Pop. Rel.*, i, 179 ; Krauss, *Sitte u. Brauch d. Südslawen*, 542 ; *Anthropos*, vii, 99 ; 658 ; iv, 710 ; v, 765 ; *Zschr. f. Ethnol.*, Bd. 6, p. 363 ; Gobhila, Gṛihyas., iv, 3.27 ; Caland, *Ahnenkult*, 8 ; 10 ; 13 ; 43 ; 73, n. 3 ; 10, n. 2 ; *Totenverehrung*, 6, 39, etc.

bees were humming. By love his soul was held, but he could not see Girikā. As he went along thus tortured with longing, he happened to behold a delightful açoka-tree ; the tips of its boughs were strewn with flowers, young shoots adorned it, and it was covered with clustering blossoms, honey-sweet was the smell of it, and it charmed by the scent of its flowers. Under this tree the prince of men sat himself down, taking his ease in the shade. But inspired by the wind, he gave himself up to the joyful lust after darkness' deed (sexual union). Then his seed spurted forth, as he tarried in the thick forest. And as soon as the seed had spurted out, the lord of the earth put it on the leaf of a tree, thinking with himself : " My seed shall not fall fruitlessly." " This seed of mine shall not have spurted forth to no end," that was his thought. " And may my wife's ṛitu not be lost," this was the thought of the ruler. As now the prince thus pondered and weighed, and as the best of kings recognized the fruitfulness of the seed, and reflected that it was the right time to send it to his wife, therefore he now uttered a spell over it with holy words, went to a swift-flying falcon that was standing afar off, and said to him, who knew the delicate essence of religious duty and of worldly advantage : " My friend, carry thou this seed into my house. Hand it over speedily to Girikā ; for now is the very time of her ṛitu." The falcon, the impetuous one, took it, flew swiftly up, hastened away with his utmost speed of flight ; thus did the air-wanderer. Then another falcon saw this falcon coming, who at once, when he saw him, swooped down on him, for he thought he was carrying a piece of flesh. Then the two started to fight in the air with their beaks. As they fought, the seed fell down into the waters of the Yamunā. And lo ! in it was living an Apsaras in the shape of a she-fish by Brahma's curse, who swallowed the seed. In the tenth month after this had happened the fish was caught and cut open. They found in its body a boy and a girl. The girl became the famed Satyavatī, at first afflicted by a fishy smell, whom then the king, her father, handed over to a fisherman, and who, while she was working the ferry for him, gave the gift of life to Vyāsa. The boy, her brother, as King Matsya (" Fish "), prince of the Fish-folk (Matsya), won himself a name (i, 63.36 ff.).

WOMAN IN HER SEXUAL RELATIONS

But sexual intercourse with the still unclean woman is strictly forbidden. To have connection with a woman during the monthly flow is reckoned among the dreadful crimes set forth in Arjuna's formula of self-cursing (xii, 73.42). To visit a rajasvalā (menstruating woman) is one of the seven things whereby a man forfeits his happiness or long life (xiii, 104.150 ; xvi, 8. 5, 6), and Brahmans who thus fall appear as sinners (pāpakarmin) in xii, 165.26. Cp. e.g. also xiii, 157.9 ff. The Apsarases by Brahma's order had to take on themselves a fourth part of the murder of a Brahman, which weighed so heavily on Indra. They besought the father of the worlds to think out some means to free them from it. He answered : " He that has connection with menstruating women, on to him will it (the Brahman-murder) immediately be transferred. Let your souls' torment forsake you ! " (xii, 282.43 ff.). He that goes to a woman that must not be visited (agamyā) shall, as a penance, for six months wear a wet garment and sleep on ashes (xii, 35.35). The agamyā are of very different kinds, but among them is the rajasvalā.[1] Cp. vii, 73.38 ff. ; Manu, xi, 171–179. The mere presence of the woman with such a stain is noxious. What she looks at the gods will not take in sacrifice (xiii, 127.13). She must not be in the neighbourhood of the ancestral offering (xiii, 92.15 ; K, xiii, 238.18), otherwise the forefathers will be unappeased even for thirteen years (xiii, 127.13, 14). For the Brahman only that food is clean on which the eyes of a menstruating woman have not fallen (xiii, 104.40 and Nīl.). Food thus spoiled is the very portion of the demons (xiii, 23.4). What the rajasvalā has prepared must not be enjoyed (xiii, 104.90 and comment.). It is even forbidden to speak with her (xiii, 104.53).[2] See also

[1] The agamyā reckoned in the law books come, indeed, mostly under the conception of incest or the staining of the teacher's marriage-bed. See, for instance, Baudh., ii, 2, 4.11 ; Nārada, xii, 73 ff.

[2] The uncleanness and danger ascribed by various peoples to the menstruating woman and her discharge is indeed well known. It strikes us then as remarkable that the Aino are not frightened by any such superstition (*Anthropos*, v, 774). According to a Red Indian tale published by Boas, *Zschr. f. Ethnol.*, xxiii, p. 552 ("Abhandlungen"), if some menstrual blood is put among the tobacco, then three puffs

iii, 221.27 ; MBh. K., xiv, 116.19 f. ; 109.22 ; 112.46 ; xiii, 161.118 ; Negelein, *Traumschlüssel der Jagaddeva*, p. 375.

from his pipe are sufficient to cause a man to fall down dead. Cp. Ploss-Bartels [4], i, 323 ff. Even the glance of the woman is at this time full of deadly poison (Hertz, " Die Sage vom Giftmädchen," *Abh. d. Münchner Ak.*, xx, 109). Cp. Thurston, *Omens*, etc., pp. 185–6. And this superstition is by no means confined to the uneducated even in our own days. Only a few years ago, I am informed by one present, the following happened in an English boarding-school for " young ladies " : The cook had her courses, and therefore did not dare to touch the meat, as it would thus be spoiled. In her difficulty she called in the head mistress. But, as it happened, she too was indisposed. She called one or two of the teachers. But a spiteful fate willed it that they, too, at that very time had to pay their debt to woman's nature. The meat, therefore, could not be cut up and made ready, to the greatest joy of the very avaricious head of this hungry institution ; and the butcher had to be told to take his meat back again for once.

In the Indian law writings, too, the precept is found that a menstruating woman must not be approached ; and whoever so offends must, according to Yājñav., iii, 288 fast and eat *ghī* for three days. The woman must not inflict her presence on others at this time; detailed rules for her behaviour are given, e.g. in Vasishtha, v, 9.5 ff. ; cp. Parāçara, vii, 9–18. She was kept away from the ancestral sacrifice (Mārk.-Pur., xxxii, 25) ; her very glance makes unclean (ibid., l, 47 ; Dubois-Beauchamp, 347, cp. 708–10) ; even speaking to her sullies (Āpast., i, 3, 9.13), and food she has touched must not be eaten (Vasishtha, v, 7 ; Yājñav., i, 168 ; Manu, iv, 208 ; Vishnu, li, 16 ; etc.). If she wilfully touches a twice-born man, she shall be flogged with a whip (Vishnu, v, 105). It should be said that Brihaspati tells us that the women " in the north " have sexual intercourse during their period (ii, 30), but this, at any rate, is probably not Aryan India. That the monthly issue is a mark of sin, but also a setting free from ill, that it is, indeed, a third or fourth part of the murder of a Brahman, is often asserted with the legend belonging thereto. So Vasishtha, v, 4 ff. ; and here the following account according to Taitt.-Samh., ii, 5, 1.2–5 is given : Indra, tortured by the murder of a Brahman, unloaded a third of his guilt onto women, but for this he had to grant them the grace that they should get children from their husbands during the ritu. On the other hand in accord with a true Indian view we are told as follows in Bhāgavatapur., vi, 9.9 : For the boon of constant enjoyment of love (or : to be allowed to live after

their own desires ? çaçvatkāmavareṇa) women took on themselves
a quarter of the sin ; this is seen in them month after month in the
form of the menſtrual blood. But the woman in this wise is fully
rid of the sins she has herself done, particularly those of sex, as has been
already eſtablished from the MBh. (p. 219). With this the law literature and the Purāṇa literature is in agreement. The monthly flow
cleanses her from married unfaithfulness (vyabhicāra), Yājñav., i, 72 ;
Agnipur., clxv, 6 f. (where we muſt read na tyajed) ; 19 ff. ; from
pollution in thought, Manu, v, 108 ; Vishṇu, xxii, 91 ; cp. Parāçara,
vii, 2 ; x, 12. Baudhāyana, ii, 2, 4.4 teaches that women have an
incomparable means of cleansing, they are never wholly ſtained ;
for month after month their sin is carried away. Exaſtly the same in
Vasishṭha, xxviii, 4, and essentially the same in v, 4 ; iii, 58. Hence,
then, comes the ordinance in Parāçara, x, 16–19 : The woman who
does wrong with a Caṇḍāla (pariah) muſt confess her guilt before a
gathering of ten Brahmans, then faſt a day and night plunged up to the
neck in a well with cow-dung, water, and mud, then shave her head
quite bald, and live outside the house praſtising further mortifications
and cleansing aſts, up to the time of her period ; then she is clean,
but muſt furthermore give food to Brahmans, and beſtow a pair
of oxen. According to 20, however, she is absolved through the
Cāndrāyaṇa vow. Vasishṭha, xxviii, 1 ff. even declares : The woman
even through a lover becomes no more unclean than water through urine
and dung, than fire through rubbish it deſtroys ; no matter how bad
she may be, or what adventures she may have experienced, let her
husband wait till she gets her courses ; through these she then becomes
spotless again. Before this, as a maid, she has already belonged to
Soma, Gandharva, and the fire god, to them that hallow, and cannot
after that be polluted by the faſt of going from hand to hand—a
conception to be discussed in another conneſtion. According to
Parāçara, x, 20, woman is like the earth, and can never become wholly
unclean. Women, water, and pearls are never spoiled, as we have
already been told. Cp. Muir, *Metrical Translations*, p. 277 f. Her
mouth, that is, her kiss, is always clean, happen what may (Manu, v,
130 ; Yājñav., i, 187 ; Vishṇu, xxiii, 49; etc.), and she herself during
the pleasures of love (Vasishṭha, xxviii, 8 ; Baudh., i, 5, 9.2). Parāçara,
viii, 34, declares that a woman, a child, and an old man are never
unclean. Çrī, the goddess of happiness, abides, indeed, in the body of
wedded and unwedded women (Vishṇu, xcix, 8 ff.). A marriageable
woman who is not aſtually having her period is the godlike draught
of immortality (Vasishṭha, v, 1). Indeed, Vasishṭha, xxviii, 9,
proclaims : Woman is pure in all her limbs, while the cow is pure
only behind (cp. Meyer, *Altind. Rechtsschr.*, 146). Then there are

227

views which also give other reasons for this monthly *purgatorium terrestre et naturale* of woman, which is generally looked on as so uncanny and fraught with evil. Mārkaṇḍeyapur., xlix, 8 ff., relates : In the beginning, women knew nothing of this contrivance of nature, but in spite of copulation they got no children. Later the passion of love (rāga) came into the world, and then, with it, both the woman's period, and offspring through the sexual union; for till then propagation had only been by means of concentrated thought (dhyānena manasā), and that very sparingly (11 ; cp. this book, p. 370). Cp. the already mentioned passage in Vasishṭha, v, 4 ff., and its source. As is clear enough from the puberty customs, savages, too, know that the monthly flow is needful for impregnation. See further *Anthropos*, v, p. 772 f. ; vi, 703. The American Indians quoted in the last-named reference share moreover the belief that this flow is first called forth through sexual intercourse. It would thus be the holy duty of the girl to indulge in love in good time. It is no wonder that evil spirits, then, disturb and destroy this blessed monthly act. See, for instance, Mārk.-Pur., li, 42 ff. ; 114 ff. Cp. also Winternitz, *Altind. Hochzeitsrituell*, pp. 92–95.

VII

The Pleasures of Sex (surata)

ON the fourth day, however, the woman becomes snātā, ṛitusnātā (one that has bathed), and thereby peculiarly fitted for the delights of love, the surata. The woman ſtands in very great need of them ; without them she pines : asambhogo jarā ſtrīnāṃ (want of sexual enjoyment is decay and old age for women, iv, 39.78b–79a ; v, 39.78, 79).[1] In the Indian view the woman has also a far ſtronger erotic disposition, and her delight in the sexual aɕt is far greater than the man's. This is shown, indeed, in the Epic, in the tale of the king who was changed into a woman. It will be given later on. We can thus underſtand Lopamudrā's whim (iii, 97 ff.) :

The great saint and artiſt in digeſtion Agaſtya wishes to wed, and woos Lopamudrā, the bewitchingly lovely princess of Vidarbha, brought up in the greateſt luxury and ease. The father is not over-delighted with the proposal, and will not agree, but is afraid of the anger and curse of this powerful one. Then his daughter comes to him in his sorrow, and speaks : " Do not diſtress thyself because of me. Give me to Agaſtya, and save thyself through me, O father." So she is wedded to the Ṛishi. But when Agaſtya had taken Lopamudrā to wife, he spoke unto her : " Lay aside these coſtly garments and ornaments." Then she, with the great eyes, with thighs like banana-ſtems, laid aside her garments so splendid to see, so coſtly and thin. Then she put on clothes of rags, baſt, and skins, and together with him led a ſtriɕt life of religion, she the lovely one with the great eyes. The beſt of Ṛishis went to Gaṅgādvāra, and there gave himself up to the hardeſt penance together with his obedient

[1] " Mankind is made old (is worn down) by care, the warrior by fetters, woman by a life without coition, and clothes by the glow of fire." Thus a saying of Cāṇakya. See Kressler, *Stimmen indischer Lebensklugheit*, Leipzig, 1907, p. 159; cp. Garuḍapur., 115.10; Rām., iv, 35.9 ; etc.

229

wife. Filled with joyful love and lofty regard she served her master, and Agaſtya, the lord, showed glad love towards his wife. Then the glorious Ṛishi saw that Lopamudrā, shining with ascetic praċtice, had already bathed some time (after her period).[1] Gladdened by her deeds of service, her purity, self-control, splendour, and beauty, he invited her to unite. Then, folding her hands before her forehead, as though filled with shame, the fair one spoke these words lovingly to the holy man : " Doubtless the husband wedded the wife for the sake of offspring. But the joyful love I bear to thee, that do thou (too) praċtise, O Ṛishi. On juſt such a couch as I had at home in my father's palace, do thou visit me. And decked with divine ornaments I would fain glide unto thee according to my wish, thou, too, wreathed and decked. Otherwise, clad in the brown-red penitential garb of rags, I will not approach thee. Of a truth this adornment (the ascetic garb) muſt not be soiled in any way whatever."[2] Agaſtya spoke : " I have not indeed such treasures for thee, Lopamudrā, as thy father has, thou slender one." Lopamudrā spoke : " Through thy asceticism thou, rich in asceticism, haſt full power to procure anything in a moment, whatsoever things there are in the world of the living." Agaſtya spoke : " It is as thou sayeſt. But through such a thing (that is, through the making use of the Yoga powers) ascetic merit is deſtroyed. Give me some bidding whereby my penitential merit shall not be loſt." Lopamudrā spoke : " Of my ṛitu time there is only very little left, O thou rich in penance. And in other wise I have not the slighteſt wish to approach thee. I would indeed in no way deſtroy thy religious perfeċtion

---

[1] Taking çl. 23 into account this is perhaps less likely thus : He saw after some time that she had bathed (bahutithe kāle). Cp. the bahutithe 'hani in i, 108.3, already known from the song of Nala (ix, 12).

[2] During sexual union the father of the family muſt have on a special garment, only to be used for this purpose. Āpaſtamba, ii, 1, 1.20. And when ſtudying the Veda he muſt not wear anything he has worn during copulation. Manu, iv, 116; Vasishṭha, xiii, 26 (here : unless it has been washed). As to ornaments at this time cp. Meyer, *Altind. Rechtsschr.*, 8; 12 f.; 376 f.; also Jolly, " Medizin " (in the *Grundriss*), p. 38.

230

(dharma), but prithee bring that about which I wish." Agastya spoke : "If thou, O lovely one, art so set in thy heart upon this wish, then I will go and seek, my loved one. Do thou stay here, and live as thou wilt."

Then the complaisant husband went off to three kings one after the other to ask for what he needed. All three welcomed him most reverently at the extreme frontiers of the land, and put all their possessions at his disposal. But each time the holy man saw that their income and their expenditure exactly balanced one another, and he had no wish to bring hurt on living beings by having in such a case taken anything for himself. Accompanied by the first king, he came to the second, then together with these two to the third ; and now together with the three and on their suggestion he went on to the exceedingly rich Daitya Ilvala, well known for his malicious wickedness towards the Brahmans. He had been angered by one of the priestly caste, who would not grant him a son equal to Indra. He now magically changed his younger brother Vātāpi into a goat, slaughtered him, made him ready, and set him before the Brahman. When the Brahman had eaten him, the other called back to life him that was eaten, and the laughing monster that came walking out from the belly naturally thereby split his host in twain. Thus did Ilvala slay many Brahmans. When Agastya, with the three kings, now offered himself as his guest, to him too did he dish up his brother, magically turned into a goat and daintily made ready, and great was the fear of the three brave warriors when the good holy man ate the dish up quite calmly. But the wicked man this time had fallen into his own trap : in answer to his wonted loud "Vātāpi, come out !" there came from under the high-souled one a wind with a mighty roar, like a thundering cloud.[1] When he went on

[1] No wonder that the genius of digestion, Agastya (Wilson's Vishṇup., iii, p. 128) shows such an overflowing health. As among the peasants in Zola's *La terre*, and elsewhere in the world, things all go their good way amid this blessed noise as the body is thus eased, so, too, the Indian sees in it a token of food well taken and of the favour of the gods, and, in fact, of general present and future happiness. See Dubois-Beauchamp [3], p. 329 ; Schmidt, *Liebe u. Ehe in Indien*, p. 397 ; E. Thurston, *Omens*, etc. (1912), p. 26.

calling to arouse his brother again, the pious belly-hero laughed him to scorn, and let him know that the brother had long ago been digested.[1] The Daitya prince was beaten and humbly offered his services. Agastya demanded for each of the three kings ten thousand oxen, and the same number of gold pieces, but for himself twice as much, and a golden chariot forthwith, with two fleet steeds before it, swift as thought. All this the poor demon had to give, and with the three kings and all the treasure the holy artist in eating and drinking drove into his hermitage. Then there was nothing more to stand in the way of the longed for love union. Lopamudrā got her princessly wish and a lusty son.

We are told, too, of a fair one who reached a remarkably high pitch of virtue in the pleasures of love. King Parīkshit rides off at full speed in the forest, lost by his retinue, and follows after a gazelle. Thus he is carried far away. Hungry, thirsty, and wearied, he sees there in the thicket an enchanting lake, covered with lotus-flowers. He throws his horse some of the lotus-stalks and sits down to rest. Then he hears sweet singing. As no human traces are anywhere to be seen, the king is filled with wonder, follows the voice, and finds a wondrous-fair maiden singing and plucking flowers. He woos her, and she consents, on condition that water must never be shown her. The king promises this, and so she becomes his wife. Meanwhile his followers come up, and she is borne in the litter to the royal city. Here Parīkshit lives with her in great joy. But the minister has a delightful grove with a splendid tank laid out, and when the king goes to walk in it with his beloved, and sees the tank, he asks her to go down into the water. She goes down below, but does not come up again. The king in despair has the water drawn off from the tank : they find only a frog. "The frogs have eaten my beloved !" the king cries, and orders a general slaughter of the frogs in his kingdom. Then the king of the frogs comes in ascetic garb, shows the prince the wrong he is doing, and tells him that the lady is his daughter Suçobhanā, who has already befooled many kings. On

---

[1] Another time Agastya drank up the ocean, and digested it, to the terror of the gods, only too quickly, so that they did not know now how they should fill the mighty bed again with water (i, 105).

Parīkshit's beseeching him, he gives her to him as wife. And when the king had received her, it was to him as though he had won the lordship of the three worlds ; for his heart was hers because of her surpassing excellences in the surata ; and with words choked with tears of joy he went down, did reverence to the king of the frogs, and said : " I thank thee " [1] (iii, 192.1 ff.).

That the disturbance of the enjoyment of sex was felt as especially inhuman can be easily understood. King Kalmāshapāda (" Pied Foot "),[2] who had had the curse of man-eating laid on him, comes upon a Brahman and his wife in the forest, engaged in the joys of love. They flee in terror before the business is brought to its end. But the man-eater runs after them and falls on the Brahman. The wife beseeches him with tears to have pity on his victim, for she is not yet satisfied, has her ritu, and wishes for a child. But the king's mind is shaken by the curse, and he eats the Brahman. Angry tears run down from the poor wife's face, and turn to fire which sets the whole neighbourhood alight. Then she curses him : " Since thou before my very eyes, before my business was done, hast eaten my husband, thou wilt leave thy life when

[1] Literally : " I have been granted a favour." This and like expressions are quite regular, and may be compared with the regular German " genade ! " (French, merci) of the Middle Ages.

[2] This prince when hunting in the forest met Çakti, the eldest son of that Vasishtha held by him in high honour. He ordered the Muni to give him the path. But the Muni insisted that under the eternal law the Kshattriya must give way to the Brahman. (Cp. Āpast., ii, 5, 11.5, and parallels). So they went on wrangling ; at length the angry king struck the priest's son with his whip " like a Rākshasa ", and had the curse put on him by the insulted man that he should eat human flesh " like a Rākshasa "—one of those curses by holy men and Brahmans which almost always bring down misfortune on the innocent. But in this case a kind of strange Nemesis was at work : the first victim of the new monster was Çakti himself, then he was followed by his ninety-nine brothers into Kalmāshapāda's maw (i, 176). According to Bṛihaddevatā, vi, 28 these 100 sons were slain by the Saudāsas (sons or followers of Sudās) ; according to Sāyana on Ṛigveda, vii, 104.2 it was a Rākshasa. Cp. Muir, *Original Sanskrit Texts*, i, p. 326 ff.

thou drawest nigh to thy wife during the ritu. But Vasishtha
will beget thee an heir." Then she throws herself into the fire
and is burned. Kalmashapāda's wife is with him, and later she
keeps him away, when he has got his wits back again, but not
the memory of this event, and now wishes to approach her during
the ritu. In his fear of dying he stands aside, and gives Vasishtha
the commission (i, 182).[1]

The, in parts very clumsy, legend of Pāndu seems to be an
imitation of this last one. The king shot at a couple of antelopes
that were just in the joys of pairing.[2] But it was really a young
Rishi, who had thus transformed himself and his wife, and was
then love-making with her. With a human voice spoke he that
had been brought to the ground : " Even they that are seized by
hot desire and rage, they that are robbed of understanding,
even men that take their delight in evil shun gruesome deeds.
Born thou wast in the glorious race of men whose soul lived
ever in virtue ; how then couldst thou, overcome by desire
and greed, so go astray in thy mind ? " Pāndu insisted he had
every right to slay the beasts of the forest.[3] But the male antelope
said : " It is not for my own sake that I upbraid thee for

[1] The same tale is, for instance, in Wilson's Vishnupur., iii, p. 306 ff.
(4th Book, 4th chapt.) ; Bhāgavatapur., iv, 9.20–39 (in both places
the explanation is also given of how the king became " Pied Fnot ").

[2] With this tale cp. Mārkandeyapur., lxxiv, 23 ff.

[3] Not only are all Kshattriyas in the Epic, and the holy kings of
earliest times mighty hunters before the Lord, but even in the midst
of a rhapsody on the ahimsā and the awfulness of killing living beings
and of eating flesh hunting is held up to praise and declared to be wholly
sinless ; for the Kshattriya while so engaged sets his own life at stake,
it is slaying foes. And moreover Agastya, the great saint, and in our
days the hero above all others, of the Tamil people, not only did hunt
himself, but also besprinkled (that is, consecrated) the beasts of the
forest as sacrifices for all the gods, and thereby made them outlaws
(i, 118.12 ff.; xiii, 115.56 ff.; 116.15 ff.; Vasishtha, xiv, 15;
Manu, v, 22). The hunt is looked on as a right and virtue
of the nobles (Mahāvīracaritam ed. T. R. Ratnam Ayar, S. Ranga-
chariar, and K. P. Parab, Bombay, 1892, p. 220 : mrigayā ca rājñām
dharma eva) ; indeed it is called their eternal law (sanātana dharma,
Mahānirvānat., xi, 142). Cp. my Daçakumāracar., p. 340 f., and
Rām., iv, 18.36 ff.

killing the antelopes. But thou shouldst out of friendly thought-fulness have taken heed that I was just pairing. For what man of sense could bring himself at such a time dear to all beings, longed after by all beings, to slay in the forest an antelope when in the act of pairing? For thee, born of the race of the Pauravas, unwearied in the doing of noble deeds, this deed is not seemly, which is cruel, unheard of, one that all men will condemn, which leads not to heaven, but to shame, and is called accursed. Thou, who understandest well the particularities and excellences of the enjoyment of women, and knowest the books of the doctrine, and the nature of religious duty and human well-being, shouldst not have done a thing which thus brings about the loss of heaven. I am a Muni purified through asceticism, my name is Kindama. It was because I felt ashamed and shy before men that I did pair with the she-antelope. Turned into an antelope, I roam about with antelopes in the depths of the forest. But as thou didst not know that, for thee it will not be as the murder of a Brahman that thou hast thus slain me, who was wearing an antelope's shape, and was mazed with love. Yet, O blinded one, thou shalt have this requital : when thou, bewildered with love, art in the embraces of thy wedded wife, thou wilt in this very state go into the world of the dead. The loved one whom thou art embracing at the time of thy death will, however, out of loving devotion, follow thee, O best of the prudent, when thou hast reached the city of the dead, into which all beings come but unwillingly." When these words had died away life left the antelope, and Pāṇḍu at once was gripped with sorrow (i, 118). From that time on he lived in strict continence as a forest penitent, together with his two wives, and he had his five sons through the gods. " One day the king with his wives was wandering through the forest in spring-time, when the forest blooms and living beings are all mazed. When Pāṇḍu beheld the forest with its bloom- and fruit-laden trees, its varied waters and lotus-clumps, love came into his heart. As now he roamed there with joy-lifted mind like an immortal, Mādrī wearing magnificent garb, alone was with him. As now he gazed on the youthful one, clad in thin garments, his love blazed up, like a fire lit in the thick forest. And as he stealthily beheld the lotus-eyed one thus alone, he was overcome with longing and could not keep back his passion. And then the king fell with force on her that was alone, although the queen kept him off, and sought with the strength of her body to wrest herself away. But his senses filled with love, he gave no thought to the curse. In love's longing, forcibly he drew nigh to Mādrī, and himself drew nigh to death, fallen under the spell of love's desire, as he bade fear begone, goaded on by fate. As Pāṇḍu, the Kuru scion of highly virtuous mind, united himself with his wife in the joys of love, he united himself with death. Then Mādrī clasped the lifeless king, and again and again uttered loud cries of woe. Kuntī with her sons, and Mādrī's two children came to where the king was lying in this state. Then spoke Mādrī in torture these words to Kuntī : ' Come thou hither quite alone ; the children must stay there.' When Kuntī heard these words of hers, she left the children there and ran quickly to her, screaming out : ' I am death's own ! ' She now upbraided Mādrī with having led the king on to being stirred with love (praharsha), and called her blessed withal in that she had gazed on the prince's face stirred with love. Mādrī told her how the king would not be held back, and Kuntī claimed as eldest wife, to die with him. Mādrī, she said, must rise, and take the children into her care. But Mādrī spoke : ' I shall follow after my brave husband, for I have not yet taken my fill of love ; let the elder one grant me this. And as he was drawing nigh to me, he lost love. How should I cut this love off from him in Yama's abode there ? And I cannot fully make atonement by having borne myself impartially towards thy sons ; and so a sin would be laid upon me. With the king's body shall this dead body of mine, well wrapped, be burned. Do this for love of me, O noble one ! And take good care for the children, and love me.[1] I do not see anything more to charge thee with.' After these words the law-keeping wife, the splendid daughter of the king of the Madras, climbed swiftly up to him as he lay on the funeral pyre." [2] See, too, Rām., i, 36.5 ff.

[1] Or : Be careful and kind with my children.
[2] As in the following chapters we are told how the penitents bring the two bodies, Kuntī, and the children to Hāstinapura and hand them

If women, then, have such a healthy and natural joy in the surata, the men indeed are in no wise behind. The frequently seen ideal of the Indian, and above all of the warrior, of the blissful life is intercourse with thousands of lovely women in the bloom of youth, smiling with long lotus-eyes at the man, winding their rounded arms about his neck, and pressing their swelling firm breasts against him—women who press great over, and how the two corpses are then burned with all proper ceremonies, this short enigmatic sentence strikes oddly. We only expect to find that Mādrī has killed herself, at least if what follows is looked on as belonging to the original, or at least to the same account. K. for this part has a true flood of words evidently from a very late period (i, 134 ff.). Kuntī here at the sight of the dead man falls to the ground like a felled tree, and gives herself up then to a long conventionally-phrased wailing. The penitents who come running up also raise cries of woe, and the five brothers come up in single file, and in the order of their ages say their little verses of lamentation. Then there follows a regular suttee scene : first the penitents do all to dissuade the two wives from offering themselves up ; they were to live in chastity and good works, and so be serviceable to their dead husband. Kuntī humbly consents to this, but Mādrī repeats her earlier declarations, solemnly makes her farewell, addresses a wise exhortation to the children, and is consecrated with pious prayers by Kuntī. The Purohita Kāçyapa has bits of gold, sacrificial butter, sesame, sour milk, rice grains, water-jugs, and an axe brought by the penitents, and has the wood-pile set alight by Yudhishthira with fire from a horse-sacrifice (!), whereupon she dedicated to death leaps into the flames (i, 135). In what follows there is then a description given, somewhat as in the Bomb. text, of the body-burning, which in both places must now be thought of as carried out only on what is left of the bones, though this does not agree very well with the actual account. The whole is probably patched together from different versions. It looks as though the idea of the burning which had taken place before this in the penitential forest were borrowed from the example of the Brahman's wife. In her case all happens naturally ; for Mādrī was the wood-pile inserted for better or worse. The fact of the penitents only reaching Hastinapura on the 17th day after Pāndu's death does not of course give any support to the text as handed down. Needless to say, however, there may have been a version of the tale in which the final burial was carried out at once in the forest, and then Mādrī's fiery death quite fits in. But there was an unwillingness, I think, to lose the solemn and splendid public ceremony. Cp. i, 150.10 ff.

237

swelling hips, and thighs like banana-ſtems againſt his body, who give lips red as the bimba-fruit to be sucked by his, and who as they glow in the surata not only receive, but also give. And thus the princes of Old India in particular were much given to the joys of love, and Indian literature tells us of many who, owing to an over-eager indulgence in the surata, fell. victims to consumption and an early death. So it was with Vicitravīrya, who secretly turned all the women's heads, and through his two big brown wives, with their black curly hair, red high-arched finger-nails, and swelling hips and breaſts, became from a dharmātman (virtuous-souled) a kāmātman (one whose soul is love, i, 102.66 ff. ; v,147. 25 ; cf. i, 119.3–4 ; v, 11.10 f.). As he died without children, Vyāsa had to call up offspring for him. The same lot of an early death, uncrowned by offspring, fell to King Vyushitāçva, only too madly in love with his intoxicatingly lovely wife, Kakshīvatī. Then after his death he brought about that which in life was not possible, as will be told later (i, 121.17 ff.). More will be said when we deal with the love life of the Epic hero. Then, too, the sexual embrace comes before us as a healing remedy : The soul has the greateſt influence on the body, " for through pain of the soul the body is heated in torment like water in a pitcher by a glowing ball of iron." [1] Skilful leeches therefore in dealing with bodily ills firſt remove those of the soul, and this is done by their providing the man with sexual enjoyment (iii, 2.21 ff.).

It is well known also that in the more formal poetry of India and in the doctrinal books various refinements play a great part in the ordinary love embrace. Of these the Epic refers to one only : in the description of the horses wandering about in a battle we find as follows : " Trampled by the hoofs of these ſteeds, the earth shone in many colours like a woman that is marked with scratches this way and that by the nails (of the lover) " (ix, 9.13). To heighten the powers of love [2] flesh

[1] " As thought, so the mind ; as the mind (manas), so the body becomes " (sick and healthy, too). Pañcaçatīprabandha ed. Ballini, p. 34.
[2] Means of heightening the sexual powers of the man, so much even that in one night he can satisfy a thousand women, are known in

has from times of old been recommended, and the Indians of the Epic, above all the Kshattriyas, are great, nay enthusiastic, meat-eaters. So even that pattern of virtue, Yudhishthira, acknowledges in xiii, 115 that he prizes flesh above everything, and would now learn the good and the evil of flesh-eating from the dying Bhīshma. And Bhīshma grants, too, that there is nothing better than flesh, and that among other things it has many advantages for those who are given up with all their

the Old Indian literature in great abundance. See Rich. Schmidt, *Indische Erotik*, 842–857 ; Garuḍapur., 182.2 ; 184.13 ; 192.20–23; 202.25–28 ; Bṛihatsaṃh., 76 ; Agnipur., 302.15–16 ; Chavannes, *Cinq cents contes*, ii, 205 ; iii, 235 ; etc. It is to be noted that onions, garlic, and beans play a part in this. Because of their magical nature onions, leeks, and garlic are foods strictly forbidden in the law literature (Āpast., i, 5, 17.26 ; Manu, v, 19 ; Yājñav., i, 176 ; Vishṇu, li, 3), and the well-known prohibition of beans would seem, seeing this effect of the anti-Pythagorean field-fruit, easy to understand. As I know from one who has lived long in India, one hears there in our days as the explanation of the onion tabu its too great likeness to flesh. But it is the well-known erotic, magical, and religious importance of the onion plants that seems to be the main reason here. Onions and garlic are found as aphrodisiacs e.g. in Samayamātṛikā, ii, 26. Garlic is among the Ainu the favourite food of the gods (*Anthropos*, v, 766) ; onions and leeks were talismans among the Classical peoples (Schurtz, *Urgesch. d. Kult.*, 599) ; and to-day among the South Slavs the garlic is " a protection against witchcraft and haunting " (Krauss, *Sitte u. Brauch*, 398 ; cp. 545 ; *Slav. Volkforschungen*, pp. 37, 66, 95, 148, 250). The fire of love, too, in Slav belief is made hotter by the eating of garlic (Krauss, *Sitte*, etc., 240 f.). Cp. further R. Andree, *Ethnol. Parallel.* (1878), i, 41–43 ; Th. Zachariae, *Kleine Schriften*, 358 ; K. E. Franzos, *Vom Don zur Donau* (1878), 1, 211 ; ii, 8 ; 80; also MBh. K, xii, 141.91 f. ; xiii, 91.38 f. That among the old Hindus, too, the onion was prized as a food, anyhow by many, seems to be shown by the tale of the onion-thief, which has wandered into the West and is known there in many places : he was caught, and was given the choice of paying 100 rupees, getting 100 blows with a stick, or eating 100 onions ; he chose at first, of course, the onions, but then, with streaming eyes and a face drawn in torment, the cudgelling, and under the pain of the first stroke quickly chose the money fine. See Hertel, *Studien z. vergl. Literaturgesch.*, Bd. 5, p. 129 ff., and especially Zachariae, ibid., Bd. 6, p. 356 ff.

soul to the " villagers' custom " (pleasures of love) ; and there is no doubt but that flesh arises out of the seed (çl. 9 ff.).[1] Çiva and his wife are the ideal figures, carried beyond all bounds, even to grotesqueness, of the Indian power of imagination, in this respect, that they can immeasurably lengthen the embraces of love. When under the mountains this god had wedded the daughter of the prince, he set himself with his wife to sporting in bed. But a long thousand years of the gods went by,[2] and the heaven-dwellers grew anxious lest the fruit of so endless a begetting should be far too mighty for the world to tolerate. They went therefore to the tireless pair, and begged Çiva that for the weal of all beings he would put a check on his manly powers. He graciously consented, but asked who should catch up the seed already aroused. The earth was chosen for this, but it filled up altogether with it, and so the god of fire was called in to help ; he penetrated this flood, and so there arose the mountain Çvetaparvata, and the heavenly cane-forest, where from the god's procreative fluid the war-god Kārtikeya or Kumāra came into being (Rām., i, 36.5 ff.).[3]

Neither myths like these, however, nor the sensuality so often blazing up, in any way alter the ethical view of the surata found in the Epic, especially in its didactic parts. Here also it comes before us as something unclean. The evil spirits Pramatha are asked by the gods, the dead, and the Rishis what it is that

---

[1] Ascetic literature lays stress in India on the view that one must abstain from eating flesh for the very reason that it hinders the control of the senses. So, for instance, Amitagati, Subhāshitasaṃdoha, xxi, 13 (also honey has an erotic effect, xxii, 18). The main reason for the turning away from flesh is suggested by me in my *Altind. Rechtsschr.*, p. 45 (middle) ; 370, note.

[2] A year for men is equal to a day for the gods (e.g. Manu, i, 67).

[3] Somadeva gives a still more drastic turn to the legend (Kathās., 20.60 ff.). According to MBh., xiii, 84.60 ff., where no mention is made of the love joys of the heavenly pair lasting so long, the gods come to them and get Çiva to promise to beget no offspring, for they are anxious lest it should be too powerful and terrible. Umā's mother-urge is thus scornfully cheated of its rights, and "since she is a woman, to the gods she utters the hot, raw words of the curse : Now ye, too, shall all be childless ! "

makes anyone ucchishṭa (usually he that has not yet undertaken
the needful washings after eating), açuci (unclean), and kshudra
(low, common), and thereby fall a victim to their destroying
power. And they answer among other things : " Through
copulation men become ever ucchishṭa, and if they have practised
the ' upside-down ' " (xii, 131.4).[1]   And in the golden age
there was no sexual union whatever. So we find in xii,
207.37 ff. : " So long as men chose to retain the body, so long
they lived ; there was no fear of death. Nor did they know
either the custom of copulation ; their offspring came into being
through the mere wish.   In the days of the Tretāyuga (silver
age) thereafter, the children were begotten by touch ; for they,
too, had not the custom of copulation.   In the Dvāpara age
arose among creatures the custom of copulation." In our own
evil or Kali age it is now needful ; but it is regulated.   It
must not be practised in the open air (ākāçe, xii, 228.45 ; cp.
Meyer, Altind. Rechtsschr., 237), and must be practised secretly
(xiii, 162.47 ; xii, 193.17 [2]) ; in the latter passage is added
that it must also be in lawful wise, which may mean the
restriction to one's own wife, but according to Nīl. refers to
the ṛitu.   Then there is only the vulva for it ; done in

[1] Adharottara is here probably an expression for " perverse " love
(viparīta surata), for the usual meaning (here also accepted by the
schol.) does not fit very well.—Here belongs also iii, 136.13 :
To the penitent Yavakrī(ta) there comes a magical being (kṛityā)
in the shape of a woman beloved by him, infatuates him, and takes
away his water-jug.   Since he is now ucchishṭa and robbed of his water-
jug, an enemy Rākshasa gets him in his power.   Then even the public
harlot washes her hands and feet after the act of love, and rinses her mouth
out (Kuṭṭanīmata, 162 f.).   A bath or wash afterwards is enjoined,
for instance, in Manu, v, 144 ; Vishṇu, xxii, 67 ; Parāçara, xii, 1 ;
Mahānirvāṇatantra, vii, 75.   Cp. Kāmasūtra, p. 179 of the edit. ;
and Wasserschleben, Die Bussordnungen d. abendländ. Kirche, 1851,
p. 216 : Maritus, qui cum uxore sua dormierit, lavet se, antequam
intret in ecclesiam.   Among the Hovas of Madagascar for one week
before the circumcision the parents and sponsors of the child to be
circumcised must abstain from coition, otherwise l'opération ne
réussirait pas bien (Anthropos, iv, 378).   And dozens of such cases.
Cp. too Thurston, Omens, etc., p. 29.
[2] Cp. e.g. Vasishṭha, vi, 9.

the mouth it is a crime (vii, 73.43). The āsyamaithuna is also named as one of the dreadful things making their appearance towards the end of the world : Bahuprajāḥ, hrasvadehāḥ, çīlācāravivarjitāḥ, mukhebhagāḥ ṣtriyo, rājan, bhavishyanti yugakshaye (iii, 188.41 ; cp. vii, 73.38 ff.).[1] So, too, homosexuality is a dreadful sin : "The blind ones, evil-livers, very foolish ones, however, who find their delight in intercourse with a base womb (especially of an animal, but also of a woman of low rank) (viyonau), and with men, are born again as men incapable of begetting" (xiii, 145.52).[2] Here, too, seems to belong the passage from the description of the evil ṣtate of things at the time when a world age is coming to its end : "Men and women will walk their ways after their own wishes, and not be able to suffer one another, when the end of a yuga has come about. Then, when the end of the world is at hand, the

[1] We are told by Nīl. : The women in Bengal (Vaṅgeshu) are known for beginning with their mouth the business of the vulva to excite the man's desires, owing to their excessive craving for the joys of love. Such a thing is, of course, ṣtrongly condemned by the law books. Whoso has unnatural intercourse with his wife, his forefathers have to live the month through in his seed (Vasishṭha, xii, 22 f.) ; according to Mahānirvāṇat., xi, 44 he is even to be punished with death. For unnatural desires, of whatever kind, the law writings and the Purāṇas lay down various purifications and penances (and expulsion from the caṣte). Anyone praċtising such lewdness or other forbidden sexual intercourse is, according to Baudhāyana, iii, 7.2, the same as a Brahman-murderer.

[2] But perhaps more likely so : "the blind ones, evil-livers, among men (persons) very foolish ones, who delight themselves with intercourse with a base womb," which then of course might be meant for sodomy; according to xii, 228.45 rather for intercourse with women of low standing. Cp. xii, 227.14, and as to viyoni also xii, 296.11 ; xiii, 104.133 ; 106.72 ; K, xiii, 53.1 f. For : maithunaṃ purusheshu compare : maithunaṃ puṃsi in Manu, xi, 68. According to this passage and Vishṇu, xxxviii, 5 by homosexual perversion the man loses his caṣte ; while Manu, xi, 175, Vishṇu, liii, 4, prescribe bathing in the clothes as the atonement. Lesbian love between girls is punished with a heavy money fine and ten ṣtrokes of the whip (çiphā) ; the married woman who thus ṣtains a maid shall be at once shaved bald, have two fingers cut off, and be led on an ass through the place. Manu, viii, 369 f.

woman will not find content with her husband, nor the man with his wife " (iii, 190.45, 50).[1] And you shall not be a thrall to the pleasures of love, when you celebrate a sacrifice to the fore-fathers (çrāddha). The çrāddhamaithunika is set before us, in vii, 17.32, as a great sinner. All those taking part are then bound to keep chaste. " It is held that on this day copulation is to be avoided. It is as one pure that you shall always partake of the death-meal (çrāddha). He that gives or shares in a death-meal, and goes to a woman, his fathers must lie that month in the seed " (xiii, 125.42, 24).[2] Further, we find (xiii, 104.29) : " In the first night of the new moon, in the night of the full moon, in the fourteenth night and in the eighth night of each half of the month you shall always practise complete chastity." [3]

---

[1] Also MBh., xii, 228.73 would belong here, if kaçcic chishyasakho guruḥ has been rightly translated by Deussen : " Now and then the teacher was the disciple's lover " (the immorality which spread among the Daityas is being spoken of). But perhaps it only means that the disciple's reverential relation towards the teacher vanished, and too little restraint, or over-familiarity, came in its stead. As an evil habit of the degenerates it may here be further mentioned that the men dressed in women's clothes and the women in men's, and they so associated with one another (çl. 68), which reminds us of other phenomena known. Cp. xiii, 104.85.—The passage in the text (iii, 190.45, 50) could, it is true, also be speaking only of adultery.

[2] The same threat is in Mārk.-Pur., xxxi, 31–34, while according to Vasishtha, xi, 37 they have to live on the seed. Cp. Manu, iii, 250; Gautama, xv, 22. The sinner himself goes to hell. Garuḍa-purāṇasārod., iv, 41.

[3] Not on the 8th, 14th, 15th day of the half month (the Parvan days) nor on the four days when the moon changes must love be indulged in. Baudh., i, 11, 21.18 (cp. 22); Vasishtha, xii, 21; Manu, iii, 45; iv, 128; Yājñav., i, 79; Vishṇu, lxix, 1; Mārk.-Pur., xxxiv, 43–44. Otherwise the sinner goes to hell. Garuḍa-purāṇasārod., iv, 41. The root of these (and of who knows how many similar and seemingly purely ethical) precepts is shown quite correctly in Baudhāyana, i, 11, 21.19 : " On the Parvan days evil spirits are in wait." Especially dangerous then are naturally an empty house, a graveyard, a tree, water, etc. (see e.g. Vishṇu, lxix, 7, 8 ; MBh., xiii, 131.4 f.; i, 170.8–11 ; 15 f.; 69; Manu, xi, 174 f. (= Agnipur., 169.36 f.)).

Cp. xiii, 104.89 ; 228.45 ; K, xiii, 211.43 ; 233.50. And for the permitted times, too, the rule holds : "Only in the evening (in the night) ! " For the morning belongs to the religious duties, midday to the worldly (artha). Cp. for inﬆance xiii, 22.27 ; vii, 73.38 ff. ; ii, 5.20, and comment. Among the moﬆ dreadful sins coition during the day is given in vii, 73.38 ff. ; so also in xiii, 93.121 ; 94.24 ; and in the self-cursing formula of Arjuna, already given (vii, 73.41, 43).[1]

---

[1] The same prohibition is in the law books. According to Mārk.-Pur., xiv, 74, 76 he that copulates by day is badly tortured in hell. So in other Purāṇas. Furthermore in the morning and at twilight continence muﬆ be observed. Mārk.-Pur., xxxiv, 82.73 ; Vish-ṇusmṛiti, lxix, 10. And in a vehicle muﬆ Venus not be sacrificed to (e.g. Manu, xi, 175 ; Vishṇu, liii, 4 ; Agnipur., 169.37 (= Manu, 175, cp. Meyer, *Altind. Rechtsschr.*, 237)). Thus then the conduﬆ of the loving couples in Flaubert's *Madame Bovary* and Maupassant's *Bel-Ami* and doubtless elsewhere, who quench their desires in the hired coach, is doubly wicked. Speaking, too, during the "work of darkness" is banned (Agnipur., 166.17a–18a), naturally, as with the other dispositions there given, so as not to arouse evil influences. A shorter compilation of rules for sexual intercourse with the wife is to be found in Manu, iii, 45 (cp. Bühler's parallels), and a good one, somewhat more in detail, in Vishṇu, lxix ; particularly excellent is Carakasaṃhitā, iv, 8, and good, too, is Garuḍapur., Pretakalpa, xxxii, 7–19 ; Bṛihat-saṃh., 78.11 ff. ; etc. Much that is beautiful is given us, for inﬆance, in Vishṇupurāṇa, iii, 11.110 ff., a passage which may here be given as an example of such similar precepts often to be found in the law books and other writings : "At the time of the ṛitu do thou, O lord of the earth, approach thy wife, happy, under a conﬆellation bearing a masculine name, at a propitious time, during the beﬆ even-numbered nights. But go not to the unbathed woman, to the sick one, to the menﬆruating one, not to her without desire, not to the angry one, not ·to one in ill-repute, not to one with child, not to one uncoṁplaisant, not to her that longs for another man or is without love (or : that is unwilling), not to another man's wife, not to one that is faint with hunger, not to one that has overeaten. Nor do thou thyself be weighed down with such qualities as these. Bathed, wearing a wreath and scented, bursting with ﬆrength (sphīta), not wearied or hungry, filled with love and tender inclination, let the man go to sexual union. The fourteenth and the eighth day of the half-month, the day of the new moon, as also the day of the full moon and also the

THE PLEASURES OF SEX

But the Epic particularly often stresses the prohibition against a man embracing any woman other than his own wife. This has already been touched on. A few more passages are given here. He who in other things is pious, and is content with his own wife, and does not even in thought covet another woman, wins a glorious lot in the other world, and the same merit even as one that offers a thousand horse-sacrifices (xiii, 107.10, 50 ff.).[1] Subhadrā bewailing her son, says in

day when the sun comes into a new house of the zodiac—these are the Parvan days, O ruler of princes. The man who on these Parvan days partakes of oil, flesh, and woman goes after death to hell, where dung and urine must be his food. . . . Neither outside the vulva, nor in the vulva of another (not human) being, nor using medicines (exciting or strengthening the manly powers), nor in the house of a Brahman, a god, or a Guru, let a man give himself up to love's pleasures, nor near holy trees (or : village shrines, caitya), nor by cross-roads, nor in places where many roads meet, nor in grave-yards, nor in groves, nor in the water, O lord of the earth. Neither on the Parvan days named, nor in either twilight, nor troubled by urine or stool, must the wise man go to the joyful union. Copulation on the Parvan days brings misfortune on men, that by day brings evil (or : sin), that done on the ground has sickness after it, and calamitous is that done in water. Let none ever approach the wedded wife of another, not even in thought, how much less in words. Not even longing (asthibandha) have those who lie with such a woman ; after death such a man goes to hell, and already here his life is shortened. Intercourse with the wedded wife of another is destruction for men, even in both worlds. Mindful of this, let the wise man go to his own wife, when she is in her ritu and free from the blemishes already told ; and if she has a longing for love, then even outside the ritu." (Translated after the Bomb. edit. Çāka 1811.) The places and times here set forth, but not exhaustively, have of course become tabu because of their magical danger. A highly instructive parallel to them is offered, for example, by the monstrously intricate rules of behaviour for the Snātaka, which take up so much room in the Gṛihya-sūtras, the law books, and the Purāṇas, and form a real store-house for the history of superstition and of mankind.

[1] But he has also the duty laid on him to speak no untruth, even for his father and mother, to sacrifice to the fire god constantly for twelve months, and to eat havis, when the eleventh day has come ; and as the two last-mentioned things are extraordinarily meritorious,

vii, 78.24 : " Go thou, my little son, to the same place whither come through their chaſtity the Munis obeying ſtriĉt vows, and whither come the men with but one wife " (cp. çl. 31.32). " The men who find delight only in their own wife, and ever aĉt towards other women as they do towards their mother, their siſter, their daughter, they whose eyes through good ways of life are shut to ſtrange women, who do no hurt to ſtrange women even in thought, even when these women approach them secretly with love—such men come into heaven " (xiii, 144.10–15 ; 33). In the long and solemn imprecatory formula wherein Bharata wishes all the moſt dreadful horrors and evils for him who has been glad to see Rāma banished, he also says : " May the evil-minded one, with whose consent the noble one went forth, set in the second place his wife that has bathed after her period and is keeping her ritu ! Given up to the pleasures of a love againſt law and virtue, blinded, may he leave his own wife on one side, and consort with other women, he with whose consent the noble one went forth ! " (Rām., ii, 75.52, 55). Mahābhārata, xii, 90.32 says emphatically : " With unknown women, with such beings as belong to the third sex, with women of loose morals, with the wives of others, and with maidens let not a man have union." Besides the unknown woman, the woman with child is named as forbidden in xiii, 104.47.[1] Furthermore, we read (xiii, 104.20 ff.) : In all caſtes a man muſt never approach the wife of another. For there is nought in the world which so shortens life as that the man on earth should visit the wife of another (= Manu, iv, 134). As many pores as are on women's bodies, so many years will he sit in

the chaſtity and truthfulness that is demanded besides them, play, anyhow in the present text, a secondary part.

[1] The prohibition of intercourse with the pregnant woman is well known to be widespread throughout the world, and of course above all because the pregnant woman is looked on as unclean and bringing disaſter. See Ploss-Bartels [4], i, 601 ff. ; Elsie Clews Parsons, *The Old-Fashioned Woman* (1913), p. 80 ff. If her bare shadow falls on a snake, it becomes blind. Crooke, *Pop. Rel.*, ii, 143. And yet Vasishṭha, xii, 24, at leaſt, brings forward an old and holy authority for women being allowed to share in the sport of love, even when far advanced in pregnancy, in virtue of a favour granted them by Indra.

hell. "Men who give themselves up to promiscuous intercourse (prakīrṇamaithuna) have, as men of vice and spurners of
order, a short life, go to hell, and invite their being
reborn impotent " (xiii, 104.12 ; 145.53).[1] He that
touches another's wife is born as a wolf, as a dog, as a jackal,
then born as a vulture, a snake, a heron, as also a crane (baka).
The blinded villain who defiles his brother's wife becomes for a
year a kokila cock. He that to slake his luſt lays hands on the
wife of his friend (cf. xiii, 101.16), of his teacher (guru), or of
the king, is born after death as a swine. He will be five years a
swine, ten years a porcupine, five years a cat, ten years a cock,
three months an ant, one month an inseƈt (kīṭa), and then,
having had these embodiments (saṃsāra, cp. iii, 183.70), will be
born in a worm's exiſtence (kṛimiyoni). In this worm's
exiſtence he will live fourteen months, and then, having atoned
for his evil (adharma), be born again as a human being
(xiii, 111.75 ff.). For five offences, indeed, there is no atonement (nishkṛiti), through them a man becomes an outcaſt,
unworthy of intercourse (asambhāshya) with forefathers, gods,[2]
and pious men, goes to hell, is roaſted there like a fish, and has
to live there on matter and blood. These are : the murder of
a Brahman, cow-slaying, intercourse with another's wife,
unbelief, and living on a woman (xiii, 130.37–40). In the
same way Rām., iii, 38.30 teaches : "There is no greater sin
than to touch another's wife." On the other hand xii, 35.25
prescribes, indeed, an atonement for him that seduces the wife
of another ; but it is noteworthy that it is the same vow of
mortification that is also laid on the Brahmṇan-murderer. The
former, however, only need keep it for a year. "Then he is
free of his sin." This punishment falls on him "as a robber of
another's property " (paradārāpahārī tu parasyāpaharan vasu).
The matter is in xiii, 129.1–4, looked at from the same, though
sharper defined, ſtandpoint : He that lies with another man's
wife has to bear the same guilt as he that takes property
away from a Brahman, which is, indeed, an offence crying to
heaven. He is equal to a Brahman-murderer (v, 35.46 ff.). But if

[1] They also fall out of the caſte (e.g. Agnipur., p. 644).
[2] The explanation of this expression given in xiii, 130.3 is that gods
and forefathers scorn his sacrificial gift.

247

the Brahman himself takes some woman who is not his wedded wife to his bed, then to atone for his guilt he muſt lie with his (bare) back on the grass (xii, 165.28), and so, and only in three years does he wipe out the sin of a night. The member of the prieſtly caſte becomes apankteya, loses his social position, if he is a pander or brothel-keeper (kuṇḍāçin), has his wife's lover living in the house (that is probably, also makes profit from him), and if he visits the wife of another. On the other hand he is deemed to be a brahmacārin or continent man, if he at the time of the ṛitu always embraces his lawful wife (xiii, 9.7 ff., 28, 29 ; 89.7–9).[1] But also the noble view that sexual self-control is the holy and pure thing finds expression. In xii, 269.27 Kapila sets forth the rule : " Let the man delight no woman that is the wife of a hero,[2] nor let him call a woman when she is not in the ṛitu ; let him keep in his person the pious vow of wedded faith (bhāryāvrata).[3] Thus will the gate of his sexual parts be warded." [4] There is then the magnificent verse, xii, 210.37, wherein the body is called "the holy city with the nine gates" (navadvāraṃ puraṃ puṇyaṃ).[5] Among the four

---

[1] That the prieſtly caſte in Old India was not so very diſtinguished for its chaſte living is shown indeed by this passage, but ſtill more so by many others in the literature. But it is well to use some care in accepting tales of prieſts not only among ourselves, but also in the Hindu land. According to an old proverb the he-goat and a Veda-learned Brahman are the lewdeſt of beings. Āpaſt., ii, 6, 14.13. In the Epic, however, what is told of them does not give a particularly unfavourable piĉture of their sexual morality. That they anyhow preached a loftier sexual ethic is also shown by numerous passages in the Epic.

[2] It would be quite easy inſtead of vīrapatnīm to read vīrāpatnīm, " let him delight no woman that is not his wife, O hero." But a hero's wife is very dangerous (xii, 82.51).

[3] So Manu, ix, 101, enjoins : " Unto death shall they keep wedded faith one to another. This in a word is what is to be recognized as the higheſt duty of wife and husband."

[4] The often-appearing thought of the gates of the human body is then dealt with in the following çloka, and appears, too, elsewhere in the Epic.

[5] What is probably meant is the nine openings (srotas, kha, chidra): mouth, noſtrils, ears, eyes, anus, penis. The wholly arbitrary interpretation of Nīlakaṇṭha is, indeed, different, and besides it there is a like one

gates that muft be watched over is found the male member, both in xii, 269.23 ff., and in xii, 299 28 ; 335.4.[1] If the wife is unfaithful to the husband or the husband to the wife, then this is an evil ftate of things which forebodes universal and dreadful disafter (xvi, 2.11). Of course, he, too, is a wicked man who helps others to adultery : " He that seduces or touches another's wife, or gets her for another, goes to hell " (xiii, 23.61).[2]

in vi, 29, 13. But later on I see that he gives in xiv, 42, 56 the same interpretation as myself. In the passage before us we could as againft the scholiaft choose rather to give the five sense organs and the five active organs according to çl. 30, but to reckon the tongue and speech as one only, thus : ear, eye, skin, tongue, nose, anus, generative member, hand, foot. This, too, seems to be pointed to by çl. 32, which then would be translated : " In perceiving tafte it is called tongue, in uttering it is called speech." Cp. xii, 210.32. Not so beautiful, but on the other hand more common, not in India alone, is the well-known view that the body and its openings are clean above, unclean below the navel. Baudhāyana, i, 5, 10.19 (= i, 5.75 ; according to Taitt.-Samh., vi, 1, 3.4) ; Vishnu, xxiii, 31 ; Manu, v, 132 ; Cp. Meyer, *Altind. Rechtsschr.*, p. 9. Therefore it is that at death the soul of the good man escapes through one of the upper openings, the soul of the bad man through the lower ones. For inftance, Agnipur., 371.3 ff ; Garudapurāṇasārod., ix, 36 f.; Crooke, *Anthropos*, iv, 468 (in the laft-mentioned that of the bad man through the anus, that of the pious man through brahmarandhra).

[1] The three others are arms (and feet), the tongue, and the belly.

[2] The views held in the law literature and the Purāṇas on intercourse with the woman that is not one's wedded wife, but particularly with the wife of another, are no less severe. Here we can only give a few inftances. The adulterer has a short life and goes to a hell of torment. Mārk.-Pur., xxxiv, 62 ; xiv, 76 ; Agnipur., 203.15, 20. He shall be put to death, unless he is a Brahman. Baudh., ii, 2, 4.1 ; Manu, viii, 539 (cp. 352 f.). In adultery the man's penis and tefticles are to be cut off, in evil-doing with a maiden his property shall be seized, and he banished from the land. Āpaft., ii, 10, 26.20–21 ; 27.1. The king muft then shield such women and maidens from ftain and hand them over to their guardian, if they promise to undertake the prescribed penances. When they have done these they muft be treated as they were before their fall. Cp. Meyer, *Altind. Rechtsschr.*, index under " Ehebruch ". Besides these, however, there are also lighter punish-

ments : chaſtity for so many years, a year of the Mahāvrata mortification, the higheſt possible and also lower money fines, and so forth. The adulterer is a thief (caura). Yājñav., ii, 301, etc. (cp. Saṃyuttanikāya, ii, p. 188). Intercourse with another's wife is reckoned among criminal deeds of violence (Nārada, xvi, 2), and according to 6, along with murder of any kind it belongs to the worſt class of all. The punishments are : Not less than 1,000 paṇa fine, confiscation of all property, banishment, branding, cutting off the offending member, death (8). Cp. Bṛihaspati, xxii, 1. So, as in robbery and violence, in adultery also the witnesses are not to be, as happens in other cases, most carefully examined firſt, but anyone can here be a witness. Manu, viii, 72 ; Nārada, i, 189 (p. 101 in Jolly's edit.) ; Yajñav., ii, 72 ; Vishṇu, viii, 6. The adulterer, indeed, is reckoned among the seven kinds of murderers (ātatāyin), as the man, too, who raises his hand to utter a curse againſt another, and he that makes use of a deſtructive magic from the Atharvaveda againſt another man ; and as a murderer he can be slain without further ado. Vishṇu, v, 189 ff. Cp. MBh. K, xii, 14.79–83. So Mahānirvāṇatantra, xi, 53 enjoins : If a man comes upon his wife in another man's arms, and kills both, then the king muſt not punish him. A memorable case out of Rājput hiſtory is told by Tod, Rājaſthan, ii, 523 : Prince Gopināth of Bundi goes in the night to a Brahman's wife. The husband takes and in the end binds him, goes to the sinner's royal father, and announces he has taken a thief who has ſtolen his honour. What did the man deserve ? " Death." The injured man hurries home, beats in the prince's head with a hammer, and throws him into the ſtreet. The king, his father, silently submits. Among the Gurkhas, who are said to descend from the Rājputs, the husband kills the adulterer publicly. Wright, Hiſt. of Nepal, 32. In the case of certain women there can be no queſtion whatever of adultery. The wives of actors and singers have already been mentioned on this point. As to the abhisārikā see later. The following can be freely visited : the public harlot (veçyā), the svairiṇī, if she is not a Brahman, and the slave-woman who is not held back (demanded) by her maſter (dāsī nishkāsiṇī " who may go out freely "). But intercourse with such women as these (bhujishyā) is adultery too, if they are the concubines (parigraha) of another man. So Nārada, xii, 78 f. But on the other hand, Bṛihaspati, xv, 7 says : He that lies with the slave-girl of a man becomes himself his slave. And in other places too she is found not without protection. Yājñav., ii, 290 lays down : In the case of confiscated serving-women and slave-women (harlots ? avaruddhāsu dāsīshu bhujishyāsu tathaiva ca) the man muſt pay a 50 paṇa fine. Cp. Kauṭilya (transl.), 311.10 ff. ; Manu, viii, 363. The svairiṇī

THE PLEASURES OF SEX

In the Epic, intercourse with the teacher's wife is often marked out as peculiarly shameful. Such a sinner is reincarnated as one without manly powers (xiii, 145.53 ; see also xiii, 111.64 ff., and cp. Manu, xi, 49 ; xii, 58). The atoning punishment here is as follows : " He that ſtains (gurutalpin) the teacher's bed shall seat himself on a glowing iron plate (çilāṃ taptām ayasīṃ),[1] cut off his own member, and go away with uplifted eyes. Freed from his body, he is freed from his

is according to Nārada, xii, 49 ff. of four kinds : (1) the woman who leaves her husband, and for love lives with another man ; (2) she who after her husband's death rejeĉts her brothers-in-law and other kinsmen of her husband, and for love unites herself with a ſtranger ; (3) she who through want, or, being bought for money, gives herself to a man ; (4) she who after a lawful marriage is made the wife of another by force. The earlier one among these four is always worse than the one following. Elsewhere the analyses of the concepts are less detailed. Yājñav., i, 67 says that her lover muſt be of the same caſte if the name svairiṇī is to hold. And the nearer determination of what adultery really is leaves nothing to wish for on the score of severity. Especially detailed are Manu, viii, 354–363 ; Nārada, xii, 62–69 ; Yājñav., ii, 283 ff. ; Bṛihaspati, xxiii, 2 ff. He that is together anywhere with the wife of another, as for inſtance at the junĉtion of ſtreams, at bathing-places, in gardens, in foreſts, speaks with her, sports with her, sends her all kinds of gifts, kisses her, winks or smiles at her, touches her on the clothes or ornaments or body, particularly at unseemly places, or lets himself be touched by her there, sits on a bed with her, takes her by the hand, the hair, or the hem of her garment, and so forth, such a one by this commits adultery, although not of equally serious kind in each case. So, too, belong here the sending of a procuress, of a letter, and like aĉtions. Indeed, if a man from vanity, blindness, or boaſtfulness himself says : " I have enjoyed this woman," then he is guilty of adultery (saṃgrahaṇa) according to the holy tradition (Nārada, xii, 69). Maithuna (copulation), indeed, is according to old Indian teaching eightfold : smaraṇa (thinking of it), kīrtana (speaking of it), keli (dallying), prekshaṇa (viewing), guhyabhāshaṇa (secret converse), saṃkalpa (firm will to copulate), adhyavasāya (resolve to do it), kriyānishpatti (the aĉtual accomplishment). Each part is in itself maithuna.

[1] This meaning for çilā is not found, indeed, in the diĉtionaries, but Nīl. anyhow gives for iii, 146.24 the explanation : çilāḥ samapashāṇāḥ çayanāsanayogyāḥ, upalās tadanye.

251

unclean deed ; women are redeemed from such-like deeds by making earnest endeavour (yatta, according to Nīl., making abstention in food and pleasure) for a year. But he who carries out the ' great vow ',[1] and gives away even all his possessions, or for the sake of the teacher is killed in battle, sets himself free of his unclean deed " (xii, 35.20 ff.). " The evil-begotten, evil-minded man that violates his master's marriage-bed is made clean by clasping a glowing statue with the shape of a woman, and so meeting death. Or let him take his penis and testicles [2] himself into his hand, and go straight off into the region of the Nirṛiti (to the south-east) till he falls down (dead), or else give up his life on behalf of a Brahman ; thereby he becomes clean.[3] Or he receives honour here and after death,

---

[1] The " great vow " (mahāvrata) is the giving up even of water for a month. Nīl.

[2] All three of which he has himself cut off.

[3] The same bloody punishment by loss of manhood, etc., is found in Manu, xi, 105 f. ; Āpast., i, 9, 25.1 ; Gaut., xxiii, 10 ; Vas., xx, 13 ; Baudh., ii, 1, 1.15 ; Yājñav., iii, 259. According to Manu, xi, 104 ; Gaut., xxiii, 8 ; Baudh., ii, 1, 1.13, the offender is to burn himself on a glowing iron bed (gridiron) ; according to Manu, xi, 1 ; Āpast., i, 9, 25.2 ; Gaut., xxiii, 9 ; Vas., xx, 14, he is to clasp the glowing iron figure of a woman ; he is to be burned in a hollow iron statue, under which fire is stirred up, according to Āpast., i, 10, 28.15 ; Manu, xi, 106 f. Yājñav., iii, 260, lets him be cleansed of his sin through mortifications ; Agnipur., 169.20 adds self-castration to this (cp. 664). Manu, ix, 237 ; Vishṇu, v, 7 ; Nārada, Pariçishṭa, 44 prescribe that the gurutalpin shall be branded with the yoni (vulva) ; so too Agnipur., 227.50. See also Meyer, Kauṭilya, and Altind. Rechtsschr., index under " Brandmarkung ". It must not be left unmentioned that this sin also, like so many others, according to Smṛiti can easily be made good so long as it is kept hidden, namely by lip-penance and purse-mortification, that is, by grinding out mantras (Manu, xi, 252), and at the same time making the pious gift of a milch-cow (Yājñav., iii, 305). But on the other hand Smṛiti speaks of many sexual offences that are the same as the staining of the teacher's marriage-bed, and a long list of women is given who are on the same level with the guru's wife. Here we give only one or two : a woman who is the man's ward, a virgin, the wife of a friend, or of the son, a Pariah woman, the sister's friend, a kinswoman

if he makes a horse-sacrifice or a gosava or agnishṭoma sacrifice in the rightful way [1] (xii, 165.49 ff.). According to xii, 165.34, this offence, along with the drinking of spirits (surāpāna) and Brahman-murder, is among the monstrous ones for which there is no atonement laid down (anirdeçya), and which can only be made good again by death (cf. Manu, xi, 55). Also for sexual intercourse with a woman of higher caste there is the sharpest punishment. In this case the sinning woman also, whose punishment in general belongs not here, but to the chapter dealing with her relations with her husband, comes under public justice : " As to the woman that sins against her husband, especially if she has been held back, she shall be made to carry out the same expiatory vow as is the man after adultery.[2] If she leaves a better bed to go to another, a worse man,[3] then shall the king have her torn (ardayet) asunder by dogs on a wide public place. But let the wise one put the man on a glowing bed of iron, and let him heap up wood, and there shall the evil-

(sagotrā), a begging nun (pravrajitā). Vishṇu, xxxvi, 4 ff. ; Yājñav., iii, 231 ff. So, too, intercourse with a woman-ascetic is in Nārada, xii, 73 held to be the same as incest (contrariwise Kauṭilya (transl.), 364.12 ff. and Yājñav., ii, 293 in this case have only a 24 paṇa fine. Cp. Kauṭilya 364.35 ff. ; and Manu, viii, 363). That incest, which is given a very wide meaning, can only be wiped out through death by fire, castration, expulsion from the caste, and the like is easily understood. See Bühler's Manu, xi, 171, and the parallels there given, as also Āpast., i, 7, 21.8 ; Nārada, xii, 73 ff. ; Vishṇu, xxxiv ; Parāçara, x, 9–11 ; Agnipur., 173.47 ff. Cp. Meyer, Kauṭilya, 263.31 ff. and addit. Violating the teacher's marriage-bed (gurutalpa) and incest are often in other places not kept apart, which is very natural. Among the four great deadly sins the gurutalpa is always found.

[1] A truly priestly addition, at any rate inserted later, but typical. But the " punishment by study " in Vasishṭha, xxvii, 19, Vishṇu, xxx, 4–8, is just as important, and many like things.

[2] Cp. Manu, xi, 177 f. Those spoken of here are not women who for once forget themselves, but those who are utterly vicious (vipradushṭā) and will have no check or bridle put on them.

[3] That is, if she is unfaithful to a husband of higher caste, especially a Brahman (according to the comment. only such a one is meant), and consorts with one of a lower caste.

doer burn " (xii, 165.63 ff.).[1] Cf. also xiii, 111.89 ff. ; xii, 165.36.

[1] The law books and the Purāṇas no less angrily brand intercourse with a woman below a man's own caſte, and particularly with one above it. The Brahman who lies with a slave-woman goes to hell (Garuḍapurāṇasārod., iv, 37) ; if he goes to a Pariah woman he becomes a Pariah himself (Baudh., ii, 2, 4.14 = ii, 2.67 ; Manu, xi, 176) ; he is the same as the defiler of the teacher's marriage-bed (Yājñav., iii, 231). The man of the three upper caſtes who lies with a Çūdrā woman muſt be banished (Āpaſt., ii, 10, 27.8). The man without honour who demeans himself to an antyā (woman on the loweſt rung of the social ladder) muſt be put to death (Vishṇu, v, 43), or branded and banished ; a Çūdra man so doing becomes himself an antya (the antya who goes to an āryā or woman of the three upper caſtes is, of course, put to death). Yajñav., ii, 294. According to Parāçara, vii, 8 the Brahman who lies one night with a Çūdrā woman muſt live for three years on alms, and recite mantras daily ; while x, 5 ff. lays down for intercourse with a Pariah woman fixed penalties, which also consiſt of gifts of oxen. It is significant that it is the Çūdra man who suffers moſt here, and so upwards to the Brahman, who only has to faſt for three nights. Manu punishes intercourse with a woman of lower caſte by heavy fines (viii, 373 ; 382–5). Āpaſtamba, ii, 10, 27.8 punishes with banishment the man of the three upper caſtes who finds delight with a Çūdrā woman. Naturally the dragging down of a woman is a ſtill worse thing. A Kshattriya, Vaiçya, or Çūdra who lies with a Brahman woman is burnt. This same fate befalls the Çūdra man who sins with a Kshattriyā or a Vaiçyā woman, and the Vaiçya man who sins with a Kshattriyā woman. Vasishṭha, xxi, 1–5. There is at leaſt this much, however, that good grass, but less so as we go down the caſtes, is used for this fiery cleansing. It is in a fire of ſtraw according to Baudh., ii, 2.52 f. that the Çūdra man suffers death ; others muſt keep chaſte for a year (but cp. the commentator). The man's death alone can atone for his intercourse with a woman of a higher caſte (Nārada, xii, 70 ; Yājñav., ii, 286). If a Çūdra has intercourse with an Āryā woman, then his penis is cut off and his property confiscated ; if the woman was a ward he is put to death. Gaut., xii, 2 f. ; Manu, viii, 374. Āpaſt., ii, 10, 27.9–10 simply enjoins execution for this case. Heavy punishment also befalls according to Manu, viii, 375, the Kshattriya or the Vaiçya man who defiles a Brahman woman, in certain circumstances even death by fire like the Çūdra man. And so on with other cases. The woman who thus lowers herself comes out of it, according to many

codes of law with very little harm, but according to others very badly. The glance of the woman who has had to do with a man from a caste below her, like the Çūdra man, makes unclean. Āpast., i, 3, 9.11–12. Āpast., ii, 10, 27.10, condemns the woman who commits adultery with a Çūdra man to fasting and mortification only. Vasishṭha, xxi, 1–5 ordains as follows : The Brahman woman who had to do with a Çūdra, a Vaiçya, or a Kshattriya man has her head shaven, her body smeared over with butter, and is led naked along the street on an ass, which is black where the intercourse was with a Çūdra man, yellow for a Vaiçya man, white for a Kshattriya man ; thus she is cleansed again. 13 prescribes, according to the caste of the fellow-offender, various mortifications (cp. 20) for the adulteress who lets herself be embraced by a man under her rank. It seems therefore to be a question whether the sinning woman has done more evil or less, as Bühler holds (cp. e.g. Manu, xi, 177, 178). So also Baudh., ii, 3.49 ff. But according to Vas., xxi, 12 a woman of the three higher castes who has received a Çūdra man can be rid of her guilt by making an atonement, only if she has not got with child thereby; and in any case, if she sinks still lower, then she must be cast out (10). If a woman does wrong with a man below her caste, she has to suffer, according to Yājñav., ii, 286, the cutting off of her ears, and suchlike punishment (= Agnipur., 258.69b). Yājñav., iii, 298 declares : The principal offences of a woman leading to loss of caste are : intercourse with the low (nīca), abortion, and murder of her husband. So essentially Gautama, xxi, 9. Parāçara, x, 16–19, as already mentioned, lets her that has been ravished by a Pariah be cleansed by the penance in the well, and rites of purification and mortification, and then by her monthly course. The same punishment as in the MBh. falls on the woman committing the crime of having connection with a man of a lower caste (nihīnavarṇagamana) according also to Gaut., xxiii, 14. According to Manu, viii, 371 f. the haughty (jñāti-strīguṇadarpitā) adulteress and her fellow are to have their reward in the way given in the Epic. For this purpose there are specially trained dogs (Manu, viii, 371 ; Agnipur., 227.42). So too Bṛihaspati, xxiii, 15, prescribes this death (or mutilation) for the bold woman who herself comes into the man's house, and seduces him ; the man thus surprised naturally comes off more lightly. The inveterate adulteress is in general put to death (Vishṇu, v, 18) ; and Yājñav., ii, 279 f. ordains : A wholly bad woman, such a one as has killed a man or destroyed a dam is to be drowned with stones round her neck, unless she be with child. Of a woman that makes poison, of one that is an incendiary, or of one who slays husband, guru, or child, the ears, nose, lips and hands shall be cut off, and she be put to death by bulls. But

255

A man shall not even look on a stranger naked woman (xii, 193.17).[1] The evil-doer who looks with sinful eyes on a naked woman is born again as a weakling (xiii, 145.51 ; 162.47) ; and he that looks on his neighbour's wife with impure eyes comes into the world blind at birth for his wickedness (çl. 50). Involuntary shedding of seed must also be atoned for,[2] husband and wife are reminded not to bring one another before the court of justice (Nārada, xii, 89). It is for the husband in the first place to punish the adulteress. Of this more will be said later. Of course the Epic, the law writings and the Purāṇas threaten the Çūdra especially, who embraces a Brahman woman, with the most awful Saṃsāra punishment ; and according to MBh., xii, 165.35, 36 if a man not a Brahman and a Brahman woman have relations with one another, loss of caste follows, as also with agamyāgamana. Cp. Meyer, Kauṭilya, 263.31 ff.

The treatment, given in the text, following xii, 165, of the woman who defiles herself with a man below her rank has particularly roused horror in Professor Hopkins. We may here be reminded of our own forefathers, who were after all very well-inclined to women. " No free maiden could marry a man of the servile class without suffering servitude or capital punishment. . . . The Burgundian law provided that both the free maiden and the slave be slain. . . . Among the Goths, if a free woman married her own servant they were both to be flogged in public and burned at the stake" (Rullkoetter, The Legal Protection of Woman Among the Ancient Germans, Chicago, 1900, pp. 58, 59). Among certain South Sea islanders the nobleman marrying a girl from the people was punished by death (Westermarck, 370 f. after Waitz-Gerland). Noblesse oblige : the heavy punishment falls on him who is high, for he must show himself worthy of the honour he gets, and avoid any debasing of himself. Among the Old Indians it is never marriage but adultery with such a man that is the object of these threats.

[1] Cp. Vishṇupur., iii, 12.12 ; Mārk.-Pur., xxxiv, 23 ; Manu, iv, 53 ; Vishṇu, lxxi, 26 ; Yājñav., i, 135 ; Gautama, ix, 48. Cp. Meyer, Altind. Rechtsschr., index under " Nacktheit ".

[2] Cp. Manu, ii, 181 f. ; Gaut., xxiii, 20 ; Vishṇu, xxviii, 51 (and the parallels in Jolly's transl.) ; Yājñav., iii, 278 ; Baudhāyana, ii, 1.28 (= ii, 1, 1.29). Onanism is also of course punished. Of special importance is this in the case of the brahmacārin (the disciple bound to chastity). According to Vasishṭha, xxiii, 4 this offence must be atoned for in just the same way as the Veda-learner's intercourse with a woman. Cp. Manu, ii, 180. But if the brahmacārin goes

and this according to xii, 34.26, is done by a fire-offering. Seed and the shedding of seed is, indeed, magically dangerous. It also belongs to full chastity, as already mentioned, that a man should not know a woman (prajānāti, i, 64.117) before she has reached puberty (aprāptayauvana). Perhaps the heights of considerate chastity are reached by Nakula, the hero beautiful, " most worthy of gaze in all the world," who goes off into banishment plastered with dust all over his body, as he does not wish to turn the women's heads on the way (ii, 80.6.18).

It is in the light, then, of the passages given on the importance of offspring that the ordinance in xii, 35.27 must be understood, which seems to be at variance with the commandments of chastity : " If a man is begged for it (bhikshite) as for a pious alms, lying with the wife of another does not put a stain on law and virtue." The commentator says : If a man is begged by a woman for the dharma's sake : " Pour in the seed ! " And as this half verse stands in a didactic discourse highly tinged with Brahman views, Nīl. is undoubtedly right, and we hardly need have in thought a generous chivalry on the man's, namely the warrior's, side, such as comes into the myth of Çarmishthā and Yayāti.[1]

to a woman (avakīrṇin), then according to MBh., xii, 24 he must be clad for six months in an ox-skin and carry out the penance of the Brahman-murderer, and also in xii, 34.1 ff. his name is given along with the slayer of a man of the priestly class and other wicked evil-doers, and prāyaçcitta (atonement) is imposed on him. Cp. v, 38.4. According to the law writings he gets cleansed again by sacrificing in the night at a cross-ways to Nirṛiti (goddess of corruption) a (one-eyed) ass. The sinner must put on the ass's skin with the hair outside, and (with a red begging-bowl) beg at seven houses, making known his deed. (He must eat only once a day, and bathe in the morning, at midday, and in the evening.) Besides this other offerings and atonement rites are also given. Baudhāyana, ii, 1.29–34 ; iii, 4 ; iv, 2.10 f. ; Āpast., i, 9, 26.8 ; Vasishṭha, xxiii, 1–3 ; Manu, xi, 119–124 ; Yājñav., iii, 280 ; Vishṇu, xxviii, 48 ff. ; Gautama, xxiii, 17–19 ; xxv, 1–5 ; Pārask.-Gṛihyas., iii, 12.1 ff. ; Agnipur., 169.15b–18a (essentially = Manu, xi, 119 ff.). Any other self-polluter comes off lightly (bathing, Vishṇu, liii, 4, etc. ; to say the Gāyatrī a thousand times, and three times to hold the breath [prāṇāyāma] in Parāçara, xii, 63 ; and so on). Cp. Baudh., iii, 7.1–7 ; iv, 2.13 ; Āpast., i, 9, 26.7 ; Manu, xi, 174 ; Vishṇu, liii, 4 ; Gaut., xxv, 7.

[1] Cp. too the words of this king in i, 83.32–34.

VIII

The Continence of Man

NOT only is the refraining from adultery a part of the five-fold dharma (xiii, 141.25), but the Epic, as does Indian literature so often, declares : " Chastity is the highest virtue " (or : the highest law, brahmacaryam paro dharmah, e.g. in i, 170.71). In this passage it is not a question of the purity of the ascetic, but since Arjuna is living a chaste life—the scene belongs to the time when the brothers are going to Draupadī's choosing a husband—he can overcome the Gandharva Aṅgāraparṇa during the night. Now Arjuna, at least later on, is no very great paragon of chastity, for during the twelve years' continence he undertakes he has various erotic adventures (with Citrāṅgadā, i, 215 ; with Subhadrā, i, 219 ff.). The instructive either-or that the snake fairy Ulūpī then forces on his conscience does not give him much difficulty : the love-fired lady puts it before him (as happened to the young hero in Barlaam and Josaphat and to others in East and West) that by rejecting her he will also have her death on his soul ; and he is at once ready to save the fair one's life (i, 214). Bhīshma, on the other hand, who for love of his father, has renounced all the joys of love and family, takes his vow very earnestly, and will not have the slightest thing to do with anything that is woman, that is called woman, or has anything whatever in common with woman. See especially v, 172.16–20, and Nīlakaṇtha's gloss. By Çiçupāla, who in this is certainly not alone, he is indeed most basely suspected because of his rare virtue (ii, 41.2, 25 ; 42.8).

Naturally in the Epic, too, the ascetic shines in the most glorious of haloes, and great is the worth and the might of his utter renunciation of sex. Bhīshma thus teaches Yudhishthira : " He that on earth from birth to death observes chastity, for him there is nothing beyond reach, know this, O herdsman of men. But many tens of millions of Rishis live in the world

258

of Brahma who take their pleasure in the Truth, ever bridle their senses, and keep wholly continent. Continence that is practised burns up all that is evil, especially in the Brahman, for the Brahman is called a fire " (xiii, 75.35 ff.). Divine in the word's deepest meaning is this virtue, but it is not an easy one. Thus in xii, 214.7 ff. we find : " As to that form of Brahman (the divine Absolute and First Cause, the Ātman) called Chastity, it stands higher than any of the virtues (religious ordinances) ; through it we come into the highest Being, into the Featureless, the Unconnected, which is taken out of the realm of sound and sensation, which, through the ear is hearing, and through the eye seeing, which as speech proceeds from speaking, and which is without manas. Let a man make the firm resolve of (this Brahman, of) spotless chastity, through the channel of the buddhi. He that lives wholly therein reaches the world of Brahman, he of the moderate life therein reaches the gods, and he that is with knowledge, who only gives himself up to the lesser practice of it, is born again as one that stands out among the Brahmans. Hard indeed is chastity. Hear, then, the way from me. The passion that has kindled and risen let the twice-born one keep under. Let him not give ear to speech of women,[1] nor gaze upon them, when they are unclothed. In some way or other through the sight of them passion may take hold of the weak man. If passion arises in him, then let him undergo mortification.[2] If he is in great erotic straits,[3] then let him put himself in water. If he is

[1] This can mean : " women's speech " or " speech about women ". The very sound of woman's voice inflames the heart, as Buddhistic tales, especially, show.

[2] Or as the commentator says : the vow of fasting, which consists in his eating only in the morning for three days, then for three days only in the evening, for three days more eating what he has got without asking, and the three last days nothing at all. Cp. Manu, xi, 212, and the parallels therewith.

[3] Mahārti. Cp. in my translation of Kshemendra's Samayamā-trikā, p. 59, note 1 ; MBh., iii, 46.44 ; Divyāvadāna (ed. Cowell and Neil), pp. 254, 255 (kleça and roga = hot desire) ; Dāmodaragupta's Kuṭṭanīmatam in my transl., pp. 59, 131. There vyādhi is anyhow = hot desire. With kaṇḍū in the same passage cp. the Finnish kutku, itching = hot desire.

overwhelmed[1] in sleep, then let him whisper in his soul thrice the prayer that cleanses sin away.[2] Thus will the wise man burn up the evil that is the inward passion, through his ever ready manas[3] bound up with knowledge."

That even the strictest penitents are not proof against woman is shown by innumerable Indian tales, and by a whole set of them in the Epic. As an irresistible power dwells in perfect asceticism, and heaven and earth are no more than clay in the hands of such a holy one, so even the gods in heaven tremble before him, and Indra, who fears to be dethroned by the mighty one, is well known to send at such times one of the unspeakably lovely fays of heaven, one of the hetæra-like Apsarases, down to the dangerous one. If he is really love-proof, he is usually overpowered by such rage that he sends forth his curse and so crashes down from his heights. It is true that the pious Triçiras ("three heads"), whom a whole troop of these courtesans of paradise seek to seduce with every wanton art, keeps an untroubled peace of soul, and Indra has to slay him with the thunder-bolt (v, 9). But what nearly always happens is that the ascetic is fired with lust, and forgets his chastity. Thus it is with the famed Viçvāmitra, who begets Çakuntalā with the Apsaras Menakā. Indra entrusts this heaven-maiden, surpassing all her sisters in loveliness, with the delicate task. But she sets before him the more than divine deeds of this royal Rishi, and says that he who by the might of his fire burns all the worlds, brings the earth to quake with his foot, can roll up (or : overturn) Mount Meru and the quarters of the world, —he that before now has made new worlds with new starry systems will destroy her by fire in his rage. Therefore the

[1] By passion. Or, by the shedding of seed, as the comment. takes it. But this second meaning would not harmonize with the passage just quoted, xii, 34.26.

[2] Or that cleanses evil away (aghamarshana). The reference is to Rgv., x, 190.

[3] The manas, the "inner sense", is the channel for the impressions of the perceptual senses, and brings about the action of the active senses ; so too it is the seat of the wishes, of desire. The buddhi is the faculty " of distinguishing, of determining, of judgment, and of decision." See Garbe, *Sankhyaphilosophie*, pp. 244–72.

king of the deathless ones muſt send with her the god of love and the wind to help. This is done ; and when the enchanting one ſtands before the penitent, the wind is wafted thither laden with foreſt scents, and blows the wanton one's garment away. She bends down haſtily after it, smiling shamefacedly. But Viçvāmitra is so carried away by the charms of her bared body that he invites her to love, " and the faultless one wishes for it, too." The two ſtay together a long age, but it goes by them like one day (i, 71.20 ff.). In the Rāmāyaṇa Menakā happens to bathe near Viçvāmitra, and overborne by love he asks her to lie with him. Ten years go by him, in pleasure and ecſtasy with her, like one day and night. Then he comes to himself, and by fresh mortification sets the gods and Ṛishis in dread. Indra now bids the Apsaras Rambhā to undertake the saving work of seduction. As she is fearful of the adventure so fraught with disaſter, he goes himself to ſtand by her, changed into a kokila-bird, and accompanied by the god of love. The ſtaunchness of the holy man is indeed shaken by the bird's sweet, heart-mazing notes, and the incomparable singing and semblance of the nymph, but he sees that it is a snare of Indra's, and falls into such anger that he curses the temptress into ſtone, and so loses his penitential powers (Rām., i, 63, 64).[1]

Particularly frequent in the Mahābh. are the tales of penitents who at the mere sight of a lovely woman are thrown into an orgasm. Çaradvant, the son of Gotama, not only highly learned in the Veda, but also an eager and skilful bowman, brings torturing pain to the prince of the gods through his asceticism. Indra sends down the heaven-maid Jānapadī to make him human. When the foreſt-brother sees the very lightly clad and enchanting creature, he ſtands there with wide-opened eyes, his bow and arrow fall to the ground, and a shudder goes through his body. He makes, indeed, a brave ſtand, but his excitement drives his seed forth without his noticing it. He leaves his beloved arrow lying there, and flees before the all too dangerous

[1] A free poetical version, fusing the two tales together, is to be found in my collection of poems *Asanka, Sudschata, Tangara und andre Dichtungen*, p. 58 ff. Good, too, is iii, 110.40 : Since Ṛishyaçriṅga in the foreſt away from the world never saw a human being (that is, no woman either) besides his father, therefore remained he so chaſte.

one. Out of his seed, poured into the cane-brake and split into two, arises a twin pair, Kṛipa and Kṛipī, who are found by King Çāntanu when he is hunting, and then adopted (i, 130.1 ff. ; cp. v, 166.20 f. ; 55.49). The zealous ascetic Bharadvāja sees the young Apsaras Ghṛitācī, who, wrapped only in her blinding naked loveliness, is bathing in the river. His seed that escapes in the love-urge he puts in a pitcher (droṇa), and Droṇa comes into being, the famous teacher of arms to the Pāṇḍavas and other princes (i, 130.33 ff. ; i, 166.1 ff.).[1] ix, 48.64 ff. tells us that Bharadvāja's seed, that came forth because of Ghṛitācī, dropped into a leaf packet and thus gave life to Çrutāvatī. Thus, too, it is Ghṛitācī who in like wise helps Vyāsa to get a son. He is juſt then busily engaged getting fire with the two rubbing-ſticks. The lovely one arouses a violent ſtorm of love in his soul, " which surges through all

[1] In this laſt-named passage also the wind carries off the lovely one's garment, while in chap. 130 the drunken wanton seems to let it fall herself on the bank. To bathe naked is, indeed, not the Indian cuſtom ; it is even looked on as a dreadful sin (originally because of the danger of spirits). See note 3, p. 203 of my *Hindu Tales* ; MBh., vii, 73.32, 82.9 ; xiii, 20.1 ff. ; 104.51, 67 ; Kuṭṭanīm., 366 ; Parāsk.-Gṛihyas., ii, 7.6 ; Açva.-Gṛih., iii, 9.6 ; Çaṅkh.-Gṛih., iv, 12.31 ; Gaut., ix, 61 ; Baudh., ii, 3, 6.24 ; Vishṇu, liv, 23 ; lxiv, 5 ; Manu, iv, 45 ; xi, 202 ; Yājñav., iii, 291 ; Mārk.-Pur., xxxiv, 34 ; Agnipur., 155.22 ; Bhāgavatapur., x, 22 (here the shepherdesses are bathing naked, Kṛishṇa carries off their clothes and says in çl. 19 that as they [here indeed as dhṛitavratā] have jumped unclad into the water, they have mocked the gods). Yet even the pious, chaſte wife of Cyavana bathes naked (iii, 123.1), and wholly unclothed bathing women are also often found elsewhere, but especially those of the band of heavenly fays, who in this, too, show the way for their siſter wantons on earth. See, for inſtance, further xii, 333.17 f., 28–30, and in my version of Kshemendra's Samayamātṛikā, p. xviii. Bathing-clothes (in the house) are called snānaçāṭī in xiii, 20.1 ff. Also sleeping naked is forbidden (e.g. Manu, iv, 75 ; Gaut., ix, 60 ; Vishṇu, lxx, 3 ; of course here, too, the fear of magical harm is the real basis). On the other hand it is well known that people in Germany, even, down to Luther's time slept without any clothing whatever, and even later than that time this cuſtom is widespread. See Stratz, *Die Frauenkleidung*, etc. [3], p. 19 ff. ; Max Bauer, *Das Geschlechts-leben i. d. deutsch. Vergangenheit* [2], p. 40.

his limbs, and overwhelms his understanding." But he holds himself in check, and although his seed falls onto the lower fire-stick, he goes on steadfastly, and so in the end twirls his son Çuka into life (xii, 324.1 ff.). Mankanaka, the forest-dweller living in the unspoiled purity of youth, puts his seed into his water-vessel, when, while he is washing in the Sarasvatī, he sees a glorious woman bathing naked, and his semen thus spurts out into the waves. Seven Ṛishis thus arise, the fathers of the wind gods (ix, 38.32). The same gift came to the Sarasvatī from the holy Dadhīca, when at Indra's bidding the Apsaras Alambushā appeared before him. But the river goddess this time took the seed into her bosom, and bore a son, whom the father later welcomed with joy (ix, 51.5 ff.). Ṛishyaçṛiṅga, whom we shall meet with again, has a like origin. But here it is the bathing Kaçyapa who is stirred by the loveliness of Urvaçī. A she-gazelle drinks up the love-sap along with the water, and bears Ṛishyaçṛiṅga (iii, 110.34).[1] Cp. Windisch, *Buddhas Geburt*, etc., p. 21 ; Chavannes, *Cinq cents contes*, ii, 283 ; iii, 234 f. ; Hartland, *Primit. Patern.*, pp. 12 ; 23 f. ; 151 f. ; Weber's *Ind. Studien*, xiv (1875), p. 121 f. ; also MBh., xiii, 85.17 ff.

[1] The same Urvaçī is seen by Varuṇa, the prince of the waters, playing with her girl-friends, who is fired by her, and seeks to lie with her. She tells him that her love, indeed, is his, but her body is Mitra's. But his fire now is too hot, and with her glad consent he discharges the seed into a pitcher, and in this the fruit is formed (Rām., vii, 56.12 ff.). Varuṇa, it is true, is no saint, and his rape of Utathya's wife will be described later on. Cp. further Hartland, *Prim. Patern.*, i, 12, 23, 151 (fertilization by drinking semen). According to K, i, 150, the king of Pañcāla lived a life of sternest penance in the forest that he might get a son. There one day he saw the Apsaras Menakā in the blooming açoka-forest. His seed fell onto the ground, and filled with shame, he trod on it with his feet. From his seed arose King Drupada, the father of Draupadī. Such tales are found already in Vedic times, as the origin of Agastya and Vasishtha shows. Cp. Sieg, *Sagenstoffe d. Rigveda*, p. 105 ff.

IX

The Pleasures of Venal Love

A WAY in the forest the penitent buried himself in the deepest mysteries, or lived piously cut off from the world, and strove earnestly, although not always with complete success, after a stainless chastity ; but in the towns and cities the harlot, often very wealthy and of great distinction and quite often very well educated, went in her splendour along the street, taking to herself the fiery eyes and hearts of the men, but above all their purses—India is the land of sharpest contrasts. And in what civilized land has not "venal love" played its part? The Hindu has always sung the praises of "the public woman" as the very type and embodiment of perfect womanhood.[1] In the Epic, too, as already in the Veda, the woman for sale is something that is a matter of course, even though the enraptured song of praise to these earthly lieutenants of the unembodied god of love, as sung especially in the artificial poetry, is here wanting. Ever since those dim days, when, according to the already told legend of the Mahābh. (i, 104.36), Dīrghatamas, saint, and poet of the Veda songs, blind from birth, brought into the world the pleasures of love granted for ringing coin, the horizontal trade had been flourishing in the land of India ; and if the "public woman, open to the visits of all' (nārī prakāçā sarvagamyā) wore a red garment, a red

---

[1] On her see my three books: Daṇḍin's Daçakumāracaritam, p. 46 ff. and 205 ff., Kshemendra's Samayamātṛikā, and Dāmodaragupta's Kuṭṭanīmatam (all published by Lotosverlag, Leipzig), where, however, I should now like to add much, and in some things to make some changes. See, too, in my Kauṭilya the passages under "Lustdirne". There is no need, perhaps, to make mention of R. Schmidt's excellent works : *Vātsyāyanas Kāmasutra*, *Indische Erotik*, and *Liebe und Ehe in Indien*. In them will be found abundant information on this leading figure in the Indian life of love, or·rather lechery.

wreath, and red gold (viii, 94.26), by this garb, recalling the god of death and the public execution,[1] she was not marked out as something criminal or ill-omened, although, of course, her class took a low rank in the social order, but it was far rather that she mu§t be di§tinguishable for the greater ease and comfort of the world of men, as for in§tance the charitable si§ters of the order of Saint Amor, in the German Middle Ages by their yellow dress so often spoken of.[2]

[1] In a model city, according to Meyer, Kauṭilya, 75.1 ; Agnip., 106.7, they mu§t dwell also in the southern part, that is, in Yama's quarter of the heavens. On red as the colour of death see the good essay of Fr. v. Duhn, " Rot und Tot ", *Arch. f. Religionswissenschaft*, Bd. 9, p. 1 ff.

[2] But the German city-fathers may usually have had quite other ends in view in laying down such marks for them. See, e.g., G. Wu§t-mann, "Frauenhäuser u. freie Frauen i. Mittelalter," *Arch. f. Kultur-gesch.*, Bd. 5, p. 469 ff.; Max Bauer, *Die Dirne u. ihr Anhang*, p. 110 ff. Mantegazza (*Geschlechtsverhältnisse d. Menschen*, p. 363, note) reports a catalogue of the sixteenth century which came out in Venice, and offered for everyone's needs the mo§t exa&t information as to the public women living in this city. Suchlike li§ts from old and from modern times are to be found in Iwan Bloch, *Die Pro§titution*, i, 491. About the red garb of the harlot see Daçakumāracar., p. 51. Red is the mo§t favoured colour on earth (Stratz, *Die Frauenkleidung*[3], p. 74), and also in India the colour of life, passion, love (*Hindu Tales*, p. 106 ; Tod, *Raja§than*, i, 612 ; red at the Holi fe§tival; and so on); it is the mo§t usual colour for women's clothing in the Epic also (e.g. i, 221.19 ; 212.9 ; xii, 296.20 ; xiii, 45.5), and then yellow. Both are very elegant, as yellow was the modish colour, too, in the German Middle Ages. Cp. Billington, *Woman in India*, pp. 76 ; 181 ; 183. Then harlots and criminals like keeping up survivals from a rougher culture, as for in§tance tattooing and a super§titious religiosity among ourselves also (cp. e.g. Maupassant's " Maison Tellier "). As red is so mighty a scarer of demons, it is no doubt on this account that it is to the liking of the always-highly-endangered lightning condu&tors of public vice. At the love visit by night, it is true, Rambhā in the Rām., and Urvaçī in the MBh. wear dark clothing, but naturally to be less seen. The white garments of the fair one ha§tening to the try§t is often mentioned in Indian literature, and made use of for poetical feats of skill. Red wreaths are worn too by the hetæræ of heaven when they make their way to the hour of dalliance (Rām., iv, 24.34),

The veçyā or strumpets are in the Epic, as elsewhere in Indian literature, an important part of the life of the city. When the great fight is to burst forth, and the armies are there fully equipped, Yudhishthira, the pious one, sends into the royal city, among many other more or less tender greetings, one, too, to these granters of delight : " My dear friend, ask after the welfare of the fair-decked, fair-clad, scented, pleasing,

as they are by the earthly abhisārikā. Although according to xiii, 104.84 no red wreaths are to be worn, but only white ones, yet red flowers may be worn on the head. But kamala and kuvalaya are to be altogether avoided. Vishṇu, lxxi, 11–12 is very strong that no red wreaths but water-flowers are to be worn. Cp. Gobhila, Gṛihyas., iii, 5.15. As, indeed, white is in general the lucky colour, and red often the colour of ill-hap, of evil magic, and of death, white wreaths are among the lucky things, red among those foreboding evil. In the main, white flowers are also to be offered to the gods, red ones and black to the spirits (bhūta), and red-flowered plants with prickles serve to bewitch foes. To the Yakshas, Gandharvas, and Nāgas let water-flowers be offered. That Kāma, however, the god of love, was worshipped with red açoka-flowers is shown, for instance, by Gauḍavaho, 754. It is natural that Çiva, the god of the souls of the dead, and of procreation, should wear red wreaths (xii, 284.147). Cp., too, Billington, p. 222 f. Flowers that have grown on a graveyard or in sanctuaries of the gods must not be brought along to the wedding or to the pleasures of love (rahas). See Rām., v, 27 ; ii, 25.28 ; MBh., xiii, 98.28 ff. ; and cp. also Zachariae, Zeitschr. d. Ver. f. Volksk., Bd. 14, p. 303 f., 397, note 3 ; Lewy, Zeitschr. d. Ver. f. Volksk., Bd. 3, p. 136 f. ; then Dubois-Beauchamp [3], p. 645 (red flowers for the bhūta) ; ibid., 388 (red flowers offered at magic rites) ; Thurston, Omens and Superstitions, etc., pp. 42, 47, 48 (white flowers lucky, red unlucky). Red turbans and red garments are to be worn by the priests at the sacrifice that is offered up as magic against foes. Baudh., i, 6, 13.9. Cp. ii, 8, 15.5. Here no less belongs the following solemn magical rite : He who in disputes fixes the boundary wears red garb and on his head red wreaths (and earth). Yājñav., ii, 152 ; Nārada, xi, 10 ; Bṛihaspati, xix, 11 ; Manu, viii, 256. Rules as to which flowers are to be offered the gods and the forefathers, and which not are given also in Vishṇusmṛiti, lxvi, 5–9. Cp. Agnipur., ccii, 1 ff. and ccxlviii, as also Mahānirvāṇat., v, 147 ff. In the third passage it is, however, at the same time taught that best as offerings are the fifteen *spiritual* flowers.

happy, pleasure-fraught women of the houses of joy (veçaſtriyaḥ), whose glance and speech glide so easily and sweetly along " (v, 30.38). Indeed, the heroes in their camps have no need to feel themselves alone : on both sides, besides other objeᶜts of a luxurious life, they have taken with them plenty of these moſt necessary supplies. When they march out to the battlefield of Kurukshetra, in the midſt of the army of the Pāṇḍavas is Yudhishṭhira, as also çakaṭāpaṇaveçaç ca yānayugaṃ ca sarvaçaḥ " carts, traders' goods, and pavilions, and the chariots and draught-animals in a body " (v, 151.57–58 ; cp. 196.26). These chariots and draught-animals are certainly for the hetæræ also, perhaps for them firſt of all, for in the Epic the better sort of women, particularly the noblewomen and the Kshattriyas, usually drive in yāna.[1] When the camp has been pitched on the battlefield, these seᶜtions take their place in the baggage-train in the rear. The enemy force under Duryodhana is accompanied by craftsmen, professional singers, spies, and gaṇikā (women of pleasure, v, 195.18, 19) ; and in çloka 12 we are further told expressly : " But Duryodhana had the encampment made like another embellished Hāſtinapura." In the Rāmāyaṇa (ii, 36) Daçaratha gives orders for a splendid

---

[1] Ratha is seldom found here. See iii, 293.19 ; iv, 22.11. Yāna, so far as I know, does not denote a litter in the MBh. ; this is called çibikā or perhaps nṛi-(nara-) yukta yāna, and is used especially for carrying out dead bodies, but also for women. See i, 127.7, 9 ; xi, 10.1 f. ; 16.13 ; xii, 37.41 ; xv, 22.20 ; 23.12 ; xvi, 7.19 : cp. xvi, 7.11 and 33. On the other hand, at leaſt Rām., vi, 114 uses yāna and çibikā as equivalent to one another. Cp. too MBh., iii, 69.21, 23. The ladies' chariot is drawn by horses, the moſt diſtinguished or typical beaſt of the Kshattriyas (cp. also Baudh., ii, 2 ; 3.4,9), and by she-mules, sometimes by oxen (the Brahmans' beaſts), asses, or camels (xvi, 7.11, 33 ; iv, 22.11), while according to the law writings the ass and the camel are tabu as draught and saddle beaſts (see, for inſtance, Vishṇu, liv, 23 ; Manu, xi, 202 ; Yājñav., i, 151 ; iii, 291 ; Jahn, Saurapurāṇa, p. 141) ; and it is an ill omen also for the man in the Epic, if he in a vision drives with asses (southwards). But see also ix, 35.23. According to the Çiçupālavadha the women ride on asses or horses in the army, or drive in light chariots (v, 7 ; xii, 20 ; xii, 14). That in particular the 'circulating beauties' (vāramukhyā) drive along in yāna we learn for inſtance from Bhāgavatapur., i, 11.20.

army to be fitted out for his son Rāma, and there says (çl. 3) : "Women that live by their beauty, those skilled in words, and rich merchants shall adorn the well drawn up troops of the prince." Even when the Pāṇḍavas with Draupadī and other women, and the burghers that wish to go with them set out in deepeſt grief to make sorrowful visit to their mother, who has withdrawn into the penitential foreſt, and their other kinsfolk there dwelling, Yudhishṭhira gives orders not only that the very splendid royal household shall go with them as a necessary retinue, but also that the " chariots, traders' goods, and brothels " shall also be taken (xv, 22.21). These women-folk were indeed an indispensable part of any expedition. Therefore the rulers took them with them when they went hunting, or took their diversion in the country, not to speak of the excursions to the pleasure-gardens. Thus Duryodhana goes hunting with his brothers and friends, and to brand the cattle in the herdsmen's ſtations away in the foreſt. It is a splendid setting out for the green depths, which is very excellently described : the wives of the Kshattriyas go with them in thousands, burghers along with their wives, then singers, too, and skilled huntsmen in crowds ; and traders and the girls of joy have their regular place (iii, 239.22 ff.). Princes that find their delight in horses, elephants, and harlots are evidently not an unusual thing (Rām., ii, 100.50). As so often in other literature, the ſtrumpet is not only the camp's ornament, but the ornament too of civic life, that lovely-coloured, scented flower that the city puts in its hair for all to see, when a feſtival or some other joyful event is being celebrated.[1] King Virāṭa

[1] It is mentioned times beyond number that the " city beauties " dance on joyful occasions. So, too, Mārk.-Pur., cxxviii, 9. The very sight of them brings good luck, while, for inſtance, the sight of a pregnant woman foretells evil. Agnipur., 230.4, 11 ; v. Negelein, *Traumschlüssel d. Jagaddeva*, p. 132 f. ; Bloch, *Die Proſtitution*, i, 474–476. Therefore the Vishṇusmṛiti (lxiii, 29) bids the father of a family : When he is on the journey—well known to be an under-taking under the threat of magic—he shall, as on Brahmans, filled water-pitchers, fire, and other things bringing blessings, so also look on harlots. Cp. Thurſton, *Omens and Superſtitions*, etc., pp. 23 ; 46 f. It is no wonder therefore that these women at public feſtivals

has with the Pāṇḍavas' help been victorious in a dreadful battle, and now sends messengers with the bidding : " Go into the city, and make known my victory in the fight. Young girls shall bedeck themselves, and come out of the city to meet me, and all kinds of musical instruments, and the beautifully adorned gaṇikā " (iv, 34.17.18). So, too, as soon as he hears his son's arms have been successful, he has him welcomed in the triumphal procession of youths and sellers of love, and by the young sister of him that is wearing the diadem of fortune, and her girl-friends (iv, 68.24, 26, 29). When Rāma is to be consecrated as the "young king", the priest Vasishtha directs the city to be given a festal garb and the things set up in it that bring good fortune, the temples of the gods and holy places to be put in order, and all other preparations to be made. Among these is a band of fair-dight daughters of pleasure drawn up within the second wall of the royal palace (Rām., ii, 3.17, 18). And in 14.33 ff. he then sends to tell the king in a long list all the holy and worldly requirements whose fulfilment he has now seen to, and of all the multitudes of musical instruments, and of the well-decked harlots (çl. 39). Rāma, instead of going to be dedicated as prince goes into long exile and to the stern fight with Rāvaṇa ; but at length he comes home again victorious, and then his half-brother, filled with holy joy, gives the command : " Pure men shall honour all the divinities and the holy places of the city with scented wreaths and the playing of music. Sūta, well-versed in songs of praise and old legends, as also all panegyrists (vaitālika), all masters of musical instruments, and the gaṇikā in full numbers, the king's wives and ministers, the soldiery and the bands of army women, the Brahmans and the nobles, and the corporations (gaṇa) with the heads of the guilds [1]—all these shall go out to behold the moonlike countenance of Rāma " (Rām., vi, 127.1 ff.). And when King Kuçika, together with his wife, comes back to his capital after a heavy trial of patience laid on him by the Rishi Cyavana, he is received by an escort of honour made up

and shows had their own particular seats for the spectacle (gaṇikānāṃ pṛithagmañcāḥ). See Wilson's Vishṇupur., ed. Hall, vol. 5, p. 24 f. ; p. 58, note ; and cp. my Daçakum., p. 50 ff.

[1] Or : with the guilds at the head ?

of the army, the great ones of his kingdom, and the hetæræ (xiii, 53.65, 66). To Janaka of Videha, the pious king who has penetrated into the deepeſt secrets of the world, Çuka is sent by his father, Çuka who came into being from the araṇī [1] and the seed of Vyāsa that fell on it, and who as a wonder-youth ſtands out through deepeſt knowledge, loftieſt purity of heart, and a mighty asceticism, is sent that the prince so filled with the knowledge of salvation may bring him into the holy of holies of that knowledge. The gueſt is welcomed with great honours ; the miniſter takes him into the third walled court of the royal abode, and there into a splendid pleasure-grove, escorts him to a seat, and goes off. " To him came running up quite fifty pleasure-girls,[2] splendidly dight, fair-hipped, young and tender, sweet to gaze on, wearing a thin red garment, decked with gleaming gold, well versed in speech and honeyed words, skilled in dance and song, speaking mid smiles, like the Apsarases in loveliness, practised in the service of love, gifted with the knowledge of the heart's ſtirrings, in all things skilful ; they offered him water for the feet, and other things, and marked him out for the tokens of higheſt honour. Then did they offer him well-taſting foods belonging to the season of the year. When he had eaten, they showed him in all its details the enchanting pleasure-wood by the women's abode. And playing, laughing, and singing gloriously, thus did the women, wise in their knowledge, wait on the youth of the noble nature. But he that was sprung from the araṇī, he the pure-minded, bare of all doubt, was set only on the work before him, and as one maſter of his senses and overcomer of his anger he took no joy,[3] nor felt anger. These glorious women offered him a heaven-like couch (çayyāsana) worthy of the gods, adorned with

[1] The lower rubbing-stick in making fire (naturally often compared to the woman).
[2] Anyhow such as the Old Indian rulers are wont to keep in their harems. Cp. my Daçakum., p. 54 ; Gauḍavaho, 161–166 (haughty and merry do bathe the hetæræ of King Yaçovarman in the pleasure-tanks of the rulers he has conquered) ; ZDMG, 60, p. 282 f. ; Meghadūta, 35 ; Karpūramañjarī, 1, 18.6–8 ; Prasannarāghava, iii, ſtr. 11 ; Daçarūpa, ed. Hall, p. 141 at top ; Çiçupālav., xi, 20.
[3] Or : was not amorously roused (hṛishyate).

precious stones, spread with priceless rugs. But when Çuka had washed his feet, and performed his evening worship, he sat himself down on a bare seat, pondering only on his task." He then spent almost the whole night sunk in his thoughts, and with holy works (xii, 325.33 ff.).

It was better than this youthful penitent, who was assuredly to be put to the test,[1] that the woman's hero Krishna knew how to appreciate such marks of hospitality as these. When he is sent by the Pāṇḍavas to the Kauravas, if possible to bring peace about, not only did Duryodhana have rest-houses with women and other needful comforts provided for him everywhere on his road thither, but Dhritarāshtra also gives orders : " My sons and grandsons, except Duryodhana, shall all drive to meet Janārdana in splendid chariots, and finely adorned. And the fair harlots shall go on foot, comely-decked, to meet the most high Keçava. And all lovely maidens, too, who wish to go forth from the city to behold Janārdana may go unhindered " (v, 86.15, 16).[2]

[1] So Marco Polo (Yule)[3], ii, p. 366 relates of the Yogis that when a man wished to be received as one of them, they first sent beautiful temple-dancers to him to make trial of his steadfastness (cp. the note there, p. 370). But following the Venetian's description, it seems to be not Brahmans who are in question, but rather Jains.

[2] In like wise Krishna when he comes back to Dvārakā (Bhāgavatapur., i, 11.20) is, among other things, given a festal welcome by the servants of love, driving in chariots; and the Abbé Dubois, moreover, tells us that " Ordinary politeness requires that when persons of any distinction make formal visits to each other they must be accompanied by a certain number of these courtesans " (p. 585). But on the next page he stresses that in public the Indian prostitutes are far better behaved than their European sisters, and are treated there correspondingly. Taken by itself, the translation could also be : " All the fair maidens from the city who wish to go to see Janārdana must go there naked." But, as already explained, anāvṛita in the MBh. does not seem to mean " unclothed ". Furthermore cp. say xv, 22.22. Then, again, such a piece of lewdness would seem to be foreign to the Indian of old, however little squeamish he often is. It is mainly confined to the West, especially to the older history of the Christian lands. There it often happened that the fairest maidens of the town or city, and these the daughters of the patricians, went to meet a distinguished guest in the costume of Eve in paradise, and escorted him in. On the

exhibition of woman's nakedness in the Middle Ages and later, see especially R. Günther, *Weib u. Sittlichkeit*, Berlin, 1898, pp. 141–163 ; and on the public exposure of the hetæræ in Greece and Rome, and other matters, see the same, p. 134 ff., Ploss-Bartels, i, 336–48.

As is well known, the vaſt numbers of proſtitutes were in the Middle Ages also, and not leaſt in Germany, well cared for by the State, looked on with favour by the townsfolk and the rulers, and the objeɕt especially of keen intereſt from the clergy and monks, and so forth. Cp. addition, 375.27 in my Kauṭilya, and as an explanation of Manu, x, 47, Agnipur., 151.14b : ſtrījīvanaṃ tu, tadrakshā, proktaṃ vaidehakasya ca. A visiting prince was entertained with the free entry into the houses of ill fame ; the public women even went to meet such auguſt lords outside the gates as his escort of honour, as was done for King Sigismund at Ulm in 1434. References are to be found in Ploss-Bartels, i, 416 ff. ; Günther, *Weib u. Sittlichkeit*, p. 197 ff. ; Weinhold, *Die deutschen Frauen i. d. Mittelalter*, ii, 2 ff. ; Schultz, *Das höfische Leben zur Zeit d. Minnesinger*, chap. vii ; Max Bauer, *Die Dirne u. ihr Anhang*, pp. 94–100. Here we give only one more passage : " Everywhere at public feſtivities, especially the reception of princes, they (the public women) were represented as a separate class beside the reſt of the people organized in corporations. When important persons were passing through, their (the women's) houses were specially ornamented and lighted to receive them ; indeed sometimes on such occasions they were clothed at the town's expense. In Zürich it was ſtill the cuſtom in 1516 that the burgomaſter, the servants of the court of juſtice, and the public women should eat together with the foreign envoys who came to the town " (Dr. C. Bücher, *Die Frauenfrage im Mittelalter*, p. 46 f.).

The counterpart to the Old Indian glorification of the gaṇikā is, as is well known, the high eſteem in which the hetæræ were held among the Greeks of old ; and in the time of the Abbasids also such ladies are said to have held a like position in Baghdad (Schweiger-Lerchenfeld, *Die Frauen d. Orients*, espec. p. 114). They are likewise held in high eſteem in Java, in many parts of Africa, and so forth. Günther even delivers himself as follows on p. 82 : " Intercourse with the hetæræ raised the man (in Hellas) quite consciously (!) onto a higher level ; for it brought out the individual in him who sought out, heedless of the State, that other individual akin to him, who brought him, over and above the sensual, a lofty spiritual pleasure." Such words would have sounded, to the ears of an old Greek, both quite incomprehensible and ridiculous. He looked for the beautiful body, the refinements of love, and entertainment. This the hetæræ offered him. He had, indeed, honour

THE PLEASURES OF VENAL LOVE

This being the actual importance and value set on the girls of pleasure, it can easily be also understood that the Epic is filled with zeal against them in its didactic parts. A vigorous saying that is found again and again goes : " As bad as ten slaughter-houses is one oil-miller's wheel,[1] as bad as ten oil-miller's wheels is an inn-sign, as bad as ten inn-signs is a harlot, as bad as ten harlots is a king " (xiii, 125.9). The ruler is then sharply told : " Drinking-halls and strumpets, as also traders and mimes, and gamblers and others like them—all these are to be held in check as harmful to the kingdom. Where they set their feet fast in the kingdom,[2] they are an infliction for honest subjects " (xii, 88.14, 15).[3]

from such unions, but mainly because he could afford himself such a luxury. This had to be dearly bought. The small townsman gave his money, the poor poet or artist the fruits of his talent. Then it was something distinguished to yield fitting homage to this the " eternal woman ". Cp. Iwan Bloch, *Die Prostitution*, i, 283 f. ; 340 ff. ; 354 ff. The same thing is probably true of Old India. Setting aside a few exceptions, there could probably be no question in either place of real " spiritual pleasures ", not to speak of all the fine things in Indian poets, and the mystic-Germanic sentimentalism about the union of souls between " kindred individuals ". More sensible here is the glowing dithyramb of Robert Hamerling in Socrates' words addressed to Theodata (*Aspasia*, i, p. 234).

[1] Because of destroying living beings. For this reason by a decree of Rana Jey Sing no oil-mill might work during the four rainy months. Tod, *Rajasthan*, i, 586. Cp. Glasenapp, *Der Jainismus*, 69. For when there is much rain there swarm huge numbers of gnats, insects, and all kinds of nuisances in the air. See MBh., iii, 182.4 ; Fuller, *Studies of Indian Life*, etc., p. 12 f.

[2] Or : become masters of the kingdom.

[3] As is especially to be seen from Indian narrative literature, the harlot and dicing go together. But when Hopkins deduces from MBh., ii, 68.1 that " loose women frequent the gambling halls ", he has misunderstood the text. In the same way thieves and other criminals are inseparable from public women, as, for instance, is so often seen from the Daçakumāracaritam. Yājñavalkya, ii, 266, therefore, among the four tokens by which the police can catch a thief gives that of living in a house of ill-fame (açuddha vāsaka) ; cp. Meyer, Kauṭilya, 335.8–336.14 ; addit. 336.34. In the Jaina tale Agaladatta, the harlots' abodes are given as the first places where

thieves are to be looked for (*Hindu Tales*, p. 249 f.). A list very like that given there of the places preferred by criminals is found in Manu, ix, 264 ff., and in it, of course, the veça (pleasure-house) has also its place. The same is true of MBh., xii, 140.41–42. Here praveçashu, if it cannot exactly mean brothel (and I do not know of any evidence in support), should anyhow be changed to ca veçeshu. But as the singular panāgāre here is in any case extraordinarily rare, we must in all probability read : panāgāreshu veçeshu. Thus, too, the parallel, in great part like-worded, in i, 140.63–65. Over and above the fact that the list in the MBh. is so like the two former, in Indian literature the wine-house and the women's house are separated from one another only by a very well oiled folding-door. Among the " open thieves or tricksters " (prakāçavañcaka, prakāçalokataskara) is the harlot, together with the gamblers and those who use false measures and weights, who demand bribes, who make attacks with violence, and who live by giving information as to lucky times and ceremonies (Nārada, Pariçishṭa, 2 and 3; Manu, ix, 256 ff.) ; and Brihaspati, xxii, 9, says : Gamesters, prostitutes, and other swindlers must be punished. Cp. Wustmann, " Frauenhäuser u. Freie Frauen in Leipzig im Mittelalter," *Zeitschr. f. Kulturgesch.*, v, p. 473. So the tale comes back then again to the ruinousness of inns, harlots, kings, and so on in Manu, iv, 85 also, and, with some changes, in Yājñav., i, 141. From the harlot the Brahman (or the father of a family) must not accept anything, nor eat any of her food. Vasishṭha, xiv, 10 ; li, 14 ; Manu, iv, 209 (cp. 85, 86) ; Vishṇu, li, 7 (otherwise fast seven days !) ; Yājñav., i, 161 (cp. 141) ; Agnipur., 168.3–9 (otherwise atonement by mortification). The man of the priestly caste must, of course, never visit her. If a Brahman goes to an hetæra, then he must carry out a heavy mortification so as to be cleansed. Jahn, Saurapurāṇa, p. 140. Intercourse with her is on a level with sodomy (Parāçara, x, 12 ; Mahānirvāṇa-tantra, xl, 43). The slaying of a woman that belongs to all is even free from punishment according to Gautama, xxii, 27. But the law writings also give them a somewhat more humane consideration. Their ornaments, being the tools of their craft, must not be confiscated, even though the rest of their property be taken from them. Nārada, xviii, 10 f. And this ". public cheat " must also act honourably. If she has received her hire from a man, and then refuses, she must pay the double as a fine. Yājñav., ii, 292. According to Agnipur., 227.44b–45a, if she has promised herself to a man, and then goes to another, then she must restore to the injured one double the amount he has put down, and furthermore also pay a fine to the royal treasury. Kauṭilya under certain circumstances even condemns her to an eight-fold restitution. See 195.8–14. If a dispute arises between public

THE PLEASURES OF VENAL LOVE

women and their lovers, then the head hetæræ and the lovers shall settle it between them. Bṛihaspati (SBE, vol. xxxiii, p. 266). Very inſtructive information is also to be found in ZDMG (= *Zeitschr. d. deutsch. morgenländ. Gesellsch.*), Bd. 60, p. 282 f.; and especially in Kauṭilya ; see index under " Luſtdirne ". In it the public " fair lady " comes off far better than in the Dharma writings. As a matter of course, and as is well known, woman and piety go readily hand in hand, and in this even the public kind of both these is no exception. Thus the holy bathing-places (tīrtha) are often known not only as places for all kinds of love-making, but also as places where light women ply their trade ; and in the Tantra literature at a Devacakra, one kind of cycle connected with the worship of a god (or Tantric-myſtic), the leading part is played, as Çakti or embodiments of the active power of the divinity, by those five well-known kinds of harlots: rājaveçyā (the harlot of rulers), nāgarī (the city harlot), guptaveçyā (the secret harlot, that is, the woman of good family who secretly follows this calling or these joys), devaveçyā (the harlot of the gods, or temple-dancer), and brahmaveçyā, that is, the tīrthagā (the harlot of the bathing-places). See Mahānirvāṇatantra transl. by M. N. Dutt, 1900, p. xxvii f.

END OF VOLUME I

VOLUME TWO

X

LOVE

IN the artificial poetry, and the text-books of poetry and those of love, as oftentimes elsewhere, the hetæra is sung of as queen in the land of love. In spite of her unmistakable importance for Indian eroticism of the Epic world, however, it would be wrong to give her such a place here, too. She is there simply an article of necessity. And if Indian literature along with those fairly numerous songs of praise for the "circulating beauties" is filled with the most splendid love stories and descriptions of the passion of sex—the glowingly sensual and the sweetly tender—the Epic in particular yields a very great number of pleasing flowers of this same kind. And these flowers have also a charm which is at least somewhat rare, in that they do not wither and die on some wild heath, but go on blooming in the garden of wedlock, and in it first reveal the full depths of their glowing colours, and their innermost, strongest perfumes. Who does not know Damayantī and Sāvitrī ! And Kālidāsa's Çakuntalā, however much she has won under the loving care of this favoured one of the god, comes originally likewise from the primeval forest of the Mahābhārata. Further examples of the mighty love of woman will be discussed in the chapter on the Wife. A long list of gods, holy men, and kings who loved their wives, and led a life of joy with them is found in v, 197.8 ff. For the Epic, too, the union between husband and wife is a picture of the tenderest human union (e.g. xii, 319.10). See, too, especially xii, 301.37–39 (the separation between man and wife is one of the most dreadful things).

The woman in Old India, as throughout the world, has far greater gifts for love than the man, that is, taking love in its nobler meaning, for that feeling which fills the whole being, is steadfast and faithful, grows ever deeper, and is strongly

277

mingled with altruistic elements.[1] But that the man, too, in the Epic is capable of a like feeling and of much romantic love is over and over again to be seen.

Romance such as this lies already before us in the earlier mentioned tale of Satyavatī, the fisherman's daughter, and King Çāntanu. For forty years he shuns women and women's love (ratim aprāpnuvan strīshu), after his dearly loved wife Gangā has vanished from his eyes, and when he then finds the gloriously beautiful, wondrous-scented fisher's maid and ferry-girl, his passion for her blazes up so fiercely that he at once woos her, and becomes quite ill and wretched because it seems as though he cannot get her (i, 100.20 ff.). Still finer rings the tale of Tapatī and Saṃvaraṇa (i, 171.6 ff.).

" He that up in the sky fills the air with brightness by his disk, the sun god, had a daughter by name Tapatī of equal rank with himself, the younger sister of Sāvatrī, renowned in the three worlds, beaming, glowing. No goddess, no Asura woman, no Yaksha or Rākshasa woman, no Apsaras, no Gandharva maid was so fair. Of the right measure and proportions, and faultless were the limbs of the peerless one, deep-black and big her eyes, good were her ways and her heart, fair to the eye her raiment. There was none here in the three worlds that the awaker of life deemed worthy as a husband for her, in beauty, character, gifts, and renown. When now she had reached the bloom of youth,[2] and he saw that he must marry this daughter away, he could find no rest through anxious thought of how to bestow her. Now at that time the son of Ṛiksha, he the strong bull of the Kurus, King Saṃvaraṇa, sought to win the graces of the sun god. Filled with loving devotion, he worshipped the rising wealth of beams with guest-gifts (arghya), wreaths and offerings, and so forth, and with sweet perfumes, his mind well held in check, pure, with vows and fasting and manifold penances, obedient, free from the pride

---

[1] The author of the Kumārasaṃbhava has rightly seen that men have greater gifts for real *friendship* : " The love of men, which towards beloved women is unsteadfast, towards friends never wavers " (iv, 29).

[2] According to K, i, 187.11 she was then 16 years old. Fifteen or sixteen was evidently also the age of Draupadī at her marriage (cp. xv, 1.6 ; 25.9 ; 29.38).

278

of the self, cleansed. Then the sun god deemed the grateful Saṃvarṇa, learned in the law, with no peer on earth in beauty, a husband worthy of Tapatī. Now he willed to give this maid as wife to Saṃvaraṇa, beſt of the shepherds of earth, the man of renowned noble blood. For as, in the sky, the beaming one caſts brightness abroad through his fiery glow, so on earth was Saṃvaraṇa full of light.[1] And as the knowers of the holy knowledge worship the rising sun, so did those among creatures that were younger brothers of the Brahmans[2] worship Saṃvaraṇa. The prince for his friends outdid the moon in sweetness, and for his foes outdid the sun in fiery ſtrength.[3] Since the lord of the earth had such gifts and his way of life was thus, so he of the glowing light resolved of himself to give him 'the shining one' (Tapatī). One day the glorious, boundlessly brave king was roving, as he hunted, through the mountain foreſt.[4] While the king was busied hunting, his incomparable ſteed died in the mountains, overcome with hunger and thirſt. Robbed of his horse by death, the prince was wandering afoot in the mountains, and then he saw a great-eyed maiden, without her like in the world. When the deſtroyer of the foeman's army, the lonely one, met the lonely maid, he, the tiger among commanders of men, ſtood there, gazing with unmoving eyes. For the ruler of men held her to be Lakshmī for her loveliness, and then again he held her to be the shining bright one of the day-

---

[1] Or : through his light.

[2] That is, all the subjeⅽts (so it could be also translated) who were less than the Brahmans ; for the king, too, is bound and is wishful to worship these latter.

[3] Although the prefix is often found, in the Epic also, separated from the verb, yet probably ati is hardly to be thus taken. Ati and lesſ often atīva in the MBh. is used like a kind of uninfleⅽted adjeⅽtive (of course with an accus. depending on it) both predicatively and attributively, and in the meaning of " ſtanding above, excelling ". See, for inſtance, i, 102.32 ; 103.2, 110.1 ; 124.18, 132.62 ; 170.28 ; 171.19 ; ii, 11.16 ; iii, 36.19 ; 163.19 ; 173.32 ; 207.99 ; v, 167.3 ; vi, 44.13 ; vii, 100.5 ; 188.43 ; xii, 12.6 ; 134.6 ; i, 155.34 ; iv, 64.32 ; 68.16 ; xiii, 33.10.

[4] Parvatopavana.

ſtar come down thither, like unto the sun's glowing beam in her wondrous splendour and dazzling light, like unto the moon's sickle in her friendliness and sweet softness. For on the mountain-ridge where she ſtood she shone and gleamed like a golden ſtatue. Through her beauty and her garb, because of her extraordinary splendour, that mountain with its trees, bushes, and creepers was turned as though into gold.[1] When the king had seen her, he despised the women in all the worlds, and believed that now only had he found profit of his eyes. All the loveliness that he had seen since his birth he deemed as below hers in rank. His heart and eye were fettered by her with the bonds made by her charms, and so he did not ſtir from that spot, and knew of nought. 'Of a surety the Maker has whirled the whole world into being with gods, spirits, and mankind, and so brought the fair shape of this great-eyed one to life.' So then King Saṃvaraṇa held the maid, for the perfeċtion of the treasures of her beauty, to be without compare in the world. And so soon as the man of glorious nobility of birth had seen the glorious one, he fell in his soul into anguished care, tortured by the arrow of the god of love. Burning with the hot fever of passion, the undismayed one to her dismayed, to the heart-entangler, said: 'Who art thou, and whose, thou lovely one with thighs like banana-ſtems, and wherefore art thou found here? And how comes it that thou roameſt alone in the foreſt empty of mankind, thou of the bright smile? For thou art in every limb without a fault; and decked with every ornament, thou art as the beauty itself that is sought in these ornaments. I hold thee to be no goddess and no Asura woman, no Yaksha nor Rākshasa maid, for no snake fay, no Gandharva woman, and no human beauty.[2] For whatever glorious women I may have seen or heard of, thou, to my mind, art like none of them, thou mazed allurer. Thou of the lovely countenance, so soon only as I set sight on thy face with its lotus-leaf eyes, which is more

---

[1] Cp. Spenser, *Faerie Queene,* canto iii, stanza 4; Swinburne, "Triſtram of Lyonesse," canto vi (*Poems* [1904], vol. iv, p. 90); Eilhart von Oberge, *Triſtan,* ed. Lichtenſtein, 6512 ff.; Lewis Truman Mott, *Syſtem of Courtly Love,* p. 124; Arnold in *Zeitſchr. d. Ver. f. Volksk.,* vol. 12, p. 166 f.

[2] Less likely : for now I set no value on (I despise) goddess, etc.

ravishing than the moon, the stirrer of the heart stirred up, as it were, my whole heart.' Thus did the warden of the earth speak unto her, but she answered not a word to him that was tormented by love in the lonely forest. While the prince was thus confused by speaking, the great-eyed one disappeared where she stood,[1] like the lightning in the cloud. Seeking her, her with the lotus-leaf eyes, the commander of men now ran all over the forest, wandering about like a madman. But when he found her not, the first among princes raised much lament there, and stood a moment without stirring. When she now was no longer to be seen, the smiter of the foeman's hosts, the love-stupefied ruler of men, fell down to earth. When he was lying on the ground, then the sweet-smiling fair one with the swelling, long hips, showed herself once again to the prince. Then the glorious one spoke with sweet voice to the herdsman of the earth, the heir of the Kurus, whose soul was smitten by love ; with a light laugh Tapatī spoke the sweet words : ' Rise, rise, I beg ! Thou tamer of foemen, tiger among princes, that standest before all eyes on earth, thou must not come to be thus overcome in bewilderment.' Thus addressed with sweet speech, the ruler of the earth now saw the wide-hipped one standing before him. Then spoke the king to her of the black eyes, his soul ringed by the fire of love, with a voice that uttered only confused sounds : ' Come, thou black-eyed one, thou mazed allurer, love me that love thee and am tortured with yearning ; for the spirits of life are leaving me. Because of thee, thou great-eyed one, who shinest like the cup of the lotus-flower, the god of love is ever piercing me with sharp arrows. Therefore, thou of the lovely face, that hast swelling, long hips, take me to thee ; for in helpless plight I am being entwined [2] by the mighty snake of desire. For on thee my life depends, O thou whose words sound sweet as the song of the Kinnaras, thou, free from fault in every limb, woman with countenance like unto the lotus-flower and the moon. For without thee, O shy one, I cannot go on living. The god of love is wounding me here, lotus-faced one ; there-

---

[1] Literally : just there, then and there.
[2] Literally : bitten.

fore take pity on me, thou woman with the all-powerful eyes. Black-eyed one, thou shalt not repulse me, who am thy servant in love, for, glorious one, thou shalt save me through a union in joy. My heart, where love has been awakened through the sight of thee, is deep shaken ; now that I have seen thee I have no wish left to see another, thou noble one. Grant me thy favour, I am in thy hands, love me the lover, thou glorious one. For since I have seen thee, thou fair-hipped woman, the ſtirrer of hearts, O big-eyed one, is piercing me sorely within with his arrows. The fire that has been kindled by love, O lotus-eye, slake it for me with the life-giving water that comes with the union in joy. Thou kindly, thou glorious one, bring the god with the flowery dart, him so hard to overcome, armed with cruel arrow and bow, that has awakened at the sight of thee, and is drawing on me with arrows beyond bearing, bring him to reſt by giving thyself to me. Come unto me after the wise of the Gandharva wedlock, thou all-excelling woman ; for among marriages, O banana-thighed one, the Gandharva marriage is held for the higheſt.' Tapatī spoke : ' I am not miſtress of myself, O king, for I am a maiden that has a father. Doſt thou harbour liking and love for me, then ask of my father. For as thy life-spirits have been taken and held by me, so by the very sight of thee have my life-spirits been borne headlong[1] away by thee. I am not now miſtress of my person ; therefore, O beſt of princes, I go not to thee ; for women are not free. For what maiden in all the worlds muſt not wish for herself the renowned prince of the nobility as shield and tender-loving husband ? Therefore, as things are thus, do thou ask of my father, the sun god, through humble showing of honour, through penance, and a vow of mortification. If he will give me to thee, O slayer of foes, then will I ever live, O king, after thy wishes. I am, indeed, Tapatī, the younger siſter of Sāvitrī, I am the daughter of that light of the world, of the awaker of life, O warrior-bull.' After these words the faultless one swiftly rose in the air, while the king fell down on the ground again where he ſtood.

The miniſter who was seeking for the king, the beſt of

---

[1] Or : so and ſtill more (liter. : more so, so ſtill more).

LOVE

princes, with an army, then¹ along with his following saw him
fallen to the ground in the great forest, like the raised banner of
Indra.² When the king's comrade saw the great bowman
lying thus on the ground like an outcast, he was kindled as
though with a fire, and he hurried towards him, seized by
a tumult of distress owing to his tender affection, and put
the prince, overcome with love, the lord of earthly rulers, on his
feet, like a father his son that has fallen. When the minister,
who was old in understanding, years of life, renown, and state
wisdom, had set him up, the feverish pain left him. And he
spoke to him that was raised with loving, sweet words : ' Fear
not, O tiger of men ; hail to thee, thou good man ! ' He
believed that the prince, exhausted from hunger and thirst,

¹ Kāle "at the time, then, now " is often found in the Epic. So,
e.g., i, 25.3 ; 49.3 ; 167.14 ; v, 91.16 ; 94.20 ; vi, 120.66 ; xii,
31.6 ; xiii, 167.25, 29 ; Rām., iii, 16.15 ; iv, 20.8 ; 22.20 ; v, 27.9.
² The favourite festival of Indra or Indra's banner is often mentioned
in the Epic. A very good description is given in a Jain tale which I
have translated in my *Hindu Tales* (pp. 142–3) ; and MBh., i, 63.17 ff.
describes how King Uparicara founded this joyous festival and first
held it. The standard was set up seven days before the full moon
of the month Āçvina (Sept.–Oct.), waved day after day in all its glory
and then on that day of the full moon was thrown down on the ground.
Before this it had been held up by cords. K, i, 64, has interesting
details, wanting in B. Because of its beautiful colours and richness
and its sudden fall to earth it is in constant use as a comparison in the
Epic. See i, 163.18, 19 ; 70.14 ; 173.1, 2 ; ii, 77.9 ; v, 59.15 ;
vi, 119.91 ; vii, 15.29 ; 49.12 ; 87.6 ; 92.66 ; 94.69, 70 ; ix, 17.53 ;
Rām., iii, 34.3 ; iv, 16.36, 37, 39 ; 17.2 ; iv, 34.3 ; vi, 45.17. By
MBh., i, 63.20, I am brought back to my suggestion expressed in *Hindu
Tales*, p. 143, n. 3, that ḍoya denotes a wooden utensil, perhaps in
particular a wooden box or basket (piṭaka). On the raising and lowering
of the Indradhvaja see also Yājñav., i, 147 ; Agnipur., 121.65 f. ;
but above all Bṛihatsaṃhitā, chap. 43, and Meyer, *Altind. Rechtsschr.*,
385 f. (note). Yantra in MBh., vii, 94.70, however, does not mean
" lever ". The meaning of piṭaka is not made clear by Bṛihats.,
43.8, 41, 50, 57, 61, 64, 41–50. The Karm festival among the Urau is
probably akin. *Zeitschr. f. Ethnol.*, Bd. 6, p. 346 (after Dalton). Both,
anyhow, are fertility festivals, as are the well-known May-tree festivals
(with them cp. Tod, *Rājasthan*, ii, 217). See also Wright, *Hist. of
Nepal*, pp. 38, 41.

283

he the destruction of the foe in the fight, had fallen to the ground. With very cool, lotus-scented water he sprinkled the king's head, tearing off his diadem.[1] Thereupon the life-spirits came back to the herdsman of men, and the mighty one dismissed his army, except this one counsellor. Then at the king's command the great army withdrew ; the king sat himself down again on that plateau. Then in those lordly mountains he stood there on earth, having acquired ritual purity, his hands folded before his forehead, and his face lifted upwards, to bring the sun god's favour on himself. And in his mind, Samvarana, the king, fled to Vasishtha, best of the Rishis, his foe-destroying house-priest.[2] As now the herdsman of men was standing at one spot day and night, the Brahmanic Rishi came to him on the twelfth day. Since the great seer with the pure soul already knew that the commander of men had been carried away by Tapatī, and had come to know this in super-mundane wise, the best of the Munis, he filled with virtue, addressed the prince that was thus fast harnessed and bridled in his thoughts, in his yearning to carry out his business. Before the eyes of the ruler of men the sublime Rishi was wafted up towards heaven, he that was gifted with the sun's brightness, to pay his court to the sun god. Then the Brahman, laying his folded hands on his forehead, came before the thousand-beamed one, and announced himself, filled with joyful love, saying : ' I am Vasishtha.' To the best of Munis said the light-spreader : ' Great Rishi, welcome to thee ! Speak thy wish. Whatever thou wishest from me, this thy desire, I will grant thee, even though it were hard to carry out.' Thus

[1] I read āsphuṭan (instead of asphuṭan) and take it as transitive. Intransitive verbs are often used in the Epic as transitive (causative). See, e.g., i, 92.7 ; 139.26 ; 153.29 ; iii, 40.19 ; 192.54 ; iv, 1.25 ; v, 75.12 ; vii, 79.31 ; xii, 242.23 ; 269.45, 68 ; 287.11 ; xiii, 164.2 ; Rām., iv, 66.7 ; vi, 114.28. K (189.10) has the straightforward reading aspṛican : without touching (wetting) (the king's diadem). Ākarshan would likewise be clear. Nīl. says : " With the other reading the meaning is clear." But he does not say which. His interpretation does not agree with mine.

[2] In the Epic also it is one of the main tasks of the Purohita of a prince to bring hurt on the prince's foes by witchcraft.

addressed by him, the seer Vasishtha answered the light-spreader, the abounding in beams, falling down, he the mighty one in penance, before him : ' It is thy daughter, Tapatī by name, the younger sister of Sāvitrī, that I woo from thee for Samvarana, O thou filled with brightness. For this king has high renown, knows the religious and the worldly duties, and has a noble mind ; Samvarana is a fitting husband for thy daughter, O wanderer through the air.' Thus bespoken by him, the maker of day resolved : ' I will give her,' and answered the Brahman with joyful consent : ' Samvarana is first among princes, and thou, O Muni, art first among Rishis, Tapatī is above all women. What else could there be, then, but to make grant of her ! ' Thereupon the shining one himself handed over the shining one (Tapatī), her without fault in any limb, to the high-souled Vasishtha for Samvarana. Then did the great Rishi take over the maid Tapatī, and, dismissed (by the sun god), Vasishtha now came back again to where that Kuru bull known to fame, the king filled with love's unrest, was waiting, and in mind was by her side only. And when he saw the maiden of the gods, the sweet-laughing Tapatī coming to him with Vasishtha, he was lit up with overflowing joy. She of the lovely brows shone exceeding bright as she was wafted down from the sky, lighting up the quarters of the world with flashes like a falling flash of lightning. When scarcely twelve days had gone by, Vasishtha, the august Rishi with the pure soul, came to the king.[1] After Samvarana had brought the god that grants wishes, the prince of the beams, the lord, to be favourable to him, he won his wife only through the majesty of Vasishtha. Then did the bull among men take hold of the hand of Tapatī in lawful wise on that prince of mountains, the resort of gods and Gandharvas. With Vasishtha's leave the kingly Rishi was minded to take his pleasure with his wife on this same mountain. Then the herdsmen of the earth left that minister (as his representative) in the city and the kingdom, in the forests and the groves.

[1] Or samāhite taken substantively : when the king (rājñah) had firmly concentrated his thoughts ? The version given in the text is perhaps better for the reason that the tale in its present, not very old form is meant to set before our eyes the greatness of the Brahmans.

Vasishtha then took his leave of the prince, and went away. The king now took his delight on that mountain, like an immortal. For twelve years did the king find his pleasure in this wise together with his wife in groves and forests on that mountain. In this king's city and in his kingdom he with the thousand eyes (Indra) did not rain in all the twelve long years. Then when this drought came all creatures fell to destruction, those that move not and those that move. While this very dreadful time thus prevailed, no dew came down on the earth, and therefore the seeds grew not. Then did mankind with minds bewildered, tormented by hunger and dread, leave their houses and wander forth to every quarter of the heavens. Then in this city and this kingdom folk gave up wife and possessions, and slew one another, released from law and order, tortured with hunger. So did this city with its hungry, foodless people, turned to (living) corpses, seem like the city of the king of the dead, filled with the dead.[1] When the holy Rishi Vasishtha

[1] This drought and its dreadful consequences came about because there was no king in the land. As elsewhere in the East, the prince according to Indian literature and particularly the MBh. is the source and origin of all that happens in his kingdom ; he is a blessing or a disaster for his land, equal to all the gods, destiny, the ladder to heaven or to hell ; he makes the sun to shine, the fire to burn, rules as the god of wind and of the sea, is Çiva and Vishnu ; he makes the four ages of the world, all power is set in him—and that by the Brahmans, and so forth *ad infinitum*. This flower of princely apotheosis had its roots, indeed, in the ground of reality. The king in Old India often made his subjects' lives very uncomfortable, and he was often of most benefit when he—slept (Cardonne, *Mélanges de lit. orient.*, 1788, p. 117) ; on the other hand he could do much good. Cp. Kirātārj., i, 17, and the precious remarks of Hopkins, *India Old and New*, p. 234. Now above all the king makes it to rain, and this not only through his fitness as a ruler, but through his magical presence itself ; where there is no king the fruitful moisture does not fall. But the king also brings the curse of drought on his land if he is evil, while under the good king the gift of rain in right measure is poured on the kingdom, which is the beginning and end of all for India, the land of agriculture. On this subject see my note on p. 344 of the Daçakum., and with it cp. Manu, ix, 246, 247 ; Tawney, Prabandhacintāmaṇi, 70 ; Vikramorv., iv, between śtr. 3 and 4 ; Jātaka, i, p. 94 ; v, 193 ; Rückert's

saw what was happening, he with the soul of virtue, the best of the Munis came thither.[1] And he had the tiger among princes, who had been away together with Tapatī far off for endless years,[2] brought home to this city. Then the slayer of the foes of the gods rained there as before. So soon as this tiger among princes had come into the city once more, the mighty one of the thousand eyes made rain to fall and so the crops to grow. Then did that city and the kingdom rejoice with joy beyond compare, raised up by this the foremost one of earthly rulers, by him that was lofty in soul. Then did the high herdsman of men, with his wife, make sacrifice for twelve years in return, as Indra with Çacī. Thus was the excelling one, Tapatī by name, the sun god's daughter, thy forbear,[3] O Arjuna, because of whom I declare thee for a child of Tapatī. By her King Saṃvaraṇa begot Kuru."

poem : " Der Fürst ritt auf die Jagd " in his *Weisheit des Brahmanen* ; Bulloram Mullick, *Home Life in Bengal*, p. 24 f. ; Temple, *Legends of the Panjab*, i, 264; Ward, *View of the Hindoos* [5], 273; Divyāvad., p. 435 (cp. Jāt. Nos. 334, 520) ; Cardonne, *Mélanges*, p. 89 ff. ; Crooke, *North-Western Provinces of India*, p. 170; etc. From the MBh. some of the passages are : i, 64.15, 16 ; 68, especially 10 ; 105.44 ; 109.1 ff. ; ii, 13.14 ff. ; 33.1 ff. ; 38.27–29 ; iii, 185 ; 207.28 ff ; iv, 28.15 ff. ; 132.15 ff. ; v, 147.25 ff. ; xii, 29.51 ff. ; 69.75 ff. ; 91.9 ; 141.9, 10 ; 223.5 ff. ; xiii, 62.43 f. The Old Indian king, too, does not know better : In the kingdom of the Kalingas there is a heavy drought; everything is ruined. The people make complaint to the ruler, who then says : " I will make the god rain," and gives himself up to good works. But as this is no good, King Vessantara's state-elephant is asked for ; where it comes, there it rains (Jāt., vi, p. 487).—To tat we can add puram. Or the liter. transl. might be : Hence it became (or : It became) in this way like the city filled with ghosts, etc.

[1] Read abhyavartata instead of abhavarshata. In itself the text, indeed, might be quite right as a senseless insertion for glorifying the Brahmans. But if we are not to reject the whole çloka, which indeed is not altogether unsuspect, then this amendment offers itself quite naturally, and is moreover supported by K, where abhyadravata is found.

[2] That is, of course : an endlessly long time.

[3] It is to him that the tale, told by a Gandharva, is addressed.

Still more splendidly than here does the man's love for his chosen one shine in the legend of Ruru (i, 8.5 ff.) : "There was once a great Ṛishi, endowed with asceticism and knowledge, famed under the name of Sthūlakeça, gladly given up to the welfare of all beings. Now at this very time the king of the Gandharvas, named Viçvāvasu, begot offspring with Menakā. The Apsaras Menakā exposed this child near by the hermitage of Sthūlakeça, when her time had come. And having left the child on the river-bank, she went away, she the Apsaras Menakā, ruthless and without shame. This girl like a child of the gods, blazing, as it were, with the splendour of beauty, that was exposed on the river-bank, and in the unpeopled wilderness bereft of her kindred, was seen by the great Ṛishi, the majeſtic Sthūlakeça. Now when the great Brahman Sthūlakeça had seen this maiden, the beſt among Munis, filled with pity, took her and brought her up. And she with the lovely hips grew up in his holy and glorious hermitage. The religious rites—the birth ceremony, and so forth—were carried out over her by the very great Ṛishi Sthūlakeça, the famous one, according to precept and in order. But she was the moſt excellent of women (pramadābhyo varā), gifted with loveliness of charaſter and form, wherefore the great and holy man gave her the name Pramadvarā. This Pramadvarā was seen in the penitential grove by (the scion of Bhṛigu) Ruru, and he with the soul of right and virtue was at once ſtruck down by love. Through his friends he then sent word of it to his father, the Bhṛigu scion Pramati, and the father asked for her hand from the high and glorious Sthūlakeça. Thereupon her father gave the maiden Pramadvarā to Ruru, fixing the wedding beforehand for the time of the conſtellation that has Bhaga for god.[1] A few days later, when the wedding was juſt nigh, this lovely-faced maiden was playing with her girl-friends, and did not see a snake faſt asleep and ſtretched right across (the path). She trod with her foot on the beaſt, since she was doomed to death and driven on by fate. The snake, goaded on by the god of death, ſtruck with its poison-smeared fangs deep into the heedless

---

[1] Uttaraphalgunī is meant. This is a lucky time for weddings often mentioned in the Epic also. Bhagadaivata also means " giving happiness in marriage " (e.g. iii, 233.8 ; 234.12).

LOVE

girl's body. Bitten by this snake, she fell suddenly to the ground, robbed of all colour and of her splendour, as her charms and consciousness fled from her. Taking all joy from her kindred, her hair unbound, abandoned by life—so was she, that was most worthy of beholding, taken from their sight.[1] And it was as though she, slain by the snake's poison, had gone to sleep on the ground ; the slender one was far more fascinating still to the heart. And her father and the other penitents saw her in her lotus-like glory fall quivering on the ground. Then came all the excellent Brahmans, filled with pity : Svastyātreya, Mahājanu, Kuçika, Çankhamekhala, Uddālaka, and Katha, and Çveta, the greatly renowned, Bharadvāja, Kaunakutsya, Ārshtishena ; then Gautama, Pramati with his son, as also other forest-dwellers. When they saw the lifeless maiden, slain by the poison of the snake, they wept for the pity that was in them ; but Ruru went forth tormented by suffering. And all those excellent Brahmans sat themselves down at that very spot.

While those lofty-minded Brahmans were sitting there, Ruru went into the depths of the forest, and wailed aloud, filled with the greatest sorrow. Sore wounded, he poured out his woe in manifold heart-moving ways, and in his pain and in his memory of the beloved Pramadvarā he spoke the words : ' She is lying on the ground, the slender one, that makes my cares to grow, and those of all her kindred. What unhappiness could be greater ! If I have given charitable gifts, if I have practised asceticism, if I have won the goodwill of worshipful men, then my beloved one shall thereby come to life again. And as surely as from my birth I have held myself in check, and kept a pious troth towards the law, so surely shall Pramadvarā here, the shining one, arise again.' While the sorrowing one in this wise was bitterly bewailing his wife, there came a messenger of the gods and spoke to Ruru in the forest : ' It is useless for thee, O Ruru, to be speaking words in thy sorrow ; for for the mortal whose life is run there is no life left, O thou with virtuous soul. The life of this poor daughter of the Gandharva and the Apsaras has run out ;

[1] aprekshanīyā. Lit. not visible, that is, gone over into the other world, dead.

therefore, my friend, do not give thine heart up at all to sorrow. But there is a remedy for it that has been already laid down by the lofty-minded gods ; if thou art willing to make use of it, thou shalt receive Pramadvarā again here on earth.' Ruru spoke : ' What is the remedy laid down by the gods ? Speak according to the truth, O wanderer through the air ! I will do in accordance with it so soon as I have heard. O do thou save me !' The messenger of the gods spoke : ' Make over, O child of Bhrigu, the half of thy life to the maiden. Thus, O Ruru, will thy wife Pramadvarā rise up again.' Ruru spoke : ' I will make over half my life to the maiden, O best of the air-rangers. Dight with love and beauty,[1] my beloved shall rise again.' Then the king of the Gandharvas and the messenger of the gods,[2] the two excellent ones, went to the king of righteousness and death and to him spoke these words : ' O king of righteousness, let his wife that is dead arise once again for the half of Ruru' slife, if so thou deemest.'[3] The king of righteousness spoke : ' If thou art asking for Pramadvarā, Ruru's wife, O messenger of the gods, then shall she, endowed with the half of Ruru's life, arise again.' So soon as he had thus spoken, the maid Pramadvarā by virtue of the half of Ruru's life arose again, as though she of the lovely face had only slept. For it was this that was written in the future for this Ruru, endowed with surpassing splendour, that from him the half of his life should be cut off on behalf of his wife, when he should be far gone in years.[4] Then did the parents on the wished for day hold with glad hearts the wedding of the two, and the two lovers took their joy, each wishing all that was best for the other." But thenceforward Ruru was a bitter foe of snakes, as is told in what follows, and to this hatred he also owes his immortalizing in the Mahābhārata.[5]

[1] Or : in festal garb, beauty, and adornment (çriṅgārarūpābharaṇā).
[2] So according to K (9.19) : devadūtaç. The Bomb. ed. has Devadattaç, which then must be the name of the gods' messenger. But it is probably a mistake.
[3] Less likely : that is thus dead . . . if thou deemest.
[4] Or : the half of the much-grown length of life.
[5] The tale itself is also to be found in a bare shortened form in Kathās. Tar., xiv, 76 ff. Cp. Mārk.-Pur., xxii–xxv ; Hemavija's

LOVE

The love romance of the Rākshasī woman Hiḍimbā is also very beautiful, to whom the whole-hearted energy of purpose in following the ways of her heart is more becoming than to many a one among her numerous Eastern sisters skilled in the campaigns of love. And with it all there is a pretty touch of adventurous humour running through this tale of a giant, which reminds us of the giant-tales of Western, especially German, lands.

The five Pāṇḍavas had escaped with their mother out of the burning house of resin, and were wandering through the forest. Bhīma the strong had at last carried all the wearied ones away, and was now watching over them as they lay asleep. Then a man-eating monster (Rākshasa), dwelling near by, Hiḍimba by name, climbed a çāla-tree, and looked about him for prey. Black he was as the rain-cloud, red-eyed, with bristling tusks and hanging belly, red stubbly beard and hair, out-standing ears, and a neck and trunk like some mighty tree ; huge were his jaws, every feature was hideous and frightful. He scratched his shaggy hair, opened his jaws in a gaping yawn, and kept on looking all round, tormented by hunger and thirst. When he smelt human flesh he was greatly rejoiced, and called to his sister Hiḍimbā : " At last I have now found my much-loved food ; my mouth is watering. Happiness is clasping me.[1] My eight sharp-tipped tusks, whose thrust none can withstand, I will at length bury in the bodies and the tender flesh. I will leap on to a human neck, tear the veins open and drink my fill of the warm, fresh, foaming blood. Go ; find out who is lying there in the forest. The strong human smell seems to refresh my nose. Kill all these persons, and bring them to me

Kathāratnākara, 106th and 183rd tales ; Fr. v. d. Leyen, *Ind. Märchen*, 136 ff. ; *Herrigs Archiv*, 11, p. 453 ; Keller's " Altdeutche Erzählungen " in *Stuttg. Lit. Verein.*, Bd. 35, p. 372 ; Meyer, *Isoldes Gottesurteil* (Berl. 1914), p. 182, and with this Chavannes, *Cinq cents contes*, No. 12 ; Schiefner, " Ind. Erzählungen," No. xvii (*Bull. d. Petersburg. Akad.*, Bd. xxiii, col. 29 ff.) ; Grimm's *Märchen*, No. 16 ; etc.

[1] Snehasravāt prasravati (printed prasavati) jihvā, paryeti me sukham. K has : Jighrataḥ prasrutā snehāj jihvā paryeti me sukhaṃ. In B one expects mā rather than me.

here. As they are sleeping in our domain, thou haſt nought to fear from them. When we have eaten to our heart's desire of the men's flesh, we will both of us dance many dances together in time." Hiḍimbā went quickly off ; but when she saw the mighty Bhīmasena watching over the sleepers, and towering up like a young çāla-tree, she fell in love with him, the one without compare in form on earth. "This dark, ſtrong-armed, lion-breaſted, lotus-eyed one would be a fitting mate for me. I could never carry out my brother's cruel order. The love for a husband is mighty beyond all, not so is the friendship for a brother. Were my brother to slay them, he would be sated but for a moment. If they live, then I have gladness for years unending." As she could change her shape at will, she put on that of a glorious human being, and softly drew nigh the long-armed Bhīmasena. As though shy, playfully, dight with divine ornament, she spoke these words, as she smiled, to Bhīmasena : "Whence haſt thou come, and who art thou ? And who are these that are sleeping here ? Here dwells the evil-minded Rākshasa called Hiḍimba. He has sent me, and means to eat you. But now that I have beheld thee, that shineſt like a child of the gods, there is none other whom I will have as a husband. Do thou love me who love, whose soul and body are wounded by passion. I will save thee from the man-eater, and we will live together in the mountain wilds." But Bhīmasena said that he could not leave his kindred to be eaten by the Rākshasa, and go off like one love-sick. She made answer : "Wake them, I will save them from the monſter." [1] "How should I wake them that sleep so calmly ? What could a Rākshasa like this do to me ? Go or ſtay, my dear, or do whatever thou wisheſt. Or send thy man-eating brother here." She drew a piĉture of the dreadfulness of the Rākshasa, and offered herself to carry them all away through the air on her hip. Bhīma once more made boaſt : "I will slay him before thine eyes. The wretched Rākshasa is no match for me. See these round arms of mine, like elephants' trunks, my thighs

[1] According to K, which as so often happens elsewhere, has many additions in this place, Bhīma points out that he muſt not marry before his elder brother, and she answers (164.45) : " I will save thee only and with thy mother. Leave thy brothers here, and mount my jaghana."

like clubs, and my mighty firm cheſt. Now thou wilt behold
my hero's ſtrength, that is like Indra's. Do not belittle me,
thou broad-hipped one, by thinking I here am only a man."
" I do not think little of thee, thou with the godlike form.
But I have seen what the Rākshasa can do to men." The giant
heard his voice and ran there angrily. When he beheld his
siſter thus in fair human shape, wearing thin garb, with a
wreath of flowers in her hair, and all decked, he opened wide
his eyes, and bitterly reproached her for being so bent on man-
hunting, putting a hindrance in his way through her blindness,
and being willing to bring shame upon the Rākshasa princes.
But as he raged on with gnashing teeth, Bhīma laughingly
said to him : " Why shouldſt thou awake these quiet sleepers ?
Set on me quickly, thou fool. Come, beat me ! Thou shalt
not kill a woman, especially when she has done thee no hurt,
but another. This maid has no power over herself : she lcves
me now, she is driven on by the god of love, who has his being
within the body. Not againſt thee has she sinned. It is love that
did the crime ; do not upbraid this woman here. When I
am there, thou shalt not slay a woman. In a moment I will
crush thy head." Then the Rākshasa uttered wild threats,
and fell on Bhīma. But Bhīma laid hold of the arm he ſtretched
out, and firſt of all dragged the ſtruggling Rākshasa a long way
off, that the sleepers might not hear the noise of the fight. A
fierce ſtruggle now was fought between the two ; like two
rutting elephants of sixty years [1] they broke down trees, carrying
away creepers with them. Kuntī and her sons were awakened
by it, and she asked the wonderful apparition ſtanding before
her who she was. Hiḍimbā told her how things ſtood, and
declared to her that, driven by the love that has its abode in the
hearts of all beings, she had chosen the other's son for her
husband. Arjuna shouted to Bhīma that he would help him,
and bring the monſter down. But Bhīma answered : " Look
thou on as one beholding only, and be not ſtirred. One that

---

[1] The sixty year old elephant as a type of huge ſtrength is often
found in the Epic. So i, 151.4 ; 153.44 ; ii, 53.7 ; iv, 13.24 ;
31.31 ; vii, 28.20 ; Rām., ii, 67.20 ; vii, 23.45. Cp. Çiçupālav.,
xviii, 6, and Mallinātha, on the passage, where the forty year old is at
the height of his ſtrength.

has once fallen between my arms stays not in this life." The brother bade him act quickly, before the east should redden, for by twilight, he said, the Rākshasas are strong.[1] Bhīmasena whirled the giant around a hundred times in the air, dashed him onto the ground, and broke him in twain at his middle, so that he met his end with a dreadful roaring. Then the brothers went quickly on, and Hidimbā followed them. Bhīma wanted to send her after her brother, fearing her vengeance and craft, but Yudhishthira prevailed on him not to murder a woman, and Hidimbā turned humbly to Kuntī : " Noble lady, thou knowest the sorrow that comes on women through love. It has come on me, and the cause is Bhīma. I have borne the utmost pain while awaiting the right moment. This has now come, and must be for my happiness. Friends, my duty and my folk I have left, and chosen the tiger among men, thy son, for my husband. If I am repelled by this hero and by thee, I cannot go on living. Therefore have pity on me, thou of the lovely face, thinking of me : ' She is blinded,' or ' given up to love ', or ' has followed him ' ". She promised the fugitives every kind of help, and pointed out that on the general view life must be preserved in any way whatever that is possible and that unhappiness is harmful to virtue [2] ; but that he who like herself keeps virtue unharmed amid unhappiness, and preserves his life in holy wise is worthy of all praise. At Yudhishthira's bidding she was then wedded to Bhīma but on the condition that she should only take her pleasure with him by day and always bring him back again at night ; and Bhīma added he would only stay with her until she had borne a son. She was content with all, and now the two lived the happiest days in a great variety of splendid places, even in the forests of the gods ;

[1] The Rākshasas and other evil spirits are especially powerful by night, particularly at midnight, but also by twilight. See, e.g., 170.8 ff., 69 ; iii, 11.33 ; vii, 156.69 ; 173.57 ; Rām., i, 26.22, 23.

[2] Also hunger destroys virtue and, as the old Upanishad so clearly teaches, knowledge and wisdom (iii, 260.24 ; ix, 51.36 ff.; xiv, 90.90, 91; cp. v, 33.101 f. ; xiii, 93.66 f.). Therefore, according to an old verse, the draught-ox, the sacrifice in fire, and the scholar must eat heartily. Āpast., ii, 5, 9.13 ; Vashishtha, vi, 21 ; Baudh., ii, 7, 13.7–8 ; ii, 10, 18.13 ; Çāṅkh.-Gṛihyas., ii, 16.5 ; K, i, 85.21.

for the beloved one, appearing in bewitching form, took the hero everywhere. But then she bore a son, and directly after she had first conceived, as is the way of Rākshasa women. And since the stipulated time was now run, she took farewell of Bhīmasena without a murmur, and went (i, 152 ff.).[1]

Among the most beautiful passages in Indian literature are perhaps Rāma's love-plaints for Sītā robbed by Rāvana, only we must thrust our Western feelings somewhat aside, and not find this delicate, somewhat feminine soul of a hero unmanly.

The beloved one is not to be seen near the leaf-hut in the forest, and he cries out that without her he cannot live, nor has any wish for lordship over the gods or the earth. And how the poor timid one will pine without him ! The hut itself is empty ; like a madman, with eyes reddened by weeping, he runs about the forest, seeking her that is lost ; from tree he wanders to tree, through the mountains, over rivers ; he asks all the trees in moving speech, the beasts of the forest, whether they have seen the much loved, the wondrous-fair one ; and in great horror he pictures to himself how the monsters have eaten her, have swallowed her bewitching limbs. And then again he cannot bring himself to believe that she could really have been taken from him ; he calls out to her that she must now put an end to her play, as he is thus suffering ; she must come forth from her hiding-place ; he can see her yellow silk robe. He lets himself be persuaded by Lakshmana that she has gone to pick flowers ; that she, who so loves the forest, has gone wandering away in it, and will surely spring suddenly out to frighten him. And once more he searches all about with his brother, but finds her not, who to him " is dearer than his own life ". Then he breaks forth wailing once more ; again he believes she is only hiding

[1] Rückert has translated this piece from the MBh. in a very much shortened and not altogether successful form : " Hidimba. Eine brahmanische Erzählung," *Gesammelte poet. Werke*, Bd. xii (Frankf. a. M., 1882). It is given in a short form in MBh., iii, 12.94 ff. According to Samayamātrikā, ii, 22, Bhīma had deeply loved Hidimbā. As we are told in K, i, 160.4 ff. she lived seven months with him before she became with child.

herself, and he calls out as before that he can see her, that the jeſt has gone on long enough. And as she ſtill does not come, he is certain she muſt be dead, for how could she, she of all, otherwise leave him without consolation. He never wishes to go back to the city again ; how can he go to meet his kindred without Sītā ? " And without her heaven itself would feel empty for me."

> " There is no other on earth, methinks, that so
> much evil in his former being has done as I ;
> for on me now there falls in one long chain
> but sorrow after sorrow, my heart and soul it crushes.
>
> My kingdom loſt, the farewell from my folk,
> my father's death, the parting from my mother—
> when I ponder on all this within me,
> then the wild waves of my sorrow are swollen.
>
> But all the sorrow died in me, O Lakshman,
> when I went forth into the foreſt, into want :
> I had Sītā ! Now it rises again
> like fire, set swiftly blazing by the logs.
>
> She so noble, so timid, by the monſter
> robbed, and snatched up into the air,
> she that else speaks in sweet notes—how muſt
> she have uttered sharp cry on cry of fear !
>
> Her face, whose lips so tenderly have spoken,
> and girt by a wealth of locks—
> it shone surely in the Raksha's claws
> like the bright moon in Rāhu's maw.
>
> With blood are flecked her rounded breaſts,
> that ever knew but beſt of sandal-wood,
> red, lovely sandal. O sure it is :
> never shall I clasp my deareſt one to me.
>
> By me forsaken in the lonely foreſt,
> ringed round and hurried away by the Rakshas,
> the woman with great, lovely eyes has in sorrow
> mourned like the hen-osprey.
>
> On this rock sat with me
> once Sītā of the glorious life.
> How sweetly did she smile and laugh, O Lakshman,
> and as she prattled, to thee said this and that.

LOVE

She might have gone into that forest
of blooming, close-set trees of many kinds,
and filled with flocks of birds.—But that too cannot be.
Left thus alone, the timid one is too afraid.

What here is done, what not, thou, O sun, knowest it,
witness to the works of truth and falsehood.
Whither then went my darling ? Did a robber take her ?
Tell me of all, who am the mark of sorrow.

Nothing, nothing is in the universe to find,
whereof, O wind, thou shouldst no knowledge have.
Tell of her that is the treasure of her house :
is she dead ? carried off ? still on the way ? "

Again he goes on looking and looking ; the river Godāvarī
gives no answer to the anguished questioner, the mountain
tells him nought ; but the beasts of the forest let him understand that he must go southwards, and there he finds traces :
flowers that have dropped from the ravished one, wreaths,
bits of ornament, other signs of the Rākshasa ; his anger
blazes forth ; he is going to destroy the whole world. Then
the prince of the apes, Sugrīva, brings him the upper garment
and ornaments of Sītā. Weeping loud he falls to the ground
and presses to his heart these ornaments and garment which
have felt the glow of her body. His thoughts henceforth
are only for his beloved ; particularly when he sees the moon
rise, do his tears well up, and sleep comes not to his bed. He
eats but at every fifth meal ; flies, gnats, and other vermin
he does not keep away from himself ; he does not mark it at all,
since his soul is busied but with Sītā ; " Sītā, Sītā ! " is the only
sound on his lips. As an earthquake rocks the mighty
mountain, so is he thrown this way and that by his sorrow.
When Hanumant brings him a token from her, who is still
pining in the captivity of the man-eating monsters, the token of
a precious stone, then he calls out with tear-filled eyes : " As
her milk flows from the tender cow for love of her calf, so
does my heart flow at the sight of this best of jewels. Yes, for
me it is as though I had my darling once again. But what
could there be more harrowing than this, that the stone born
of the sea comes to me again, but without her of the black
eyes ? " She can only live, he says, a short time longer without

him, and amid the cruel wretches. And now he overwhelms the messenger with queſtions about her welfare, and wants to know every word she has uttered ; for that, he says, will give him life, like medicine to the sick man. At laſt the army is camped on the sea-shore over againſt Laṅkā, the city of the Rākshasas, where Sītā is being held a prisoner ; and Rāma breaks out into the words : " They say that sorrow dies with time ; but in me, who do not see my beloved, it waxes day by day.

> Blow, O wind, where my beloved tarries,
> touch her firſt, and then me, too.
> In thee our bodies touch one another,
> in the moon our glances are united.[1]

> I dive into the waters of the sea
> and sleep deep alone ;
> there love's torments burn not
> the sleeper with glowing fire.

This it is that for the lover means much, and it is through this that he can live—that I and she of the lovely thighs are on one ſtretch of land. When shall I tilt lightly upwards her lotus-like face, lit by its lovely teeth, and drink, as the sick man drinks the draught of life ? When will the quivering breaſts of the laughing one, pressing againſt one another, swelling, like unto the wine-palm's fruit, when will they but clasp me ? Alas ! the black-eyed one who has me to shelter her, can find no rescuer, like one that is shelterless. When at laſt will Sītā, the kind, she like a daughter of the gods, twine herself round my neck, filled with longing, and shed tears of joy ? When shall I of a sudden caſt off this dreadful pain, that comes of my separation from Sītā, like a sullied garment ? " (Rām., iii, 58, 60–64 ; iv, 6.11 ff. ; 27.30 ff. ; v, 35.38 ff. ; 36.40 ff. ; 66.1 ff.).

Bhīmasena, by far the moſt humanly attractive of the five brothers, shows, too, in his relation towards Draupadī, his deeper and passion-filled soul. " In this hermitary dwelt the tigers among men (the Pāṇḍavas robbed of Arjuna) for six days, earneſt in the loftieſt purity, and filled with

[1] Because they both look, parted from one another, into the moon. This is againſt the miſtaken interpretation of Nīlakaṇṭha (vi, 5.6).

longing to see Arjuna again. Then the wind wafted out of the north-east happened to bring there a divine lotus-flower, like unto the sun. This wind-wafted, pure, water-borne thing, heavenly-scented, gladdening the heart, was seen lying on the ground by the princess of Pañcāla (Draupadī). When the shining one had found this shining thing, the surpassing lotus-flower,[1] she was right glad, and spoke to Bhīmasena : ' Look, Bhīma, at the heavenly, brightly shining flower without compare, perfect in scent and shape, a delight for my heart ! . . . If I am dear to thee, O son of Pṛithā, then get me many like it ; I will take them with me back again into the hermitary Kāmyaka.' When she with the lovely eyes, she free from any fault, had thus spoken to Bhīmasena, she went and took away the flower for Yudhishthira.[2] At once when the bull among men, Bhīma, the powerful strong one, had learned the wishes of his beloved wife, he went off filled with the yearning to do something after her heart. Facing the wind, he strode swiftly along towards whence this flower had come, wishing to bring more flowers, and grasping his gold-backed bow and the snake-like arrows, like the angry king of beasts, like a rutting elephant. All beings saw the bearer of the arrows and the mighty bow. Neither weariness nor weakness, neither fear nor bewilderment ever befell the child of Pṛithā, the son of the wind. Striving after that which was dear to Draupadī, trusting in the strength of his arms, shunned by anxiety or numbness of senses, the strong one flew along on the mountain. The destroyer of foes ranged the glorious mountain-top, clothed in trees, creepers, and bushes, paved with dark stones, the wandering-ground of Kinnaras ; it showed bright, with many-coloured minerals, trees, beasts, and birds, and was filled with every beauty, and raised up like an arm of the earth. While his eye clung always to the ravishing ridges of the Gandhamādana, and he was pondering his purpose in his heart, and his ear,

[1] Saugandhika in this meaning is often found in the Epic. So iii, 146.2, and over and over again afterwards ; 152.13 ; 153.6 ; 154.2 ; 155.13 ; Rām., iii, 75.20 ; iv, 1.63.

[2] In the doublet of this tale in K, iii, 161 (= B, 160) Draupadī says to Bhīma she will be his in love, when she has had these flowers.

heart, and eye were held captive by the notes of the male kokila-bird, and the working of the bees,[1] he went striding along in his unbounded heroic strength. Scenting the perfume wafted up from the flowers that bloom at all seasons of the year, unfettered in the forest as a rutting elephant, fanned by the wind from Gandhamādana,[2] very pure, filled with sweet scent from various flowers, cooled through having touched its father, he freed from weariness by his father,[3] his body clothed with fine hair ruffled with joy—thus did the so mighty queller of foes search the mountain, haunt of Yakshas, Gandharvas, gods, and Brahmarshi-bands, to find the flower. This mountain was wrapped in the headlong waters of the waterfalls as in threaded pearls, filled with the splendid peacocks brought to dance by the sounds of the anklets of the Apsarases, and the robe seemed to be gliding down from it in the form of the hurrying [4] waters streaming from the rivers. With young torn-up grass in their mouths, calm, keeping near him, unknown to fear, the gazelles gazed at him ; in his headlong career he set the tangle of creepers quivering in great clumps, he sported with merry heart, and so the son of the wind went along, he of the beautiful eyes, eagerly bent on fulfilling his loved one's wish, tall, in golden splendour, the youth with the stout limbs of the lion, with a hero's might like a rutting elephant, headlong as a rutting elephant. Representing,[5] as it were, a new Avatāra of beauty, thinking of the various miseries caused by Duryodhana, full of eagerness to do something pleasing for Draupadī living in the forest wilds, filled with the thought : ' How can I very speedily get the flowers ? ' —so did he range along the glorious ridge of Gandhamādana.

[1] Or : by the (mountain-ridge) filled with the kokila's song, haunted by the bees.

[2] The wind is cool since it comes from the scented forests (sandal-wood groves) and lotus-clumps of Gandhamādana. By " father " this place of origin is meant here.

[3] That is, the wind, who is Bhīma's begetter.

[4] Ākshobhya (has this meaning once or twice). I have considerably shortened down the description, too.

[5] With vikrīdati, to play, that is, represent (by playing), cp. vikrī-date panyam, to trade (iii, 188.53).

LOVE

Draupadī's word was his journey's food ; swiftly ran Bhīma,
like the storm-wind at the time of the Parvan days,[1] and the
ground shook under his feet. The herds of elephants were
terrified by him, swift as the wind ; lions, tigers, and antelopes
were trodden down by the strong one ; great trees were
uprooted and dashed to pieces by the mighty one in his headlong
course ; creepers and climbing plants he tore off along with
him in his wild career ; loud he roared like the lightning-
riven cloud. At this loud din raised by Bhīma the tigers
woke, and left their lairs, the forest-dwellers were filled with
fear, the birds flew up in terror, and the herds of gazelles fled.
Many elephants, tigers, and suchlike beasts fled, others attacked
him with loud and angry roars. Then in his rage the son of
the wind with the strength of his arm with one elephant
put the others to flight, with the lion he put the lions to flight,
other beasts with his open hand. Waterfowl terrified by the
din flew up in thousands with wet wings, and when the Bharata
bull followed after them he saw a very great and pleasant
pond with stirring waters,[2] fanned by golden clumps of banana-
trees waving in the wind, and stretching from one bank to
the other. Into this pond, studded with many day-lotuses
and blue lotuses, the strong one climbed down, and played in
it, full of wild strength like a frolicsome elephant. When he
went on his way again, the strong Bhīma winded his war shell-
trumpet with all his might and with a loud note, and beat on his
arms, so that the lands of the world resounded. With the notes
of the shell and Bhīmasena's shouts, and the mighty cracks
of his arms, the caves of the mountain seemed to resound.
When the lions asleep in the mountain-caves heard this great
cracking of his arms as he hit them, like the fall of the thunderbolt, they uttered loud roars. And then the elephants,
frightened by the roaring of the lions, started a mighty
trumpeting, which filled the mountain."

After a truly Indian adventure with his half-brother,
Hanumant, he went on his way again to search "with Draupadī's
word as food for his way ", and at length beheld a mighty
river, and in it a grove of those particular lotus-flowers that his

[1] Probably at the time of the equinox.
[2] Ākshobhya.

301

wife yearned after, shining like the newly risen sun. " When he had seen it, he felt in his heart that he was at the goal of his wishes, and in his thoughts he hastened to his beloved, sore worn as she was by her life in the forest." Near here, too, was the wondrous-fair lotus-pond of Kubera the god of wealth, whence that flower had come ; and this pond was covered by those rare golden lotus-flowers, resting on stalks of cat's-eye stones. They sent forth the sweetest scent, and, whirled up by the waterfowl, their pollen flew through the air. The bold hero now at once drank of the water, and wanted to take the flowers ; the watching spirits, however, angrily stopped him, and demanded that he should first ask the owner, Kubera, as did even gods and holy men. But he told them proudly that he was the Pāṇḍava Bhīmasena, and had come at the sweet bidding of his wife. " Kings do not beg, that is the everlasting law. And I can in no wise set the custom of the Kshattriyas behind me. And this lovely lotus-clump grew up by the waterfall in the mountain ; it belongs to all beings as much as to Kubera." They came to blows, but Bhīma with his huge club overcame his attackers, and put them to flight ; he drank his fill of the nectar-like water, and plucked of the wonderful lotus-blooms to his heart's desire. Kubera, who was at once told of the matter, laughed and was content withal (iii, 146 ff.).

If we are reminded by this haughty strong man, fighting in the service of his lady-love against giants and spirits, and fetching her the golden flower, of a lover from knighthood's days, so he, too, shows knightly feelings towards Draupadī. It is he only of the brothers that is aroused by the shame put on the proud princess of Pañcāla by that disastrous game of dice, and so deeply aroused that he angrily reproaches his eldest brother, when this brother has played away his wife. That Yudhishthira has wagered and lost all their possessions, and then the four brothers themselves, he is quite willing to forgive ; for he is their lord. " This it is I hold for a sin, that Draupadī was made a stake ; for this youthful woman, who has been given the Pāṇḍavas, is through thy fault tormented by the low, cruel, rough Kauravas. Gambling ruffians have evil wives in their homes, O Yudhishthira, but for them they

do not play ; for they feel a loving sympathy even for them."
And since he cannot pour his anger out on the hallowed head
of his eldeſt brother, he is minded to burn his own arms in the
fire, before Yudhishthira's eyes—a truly Indian way of revenge
and branding (ii, 68.1 ff.).[1] In full sight of the brothers
Duḥçāsana drags the but partly clad woman into the hall
before all the men, and tears her clothing off her ; but Bhīma
blazes up, and with quivering lips and hand pressed againſt
hand swears for this to drink the blood from the shameless
man's breaſt (ii, 68.50 ff.). And when Duryodhana shows
her his bare thigh, flames of fire come out of every opening
in the body of the giant Bhīma mighty in anger, as from the
hollows of a burning tree,[2] and he swears by all his
bliss to shatter with his club, in the fight, the insolent
one's thigh (ii, 71.13 ff.). And both these dread deeds
he carries out afterwards.[3] But he can never forget what
has been done to Draupadī, and his soul is filled with pity
for her that she muſt bear so heavy a burden (cp. too iii,
312.2 ; vii, 79.4; xi, 15.6–9 ; xii, 16.18, 21, 28 ; xv, 11.21 ;
etc.). Afterwards all her sons fall at the hand of the foe,
and in her agony she falls to the ground. Bhīma clasps her
in his arms, lifts her up, and utters consoling, loving words

---

[1] Cp. the prāya (prāyopaveça, dharna) and Billington, 248 ff.
Devendra Das, *Sketches of Hindoo Life*, 180 f. Tod, *Rajaſthan*, i,
740–2 ; ii, 182–3 ; 674–7 (here the Bhāts are discussed, who are
related to the Kshattriyas, and probably descend from them); Devendra
Das, 205 (fakirs light a fire and threaten to burn their arms, if their
wish is not fulfilled); and so forth. Cp. Crooke, *Popul. Relig. and Folkl.*
etc.[1], p. 122 ; Jolly, *Sitzungsber. d. bayr. Akad.*, 1877, p. 316;
Zachariae in *Zeitschr. d. Ver. f. Volksk.*, 1925–1926, p. 149 ff. ; E.
Thurſton, *Omens and Superſtitions of Southern India* (Lond., 1912),
p. 144 f. ; Hopkins, JAOS, vol. 21, 2nd half (1900), pp. 146–159 ;
also Āpaſt.-Dharmas., i, 6, 19.1. For the dharna cp. Schurtz,
Urgesch. d. Kultur, p. 615.
[2] Cp. ii, 72.14; iii, 277.51 ; viii, 91.19, 20 (Rām., vii, 68.9).
[3] In the same way King Dama wants to drink the blood of a low cunning evil-doer whom he has cut down in battle, but is ſtayed by the gods,
Mārk.-Pur., cxxxvi, 34. The drinking of a slain man's blood, indeed,
is a wide-spread cuſtom, found also in Germanic olden times. As
is well known, it has, mainly, other motives than that of angry revenge.

to her. It is he then who takes on himself the charge from his mother, burning for expiation, to take revenge on the murderer of the five (x, 11.8, 9, 20 ff.). He also takes wrathful vengeance on King Jayadratha, when the latter has carried off Draupadī (iii, 264–272.24, especially 272.7 ff.). He alone, too, steps into the lists on her behalf, when the Lothario and royal favourite, Kīcaka at Virāṭa's court tries to rob her of her honour, a truly captivating chapter, inviting us to a more particular examination (iv, 14–24).

According to the agreement the Pāṇḍavas have to spend the thirteenth year of exile somewhere in hiding and unknown. They hire themselves out in various positions at the court of King Virāṭa : Yudhishṭhira as steward of the prince's gambling-house (sabhāstara), Bhīma as his cook, and circus wrestler, Arjuna as a eunuch in woman's clothes, and as teacher of dancing and music to the young princess and her companions, and so forth. Draupadī goes as chambermaid and *coiffeuse* into the service of Queen Sudeshṇā; and they succeed in keeping quite unknown. But at the end of ten months Kīcaka, the queen's brother, the leader of the army, and all-powerful favourite, gets to see the dazzlingly beautiful maid, and is fired with love for her. In glowing words he sings the praises of all her charms from the eyes down to her pubic parts, vaulted like a river-island, paints his agony of love, beseeches her to save him, and shows her how mistaken she is to wish to live as a lowly maid. He offers himself to her as husband and slave, and says he will cast off his wives, and make them the servants of the servant that now is, and give her all the earth's delights to taste. He is, he tells her, the real ruler in the land, and none on earth is his equal in beauty, youthful bloom, success with women, wealth, and other splendid things. But she bids him bethink himself what a heavy crime, what a shameful deed, and how dangerous a thing it is ever to touch another's wife. Moreover, she says, she is the wife of five hot-tempered Gandharvas, who would kill him. Whether he were to penetrate into the earth, or fly up into the air, or flee to the other shore of the sea, he cannot escape these all-destroying sons of the gods, these cleavers of the air. He is as the child sitting in its mother's lap and wanting to clutch the

moon. Kīcaka now took refuge behind his sister, and by his
desperate plaints moved her to take pity and help him. Following
her directions he made a feast ready, and set out much food
and heady drink. Then Sudeshṇā bade her maid : " Arise
and go into Kīcaka's house, O kind one, and fetch me something to drink ; I am tortured by thirst." Draupadī answered :
" I would fain not go into his house. Thou thyself, O queen,
knowest well how shameless he is. And I wish not in thine
house to follow the lust of the flesh, nor sin against my husband.
Kīcaka, indeed, O thou with the lovely hair, is blinded, and
over-daring in love. He will bring dishonour on me, if he
sees me. I shall not go there, O fair one. Thou hast many
serving-women standing at thy bidding. Send thou another,
for he will show me the little esteem he has for me." Sudeshṇā
spoke : " He will never do thee any hurt, if thou art sent by
me." With these words she gave her the golden vessel, fitted
with a lid. Weeping and filled with fear, Draupadī went.
Kīcaka called out to her right gladly :

> " Welcome, lady with lovely hair !
> How bright the night is lit for me !
> Hither as my lady thou dost come.
> Be kind, fulfil my longing.

> Gold wreaths shall to thee be brought
> and wondrous ornament of silken robes,
> gold rings, shells, stone jewels ;
> a divine bed stands ready for thee ;
> come hither and with me sip
> the sweet glory of the intoxicating drink."

> " 'Twas for spirits that the king's daughter
> sent me hither to thine house.
> ' Bring me to drink at once ;
> I am athirst.' Those are her words."

The lover answered that the queen had other serving-women,
and took hold of her garment ; but she pulled it towards
her with all her strength, and so pulled him to the ground.[1]

[1] In the same way she pulls Jayadratha onto the ground, when he
takes hold of her, the lonely one, in the forest of banishment, and tries
to carry her off (iii, 268.24).

Then she ran for protection into the sabhā,[1] where Yudhishthira was. Kīcaka ran after her, caught hold of her by the hair, threw her down, and kicked her. But then a Rākshasa, whom the sun god had sent Draupadī, after her prayer, to stand by her unseen, headlong as the wind took him off, and flung him to the ground. Yudhishthira and Bhīma saw what happened ; over Bhīma's eyes there passed a misty shadow, the sweat broke out from the dreadful wrinkles on his forehead ; hand to hand he pressed, and ground his teeth in fury. His eyes were fastened on a tree standing near. But Yudhishthira was anxious lest it should be found out who they really were, made him a sign, and said : " O cook, an thou need wood, then go outside (beyond the city), and bring down trees for thyself."[2] Draupadī controlled her countenance, but threw dreadful, almost burning glances at her husbands, and bitterly bewailed the fact that this son of a Sūta dared kick her, the wife of such mighty heroes, with his foot, and that, coward-like, they stood not by her ; King Virāta, too, she felt, and his counsellors were shamelessly neglecting law and justice; they were calmly looking on at the crime against an innocent woman, they were acting like thieves and robbers. But

---

[1] The sabhā serves both as gambling-house and as the place of justice ; cp. çl. 43. The sabhya and sabhāsada (çl. 33, 36 ff.), and the men who sit in the rājasaṃsad (31, 43) are both law and gambling confrères of the king. H. Schurtz would see in the sabhā the well-known " unmarried men's house ".

[2] Vrikshān nigrihyatāṃ ; we should expect perhaps : nikrityatāṃ. K (19, 36) has samūlaṃ çātayer vrikshaṃ, which reads smoothly enough, it is true, but is anyhow not in the original, as, indeed, the whole Kīcakaparvan in K shows many insertions and changes of an evidently later date. The passive with the accus. has many parallels in the Epic. The nearest to our case is Rām., vii, 59.2 : Madarthaṃ pratigrihyatāṃ jarāṃ paramikām ; and the accus. with the gerundive : kiyad adhvānaṃ asmābhir gantavyam imam īdriçam = " how far must we go along this road made thus " (xviii, 2.16), where probably we hardly have simple Prakrit neuters, although the neuter adhvāna is often found in the MBh. Cp. too the accus. with the pass. infin. in ii, 48.17 (liter. indeed : " I know by what the overcoming of Y. is made possible."). See e.g. also iii, 68.25 ; xii, 215.14 ; xiv, 29.22 ; 71.14 ; 87.12 ; xv, 3.59 ; etc.

LOVE

Yudhishṭhira showed her she muſt put a check on herself; he told her that her Gandharva husbands did not deem it now the time to take revenge, and would see to that by and by. Draupadī cried out : " I am but too considerate for these weak-souled men. The firſt-comer may beat [1] them, whose eldeſt is a dice-player." After these words she ran weeping and with ſtreaming hair into Sudeshṇā's abode. She purified herself, washed her limbs and her clothes, and considered what she should do. She decided that only Bhīma could and would help her. So in the night she crept to him in the kitchen, clasped him as a creeper does the tree, and awoke the sleeper : " Rise, rise, wherefore doſt thou lie sleeping, O Bhīmasena, like a dead man ! For no evil man touches the wife of a man that is not dead, and ſtill lives." Bhīma ſtarted up, and asked her what was diſtressing her. She burſt into bitter complaints of what she had already had to bear, and that now at the fresh insult her heart was ready to burſt. But what else could she expeçt, since Yudhishṭhira, the evil dicer, was her husband, the man who had brought himself and all belonging to him from kingly pomp and splendour into the very depths of poverty and contempt ! [2] She now drew a piçture of the degrading life the brothers led ; and she

[1] Or : slay.

[2] In K. she expresses herself far more emphatically ſtill. There among other things she cries out (22.45 ff.) : " Be thou my ſtay ; I do not wish to turn to Yudh., the man without ſtrength of will, without the passion of revenge (amarsha), without manhood. Oh ! may no woman bear such a son ! . . . As the rutting lord of the herd, the sixty year old elephant, tramples with his feet on the bilva-fruit fallen to the ground, and squashes it, so do thou, O man-tiger, pound in fragments Kīcaka's skull, after thou haſt flung him to the ground. If Kīcaka rises to-morrow morning, and when the night has grown light [accus. absol. çarvarīṃ vyushṭāṃ, as, for inſtance, in v, 194.2 ; vi, 3.35 ; 60.1 ; vii, 74.46 ; 76.27 ; 29.44 ; ix, 30.21, like the not unfrequent prabhātāṃ çarvarīṃ], sees the rising sun, then I can no longer live. . . . And put the blame on thine eldeſt brother, the evil dice-player, through whose fault I have been brought to this boundless sorrow. But they, whose head and eldeſt is a shameful ſtain on his family, will probably, as men of humble spirit, follow after their excellent brother."

herself, she said, was a slave ; she, the once proud daughter of a king, she a queen, whom the sea-ringed earth had obeyed, muſt wait in awe on her miſtress, with her delicate hands pound sandal-wood and prepare salve, and tremble to see whether it was to the liking of her lady. And she showed Bhīma her hands all horny. Bhīma raised her hands to his lips, and wept with her. Then he explained to her that he himself had wished to take a bloody vengeance at once, but Yudhishṭhira had ſtood in the way ; she muſt have patience only a little while longer, until they could come forth before the world. But she made him see that the danger from the all-powerful woman-hunter was too great, and that the warrior has no other duty but to deſtroy the foe. As so often before, so now again Bhīma muſt save her. " Break this man mad with love, like a pitcher on the ſtone ! If to-morrow morning the sun rises on him, who has brought me so much unhappiness, as on a living man, I shall mix myself poison, and drink it ; but I will not fall into Kīcaka's power. It is better I should die here before thine eyes, Bhīma." Weeping, she leant againſt his breaſt, and he spoke loving words of consolation to her. Then he wiped away her tears, licked the corners of his mouth [1] with rage, and spoke : " I will slay him even to-day together with his kindred. Give him a tryſt this evening. There is the dancing-hall, built by the king of the Matsyas. By day the maidens dance there, at night they go home. In it there is a heaven-like, firmly made bed. On it I will show him his forbears that died before him. Look to it that thou art not seen speaking with him, and that he comes there."

Next morning Kīcaka spoke scornfully to Draupadī : " Before the king's eyes did I throw thee down in the sabhā, and kick thee with my feet, and there was none to save when a ſtrong man laid hold on thee. It is I who am really the king of the Matsyas. Do thou take me joyfully, and I am thy slave. I will give thee forthwith a hundred golden nishkas, a hundred slave-girls, and as many slaves, together with a chariot drawn by she-mules." She made answer :

---

[1] An angry man's geſture often mentioned (so, e.g. iii, 157.50, 52; v, 162.17 ; vi, 84.12 ; 94.5 ; 96.22 ; 102.29 ; 111.11 ; xii, 8.2).

LOVE

" Do thou now make this condition with me, O Kīcaka :
no friend or brother of thine muſt know that thou meeteſt
me. If there is evil speech of me, I am afeard of the glorious
Gandharvas.[1] Promise me this, and I will do as thou willeſt."
Kīcaka spoke : " Thus will I do, as thou sayeſt, O thou with
the lovely hips. Alone I shall come into thy lonely abode,
to unite with thee in the madness of love, so that the Gandharvas, shining as the sun, may not see thee." " Come thou
by darkness into the dancing-hall that was built by the king
of the Matsyas. By day the maidens dance there, at night
they go home. This the Gandharvas will not remark.
There of a surety we shall avoid any harm." As Draupadī
talked on of this thing, to Kīcaka the half-day seemed as a
month.[2] Then Kīcaka went back to his house, overwhelmed
with joy ; in his blindness he marked not his death in the
form of the waiting-maid. Being much given to scents,
ornaments, and wreaths, he haſtily adorned himself, mazed
with love. While he was thus busied, the time seemed to
him very long, for he thought but of that great-eyed one.
Right splendid did he look, juſt when he was to leave his
splendour behind, like a light when it is about to fade away,
and ſtrives to use up its wick to the end. Draupadī slipped
away to Bhīma, told him all, and once more with ſtrong words
called on him to bring the haughty one, who used contemptuous
words about her Gandharva husbands, to his end. Wild with
rage, he boaſted he would tread down Kīcaka's head, as the
elephant does a bilva-fruit, and slay all the Matsyas, and then
Duryodhana, and rule over the earth ; Yudhishṭhira could
ſtay on as a servant to his heart's desire. But she impressed
on him that he muſt carry out the vengeful deed in secret.
In the night the thirſter after love came into the hall deep in
darkness, and spoke with a heart ſtirred with joy : " Mine

[1] Probably less likely : I am afraid of evil speech about the Gandharvas (anupravādād bhītāsmi gandharvānām yaçasvinām). In view
of what follows the meaning might rather be : I am afraid that the
Gandharvas will upbraid me.
[2] The inſtrumental, probably liter. : " became through Kīcaka,
in K.'s eyes " ; or the modal : " according to K., in K.'s opinion."
Kīcakasya in K. is probably a reading which has been touched up.

house and my women's apartment, adorned with fair-shaped, most pleasing young women, and bright with merriment and love's pleasures—all this I have left for thy sake, and have come hither.[1] Quite of their own accord (akasmāt) the women that are in the house do constantly sing my praises : ' Fair-clad, and a sight of splendour art thou, and no other man is equal to thee.' " Bhīmasena called out :

> " Luck be with thee, thou vision of all splendour !
> Luck be with thee, thou singest thy loud praises !
> Now will something be brought thee
> such as thou never yet hast touched.

> Contact thou dost know, thou hast been distilled
> with every kind of water, and art well skilled
> in the way of love, thou delight of women ;
> no man can here be seen like thee." [2]

Saying this, he sprang up and laid hold of his wreathed hair, But Kīcaka clasped him with his arms. And now began a long, hard-fought wrestling-match between the two stout opponents. But at length Bhīma overbore him, squeezed his throat, and strangled the life out of him like a beast.[3] Then with awful strength he rammed arms and legs, head and neck into his trunk, so that only a shapeless lump of flesh remained. He then called Draupadī, kindled a light, and showed her the sight. Full of joy she ran and told the wardens of the sabhā that the Gandharvas, her husbands, had slain Kīcaka, the luster after women. The kindred, and followers of the murdered man came, and wanted to vent their rage on Draupadī.

[1] I would read saṃhāyāhaṃ instead of sahasāhaṃ. It is hardly : Allotting thee . . . my house, I have come at breathless speed.

[2] Or perhaps better : " as the delight of women no man can here be seen like thee."

[3] It is only by the sanctifying death from the weapon (çastrapūta) that the warrior comes into heaven, as the MBh. tells us over and over again. The hero, therefore, likes to slay a specially hated foeman in such a shameful way (paçumāraṃ mārayati), so that the wretched man may thereby lose paradise. Moreover, it is also awkward if we, like Yudhishthira (xviii, 1), see C. F. Meyer's words coming true : Even in heaven we may meet a man we cannot bear.

LOVE

They laid hold of her and dragged her with them to the place of the burning to give her to the flames along with the lover, and so do him a loving service even in death. Loudly she cried out for help, and Bhīma leaped over the wall, and fell on the Sūtas, tearing up a mighty tree, and swinging it as a weapon. In terror the men let the girl go, and fled before the supposed Gandharva. But he killed a hundred and five, "this made with Kīcaka a hundred and six." Filled with fear and terror they now importuned the king to take all care left his kingdom should fall a prey to deſtruction ; for the Gandharvas, they said, were so ſtrong, and the waiting-maid too fair ; and such a lovely objeſt for the senses attraſted men all too ſtrongly to the pleasures of love. Virāṭa now exhorts his wife to send away the waiting-maid, saying he could not tell her for fear of the Gandharvas,[1] while a woman would not come by any harm if she did it. Meanwhile Draupadī came home again, and the girls, who were being taught by Arjuna disguised as a eunuch, came out and congratulated her ; but the queen asked the dangerous one to go away. Draupadī begged to be allowed to ſtop another thirteen days (iv, 14–24).[2]

[1] Naturally tām is to be read inſtead of tvām (24.10).

[2] With our tale compare above all Holtzmann, *Das Mahābhārata u. seine Teile*, iv, 98 ; Daçakumāracar., p. 172 ff. (Pushpodbhava's adventure), espec. 176 ff., and my note on p. 178 ; Daçāvatāracar., viii, 555 (a woman may have Gandharvas as husbands ; these then kill any man touching her) ; Weber's *Ind. Studien*, xv, 337 (in the Siṃhāsanadvātriṃç., a Rākshasa even lays hold of a surpassingly lovely hetæra) ; Kuṭṭanīmatam, 347 (a demon has a woman in his possession and slays her lover). Daṇḍin's tale is assuredly not unconneſted with the Kīcakaparvan.

The Gandharva, and later the Gandharvas, as owners before marriage, and afterwards lovers of the wife, and other luſtful spirits have been alive in Indian thought since Vedic times, and, as is well known, there is nothing singular about this faſt ; for monſters, and supernatural beings of every kind, even Chriſtian saints, know only too well how to appreciate fair women, and often bring down misfortune or deſtruſtion on the mortal man who is the mate of such a one. See the St. Petersburg diſtionaries, and Monier-Williams, under " Gandharva " ; Pischel u. Geldner, *Vedische Studien*, i, 77 ff. ; L. v. Schroeder, *Myſterium u.*

311

Mimus, p. 60 ff.; 309 f.; 324; Bṛihadāranyaka-Up., vi, 4.19; Divyāvadana, p. 1; Crooke, *Pop. Rel.,* i, 243, 264; Garnett, *The Women of Turkey,* etc., ii, 92 ff.; 378 ff.; Dunlop-Liebrecht, 68, 468, n. 126; *Revue des trad. popul.,* 14, p. 480; Basset, *Contes popul. d'Afrique,* 151 ff.; Ploss-Bartels [4], i, 391 ff.; Meyer, *Isoldes Gottesurteil,* note No. 214; *Altind. Rechtsschr.,* 373; Reitzenſtein, *Zeitschr. f. Ethnol.,* vol. 41, p. 657 f. The woman belongs firſt to Soma, Gandharva, and Agni, and only afterwards to her husband. Thus she can never be sullied; Soma (the moon) gives her purity (çauca), Gandharva (probably a genius of fertilization) her sweet voice, and the fire god gives her the ſtainlessness (to be taken aĉtively and passively, " cleanness," sarva-medhyatva) in her whole body and being. Rigveda, x, 85.40–41; Pāraskara's Gṛihyasūtra, i, 4.16; Hiraṇy-Gṛihyas., i, 20.2; Vasishṭha, xxviii, 5–6; Yājñav., i, 71; Baudh., ii, 2, 4.5; Jolly's note to Nārada, xii, 28, in SBE, vol. xxxiii; Agnipur., 165.9, 19–21a; Meyer, *Altind. Rechtsschr.,* 22 f.; 229; 373–375; Winternitz, *Die Frau in d. ind. Religionen,* i, p. 33 [7]. Probably this belief that the spirits feel thus drawn to earthly women is not without its influence on the origin of the widespread Tobias nights, and the tale in the Biblical book is therefore worthy of all attention. On these nights see e.g. Weber, *Indische Studien,* v, 325 f.; 330 f.; 347; 359 f.; 368; 375; 377; of the Gṛihyasūtras: Çāṅkhy., i, 17.5; Açval., i, 8.10 f.; Gobh., ii, 3.15; Pārask., i, 8.21; Hir., i, 23.10; Āpaſt., iii, 8.8; Meyer, *Altind. Rechtsschr.,* 373; Garnett, *The Women of Turkey,* i, 240; Schmidt, *Jus primae noĉtis,* p. 149 ff.; Mantegazza, *Geschlechtsverhältnisse,* 252, 289–90; Henne am Rhyn, 28; McLennan, *Primitive Marriage,* 181; L. von Schroeder, *Die Hochzeitsgebräuche d. Eſten,* 192 ff.; and of course Ploss and Weſtermarck. An intereſting case is found in the *Tavola ritonda,* ed. Polidori (Bologna, 1864), p. 93. At a feaſt at the court of King Marco the lovely Donzella dell'Aigua della Spina and Triſtano ogle one another and fall in love. As a typical lady of the Middle Ages, after leaving the table the ſtricken lady goes at once to the hero, offers herself to him, and then by a message sends for him to come by night to her chamber. Then it goes on : Triſtano entra nel letto con lei, e ſollazono e dánnosi piacere e diletto. Vero è che la donzella avea preso marito di sedici giorni dinanzi, non che ancora si fossono congiunti insieme : imperò ch'egli era usanza a quel tempo, que quando gli cavalieri prendeano dama (a wife) egli ſtavano trenta giorni inanzi ch'eglino si congiugnessono insieme ; e ciascun insieme udivano messa ; acciò che Iddio perdonasse loro l'offense, e anche perchè perdeano la loro verginitade e venivano al conoscimento carnale; e pregavano Iddio che di lor uscisse fuori frutto che fosse pro al mondo e grazioso alla gente e degno a Dio e che portassero loro matrimonio con leanza.

Anyone with a knowledge of the sexual ways of the Middle Ages smiles at this meaningly to himself, as also at the words of Schweiger-Lerchenfeld which he regales us with in his description of Indian wedding customs : " The abstinence, too, by the newly wedded couple, for three whole days, has come down to us as a shining symbol from the mists of antiquity with its lofty conceptions of chastity " (*Die Frauen des Orients*, p. 591).

The first and main reason for this phenomenon, as also for the so-called " romantic reserve " of the newly wedded connected therewith, that is, the secret visits of the young husband, is to be sought, however, elsewhere than in that union of spirit-beings with the earthly woman. Nor does " marriage by capture " (McLennan and others), " paying the price of maidenhead " (Ploss-Bartels and others), " furthering fruitfulness " (Günther, 85–86), or the various other suggestions of this kind meet the case. The feeling of the sinfulness of coition which Westermarck calls in is too little prevalent, and also in the main of too late a period to give an explanation. Thus we ask : Why is coition outside wedlock not dangerous because of its uncleanness ? And why is continence only kept for so short a time ? To me the matter presents itself thus : The coition which we call unlawful, lechery or fornication, is in general practised without any hesitation among very many peoples and tribes. It is no more than a pleasant sport, and of no importance. Thus the mysterious powers do not give any heed to it, either. But marriage is a thing of great importance, indeed it is a downright injury done to nature and to the beings which hold sway in the darkness of nature, and especially in woman. Up to now they have been the owners of the woman. Now a man becomes her private owner. This is a robbery done to them. Thus with marriage —but not with sexual intercourse outside marriage—the man is threatened by the sharpest malice of magical powers. But the demons are very stupid. So they only watch the door (Jāt., ii, 79, introduct. ; Dubois-Beauchamp [3], p. 499 ; *Zeitschr. d. Ver. f. Volksk.*, 11, p. 268 ; *Zeitschr. f Ethnol.*, Bd. 30, p. 353 ; Ploss-Bartels, i, 560), believe that if the child has an ugly name, or is spoken of slightingly, then nothing will happen, and so on. If then the newly wedded refrain at the beginning, these simple fools of spirits imagine that it will go on in this way. Among many peoples and tribes a short time only of chastity is enough to trick the evil powers, among others due trouble must be taken. Thus it is that those, too, who have not been long married come together by stealth, or in the forest, in the open, for the spirits only watch the house and what goes on in it, especially in such a case as this. In other places, indeed, the young married couple muſt for a long time keep themselves carefully shut in, particularly by night, but this, too, is only because of the spirits who are then so powerful. See, for example, Weber's *Ind. Studien*, v, 331, 347 ; Garnett, i, 241–2, 324 ; ii, 257 ; Mantegazza, 256 ; McLennan, 181, 186–7 ; Weſtermarck, 151–2 ; *Anthropos*, iii, 185. When the demands on the woman's purity are more highly developed, there is furthermore the superſtitious dread before the myſtery of the firſt blood, which gives an opening for the demons—the firſt cause of the so-called " right " of the firſt night. This laſt also is primitive, and at firſt an evil necessity ; the slave and the ſtranger, the latter as a foe or one of no account, not indeed, as the fable has grown up, as the representative of the god, are called in for the task ; the kinsfolk or the girl herself has to see to the defloration as a duty ; it falls to the lot of the shaman, the prieſt, or of the chief or ruler, who is more or less proof againſt the spirits. In the case of the Tobias nights, the thought may then at an early ſtage have been present, that through self-denial or even self-torture the demons (and the gods also) are won over ; there may also be other ideas. But we muſt not forget that it is the husband who is the one threatened by the greateſt danger ; others are not so ſtrongly, or not at all, affeéted by the myſterious powers as such. Thus the Kamchadale widow muſt firſt lie with another man so that the ghoſt of her firſt husband may not kill his successor (Hartland, *Prim. Patern.*, ii, 183) ; and the husband of the adulteress among some tribes on Lake Nyassa cannot approach her again before another man has lain with her ritually (Hartland, ii, 122). Hence, too, the girl's " preliminary husband ", used as a lightning-conduétor. See R. Wilhelm, *Chines. Volksmärchen*, p. 236. And so on for other cases. A like superſtition is very likely at work in the case of the " firſt night " also, but certainly in other cases belonging here. Among the South Slavs inſtead of the bridegroom it is the groom's men, the mother-in-law, and the siſter who during the firſt night share the bed of the newly wedded wife. Krauss, *Sitte u. Brauch*, 382, 456. And if we find that among them the young wife muſt not, for a whole year, refer to her husband by his name, this has probably a like cause : the name, in accordance with a well-known belief found all over the world, as part of a person's being, gives a hold to the hoſtile powers ; the young husband muſt at firſt, therefore, keep a ſtrict incognito. To see so confidently in this only the trace of earlier " hetærism ", as is the cuſtom, seems to me very ill-founded. " Evil, harm " and " sin " often coincide in thought and in speech. The Russian " gryekh " (" sin "), too, denotes likewise " harm, hurt ". Might not in the same way the corresponding South Slav word, provided always that purely

LOVE

Now Kīcaka, who in spite of his coxcombry, was a stout warrior, as K. at least, proves in a special chapter on his descent and doughty deeds, does indeed show a certain romanticism in his passion of love, anyhow in his relations with Draupadī ; for as she herself shows him clearly, it means a sacrificing of his own advantage that he should want to make her, the unclean waiting-woman, his wife. Otherwise, however, he is evidently a typical representative of a class of

Christian ideas are not at work, have nothing about it of what Krauss sees in the "child through sin", but rather might there not be a glimmer of the primitive meaning of the magically dangerous? And such customs as the handing over of the bride to the wedding-guests may well, in so far as it is not hospitality towards the guests, in many cases have as first purpose the most thorough securing of the husband against the mysterious powers that are thus tricked. Many wedding customs, such as the well-known flight of the bride, her struggles, the pitched fight with the bridegroom, the keeping back of the bride, and so on, have been traced back to marriage by capture. Here and there it may be that one at least of the reasons is to be found in this. But originally probably there was often the purpose of throwing dust in the evil spirits' eyes. Anyhow there are a few, very few, cases where force has to be used on the bridegroom. So it is among the Garos (Maj. A. Playfair, *The Garos*, Lond., 1909, p. 67 ; Crooke, *Pop. Relig. and Folk-Lore*, etc., i, 121 f. ; Westermarck, 158 f. ; Finck, *Prim. Love*, 649). It must be noted that among them only the girl may propose marriage, and if a love-blinded young man lets himself be carried away into doing such a thing, it is a great insult to the whole family. *Zeitschr. f. Ethnol.*, Bd. 5, p. 268 (after Dalton). Also among the gipsies in India we find the bridegroom's "mock refusal" at the wedding. Devendra N. Das, *Sketches of Hindoo Life*, p. 238. Among them the girl has sexual freedom, and makes her own choice in marriage. Ibid. 237. In the end we find it true here too that man, above all, more primitive man, is after all no memory-mechanism. Even among the beasts the male must often get the female as his hunting-booty, and overcome her while she struggles, and so on. And every woman is a Sabine, as Olaf in Johannes Linnankoski's great novel *Laulu tulipunaisesta kukasta* (Song of the Fire-red Flower) says ; she wishes to be carried off. Is it likely that so strong an instinct in more primitive man—for imitation, for play, for the symbolical and the use of his powers of imagination—would have slumbered at the wedding above all ?

315

men who are seen everywhere in the Epic, especially among the Kshattriyas.[1]

It is true the assertion is made of the barbarians (Yavanas, Pāradas, Çakas, and Bālhikas) that they are woman-mad (vii, 93.42) ; but the wail of the noble wife (i, 158), whose husband muſt go forth to the monſter as the tribute-prey of the Rākshasa, is not only the fantasy born of her anguish. She shows him how men will fall upon her and their daughter in their blind greed, and mishandle them for their own ends, so soon as their protector is gone. They will not, in short, be left to ſtay on the path of virtue. " As the birds swoop down on a piece of flesh thrown on the ground, so do all swoop on a woman that lacks her husband " (çl. 12).[2] A woman, especially, in a menial position, was naturally in Old India always in danger, although, to all seeming, not the outlaw she is in Europe ſtill to-day, or anyhow in German lands. As it naturally cannot be expected of princesses to underſtand anything else, but juſt to be princesses, Draupadī as well as Damayantī has to condescend in misfortune to take service as a chambermaid ; for she already knows something of wreaths, perfumes, ornaments, and fine clothes. But she reminds Yudhishṭhira : " Chambermaids are unprotected in the world, they are slave-girls, O Bhārata " (iv, 4.15 ff.) ; and the future was to bring what she feared, as we have juſt seen. The man wants only to enjoy a woman, not to marry her, as, for inſtance, Rām., vii, 79–81 : Daṇḍa, the ſtupid youngeſt son of King Ikshvāku, sees the young and lovely daughter of a holy man, and is fired with a passion for her. She warns him of the fatal anger of her father, and that he muſt ask for her as his wife ; but he forthwith ravishes her. The holy man makes a seven days' rain of ashes to fall on the place ; so everything lies dead there, and this is the Daṇḍaka foreſt.[3] " The man would not come to the taking home

[1] " He was one that mowed down soldiers, and an evil adulterer," we find said of him in iv, 25.3.

[2] It is noteworthy that as to her daughter her anxiety is, above all, leſt Çūdras and others not worthy of the maiden may ask for her in marriage.

[3] Cp. the end of Jāt., 497, and 522 towards the end ; Meyer, *Hindu Tales*, 114 ff.; and further Dvārakā's fate, which has so many

LOVE

(as bride) of a maiden did not the 'ſtick' (daṇḍa, the juſtice that punishes) proteĉt " (xii, 15.37). But the daṇḍa, according to the much-preached Indian view, indeed brings about all moral order whatever in the world ; and on the other hand the men in Old India were juſt the same as men throughout the ages. It is so, too, that King Dhṛitarāshṭra muſt naturally be judged. He has a moſt excellent wife, Gāndhārī, but also from a Vaiçyā woman a son Yuyutsu. His descendant Janamejaya asks Dvaipāyana, the relater of the Mahābhārata : " Why did he hurt her by unfaithfulness ? " The answer goes : " Since the belly of the (pregnant) Gāndhārī waxed and pained for so long a time, a Vaiçyā served him, and from her was the son born " (i, 115.4, 5, 41, 42). On the other hand, the note of wonder in Janamejaya's queſtion might well be looked on as illuminating. Even holy men and penitents are no spoil-sports there, but we see them even as brothel-keepers of a kind, or rather, as the hoſts presiding over free tables of love in moſt magnificent ſtyle. When Bharata went forth to fetch back the banished Rāma, he came with his mighty army also to the hermitage of the Ṛishi Bharadvāja. This Ṛishi by his miraculous powers entertained the whole crowd of warriors in a way that was a real dissipation of the senses : from out of Indra's paradise he called down the whole hoſt of the Apsarases, and from other heavens other divine women. Twenty thousand of these wondrous beauties were sent by Brahma, twenty thousand by Kubera, twenty thousand by Indra ; even the creepers in the foreſt did the yogi turn into delightful women. Seven or eight of these charming examples of ravishing womanhood gave each warrior, moſtly married (cp. Rām., 33, 82.25 and 26), their services for the bath, and offered him heady drink—spirits and spiced liqueur (maireya),[1] whereof there were whole ponds

parallels in Eaſt and Weſt. It went ill, too, with Yavakrī(ta), the insolent son of a penitent, who ravished (majjayāmāsa, MBh., iii, 136) the daughter-in-law of Raibhya againſt her will. See also Tod, *Rajaſthan*, ii, 39.

[1] The scholiaſt says in MBh., vii, 64.6, that this word means a mixture of spirits (surā) and āsava (rum) ; in xiv, 89.39, that it means a " heady drink coming from the tree " (vṛikshajaṃ

and rivers, and the flower-cups of their divine bodies—to say nothing of the heaps of rare meats, and other choice foods, and carnal pleasures. It is no wonder that the soldiery danced, and laughed, and sang there, and to this air :

> " This is heaven ! Hail to thee,
> O Bharata ! Here we ſtay ! "—(Rām., ii, 91.)

Among the gods there are by no means few who show mortals the beſt example. " Bhadrā was the daughter of Soma (the moon god), held to be firſt among women for beauty. Soma deemed Utathya a husband worthy of her. And she, the peerless, the glorious one, for Utathya's sake gave herself up to ſtriɕ penance, praɕtising the loftieſt mortification, she with the lovely limbs. Then Soma called Utathya to him, and gave him the splendid one to wife, and the pious man took her in lawful wise. But already before this the lordly Varuṇa had loved her, and he came to Vanapraſtha [1] on the Yamunā, and carried her off. And when the lord of waters had carried her off, he brought her to his city, which is a wonder beyond compare to the eye, to the place of the six thousand lakes. For no other splendid city is fairer than this, which shines with palaces, Apsarases, and heavenly delights. Then the god, the lord of the waters, took his delight with her. Then the news was told Utathya of this shame done to his wife.[2] So soon as Utathya had heard all this from Nārada, he spoke unto Nārada : ' Go, speak these sharp words to Varuṇa : Give up my wife at my bidding ! Why haſt thou carried her away ? Thou art a warden unto the worlds, not a world-deſtroyer. Soma gave me my wife, and now thou haſt robbed me of her.' Thus at his bidding was the lord of waters addressed by Nārada : ' Give up the wife of Utathya ! Why haſt thou carried her off ? ' When Varuṇa had heard these his words, he spoke : ' She is my much-loved wife ; I cannot give her

madyam), that is, palm-wine ? fruit-liquor ? Much better information is given as to the ingredients by Kauṭilya (transl.), 186.17–187.3 ; Yaçodhara in Kāmasūtra (Durgaprasad's ed.), p. 54.

[1] Or : into the mountain foreſt.

[2] Patnyavamardana ; perhaps simply : coition with his wife. Cp. abhimardana, rubbing, coition, in Divyāvad., p. 624.

up.' Having been thus addressed by Varuṇa, Nārada now came to the Muni Utathya, and spoke with heart not at all gladdened : ' Varuṇa took me by the neck and threw me out, O great Muni. He will not give thee thy wife. Do what thou muſt do ! ' When the Aṅgiras had heard Nārada's words he was angered, and drank, as a great penitent, the water through his sublime ſtrength, holding it up.[1] Although now all the water was drunk up, and the lord of water was besought by his friends, yet he did not give her up. Then spoke Utathya, the beſt of the Brahmans, hot with anger, to the earth : ' My dear friend, do thou make the place of the six thousand lakes to come forth as dry land.' Then did it become a salt desert, as the sea flowed away from that place. And to the river [2] also spoke this moſt excellent Brahman : ' Thou timid one, flow unseen towards the sand-waſte (marūn prati), O Sarasvatī ; unhallowed be this place when thou haſt left it, thou kindly one.' When this land was now dried up, the warden of the waters came with Bhadrā, and gave the scion of the Angiras his wife, taking refuge with him. Utathya welcomed his wife, and was very glad, and he set the world and Varuṇa free from afflicʈion. What he with the knowledge of the law, the very mighty Utathya, spoke to Varuṇa, when he had received his wife, do thou now hear, O herdsman of men : ' I have won her through the might of my asceticism, while thou art moaning, O water king.' " After these words he took her and went to his abode (xiii, 154.10 ff. : cp. 153.3–5).

But a regular Don Juan from heaven is Indra, like the Greek king of the gods, his colleague.[3] In days of old he ſtarted

[1] So according to ix, 29.54 ; 30.8, 44, 56, 63, 66 ; 31.2, 4, 20 ; 32.38 ; 54.31 (cp. i, 1.209 ; 2.283), where Duryodhana flees into the pond, and by his magic powers heaps it up about himself, in like wise, probably, as it happened for the children of Israel. In the following he is always seen as being in the water. In our passage perhaps vishṭabhya might in itself be more naturally translated : suppressing it ; that is to say, he made it vanish, dry up. An acʈual drinking dry, as in the case of Agaſtya, is probably not meant ; but cp. xiii, 153.3 ff.

[2] Feminine in the Sanskrit.

[3] For him too the god of love makes the coy ones yielding, as for Zeus. Kumāras., iii, 14, 15 ; Pārvatīpariṇayanāʈ., ii, ſtr. 8.

319

to win laurels in this field, and the later literature often tells of his love affairs (cp. Wilson, *Selected Works*, iii, 35 ; Weber's *Indische Studien*, v, pp. 249–50). In spite of his faithful wife Çacī, who, however, was kept very wan and haggard, and in spite of his host of heavenly hetæræ, the Apsarases, he is drawn to the women of the earth. Everywhere he lies in wait for beautiful women, and changes himself into every kind of shape so as to enjoy them, just like his more majestic but correspondingly craftier brother of Olympus, or like Odin in Germanic mythology. Just as Zeus once came to Amphitryon's wife in the shape of her husband, so did Indra come to Ahalyā, as we have already touched upon (xii, 266 ; Rām., i, 48 ; vii, 30.20 ff.).[1] After he had given the bad example, had brought love-making with other men's wives into the world, this also spread among mankind (Rām., vii, 30.33). To what a pitch of cunning invention he had reached in the seduction of women will be shown shortly in another connection. And in other ways, too, this heavenly libertine is fond of playing all kinds of tricks on women, as is to be seen from the tale of Devayānī and Çarmishthā.

Thus, too, we find it given as the pride of the earthly warrior, and the picture of mortal man's glory " to press the breasts of loving women, to make gifts, and to slay foes " (viii, 83.23 ; 94.46, 47). So Bhūriçrava's wife, when bewailing the dead man, boasts thus of his hand that Arjuna has shot away : " This is the hand which slew heroes, and gave security to friends, which gave thousands of cows, and dealt death to

[1] In the account of the Rām. (i, 48.19 ff.), it is true, Ahalyā very well recognizes the ruler of the gods with all his disguise, and gladly welcomes the change for the more voluptuous entertainment it will bring ; and in the account in the Kathāsarits. (tar. 17, çl. 137 ff.) she even encourages her lover ; a change of shape is thus not really needed. Cp. Zachariae, *Zeitschr. d. Ver. f. Volksk.*, Bd. 16, p. 131 ; Toldo, ibid., Bd. 15, p. 367 ff. That supernatural beings take on the outward appearance of the husband, and so lie with the wife, is indeed a wide-spread belief (see Ploss-Bartels, i, 392) ; and earthly men have often reached their object in the same way, by magic or otherwise. King Arthur, indeed, is the fruit of such a trick (Malory, *Morte d'Arthur*, i, 2).

Kshattriyas. This is the hand that took away women's girdles, pressed swelling breasts, felt navel, thigh, and secret parts, and loosened aprons" (xi, 24.18 ff.).[1] Cp. too, Gāndhārī's lament for her fallen sons in xi, 19.14, 18. The same ideal for princes is found in ii, 54.11. The happy man has fair women, and rice with meat (ii, 49.9 ff.). See e.g. also ix, 56 f. ; vi, 17.8 ff. ; xiii, 57.13 ; 106.22, 30, 32 ; K, xiv, 103.71.

Now everything on earth is limited ; so, too, the supply of beautiful women for each man, and no less so his strength for enjoying them. In heaven it is otherwise. Times beyond count the Epic emphatically says that the doughty man is rewarded in the world beyond with boundless joys of love, and hosts of wonderful women. In particular the Apsarases are often mentioned as a kind of Indian valkyries, or rather, houris of paradise, and the welcome is painted which they give the hero fallen in the fight.[2] As an ever-present spur in the fiery speeches of the battle-leaders, and in the thoughts of the warriors, we find the glorious prospect of this unmeasured bliss. But all other good deeds as well, and all the virtues are rewarded in this way : asceticism, fasting, alms-giving, gifts to the Brahmans, and so forth ; and the member of the priestly caste must naturally in this not be left behind others, although the warrior, indeed, in these, anyhow mainly, warlike poems comes before us as the chief candidate for those very willing ladies of heaven. Here we only mention a few passages : xiii, 96.18, 19 ; 82.85, 86, 88 ; 64.17, 30 ; 106.53 ff. ; 107.6 ff. ; iii, 186.7 ; viii, 49.76–78; xii, 98.46 ; 99.4 ; Rām., iv, 20.13 ; 24.34 ; Holtzmann, ZDMG, 33, p. 642.

---

[1] Proudly Duḥçāsana, hurled to the ground, still shouts out in the shadow of death : " This is the hand that has pressed swelling breasts, that has given thousands of cows, and has dealt death to Kshattriyas " (viii, 83.22). See also especially Duryodhana's great speech in ix, 5.22 ff. This hero's body above the navel is made of diamond, but below it of flowers for the delight of women (iii, 252.5 ff.).

[2] The later artificial Epic, as is well known, is lavish with similar descriptions (e.g. Raghuv., vii, 50 ; Kumāras., xvi, 36, 48 ; Çiçup., xviii, 60, 61). Cp. Daçakum., p. 144.

And thus much more evidence could be brought forward showing the delight in woman and woman's love which is part of the Epic heroes' life. And as in the later and the erotic literature, the public gardens and pleasure-groves are a chosen place for tender adventure. There in the evening men and women seek their pleasure, and attend the joys of love in the shelter of the trees and bushes (Rām., ii, 71.22, 25, 26).[1] In swift carriages the upper world of love, too, drives out, modish and dashing, to the tangled foreſt (Rām., ii, 67.19). Picnics in the foreſt and park are often found in the Epic. All kinds of choice foods are taken, but above all intoxicating drinks, for juſt as the Hindus in the narrative parts of the Epic know nothing of the Brahmanic horror of flesh—indeed that moſt ſtrict Brahman, the pious Rāma, is a very great connoisseur in this matter (Rām., ii, 91.1 ff.)—so also they show themselves to be very fond of intoxicating drinks, particularly of the surā which is so heavily condemned by the law books and the ascetic writings. And the women, the nobleſt among them, too, are quite a match for them. Bacchus and Venus as elsewhere in India, so also in the Epic, show themselves as brother and siſter.[2] We have already been told how the haughty and high daughter of a Brahman, Devayānī, and the royal princess

---

[1] It is no wonder that Smṛiti forbids the delights of love in park, garden, or foreſt.

[2] Cp. Raghuv., vii, 11 : my Daçakum., 64 ff. ; 231 ; Amitagati, Subhāshitasaṃd., xx, 24 (ZDMG, 61.119) ; Rajendra Lala Mitra in the *Journ. of the Roy. Asiatic Soc. of Bengal*, 1873, Part 1, No. 1 : " Indo-Aryans," i, 389 ; Phear, *The Aryan Village in India and Ceylon*, 90 ; R. Schmidt, *Liebe u. Ehe in Indien*, 44 ff. Especially good descriptions of drunken and therefore extraordinarily attractive and amorous women are given in Kirātārj., ix, 51 ff. ; Çiçup., x, 1–38. —Beſt of all things on earth is the taſte of vāruṇī and latvākā-birds (MBh., xii, 180.31). Only the Brahmans were forbidden spirits by Çukra, as we have been told, and although they do not always abſtain from it in the Epic, yet abſtinence ſtruck root among them from early times ; and how great an abomination was intoxicating drink to the members of the prieſtly caſte later on, is shown even by Vidūshaka in the Nāgānanda (see my Samayamātṛikā, pp. xxvii, xxx). The original grounds for this horror are pointed out by me in *Altind. Rechtsschr.*, pp. 25 f. ; 352.

LOVE

Çarmishṭhā with their girl-friends and serving-women make a merry foreſt picnic, and how they there quaff sweet intoxicating drink (madhumādhavī) (i, 81.1 ff.). A quite classic description of such a river and foreſt outing is given in i, 222.14 ff. : Some days later Arjuna said to Kṛishṇa : " It is now the hot days ; let us go to the Yamunā. When we have taken our pleasure there together with our friends, we will come home again in the evening ; be pleased to do this, O Janārdana." Kṛishṇa spoke : " O son of Kuntī, it is also pleasing to me that we should take our pleasure together with our friends by the water to our heart's desire." When they had taken leave of Yudhishṭhira, and had got his consent, the two, the son of Pṛithā, and Govinda, then went, accompanied by their friends. Speedily the women's band (antaḥpura) of Kṛishṇa and Arjuna, in all their manifold shining jewels came upon the scene, when they had reached the incomparable pleasure spot. This was covered with all kinds of trees, furnished with all kinds of houses, comparable with Indra's city, provided with many kinds of well-taſting and rare meats and drinks, as too with wreaths and manifold perfumes. And all did make merry after their desire. And the broad-hipped women with enticing, swelling breaſts, and lovely eyes did sport around, with drunken, ſtumbling gait. Some of the lovely ones of Kṛishṇa and Arjuna sported in the foreſt, others in the water, others again in the houses, according as the place disposed, as their pleasure urged them. Draupadī and Subhadrā, both merry with drink, beſtowed clothing and ornaments on the women. Some danced in unbridled gladness,[1] others shrieked and screamed with joy ; some among the glorious women were laughing, and the others drinking the beſt of rum (āsava). Here some were clutching hold of one another,[2] and ſtriking each other, others again were talking their secrets over among themselves. Houses and foreſt were filled everywhere with the sound of the sweet flutes, lutes, and tambourines, in glorious splendour beyond words. Arjuna, too, had juſt received as a wedding-gift from Kṛishṇa a full

[1] Or : in wanton excitement (prahṛishta).
[2] Were holding one another faſt? barred one another's way (ruddh) ?

323

SEXUAL LIFE IN ANCIENT INDIA

thousand of most delightful girls of still tender years, to wait
on him at bathing and drinking entertainments (i, 221.49–50).
Then there were all kinds of entertainments, where drinking
and other merry-making played a great part. So the festival
already mentioned in honour of the mountain Raivataka in
Krishna's kingdom. " And this mountain was adorned ;
it shone, covered with the most manifold, many-coloured
treasures made of precious stones, with the most splendid
gold wreaths, as also with flowers and garments and wishing-
trees.[1] And always decked with golden branched lights,
it blazed like the light of day, in its caves and waterfalls. It
was as though it sang, when many-coloured banners bearing
small bells, and men and women filled it everywhere with
sounds. A sight of splendour beyond words did it offer,
like Meru with its bands of Munis. The din from the drunken,
merry, singing women and men rose even into the sky, con-
fusedly filled with the merry shouting and screaming [2] of the
roaring, drunken men and women, crazed with delight. Thus
did the mountain delight the heart with the sounds of joy,
furnished, too, with chapmen's booths and markets, enticing
the heart, abounding in all kinds of food and pleasure haunts,
covered with a great array of cloths and wreaths, resounding
with lutes, flutes, and drums. Great magnificence was given
to the festival of the mighty mountain, by the unending bestowal
on the poor, the blind, the needy, and so forth, of hard and soft
foods, together with spiced liqueur (maireya) and spirits
(surā) " (xiv, 59.5 ff.).

Not less so did the great sacrificial gatherings also offer

[1] Probably natural trees, or ones set up (poles), hung with all kinds
of splendid things (kalpavriksha).
[2] Read utkrushṭa.—Kshvedita, kshvedati is very often found in the
Epic, and especially of the sounds of lusty fighting, of courage and
defiance in battle, and so on. Although it is found very often in the
MBh. with this meaning, yet Nīl., so far as I know, does not give a true
explanation anywhere. But in the Rām. there is several times to be
found very useful matter. So kshvedita and kshvedā = siṃhanāda
(v, 4.12 ; vi, 4.26) ; and better still, though a little indefinite, in vi,
59.8 ; kshveditāni = svaçauryaprakāçakaçabdāḥ (in the text along with
siṃhanāda, as also often elsewhere).

324

opportunity enough for women's drinking. Thus we find at the end of the description of the horse-sacrifice made by Yudhishthira (xiv, 89.39 ff.) : " So was the sacrifice of the wise king of justice and truth a flood of many foods and precious stones, a sea of spirit-drink and spiced liqueur (maireya). At it were ponds whose mud was made of molten butter, mountains of foods, rivers whose mud was of curdled milk with sugar and spices. Folk saw no end there to the cakes and sweetmeats [1] that were made and eaten, nor to the beasts slaughtered. Pleasant it was there with the sounds of drums and shell-trumpets, with all the drunken, noisy, happy folk, and the crowd of right merry young women." [2] But at ordinary times, too, fair ladies were much given to heady drink, as it is to be gathered from various passages ; and in the description of Rāvaṇa's flock of women (Rām., v, 9 ; 10.30 ff. ; 11.2 ff. ; 18.10 ff.), reference is often made to their love of drinking. Even Sītā, that pattern of Indian womanhood, is no exception here, although naturally she keeps away from a pleasure such as this in her captivity and separation from her husband. But when she is again united with Rāma, she makes up for it. " When the son of Raghu had come into the thick açoka-grove, he sat himself down on a seat splendid to behold,

---

[1] Nīl., however, thus explains rāgakhāṇḍava : " Bean soup with pepper and ginger is khāṇḍava ; if sugar is added, then it is rāga-khāṇḍava." So, too, referring to xv, 1.19. On the other hand in vii, 61.8, he gives it = guḍodana. In vii, 64.8, rāgakhaṇḍavapānakān, therefore in all probability rāgakhāṇḍava, appears as a kind of drink, or an ingredient of a drink.

[2] So, too, the religious festivals (melā) in our days are merry fairs ; and at sacrificial festivals, even the death-meals (çrāddha), there are wild goings on ; and so on. S. Devendra Das, *Sketches of Hindoo Life*, 70 ff. ; 122 ff. Bose, *The Hindoos As They Are*, 258 ff. It is not without reason that the law writings ordain that the guests (Brahmans) at the çrāddhas shall eat in silence. So Manu, iii, 236 ; Yājñavalkya, i, 238 : Vishṇu, lxxxi, 11, 20 ; Saurapurāṇa, xix, 28. And the old Greek hecatombs are " really nothing but a great popular festival to which a fair is added ". E. Meyer, loc. cit., p. 105. So, too, to the banquets to Brahmans given by women it is especially women that come, and they give themselves a good time, and even get drunk (i, 147.5 ff.).

decked with many flowers and strewn with kuça-grass, and he took Sītā by the hand and gave her pure, sweet heady drink to quaff, as Indra did to Çacī. The tenderest meat and various fruits were quickly brought by the servants for Rāma to eat ; and before the king, bands of Apsarases and snake-fays, well versed in dancing and singing, surrounded by Kinnarīs, did dance ; and skilled women with the gift of beauty, under the spell of heady drink, and trained in dance and song, danced before Kākutstha. These heart-gladdening women did Rāma ever fill with gladness, he the best of gladdeners, he with the virtuous soul, he filled them with gladness, them the preciously adorned. Sitting with Sītā, he shone with sublime splendour, like Vasishtha sitting with Arundhatī. Thus did Rāma, attended with joy, delight Sītā day after day like a god, Sītā like unto a daughter of the gods, the princess of Videha " (Rām., vii, 42.17 ff.). It seems, then, quite natural that she who had been carried off by the monster should speak scornfully to him : " There is the same difference between Rāma and Rāvaṇa as between the lion and the jackal, between a brooklet and the great sea, between sour rice-gruel (sauvīraka and choice spirits " (Rām., iii, 47.45). And so, too, she throws at him in Mahābh., iii, 278.39, 40 : " How could a cow-elephant after having come to a rutting, noble, forest-roving giant bull-elephant, touch a pig ? How could a woman that has drunk mādhvīka and madhumādhavī feel any longing after sour rice-gruel ? " [1] The lovely drunken woman is often used in comparisons also, for instance, in vi, 75.34 : " So did thine army, ravaged by Bhīma and Arjuna, reel hither and thither, like a drunken woman " (cp. vi, 77.61 ; vi, 100.19 ; ix, 9.37 ; xii, 164.63).[2]

[1] Nīl. says that mādhvīka is an intoxicating drink got from flowers, madhumādhavī one made from honey.

[2] Cp. R. Schmidt, *Ind. Erotik*, 190–193. The Gaṅgā rushing down from the sky, likewise is seen as a tipsy woman (iii, 109.10). Cp. e.g. iii, 187.44. Even the so-called lifeless Nature feels the spell of intoxicants on lovely lips ; according to Indian poetic convention, the bakula (or kesava) cannot bloom unless its stem has been besprinkled with such moisture from the mouth of a young and pretty woman (e.g. Raghuv., ix, 33 ; xix, 12 ; Lokaprakāça, *Ind. Stud.*, vol. 18,

LOVE

And indeed the woman drinks, muſt drink, and looks so delightful under the effects of intoxicating drink, because by it love is helped, as, too, the Indians often say. The Epic also often hints at this, or lays ſtress on it. Here we give only one or two passages. Woman easily becomes shy and ashamed, but under the effects of drink, she puts her arms round her beloved (xi, 20.7 ; cp. xii, 167.38 ; Rām., iv, 1.85).[1]

p. 325 ; Pārvatīpariṃ., iii, 6). A pleasant womanly impression also is made by the cuſtom of putting flowers, especially lotus-flowers and those of the sahakāra-mango, in the intoxicating drink (Kāvyā-darça, ii, 157 ; Kirāt., ix, 56 ; Çiçup., viii, 52 ; x, 1, 3, 5, 8, 11 ; xv, 12 ; Rāvaṇavaha, xii, 14). Flowers and shoots, indeed, keep evil away, and bring good, e.g. ii, 21.51.

[1] When drunk a person shows his true nature (Çiçup., x, 18 ; Rāvaṇav., x, 80). And woman's nature and calling is love, and : " Every woman is at heart a rake," as Pope says. This, acccording to Kirāt., ix, 54, is brought out by intoxicating drink. But it shakes the morality of the fair (MBh., vi, 77.61).—According to Gobhila's Gṛihyasūtra, at the wedding the bride, after the wedding oracle, is sprinkled with surā, so that her whole body is moiſtened with it, and at the same time this formula is spoken : " Kāma, I know thy name, intoxication is thy name." On the Brahmanic view, indeed, not only is spirit-drinking (surāpāna) in itself one of the four deadly sins, and holding the threat of dreadful punishments in this world and the other, but also women's offending is heavily condemned. A woman who partakes of spirituous drink is set on the same level as the murderess of her husband, or as one using abortion, and so forth ; and for her, as for the suicide and other great sinners, no death-gift muſt be made (Manu, v, 89 f., cp. ix, 13.80). The Brahman woman who thus sins cannot come after death into the world of her husband, but is caſt out into the loweſt births of all (Vasishṭha, xxi, 11). And intercourse with a spirit-drinking woman is a serious offence (Vishṇu, xxxvii, 33 ; cp. Vas., xxi, 15) ; and he who sees a woman of good family (kulaſtrī) drinking surā, muſt look at the sun to cleanse himself, utter Vishṇu's name, and bathe iṅ the clothes he has on his body at the time of the ill-omened sight (Mahānirvāṇatantra, xi, 163 f., cp. 122). This laſt-named, highly inſtructive work, translated by Manmatha Nath Dutt (better by Arthur Avalon, with an excellent introduction, Luzac and Co., 1913), as a Tantra book, praises surā, indeed, in the moſt dissolute phrases—this freer of living beings, this annihilator of all sins, this mother of pleasure and release, this augmenter of under-

327

Thus Tārā, Vālin's widow, who is set forth as a pattern, when she goes over to the conqueror Sugrīva, first makes herself tipsy before beginning the new pleasures of love (Rām., iv, 33.38 ff.).

Further love-kindlers are the beauties of nature, and spring with all its signs of bursting life : the green of plants and splendour of flowers, bird-song, and the humming of bees, and all the rest ; and the wind, particularly the spring wind, is the arousing friend not only of fire, but also of Kāma. This is more particularly described in the account already given of how Pāṇḍu finds death in the way Ovid wished for, and that Frenchwoman in Brantôme ; and is touched on or told at length in other tales. Here we may recall, too, the æsthetically so well thought out description of the forest glories in the old saga of Dushyanta and Çakuntalā, which introduces in a two-fold meaning the love scenes that follow it. Cp., for instance, also iii, 136.1–3 ; 158.67–69. But a *locus classicus* is to be found in Rām., iv, 1 ff.

" When Rāma, together with Lakshmaṇa, went to that lotus-lake (Pampā) filled with day-lotuses and blue lotus-flowers, he bewailed himself with mind awhirl. Scarce had he seen it but his senses quivered for joyful excitement ; fallen under the power of the love god, he spoke these words to the son of Sumitrā : ' Son of Sumitrā, Pampā is shining with its water clear as the cat's-eye jewel, with its wealth of blooming day-lotuses and blue lotus-flowers, adorned with trees of many kinds. Son of Sumitrā, behold the grove of Pampā, so glorious to see,

standing, science, and knowledge, and so on, but at the same time condemns excess in biting words (e.g. xi, 105–123), and gives this drinking rule for the Kaula-rites :—

> So long as the steadfast look wavers not,
> So long as the mind's light flickers not,
> For so long drink ! Shun the rest !
> Whoso drinks still more is a beast.—(vi, 196).

According to Baudhāyana, i, 1, 2.1 ff., it is the custom " in the north " to drink intoxicants, and in particular Bṛihaspati, ii, 28 ff., records it of the women there. This is in order there, for it belongs to the custom of the land ; for in Old India also, as is well known, customary law prevails (dharma = custom, usage, law, right).

LOVE

how the trees, rising as though to mountain-heights, stand up like rocky steeps. But I, who am parched through with sorrow, I am tortured by agonies of soul in my grief for Bharata, and for the raped princess of Videha. The flower-crowned creepers around us clasp everywhere the flower-laden trees. This season with its grateful wind, the scented moon of spring, when flowers and fruits have come forth on the trees, kindles a strong love. Behold, O son of Sumitrā, all the shapes of the rich-flowered forests, that shed a rain of flowers, as the clouds shed water. And on the lovely plains all the manifold trees of the grove, shaken by the strength of the wind, bestrew the earth with blossoms. The wind blowing forth from the mountain-caves seems to sing, through the notes of the drunken kokila-bird, bringing, as it were, the trees to dance. How grateful is its touch as it blows along cool as sandal-wood, carrying hither a pure scent and bearing weariness away. The trees seem to sing with their wreaths of bees ; their tops are roofed with flowers, much shaken by the up-tossing wind. The joyfully stirred water-cock by the enchanting waterfall, sets me, a prisoner of love, sorrowing with his notes. Ere now in the hermitage my beloved heard his call, called me to her in delight and welcomed him in utmost joy. With the water-cock's cry of love's delight, and the song of the male kokila-bird these trees resound, setting the passion of my love afire. This fire—the spring, whose (glowing) embers are the flowery clusters of the açoka grove, whose crackling and roaring are the notes of the bees, and whose red flames are the young shoots—this fire will burn me up. For life has no meaning for me, O son of Sumitrā, if I do not see this woman with the soft-lashed eyes, lovely hair, and gentle speech. Look, O Lakshmaṇa, the love-racked peahen dances on the mountain-top to the dancing peacock, her mate, and the peacock hastens, filling with longing, to the darling one, spreading his shining wings, and, as it were, laughing while he calls. Clear it is that the Rākshasa has not robbed the peacock in the forest of his beloved. And to me, too, would come the great-eyed daughter of Janaka in welling maze and love, were she not robbed from me. Even if 'tis spring there where my darling is, yet Sītā, in the power of another, will of a surety be mourning just as

I am. But without a doubt spring does not touch that place; for how could she with the black lotus-eyes go on living without me ! For of a truth Sītā's soul is sunk in me, and my soul is utterly sunk in Sītā. This coolness-bringing wind, scattering the flowers, and softly caressing, is for me, who am thinking of my sweet one, as fire. I could bear the love that came to me, were it not that spring, which brings the trees to blossom, were wounding me. My eye believes it sees the petals of the lotus-cups—ah ! Lakshmaṇa, so do the flower-cups of Sītā's eyes indeed appear. Mingled with the threads of the lotus-flowers, and coming through the trees, the delightful wind blows hither like Sītā's breath.[1] The creepers follow after (the loved ones) like drunken women, climbing from tree to tree, from rock to rock, from forest to forest. Without compare shimmers the dark-green and yellow sward, bespread with the various flowers of the trees as with rugs—it stretches away like a bed. If but my beloved were to be seen, if we could both dwell here, then should I not envy the king of the gods, nor Ayodhyā. For if I could take joy together with her on this delightful grassy floor, then should I be filled with care no more, nor any longing after other things. See, the he-gazelles that rove with their mates this way and that, on the many-coloured mountain-tops, rend my soul, for eyes like the young gazelle has the princess of Videha from whom I am parted. Ah ! Where is Sītā now, my darling one, who, obedient to virtue, came slowly after me, when I was sent into the forest by my father ? To me, who am now consumed by love, she spoke kind words, she, the brown one, the kind one, although in the depths of the forest and suffering, and as if free from pain, and filled with joy.' "

Now in spring alone, that flighty youth, and all its glory, and in nature with its splendour, reliance or something like it is not always to be put. Moreover, it is not everyone that is susceptible to such. Thus, in India, the land of magic, the love-charm in its most various shapes flourished from Vedic times.[2] The women, of course, practised it particularly, and, above all, to

[1] Or : sighing breath.

[2] See Weber's *Ind. Studien*, v, 218 ; Winternitz, *Altind. Hochzeitsrituell*, pp. 26, 97 ff.

the end of getting their husband's love, and keeping it, and of bringing him under their sway, but above all else to the end of wreśting him from the rival, and keeping her away or deśtroying her. What is to be found in the Epic on this subjeét will be told later in another chapter.

And why should mankind at all times and among all peoples not try every possible means to win the love of one desired ? Love and the joys of love are often deemed to be the higheśt of all earthly blessings, and, indeed, not only among the Indians. Often these latter ponder the queśtion : Which of the three ends of life : dharma (duty, religion, virtue), artha (worldly advantage, wealth, high position, etc.), kāma (desire, enjoyment, love) is the higheśt ? Thus, too, the five sons of Pāṇḍu discuss this hard riddle (xii, 167). Each one gives his opinion. Bhīma speaks : " Without kāma a man has no wish for worldly profit, without kāma a man does not śtrive after the Good (dharma), without kāma a man does not love ; therefore kāma śtands above the others. For the sake of kāma the Ṛishis even give themselves up to asceticism, eating the leaves of trees, fruits, and roots, living on the air, and wholly bridling their senses, and others bend all their zeal to the Vedas and lesser Vedas, making their way through the whole of the holy śtudy, as also to anceśtral offerings, and sacrificial aéts, to alms-giving and alms-taking. Traders, husbandmen, herdsmen, craftsmen, as also artiśts, and those that carry out aétions consecrated to the gods, give themselves up to their works because of kāma. Others, again, take to the sea filled with kāma ; for kāma has the mośt varied forms : everything is śteeped in kāma. No being ever was, or is, or will be, higher than the being that is filled with kāma. It is the innermośt core (of the world), O king of righteousness ; on it is founded dharma and artha. As butter from sour milk, so kāma comes forth from artha and dharma.[1] For oil is better than the squeezed oil-cake, and better melted butter than butter-milk. Better is the flower and the fruit than the wood, kāma is more excellent than artha and

[1] It is the flower that blooms from them ; they are both only praétised to win the gifts of kāma. But the literal translation is perhaps : " As butter is better than sour milk, so is kāma better than artha and dharma."

dharma. As honey is the sweet juice from the flower, so kāma is from these two, according to the teaching of tradition. Kāma is the womb of dharma and artha, and kāma makes up their essence. Without kāma the manifold workings of the world would not be thinkable.

> Give thyself up to kāma, take thy joy with women
> In fair garb and ornament, and sweet to behold,
> With young women loosed with the madness of drink;
> For kāma, O king, for us is greateſt of all." [1]

All-powerful is love. " If the god of love draws nigh a man, there is no gainsaying him, although he has no body " (v, 39.45, 46). Kāma is one form of Agni, an all-penetrating, devouring fire, Kāma the unspeakably great and lovely. " He that in form has not his like in the heaven of the gods, the god of fire, has been named Kāma by the gods for his peerlessness " (iii, 219.23).[2] Therefore, too, the man in love is not

---

[1] Countless Indian passages teach the same thing. Here we give only a few: Kuṭṭanīmatam, 801; Kathākautukam, i, 30; 67; 70–71 (love is the higheſt thing); Mārk.-Pur., lxv, 33 ff. (the world is made up of kāma). Therefore, too, the full enjoyment of love and the world of sense is a right of mankind. King Yayāti is cursed by Çukra to grow old at once, for having aĉted so ill by Devayānī. But he has not yet taſted kāma and youth to the full, and therefore begs his sons in turn to take on themselves his old age for a thousand years, and lend him their youth for such time, but each finds old age too ugly and joyless; only the youngeſt, Pūru, is ready at once. Yayāti delights himself for a thousand years with his beloved wife Çarmiṣṭhā, and enjoys the objeĉts of sense also, but in virtuous wise. At the end of the thousand years he gives his son youth, takes over old age, and acknowledges that kāma is never ſtilled by kāma (i, 83 ff. Cp. Rām., vii, 58, 59, where the same tale is found again somewhat different; elsewhere, too, it is found with differences again; cp. Wilson's *Seleĉt Works*, ed. Roſt, vol. iii, p. 36 f.). Sexual union is (together with sleep and food) the law and the right of the body (dehadharma, Rām., iv, 35.1).

[2] Cp. the great St. Petersburg Diĉtionary, Bd. ii, col. 218; Weber's *Ind. Studien*, v, 225, 226; and MBh., xiii, 85.11, 16 f., 22, where Kāma is seen as the eternal, great original godhead, and is also identified with Agni. Cp. Ṛigveda, x, 129.4; Ath.-Veda, x, 2.19. The world is made up of Kāma. Mārk.-Pur., lxv, 33 ff.

responsible ; he is in the hands of a higher power. So Bhīma reminds Hiḍimba : "This young woman has no hold over herself ; she now loves me. She is driven by the god of love, and it is on him the blame falls " (i, 153.25 ff.). As by sleep (x, 4.22), so is shame taken away by love (v, 35.50 ; 37.8). Rām., iv, 33.54-57 paints in the same way the all-conqueror, love. The lover knows no law, no virtue (dharma), and he muſt be shunned (v, 33.101 ff.). He that leaves kāma behind himself, reaches to profit (iii, 313.78). It is in tender love (sneha) that sorrows have their root,[1] from it comes all anguish ; joy and sorrow and suffering—all springs from it. Juſt as a fire in the hollow of a tree burns up the prince of the foreſt, roots and all, so does even the lighteſt passion deſtroy what is good and useful. Overwhelmed by passion, man is dragged about by kāma. The wise man shuns a tender inclination, whether it be for friends, for worldly good, or for a woman (iii, 2.27 ff.). Indeed, Kāma (luſt, love) is the ally of Mṛityu, the goddess of death (xii 258.35 ff.). Apart from the deſtruction it otherwise brings, it is also saṃsārahetu, the cause of the continuance of this world of pain and death (iii, 313.98). Between such ascetic doſtrines, that are so often found in India, and the glorification of love as the one and only thing, there is also in the Epic the wise teaching : Enjoy love with discretion (e.g. xii, 140.26). It is often insiſted, especially for the king, that not the morning, but only the evening muſt be given up to women and love (so, ii, 5.69). It was indeed among the Old Indian rulers that there were very many, as already hinted, whose divinity was the vulva (bhagadeva, xiv, 43.15). Rules for love and wedlock from the ſtandpoint of long life are set forth fairly numerously. " Let a man not go during the day to copulate, nor to a maiden, nor to a bad woman, nor to an unbathed (ſtill menſtruating) woman ; thus shall a man have long life " (xiii, 104.108 ; cp. 150.151). " Let not a man draw nigh unto women that may not be visited, nor unto the wife of a king, nor unto his woman friends (or : not to woman friends) ; not unto the wives of physicians, youths, and old men, of servants, kinsmen,

[1] Snehamūlāni duḥkhāni (cp. e.g. Laghucāṇakyam ed. Teza, vi, 11 ; Çivadāsa's Vetālap. ed. Uhle, p. 53, ſt. 17 ; Dhammapadam, 210 ff.).

333

Brahmans, seekers of protection, kinsmen by marriage ; thus shall a man have long life " (xiii, 104.116 ff.). It brings well-being to wed a grown (vayaḥsthā) girl, born in a noble family, held in praise, favoured with the bodily marks of happiness (xiii, 104.123, 124, 135). Then (131 ff.) a whole set of women are named that a man must avoid, as in the law books ; and, further, it is taught that a man must protect women, indeed, but must never harbour jealousy for their sake, since this shortens life, as does lying with another man's wife. Cp. the already discussed passage in i, 64.5 ff., and especially the chapter on the surata.

But love must be on both sides, and lead to the pleasures of sex ; for love has, as its natural fruit, sexual pleasure (kāmorati-phalaḥ, xii, 123.6). " If a man and a woman that yearn for one another reach their goal, then that may be compared with Amṛitam ; but if a lover cannot reach the goal of his wishes, then that is a misfortune which is the same as the poison-plant " (xii, 320.69, Deussen's transl.). " If a man love a woman who loves him not, then his body glows in torment ; a man has then joy when he loves her who wishes for him " (Rām., v, 22.42–43). " Two kinds of human beings call forth trust from others (or : the highest trust) : women that are loved and love, and folk that honour the honoured.[1] Two kinds of human beings are sharp thorns, destroying the body : he that is poor and yet loves, and he that is weak and yet is angry " (MBh., v, 33.55, 56). But he is loved who is near : " Love goes to him who is seen ; there is no leaning towards him who is not seen " (Rām., v, 26.39), which is what we read as boys, in Cicero.[2] Cp. e.g. MBh., iii, 71.6. For the woman particularly this is true ; for, like the creeper, she twines round the very nearest tree, the Indian says. Love does not at all go to the worthiest object : " We see a good woman in glorious beauty

---

[1] But after all this saying does not fit in with the following one, and is to be rendered : " Two kind of human beings put their trust in others : women that love a loved one (are loved and love)," etc. The pūjitapūjaka, he that praises and honours together with the multitude, is often condemned in the MBh.

[2] Cp. Bhartṛihari, i, 42 (ed. Gopinath). Also Heinrich von Freiberg holds : Separation cleaves the heart's love (Triſtan, 319).

going away unloved, and another without diſtinction (alakshaṇā),
and ugly, sitting there on the heights of love's happiness "
(xii, 224.34).[1]

But if the woman is in love, and, anyhow, believes herself
loved, then in Old India, as is well known, she usually goes
herself to the house of her loved one for her purpose.[2] Of this
a good example in Urvaçī, the heavenly hetæra, is given by the
Epic (iii, 45, 46), which, indeed, here also, is far removed from
the over-refinement of the classical literature, and chooses
to make Kīcaka go into the house of the chambermaid Draupadī.
Arjuna's eyes during his visit to Indra's heaven have been
unwaveringly fixed on this Apsaras, and his very indulgent
father, Indra, so versed in the things of love, is gladdened
by the son who evidently has not fallen away, and who as a gueſt
muſt be provided with what he needs in this direction. Therefore
through the Gandharva Citrasena as messenger and pander,
he suggeſts, as already told, to this Ninon of heaven that she
should make Arjuna happy. By the description of the manly
beauty of this youth recommended to her favour, she, too, is
fired with a hot love, and gives her consent. She bathes and
then adorns herself moſt splendidly, filled with the moſt ardent
yearning for the hero. " When the moon had risen, and early
night had come, the broad-hipped one went forth and sought
out the house of Pṛithā's son. Shining in her soft, curly, long
hair, wherein she wore many jasmine-flowers, the heart-breaker
went her way. With the moon of her countenance, and the
delight of the movements of its brows, and the sweetness of the
words tripping from her mouth, with her charm and her soft
loveliness, she seemed to be challenging the moon as she walked
along. As she went along, her breaſts, scented with a heavenly

---

[1] This is ſtill truer of the man : he is generally the more loved by
women, the less he deserves it. Leminkäinen, the merry bully, drunkard,
and woman-hunter of the Kalevala is everywhere the cock of the walk
with the hens fluttering and clucking around him in love ; the wise
and noble Wäinämöinen, bringing happiness to mankind, can only
speak of ill-luck in love.

[2] But alas ! poor woman, and cunning man ! If the woman comes
herself into the house of her beloved, then he does not commit adultery
(Nārada, xii, 60) !

salve, black-nippled, rubbed with heaven's sandalwood, and shining from her necklace, were shaken up and down. Through the upborne burden of her breasts, and the sharp movements of them she was bowed down at every step,[1] she with the surpassing splendour of the centre of her body,[2] gloriously girdled around by the three folds. Below shimmered, spread out like a mountain, swelling on high like a hill-side,[3] the place of the temple of the god of love,[4] ringed by dazzling splendour, adorned by the girdle's band, tempting with heart-stirrings even the divine Rishis, the faultless seat of shame, wrapped in thin garb. Her feet, in which the ankles were deep imbedded, and whose toes made red and long-stretched expanses, glittered, being hung with small bells, and arched like the turtle's back. Her appearance was made still more captivating by her having partaken of heady drink, and by her contented joy, by the love within her, and by her various sweet wiles. With Siddhas, Cāraṇas, and Gandharvas the coquettish beauty went along, even in heaven, of a truth, where there are many wonders, a figure right worthy of remark, with her thinnest of upper garments that shimmered with the colours of the clouds, and like unto the slender sickle of the moon in the sky, as it rides along, wrapped in clouds. Then did the brightly smiling one reach, in but a moment, the abode of Arjuna, son of Pāṇḍu, hastening like the spirit, like the wind. When she had come to the gate there, Urvaçī, she with the lovely eyes, was announced

[1] This is well known as an ever-recurring conception among the Indians. But such as it is, it does not sound more unreasonable than, say, the following passage, for which probably very many parallels could be found in the West: " She wore her deep-black hair in astounding quantity wound several times around the back of her head, and it was as if she had trouble to keep her delicate head raised under the heavy burden." F. K. Ginzkey, *Jakobus und die Frauen*, 1908, p. 107. Yet many women that are blessed with thick hair do say that it is a dragging burden.

[2] But probably çobhitā is to be read instead of çobhinā.

[3] Or : swelling on high with its buttocks.

[4] In the same way this " high altar of the senses' pleasure " (Viereck, *Niniveh*, etc., p. 79) is called " the most splendid sacrificial offering to rati (love's pleasure) ", Rām., vii, 26.16.

to Arjuna by the gate-keepers. She came into this faultless house, that was very delightful to the heart. With a mind filled with anxious doubts he came to meet her in the night. And so soon as Prithā's son had seen Urvaçī, his eyes were dimmed with shame, and as he greeted her, he showed her the respect that is shown to those of high station. Arjuna spoke : ' I bow my head before thee in greeting, thou most excellent of the most excellent Apsarases. Command me, goddess ; I have come to thee humbly as thy servant.'" Urvaçī was utterly taken aback by these words, and explained to him at some length that at the singing and dancing which the Apsarases had performed in his honour, he had steadily gazed at her and her only, and that his father, her lord, had sent her. " In obedience to him I have come to thee, O queller of foes, drawn by thy charms and by my heart, and having fallen into the power of the god of love ; for I, too, O hero, have for long been cherishing this wish." But Arjuna, seized with shame, stopped his ears so as not to hear such words, and declared that he had looked on her thus respectfully as being the ancestress of his family, and that for him she was the wife of a high personage. " Urvaçī spoke : ' We are all free and unfettered,[1] O son of the king of the gods. Do not allot me the position of one of high standing, O hero ; for all sons and grandsons in Puru's race that come hither delight us (Apsarases) through their ascetic merit, and do no wrong by it. Therefore be kind, and send me not away in my need ; love and enjoy me, who love thee, and am fired with passion, O thou my pride.' But Arjuna was not to be shaken, and honoured her as his mother. Then was Urvaçī overcome with rage ; quivering, with brows drawn awry, she cursed the winner of booty : ' Since thou wilt not give me welcome, me who had leave given me by thy father, and have come to thy house of my own accord, under the sway of the god of love, therefore, O son of Prithā, shalt thou live as a dancer amidst women, bereft of honour, known as a eunuch, living as an impotent man.' When she had thus laid the curse on Arjuna, Urvaçī went swiftly, with twitching lips and breathing heavily, back into her abode." When Father Indra learned of the business, he spoke with a smile to his virtuous son : " In thee Prithā has a good son ; thou hast outdone even the holy men

1 Or : not forbidden (anāvrita).

with thy ſtaunchness." This tale, however, once more shows :
If a foolish man will not when a foolish woman will, then he has
to pay for it heavily (cp. Mahābh., xiii, 23.75).
" Now love itself springs from the idea (saṃkalpāt, xii,
163.8 ; cp. e.g. Manu, ii, 3), and sexual excitement (harsha)
is born of the idea (saṃkalpa), and is born from sound, and is
born, too, from taſte, and is born, too, from form " (xiv,
24.5).[1] As an explanation of the concept, iii, 33.30, 37, 38
gives the following : kāma, this wishful conception of the mind
(cittasaṃkalpa), is the joy that arises at the union by touch with
material things (dravyārthasaṃsparça), when the five senses,
the mind (manas), and the heart are taken up with an objeĉt
of the senses. Finally it muſt be mentioned further that we find
no trace in the Epic of the exaĉt classifications of lovers and their
counterparts among women, such as appear in the erotic and
rhetorical treatises. The man who is called to high
things and to good fortune has a thin, short member, a smooth
glans, and hanging teſticles (Rām., v, 35.17 ff.). Cp.
xii, 335.11 ; 343.36, 46–50.[2]

[1] That is to say, of course, through the mind, the ear, the mouth
(the tongue), and the eye, all of which have a share in the beloved
being. We miss the smell, and the moſt important sense of all for love :
sparça, the touch, the sense of feeling. K. (25.5) then adds : " and
is born, too, from the touch, and is born, too, from the smell."—As to
saṃkalpa " idea, conception " cp. p. 309 of my Daçakum., as also
MBh., iii, 298.36 ; xiv, 22.20, 27 ; Nil. on xii, 248.1. With the
riddle set in Daçakum., 297, 306 ff., and the tale itself : " Love is an
idea," may be compared : Avaçyakaerzählungen, ed. Leumann, i,
p. 26 ; Prabandhacintāmaṇi, p. 80, and Tawney's note ; Stricker,
Das Bloch (ed. Lambel in the Deutsche Klassiker des Mittelalters,
Bd. xii, p. 103 ff. = Hagen, Gesamtabenteuer, ii, 171 ff.) ; Bandello,
i, 22 ; F. T. Vischer, Auch Einer [3], Bd. ii, p. 227 ; Novalis (ed.
Heilborn, 1901) ; H. von Ofterdingen, p. 139 (" Where is love ? In
the imagination ") ; Chauvin, vi, 15 ; Zeitschr. d. Vereins f. Volksk.,
vol. ii, p. 300.
[2] Cp. e.g. Garuḍapur., 64.7 f.; 65.10–14. Phallic worship or
linga-worship in the Epic comes, of course, from a later time, and is
an interpolation, as is somewhat needlessly shown in JRAS, 1907,
p. 337 ff. The following are a few details : Çiva's member is always
ſtiff, and this because of his unbroken chaſtity ; therefore it is
worshipped by the world. It is always kept ſtanding fixedly up ;

he has a great, upstanding, pleasing linga ; he is head warden of the phallus, and appears in the penis, as being his origin (medhraja) ; the all-shaped god is in the linga, and through all the ages of the world he has been worshipped by the other gods, by the spirits, and the seers, in the linga ; the phallus-worshipper wins the highest happiness and Çiva's whole approval. Because his linga stands up, he is called the " standing stump " (Sthāṇu) in vii, 201.92, 93, 96; 202.124, 133, 140; xii, 166.48 ; xiii, 17.46, 60, 77, 128; 161.11–18. See, too, xiii, 14.161, 227–235. We may look on x, 17.8 ff. as a kind of history of the origin of linga-worship : Brahma begs Çiva to make the beings of the world, and he consents. But he then gives himself up to an endless tapas in the water. Brahma finds it too wearisome ; he leaves him to it as useless, and has the creation seen to by seven Prajāpatis. Çiva gets into such a fury about this that he literally " pulls out his own tail ", and throws it away ; the member drives into the earth, and sticks in it (in çl. 23 read utpātya for utpādya). This tale is worthy of note ; for in the phallic cults and phallic myths of the world emasculation (castration) plays a great part, but above all self-castration. See Dr. W. Schwartz, " Der (rothe) Sonnenphallos d. Urzeit," *Zeitschr. f. Ethnol.*, vi, p. 172 ff. (his sun and thunder theories may, indeed, be left to look after themselves). Castration, although not the probably more primitive self-castration, offers also another legend of the origin of the linga-worship, which is given us in a simpler and certainly older form by the Saurapurāṇa (lxix, çl. 35–55), and then, following Sonnerat, by Schmidt, *Liebe u. Ehe in Indien*, p. 23 ff. ; and in weak colours it seems to glimmer through still in the myth which Dubois, ed. Beauchamp[3], p. 629 ff., repeats after the Linga-purāṇa. In this last form Çiva and Pārvatī die in the midst of their love embrace, and come to life again in Linga and Yoni. On this tale and the origin of the linga-cult cp. Jahn, " Die Legende vom Deva-dāruvana," ZDMG, 69, p. 529 ff. ; 70, p. 301 ff. ; 71, p. 167 ff., and also Deussen, 71, p. 119 f. In the end, however, this dying is itself the older element, and the emasculation or castration, both of the god of procreation himself and of his priests, denotes only a kind of death ; for the death and coming back to life of the genii of fruitfulness is a very widespread conception. Thus it appears as quite natural in the case, too, of these two Indian godheads of the sexual life. Further-more I of course hold the passages in the Epic where phallus-worship is referred to to be late. This worship itself is likewise in India of very great antiquity.

[From Melanesia the tale of the phallic snake Pauravisia given in G. C. Wheeler, *Mono-Alu Folklore*, Lond., 1926, p. 37 f., 201 f. has certain points of likeness with these Çiva and Pārvatī myths. (Translator)]

XI

WOMAN AS WIFE

IF the man in the Old Indian Epic in his life of love, in spite
of many beautiful exceptions, and in spite of the noble,
often-ſtressed view that the man muſt be as chaſte as the woman,
nay, that his duty is even to surpass her, the weaker vessel, in
this virtue also—if in spite of this he actually felt himself
evidently very free, yet for the woman on the other hand
there was a far ſtricter moral law : it was only as a wife that
she had any real right to the joys of love ; it is only for the wife
that life has worth, and it is only the wife that has any worth
for life, that has a right to life and its gifts. For the maid also
is, above all, a wife, even if it is firſtly the future wife ; she
is but a pledge entruſted by the Maker, which the father muſt
carefully keep for the husband to be (i, 157.35). On
woman as wife, therefore, falls the fulleſt and moſt
wonderful glory of the nobleſt Indian poetry, especially of the
Epic. Figures such as Damayantī and Sāvitrī will " have
undying life ", for they also " were made by the heart ", not
by the mere selfishness of the man, setting a pattern before the
woman only for his own advantage and good, as Finck, for
inſtance, believes. The Epic is filled with the praise and the
examples of womanhood faithful in wedlock ; and from the
two mighty poems there could be gathered a collection of such
pictures, great and small, of Old Indian women, and one by no
means lacking in variety.

And thus Çakuntalā speaks (i, 74.40 ff.) : " She is a wife
who is skilful in the house ; she is a wife who has children ;
she is a wife whose life is her husband ; she is a wife who keeps
a holy troth with her husband. The wife is the half of a man ;
the wife is the beſt friend of all ; the wife is the root of the three
ends of life [1] ; the wife is the root of what will save

---

[1] Cp. e.g. xiv, 90.47, 48. And so times beyond count in Indian
literature.

340

there.[1] He that has a wife accomplishes deeds [2] ; he that has a wife is a householder ; he that has a wife has joy ; he that has a wife is accompanied by happiness. They are the friends that in loneliness speak of love, fathers at the calls of duty, mothers for him that suffers, rest even in the wilds of the forest for the way-wearied wanderer. He that has a wife finds trust [3] ; therefore the wife is the surest refuge. Even when the husband crosses over into another birth, when he dies, hurries along rough paths alone, the faithful mate follows ever after him. If the wife has died first and gone away, then she awaits her husband, and the good woman follows the husband that has died first (paccāt sādhvy anugacchati). For this reason it is that a man wishes to marry, that the master may have a wife in this world and the other. The self begotten by the self is by the wise called ‘ son ’.[4] Therefore let the man look on his wife, the mother of his son, as his own mother. As does the doer of good deeds when he comes into heaven, so does the begetter feel comfort within him when he beholds the son, begotten by him in his wife’s womb, as it were his own countenance in the glass. If the man is burning in sorrows of the soul, and is sick with bodily ills, then does he find comfort by his wife, as he that is tortured with heat does in water. Even the man in the clutches of hot rage will do nothing harsh to women, if he considers that on them depend the pleasures of love, joy, and what is good. As the field on which the self grows up, women are an ever-holy thing [5] ; for what power have even the Rishis to produce children without a woman ! ”—Over and over again the wife is called the friend, the friend determined by fate, the best among friends, and so on. So in iii, 313.72, cp. çl. 63–64 ;

[1] Above all in the other world. Less likely : of him that wishes to sail across (across all kinds of harm, especially that threatening in the other world).
[2] Or : the religious celebrations.
[3] That is, he is worthy of trust (viçvāsya) ; but here rather : he can find consolation and courage (through his wife, of course).
[4] Often in the MBh. as elsewhere. Hartland, *Prim. Paternity*, i, 195 ff. ; 208, and others, take this literally !
[5] Or : Women are the holy (pure) everlasting field of the birth of the self.

iv, 2.17. No friend is like her ; she is the beſt herb of healing for him that suffers (iii, 61.29, 30). In this meaning likewise, not only in the erotic or culinary, she belongs to the care of the body (çarīrayātrākṛiti, xiii, 145.13). An abundance of earthly goods, laſting health, and a beloved sweet-spoken wife, and an obedient son, and knowledge that fulfils its end [1]—these are the six blessings of the world of mankind (v, 33.82).[2] In the good wife the three goals of life, which otherwise are endlessly at feud, are at one together (iii, 313.102) ; on the wife, indeed, this trinity depends, as, too, dutiful service, the propagation of the family, the good (dharma) of the forefathers and of the self (of the man, xiv, 90.47, 48), which is felt in the world beyond. The good wife is not only joy and peace, but house and home, too. Thus the anxious bird-husband whose wife does not come home in the evening calls out (xii, 144.3 ff.) : " There was a heavy rain with ſtrong wind, and my loved one does not come. Why is it that she does not yet come back ? I wonder if it is well with my darling in the foreſt. Without the wife the house of one dwelling in it is utterly empty, even if it swarms all over with sons, grandsons, daughters-in-law,[3] and servants. It is not the house that is called house, it is the miſtress that is the house ; but a house without the miſtress is the same as the lonely foreſt. If this darling of mine with the round eye-margins, the lovely body, and the sweet voice does not now come, then I have nothing left in life. She, the ſteadfaſt in virtue, who eats not before I have eaten, bathes not before I have bathed, ſtands not unless I ſtand, lies to reſt only when I lie, she is not glad if I am not glad, she frets if I am fretting ; if I am away on a journey, then her face is mournful, and if I am angered, then she speaks sweet words. True to her husband, devoted to her husband as to her one refuge, finding her delight in that which is dear and wholesome for the husband—he who has a wife such as this, that man is blessed

[1] Or : that is of some use (arthakarī).

[2] Like other truly wise men, this one, therefore, could not reckon well.

[3] Vadhū " daughter-in-law " is often found in the MBh. (e.g. i, 106.1, 22 (cf. 13) ; 177.11 ff. ; 212.16 ; ii, 72.27 ; iii, 280.60 ; 296.28 ; 298.9 ; v, 37.5 ; xii, 228.96 ; xiv, 90.67, 80).

on earth. For the dutiful one knows when I am wearied and racked by hunger—filled with heartfelt affection, ever attached to me by love, and tender is my glorious one. He for whom a beloved wife lives, he has a home there, even if it be only on the root of a tree ; even a palace without her is a wilderness, that I am convinced of. Whether it be the time for fulfilling a pious duty, or for acquiring worldly goods, or for love, man's comrade is his wife ; and if he must go abroad, then she bestows solace and trust on him. For the wife is called here on earth the highest gift of happiness,[1] the mate of the mateless on life's way.[2] Even so for the man laid low by sickness and ever suffering, for the afflicted one, there is no healing like his wife. There is no kinsman like the wife, no comrade in the world like the wife, where it is sought to win pious merit. He that in his house has no good and sweet-speaking wife, let him but go into the lonely forest ; his house is as the lonely forest " (xii, 144.3 ff.).[3] In harmony with ideals such as these, even tender daughters of kings, like Draupadī and Damayantī, used to the most delicate luxury, go into wretchedness along with their husbands who have come to grief through their own fault ; and the queen herself faithfully follows her lord, who has been changed into a man-eating monster, on his wanderings through forest and wilderness (i, 182.6 ff.).

[1] Or : the highest end (the highest thing, artha).

[2] Or : the pilgrimage through the world (lokayātrā) ; cp. tīrtha-yātrā, and Rām., ii, 109.27, where the word has probably the same meaning; also MBh., v, 192.33 ; xiii, 13.1 ; as also e.g. Manu, iv, 242.

[3] As against these passages (to which many could be added from Indian literature) there are many bitter attacks also to be found : such is the verse in an ascetic didactic discourse which calls wife and child leeches (xii, 301.70). Then in one of the many strophes of the MBh. preaching unlimited individualism, we find : " The wife is all-devouring wear and tear (jarā), the son but a seed, the brother a foe, the friend only something to give gifts to (klinnapāṇi, elsewhere also ārdrapāṇi in the Epic), only the self is the enjoyer of pleasure and pain (xii, 139.30). The evils that come towards the end of the world are also to be seen from the fact that men take their wives as friends (iii, 190.19, 20). They cannot find or value anything better, and women's respect is gone.

343

Terribly hard and noble beyond words is the task of the good woman already as a daughter, and still more so as a wife, as is explained in iii, 205 ff. "Then did King Yudhishthira put to the famous and mighty Mārkaṇḍeya a question on virtue, right hard to decide (dharmapraçnaṃ sudurvi daṃ). ' I would fain hear set forth by thee in its true nature the nobility and dignity of women, this thing above all others, fair, and holy and good (dharmya). Clearly before us we see here, O priestly Rishi, the gods, the sun, the moon, the wind, the earth, and fire, O best one, and father and mother, O holy one, and the teacher, O best one, and whatever else there is, that which has been created, that, too, O son of Bhṛigu. All persons of standing especially must be given honour, and then those women who know only one man ; the obedience of faithful wives seems to me a hard thing. Do thou, my lord, set forth to us the high dignity of faithful wives that keep a check on the host of the senses, and a restraint on the heart, and ever bethink themselves of their husband, as of a god. O lord, thou glorious one, this seems to me a heavy task. Women, O twice-born one, are obedient to mother and father and husband. Compared with the so awe-inspiring duty and virtue (dharmāt sughorāt) of women, there is, indeed, so far as I can see, none other whatever that is burdensome. For it is with virtuous ways, and ever attentive, that women have their work to do ; truly they have a heavy task towards father and mother [1] ; and the women, too, who know only a husband, and who speak the truth, and who carry the fruit in their body for ten months, and so live beside death— what could there be that is more wonderful ? And women come into the utmost danger and pain beyond compare, and so

---

[1] In a literal translation çl. 9 is perhaps to be thus combined with what is before : (heavy, compared, that is to say, with that) which good women do who lead a good life, and are ever attentive. Or less likely, taken together with 9b : what . . . do, they have a heavy task therewith towards father and mother. Kṛi with the accus. of the person = do, do towards, treat, handle, is often found in the Epic. So vi, 79.6 ; vi, 64.16 f. ; vii, 21.1 ; viii, 68.23 ; xii, 175.5 ; Rām., iv, 5.30 ; cp. MBh., vii, 12.3 ; Rām., iv, 18.47 : tatrāpi khalu māṃ doshaṃ kartuṃ nārhasi, Rāghava " therein also thou must see no blame for me ".

bear their children in great torment, O my lord, and rear them with true and tender love, O bull among the twice-born. And they, living amidst all the cruel conditions,[1] looked on with loathing, fulfil their duty always—this I deem to be a hard thing. Show unto me, O twice-born one, the true essence of their way of life, based on that of warriors and with warriors' duties ; hard to attain to, O Brahman, is the virtue of the very glorious ones because of (all) the malice (cruelty).[2] As to this I would fain hear, holy and august one, as to this question, thou most excellent of those wise in questions, foremost of the race of Bhṛigu. I am hearkening unto thee, thou pious man.' Mārkaṇḍeya spoke : ' 'Tis well, I will enlighten thee according to the truth on this question, which is very hard to explain. Hearken unto it from me, while I speak of it. Some grant the greater respect to the mothers, others to the fathers.[3] The mother, who brings up the children, carries through a heavy task. Through asceticism, sacrifices to the gods, worship, patience, magic, and other means the fathers seek to get sons. When thus they have won the son, so hard to obtain, then they are ever thinking, O hero, what kind of man he will become. For the father and mother hope from their sons for fame, glory, and power, offspring, and religious merit, O child of the

---

[1] Or : " men " (krūreshu sarveshu) ?

[2] Note that the whole extract deals with the māhātmya, the glory of woman, and that the text speaks much of all the cruelty (or baseness, nṛiçaṃsa) that works against women on earth. My rendering, therefore, fits in excellently with the context and with the truth and reality. The child-bearing woman and the warrior are especially linked together in the popular mind in other parts of the world also. Here samācāra can be taken either as sam or as sama + ācāra ; the genit. mahātmanām probably refers back to the first half of the çloka. From the point of view of the language the most obvious, indeed, would be : " Show unto me the true essence of the way of duty of the Kshattriyas ; the virtue of the high-souled is for the lowly man hard to win." But then we should here have to reject the whole çloka. Kshettra could also be read instead of kshattra, and " fruitful field " be put = wife. But for all that this idea is very usual, yet there are some difficulties here about the matter (xii, 205.14).

[3] More literally : Some from the standpoint of the venerable have been on the mothers' side, others on the fathers' side.

Bharatas. He that lets their hope bear fruit is one with a knowledge of duty, and he from whom the father and mother have ever joy, O ruler above kings, has here in this life and after death fame and everlasting virtuous merit ; no sacrificial deeds, no gifts to forefathers, no fasting is like this.[1] But through

[1] So, if naivaṃ were read for naiva. But after all it is better to keep to naiva, and to join çl. 22b with 22a : (" For the woman) there is (is of avail) neither any sacrifice, nor gift to the dead, nor fasting, but through obedience towards her husband she wins heaven." This reading is the more likely in that this saying with fixed variations is often found. So, for instance, Vishṇusmṛiti, xxv, 15 :
Nāsti strīṇāṃ pṛithagyajño, na vrataṃ nāpy uposhitam ;
Patiṃ çuçrūshate yat tu tena svarge mahīyate.
Mārkaṇḍeyapurāṇa, xvi, 61 :
Nāsti strīṇāṃ pṛithagyajño, na çrāddhaṃ nāpy uposhitaṃ ;
Bhatṛiçuçrūshayaivaitān lokān ishṭān vrajanti hi.
Cp. e.g. MBh., i, 158.24 ; xiii, 8.20 ; 40.11 f. ; 59.29.
On pṛithagyajño there is a strong stress, and even in the house the woman according to her standing in law has no importance at all in herself. The woman throughout her life is dependent, and therefore also she is not entitled to hold property, as is often laid down. In childhood she is under the rule and protection of her father, in the flower of her age under her husband's, and if the husband is dead, under her sons'. She can never enjoy freedom to dispose of herself. See e.g. Manu, v, 147 f. ; Vas., v, 1–2 ; Yājñav., i, 85 ; Nārada, xiii, 28–31 ; Vishṇu, xxv, 12–13 ; Mahānirvāṇat., viii, 106 ; Baudh., ii, 2, 3.44. In the last two passages the well-known pronouncement is found in immediate connexion : " Through obedience to her husband she wins heaven." And for the gods she is only a—woman. Only together with her husband can she do pious works, only together with her husband can she come into paradise. And there, too, the stone wall stares before her with the flaming inscription : Asvatantrī dharme strī " The woman has no independence in virtue, religion, or law " (Gautama, xviii, 1). It is only over the gates of hell that for the Indian woman who may thirst for freedom there stands the direct opposite of those famous words of Dante. Bitterly, but with truth Ramabai Sarasvati calls out : " The only place where she can be independent of him is in hell " (*The High Caste Hindu Woman*, p. 41). So the woman must not go on a pilgrimage either ; her place of pilgrimage is her husband, and good works are done at home. Mahānirvāṇatantra, viii, 100 f. Cp. here the splendid words of the

obedience towards her husband—through this she wins heaven.
As to that which relates to this chapter, O King Yudhishṭhira,
with heed hear then of the firm-set virtue of faithful wives.
There was one moſt excellent among the twice-born, given up
to Veda ſtudy, rich in penance, of virtuous charaĉter,
Kauçika his name, O child of the Bharatas. The beſt among the
twice-born ſtudied the Vedas, together with the knowledge
helpful to them and the Upanishads. (Once) he was by the root
of a tree, repeating the Veda aloud. Up in the tree a hen-crane had
perched, and let its droppings fall on the Brahman. When the
angry twice-born one saw her, he cursed her in his thoughts. With
the eye of the hotly angered Brahman on her, and cursed in his
heart, the hen-crane fell down onto the ground. When the
twice-born one saw her lying there, lifeless, and bereft of consciousness, he bewailed her, seized with a burning pain through
pity : " I have done evil, overcome by anger and passion."
So spoke the wise one many times, and then went into the village
to beg, calling on the pure families in the village, O bull among
the Bharatas. When now he came into a house, where he had
already visited before, and made requeſt " Give ", the woman
said to him : " Wait." While the lady of the house was now
seeing to the cleaning of the crockery, her husband suddenly
came in with the pangs of hunger on him, O beſt of the Bhāratas.
And when the good wife saw her lord, she left the Brahman
ſtanding there unheeded, and handed her husband water for
washing the feet and rinsing the mouth, and a seat, and
reverently did the black-eyed one then wait on her husband,
with very delicious food, hard and soft ; what her husband
left over she was wont to eat, she with the pure soul, O
Yudhishṭhira. And she looked on her lord as a god, fitting herself
to her husband's thoughts ; in deeds, thoughts, and words she
took her course from her husband alone, not giving a thought
to any other, devoted to him with all her being and life, finding

wonderful Berthold von Regensburg, which I have given in the note
on Daçakumārac., p. 50. In the same way as Berthold, and as Luther
in his epiſtle to the nobles, Mahānirvāṇat. (viii, 97 ff.) and Baudhāyana, ii, 3.16, as also Manu, xi, 10 condemn pilgrimages to holy
places, and pious works in general, if thereby a man in any way ſtints
his family.

her pleasure in obedience to him, leading a good life, pure, active, and skilful, thinking always of her family's welfare. And whatever was wholesome for her husband, that she lived for always, ever taken up with the humble service of the gods, guests, and servants, as, too, of her mother-in-law and father-in-law, and ever with a bridle on her senses. While now the bright-eyed one was giving obedient service to her husband, she saw the Brahman standing and asking for alms, and bethought herself of him.[1] The good woman was then taken with shame, O best among the Bhāratas, took alms for the Brahman, and went out, the glorious one. The Brahman spoke : 'What does this mean ? "Wait" thou didst tell me, O fair lady, and then keep me to my loss and not send me away.' Mārkaṇḍeya spoke : 'When the good woman saw the Brahman, aflame with anger, flare up, as it were in a mighty fire, soothingly she said these words to him : " I beg thee, forgive me, O wise one ! My husband is my great godhead. And he arrived hungry and weary, and therefore was waited on by me." The Brahman spoke : " Thou didst not hold the Brahmans as being more worshipful, thou didst hold thy husband as more worshipful ; although thou livest in householder's rank, thou dost despise the Brahmans. Even Indra bows himself before them. How much the more so a human being on earth ! Thou haughty one, dost thou not know and hast thou not heard from the old that the Brahmans are like fire, and could burn up even the earth ! " The woman spoke : " I am no hen-crane, O Brahmanic Rishi. Put away thine anger, O thou rich in asceticism. What wouldst do, angry one, to me with this angry look ? I do not despise the Brahmans, those wise ones, like unto the gods. Do thou forgive me this slight, thou blameless one. I know the greatness of the Brahmans, for by the anger of the Munis of just such glowing asceticism

---

[1] Perhaps I should have kept, however, to my first version : " And what was wholesome for her husband, for the gods, the guests, the servants, and for her mother-in-law and father-in-law, this she lived for always. While she that strove only and always for obedience, and had always her senses bridled, she the bright-eyed one, was carrying on the service of her husband, she saw the Brahman," and so on.

and purified soul,[1] of the Munis, whose fiery anger is still
to-day unquenched in the Daṇḍaka forest [2]—by their anger was
the sea made undrinkable and salt-watered. Because the very
evil-minded Vātāpi harmed the Brahmans, the cruel and huge
Asura, when he came to the Ṛishi Agastya, was eaten up and
destroyed. We are told of many mighty doings of the Brahmans,
the high and glorious ones. Full of power is the anger of the
high-souled ones, and their favour, O Brahman. But this
offence, O Brahman, thou without fault, do thou forgive unto
me. The virtue arising out of obedience to the husband is
pleasing to me, O twice-born one. Among even all the
divinities my husband is the highest for me. In all circumstances
I would fain fulfil my duty to him. See, O Brahman, what the
fruit is of faithful service to the husband : Thou didst burn
up the hen-crane out of anger ; that I know. Anger is a foe
to man that dwells in his (own) body, O best of Brahmans. He
that puts anger and blindness behind him is known by the gods
as a Brahman. He on this earth that always speaks the truth,
and makes those worthy of respect content, and, if he is harmed,
does no harm, him the gods know as a Brahman. He that has
overcome the senses, is given up to virtue, finds his delight in
holy study, is pure, and has love and anger under his sway, him
the gods know as a Brahman. He to whom the world is as his
own self, he that knows the good, and is wise, and finds his
joy in all the virtues, him the gods know as a Brahman." ' "
She then explains still further to him what virtue is, and how
little he understands about it, and sends him to Mithilā to
the pious butcher that the Brahman may learn it from him
(iii, 205, 206).[3] Cp. especially MBh., K, xiii, 249.16 ff.,
a kind of Martha and Mary tale.

[1] Or : For in this same way the sea became undrinkable, salt-watered
through the anger of the Munis of shining asceticism, etc. Cp. with
this passage Manu, ix, 314, and Bühler's note, SBE, xxv, p. 398 ;
as also MBh., xii, 342.61 f.; xiii, 34.27 ; 151.17 ; 153.7, 11.
[2] The Epic, too, tells this tale, which was remodelled as a motive
by the Buddhists and the Jains. See Rām., vii, 80 f.
[3] This tale, as also that of Dharmavyādha, is also in the 56th Tar.
of the Kathāsarits., and separately in the Parrot Book (Rosen,
Tutinameh, ii, 232 ; ZDMG, xxi, 543). Cp. Çukas., Introd.

So, too, the Brahman Uttanka cannot even see the faithful wife of King Paushya, and thinks he is being tricked by the ruler, as being he that brought him to her ; because of this virtue she is invisible to anyone that is not wholly pure, and the holy man in the haſte of his journey in the morning has forgotten to carry out the ritual purification (i, 3.101 ff.). " The chaſtity and goodness of a woman brings all knowledge, it has power over life and death, heaven and hell. Utterances such as the touchingly simple one in Rām., vi, 111.67 : ' It is not in vain that the tears of faithful wives fall to earth ' are tame indeed compared with what, as is well known, we so often find." [1] For a faithful wife is a sin-cancelling means of grace (tīrtha), juſt as much as asceticism, etc. MBh.K, xiv, 118.8 ff.

Very frequent in Indian literature, and often found in the Epic also, is the " aĉt of truth ", especially in the case of pure wives. In later Hindu tales this is, indeed, often undertaken without good reason.[2] But the Epic knows nothing of cynical jeſts such as these. Thus, for inſtance, Sītā also proteſts her obedience and her faithfulness to Rāma, and so forces the fire on Hanumant's tail, in spite of all its glow, to be quite cold (Rām., v, 53.25 ff.).

But above all it is of course in the beyond that the faithful wife is rewarded. She goes into the world of her husband (xiv, 20.4) ; there are, indeed, various worlds, the higheſt heavens of the pious, that are seen only by Brahma, holy Ṛishis, Brahmans with a pure spirit, and faithful wives, and which are for ever shut even to the eyes of the king of the gods (xiii, 73.2 ff.). Nay, more : Far away beyond the heaven of those that are absorbed in holy meditation (brahmasattrim) lies the world of

---

[1] Daṇḍin's Daçakumārac., p. 40. Cp. e.g. in Tawney's Kathākoça, the tale of Davadantī, p. 195 ff., espec. 207 ; Prabandhacint., p. 64 ; Bhojaprabandha, ed. Vidyasagara, p. 90; Mārk.-Pur., xvi, 27 ff. (faithful wife ſtops the sun from rising) ; etc.

[2] Cp. the case referred to by me in Daçakum., p. 40, where the 80,000 wives of the king along with all the women of the city cannot bring a dead elephant back to life again (Kathās., Tar. 36),and with that Rājatar., i, 318. Schiefner, *Bulletin de l'Acad. Imp. des Sciences de St.-Pétersbourg*, vol. 21, col. 479 ; J. J. Meyer, *Isoldes Gottesurteil* (Berlin, 1914), p. 277 f. (note 176).

faithful wives ; beyond that again lies only the formless, the domain of ultimate being. ix, 50.41–48.

It is truly not made very easy for the woman of Old India to win for herself the name of a true and seemly wife. That has already been seen from much that has been ſtated. Here we give a few special passages. " This only is what the good call the oldeſt law : what the husband says to the wife, whether right or wrong, that she muſt do exactly ; thus do the knowers of the holy knowledge know " (i, 122.27, 28). " This is the higheſt and everlaſting task of the woman in the world, that she do all that is beſt for her husband, even at the coſt of her life " (i, 158.4). " Truth, and the joy of love, and heaven won by excellence, and whatever is wished for is for women dependent on the husband. Menſtruation (which is needful for conception) comes from the mother, the seed from the father, the higheſt god is the husband ; through the husband the goal of life for women, made up of the pleasures of love and children, is thus reached " (xiv, 90.50 ff.). " But the husband, be he virtuous or not, is for those women that heed the moral good the visible godhead " (Rām., ii, 62.8). See also MBh., xii, 145.3 ff. Anasūyā says in Rām., ii, 117.22 ff. : " Thy kinsfolk, O Sītā, thou rich in honour, and honour and prosperity thou haſt left behind, and followeſt Rāma banished in the foreſt. Good fortune be thine ! Those women whose husband is dearly loved, whether he live in city or foreſt, be he good or bad, theirs are the worlds of high happiness. For women of noble charaċter the husband is the higheſt godhead, although he have a bad charaċter, or live after his luſts, or be bereft of worldly goods." [1] Thus, too, her lord is more for the wife than her own child. Arjuna's wife, Citrāṅgadā, whom her hero-husband has made, indeed, with child, but soon left,[2] believes her lord and her son

[1] In the following sarga Sītā expresses her whole-hearted agreement, and lays ſtress on the doċtrine often found that the woman's tapas is wholly and alone obedience to her husband.

[2] I had firſt written : " twice made with child." But in spite of Jacobi also in his Mahābhārata so taking it, it is wrong. Arjuna leaves C., when she has become with child by him (215.27), and goes forth adventuring. Then he comes back for a short and laſt visit, and he finds there (217.23 ff.) the son who has meanwhile been born,

are dead, and is ready to let the son be lost, but not her husband, and wishes to see him called back to life ; " for this friendship has been made everlasting and imperishable by the creator " (xiv, 80.15). And in the Rāmāyaṇa (ii, 39.29–30) it is said : " Without a string there is no lute, without a wheel no chariot, without a husband no woman is happy, even though she have a hundred sons. For what the father gives has bounds, what the brother gives has bounds, what the son gives has bounds ; but him that gives the unbounded, the husband, what wife should not honour him ! " [1]

Like many another god, so this god of the wife was particularly great at asking. Above all the holy men in this also showed their very famous—holiness. Jaratkāru, who sees his forbears hanging in the cave, resolves therefore to get married to save them, and at length in spite of his strange demands finds a wife, the snake fay Jaratkāru, in fact, Vāsuki's sister, and lives after the wedding in his brother-in-law's palace amid great splendour and magnificence. " There the best one made this covenant with his wife : ' Thou must never do or utter anything that is unpleasing to me. If anything unpleasing happened to me, then I should sever myself from thee and no longer dwell in thy house. Take what I have spoken unto thine heart.' Then did the much afeared sister of the prince of snakes speak unto him these words in exceeding great sorrow : ' Thus shall it be.' And strictly thus (as was agreed) did she wait on her husband in ways that are as rare as white crows, for the glorious one yearned to offer him what was pleasing.

Babhruvāhana, whom he " had begotten with her " (or " begot ", çl. 24). The context in the last-named passage, and various other circumstances force us to this reading.

[1] So, too, MBh., xii, 148.6, 7. Cp. e.g. iii, 234.3. A woman in Bhoja's capital was holding her sleeping husband on her lap, and her small child crawled into the fire. So as not to awake her lord, she sat still, but besought Agni for the sake of her faithfulness to her husband not to burn the child. It was done as she begged. When the man woke up, she quickly took out the child, who was sitting smiling in the flames (Bhojaprab., ed. Vidyasagara, p. 90). The woman left by her husband has fallen from the world of holiness and of salvation (puṇyasthāna), and cannot come into heaven (iii, 230.3, 5).

Now once when Vāsuki's sister had just bathed herself at the time of her courses, she approached, as is seemly, her husband, the great Muni. Then there came into being in her a fruit of the body like unto fire, exceedingly endowed with brightness, full of light as the god of flames. As the moon in the bright half of the month, even so did this fruit grow. A few days later the greatly famed Jaratkāru was lying wearied asleep, having laid his head on her lap. And as this prince among Brahmans slept, the sun came to the mountain of its setting. As the day was now about to vanish, the wise sister of Vāsuki thought to herself, filled with a dread of the holy law being broken : ' What would be a good deed for me : to wake my husband, or not ? For he with the soul of virtue is angry-minded. How shall I do so as not to give him offence. Either the man of virtuous character will be angered, or he will break the holy law. The breaking of the holy law would be, indeed, of greater moment.' So she came to a decision. ' If I awake him, he will certainly fall into a rage. But he will inevitably fall into breaking the holy law, if he misses the twilight prayer.' [1] So soon as the snake fay Jaratkāru had thus decided in her mind, the sweet-speaking one spoke the following gentle words to this Rishi of flaming asceticism, to him like fire, who was lying there asleep : ' Arise, O high and glorious one ; the sun is setting. Perform thou the evening worship, O august one, as a strait observer of religious duty, having carried out the washing. The sweet and awful moment has come that brings the fiery sacrifice with it. [2] The evening twilight is now coming up in the west, O lord.' Thus addressed, the holy and august Jaratkāru, the mighty one in penance, spoke these words to his wife, with quivering lips : ' Hereby thou hast slighted me, O snake fay. I will no longer live with thee ; I will go thither whence I came. The sun has no power to set at its usual time, if I am asleep, O thou with the lovely thighs ; so I know in my heart. But none would choose to dwell here, having been slighted ; how much less would I, the man of virtuous character, or one of my kind.' Thus addressed by her husband with words

[1] See J. J. Meyer, *Altind. Rechtsschr.*, the passages under " Dämmerungsandacht ".
[2] Literally : into view.

that set her heart quaking, Jaratkāru, Vāsuki's sister, spoke there in his abode : ' It was not out of slighting scorn, O Brahman, that I awoke thee. I did so that thou mightst not become guilty of any offence against the holy law.' Thus addressed, he spoke to his wife, he the great penitent Jaratkāru, the Rishi overcome by anger, who wished to leave the snake fay : ' My tongue has never yet spoken an untruth. I shall go, O snake fay. This mutual agreement I made with thee before. I have dwelt here pleasantly, my dear one. Tell thy brother, thou good one, when I have gone hence, thou timid one : " The holy man has gone." And thou thyself have no care, when I have gone away.' Thus addressed, she of the faultless limbs now spoke to the Muni, to Jaratkāru, she Jaratkāru with the lovely hips, sunk in sorrow and pain, with tear-stifled voice, parched mouth, hands folded before the forehead, and eyes wet with tears, as she with the lovely thighs firmly gathered up all her courage, while her heart shivered— she spoke : ' I beg thee, thou with the knowledge of virtue, do not leave me who am guiltless, thou that abidest ever in the holy law leave not me who abide ever in the holy law, who find my delight always in what is pleasing and wholesome for thee.' " She implored him to stay, since for the welfare of her kindred and of the world of the snakes she must first have a son by him. But he assured her that the fruit of her body already conceived would be a fire-like Rishi, mighty in knowledge, and he went away (i, 47).

Like him in holiness, penitential might, and irritability was the great Muni Jamadagni, and at the same time a master of bowmanship. "Once the holy man, the Bhrigus' son, was amusing himself by fixing and then shooting one arrow after another. These shining, flaming arrows, shot off by him were brought back again in quick succession by Renukā (his wife), and given to him. At the sound of the bow-string and the arrows he was joyfully stirred, and went on shooting, and she brought them back again to him. Then, when the sun, now in the summer month of Jyeshtha, had climbed the heights of midday, the Brahman who had sent forth the arrows said these words to Renukā : ' Go, big-eyed one, and bring hither those arrows that have sped from the bow, that I may shoot them off again

354

at once, O thou with the lovely brows.' On her way thither
the glorious one went into the shade under a tree, for her head
and her feet were burning hot. But when she had been ſtanding
a moment, the pure, the black-eyed one went on her way,
fearing her husband's curse, to fetch back the arrows ; and the
shining one came back with the arrows in her hand. Wearied,
indeed, and keeping down her pain, she with the lovely limbs
walked up to her husband, trembling with fear of him. Then the
angry Ṛishi kept on saying these words to her with the shining
face : ' Reṇukā, wherefore art thou so late in coming ? '
Reṇukā spoke : ' My head and feet are truly burning, O thou
rich in asceticism ; being weighed down by the glow of the
sun, I took shelter in the shadow of a tree. This is why, O
Brahman, I took so long. Now that thou haſt heard this, O lord,
be not angered, O thou rich in penitence.' Jamadagni ſpoke :
' Now will I shoot down him with the flaming beams who has
brought pain on thee, O Reṇukā ; the sun god with my
arrows by the fiery ſtrength of the bolt [1] will I shoot
down.' " The sun god, whether he likes it or no, now has
to submit : he makes his appearance in the shape of a
Brahman, and firſt tries to show the angry man that the sun muſt
shine thus for the good of the world ; and when the ſtubborn
fellow will not liſten, he soothes him with humble words
and geſtures, and gives him a pair of sandals, and a sunshade
againſt the heat of the day-ſtar. Thus did these two useful
things originate. But whether the poor woman also had any
service from them is not clear from the account, which, indeed,
has for its objeＣt only to fire men on to give the Brahmans
sunshade and sandals (xiii, 95, 96). But here, too, we are
reminded of Dushyanta's words : " By patience with their
husbands women reach the virtue of faithfulness " (K., i,
100.28).

Many, it is true, find it too much. A great number of the
men of whom the Epic, too, tells us are mighty in asceticism ;
the conqueſt of the senses then appears as the higheſt end.
Woman wants love ; and she wants to see the man using
his ſtrength, even if it be savagely or even brutally, not in the
pure ether where passion is not. " This old legend, too, is

[1] Of the arrow magic (aſtra) ?

told, the discourse which was held between husband and wife. A Brahman woman spoke to a Brahman man who had reached the further shore of holy and worldly knowledge, and whom she saw sitting there alone, the wife spoke to the husband : ' Into which world (of heaven) shall I now come, who am allotted to thee as wife, to one that has cast aside all active work, and squats there, a stupid, miserable wretch (kīnāça) ? Wives come into the worlds made ready by their husbands, so we have been told. To what place shall I now go, who have fallen to thee as my husband ? ' " (xiv, 20.1 ff.). See, too, how King Janaka of Videha who has become a monk is upbraided by his wife as one that has forgotten his duty (xii, 18). The wife of Dīrghatama has to support him, but rids herself, as we saw, of a master who is in many respects unpleasant (i, 104.30 ff.). From the holy Atri his wife runs away and cries out : " I will no longer be subject in any way to this Muni ! " (xiii, 14.95). How others, while keeping faithfully by the husband, yet give utterance to their discontent with him, of this we have already found an example in Draupadī. More will be said later. So also in the chapter on the ideal woman something more will be found on the relation of the wife to the husband. Here we give only three further examples of wedded faithfulness. Çacī is proverbial for her chastity, the wife of the woman-loving king of the gods. How she was put to a hard test is told in v, 10 ff. Indra had slain Vṛitra, and thereby burdened himself with the guilt of Brahman-murder. He therefore crept away into the water at the edge of the world. The whole world suffered most dreadfully, since now there was no Indra. The gods then appointed Nahusha, the pious guest of heaven, as his successor. But he now became an insolent ruffian, giving free rein to his lusts. All the hosts of Apsarases and houris of the gods were not enough for him : as soon as he had seen Çacī he wanted her. The gods represented to him the shamefulness of touching another man's wife, but he made them remember that they had held their tongues quiet enough when Indra was raping Ahalyā, and doing his other foul deeds. The poor harassed queen of heaven had at last to submit, and take herself in fear and trembling to the tyrant, and ask a respite of him.

She knew not at all, she said, what had become of her lord. Nahusha consented, and in tears she set about her search, calling after Indra, and through her womanly purity she managed it so that the goddess of oracles, Upaçruti, showed herself to her in bodily shape, and took her northwards to the Himālaya, where in a great lake a mighty lotus-flower towered up. The two went into its stalk, and there found Indra, who had taken on a slender, small shape, and hidden himself there. Çacī besought him to save her from shame. But he answered that Nahusha was too strong, and told her of a trick by which she should fool her lover. So she had to go back alone, and expose herself once more to the profaning looks and words of the burning lover. But the trick was successful, the bold rascal was overthrown, and the two rulers of the gods once more united (cp. xii, 342.28–53).

Nārada, the great seeker after new things in heaven and on earth, once goes forth together with his nephew on a very diverting ramble through the lands of the earth. They make the agreement that " whatever wish the one may have, he must let the other know of it, be it good or evil ; otherwise the curse will light on him for an untruth ". They invite themselves as guests of King Srñjaya for an indefinite time. The king one day says : " I have a daughter with a fair face. She is my only girl. She shall wait on you. She is lovely to look on, with a faultless body, wholly given to virtuous ways, a tender maid, bright-shining as a filament of the lotus-flower." " That is a friendliness without compare," said the two. The king gave her his bidding : " Girl, wait on the two Brahmans, as though they were gods or thine own fathers." The maiden, she that lived after the law, said " Yes " to her father, and did honour and service to the two according to the king's bidding. Because of her service and her peerless beauty love came swift and sudden on Nārada. And passion waxed in the heart of the high-souled one, as the moon waxes step by step, when the bright half of the month has come. But for shame the knower of the law did not tell his nephew of this violent love of his, did not tell the high-souled Parvata." But Parvata noticed all, and on the close one put the curse of becoming an ape. Nārada got his beloved one as wife, but the

357

curse was also fulfilled, and, indeed, directly after the wedding. But she loved him even thus, and kept strict faith with him (xii, 30 ; cp. vii, 55).

The king's daughter, Sukanyā had aroused the anger of the old and ugly penitent Cyavana, and was given him to wife that he might forget his deadly wrath. The two Açvins saw her bathing unclad (kritābhishekāṃ vivṛitāṃ), like a daughter of the ruler of the gods, and told her how foolish she was to waste her wonderful beauty and her blooming youth beside her withered old husband, who could not protect or support her either ; she must choose one of them for a husband. But she spoke : " I am content with my husband Cyavana ; do not, I beg you, believe such evil of me." Then these two physicians of the gods offered to make the old man a handsome youth ; then she should pick out one of the three for herself. All three dived into a pond, and came up in a moment exactly alike in youth, beauty, and form. Each one shouted : " Choose me ! " But she with her mind and her heart still found her husband out, and chose him (iii, 123).[1] Cp. iv, 21.10–14.

[1] Cp. Hopkins, " The Fountain of Youth," JAOS, 26, p. 44 ff. ; Crooke, *Popul. Relig.*, etc., i, 59 f. ; Bhāgavatapur., ix, 3.1 ff.

XII

Woman as Child-bearer : The Origin of Man

ALL the virtues of the wife are still uncrowned if she bestows no children, especially no son, on the husband, as has already been said. The wife as a child-bearer, therefore, stands first and foremost. What now does the Epic teach us as to procreation, pregnancy, and birth ?

The juices [1] nourish the body of man through the networks of veins, wind, gall, mucus, blood, skin, flesh, sinews, bones, and marrow. It must be known that there are ten small tubes in it bringing their powers [2] to the five senses, and from them spread other small tubes in thousands. In this wise these veins—the rivers that here carry juices as water—feed the body's sea, each in its time, as the rivers feed the sea. And in the middle of the heart there is a vein Manovahā (the bearer of the manas, the appetitive and concept-building faculty of man), which sets free from all the limbs the seed of men, born of the yearning concept. For the veins that branch off into all the limbs have their outlet in it. Carrying the fiery matter,[3] they run from and to the eyes. Just as the butter that is in the milk is twirled out by the churn-staff, so is the seed

[1] More precisely : food-juices (rasa, chyle). Cp. xii, 185.9.
[2] More literally : their constituent of strength, of energy ; or their element (guṇam). Nīl. = svasvavishayagrahaṇapāṭavam.
[3] Or : the fiery part ; or : the light-element (taijasaṃ guṇam). Tejas is here probably to be taken in a twofold sense : first, as light, for the eyes are the instrument of seeing, which is dependent on light ; second, as fire, glow, passion, for from the eyes also, and from them first of all, love and erotic excitement is born, as may be likewise read in Indian literature. It would be possible to take taijasaṃ guṇaṃ = rājasaṃ guṇam = " carrying the material ingredient, passion (rajas)." " The senses are tejas-natured, that is, rajas-natured " (Saurapurāṇa, xxi, 9).

359

twirled out by the churn-staff of the appetitive ideas in the body (dehasaṃkalpajaiḥ khajaiḥ). And as in this wise even in sleep the passion born of the appetitive ideas of the manas streams hither, the manovahā discharges the seed from man's body that is produced through the appetitive idea.[1] The great Rishi Atri, the holy and august one, knows of this origin of the seed, which origin has three sources, and Indra for its god ; therefore, too, do we say indriya " (xii, 214.16 ff.).[2]

Yudhishthira spoke : " This hast thou shown, august one, how merit by works follows. But I would fain know this other, how the seed is produced." Brihaspati spoke : " What the godheads that are in the body eat for nourishment, O lord of men : the earth, the wind, the ether, water, light, and the manas—when these five elements, with the manas as sixth, have become sated therewith, O prince of kings, then the seed is brought into being, the momentous seed,[3] O man of the pure soul. From it then arises the fruit of the womb upon the union of woman and man, O prince. Thereby I have set forth all to thee. What wouldst thou still hear ? " Yudhishthira spoke : " Thou, holy man, hast told me how

---

[1] Or : And as in this wise even in sleep the passion born of the idea comes by way of the manas (the organ of perception, ideation, and desire), the manovahā sends (sṛjati) the seed born of the idea out of the body. This reading, however, seems to me not so good a one. The manovahā in its function of setting free the seed from all parts of the body is helped by the erotic feelings and ideas. There seems to be no thought here of the pouring forth of the seed. This Indian theory of the manovahā comes up again perhaps in the " Tavola ritonda ", which has many Eastern elements in it : La infermità dello amore si èe in una vena la quale vae per mezzo lo cuore, cioè che si muove dalla cima del cuore e gira tutte l' altre circustanze del corpo ; sicchè, essendo il cuore dello amadore tristo, dolenti e malinconichi stanno tutti gli altri membri ; e perchè la infermità dello amore è più forte e più è pericolosa di tutte l' altre, tanto è più acculta e nascosa (ed. F. L. Polidori, p. 250). See also Brihadāraṇyaka-Up., ii, 1.19 ; iv, 2.3 ; 3.2c ; Chānd.-Up., viii, 6.1–2.

[2] " Indra-strength," manly strength, seed. The three sources are : the food juice, the vein manovahā, and the idea (saṃkalpa). So the comm. rightly says. Cp. Aitareya-Up., ii, 1 ; Yājñav., iii, 71.

[3] This is hardly : in plenty (mahat).

the fruit of the womb comes into being. But how it is with the unborn Purusha [1]—let that be told." Brishaspati spoke : " The Purusha is but in the neighbourhood, and so is taken hold of by these elements (bhūta), and when separated from these elements, it goes again to another exiſtence. Bound up with all the elements, it partakes (of a new embodiment) as an individual soul ; then the godheads dwelling in the five primary elements see its work (karman), be it good or bad. What wouldſt thou hear further ? " Yudhishṭhira spoke : " When the individual soul has left skin, bones, and flesh, and is freed from these primary elements (bhūta), where does it then know pleasure and pain ? " Bṛihaspati spoke : " Bound up with the karman, it goes swiftly into seed-ſtate (retaſtva, ſtate, or being, as seed), and then, after it has met the menſtrual blood (pushpa) of women, is born at its time, O son of the Bharatas. Torment at the hands of Yama's servants, hurt at the hands of Yama's servants, and the painful wheel of the Saṃsāras—torment the human being goes through. And in this world here the living being from birth onwards, O lord of the earth, enjoys what good it has done by works, as a result of the fruit of merit through works " (xiii, 111.27 ff.). " Out of the idea arises sexual excitement [2] ; it arises also from the tone ; it arises also from the taſte ; it arises also from the form (it arises also from the feeling with touch ; it arises also from the smell). Out of the seed mingled with the blood (of the woman) comes forth firſt the Prāṇa. When the seed has been altered by the Prāṇa, then the Apāna comes forth. It is formed out of the seed, and it is formed out of the menſtrual fluid ; the pleasure aroused during union, that is the figure of the Udāna. Out of the yearning of love is the seed born ; out of the seed is sexual passion born. But seed and blood had been brought into being in the same fashion, through the Samāna (which digeſts the food), and the Vyāna (which

---

[1] Probably we muſt read yathā, which K also has. B has literally : " Thou haſt set forth to me that the fruit of the womb thus comes into being." Purusha is the eternai Ātman, the soul. Both texts have yathā jātas tu ; I join together to make yathājātas.

[2] Cp. xii, 163.8 : " Love springs from the idea (saṃkalpa)."

assimilates the food fluid) " (xiv, 24.5 ff.).[1] " How man, penetrated by his karman, filled with love and hate, comes into the mother's womb—hearken to this fully. The seed mingled with the blood (of the woman) which has come into the womb as holder, obtains thereby a field (abode, body), a good one or a bad, as his karman may bring. As a result of its tenuity and undeveloped state, and if it, as a Brahman (in the word's true meaning) has attained to its wish (the redeeming knowledge), thereby it cleaves nowhere—the eternal Brahman (neuter). This is the source (bīja) of all beings ; through this it is that creatures live. When this soul has penetrated all the limbs of the fruit of the womb, part by part, it at once gives it the gift of consciousness, taking up its place in the abodes of the breaths of life. Thereupon the fruit of the womb, endowed with consciousness, moves the limbs. . . . As fire makes its way into the lump of iron, and brings it to glow all through, so do thou look on the soul's going into the fruit of the womb " (xiv, 18.4 ff.). Yayāti spoke (to Ashtaka) : " He (he that takes on a body, that is, the soul) accompanies the tear-drop, the seed poured forth by the man, bound up with the fruit of the flower (with the karman) ; he meets her (the woman's) menstrual blood ; having become the embryo,

---

[1] Prāṇa, Apāna, etc., are the five " breaths of life ", in medicine forms of the wind, which is one of the three basic substances of the body, physiologically active life-forces. The last sentence is Deussen's translation (*Vier philosophische Texte des Mahābhārata*, p. 918). After wrestling long with the here very illogical text I have resolved simply to give this again instead of bringing up other possibilities. The Sanskrit text of the preceding sentence is : kāmāt samjāyate çukram, çukrāt samjāyate rajaḥ. I have taken rajas = rāga, as it is used, for instance, in xii, 213.9–10 ; 214.11–14. Materially the rendering is quite the right one. But here it does not fit properly. According to the context rajas should mean menstrual blood. But çukrāt stands in the way of this. Deussen changes to kāmāt ; this is too violent in the face of all three texts. Seed is also indeed ascribed to the woman just as among the old Greeks and Romans ; therefore : " out of the (female seed) arises the menstrual blood ? " Or : " as a consequence of the male seed (that is, because it exists, and the woman yearns for it) the menstrual blood arises ? " This in meaning would = kāmāt.

he there goes in.[1] Into the trees, into the plants they (the souls) go, into the water, into the wind, into the earth, and into the air, into the four-footed and two-footed—into all things they go[2]; in such an existence (evaṃbhūta) they become embryos." Ashṭaka spoke : "Does it (the soul) make for itself here another body (vapus), or does it make its way in its own body (kāya) into the womb, when it comes into human existence? Let me know of this ; I ask in doubt. In what way does it come unto the various bodies, and all else that grows,[3] the eyes and ears, the consciousness? Make known, thou that art put to the question, this whole matter ; we all hold thee for one that knows the field." Yayāti spoke : "The wind at the time of the ṛitu carries the seed up to the womb, mingled with the menstrual fluid ; there it makes the embryo gradually to grow, wielding sway over the atoms. When the human being has now taken the material to himself, and is born, then he takes his place in his consciousness,[4] and so hears sound with his ear, sees shapes with his eye, smells with his nose, and tastes with his tongue, feels touch with his skin, and perceives his condition with the manas" (i, 90.10 ff.).[5] "Thirty parts[6] there are according to the tradition. Where these all are found, there there is a body,

[1] Or : The seed bound up with the fruit of the flower (with the karman), united with the Purusha (or: sent forth by the man) makes its way to the menstrual blood ; it (the purusha, or : he that incarnates himself) meets her blood, etc. In view of çl. 14 it seems, however, as if we must translate : "He (he that takes on a body) goes into the tear-drop (the seed), which mingles itself with the product of menstruation (pushphaphala)," etc. See also K., i, 84.14, where pushphaphala is found instead of the pushparasa in B., 90.14. With asra cp. bindu "seed".

[2] Atisarvam. Perhaps api sarvam : and into all ? Or atisarvam together with dvipadaṃ, and this then = human being, that is : "excelling all ? "

[3] Builds itself up, develops (i, 90.13). Cp. Rām., vii, 81.10 : sarvaṃ samucchrayam, all that grows, all living beings.

[4] Makes use of his consciousness (saṃjñām adhishthāya).

[5] It is said also of the wind in the 18th strophe that it escorts as a guide the soul that has fled from one body to a new one.

[6] They are set forth earlier. Deussen : "qualities."

so it has been handed down to us. The one takes for his own, as something that cannot be perceived, the (basic) matter (prakṛiti) of these parts, and in like wise, as something that can be perceived, the other, who has a coarse underſtanding. To be perceived or not to be perceived, twofold or fourfold—they that have pondered on the world-soul see matter in all beings. The matter which (in itself) cannot be perceived has through its (incarnated) parts taken on perceptibility : I and thou, O king, and all other corporeal beings there are. With the pouring in of the drop (of the male seed) those conditions begin that arise out of the male seed and out of the (woman's) blood, and through their appearance the kalala [1] comes into being ; from the kalala develops the small bubble (budbuda) ; and from the small bubble the lump of flesh (peçī)—so tradition teaches us. But from the lump of flesh the limbs come forth, and nails and hair from the limbs. After the ninth month is fulfilled, O king of Mithilā, name and form (the individuality) comes into being of the child begotten, a little woman or man according to the marks of sex.[2] Although a man sees his (of one new-born) shape equipped with red nails and fingers direℭly after birth, yet he does not observe that in his own shape, when it has received the shape of childhood's years. And from childhood's years into the years of youth, and into advanced years from the years of youth—in these successive ſtages a man never perceives again what has gone before. A change in the conſtituents and the various things belonging to them [3] is happening each inſtant in all beings; but because of their fineness it is not perceived. Nor is their passing away noticed, and their coming into being in one ſtate after another, no more than in a light is noticed what happens with the flame.[4] Since this whole world, which has this for its charaℭter, is ever haſtening on like a good

[1] More or less = dot, jutting point ; probably from kal, to drive. Cp. Windisch, *Buddhas Geburt u. d. Lehre von der Seelenwanderung,* p. 86 at bottom ff.
[2] This is the obvious rendering. But compare note 4 on p. 366.
[3] As form, etc. Nil.
[4] It is really different at every moment from what it was at the moment before.

steed, whence then springs a man, and whence does he not spring ? To whom belongs anything definite, and to whom does it not belong ? Whence does it come, and whence not ? What connection have beings here on earth even with their own limbs ? As fire out of the sun, the precious stone, plants, so do beings arise out of the union of the (thirty named) components. Why, just as thou seest thine own self in thyself through thy self, dost thou not see thine own self in others through thy self ? " (xii, 320.111 ff.).[1] Through a blinding of perception do men fall into desire (kāma). From desire men come into anger,[2] then into greed and blindness, into self-confidence and pride, and into self-seeking, from self-seeking then into works, through works into bonds of love,[3] through love at once into suffering,[4] and thus giving occasion for birth and death [5] by undertaking works leading to pleasure and pain, they come to that dwelling in the womb which begins with the begetting, and is brought about by seed and blood, is moist with excrement and water, and fouled with the products of the blood. Overwhelmed by the thirst for life (trishnā), bound by these things, ever and again led off astray to them,[6] let man know that women are the continuers of the web of the Samsāra. They are the ploughed field of nature (of matter, prakrityāh kshetrabhūtās), men manifest themselves as the soul ; therefore let the man before all things leave them behind him, one and all. They are witches of a dreadful kind, they bewilder those without understanding, they are the ever-abiding, passion-bewoven embodiment of sensuality (indriyānām).[7] Therefore are the children born

[1] The line of verse left out by me in the translation I have always held to be a baseless insertion, and I now see that it is not found in K.—The " self " is in all beings the same, the eternal Ātman.

[2] Translated in accordance with K. (K., 215).

[3] Read snehasambandhān. Also -sambandhāh or -sambandham would be possible. K has -sambandhah.

[4] Or : into the suffering that is immediately bound up with it.

[5] To come to their help ; that is, they being subject to birth and death through the undertaking of the works.

[6] Literally : swimming about (= drifting) to them.

[7] That is, they live and weave in passion, and as they are glorified by sensuality, their hidden (antarhita) true nature is not recognized.

from passion, animated in them, as the source. Just as the vermin (such as lice, etc.) which has come into being from our own bodies, and yet is not deemed our own property [1] is put away from our bodies, so let the vermin also which is looked on as our own property, and yet is not property of ours,[1] and is called " children ", be put away from us. Through seed and (menstrual) fluid children are born from the body, of themselves (svabhāvāt), or through the working of the karman—let the wise man look beyond them. . . . Whatever instrument of the mind is put forth in the fruit of the womb by the karman, which forms the germ, this arises out of the impulse of the self [2] through the spiritual element accompanied by the urge of passion. From the urge of passion after sound the ear comes into being of him whose self is developing, from the urge of passion after shape the eye, the nose from the wish to perceive smell, the skin for touch (for the feeling brought about through touch, and its objects). In like wise the wind is in the Prāṇa and Apāna, it is Vyāna, Udāna, and Samāna, the fivefold function of the body.[3] Wrapped round with the limbs born with him, born out of the karman, as his body, man is born, with the limbs of body and soul, which have their beginning and end in pain, and in pain their middle course " (xii, 213.3 ff.).[4]

Indeed, antarhita probably = antarita, as this is used in ii, 68.46: dharmāntarita, hidden in virtue, gone into virtue, become the essence of virtue. Cp. Rām., v, 9.23. Instead of " witches " perhaps rather : " magic forces," embodied curses, etc. (kṛityā).

[1] Probably less likely : our own self. Sva = ātman (cp. J. J. Meyer, Dāmodaraguptas Kuṭṭanīmatam, p. 108, n.) is not seldom found in the Epic (e.g. i, 111.2, 12 ; ii, 49.51 ; iii, 150.48 ; 207.54 ; v, 43.60 ; Rām., vi, 34.6 even : sā pravishṭā tatas tatra dadarça Janakātmajāṃ pratīkshamāṇāṃ svām eva bhrashṭapadmām iva Çriyam).

[2] Ahaṃkāra.

[3] Literally : in fivefold wise keeping the body in action (dehayā-pana).

[4] Or, as Indians, so far as I know, do not speak of spiritual limbs, better after all would be : With the limbs born with him is man born, wrapped in the body, with conditions of body and mind which have their beginning, end, and middle course in pain.—As to birth we are

told : "After the fifth month the fœtus has all its limbs; through the strength of the wind it is driven to the mother-gate (yonidvāra) and born, with the legs up, the head down" (xi, 4.2 ff.). xii, 320.17, therefore, should probably, instead of "After the ninth month is fulfilled, name and form comes into being, etc.," which indeed sounds strange, be translated : "When the child after the ninth month is fulfilled has been born, then its individuality becomes known, whether it is a boy or a girl, according to the marks of sex." Jāyate therefore = comes to light (or perhaps is to be altogether changed to jñāyate); hardly: "it is born into individuality (or even: the phenomenal world)," although jāyate with such an accusative would not be un-Epic.

There are many correspondences with the teachings of the Epic just set forth to be found in the discourses on reincarnation, procreation, growth of the fœtus, and birth in the Garbha-Upanishad (transl. by Deussen, *Sechzig Upanischads des Veda*); Yājñavalkya's law book, iii, 67 ff.; and the Purāṇas. These also repeat the doctrine of the Upanishads : The child in the womb remembers its former existences, but through touching the wind of the outer world is at once deprived of its knowledge, after having been driven forth by the Prajāpati or birth wind, a doctrine which in its essentials corresponds to a Jewish one (see Wolfg. Schultze, *Dokumente d. Gnosis*, Jena, 1910, p. 4 ff.). See e.g. Wilson's Vishṇupur., vol. v, p. 203 f.; Agnipur., 369.19 ff.; Garuḍapur., Pretakalpa, xxxii; Mārk.-Pur., x, 1–6; xi (according to çl. 18 the new-born child at once loses its supernatural knowledge through Vishṇu's bewildering māyā or magic powers); Bhāgavatapur., iii, 31 (according to çl. 1 man [jantu] comes into the mother's womb, borne by the male seed, retahkaṇāçraya = Garuḍapurāṇasāroddh., vi, 5); Garuḍapurāṇasāroddh., vi, 5 ff.; Abegg, Pretakalpa, vi, 5 ff. (in p. 92, note 5, Abegg gives a number of references); xv, 15–18; Carakasaṃh., iv, 4; Windisch, *Buddhas Geburt*, etc., p. 12 ff. How wonderful and mysterious the origin of man was in the eyes of the Old Indians the Epic has already shown us. In the Mārkaṇḍeyapurāṇa, pregnancy is called something holy and meritorious (x, 10); and procreation is in the Vedic view an act of sacrifice, a worship of God (see e.g. Chānd.-Up., v, 8; Bṛih.-Up., vi, 4.3). How piously and solemnly, and how ceremoniously it must be entered upon, we are taught at the end of the Bṛihadaraṇyaka-Upanishad (vi, 4.13 ff.) with a pure and elevating, a noble and simple earnestness. And so it goes on, although not with such simplicity, down to the Mahānirvāṇatantra (ix, 94–116).

Very important, however, is now the question : How are boys begotten and how are girls ? The matter has already been touched on at the beginning of this book. Nīl. in discussing i, 90.14 repeats the Indian theory : If there is an over-measure of male seed, then it will be a boy, if an over-measure of menſtrual blood, a girl ; if the two are equal, an hermaphrodite; if the seed splits, twins. There would then be no deliberate determination of sex, about which popular belief elsewhere believes it knows so much. For the Mahābhārata itself takes its place with the many examples which are to be found in this matter in Indian literature since the days of the Brāhmaṇas, and assures us in xiii, 87.10, 11 that if the forefathers are worshipped with Çraddhas on the second day in the half of the month with waning moon, then there will be girls ; if they are worshipped on the fifth day, then many sons will be begotten (cp. Āpaſt., ii, 7, 16.8, 12 ; Vishṇu, lxxviii, 37, 40). xiii, 104.151 sounds more reasonable, and not unlike a view often found among ourselves : " Let the wise man go in the night to his wife, when she has bathed on the fourth day (after the ſtart of her period) ; on the fifth day it will be a girl, on the sixth a boy." However we may here have only the well-known Indian belief : On even nights it will be a son, odd nights a girl (Carakas., iv, 8.6 ; Garu-ḍapur., Pretakalpa, xxxii, 12 ; Abegg, Pretakalpa, xv, 10 ; Agnipur., 153.2 ; Manu, iii, 48 ; Bṛihatsaṃh., 78.23 ; etc.). Another view which is often held in later times would seem to show itself already in Yājña-valkya, i, 80 : The man muſt on an even night, etc., approach once his *emaciated* wife (kshāmā), then he will beget a son. But perhaps the reference is only to the waſting effeċt, anyhow presumed, of the woman's period. There is probably an inkling of the truth in Bṛihat-saṃh., 68.14–16 (almoſt wholly = Garuḍapur., 65.19b–22a) : the matter depends on the nature of the man's seed. In the marks, too, that show the sex of the child in the mother's womb India finds itself on the same ground as the Weſt. The beautiful, blooming complexion, that is to say, of the mother, is spoiled by a female fruit in the womb, probably from envy ; while the complexion keeps its freshness and beauty when a boy is on the way. This is too the teaching of the Old Indian physicians. The Hindus are in agreement also with the Greeks, Romans, Jews, older Germans, Slavs, etc., in naturally allotting the preferred side, the right, to the male sex. So we find in Divyāvadāna, pp. 2, 98 and in other places in this colleċtion of Buddhiſt legends : " Five particular charaċteriſtics has a wise woman : (1) she knows whether a man loves her, she knows whether he does not love her ; (2) she knows the time, she knows the period ; (3) she knows if she has conceived a child; (4) she knows by whom she has become with child ; (5) she knows whether it is a boy, she knows whether it is a girl —if it is a boy, then it ſtays curled up on the right side of the belly, if it is a girl, then on the left side. So too in the Avadānaçataka ; see Feer, *Ann. Musée Guimet*, vol. xvii, p. 5, and in Schiefner's *Indische*

What each one of the two parents contributes to the building
of the body we are told in xii, 305.5 f. "Bones, sinews,
and marrow we know as the parts that come from the father ;
skin, flesh, and blood—these come from the mother, so we are
told.[1] Thus, O best of the twice-born, is it laid down in
the Veda, and in the didactic books." But we have already
been told that the flesh arises out of the seed, and so we read
also in xiii, 116.13. But of course there the formation of
the fruit of the womb is not under discussion.[2] Also the sons
take after the father, the daughters after the mother, this being
according to a popular proverb (pravādo laukikaḥ in Rām., ii,
35.28). Opposed to this there is another world saying
(lokapravāda), given in Rām., iii, 16.34 and there endorsed
on the whole, that human beings in their character do not

Erzählungen, No. xlvi ; *Bull. de l'Acad. Imp. des Sciences de St.
Pétersbourg*, vol. xxiv, col. 483 ff. In the last-named is told the well-
known test of skill for the young physician Jīvaka, taken from the journey
of the sons of King Serendip. However, the matter seems exactly
the opposite in Chavannes, *Actes du XIV. Congr. intern. des oriental.,
Cinqu. sect.*, p. 136 ff. (here the foot-marks on the left are deeper, and
therefore a male offspring is inferred). But cp. Chavannes, *Cinq cents
contes*, i, 379–381. See also Agnipur., 369.21b–22a, and especially
Windisch, *Buddhas Geburt*, p. 19. All kinds of cabbalistic means
for finding out a child's sex in the mother's womb are given e.g. in
Agnipur., cxli, 3–5.
[1] According to Agnipur., 369.31–32 ; 370.19b–20a, from the
mother comes heart, skin, flesh, colour, navel, mucus, fat, belly,
pancreas, and the black of the eye ; but from the father : veins, arteries,
nerves, seed, etc., as also the white of the eye. Carakas., iv, 3, 5.1,
is partly different. See espec. Jolly, *Medizin*, p. 55 middle, and cp.
here, as for the whole chapter, R. Schmidt, *Liebe u. Ehe in Indien*,
489 ff.
[2] On the other hand Cirakāri, xii, 266.25, 26 says tersely : " Man
has from the mother the conglomerate in mortality, made up of the
five elements," that is, at least in first place, the body ; from the father,
therefore, presumably the " soul ". This was the belief also of the
Naudowessies (Westermarck, 105–106 ; Mantegazza, *Geschlechtsverhältnisse*, 231). But Cirakāri shortly before this (çl. 18)
declares that to the father is due " the body and the rest " (çarīrādīni).
Possibly, however, body here is to be taken = life.

take at all after the father, but only after the mother. However, neither the one nor the other of these popular beliefs agrees with the teaching of the Mahābhārata ; for since the soul and the karman are bound up with the seed, and thus are contributed by the man, therefore as a necessary consequence the father, and none other, muſt be responsible for the charaćter of the children, which view as is well known, is Schopenhauer's.[1] The view, of course, is often found also that for a man's nature the father and mother muſt both be taken into account. See e.g. xii, 296.3 f. ; Agnipur., 151.18b ; Meyer, *Altind. Rechtsschr.*, pp. 263–65.

Procreation outside wedlock has, according to Bhīshma's reproachful words about Karṇa (vi, 122.11 f.), an unfavourable effećt on the charaćter.[2] Fivefold is the way whereby the gods can beget : through the simple wish, through the word, the look, the wholly outward touch (sparça), and " rubbing " (saṃgharsha, coitus, xv, 30.22).[3]

The sojourn in the mother's womb is looked on too as something nauseating and gruesome in the Epic, as has already been mentioned, and as such it is even made use of figuratively (ix, 56.32, as often in Indian literature elsewhere). The womb thus is even called in MBh., K, xii, 215.7 narakagarta

---

[1] The ſtress lies on karman. For what we call soul, that is, perception, conception, thought, will, etc., belongs on the Indian theory, especially that of Sānkhya—and the Epic is dominated by this— to the domain of matter, that is of the woman. The Jīva or Purusha ("soul" in the Indian meaning), which corresponds to the man's nature, has really no connećtion whatever with anything of this.

[2] On the other hand this opinion uttered in a personal reprimand has little value. Karṇa, indeed, and other "love children" in the MBh. itself refute it.

[3] Cp. Jacobi's Tattvārthādhigama, iv, 9 (ZDMG, Bd. 60) ; Glasenapp, *Der Jainismus*, p. 241 ; Henne am Rhyn, *Die Frau. i. d. Kulturgesch.*, p. 50. In the beginning beings propagated themselves wholly by look, touch, tapas, simple will, etc. Coition did not appear till later. Wilson's Vishṇupurāṇa, ed. Hall, vol. ii, p. 10 ; Mārk.-Pur., xlix, 8 ff. ; Saurapurāṇa, xxv, 20–28 (Jahn, p. 69). Cp. Hartland, *Primit. Patern.*, i, 18 ff.

[For such a ſtage earlier than coition cp. perhaps from Melanesia, G. C. Wheeler, *Mono-Alu Folklore*, pp. 42–3, 242 ff. (Translator.)]

(hell's pit). In the Epic, too, it lasts generally ten months (iii, 134.17 ; 205.10, etc.). But we repeatedly meet with far longer pregnancies in the Mahābhārata.[1] It is for three years that Çakuntalā bears Bharata in the womb, and that which took a long time, even here turns out well (i, 74.1–2). Gāndhārī has been now with child for two years, her womb is hard, and she learns with sorrow that Kuntī has given birth ; then with great torment she sets to thumping (ghātayāmāsa) her belly, and brings forth a lump of flesh as hard as a ball of iron. At Vyāsa's order she pours cold water over it, whereupon it falls into one hundred and one pieces, which she puts in a vessel with melted butter ; a hundred sons and one daughter thus come into being (i, 115.1 ff.). The same thing happens, too, to the wife of King Kalmāshapāda : she frees herself after twelve years from the fruit of her womb, which the Brahman Vasishtha has begotten in her, by opening her own body with a stone ; hence her son is called Açmaka (" Stoneling ", i, 177.44 ff.). Vasishtha's daughter-in-law Adriçyantī in the same way for twelve years shelters under her heart Parāçara, who was later to be the holy man. He spends his time, during this very thorough preparation for coming into life, in studying the Vedas aloud (i, 177.11 ff. ; 43 ff.). Lopamudrā, Agastya's wife, carries for seven years, and then bears her son, but a wonder-child likewise (iii, 99.24 ff.). A hundred years even does a Bhrigu woman carry Aurva, and that in her thigh. Then the child is to be slain by the hostile Kshattriyas, and comes out of the thigh with such sunlike brightness that the evil-doers all lose their sight (i, 178. 11 ff.). This cunctator, too, knows the whole Veda before his birth. On the other hand, the Rākshasa women bring forth at once after conception, as Satyavatī does Vyāsa, and as, according to Jean Paul, the Talmud teaches as to Jewish women in heaven (i, 155.36). This is a special grace which Umā or Kālī has bestowed on the Rākshasī (Rām., vii, 4.30, 31).

---

[1] See Hopkins, JAOS, 24, p. 19 ; 392 ; Wilson's Vishnupur., iii, p. 290 (7 years) ; iv, 87 ; Mārk.-Pur., cxxxiii, 2 f. (9 years) ; Vishnupur., vol. iv, p. 87 (15 years) ; Chavannes, *Cinq cents contes*, i, 200 ; iii, 136 ; etc.

Pregnancy at a very tender age is one of the signs of the on-coming end of the world (iii, 188.60 ; 190.49). Juſt as dreadful is the killing of the fruit of the womb. This crime, which is so often moſt ſtrongly condemned by the Indians, and which is heavily punished in the law books, can according to the Mahābhārata only thus be atoned for : " The fœtus-slayer is cleansed of his sin if in the midſt of battle the weapon lights on him (and kills him), or by his sacrificing himself in a kindled fire ; thereby is he cleansed of his sin " (xii, 165. 46, 47).[1]

That the man should need a very long time to bring a child into the world, when he becomes pregnant, seems easy to underſtand.[2] There once lived a king, mighty in sacrifices, of the line of Ikshvāku, Yuvanāçva his name. " As this very glorious and pious one had no offspring, he handed over the kingdom to his miniſters, and gave himself up to life in the foreſt, plunging his soul, he that had his soul under his control, in reflec\tion in the way laid down by the books of inſtruc\tion. One day, the prince, tormented with faſting,

---

[1] The slaying or making away with the fruit of the womb is one of the sins that cannot be atoned for on earth (Dubois-Beauchamp [3], 197) ; it is equal to the murder of a Brahman and to be atoned for in the same way (Āpaſt., i, 9, 24.4 ; Vasishṭha, xx, 23 f. ; Gautama, xxii, 12–13 (here when it is the embryo of a Brahman) ; Vishṇu, xxxvi, 1 ; l, 1–99 ; nay, it is twice as wicked and allows of no atone-ment, but the woman muſt be caſt out (Parāçara, iv, 18), or driven out of the city (Nārāda, xii, 91 f.). Along with the murder of a husband and connexion with a man of low birth it is one of the three greateſt crimes in a woman (Yājñav., iii, 298) ; ſtands in the same line with the moſt dreadful sins, and leads to loss of caſte (Āpaſt., i, 7, 21.8 ; Vasishṭha, xxviii, 7 ; Gautama, xxi, 9) ; is the type of moſt dreadful sin (Mahānirvāṇat., iii, 153) ; and so on. Naturally awful punish-ments are, especially in the Purāṇas, threatened after death. This very zeal shows, however, that this sin was not an uncommon one in Old India, either. But whether it is so very common among the Hindus and particularly on the part of the widow, as some observers declare, is a matter of very great doubt.

[2] For the reason, too, that he is generally used to do things more thoroughly and better ; for the long pregnancies that are found in other cases lead to human beings beyond the ordinary.

parched within by thirst, came into the hermitage of Bhṛigu. On this very night the high-souled, great Ṛishi was carrying out a sacrifice for Yuvanāçva, that he might get a son. A great jar, filled with water purified with holy words, stood there; it had been made ready before, that the wife of Yuvanāçva might drink it, and bear an Indra-like son. The jar had been set down on the sacrificial altar by the great Ṛishis, and now they were sleeping. Yuvanāçva went by these men wearied by the night watch; with dry throat, tortured by thirst, filled with a great yearning for water, he that was filled with peace of soul made his way into the hermitage, and asked for water. As the wearied one with parched throat now moaned tearfully, no one heard him, just as though it were the cry of a bird. So soon as the prince saw the jar filled with water, he ran impetuously up to it, drank it dry, and set it down again. When the thirst-tormented ruler of the earth had drunk the cold water, the wise one felt the bliss of the quenched glow (nirvāṇam agamat), and was very happy. Then those Munis and the penitents awoke, and they all saw that the jar of water was emptied. 'Whose deed is that?' those asked who came up. Yuvanācva acknowledged the truth, and said : 'Mine.' 'That is not well,' then said the holy son of Bhṛigu to him ; 'that thou mayest get a son, I have set the water there, and made it fitting through my asceticism. I have put into it the holy power,[1] having given myself up to dreadful penance, that thou mayest obtain a son, O kingly Ṛishi of great might and bravery. (It was to be) a son of great strength, of great heroic valour, and ascetic power, who with his heroic courage would bring even Indra into Yama's abode. Through this holy action I have brought this about. In that thou hast now drunk the water thou hast not done well, O king. But now we cannot make this otherwise than it is. It is undoubtedly a disposition of Providence that thou hast thus acted. Through this water that thou didst drink in thy thirst, which I had marked off by ceremony and prayer, and made ready through the power of my penance, thou thyself wilt bear such a son. I will then carry out for thee a most wonderful

---

[1] That is, the Brahmanic power. Hardly : the holy Veda word (brahman). Cp. xiii, 4.38, 60 f.

sacrifice, that thou with hero's strength, thou mayest bring forth an Indra-like son, and also need suffer none of the ills arising from the carrying of the womb's fruit.' Then at the end of a hundred years the son there, who was like a sun, split the left thigh of the high-souled king, and came forth, he the most powerful ; and King Yuvanāçva was not taken by death ; that was very wonderful."—Wonderful, too, was the child, Māndhātar, of whom not only the Brahmans but the Buddhists also have told many tales (iii, 126).[1] According to vii, 62, indeed, the two Açvins have to do service here as midwives ; they pull Māndhātar out of his father's womb (garbha). Here the king while hunting came thirsty to a sacrificial offering, and drank the sacrificial butter. In xii, 29.81 ff., too, Māndhātar comes into being in his father's belly, and in this passage, indeed, also through sacrificial butter being consumed. Here the wind gods took the child from his father's side.[2] Also the pious king Cibi Auçīnara bears a son from out of his side (iii, 197.26 ff.).

A *generatio aequivoca* is likewise related in the old Purūravas saga. The Mahābhārata gives the following account : All the sons of Manu perished through strife. "Then was Purūravas born of Ilā ; she was both his mother and his father ; so we have been told " (i, 75.18, 19). On the other hand, according to Rām., vii, 87 ff., he is the son of Ilā and Budha in the ordinary way. Ila, the very mighty king of the Bāhlīka was roving on the hunt through the forest in the heart-delighting spring-time. At this same time Çiva together with his wife was taking his delight on the mountain where Kārttikeya had been born, and for her he changed himself into a woman ; all the other male beings, too, which were

[1] In what follows there his greatness is shortly described, and more fully in other parts of the MBh. A poetic rendering of the Jātaka tale about him is to be found in my *Kāvyasaṃgraha, metrisch. Übersetzungen aus indischen u. anderen Sprachen*, p. 35 ff. Cp. Schiefner, *Bullet. d. Petersburger Akad.*, vol. 24, col. 458 ff.

[2] In Vishṇupur. (Wilson), iii, p. 267, Māndhātar splits his father's right side, so in Bhāgavatapur., ix, 6, 30, the right side of the belly, and so comes out. With his birth out of the thigh, cp. *Zschr. d. Ver. f. Volksk.*, Bd. 4, p. 48 ff. ; 157 ff.

already there, even the trees, and all that came thither had to take on woman's sex. As soon as Ila reached there, this divine spell worked itself on him also and his following. He was deeply troubled at this, and made his appeal to Çiva, who laughed him to scorn. The god's wife, however, showed herself more compassionate : through her grace Ila was allowed always to be a woman for a month, and for a month a man, and in neither state did he remember the other. Ilā, so the new woman was called, now roved through that forest, free and merry, with her following, which was likewise feminine, and she came once to a glorious lake. In it Budha, the moon's son, was giving himself up to asceticism, but through the sight of the bewitchingly lovely wanderer of the wild he was so fired by love that he could no longer restrain himself ; he turned her attendants into Kimpurushī, and told them that as these they would find husbands ; while to Ilā, who thus saw herself robbed in the lonely forest of her following, he offered himself as a loving husband, and with this she was glad. With her he spent the whole of the spring moon in such delights that it flew by him like a moment. But when the month was at an end, Ilā awoke in the morning as a man again, and called to the son of Soma : " I came into these mountain wilds with a great following. Where are my attendants, then ? " " A rain of stones has killed them." " Then I who have lost my wives and people will no longer be king, either, but hand over the rule to my son." But Budha prevailed on him to stay there for a year ; then he promised to do his best. To this the herdsmen of the earth agreed. " For a month he was now a woman, and gave himself up to his pleasure without a break ; for a month he gave himself up as a man to pious ways and thoughts." In the ninth month as Ilā he then bore Purūravas. By a horse-sacrifice Çiva was then put in a gracious frame of mind by Ila's kindred, and gave him back his manhood.[1]

[1] Cp. Hertel, " Die Geburt des Purūravas," *Wiener Zeitschr. f. d. Kunde d. Morgenl.*, xxv (1911), p. 135 ff. According to Vetālapañcav., No. 15 (quoted Daçakumāracar., p. 85) it was Gaurī's curse that changed King Ila into a woman ; according to Mārkaṇḍeyapur., cxi, 12, Maheçvara's anger ; the Bhāgavatapur. (ix, 1.23 ff.) makes the

A like change of sex is related in Mahābhārata, xiii, 12 (K., 34). "Yudhishṭhira spoke : 'Which of the two has the more glorious feeling from the touch, when a woman and man unite ? As to this doubt, do thou, O king, give me right inſtruction.' Bhīshma spoke : 'Of this too, this old tale is told, how, once before, Indra bore an enmity againſt Bhaṅgāsvana. Once upon a time there was an exceedingly pious Ṛishi king called Bhaṅgāsvana ; as he had no sons, O tiger among men, that he might get a son he made the Agnishṭut sacrifice so hateful to Indra, he, the moſt mighty Ṛishi king. This is prescribed for atonements, and if a man wants a son for himself. But when Indra, the moſt excellent ruler of the gods, learned of this sacrifice, he sought an opportunity to lay hold of this royal Ṛishi, who ever kept himself in check. And he could see no weak spot in this high-minded one, O king. Some time after, the herdsman of men went out hunting. 'This is a chance,' thought Indra, and he perplexed the king : then the royal Ṛishi did nothing but wander about with his one horse, and, tormented by hunger and thirſt, the prince could not find his way in the quarters of the heavens. And as he was galloping this way and that,[1] he saw a gloriously shining lake full of splendid water. He rode to the lake,[2] my friend, and watered his ſteed. When his horse had drunk,

change come about as in the MBh., but tells of another cause why Çiva laid this spell : Once he was visited by pious Ṛishis, who found his wife naked in his arms. She was very much ashamed, and therefore the god thus spoke for her sake : " Whoso comes into the foreſt shall become a woman." In the two sections of the Purāṇa Manu through a miſtake of the sacrificing prieſt gets a daughter, Ilā, inſtead of a son ; through special favour she becomes a man, named Sudyumna, and he then becomes a woman through the power of the god, etc. Cp. Harivaṃça, x, 615 ff. ; Crooke, Pop. Rel., ii, 7.

[For Melanesian ideas on changing of sex cp. G. C. Wheeler, Mono-Alu Folkl., pp. 19, 20, 21, 62, 276.]

[1] So according to K., where we find itaç cetaç ca dhāvan vai. In the Bomb. text we can join itaç cetaç ca either with bhrānta, whicḥ would be very ſtiff, or take it as a lively sentence without a verbal form.

[2] Or : " he rode into the lake " (lit. dipped). I would read avagatya inſtead of avagāhya, and have translated accordingly in the text.

the moſt excellent herdsman of men tied it to a tree, and plunged
in. But as soon as he had bathed there, be became a woman.
When he now saw himself turned into a woman, the beſt
of princes was ashamed ; his whole soul was filled with
mournful sorrow, and his mind and heart were troubled. ' But
how can I mount my horse ? how go into the city ? And through
the Agnishṭut sacrifice which I made a hundred ſtout sons of
my body have been born to me. But what shall I say to them ?
And what shall I say among my wives, and the townsmen
and the country-folk ? Tenderness and weakness and a
faint heart withal are the marks of women, as the Ṛishis
have declared, who know virtue, truth, and profit. Manly
ſtrength put forth, ſternness, and bravery are the marks of
a man.[1] My manhood is gone, through some way or other
I have become a woman. And since I am a woman, how
can I mount my horse again ? ' With great trouble, however,
the firſt herdsman of men now mounted his ſteed,[2] and went
back into the city, turned into a woman, he the beſt of
princes. But his sons, wives, servants, townsmen, and country-

---

[1] So according to K. The Bomb. Text has : In bodily exercises
(or : in battle) ſtaunchness (ſternness, hardness) and a hero's courage—
these are the marks of the man.

[2] Reputable women according to this passage do not ride in Old
India ; for whatever goes with the army, riding on horse or ass (Çiçupālav., xii, 20 ; v, 7) is, anyhow in moſt cases, light goods. But probably
the widow who is going to let herself be burnt with her dead husband
often rides there on horseback. See Zachariae, *Zeitschr. d. Ver. f.
Volksk.*, Bd. 14, p. 208, note 2 ; 209 ; 302 ; 305. She has come away
from the ordinary laws. Or was the horse so often chosen by her as
being a beaſt that frightens away the spirits, brings luck, and is
prophetic ? Cp. Negelein, " Das Pferd in Seelenglauben u. Seelen-
kult," *Zschr. d. Ver. f. Volksk.*, Bd. 11, p. 406 ff. ; Bd. 12, p. 14 ff. ;
377 ff. ; especially Bd. 11, p. 406 f. ; 409 ff. ; Bd. 12, p. 384 ;
MBh., iv, 39.6 ; 46.25 ; K., 46.8 ; etc. ; Tod, *Rajaſthan*, i, 592
(the Rājputs to-day ſtill see an omen in the horse's neighing); Schroeder,
Myſterium u. Mimus im Rigveda, 429 ff. ; George Wilke, *Kultur-
beziehungen*, etc. (Würzburg., 1913), p. 122 ; Fr. S. Krauss, *Slav.
Volkforsch.*, 130. As widow-burning probably originated with the
Kshattriyas, it may be indeed that therefore this warrior-animal
kept true to the Satī.

men fell to the greateſt wondering, when they learned of it, and spoke : ' What is this, indeed ? ' Then said the royal Rishi, beſt of all speakers, that had become a woman : ' I rode out to hunt, surrounded by ſtout soldiers. Losing my way, I found myself, driven on by fate, in a dreadful foreſt. And in this moſt dreadful foreſt, racked by thirſt, and bereft of my senses, I saw a moſt fair shining pond, covered with fowl. When I plunged into it, I was by the hand of Providence turned a little while ago into a woman.' And giving the names and families of his wives and miniſters,[1] then did this beſt of princes speak to his sons : ' Do ye enjoy in gladness and friendship the kingly rule ; I am going away into the foreſt, my little sons.' When he had thus spoken to his hundred sons, he did indeed go off into the foreſt. And after this woman had gone into a hermitary, she found a penitent. From the penitent she had a hundred sons in the hermitary. Then she took them all with her, and spoke to her earlier sons : ' Ye are my sons from the time when I was a man, and these are my hundred sons which I have got as a woman. Enjoy ye, at one in brotherly hearts, the kingly rule, my dear sons.' Then did these brothers enjoy together the kingly rule. When the king of the gods saw them now ruling over the moſt excellent kingdom with brotherly hearts, he thought to himself, overborne by anger : ' I have done the king a good deed, not an evil.' Then went the ruler of the gods, Çatakratu, in the shape of a Brahman, to the city, and ſtirred up these sons of the herdsman of men : ' Among brothers there is no good brotherly underſtanding, even when they are sons of one father. For the sake of the kingly rule the offspring of Kaçyapa, the gods and the demons, fell to ſtrife. Ye are the offspring of Bhaṅgāsvana, the others are the sons of a penitent. But the gods and the demons are alike Kaçyapa's sons. Your father's kingdom is being ruled by the penitent's sors.' Stirred up by Indra, they slew one another in the fight. When the penitent's wife heard of it, she broke into tears, ſtabbed through by sorrow. Indra, disguised as a Brahman, now came to her, and asked her : ' What is the sorrow tormenting thee, that thou weepeſt, O lovely one ? ' Then

[1] This was, of course, to show he was King Bhaṅgāsvana.

the woman looked at the Brahman, and said with mournful voice : ' Two hundred sons of mine have been stricken to earth by destiny. I was a king, O Brahman ; a hundred sons were born to me before, shaped like me,[1] O best of Brahmans. One day I went hunting, and lost my way in a deep forest. And when I dipped in a lake, I became a woman, O most excellent Brahman. Then I set my hundred sons in the kingly rule, and went into the forest. As a woman, I bore a great-souled penitent in the hermitary a hundred sons, O Brahman, and these I took into the city. An enmity has by the dispensation of the gods arisen among them, O twice-born one. It is for this I mourn, O Brahman, overwhelmed by the waves of destiny.' When Indra saw her sorrowing, he spoke these harsh words to her : ' In days gone by, my friend, thou didst do me evil truly hard to bear, offering the sacrifice hateful to Indra, without inviting me, who hold the first place. I am Indra, thou fool, I have cast my hatred on thee.' But when the royal Rishi saw it was Indra, he bowed his head to Indra's feet : ' Be gracious, best of the thirty-three. I made that sacrifice in my yearning after sons, O tiger among the gods ; do thou forgive me this.' Rejoiced by his humble expression of reverence Indra granted him a favour : ' Which of thy sons, O king, are to live—tell me this— those thou didst bear as a woman, or those that came to thee as a man ? ' Then spoke the penitent's wife to Indra, folding her hands before her forehead : ' The sons I bore as a woman are to live, O Vāsava.' But Indra heard this with astonishment, and once more asked the woman : ' How comes it, then, that the sons begotten by thee as a man are hateful to thee ? Wherefore harbourest thou the greater love for those thou didst bear as a woman ? I would fain hear the reason. Tell it to me here.' The woman spoke : ' The woman cherishes a more tender love, not so, indeed, the man. Therefore, O Çakra, let those live that were born to me when I was changed into a woman.' " Bhīshma spoke : " Thus addressed, Indra then joyfully uttered the words : ' They shall all live, all of them, thou speaker of truth. And choose thyself a favour,

[1] Or according to K. (surūpāṇām instead of svarūpāṇām) : " well-shaped." This is smoother, but perhaps not so old.

O prince above kings, which thou, O pious one, doſt wish :
thou mayeſt be either a man or a woman, whichever thou wouldſt
have of me.' The woman spoke : ' I choose to be a woman,
O Çakra : I have no wish to be a man, O Vāsava.' But, thus
addressed, the ruler of the gods made answer to the woman :
' Wherefore doſt thou scorn to be a man, and insiſt on being
a woman, O ruler ? ' To these words made answer the beſt
among kings, that had become a woman : ' The woman has
in the union with the man always the greater joy. That is
why, O Çakra, I choose to be a woman. I feel greater pleasure
in love as a woman, that is the truth, beſt among the gods.[1]
I am content with exiſtence as a woman. Do thou leave me,
firſt herdsman of the heavenly ones.' ' So be it ! ' he spoke,
took leave of her, and went back into heaven. So it is said
that the woman feels the greater love and pleasure." [2]

[1] According to K. (ramāmi). But the Bomb. reading has the same
meaning.
[2] Cp. Winternitz and Caland in the 17th vol. of the *Wiener
Zeitschr. f. d. Kunde d. Morgenl.*; Hertel, *Ind. Märchen*, p. 48 ff.;
371 ; and on change of sex note 200 (p. 282 f.) in my book *Isoldes
Gottesurteil.* The view that the woman has greater passion in love and
a ſtronger pleasure in the aĉt of union is not confined to India. There
a proverb often heard says that the power of eating in the woman is
twice as great as the man's, her cunning (or : her bashfulness) four
times as great, her decision (or : boldness) six times as great, and her
impetuosity in love (her delight in love's pleasures) eight times as
great. Garuḍapur., 109.33 ; Schmidt, *Indische Erotik* [1], p. 132 ;
Böhtlingk, *Indische Sprüche*, 412 ; Kressler, *Stimmen ind. Lebensklugheit*, p. 153 ; Benfey, *Pantschatantra*, i, 49. So too the Chinese
hold woman to be more passionate. Guſtave Schlegel, " La femme
chinoise," *X. Congrès intern. des orient.*, Seĉt. v, p. 117. And the
Arabs say : Les femmes ont en effet les passions plus violentes que les
hommes, parce qu'elles ont l'intelligence plus faible. Basset, " Contes
et légendes arabes," *Rev. des tradit. popul.*, xiv, p. 486, cp. 118.
Much more of this kind could be quoted. Konrad von Würzburg is
of another opinion, who sings that the man's love-pangs are twice as
cruel as the woman's (*Engelhard*, ed. by Haupt, 1932 ff.). But medieval
literature does not support him, not even the German. For there too
the fair one herself is usually the leader in love, driven on by a violent
ſtrength of impulse, when as a rule she is wanting in all shame or
bashfulness, and almoſt always in any reserve. Her hot passion and

THE ORIGIN OF MAN

The moſt celebrated case of change of sex is that of
Çikhaṇḍin, and the Mahābh. often returns to the subjeft of
this transformation. The fulleſt account is found in v, 173 ff.,
and the tale throws much light on woman in the Epic. As
has been already mentioned, Bhīshma went to Kāçi, carried off
the three daughters of the king there, who were juſt holding
their Svayaṃvara (self-choice), and brought them to Hāſtinapura
to marry them to his half-brother. He tells us of this himself
in our passage, and thus goes on (v, 174.4 ff.) : " When now
with Satyavatī's consent the wedding had drawn nigh, the eldeſt
daughter of the king of Kāçi spoke these words shamefacedly :
' Bhīshma, thou knoweſt the law, thou art well versed in all
the books of inſtruſtion. And when thou haſt heard my law-
abiding words, do thou aft accordingly. I have already chosen
the king of the Çālvas in my heart as my bridegroom, and I
have already been chosen by him in secret, without my father

sensuality is often quite repulsive. An inſtruftive compilation is
given us by Th. Krabbes (Marburg, 1884) on the bearing of the
" *Frau im altfranzösischen Karls-Epos* ". It is very well put
in the Busant (Hagen's *Gesamtabenteuer*, i, p. 34) : " She offered
her mouth, he gave the kiss "—the woman woos, as among the French,
the man grants, is " drawn on by the eternal woman ". It is probably
indeed more or less the same elsewhere, too, in the world : " Thou
thinkeſt to push, and thou art pushed." But with this long array of
medieval ladies it goes much too far, who of course are all highly praised
for their chaſtity and purity. It was truly no easy thing in the Middle
Ages to be a famous hero. If such a one came to a ſtrange caſtle and
was lying tired out at laſt in bed, thinking like Wallenſtein to have a
good sleep, then suddenly there appeared the daughter of the lord
of the caſtle or of the prince, or the lady of the caſtle herself, and
sank aflame with passion into the arms of the warrior, quite unknown
to her till now. A very long liſt of such maidens and married
women extraordinarily forward in things of love is given by Schultz,
Das höfische Leben, i, 595–8, and it is not at all complete. How
skilled in the attack, nay shameless, women in love among various
peoples, especially the more or less uncultured—as to this there
are intereſting accounts to be found, for inſtance, in Finck, *Primitive
Love*, 109 ff. ; 380 f. ; 476 f. Among the old Greeks also the woman
is seen to be far more greedy of love, and far less reserved than the man.
Rohde, *Der griech. Roman* [1], espec. 34 ; 35 ; Finck, 114 ff.

knowing of it. How couldst thou, then, go beyond thy kingly duty, and make me, O Bhīshma, who love another, dwell in the house here, especially as thou art a Kaurava ? When thou hast decided this thing in thy heart by means of thy mind, then do thou take those steps here which seem to thee fitting. The king of the Çālvas assuredly awaits me. Therefore, O best of the Kurus, give me leave to go. Show pity on me, strong-armed one, best of the upholders of the law. For on earth thou art held to be the soul of truth, so we have been told.' Then I won the leave of Kālī Gandhavatī (Satyavatī), and that of the ministers and the high priests, and that of the house priests, and released Ambā, the eldest maiden. When the girl had received permission, she went to the city of the king of the Çālvas in the care of old Brahmans, and accompanied by her nurse.[1] When she had made the journey, she reached the prince.[2] When she had come to the king of the Çālvas, she spoke unto him the words : ' I have come for thy sake, O long-armed great-souled one.' To her spoke the lord of the Çālvas, smiling somewhat : ' I desire thee not as wife, that hast first belonged to another, O thou of the lovely face. Go, my good friend, back again to thy sweetheart Bhīshma. I will not have thee after Bhīshma has taken thee by force. For thou wast carried off by Bhīshma, and taken by him as a woman rejoicing in her love, after he had taken hold of thee, and overcome the kings in a great battle. I have no yearning to have a wife in thee, that hast already belonged to another, O lovely-faced one. How could a king such as I bring home a woman that has had to do with a stranger, for I have the knowledge and teach the law to others ? Go just as thou wishest, my friend ; let not this time go by thee unused.' Ambā spoke to him, tormented by the arrows of love : ' Speak not thus to me, O herdsman of the earth. It is in no wise so. I was not carried off by Bhīshma, rejoicing in my love, O harasser of thy foes. By force was I carried away by him, as I wept, and he put the princes to

---

[1] Whom we must thus think of as having been carried off with her. Quite possible, however ; for the nurse bears her charge company at the Svayaṃvara, too, as is here and there mentioned. So xii, 4.10.

[2] K. has the smoother reading : āsasāda narādhipam.

flight. Love me, O lord of the Çālvàs, who love thee, and am young and innocent. For to repel those that love one is a thing not praised in the laws. I made prayer to Gaṅgā's son, to him that never turned his back in the fight, and with his leave I came hither at all speed. Bhīshma, the strong-armed, wants me not ; it was for his brother's sake that Bhīshma's deed was done, so I have been told. My two sisters, Ambikā and Ambālikā, whom Gaṅgā's son carried off, he handed over to his younger brother Vicitravīrya. I touch my head, O lord of the Çālvas, as I swear that but for thee, thou man-tiger, I have never thought, nor think, of another bridegroom. And it is not as one that has already had to do with another man that I have come to thee ; I am speaking the truth, and as I swear this oath I touch my own body.[1] Take me in love, O great-eyed one, me that came herself to thee as a maid, that have never belonged to another, and that yearn for thy tenderness.' But Çālva gave no more heed to the daughter of the lord of Kāçi, who thus spoke, than does a snake to its sloughed skin. Although the prince was besought by her in this wise with many words, yet did he not believe in the maiden. Then spoke the eldest daughter of the king of Kāçi, filled with anger, her eyes weeping, her voice choked with tears : ' Repulsed by thee, I go into the wide world. There may the good be my refuge, as truly as truth stands firm.' But while the maiden thus spoke, and bitterly wailed, the lord of the Çālvas was making renunciation of her. ' Go, go,' the Çālva kept on saying to her ; ' I fear Bhīshma, O thou with the lovely hips, and thou art Bhīshma's own.' Thus addressed by the Çālva, him the short-sighted one, the mournful one walked out of the city, wailing like a sea-eagle. But as she walked out of the city, she was thinking to herself in her dreadful sorrow : ' There is no young girl on earth who could be worse off than I am. I am bereft of my kindred, and I have been repulsed by the Çālva ; and I cannot go out again to Hāstinapura, after Bhīshma for the

---

[1] This is the most usual formula for an oath in the Epic. The warrior, of course, often swears by his weapons, as elsewhere (e.g. Manu, viii, 113 ; Nārada, i, 199 ; Tod, *Rājasthan*, i, 80 ; 625). See Meyer, *Altind. Rechtsschr.*, p. 222.

Çālva's sake has let me go away. Whom shall I now upbraid : myself or Bhīshma, whom it is hard to get near ? Or my blinded father, who held my Svayaṃvara ? I have brought this evil on myself, since I did not throw myself then from Bhīshma's chariot while the dreadful fight for Çālva was going on ; this is the result which now shows itself—that I have come to the wretched plight of some blind woman. Shame on Bhīshma ! Shame on my foolish father with his blinded mind, who has put me on offer like a public harlot for the purchase price of heroic strength ! [1] Shame on myself ! Shame on the king of the Çālvas ! Shame, too, on the Maker ! For through their evil conduct [2] I have fallen into the very depths of disaster. Come what may, man gets his allotted fate. But the beginning of this misfortune of mine is Bhīshma, son of Çāntanu. I look on it as right and fitting to make Bhīshma pay for it, whether my instrument be asceticism or the fight ; for I hold him to be the cause of my suffering.' "
She went off into a penitential forest and overwhelmed with sorrow she complained of her grief to the dwellers there. But they said they could be of no help, and she asked to be made a nun that she might undertake a heavy penance. For she said she could not go back to her kith and kin. The ascetics now held a council. Some said : She must go back again to her father ; others blamed Bhīshma ; others again held that the Çālva king must be brought to take her. This was opposed by others, since he had rebuffed her. In the end they made known to her that she must go to her father : " The father or the husband is the woman's refuge : the husband when all is well with her, the father when it goes ill with her. The penitent's life is hard, especially for a delicate daughter of a prince ; and if the kings see thee here alone in the deserted forest, then they will harass thee." But she insisted that she could not go home, that

---

[1] Cp. Hera's words at her " self-choice " in Spitteler's *Olympischer Frühling* (1910), Bd. i, p. 34.

[2] Liter. : their unmannerliness (durnītabhāva). In India the Creator is quite used to all kinds of abuse on his evil ways. The " old sinner " has to put up with very much too e.g. in the proverbs of the Christian and reverential South Slavs. Krauss, *Sitte u. Brauch*, etc., p. 613.

she would be scorned there ; she wished, she said, to lead an ascetic life, so that so evil a fate should not be thruſt on her again in another life.[1] Then her mother's father happened to come thither, the royal Ṛishi, Hotravāhana. When he had heard her tale, and learned who she was he spoke trembling and sorrowful to the tortured maiden : " Go not to thy father's house. I am thy mother's father. I will turn away thy unhappiness. Stay by me, my child, let thy desire reſt[2] thus to pine away." He advised her now to seek out his friend Paraçurāma, mighty in arms and penance, and to make requeſt of him ; he would slay Bhīshma, if he did not do as she said, and would set her free from her sorrow. Meanwhile, a comrade of Paraçurāma came into the penitential foreſt. The matter was put before him, and Ambā declared that Bhīshma had not known that she loved the king of the Çālvas, otherwise he would not have carried her off ; but that the ascetic muſt decide. He held that Bhīshma was the cause of it all ; for had he left her alone, then the Çālva would have been content with her. Ambā spoke : " In my heart also does this wish ever lie, whether I could not slay Bhīshma. Him on whom thou layeſt the blame, him do thou chaſtise, for I have come because of him into deep suffering." Then later came Rāma himself ; full of pity and love he hearkened to the lovely, tender young granddaughter of his friend Hotravāhana, who was begging help of him in tears. His wish was now to clear everything up through a kindly message to Bhīshma, or to the Çālva, while Ambā declared that the Çālva had sent her away through diſtruſt in her purity ; Paraçurāma muſt make away with Bhīshma, the root of her unhappiness. He reminded her that he would only take up arms on behalf of the Brahmans. But she always came back to insiſting that he muſt kill Bhīshma, the cause of all her woes. Then his comrade reminded him that he muſt help her that asks ſ r proteÅtion, and that, moreover, he was bound by an earlier vow, and therefore he

---

[1] Pare loke. Cp. my transl. of the Kuṭṭanīmata, pp. 118 and 149 ; in Petavatthu, ii, 9.44, pare = paraṃhi. In the Epic this locat. pare (apare) is often found (e.g. i, 76.67 ; ii, 44.28 ; v, 176.14 ; vi, 3.49 ; vii, 80.6 ; 151.16 ; xii, 139.66 ; 143.26 ; Rām., vii, 33.2).

[2] Paryāptaṃ te manaḥ. Cp. e.g. v, 185.13 f.

muſt fight in this case. So Rāma went to Kurukshetra with his band of disciples and the maiden, and from there a further couple of days' journey on, and solemnly asked Bhīshma, who came to meet him at the frontier respeċtfully : " Bhīshma, what was it that made thee carry off the daughter of the king of Kāçi that time againſt her will, and then let her go ? For now the glorious maid is left through thee bereft of her rights (marriage) ; for who could here on earth approach her, whom thou, a ſtranger, haſt touched ? The Çālva has rejeċted her, because thou didſt carry her away, O Bharata. Therefore do thou at my bidding take her back again. This king's daughter, O tiger among men, muſt be given her rights. It is not seemly in thee to hold kings to scorn and insult." But Bhīshma made answer : " I could in no wise give her to my brother, O Brahman. ' I belong to the Çālva,' said she to me myself before this, and it was with my leave that she went to the city. Neither from fear nor pity nor greed, nor to please anyone will I be unfaithful to the warrior's laws ; this vow I did undertake." But Rāma was angered, the more so since Bhīshma had been his disciple, and was thus under the duty of obedience to him. The unshakable one, however, for all his reverence for his teacher ſtood his ground : " Who would want to take into his house a woman that loves another man, and bears herself like a snake-woman, if he knows of it ? A fault in women [1] brings great harm. If the teacher is overbearing, if he knows not what muſt be done, and what muſt be left undone, if he goes aſtray, then according to the holy ordinance he shall be given up." After further proud and challenging words between the two, they made ready to fight. Bhīshma's mother tried to reconcile them, but without success. Through many days laſted the ſtruggle between the two picked fighters, but in the end Rāma had to declare himself beaten. Thus had Ambā's thirſt for vengeance been left unquenched. But she did not yield, but with rage in her eyes she exclaimed : " Then I will go whither I myself shall bring down Bhīshma in the fight." For twelve years she submitted to the moſt dreadful chaſtisements in the Indian liſt of penances, then visited various holy bathing-places, and there carried out cleansings. After that

[1] Or : a fault (offence) againſt women.

386

she was changed one half into an evil river, the Ambā, but as for the other half she was ſtill the former maiden, and gave herself up to further penances. The ascetics surrounded her, tried to hold her back, and asked her why she was doing all this. Then spoke the maid to the Ṛishis rich in penance : " I have been treated by Bhīshma with despite, cheated of the rights bound up with the husband. It is to slay him that I have given myself to asceticism, not to come unto heaven's worlds. When I have slain Bhīshma, then shall I find peace. This is my resolve. I shall not ſtop until I have slain Gaṅgā's son in the fight, because of whom I have been brought to where I now am, thus to dwell in never-ending sorrow, robbed of the blissful world of a husband, here on earth neither wife nor husband. I am wearied of life as a woman ; I am firmly resolved to become a man. I mean to take retaliation on Bhīshma ; none shall ſtay my hand." Then Çiva appeared to her in his own shape, and offered her a favour. She chose victory over Bhīshma. " Thou wilt slay him." " How should victory in the fight fall to me, a woman ? And as I am a woman, my heart is very mild.[1] And yet, O lord of beings, thou haſt granted me to overcome Bhīshma." Çiva answered : " Thou wilt overcome Bhīshma in the fight, and become a man. And thou wilt remember all this, when thou haſt gone into another body. Thou wilt be born in Drupada's race and become a great chariot-warrior." When Çiva had vanished again, Ambā gathered wood together out of the foreſt, made a great pile before the penitents' eyes, and kindled it. Then, her heart ablaze with anger, she leapt into the flaming fire with the cry : " Death to Bhīshma ! "

At this time the childless King Drupada was practising a dreadful asceticism that he might have a son. But Çiva granted him only a daughter, but told the discontented king that she would become a man. And the queen then later bore a lovely girl. The parents gave out that it was a boy, kept the matter a

---

[1] This seems to me to be one of the slily humorous passages in the Epic. Or else we could separate na : in life as a woman my heart no longer finds any great peace whatever, that is, I am heartily sick of it. Or are we to read çrāntam inſtead of çāntaṃ ?

secret from all, had all the rites laid down for a boy carried out on the child, and named it Çikhaṇḍin. Bhīshma alone learned of the whole matter through a spy, the divine Rishi Nārada, as also of the discourse between Çiva and Ambā. When the girl had come to marriageable years, her father was in great distress as to how he should marry her, and he took counsel with his wife. But she spoke confidently : " Çiva's words will soon be fulfilled ; the maker of the three worlds cannot lie. Therefore do thou get her a wife according to the law." Drupada after long inquiries decided for the family of Hiraṇyavarman, the ruler of the Daçārṇas, and sought the hand of his daughter. But the poor bride found herself sorely undeceived after the wedding, and full of shame told her girl-friends and nurses that her husband was a woman. Her intimates sent word of this at once to her father, who, blazing with anger, sent a messenger to Drupada. The envoy took the evil-doer on one side and gave him the message in secret that Hiraṇyavarman because of this disgraceful fraud would destroy him, and his people and ministers. Drupada stood before the messenger like a thief caught, and not a word came from his lips. He sent back word to the bride's angry father that the report was utterly untrue. But as the latter knew better, he gathered his army and vassals together, and these spoke : " If it is so, if Çikhaṇḍin is a maiden, then we will kill Drupada together with Çikhaṇḍin, and make another one as king among the Pañcālas." So a fresh message went off to the sinner : " I am going to make away with thee ; pluck up thy courage." His wife put heart into the frightened king, telling him to do honour to all the gods and worshipful persons and make sacrifice in the fires, but also to have the city fittingly defended ; for fate and manly staunchness, when joined together, was what brought good fortune. While the two were anxiously speaking with one another, their daughter came up to them and seeing how because of her such ill-hap had come on them, she resolved to kill herself. So he went forth into the thick forest, where a Yaksha, Sthūṇākarṇa by name, dwelt, whom folk avoided out of fear of the monster. Here she meant to starve herself to death. But the Yaksha came to her, and asked : " What is the object of this deed of thine ? I will accomplish the business.

Speak without hesitation." " Impossible ! " she kept on saying to the Yaksha. " I will do it," the Yaksha quickly answered. " I am a servant to Kubera ; I am a bestower of boons, O king's daughter. I grant even that which cannot be granted." Then the princess disclosed to him the plight in which she found herself ; and as the forest-spirit had given his promise so solemnly and sacredly, he had, indeed, to fulfil it. He spoke : " I will give thee my man's sex [1] for a time, and take thy woman's sex. Then thou must come hither at the proper time again. Swear it to me." Çikhandinī swore that she would become a maiden again, and give the Yaksha his manhood back again, so soon as the king of the Daçārṇas had gone away. " So the two in this plight came to a solemn agreement with one another, and then made the exchange.[2] The woman's mark of sex was borne now by the Yaksha Sthūṇākarṇa, and Çikhaṇḍinī got the Yaksha's shining mark of sex." [3] Greatly rejoicing the new man now went back to his father, who at once sent off a message to Hiraṇyavarman that his son was indeed a man, and after long negotiations the ruler of the Daçārṇas, who was still bent on destroying the deceiver, agreed to an examination ; he sent " the most excellent, very fair-formed women " that they might personally convince themselves whether it was a man. Their report was to everyone's joy an affirmative one, the father-in-law came with glad heart to the

[1] Or perhaps literally : " my man's member " (puṃliṅga). Cp. v, 192.40 f.

[2] According to the comment. : They exchanged their generative members. But as yet I do not put much trust in his suggested meaning of the word abhisaṃdeha, but take it as loc. sing., and = doubt, suspicion. It must be said, however, that saṃkrāmayatām without an object makes a certain difficulty, though not without other examples. The variant mentioned by Nīl., abhisaṃdohe might mean " agreement ". K. has anyonyasyānabhidrohe, thus also referring it to the first half-çloka.

[3] So certainly is yaksharūpa to be taken here ; for that Çikhaṇḍinī took over the Yaksha's form is out of the question. Rūpa = cihna, mark, token, first mark, forewarning is a good Epic usage (ii, 80.9, 27 ; iii, 155.8 ; iv, 39.7 ; v, 73.39 ; vi, 3.65 ff.; vii, 192.14 ; xii, 102.8 ff.; 228.1). Also it = symbolic action, bearing (ii, 80.9, cp. with 80.24).

city, gave very rich gifts to his son-in-law, and parted from his daughter with stern rebukes. But about this time the lord of the Yakshas, Kubera, happened to make a visit to Sthūnākarṇa, and as his servant, who was deeply ashamed of his new sex, did not come to meet him, but kept hidden, the god gave notice to his following of a heavy punishment for the offender. They told him why the poor wretch was not doing his duty. Angrily the god of wealth had the thus transformed man brought to him, and condemned him for his wicked change of sex, which was an insult to all Yakshas, to remain a woman always. But on the intercession of the Yakshas he ordained that Sthūnākarṇa on Çikhaṇḍin's death was to have his original sex back again. When Çikhaṇḍin later appeared, true to his promise, to hand over to the helping spirit his manhood again, the latter was greatly gladdened by his honesty, and told him of what had happened. High rejoicings now held sway in Drupada's house, the prince was handed over to learn the art of arms, and came to be a distinguished warrior-hero. Later he did indeed bring about Bhīshma's death in battle, for Bhīshma had sworn not to make use of his weapons against any woman, or against anyone that had ever been a woman, and knew full well, as did everyone, how the matter really stood.[1]

---

[1] Cp. Hemavijaya's Kathāratnākara, 118th Tale; Hertel, *Wiener Zeitschr. f. d. Kunde d. Morgenl.*, xxv, p. 168 ff.; Crooke, *Pop. Rel.*, ii, 7; and on change of sex in general *Isoldes Gottesurteil*, note 200 (p. 282 f.); Weinhold, *Zeitschr. d. Ver. f. Volksk.*, Bd. 5, p. 126 ff. K., i, 109.66, has much that is not found in B., and brings out still more strongly how holy the girl's inclination and her secret promise of marriage were, at least for the warrior caste. Ambā here for six years is sent to and fro between the Çālva and Bhīshma. One of them must marry her. Then she gives herself up to the sternest penance. The god Kumāra brings her a wreath; whoever wears it, he says, can slay Bhīshma. She now makes a round of the kings with her wreath and prayer for revenge. But none dares. [For spirits with changing sex in Melanesia, see G. C. Wheeler, *Mono-Alu Folklore*, pp. 21, 62 (Translator).]

XIII

WOMAN LYING-IN

LIKE Ambā in the tale we have juſt given, the Hindu says : The woman that is excluded from marriage must be looked on as an unhappy hermaphrodite. In marriage and in love, however, as the Epic again shows, the man seeks pleasure, but the woman seeks the child. And the half-pitying, half-proud smile of the ſtronger sex at the child-bed ſtories of women is hardly called for. The heroes, indeed, of the Mahābhārata in their converse tell one another of their victories and fights. Should the woman, then, not speak of her own, and of her " dwelling with death " ? The woman in child-bed, indeed, has by the Hindu also, from ages paſt been held to be an important, even if at the same time unclean, being. One that is unclean in any sense gives the evil powers that are ever lurking about mankind a dangerous opening. Thus, too, swarms of monſters are on the watch to do hurt to the mother and new-born child. A number of them, and also such as are dangerous to women with child are given in iii, 230.24–45 : they carry off children, eat them, for ten nights they are ever to be found in the lying-in room ; a female snake-demon penetrates into the mother's womb, and there devours the fruit, the woman then brings forth a snake [1] ; the mother of the Apsarases takes the fœtus away, and people then say : " She has loſt her child." So, too, in iii, 228.1 ff., we are told of evil spirits who carry off children after birth or even in the womb.[2]

[1] [For women and snakes in Melanesia cp. G. C. Wheeler, *Mono-Alu Folklore*, pp. 13, 36, 37 (Translator).]

[2] The children's female demon Pūtanā gives her breaſt to the suckling during the night, and those that drink of it die at once. Vishnup., vol. iv, p. 376 ; Bhāgavatapur., x, 6. Evil spirits kill the fruit of the womb, exchange those of two pregnant women, if these come near trees, mountains, embankments, ditches, cross-roads, burning-grounds, or the sea (water), where a spirit of this kind dwells (Mārk.-Pur., li,

8, 14, 21–22, 64–65, 77–80); they carry off the new-born child (ibid., li, 105–107). Cp. further Crooke, *Pop. Rel.*, i, 264 f.; Thurston, *Omens and Superstitions*, etc., 246; Chavannes, *Cinq cents contes*, iii, 42; 115; Jātaka, Nos. 510, 513, 540; etc. A long list of supernatural beings that also do harm to children is given in Agnipur., xxxi, 29–31 (Dutt, p. 125), so too in ccxcix, such as especially lie in wait for the young child, and this until the seventeenth year of life. The Bhūtas, Pretas, Piçācas, and Vetālas are foes of conception (cp. Mārk.-Pur., li, 46, 114 ff.) and dangerous to the fœtus (Mahānirvāṇatantra, ix, 124). Mārkaṇḍeyapur., lxxvi, 6–19 is worthy of remark here : Jātahariṇī (a female robber of new-born children) always first steals two children, and exchanges them with one another, then she steals a third, and eats it. When doing this she takes the shape of a cat, and so awaits near the child her opportunity. Among the Urau (in Bengal) the evil spirit Chordeva, turning into a cat, creeps into the house, and during the birth and for fifteen days after seeks to harm the mother. Therefore the husband must keep watch, and a fire always be kept up. *Zeitschr. f. Ethnol.*, Bd. 6, p. 343 (after Dalton). Cp. Crooke, loc. cit., p. 271; Elsie Clews Parsons, *The Old-Fashioned Woman*, p. 57; etc. In the West, too, this witch-beast is dangerous to the woman lying-in. See Zachariae, *Zeitschr. d. Ver. f. Volksk.*, Bd. 22, p. 235 f. But on the other hand Shashthī also, the friendly goddess of the sixth night after the birth, rides on the back of this witching beast (Crooke, *Pop. Rel.*, ii, 241); and in general this tailed creature of magic is in near relation with the sexual life of woman. Cp. also Thurston, *Omens and Superst. of Southern India*, p. 77. Like the witches and goblins, the old German wood-spirits also are fond of turning into cats (Mannhardt, *Wald- u. Feldkulte*, i, 89, 112, 146; E. H. Meyer, *Mythol. d. Germanen*, 140); and to the Indians also they are magical beings or witch-beasts (Stokes, *Indian Fairy Tales*, 15, 18, 19, 255).

Superstition of this kind is well-known to be spread throughout the world. Witches steal small children, and eat them or use them for their magical purposes ; all kinds of spirits do harm to the mother, carry off the small beings, and put their changelings in their stead, suck children's blood, and so on. Garnett, *The Women of Turkey*, etc., 1, 13, 70, 231, 315; ii, 22, 245 (and on this *Zschr. f. Ethnol.*, Bd. 26, p. 560); Żmigrodski, *Die Mutter bei d. Völkern d. arisch. Stammes*, 124 ff.; Hartland, *The Science of Fairy Tales*, New York, 1891, pp. 93–134; Fr. S. Krauss, *Slav. Volkforsch.*, 60, 64, 66, 67, 68, 72, 146, 148, 153 ff.; etc. As probably most primitive peoples believe that a man can make only one child, and that with twins there must be either an uninvited fellow-worker or a supernatural being at work, so in one of the twins there is often seen a supernatural visitor from magical realms. But as it is not known which is a man's own child, both of them are often reared. But in other places, indeed, both are forthwith killed, or there is means to find out which is the intruder, exactly like the real changeling in European tales. There is a great number of these tales of changelings. As an example let only Kirchhof's *Wendunmuth*, iii, 516 f. be given. A delightful account of the wise oracular utterances which are made especially by the swarm of aunts, godmothers, and woman-neighbours about a supposed magical being of this kind, is given by Juho Reijonen, a pleasing Finnish novelist of our day, in his *Vaihdokas* (The Changeling). Indeed, Żmigrodski states : " Witch and lying-in woman are in Aryan tradition almost one and the same " (*Die Mutter*, p. 177). The death of a woman in child-bed is always a magically dangerous misfortune in India (see e.g. *Anthropos*, vi, 872 f. ; vii, 85 f. ; iv, 68) ; she becomes, at least in the belief of some primitive tribes, a very evil spirit, called Churel or Chorail, which wanders about with the feet turned backwards. Billington, *Woman in India*, p. 100 ; Crooke, *Things Indian*, Lond., 1906, p. 131 ; *Popul. Relig.*, etc., i, 269–274 ; *Anthropos*, iv, 679 (Pahariya) ; vii, 649, 659 (Khond) ; *Zeitschr. für Ethnol.*, Bd. 6, p. 344. Cp. Ploss-Bartels, ii, 579 ff. ; Żmigrodski, 148 ; E. H. Meyer, *Mythol. d. Germanen*, 31 ; 56 ; 101 f. ; cp. 43 ; A. Jeremias, *Allgemeine Religionsgesch.* [2], p. 53 (among the old Babylonians). In the belief of the Urau they are clothed in white, and have a pleasing face, but a coal-black back. *Zschr. f. Ethnol.*, Bd. 4, p. 344 (after Dalton). Like those who have met an accidental death, women that die in child-bed are buried by the Nāgas in the jungle without any rites. And yet the Empêo at any rate among them believe that only women dying in child-bed, and men that have fallen in the fight or been killed by tigers are allowed to go forthwith to the highest god. *Zschr. f. Ethnol.*, Bd. 30, p. 353. This reminds us of the Breton belief : A mother who has died in child-bed need only fly through purgatory, and then goes straight into heaven. Żmigrodski, *Die Mutter*, p. 142. A like belief is found, too, among the Mohammedans, in old Mexico, in Sumatra, in Steiermark, and so on. The uncanny and the holy or the divine are very near akin not in India only. The woman thus snatched away was at that very time highly unclean, and she also suffered an unnatural, premature death, as do for instance the criminal and the soldier, together with whom she often appears. The ghost of a person that has thus died is, however, powerful and often malicious. In India, indeed, the robber or murderer that has been put to death becomes a kind of god. See my Daçakum., pp. 31, 358, and on that Bhāratīyanātyaçāstra, iii,

40 ff.; the eerie tale "The Cry from the River" in R. W. Frazer, *Silent Gods and Sun-Steeped Lands*, Lond., 1906, p. 90; Crooke, *Popul. Relig.*, etc., i, p. 228; ii, 199 (also Dubois-Beauchamp, 449; 548; Fuller, *Studies of Indian Life and Sentiment*, p. 95, and especially 96); and Thurston, *Omens and Superstitions*, etc., pp. 162, 178, 179, 209. With the Indian doctrine that punishment atones, blots out any guilt and reproach, is probably connected on the other hand the teaching of the old verse which I quoted in that note to the Daçakum., and which, for instance, is also found in Vasishtha, xix, 45; Manu, viii, 318; Nārada, Pariçishta, 48 : The criminal punished by the king goes without a spot into heaven, like the pious man. Cp. my *Hindu Tales*, pp. 9–10 (note). In Sicily, too, as I point out in the Daçakum., executed criminals are prayed to and worshipped. Cp. Hartland, " The Cult of Executed Criminals at Palermo," *Folk-Lore*, vol. 21, p. 168 ff.; vol. 7, p. 275; *Primitive Paternity*, i, 77. And in general anyone meeting his end by violence is outside the course of nature, and becomes a god, an evil spirit, etc. " There is a deified Pootra in every Rajput family—one who has met with a violent death." Tod, *Rajasthan*, i, 298, note; cp. 659–60; Hartland, i, 77; *Zschr. d. Ver. f. Volksk.*, Bd. 2, p. 185; *Zschr. f. Religwissensch*, Bd. 8, p. 258. Much valuable information is given especially by Crooke, *Pop. Rel.*, i, 43, 44, 46, 62, 96, 99, 115, 119 129, 138 ff., 147, 189 ff., 230 f., 234 ff.; Crooke, *The North-Western Provinces*, 252. Here we find included the suicide, who in the law writing, the Purāṇas, and elsewhere is branded as evil; even the attempt at suicide is, indeed, to be heavily punished (Mahānirvāṇatantra, xi, 72 f.), and as an offence bringing loss of caste must be atoned for by works of mortification and " Penance of the Purse ", that is, by giving cattle (Parāçara, xii, 5–8; cp. Vasishtha, xxiii, 18 ff.). If a kinsman loses his life by his own hand, or in some other "unnatural " way (execution, water, fire, lightning, a beast, battle, accident, etc.), then his death does not make his kinsfolk unclean, and for the suicide there must be no pyre, no tears, no death-gifts, nor any other pious rite, otherwise heavy vows of mortification must be undertaken, as must no less be done by him who even cuts the cord of a hanged man. Gautama, xiv, 9 ff.; Manu, v, 89, 95, 98; Vishṇu, xxii, 47, 56, 58–60; Vasishtha, xxiii, 14 ff.; Yājñav., iii, 6, 21, 27; Parāçara, iii, 10; iv, 1–6; Kauṭilya, transl., 341.23 ff.; Garuḍa-Pur., Pretakalpa, 4.104–112, 160; 40.4 ff.; 44.24–29; 44.1–5; Baudh.-Gṛihyas., Pitṛimedhasūtra, iii, 7.1 ff.; Mārk.-Pur., xxxv, 45; Agnipur., clvii, 32; 159.2–3; 158.37, 39–41; often in the Vishṇupur.; etc. How uncanny the man is who has died by his own hand, is seen clearly also from Parāçara, v, 10 ff. The Çraddha on the 14th day of the half-month is forbidden for

the ordinary dead, but prescribed for him that has been slain with a weapon. Yājñav., i, 263 ; Caland, *Totenverehrung*, bottom of 44 to 45. Sacer means " holy " and " cursed "—he that has been raised above sin and earthly mankind through blissful death in battle, and the shameful outcaſt from the caſte appear side by side in the laws we have quoted ! Cp. with this subjeƈt of death by violence, for inſtance, *Zschr. d. Ver. f. Volksk.*, Bd. 14, p. 31 ff.; 322 f. (and the references there) ; Caland, *Totenverehrung*, 74; *Zschr. f. Ethnol.*, v, 187; Crooke, *Anthropos*, Bd. 4, p. 68 (Nāga) ; ibid., 464 (Dravidian peoples); Hoſten, ibid., p. 682 (Pahariya, India) ; *Anthropos*, Bd. vii, p. 649 (Khond) ; Hartland, i, 182 (Pahariya). And the very animal one kills can become a deſtroying being. So the Hindu, when a snake has been killed, carries out the same death rites as he does in honour of a kinsman (Rāmakrishṇa, *Life in an Indian Village*, 1891, p. 135, from south India ; Thurſton, *Omens and Superſtitions*, etc., 1912, p. 123) ; and these often discussed ideas are very well expressed in the 46th rune of the Kalevala, where the bear, the ſtrong king of the Finnish foreſts, is appeased with the moſt reverential ceremonies and the moſt honeyed words, and he is told that it is not men who have taken his life, but that he fell himself out of the fir-tree to his death. Cp. Crooke, *Pop. Rel.*, ii, 212. The appeasing of the captured bear here referred to seems, however, to fit in firſt of all with the bear-worship of the Aino, the Gilyaks and other Amur peoples, which finds its higheſt expression in the famous bear-feſtival of the Aino and the Gilyaks. Of this feſtival among the laſt-named people, and what is conneƈted with it Leo Sternberg has given a very good account in his excellent article on the religion of the Gilyaks, *Zeitschr. f. Relgnswiss.*, Bd. 8, p. 260 ff.; see especially 272 there. The bear-cult of the Aino and a long set of details belonging to it, as also the ideas lying behind it are treated at length by Frazer, *Golden Bough* [2], 1900, Bd. ii, 374 ff.

It can be underſtood that the woman dead in child-bed seeks above all to harm those of her own sex, or her husband, or young men : her envious revenge is direƈted againſt those who in things of sex are so much happier than she has been. Therefore they also annoy women in child-bed. R. Schmidt, *Liebe u. Ehe in Indien*, p. 520. In India such a ghoſt, as a handsome woman, also draws on young men by night into deſtruƈtion. Crooke, *Pop. Rel.*, i, 253, 270 ff. Cp. e.g. R. Andree, *Ethnogr. Parallelen*, i, 92 f. In the same way in India the tiger that has eaten a man is always accompanied by the ghoſt of its viƈtim, and led by him to other human beings that it may also slay them. Sleeman, *Rambles and Recolleƈtions*, i, 154; Crooke, *Pop. Rel.*, i, 267; ii, 210 ff.; *Anthropos*, vii, 651, 660; and the thrilling tale of " The

Various means, ceremonies, and magics for driving off these evil influences are, of course, of great antiquity, and make their appearance already in Vedic literature. Then the Gṛihyasūtras also deal with this subject, although not at great length ; further there are the medical works, etc. A fairly clear description of the lying-in room of an upper-class woman of Old India is given in xiv, 68. It is hung with white, luck-bringing wreaths ; vessels filled with water stand everywhere towards the different quarters of the heavens, and melted butter, brands of tinduka-wood, and mustard-seeds ; round about are set naked missiles and lighted fires. Old women run around on all kinds of services, and equally skilled physicians. Everywhere the eye meets the magical things which have been set out about the place by experienced persons according to the prescript, and which rob the spirits of their evil.—So soon as Sītā has brought forth her twins, the holy Vālmīki is called in to see to the spirit-banning, protective measures. And he also drives away the rakshas and bhūtas. As being especially powerful, the holy kuça-grass is, of course, used here also (Rām., vii, 66).

Most important of all is the fire (sūtikāgni) that still burns to-day in the lying-in rooms of India. It must be kept always burning (xii, 69.49), as, indeed, for keeping off the dark powers in general the warding flame of fire must be kept up day and night [1] (cp. xiii, 131.7 ff., where as remedies against the eerie Tailless Tiger " in Frazer's *Silent Gods and Sun-Steeped Lands*, p. 11 ff. Doubtless among other things the belief also enters here that anyone killed by a beast becomes this beast himself. So also the Gilyaks believe of the human prey of a bear (Schurtz, *Urgesch. d. Kultur*, p. 570). Finally there is probably another belief at work in the dread with which a woman carried off in child-bed is looked on : The woman that was so little fitted for her natural calling is a wretched being, nay, an offence against her lord and master, and a shame on her family. How should she, then, but have to go about as an evil ghost, herself unhappy, and to others bringing unhappiness ! With more advanced views she has also done wrong to the child, and has to come back to it, suckle it, care for it, and so on. Mother love as a motive probably belongs to a higher developed set of ideas. [For child-stealing spirits in Melanesia cp. G. C. Wheeler, *Mono-Alu Folklore*, pp. 60, 61, (Translator).]

[1] Billington, *Woman in India*, 1 ff. ; 99 ; Hartland, *Science of Fairy Tales*, 96 ; etc. The woman who is unclean and makes unclean must stay ten days in the lying-in room. Manu, vi, 217.

spirit-beings Pramathas the following are also given : hyena skin, hyena teeth, mountain tortoise, the smell of butter, a cat, a black and a red he-goat). Like the fire that comes into contact with other unclean objects, as for instance the lich-fire, the sūtikāgni is unclean (iii, 221.31 ; cp. e.g. Hiraṇyakeçin's Gṛihyas., ii, 1, 3.4 ; 1, 4.8).[1]

[1] Down to to-day in India, or at least here and there, the husband also is made unclean by the wife's child-bed, and thus exposed to magical influences (Billington, 4–5) ; and the Gopa (" herdsman ") in Bengal is forty days unclean then, just as in case of a death (*Zeitschr. f. Ethnolog.*, Bd. 6, p. 372, after Dalton). The same belief is witnessed to for us by the old law books. As by the death of one of his kindred, so through the birth of a child the Brahman becomes unclean for ten days, the Kshattriya twelve, the Vaiçya fifteen, the Çūdra a month. Vishṇu, xxii, 1–4 ; Parāçara, iii, 4. According to Vasishṭha, iv, 20–29 the dark ban lies on the Kshattriya even fifteen days, on the Vaiçya twenty days. Cp. Gautama, xiv, 14–16. Indeed, in the matter of the disputed question touched on here and by Vasishṭha there were, according to Baudhāyana, i, 5, 11.19–23, those who maintained that only the father, as the main originator, was made unclean through the child's birth. Cp. Bühler's note SBE, xiv, p. 180; Agnipur., 158.60 f.; Garuḍapur., Pretakalpa, 39.9, 11. But Baudh. decides like others : " both parents." See also Manu, v, 77, 79; Agnipur., p. 608 ; Schmidt, *Liebe u. Ehe in Indien*, p. 530 ff. (also 503 ff. ; 509); Crooke, *Pop. Rel.*, i, 274–277. In the fact that the father is thus exposed to the evil-minded powers I see the most primitive and main cause of the Couvade, for which so many interpretations have been given. Max Müller's way out of it all is most extraordinary. It is in general explained as a survival from the times of mother-right; the husband wanted, it is said, to make known in a very evident way his claim on the child. So, too, Ploss-Bartels, Henne am Rhyn, Westermarck, Ed. Meyer, and others, to say nothing of those with a fad for the matriarchate. But even where mother-right actually prevails, the husband in many, but by no means in all, cases is deemed to be the natural owner of each child which his wife, that is, his property, brings forth, even when he himself and everyone else knows that he has nothing to do with it ; and under father-right this is the universally held view. Among many Brazilian tribes that have the Couvade it is to the father only that the origination of the child is ascribed. Kunicke, *Zeitschr. f. Ethnol.*, vol. 43, p. 553. Cp. there 547–8. Now for the man there is nothing more dreadful than to be in any

way put on a level with the so very contemptible, and often mysterious woman, or to be in any way like her. There is, therefore, in truth a much stronger motive needed, for making a lying-in woman of the husband, than the wish to see the children of his wife looked on as his own. Superstition filled with the thought of the precious self holds all the primitive peoples in its bonds, and an even relatively important freedom from it, such, for instance, as we meet with in the book of the two Seligmann's on the Veddas, or as is here and there reported of the Aino, arouses the greatest astonishment. On the other hand the universal development of marriage by way of hetærism and matriarchate cannot be proved. For then all the peoples with the Couvade would have to be patriarchal now, and before they had the men's lying-in they must have had mother-right. But even the first of these two does not hold, to say nothing whatever of the proof of the second. And the selfishness of the man is a truly "cosmic" element. I should like, then, as against this explanation and the other one to be immediately discussed, to point to some words of Fr. S. Krauss that are to be found somewhere in a note on the customs and habits of the South Slavs, and are worth more than many a long ethnological treatise. They are somewhat as follows: " If to-morrow the men had to bear the children, then the social question would be solved at one stroke—mankind would at once die out." Children are indeed often very valuable to primitive man ; but he does not take to the child-bed for *their* sake. But this is just what Starcke holds : " The well-being of the child is the object; the father's powers of endurance are displayed on such occasions, and might thus be assured to the child, for no one who was deficient in courage and endurance would submit to this custom " (*Primit. Family*, p. 52). Primitive man is indeed not so careful and self-forgetting for the sake of his offspring. We are, it is true, often told of the foolish fondness shown, or said to be shown, by savages towards their growing children. But when we are told how general it is for the new-born to be killed off, and when we think how despised the father would become, if he took much heed of a brat like this, usually left only to the care of women, or even of fate—then we cannot believe that he would hand over his very important self to the shame and the discomforts, and even the pains of a couvade, only that it may go well for the little helpless creature. The statement in Dobrizhoffer from the relatively highly developed Abipones is worth nothing. No; superstitious fear of the harm that might come to a man's own much-threatened personality, this only is the root. Primos in orbe deos fecit timor, as we may read also in the MBh., xii, 15.13–19; K, iii, 28.16. Dark beings and forces lurk round the father, who is likewise made unclean, far more than round the mother or the child ; for, as a man, he seems so immeasurably more important, in the eyes of the ghostly powers also, than the wretched worthless woman. The man's child-bed is probably, anyhow where it is bound up with torments of any kind, at the same time a magical matter, and bestows charmed and magic strength. And probably it makes a part of the magical homœopathy of primitive man.

Note in Proof.[1]—The well-known article by Ling Roth in the *Journal of the Roy. Anthropol. Inst.*, vol. xxii, p. 204 ff., was deliberately not read by me till the last, so that I might not be influenced by it. But unfortunately I only saw it after sending off my MS. He brings forward a good many cases where the welfare of the child is given as the reason of the couvade (pp. 209–11, 214 f., 217 f., 219 ff.). This standpoint has therefore undoubtedly not been without influence. The man's lying-in is found neither among the lowest, nor among the civilized peoples (of to-day) (p. 222). The Australians living under mother-right believe that the child really comes only from the father (225 f.). Mother-right and Couvade are met with together among the Arawaks, and in Melanesia (227 ; cp. 238 f.).

[1] [Of the original.]

XIV

WOMAN IN THE HOUSE

NOR is the careful, busy housewife left altogether out of account in the Epic. While the brothers are living in banishment in the forest with Draupadī, the idea comes one day into the head of the divine holy man Durvāsas—who on the slightest grounds will break out into an anger full of mighty curses, and finds a cannibal-like joy in scratching others till they bleed [1]—the idea comes into his head to lead the Pāndavas and their wife into some very evil plight. With a huge crowd of disciples he comes to them as a guest just as their meal is over. Draupadī now does not know what to do. The wonderful cooking-pot (sthālī) given by the sun god bestows indeed every kind of food, but as Draupadī has eaten last, it will give out nothing more for this meal.[2] She, too, has

[1] On the spiteful ill-nature of this "holy man with the purified soul" besides what has been already told and our passage see especially iii, 262.7–15; xiii, 159. In hotness of temper his no less pious brother-hermit Bhūti may be compared with him : in Bhūti's hermitage the wind therefore did not dare to blow strongly, the sun to shine hotly, the rain to cause any dirt ; even the water he drew in his pitcher was afraid of him. Mārkandeyapur., xcix, 2 ff. Cp. MBh., iii, 110.9 ff. Durvāsas was, however, in our case put up to it by Duryodhana (iii, 262.16 ff.).

[2] This wishing-pot is only one variety of the jewel of the sun god, the Syamantaka, which we are often told about in the Purāna literature. This Syamantaka bestows gold (eight loads every day), grants every blessing, keeps all evil away, etc. But in Krishna's words it must be in the keeping of a wholly pure and always chaste man ; then from the noble treasure there goes forth welfare for the whole land. But if it is entrusted to a bad man, then it kills him (etat sarvakālam çucinā brahmacaryena ca dhriyamānam açesharāshtrasyopakāram, çl. 69). Vishnupur., amça 4, adhyāya 13. It is thus a Holy Grail in this also, that it makes such great demands on its warden. It is to be noticed that in Wolfram von Eschenbach the Holy Grail is not a vessel, but a

now already eaten her meal. But the artist in curses and his following must be fed. In her difficulty she calls on Krishna, who comes and gives the guests their fill in supernatural wise without their having eaten at all (iii, 263).

A kind of beatification of the housewife wrapped up in her cooking is given in ix, 48.33 ff. Arundhatī, the companion of one of the seven Rishis, and so famous for her wifely faithfulness, likewise stood out by her asceticism. A twelve years' drought came on them. Then Çiva, gladdened by Arundhatī's piety, came there in Brahman's shape, said he was hungry, and begged for alms. "The food is used up, O Brahman; eat these badara-fruit" (the fruit of the jujube-tree). "Cook them." She now cooked and cooked the fruit for twelve years, and while she was so busied, and meanwhile listening to the heavenly discourse and tales of the guest, the drought went by : twelve years had gone by her without her marking it, and she had not

---

costly precious stone. Schroeder could without more ado have referred to our Purāṇa passage (cp. "Wurzeln d. Sage v. hl. Gral", *Wiener Sitzungsber.*, Bd. 166, pp. 4–5). The Christian stone thus probably comes from India. Mention must be here made also of the well-known breast-jewel of the sun god Vishṇu-Krishṇa, the Kaustubha. This might probably likewise be set beside the Brising-gamen, often identified by Schroeder with the sun. From the Epic much other matter could be adduced. Here we only mention those "ear-rings of precious stone" (akin to the ear-rings of the sun god) which for the wearer drive away hunger, thirst, danger from poison, fire, and from wild beasts, sweat (syand) gold, suck up by night the brightness of the stars, and so on. With them too care must be taken (xiv, 57.22 ff.). Truthfulness, honour, faithfulness, chastity, etc., are, indeed, very often demanded in the case of these fairy things, and in Old India also this was so well known a conception that the rule imagined for the "pearl of a leather pouch" in Apahāravarman's adventures seemed quite in order (my Daçakumārac., p. 224). Is it the pure and purifying light of their mother, the sun, that ever shines on them, even on the chastity—and kindred beakers, as on the renowned beaker of Djemshid, which also was made of a jewel ?—Schroeder, anyhow, has been more right than I in deriving the cooking-pot bestowed by the sun god on Yudhishṭhira directly from the old conception of the sun as a pot ("Sage vom hl. Gral," p. 16). In iii, 3.172, it is called a tāmra piṭhara (copper pot).

eaten a bite but only cooked and listened. Then the god showed himself in his own shape, and spoke to the seven Rishis : " The tapas (asceticism, ascetic merit) that ye have heaped up on the ridge of the Himālaya is in my belief not so great as the tapas of this woman. For this poor woman (or : woman rich in tapas) has practised a tapas hard indeed to carry out : fasting and cooking, she has spent twelve years."—Earlier the same chapter gives another form of the same legendary account, which was thought out to explain the badarapācana (badara-cooking) of Tīrthanamen. Çrutāvatī, the virginal and peerlessly lovely daughter of the holy man Bharadvāja, undergoes a strict penance to win Indra for a husband. In the shape of the Brahman Vasishtha he at last visits her hermitage, and is hospitably welcomed by her ; but she cannot give him her hand to take, because she is wholly dedicated to Indra in worship and love. The disguised god smiles, and offers her five badara-fruit with the bidding to cook them. The whole day long she cooks them, but the heavenly one has made the fruit impossible to cook so as to make trial of the pious woman. The day comes to its end, and her supply of wood is used up. But she is bent on faithfully carrying out her cooking duties, puts her feet in the fire, and keeps on pushing them further in when a bit is burnt off. Not a muscle does she move, there is no dejection in her soul, in her heart abides only the guest's bidding, although the fruit will not get cooked. Mightily rejoiced, Indra now reveals himself in his glory to the maid ; she lays aside the shell of the body, and goes with him to dwell as his wife in heaven. To the glorification of this housewifely self-denial the bathing-place where it happened is still world-renowned to-day ; to bathe there wipes out all sins, nay, whoever spends but one night there and carries out his washing attains to heavenly worlds hard to attain to.

The housewife must also see to strict order, see to it that spade, sickle, basket, brass vessels, etc., do not lie about (xii, 228.60). " Where earthenware is strewn about or there are broken utensils or seats, in such a house, ruined by sinful dirt, the women perish (hanyante). The gods and forefathers go back again hopeless on festivals and holy days from the house of sinful dirt (because they cannot accept anything there).

Broken utensils and bedsteads, cock and dog, and a tree growing by the house—these are all things bringing misfortune. In broken vessels dwells strife, the saying is, in the bedstead decay of wealth, in the presence of the cock and the dog the gods eat not the sacrificial food, in the root of the tree dwells assuredly a goblin ; therefore the tree shall not be planted " (xiii, 127.6, 7, 15, 16). Women that are not troubled by implements and crockery being left about are shunned by the goddess of happiness and beauty ; on the other hand, she dwells in and with those that in this and other things live up to the pattern for the woman (xiii, 11.10 ff.).[1]

Carefully to administer the household is thus the task of the wife. But does she rule, too, in the household circle ? " Be mistress over thy father-in-law, be mistress over thy mother-in-law " the bride, indeed, is told in the wedding hymn (Rigveda, x, 85.46), and the same thing is elsewhere also held out to her in prospect. But to a woman and at a wedding one may lie, the Mahābh. says more than once. Whatever of truth may at some time have lain in those anyhow noteworthy verses of the Veda, in the Epic we find it to be the duty of the young house-wife, who under Indian conditions usually lives under one roof with her parents-in-law, to be subject to these persons, who even for her husband are worshipful and authoritative. The daughter-in-law is to fear the father-in-law, and a dignified gravity must be the rule between the two (v, 37.5). Her bearing towards him shall be kindly and friendly (v, 30.35). " Since thou art the guru (dignitary) of my guru (that is, of my husband), so art thou to me the god of gods, the over-god of the gods," says a pious daughter-in-law to the father-in-law (xiv, 90.76). The daughter-in-law, therefore, must not give orders to the servants in the presence of the mother-in-law and the father-in-law (xii, 228.76). Evil-speaking against her mother-in-law

---

[1] Cp. Mārk.-Pur., l, 86 : Where utensils are strewn about the house there dwell ill-boding powers ; Vishṇusmṛiti, xxv, 4 ff., and Yājñav., i, 83 : Women must keep the pots and pans and the household things in good order. If they do this, and are otherwise virtuous and have sons, then the goddess of happiness dwells ever with and in them (Vishṇusmṛiti, xcix, 21 ff.). " Indian houses are kept beautifully clean," Fuller, *Studies of Indian Life*, etc., p. 151.

is a shameful sin for the wife (xiii, 93.131 ; 94.38), and she muſt appear before her only in modeſt, seemly clothing (xi, 10.14).

But of the well-known tabu relation between father-in-law and daughter-in-law, to which Buddhiſt writings also allude, the Epic knows nothing.[1] On the other hand it has already been mentioned as a cuſtom of the daughter-in-law to seat herself on the right thigh of her father-in-law, juſt like his own children (i, 97.9). And, in faᵉt, the Epic shows us the moſt beautiful relations between the parents-in-law and the daughter-in-law. Especially with her husband's mother the younger woman has affeᵉtionate, and even intimate relations. The Epic poetry often touches on this subjeᵉt, and there is never heard one note of that song of the mother-in-law that we know so well. Whether the then Indian daughter-in-law was really so much better off than is often her later siſter cannot, of course, be quite definitively decided. But if we bear

---

[1] Cp. Majjhimanik., i, 190; WZKM, xvi, 100 ff. ; xxvii, 474 ff. ; Lang, *Myth, Ritual, and Religion* (1899), i, 100 ; Ploss-Bartels [4], ii, 244 ; Rich. Andree, *Ethnogr. Parallelen*, i, 159 ff. ; Schrader, *Die Indogermanen*, p. 108. While the champions of woman-capture look on this inſtitution as a survival from the time of that method of getting wives (e.g. Dargun, *Mutterrecht u. Raubehe*, etc., 90 ff., 108 f.), Max Müller, Mantegazza (*Geschlechtsverhältnisse*, 276 ff.), Henne am Rhyn (p. 20) see the grounds, probably more rightly, in jealousy. But is this enough, particularly as the more primitive peoples often show so little of that " passion " ? Since the tabu relation is indeed found between father-in-law and daughter-in-law, but ſtill more between mother-in-law and son-in-law, where yet the danger of sexual intercourse is smaller, a derivation from mother-right would seem much more likely ; the mother, either as the aᵉtual owner of her daughter, or as representative of the clan would have the moſt reason to look with hoſtile eyes on the man taking this property away. Among many Vishṇuitic seᵉts the daughter-in-law muſt never speak to her mother-in-law. Dubois-Beauchamp, p. 349. This, indeed, is easier to underſtand. But this tabu inſtitution is otherwise ſtill very much in the dark. But what is seen clearly seems to be this, that powerful superſtitious ideas muſt form the main background. The explanation also which K. Th. Preuss gives in *Die geiſtige Kultur der Naturvölker*[2], p. 73 does not seem to satisfy.

in mind how often, in the Epic, ftrife between the various wives of a polygamous husband comes to be spoken of, we feel inclined from the silence on the one hand, and the very clear indications the other way to draw here very favourable conclusions at leaft for the old conditions among the Kshattriyas. Kuntī's love for Draupadī may be taken as giving the charaðeriftic. She says : " Dearer to me than all sons is Draupadī " (v, 90.43) ; and her particular disguft and sorrow is aroused by the faðt that it is Draupadī that has been so badly treated by her enemies, has suffered so much misery, and goes on ever suffering (v, 90.43 ff., 85 ; xv, 17.9 ff.). She acknowledges that she no longer had any love whatever for her sons, when Draupadī was dragged into the hall, and all looked on without ftirring (v, 90.49) ; and she reminds Arjuna and Bhīma through Kṛishṇa what a shame lies on both, that Duḥçāsana, Karṇa, and Duryodhana should have done this to the poor woman (v, 90.80–82). This love comes out in special beauty when Draupadī has to go off with her husband into the foreft of banishment (ii, 79), and she mourns very deeply when her mother-in-law has gone off into the penitential foreft (xv, 22.14–17). Gāndhārī, all of whose sons have been slain, does not bewail this so much as the sorrow of her widowed daughters-in-law (xi, 18.2 ; cp. 17.24 ; 18.6 ; 22.15 ; 24.6 ff.). On the tender regard between Sītā and her mother-in-law some light will be thrown by and by in another conneðion.

XV

The Widow

DREARY, on the other hand, is the lot of the widow in the Epic. Firſt and foremoſt the husband is the food-giver to the wife (the bhartar of the bhāryā). True, we read in xiii, 167.2 of Yudhishṭhira after the great fight : "Then did Pāṇḍu's son, the king, console with rich gifts the women whose hero-husbands, their lords, had been slain " ; and in ii, 5.54 it is laid down as the ruler's duty that he shall maintain the wives of the men that have loſt their lives or come to misfortune in his service.[1] But even if the ruler should have been true, oftener than may be presumed, to this virtue of the father of the land, it would have been only a relatively small part of the exiſting widows that were helped by such a prescript, and a grant or pension of this kind. Even where the husband was wealthy he could not at his death leave much to his wife as her personal property. "Three thousand is the moſt that a man can give his wife in money ; and this property given her by her husband she shall enjoy, as is fitting. According to the tradition the woman has the usufruſt of the property left behind by her husband. In no wise shall anything of the husband's property be taken away from her " (xiii, 47.23 ff.).[2] This laſt ordinance would indeed be a very friendly one, but, of course, can only be meant to hold if there are no sons.[3] But man, and

[1] Cp. Kauṭilya, transl., 384.6–10 ; addit., 384.32.

[2] Cp. Kauṭilya, transl., 244.7 ff. ; addit., 244.47.

[3] The woman is often found inheriting her husband's property in spite of many opposed views. The wife inherits the property of the sonless man : Bṛihaspati, xxv, 46–50 (but cp. the partly contradiſtory provisions, which yet follow immediately thereafter, 53 and 54 ; they look, indeed, like an interpolation, especially as againſt 55) ; Vishṇu, xvii, 4 ; Yājñav., ii, 135 f. (= Agnipur., 256.22 f.). Cp. Mahānir-vāṇatantra, xii, 23, 27, 28, and the passages quoted in the discussion of the inheritance rights of the maiden, especially the claim of Vishṇu

THE WIDOW

especially woman, does not live on bread alone, but also from sunshine and from love. The widow of Old India, indeed, who was not left childless had something more for which to live, and for which she was assuredly often glad to live on ; and given the beautiful relations of the children to the mother, it muſt seldom have been that she was without regard and affeċtion in her own house. But from a new marriage she was, anyhow in the upper classes, shut off.[1] Therefore does

that the mother shall inherit in proportion to her sons' (or her son's) share (xviii, 34 f.). According to Nārada, xiii, 12, and Bṛihaspati, xxv, 64 the mother has the same share as a son ; according to Gautama, xxviii, 21 the widow of a sonless man shares his eſtate with the kinsfolk. Cp. Jolly, *Recht u. Sitte*, espec. 85, 86 ; " Rechtl. Stellung d. Frau bei d. alten Indern," *Münch. Sitzungsber.*, 1876, p. 452 f., especially, however, the more precise account in Meyer, *Altind. Rechtsschr.*, p. 78 foot–81 ; also Kauṭilya, 243.17–245.18. Mention muſt be made also of the old wise man Yājñavalkya. When he leaves his house for a Saṃyāsin's life, he wishes beforehand, as something calling for no remark, to divide his belongings between his two wives left behind. Bṛihadāraṇyaka-Upanishad, ii, 4.1. If a man dies, leaving neither wife nor offspring behind him, his property goes to his mother. So Manu, ix, 217; Bṛihaspati, xxv, 63. According to Vishṇu, xvii, 4 ff. only when his father also is dead ; and Manu, ix, 185 only names the father and brothers. The sonless widow is by Nārada, xiii, 28–31, left wholly to the mercy of the husband's kinsfolk.
  [1] That is to say, this is the view which governs both Epics. In the higher caſtes, at leaſt in the noble and the Brahmanic caſte, this was also what was demanded by the higher rule of conduċt at the time when the Epic was built up. Besides this it ſtill refleċts here and there other and probably older conditions, where in these circles also, or at leaſt among the Kshattriyas, a fresh marriage of the widow or of an outcaſt woman was the cuſtom. Thus it appears a matter of course for Damayantī to take another husband, when Nala has disappeared (iii, 70 f.). In this case they had been parted only three years in all (iii, 76.37, 51). The course of development here set forth is ſtill going on to-day : so soon as a caſte begins to rise in our day, it sees the firſt token of its rise in the marriage of widows being forbidden. Billington, p. 113 ff. ; Crooke, *The North-Weſtern Provinces of India*, 211 ; Fuller, *Studies*, etc., 162.
  The old law writings, which are, however, meant above all for the twice-born, that is, the three higher caſtes, likewise give quite another

SEXUAL LIFE IN ANCIENT INDIA

piↄure than the well-known mournful one. They can tell of quite
a number of cases where a fresh marriage of the woman already married
is allowed or ordained. If the husband has gone away on a journey,
and not come back, then the grass-widow according to Nārada, xii,
98 ff. muↄt firↄt wait—the Brahman woman with children eight years,
the childless one four, the Kshattriyā woman with children six years,
the childless one three, the Vaiçyā woman blessed with children four,
the childless one two ; for the Çūdrā woman no time is laid down.
Then the woman can marry any other man. On the other hand
Vasishtha, xvii, 78 ff. says emphatically that she muↄt be given only to
a member of the family, so long as there is one such. In him the time
of waiting is for the Brahman woman five and four years, according
as there are children or not, for the Kshattriyā woman five and three,
for the Vaiçyā woman four and two, for the Çūdrā woman three years
and one. See also MBh., iii, 71.6–7. If there is tidings of the traveller,
then the grass-widow muↄt let twice as long an interval go by. Manu,
ix, 76 says in general that she muↄt wait eight years if her husband
is gone abroad on holy works (dharmakāryārtham), six years, if for
the sake of knowledge or renown, and three, if it is on the hunt after
pleasure (kāmārtham, as several commentators say, on love adventures).
Gautama, xviii, 17 lays down for the second of these cases twelve
years ; as to the others he says nothing. Furthermore we are taught five
cases where the wife may marry without more ado : when the husband
is missing (nashta), or dead, or has become an ascetic, or is impotent,
or has loↄt his caↄte. Nārada, xii, 97 ; Parāçara, iv, 28 ; Agnipur.,
154.5–6 (= Garuḍapur., 107.29b–30a, and Nārada, xii, 97).
Parāçara, indeed, in what follows promises the widow the higheↄt
of rewards in the world beyond, if she leads a life of ↄtriↄteↄt chaↄtity,
or even lets herself be burnt with the body—certainly a late interpolation. If a spotless maid (nirdoshā) has been unwittingly wedded
to a man who is afflicↄed with a laↄting or hateful sickness (dīrgha-
kutsitarogārta), misshapen (vyaṅga), out of his mind, fallen from his
caↄte, homeless, persecuted by misery (or : repulsive, durbhaga), or
rejeↄted by his kinsfolk, then not only may she, but she muↄt leave
him, and choose another. Nārada, xii, 36–37 and 96 ; cp. 31. So
also Mahānirvāṇatantra, xi, 66 emphatically declares : She that has
been wedded to one that cannot beget shall be separated and married
again. For the field muↄt be given to him that has the seed. Nārada,
xii, 19. Cp. espec. Meyer, Kauṭilya, 244.18 ff. ; addit. 244.17–21 ;
254.18 ff., 45 ff. ; 254.3–17 ; addit. 254.3–17 ; also 296.16–297.4 ;
addit. 296.47 ; Agnipur., 227.15b–16a. Hence also Yājñav., i,
55 ordains that the bridegroom is to be examined carefully as to his
manhood before the wedding (yatnāt parīkshitaḥ puṃↄtve) ; and

408

Nārada, xii, 8–19 insists on the same thing, and gives highly interesting marks of the man fit for love's duties, and a still more interesting catalogue of impotent men together with methods for cure in the curable cases (among them the mukhebhaga, and the man that has his powers with other women, but not with his own wife). Cp. Kauṭilya, 305.11 f.; addit., 305.30; 296.16–297.4; addit., 296.47; Agnipur., 227.15b–16a. Nārada, xii, 61 also lays down : If a man lies with the willing wife of a man that has left his spotless (chaste, adushṭā) wife, or is impotent or consumptive, then that does not constitute adultery. If this passage is taken together with the others in this law work, then according to it it would seem that at least the forsaken wife may marry again. The right to her has evidently been lost altogether by the husband. According to Vishṇu, v, 163 the man who leaves his wife (patnīm parityajan) shall be punished like a thief. However, nirdoshāṃ is probably to be supplemented from the preceding Sūtra ; thus : " if she is free of worse failings and unchastity." Āpast., i, 10, 28.19, makes the demand : He who unjustifiably forsakes his wife shall put on an ass's skin with the hair outwards, and beg in seven houses with the words " Give alms to one that has left his wife ". Thus must he support himself six months long. Cp. Manu, viii, 389. Among the Ghasias in the United Provinces, where as among many other tribes the girl makes the marriage proposal, the wife can leave the husband and of course marry another, if he becomes mad, impotent, blind, or a leper, or if he has to do with other women ; while the husband has not the same right against the adulteress. Hartland, *Prim. Paternity*, ii, 40 (on like and still greater privileges of the woman, and the prejudiced position of the man particularly in his relations with the other sex cp. ii, 67, 106, 124–128 ; 154 f., also 72 ff., and especially 78–82 ; further ii, 5–7, and in reference to this Welhausen, *Gött. Nachrr.*, 1913, p. 465 ff.). Cp. also W. I. Thomas, *Sex and Society* (1907), p. 73 f.; 79. If the husband has been missing for nine years, the wife in Montenegro (Crnagora) may wed again (Krauss, *Sitte u. Brauch d. Südslawen*, 229 f.). And so for other cases.

As furthermore the booty belongs to the conqueror (Gautama, x, 20), and the woman is moreover especially called the rightful property of the victor (Manu, xii, 96 ; cp. Richter, v, 30), it does not astonish us when at least the bird king Kandhara weds the wife of the Rākshasa Vidyudrūpa, whom he has slain (Mārkaṇḍeyapur., ii, 28 ff.), and when Agnipur., 236.63 also utters the special reminder : The wives of conquered kings do not become the conqueror's, but he must protect them carefully. But a love affair with a widow brings down punishment, and according to Parāçara, x, 25 a widow who becomes with child by her lover must be banished from the land. Even to-day

Duryodhana declare : " I can just as little enjoy the earth whose precious stones are gone, and whose Kshattriya heroes are slain, as can a widowed woman " (ix, 31.45). A remarkable exception is here given us in the wife, who is drawn as very loving and as a pattern, of the ape prince Vālin. At first, when it is suggested to her that she must care for the dead prince's son, she cries out : " What to me is the son or the kingdom ? What to me is my own self ? I will follow on the footprints of the slain." But these are but the words of the first sorrow. She then bewails her widow's lot : " A woman robbed of her husband may have sons and be rich in money and corn, but a widow she is called by the wise." Most bitterly she wails by the body, will not let herself be parted or consoled, strives to wrench herself from the arms of those who are taking her away by force, and beseeches Rāma to kill her as well. " I will go to him, for without me he has no joy. Even in heaven without me he walks in sorrow and with a wan countenance, and has no wish to clasp the Apsarases. Think to thyself : ' She is his own self,' and so slay me ; it will be no woman-murder. According to the books of doctrine and the Vedas, the wife is one body with the husband ; compared with the gift of a wife there is in the view of the wise no other gift in the world." But Vālin is buried in the most magnificent way, and the new king Sugrīva, brother to the slain man, from whom Vālin has earlier taken away his own wife, makes the widow his wife, and loves her greatly. She seems to be most tenderly attached to her husband's murderer ; anyhow, she takes on herself a difficult mission for him. Her son, at least, is not

the celibacy of widows has not yet made its way everywhere. Crooke, *The North-Western Provinces*, 228 f., writes of this part of India : " Recent enquiries show that out of a population of 40,000,000 of Hindu, 9,000,000 or 24 per cent prohibit widow marriage, while 30,000,000 or 76 per cent both permit and even encourage the practice. . . . As a matter of fact, among all but the very highest castes, every young widow finds another mate, and the levirate, or custom by which the younger brother-in-law takes over the widow of his older brother, widely prevails." Cp. too Chavannes, *Cinq cents contes*, ii, 293 ff. (the wife of a man that has vanished weds again) ; Bulloram Mullick, *Home Life in Bengal*, p. 123.

pleased, indeed, with the new marriage, but he only blames the uncle, and this because he has taken for himself the wife of his elder brother, her who for him is the same as a mother—a standpoint which shows a nobler, and probably for the Aryan more natural feeling than the view we found in discussing polyandry in the Mahābhārata (Rām., iv, 19.10–25 ; 29.4 ; 31.22 ; 46.9 ; 33.38 ff. ; 55.3, 14).[1] That here also the wife of the dead foe falls as natural booty to the conqueror is on the other hand probably a reflection of the older conditions, and is not to be looked on as a kind of " apish custom ".

Touching is the plaint of the pious dove that has lost her husband in the heart-snaring tale edited by M. Haberlandt in his *Indische Legenden* : " ' I cannot remember thee ever doing me an unkindness, O beloved, and every widowed woman mourns, even though she have many sons. Pitiable to her kins-folk is the poor woman that has lost her husband. And I was ever fondled by thee, and honoured because of thy esteem. Amid sweet, tender, fresh-gushing, heart-delighting words I have taken my delight together with thee in the caves of the mountains, and by the waterfalls of the rivers, and on the pleasant tree-tops, and flying through the air I have found sweet joy with thee. Once I had my delight, O beloved ; that is no more. For what the father gives has bounds, so what the brother gives, so what the son gives—what woman then should not worship the giver of what knows no bounds, the husband ?[2] There is no stay like the husband ; there is no happiness like the husband. All money and goods the woman leaves behind her, and finds her refuge in her husband. Without thee, my treasure, there is nothing left for me in life. What good wife could live without her husband ? ' After this woman, weighed down by deep sorrow, had thus wailed piteously and long, faithful to her husband, she went into the flaming fire " (xii, 148.2 ff.). Yudhishthira calls out at the side of Duryodhana, who is wounded to death : " How can I again behold my

[1] Cp. Schmidt, *Liebe u. Ehe in Indien*, p. 358 f. Tārā according to MBh., iii, 280 was first Sugrīva's wife, and was taken by force by Vālin.

[2] This strophe, which is identical with Rām., ii, 39.30, I have already taken from that.

brothers' and my sons' widowed wives, reeling in sorrow, with sorrow overwhelmed ? For thee alone, O king, is it well ; for thee stands open in heaven a sure abode. We shall come to dreadful sorrow, that is to be called a hell ; and the sorely stricken wives of Dhritarāshtra's sons, and his grandsons' wives, those widowed, sorrow-harrowed women, will of a surety upbraid us " (ix, 59.29, 30). The dying Duryodhana himself first bewails his sister, that she has lost her husband and brothers (ix, 64.35, 36). Cp. xii, 1.16. The daughter of the Rākshasa, Kumbhīnasī, has been carried off by the Daitya Madhu, and her kinsman Rāvana sets out in anger to chastise the insolent one. At first he finds only the "sister", who, however, weepingly beseeches him : "Slay not, I pray, my husband. For for women of good birth there is here on earth no horror like this. Among all horrors widowhood is the greatest stroke of evil " (Rām., vii, 25.42 ff.). Cp. ix, 42.15 f. Therefore, too, Mahābh., i, 158. 22 declares : "The highest reward of women is to go, before the husband, to that most glorious abode in heaven for those gifted with sons ; thus do they know it, those with the knowledge of the holy law."

And yet widow-burning is really foreign to the Epic ; the cases which do happen to be found are rare exceptions, and undoubtedly belong, at least in far the greatest part, to later revisions. The Rāmāyana, tells of but one woman, a Brahman, that gives herself to be burnt in the flames along with her dead husband, and this in the regular way of satī (Rām., vii, 17.14). But the seventh book does not belong to the original poem, and this legend seems to be of especially late date. Now the Rāmāyana also would have had opportunity enough for widow-burnings. But the conclusion that, because they are not found in this Epic, it is older than the Mahābh. is quite without justification. That the original form of the Mahābhārata as an Epic is from an earlier time than the original form of the Rāmāyana is for me, at least, beyond any doubt. The whole spirit of the two poems, and many details, point even to a far greater age for the Mahābhārata. But this latter has had to suffer far more from revisions than has the poem of Rāma and Sītā, which from the very beginning was far more Brahmanic than the originally unpriestly, wholly warrior-like

The Widow

Mahābhārata poetry. Furthermore, the Mahābh. is also so much longer, and thus offers more room for widow-burnings. Finally, the difference of place between the two muſt not be left out of account either. Assertions that it is the duty and nature of a good wife to follow her lord in death can be found often enough in both poems, although, as is natural, oftener in the Mahābh., but they yield no proof, since they all might be referred to later revision. In isolated cases, or locally, moreover, such a death by self-sacrifice of the woman undoubtedly happened from early times in Aryan India, too, and the Kshattriyas in particular, the forefathers of the Rājputs, who are endowed with the ſtrongeſt feeling for private property in regard to their wives, may have known it.[1] Yet even the cases actually told of widow-burning in the Mahābh., where, furthermore, so many husbands meet death, and only very few

---

[1] A good example from Rājput hiſtory, which in many ways reminds us of the MBh., is given by Tod, *Rājaſthan*, ii, 102 ff. The glory of the satī, the meritoriousness of the widow's death, and the way in which she shall burn herself are described, e.g. in Garuḍapurāṇasārod., x, 35–55. On the other hand the Mahānirvāṇatantra moſt emphatically curses this "wife's faithfulness": every woman is a picture of the great goddess, and if a woman in her blindness climbs onto the dead lord's pyre, then she goes to hell (x, 79–80). Cp. herewith Zachariae, *Zſchr. d. Ver. f. Volksk.*, Bd. 14, p. 204, n. 2. A moſt excellent essay on Indian widow-burning has been given by this scholar in this same periodical Bd. 14, p. 198 ff.; 302 ff.; 395 ff.; Bd. 15, p. 74 ff. A kind of tale, though probably quite a modern one, of the origin of the cuſtom is given in *Anthropos*, ii, p. 277 ff. The roots of the cuſtom probably lie not only in the idea that the departed one muſt not go into the other world as a wifeless wretch, but also in the superſtitious fear of his vengeance, if this property of his is withheld from him, or even taken over by a successor in marriage. On this fear of ghoſts, which send his possessions after the dead man, cp. e.g. Schurtz, *Urgesch. d. Kultur*, 155 ff.; 221, 567; Crooke, *Anthropos*, iv, p. 469 ff.; *Zſchr. d. Ver. f. Volksk.*, Bd. 15, p. 232; Andree, *Ethnol. Parallel.*, i, 26–29; *Anthropos*, vii, 659; etc. Worthy of remark here is the explanation of the Mishmi in the border hills of Assam, that they give the dead man his things in the grave not because he needs them, but because they look on it as unseemly to enrich themselves with his property (*Zſchr. f. Ethnol.*, v, p. 193).

413

widows " die afterwards ",[1] do not all show the true satī (suttee). We have spoken of the contest between Pāṇḍu's two wives, how each wished to let herself be burned with the husband's body. But of this there is no trace in the account itself. Kuntī's offer to " follow " her husband is hardly the first outbreak even of womanly overwrought feelings, as, say, in Tārā, Vālin's wife, but sounds exactly as if all was happening only for the sake of the sad widow's good appearances. And Mādrī, who is in real earnest, has not the reasons for an Indian satī. She says : " I have not yet enjoyed love to the full. And in the midst of pleasure's union he went away from love in death.[2] How might I now cut off his longing in the abode of Yama ? " The warrior that falls by the weapon comes into paradise, where with heavenly companions in pleasure he gives himself up to the intoxication of the senses. On this Pāṇḍu, who was killed by the sexual union, has no claim, and therefore must starve in the other world. Yet even if this view should not come into the case, it is natural that Mādrī in this peculiar case, should see herself driven to take her step from the feeling of guilt (i, 125.23 ff.). That in itself this manifestation of wifely faithfulness by Mādrī is looked on as something unusual and peculiar is shown by the words addressed to his slayer by the penitent when he is pairing as a gazelle with his wife, and is so slain by Pāṇḍu : " The loved one with whom thou art lying at the time of thy death will follow after thee out of loving regard, when thou hast reached the city of the king of the dead, whereunto all cross only with reluctance " (i, 118.31, 32).[3] .

The only true case of satī is found in a very recent part, where the four wives of Vāsudeva : Devakī, Bhadrā, Rohiṇī, and Madirā mount onto the pyre with his dead body (xvi, 7.18, 24). On the other hand, Rukmiṇī, the well-beloved, Gāndhāri, Çaibyā, Haimavatī, and Jāmbavatī, five of

[1] So, e.g. the widows of Droṇa, Drupada, and the still so young Abhimanyu go on quietly living (ix, 23.37 ff. ; xi, 25.19 ; 20.23-28), to say nothing of others.

[2] Less likely : perished through love.

[3] Cp. in the treatment of the surata how the wife of the Brahman eaten by Kalmāshapāda follows him in death (i, 182), and what was said there about the self-burning of Mādrī (p. 233).

Kṛishṇa's wives, burn themselves, not with the soulless body of their lord, but only later on, after a very bad experience. Satyabhāmā and other highly-revered life-comrades of the Crœsus in wives go off, on the other hand, into the forest, and become penitents, just like the wives of Akrūra, whom likewise it is wished to hold back from doing so (xvi, 7.72 ff.).[1] As against this it is related in xviii, 5.25, 26 as follows : The 16,000 women, the wives of Vāsudeva, plunged at the proper time into the Sarasvatī. There they laid aside their bodies, and mounted up to heaven, and they became Apsarases, and went to Vāsudeva. A like anumaraṇa is also described in xv, 33.17 ff. : The miraculously strong Vyāsa makes the mourning wives of the heroes fallen in the battle—all that wish to do so—plunge into the Gaṅgā, and so come into the world of their husbands ; rid of the human body, shining in divine shape, decked with the adornment of heaven, freed from sorrow, and in joyful delight, they unite in the heavens with their beloved lords.

Already before this rising into heaven through the instrument of magic, Vyāsa bids all who are mourning for their dead, man or woman, to come to the Gaṅgā. Those taking part in the truly poetical spiritualist seance wait on the bank till nightfall. Then the mystagogue plunges into the water and calls up all the dead heroes from their various worlds. Through the divine penitential power of the holy man all those that were slain in the battle now rise up from the river exactly as they were in life, but glorified and surrounded with heavenly adornment

---

[1] It is instructive to find that it is only after Pāṇḍu's death, when Vyāsa so orders her, and tells her what dreadful times are coming that Satyavatī with her widowed daughters-in-law, and therefore as one far stricken in years with these no longer young women, goes off into the penitential wilderness (i, 128, 1–13) ; and that Kuntī, too, only takes this step with Dhṛitarāshṭra and Gāndhārī at an advanced age. Yudhishṭhira and Bhīma try as best they can to persuade her not to go, all her sons follow her with tears in their eyes, and her daughters-in-law Draupadī and Subhadrā go a stretch of the way with her, weeping and in despair, but she will not let herself be held back, but means by humble service to her " parents-in-law " and asceticism to earn her entry into the world of her husband (xvi, 16, 17).

and heavenly following, especially the bands of Apsarases, and the whole night long a blissful reunion is celebrated. All grudges of former days are forgotten. Parents and children, brothers and sisters, and other kinsfolk clasp one another. " United to their fathers, brothers, husbands, and sons, the women felt the utmost joy, and left sorrow behind. After the heroes and their wives had taken their delight for the one night, they bade one another farewell, clasped one another, and each went off again whence he or she had come " (xv, 31.19 ff.).

Of real intercourse with the dead husband, and children thus begotten, we are told in a " tale from days of yore " (paurāṇī kathā) [1] : " There was once a king, renowned under the name of Vyushitāçva, most rich in virtue, a successor to the blood of Pūru. When this man of virtuous soul, the strong armed one, sacrificed, then came thither the gods together with Indra, and the godlike Ṛishis. Indra became drunk with the soma, and the Brahmans from the wages of sacrifice at Vyushitāçva's sacrifice, the high-minded royal Ṛishi's. The gods and the Brahman Ṛishis carried out the sacrificial rite at that very place. Hence Vyushitāçva shone upon mortal men as the glowing son shines on all beings at the time when winter is over. This best of princes overcame the kings in the east and the north, in the west and in the south, took them captive, and led them forth with him to the great sacrifice, to the horse-sacrifice, Vyushitāçva the splendid. For this king was gifted with the strength of ten snake spirits . . . A daughter of Kakshīvant was his wife, held by him in high honour, Bhadrā by name, peerless on earth for her beauty. And the two loved one another. So it is told. Wholly overcome through his love for her, he was taken by consumption. In a short while as the result of this he went to his home like the sun. When this ruler of men was dead, his deeply saddened, childless wife broke out in a moaning (so we have heard), Bhadrā, she that was tortured by bitterest sorrow (Hear this, O high herdsman of men) : ' Any wife

---

[1] Formalized expressions of the old bardic poetry often appear in it, and in other ways also it bears the stamp of an independent and older tale, but one later given a somewhat Brahmanic colouring. It is seen to be also a tale of the origin of the Çālvas and Madras.

robbed of her husband, O knower of the highest law, that lives without her husband, she does not truly live, the sorrow-burdened one. Death is better for a wife without her husband, O warrior hero. I will go whither thou art ; be gracious to me, and lead me thither. Parted from thee, I cannot even live an instant. Show me favour, O king ; take me quickly hence. On smooth paths, and on rough I will follow after, O tiger king, that goest but comest not again. Following thee like thy shadow, O king, ever subject to thee, I shall everlastingly find my delight in thy welfare, O tiger among men. Henceforward, O king, pitiable, heart-withering agonies of soul will come upon me, that am without thee, thou lotus-eyed one. It must be that I, a wretched one, have (in an earlier existence) sundered some that were mated ; therefore it is that this parting from thee has befallen me. But even if a woman, parted from her husband, live but a moment only, yet this wicked one can hardly be said to live at all, like one that is in hell, O ruler of the earth. I have in a former body torn asunder those that were intimately bound together ; hence, O king, has this sorrow taken me in its grasp, springing from my separation from thee, and heaped up in earlier bodies through evil deeds. From now on, O king, I shall lie on a bed of kuça-grass, bathed in sorrow, filled only with the yearning to see thee again. Show thyself to me, O tiger among men, counsel me, who have ever an aching heart within me, wretched and piteously mourning thee, O ruler of men.' As she thus in manifold words kept ever bewailing, and clasped the dead man, the voice of one hidden [1] spoke :—

> ' Arise, thou good one, go from here ;
> I grant thee a favour :
> I will beget unto us a group of children
> With thee, thou lovely one with smiling lips.
>
> Thou woman with the glory of high hips,
> Sleep thou on the moon's fourteenth night,
> Also the eighth, cleansed in the bath,[2]
> On thy bed with me united.'

[1] Literally : a hidden voice.
[2] Literally : having bathed after the monthly cleansing.

Thus addressed, the queen so did, she the faithful wife; exactly as the words did tell her, did Bhadrā, yearning after children. The queen bore three Çālvas and four Madras as sons by the dead man " (i, 121.7 ff.).[1]

[1] That the dead husband or wife can come back and have sexual intercourse with the surviving wife or husband, and even beget or bear children is a belief found elsewhere, too. Ploss-Bartels, ii, 589 ff.; Kirchhof, *Wendunmuth*, ed. Oesterley, iii, 515 ff.; Jülg, *Die Märchen d. Siddhi-kûr*, Leipz., 1866, 9th tale; Crooke, *Pop. Rel.*, etc., i, 118; *Zschr. d. Ver. f. Volksk.*, ii, p. 299 (Herod and the dead Mariamne); viii, p. 335 (South Russian vampire); x, p. 124 (Icelandic); xiv, p. 322 f.; Krauss, *Slav. Volkforsch.*, 130, 135; Elsie Clews Parsons, *The Old-Fashioned Woman*, p. 110 f.; Goethe's *Braut von Korinth*; Helgi's return in the Edda; etc. It is here that the many vampire and Leonora tales belong. Much literature will be also found, at several of the places quoted in Krauss, as to the man who cannot part from his lifeless wife (a few Indian examples in J. J. Meyer, *Hindu Tales*, p. 77; see also Chavannes, *Cinq cents contes*, ii, 221 f.). Best known of all is the commerce with the dead woman magically kept from decay after the example of Charlemagne. Hagen's *Gesamtabenteuer*, ii, p. 631 ff., iii, p. clxii f.; Weinhold, *Die deutschen Frauen i. d. Mittelalter*, ii, p. 8. This view must be particularly kind for Albanian women. There, when a woman after years of widowhood bears a child, we are told: " Her dead husband is a vampire and has visited her by night." *Zeitschr. f. Ethnol.*, " Abhandl." Bd. 26, p. 561. There is an interesting case in the Paramatthadīpanī, iii, p. 144 ff.: A vimānapeta induces the bride whom he has left by death to give a Buddhist begging monk a ball of thread; through this pious deed it becomes possible for her to taste divine pleasures. He fetches her in his heavenly chariot (vimāna); for seven hundred years, which to her seem seven, she is with him. When she leaves him the blooming wife becomes an old woman. By these last features this peculiar Indian Leonora belongs also to other cycles of tales, especially to that immensely extensive one which is best known to us by such tales as Wolfgang Müller's *Mönch von Heisterbach*, or Irving's *Rip Van Winkle*, and of which Hartland, *The Science of Fairy Tales*, (under "The Supernatural Lapse of Time in Fairy Land", pp. 166–195) gives a good, though of course highly incomplete survey. [From Melanesia for the case of marriage between a living man and a ghost woman cp. G. C. Wheeler, *Mono-Alu Folklore*, pp. 55–6, 188 (Translator).]

XVI

Woman in Misfortune and in Sorrow

A S on the widow, so the Epic, often too, beſtows beautiful and heartfelt words on the woman in sorrow, and eloquently paints the misery of her that is filled with suffering. Only one or two of these many passages will be mentioned. Bitter sorrow is laid on Draupadī when Arjuna muſt go off for a long time, and she calls down on him the favour of all beings and gods (iii, 37.24 ff.). Deeply moving is Kuntī's farewell to her sons and daughter-in-law. Through Yudhishthira's foolishness they have loſt all, and muſt wander into misery for thirteen years. In burning sorrow Draupadī clasps her woman-friends, loud cries of woe are heard in the women's house. Kuntī can hardly speak for sorrow, and says to Draupadī : " To thee, my child, I need give no counsel ; thou good and perfeƈt one, thou art an ornament to thy father's house, and thy husband's, and no sorrow can befall faithful wives. Walk thou paths of happiness, ſtrengthened by the thought of me." She sees her sons ſtanding there, who lower their faces for shame, are surrounded by gloating foes and weeping friends, and have been robbed of all their ornaments, and their good garments ; and she bewails the weary lot that lies before the banished in the wilds of the foreſt, and the injuſtice of the fate that groundlessly persecutes such glorious, such pious men, and she calls Pāṇḍu and Mādrī blessed, in that they are no longer left on earth to experience these awful things. After the laſt embrace they go forth, Draupadī in her only, dirty garment ; and the mother senseless with sorrow is led into her house by the arm of a loving kinsman (ii, 79). Cp. e.g. v, 90.

How can the descriptive powers of the poet, indeed, find scope in the crowded deaths of the great song of the bloody national ſtruggle between the Kauravas and the Pāṇḍavas ! The moſt dreadful scenes come before us there on the field after the battle ; terrible there is the sight of the dead heroes ;

419

gruesome the ways of the beasts devouring the dead bodies ; heart-rending the grief and the tender love that breaks forth from wife and mother. Vast pictures of terror in which whole hosts appear, and pictures where individual grief vents itself to the full are set before us. A whole book of the Mahābhārata, the Strīparvan, " the section of the women," is mainly given up to this theme. " Women can only seldom act with you, but to suffer with you they are always there." And elsewhere, too, in the course of the narrative the poem dilates on such episodes. We may mention above all the dreadful torment of Gāndhārī, to whom Vyāsa grants supernatural powers of sight, and who now looks out over the whole battlefield, and describes it (xi, 16 ff.) ; then Subhadrā's and Uttarā's lament for Abhimanyu, cut off in tender years (vii, 78 ; xi, 20 ; xiv, 61.24 ff.) ; lastly the descriptions in iii, 172.21–25 ; 173.61–64 (these two passages are particularly impressive) ; xi, 10.7 ff. ; 16.48, 55 ; 17.30 ; 29.68 f. ; xv, 15.35 ff. ; xvi, 7.15 ff. To dwell on details would take us too far. And much that is conventional often slips in, too. On the other hand, this utterance is worthy of remark : " The sorrow to which men give themselves up all too much in their heart, arouses burning grief in the forbears that have gone before " (xiv, 2.2).[1]

---

[1] This reminds us of the beautiful verses from Kālidāsa's Raghuvaṃça which are to be found in the poem of Aja and Indumatī, one of the very finest in Oriental literature, and which are spoken by the Guru to Aja bewailing his dead, deeply beloved wife :—

> Now bestow on the sorrow for thy wife an end.
> And grant her the grace of the death-gift ;
> For the hot tears that are shed by a loved one,
> They do scorch the dead, if they for ever flow.

Cp. Nītivākyāmrita, 103.7–8.

This idea is perhaps best known to us from Chamisso's poem, where the dead child comes to the weeping mother, and amid other things reminds her as follows :—

> I feel thy tears flow
> To me without a stop ;
> My little shift and linen,
> They are therewith so wet.

WOMAN IN MISFORTUNE

So, too, in Hoffmann von Fallersleben " the dead child " utters the prayer :—

> O mother dear, do stop !
> Why weepeſt thou ever ?
> The tears come through my grave,
> My clothes do not get dry.

And so in Otto Haendler's " Totenhemdchen " :—

> Ah, mother dear, now weepeſt thou,
> And in the grave I have no reſt ;
> It all is flooded o'er with tears,
> And my shroud grows never dry.

(In the colleƈtion of poems *Herbſt*.)

Cp. Weinhold, *Die deutschen Frauen*, i, 242 ; Lüders, " Die Jātakas u. d. Epik," ZDMG, 58, p. 706 f. ; Ralſton, *Songs of the Russian People*, p. 316 ; Fr. S. Krauss, *Slav. Folkforsch.*, p. 113 ; F. v. d. Leyen, " Entſtehung d. Märchens," *Herrigs Archiv*, Bd. 114, p. 12, and the references there ; " Den heiligen Petrus u. d. trauernde Mutter " in the splendid *Sagen u. Märchen d. Südslawen* of Fr. S. Krauss, 1884, Bd. ii, 307 ff. ; *Zschr. d. Ver. f. Volksk.*, Bd. 3, p. 151 ; Caland, *Toten- u. Beſtattungsgebr.*, p. 74. Often found in India is the belief beſt expressed in Yājñavalkya, iii, 11 (= Garuḍapur., Pretakalpa, 4.80b–81a ; xv, 58) : " Since the poor dead one has to drink the tears shed by his kinsfolk together with the mucus, we muſt not weep ; we muſt, so far as we can, carry out the works that fall to our duty." By this are meant, anyhow in the firſt place, the death rites that are helpful to the welfare of the dead one. But a further thought that finds expression in the burial-songs of the Veda —those that are ſtill alive belong to life with its business and its joy— may also be found here. The same saying is found again, e.g. in Garuḍapurāṇasārod., xi, 4, only that here the laſt pāda is altered to say that all grieving is useless after all, a view ſtressed in India countless times on such occasions. Weeping for those snatched away is over and over again forbidden in the law writings, especially at the celebration of the death rites. Whoever in spite of this gives way to this weakness muſt cleanse himself by bathing. Vishṇu, xxii, 61 f. ; Parāçara, xii, 28. The basis here again is a superſtition direƈted towards the precious self : tears along with seed, sweat, nail-cuttings, etc., belong to the " unclean ", that is, magically baneful produƈts of the human body, which leave one accessible to the evil powers. Manu, v, 135 ; Vishṇu, xxii, 81 ; xxiii, 1. They are calamitous (açiva MBh., iii, 28.18), and an evil omen (Rāvaṇavaha, xi, 124 ; xv, 43), a conception also found in Germanic lands and among the

In the Rāmāyaṇa it is naturally above all the luckless heroine
Sītā herself in whose mouth the poet puts affectingly beautiful
words of grief. Worthy of especial mention, perhaps, is her
sorrow, when Rāma has at length come to set her free, and she,
as the result of a magical trick played on her, believes that
Rāma is dead, and has to conclude that he has been murdered
in his sleep. "Why doſt thou not look at me, O king?
Why doſt thou not answer me, whom thou, the childishly
youthful one, didſt win as a childishly youthful wife, as a life-
comrade? Think of what thou didſt promise, when thou
didſt clasp my hand : 'Now will I live my life with thee,'
and take me away, who am ſtricken by sorrow. Up, Rāvaṇa !
Kill me, too, swiftly, the wife together with the husband ;
by this win for thyself the higheſt virtuous merit, and for me
the greateſt happiness." And her saying may here be given :
" It is said, if the husband dies firſt, then it comes about that
the wife has no worth [1] : and it is before me who lead a good
life that thou art gone hence, who didſt walk the path of
excellence " (Rām., vi, 32.9). It is worthy of remark that she
so often thinks of her mother-in-law : " I pity neither Rāma
nor Lakshmaṇa, the great chariot-fighter, nor myself so much
as my poor mother-in-law. For she ponders ever : When

Mohammedans, the Mandæans, the old Greeks and Romans, and
elsewhere, and a conception which probably is the firſt root of the
cuſtom of wrapping or covering the face when weeping, which, indeed,
is also done in the Epic (ix, 63.68 f. ; xi, 15.34 f. ; etc.). Sorrow itself
(çoka) is magical uncleanness (açauca), but joy and an uplifted soul
are magically salutary (çauca) (MBh., K, vii, 71.20). Food onto which
a tear has fallen is nourishment for the ghoſtly beings (ix, 43.26 f. ;
Manu, iii, 230). And so on. As a counterpart the fine Buddhiſt
saying may here be quoted : " What is united muſt divide ; we are
indeed pilgrims. Mourn not for that which is vanished ; love all
that is ſtill here " (Jātaka, Bd. iii, 95).

[1] As is well known the widow ſtill has to hear this to-day among
the Indians, as also among many other peoples and tribes. The
natural reading of the words of the text would be : " The wife's
firſt death, it is said, is the incapacity of the husband ; thou, who
didſt live gloriously art gone hence before me, who, too, lead a good
life." This meaning, however, does not fit in well, and close con-
ſtructions are not seldom found in the two Epics.

after the fulfilment of their vow shall I once more see Sītā
and Lakshmaṇa and Rāma ? But I believe that Kauçalyā's
heart will spring asunder, when she, that has but one son, learns
that he has perished in the fight. For, weeping, she will
call to mind the birth and the childhood and the youthful
years, the good deeds, and the beauty of the lofty-minded one.
When she has made the death-offerings for her slain son,
hopeless, robbed of her senses, she will assuredly go into the
fire or into the water " (see Rām., vi, 32, 48 ; 92.44–46).

Among the finest passages in the Rāmāyaṇa is perhaps the
extract where Rāma tells Sītā that he is going off into the forest
for fourteen years. He wishes to take leave of her, and gives
her counsel as to her behaviour during his long absence. But
with angered love she cries out : " What art thou saying
there ? The father and the mother, the brother and the son,
each has his own destiny : the wife's destiny in this world
and the other is the husband only. If thou goest into the
forest, I shall walk before thee, and trample down thorns
and sharp grasses before thy feet. As in my father's house,
I shall live along with thee in the forest, and shall think of
nothing in the three worlds but of my duty towards thee.
How fair will it be in the forest together with thee ! I have
long been yearning for its mountains, lakes, and lotus-ponds.
With thee so will I live a hundred thousand years in utmost
joy, and I shall not mark their flight. Thou alone art my
love, to thee alone does my heart cling ; sundered from thee,
I am resolved to die. Take me with thee ; I shall be unto
thee no burden." Rāma unfolds before her all the horrors,
hardships, and torments of life in the forest. But she answers :
" The wild beasts will run off when they but see thee. I
have long known of the forest life from the tales of a nun that
came on a visit to my mother. I am burning with longing to
go off to the penitential settlement, and to serve thee, the hero.
Through my love for thee I shall be freed from sin, following
my husband, for he is the highest godhead ; to him belongs
the wife in death also. Take me, her that is truly devoted
to thee, deeply sorrowing, a faithful wife, take me with thee
into the forest. If thou do not, then shall I seek refuge
in poison, in fire, or in water." Bathing the earth with her

tears, she sinks to the ground ; anger comes upon her, and
Rāma mu&t soothe her. She beseeches him once more :
" Go not into the fore&t without me ! The pains of penance,
the fore&t wilds, or heaven—all but with thee ! I shall not
weary, if I walk behind thee. The sharp grasses and thorns
on the way will be to me as soft cotton, the du&t &tirred up
by the &tormy wind as precious sandal-powder. When I am
lying then on the fore&t turf, even a bed spread with hand-
some&t rugs cannot be more blissful. Reach me the smalle&t
root or fruit which thou ha&t brought me thyself, and it will
be sweet to me as the food of the gods. I shall no longer
remember father, mother, or home. Where thou art, there
is heaven ; without thee it is hell. If I am forsaken by thee,
O thou my treasure, then it is better I die. Not a moment
can I bear this sorrow, how much less for fourteen years."
Loud and piteously she cries out, and twines her arms fa&t
round her beloved. Then he embraces her, utters consoling,
tender words, and tells her she can go with him : " At the
price of thy sorrow, O queen, I would not buy heaven itself.
It was only that I did not know thou wa&t so firmly resolved.
Follow me and be my life-companion in the fulfilling of duty. A
fair deed ha&t thou done, and worthy of my house and of
thine. Make thyself ready for the journey. Now were
heaven itself nothing to me without thee." And filled with
joy Sītā be&tows her ornaments, her clothing, all the beautiful
and loved things she possesses on servants and the needy,
and goes off with Rāma into the fore&t (Rām., ii, 26.8–30).[1]

Very pleasing there, too, are chapters v, 15–43, which
tell of Sītā held captive by Rāvaṇa, her ill-treatment by the
mon&ters, her heroic endurance of all sufferings, her proud
reje&tion of the enamoured prince of Laṅkā, her conversation
with Hanumant, Rāma's envoy, and of her unwavering love
for her husband. The poet here has poured forth a whole
wealth of poetry of Indian hue, without, however, reaching
that effe&t on our feelings which belongs to the simple loftiness
found in the se&tion just discussed of the second Book. The
Hindu may think otherwise. Hanumant finds the captive
in the glorious açoka-grove of Rāvaṇa. On her, indeed,

[1] With Sītā's words cp. especially those of the " Nut-browne
Maide " in the celebrated English ballad of about 1500.

all the splendour is lost : she is sunk in a sea of sorrow in the midst of the loathsome man-eating monsters. In the night comes the ruler of this hostile world, surrounded by his bands of wives, and the splendour of his court. She is not completely dressed. "When the princess of Videha saw Rāvaṇa, the prince of the Rākshasas, she trembled like a banana-tree in the wind. With the thighs did the great-eyed lovely one cover her belly, and with the arms her breasts, and crouched down on the bare earth. To the tiger among kings, to Rāma, she was hastening on the chariot of her wishes harnessed to her thoughts. With one long braid of hair she stood out easily, like the earth when the rainy time is over stands out with a dark belt of forest." Rāvaṇa in eloquent words offers her all his splendour, the position of chief wife, and his glowing love ; she is not to let her precious youth thus go by in misery. What does she want then with the strengthless penitent Rāma, who after all is dead and gone ? But she lays grass between herself and the polluting stranger, and upbraids him for his unseemly words. Great misfortune, she tells him, comes on all that lust after the wives of others. Rāma will come, she says, and destroy Lankā, slay them that carried her off, and set her free. Before him will Rāvaṇa as little be able to stand his ground, as the dog before the tiger. But he threatens her : " I give thee another two months, then either thou comest onto my bed, or my cooks will cut thee up into pieces for my breakfast." The divine and Gandharva maidens that have been carried off by the woman-lover hearten Sītā by gestures with lips and eyes, and now she flings angry, confident words at him. He goes off, filled with rage, and bids the giantesses make her compliant by friendly means or by chastisement. The Rākshasī women now beset her ; bathing her broad breasts with tears, quivering like a gazelle lost from the herd, or torn by wolves, but firm and strong, she proclaims her will to be faithful to her husband, as Çacī to Indra, as Lopamudrā to Agastya, as Rohiṇī to the moon, as Sāvitrī to Satyavant. " Cut me up, tear me to pieces, make shreds of me, burn me in the glowing fire—I will not come to Rāvaṇa. Why will ye speak so long ? " She cannot understand wherefore Rāma does not come and set her free. Perhaps he does not know where she is. Perhaps his foes have murdered him in his sleep. Or is it that he loves her no longer ? But of a certainty her wish will be fulfilled : " Rāvaṇa, the evil ruler of the Rākshasas will be slain, and the island so hard to win will wither away like a widowed woman." She ends thus :

> " My heart, robbed of happiness, with much sorrow
> Overwhelmed, is of a truth unyielding ſtaunch,
> That it splinters not in a thousand pieces,
> Like some mountain-ridge ſtruck by a thunderbolt."

Hanumant, who, up till now hidden in a tree, has been a witness to all, discovers himself to her, and gives news of Rāma, and how he is on his way to rescue her. At firſt she is filled with fear, will not believe the messenger, and holds him for a phantom shape of Rāvaṇa ; he calms and convinces her, and tells her of Rāma's sorrow and love. Then she believes, falls into joy beyond words, and sheds tears of bliss. But now she has many queſtions to put to him : how it is with Rāma and his brother, whether her loved one is not sad, does not torment himself, or whether he has loſt his love for her, he who for her sake has gone through so much suffering, whether he no longer thinks of her, and has no wish at all to set her free. Hanumant assures her : " No sleep comes to Rāma, and if he once goes really to sleep, then he wakes up again with the word : ' Sītā ! ' If he sees a fruit or a flower or aught else that delights the heart of women, then he sighs long and says : ' Woe is me, Sītā ! ' " (cp. ii, 55.26 ff.). She makes answer : " Nectar mingled with poison are thy words—Rāma thinks of no other, and he is overwhelmed with care." Hanumant wants to carry her on his back at once to Rāma, and persuades her that he is ſtrong enough. But she finds this to be dangerous for herself and him, and through this Rāma's honour would suffer ; he muſt overcome the evil-doer in battle, and bring her home ; this alone, she said, is worthy of him (39.29–30 ; cp. MBh., iii, 150.18 ff.) ; and she will and may touch no man's body but her husband's. Over and over again she charges the messenger that Rāma muſt set her free in a month ; longer she cannot live. As credential she gives him a precious ſtone that Rāma had beſtowed on her, the sight of which has consoled her up till now in her wretchedness, juſt as though she had seen the beloved giver himself.

XVII

THE IDEAL WOMAN

SĪTĀ is wholly the Indian ideal of a woman : tender and mild, soft and dreamy as moonlight, self-forgetting, filled with love, devotion, sincerity, faithfulness, and yet, where it is a case of defending womanly virtue, nobility of soul, and purity of body, a ſtrong heroine, great above all in long-suffering, but great, too, in her unyielding, daring pride.

And what a tender soul and ſtout heart together is shown, too, by Gāndhārī ! This princess is promised by her kinsfolk to the blind Dhṛitarāshṭra. She hears of it, and herself ties a cloth about her eyes : " I will let no dislike towards my husband rise up in me " (i, 110.9 ff.).[1] A wonderful fineness of feeling and ſtrength of soul is shown by the pearl of all Indian women, Sāvitrī. At her father's bidding she goes forth, filled with shame, to choose herself a husband ; the dreadful fate that lies before her she locks in her heart without a word ; tender and noble, and yet with a hero's ſtrength, she carries everything to a happy ending (iii, 293 ff.).

The Indian paragon of a woman, whose features have often emerged in the course of our treatment, is summed up also in Mahābh., xiii, 123 : " To the all-knowing, wise Çāṇḍilī, fathoming all truth, the Kaikeyī, Sumanā by name, put this queſtion in the heaven of the gods : ' Through what way of life and through what aćtions haſt thou shaken off all sin, and come into the heaven of the gods ? Thou shineſt in thine own brightness like a tongue of fire, like the daughter of the ruler of the ſtars, her whose footprints have left brightness in the sky. Clad in duſtless garments, free from weariness, ſtanding in a heavenly chariot, thou shineſt, glorious a thousandfold in

[1] An ugly knight has a beautiful wife who loves him greatly. He loses an eye in the liſts, and now does not wish to go back again to her thus ; she puts out one of her own eyes, too, that he need not be ashamed before her. Hagen's *Gesamtabenteuer*, i, 249 ff.

power. It is not through moderate asceticism, open-handedness, or piety that thou art come into this world. Say unto me the truth.' Thus put to the question by Sumanā, the sweet-smiling Çāṇḍilī calmly spoke these friendly words to her : ' Not because I had been wrapped in the yellow-red garment, nor because I had worn bast garb, nor because I had walked with bald head, nor because I had had penitent's tresses did I come unto an existence of the gods. Never did I speak evil and rough words to my husband, nor forgot my duty to him. I was ever watchful and eager in the worship of the gods, the forefathers, and the Brahmans, and treated my mother-in-law and father-in-law well. I uttered not calumny against others, nor did it come into my soul ; I stood not where there was no door, nor told long tales.[1] I gave myself up in no wise to unkind laughter of any kind, nor to hurtfulness in deeds, whether secretly or openly. If my husband had been out on business, and now came back home, I put a seat for him, and waited on him attentively. If he did not approve of some food, or did not like a dish, whether it was something to eat or to drink, then I avoided all such. If in the house-

---

[1] It strikes one as a little strange that Indian literature, which scourges woman's failings so heavily, does not pillory her talkativeness more. In this the Hindu is perhaps far surpassed by other peoples. Is it that the woman in India gives less ground on this point ? Worthy of note, too, because of the chance coincidence, is the explanation here of why no beard grows on women. The Finnish poet of the peasantry, Jaakko Räikkönen, who was also more than ordinarily capable in the affairs of life, in his poem Tyytymättömät (printed in the Wäinölä Collection, p. 229) expresses exactly the same thought as the English verse which Thiselton-Dyer, *Folk-Lore of Women*, p. 68, brii. from the neighbourhood of Salisbury :—

> " Nature, regardless of the babbling race,
> Planted no beard upon a woman's face ;
> Not Freddy Keen's razor, though the very best,
> Could shave a chin that never is at rest."

Why the woman's tongue is always wagging is explained by the merry tale of the creation of the dog's tail, which Hans Sachs has also taken as his theme. Krauss, *Sitte u. Brauch*, p. 184 ; *Zschr. d. Ver. f. Volksk.*, Bd. 11, p. 255 f. ; Bd. 18, p. 224.

hold any duties had piled themselves up,[1] then I rose early and had everything carried out, or did it myself. When my husband went away on any business, then I practised many luck-bringing things with the utmost care. When my husband was away, I gave up black eye-salve, orpiment, bathing, wreaths, ointments for the body, and ornaments. I never awoke my husband, when he was quietly sleeping, even if there was business calling [2] ; in this my heart grew joyful. I never wearied my husband with household matters ; I always kept that secret which should be hidden, and the house was fair and clean. If a woman thus keeps the path of virtue carefully before her eyes, she is raised high in the world of heaven, as Arundhatī among women.' "[3] The same teaching is found in xiii, 146.33 ff. : The woman's law and virtue, which are laid on her before the fire, and which make of her a sahadharmacarī, " the man's life-comrade in the fulfilling of the holy duties," are among other things : a friendly mind, friendly speech, a friendly eye, to think of none but the husband, to look on his face as on the son's. " The woman that shows her husband a bright and friendly countenance, when he addresses her with harsh words or gives her angry looks, she is a faithful wife. The woman who waits on her poor, suffering, sorrowful, way-worn husband as on a son, is one gifted with virtue. The woman who, filled with deep heedfulness, busily astir, and skilled, with the blessing of sons, is dear to her husband, has her life in her husband, is one gifted with virtue." Further, she must rise early, see to the service of the holy fire, make the flower-gifts to the gods, make the house clean, spread the cow-dung, give food to Brahmans, the weak, the helpless, the forlorn, the poor, carry out vows of mortification,

---

[1] Or : come to a standstill (samānīta).

[2] Āntareshv api kāryeshu. Perhaps rather : " when matters of business referring to his very near neighbourhood (or : touching him very near) came." Cp. Ābhyantara in my Kauṭilya.

[3] The name Sumanā first of all, then the language and the matter, lead us to think of a Buddhistic origin for this legend. Cp. v, 113 ; x, 54.6 ff.

and so forth. " This is holiness, this is asceticism, this is everlasting heaven, when a woman sees her highest good in her husband, is devoted to her husband with a religious zeal, and is good and chaste. For the husband is the woman's god, the husband is her kinsman, the husband is her refuge, the husband's regard is her heaven." [1]

Beauty of soul and of body go hand in hand ; where the one is, there is the other, too : Yatrākritis tatra gunā iti loke pi gīyate, says Hemacandra in Pariçishtap., ii, 233 (cp. Brihatsamh., 70.23 ; Garudapur., 65.121 ; Agnipur., 244.6) ; and in the Uttararāmacaritam (iii, 21) we find the exclamation : Bhidyate vā sadvrittam īdriçasya nirmānasya ! (cp. my Daçakumārac., p. 301, where many more illustrations from popular sayings, poetry, and even the philosophical literature of the world could be given). Here we will make only a few particular remarks as to the Indian ideal of womanly beauty, which is fairly generally known. Much is to be gathered already from the descriptions of the various heroines of whom we have already spoken. Draupadī has black curling hair, long eyes like the leaf of the autumn lotus, a scent like the autumn lotus ; her face is like the lotus-flower, like the jasmine-flower, when it is covered with sweat ; slender is her waist, her hair is long, her mouth is red. She is neither too tall nor too short ; she has beautiful hips ; she is not thin, not too red, and not too hairy (ii, 65.33 ff.; cp. 67.157 ff.). At the sacrifice she comes forth from the middle of the altar as a wondrous-lovely maid : dark, with black and long eyes, red, high-arched nails, beautiful brows, lovely swelling breasts, and so forth ; a scent as of the blue lotus is wafted from her a kroça's distance (i, 167.44 ff. ; cp. 168.6 ; 183.7–10).[2] She is of course without compare on earth for beauty, like a maiden of the gods, like a wonderful apparition ; whoever sees her folds his hands reverently before his forehead ; and more of the same kind. Even as she goes along as a poor chambermaid wearing dirty clothes, men and women run up to where she is seen. Queen Sudeshnā sees her from her palace, and, wondering greatly, describes her

---

[1] Cp. e.g. Vishnu, xxv, Solomon's Proverbs, 31.10 ff.

[2] This far-wafted wondrous scent of Draupadī, already known to us from Satyavatī, is often referred to (so, e.g. i, 197.36 ; 183.10).

beauty in these words among others: " Her ankles do not stand out (but are imbedded in the flesh, a thing which in the Epic is often mentioned of the fair), and her thighs are firm and hard. Three things in her are deep (voice, understanding, and navel), six high-arched (nose, eyes, ears, nails, breasts, the joint of the neck), five red (the palms of the hands, and soles of the feet, the corners of the eyes, the tongue, the nails) ; she speaks unclearly as the swan, her brows and eyes are round-arched, red as the bimba-fruit are her lips, her neck is like shell, her veins are hidden, her face is like the full moon, and so on. Glorious she is as a mare from Kashmir." Still more glowingly does Sudeshṇā express herself in K.: "For the man thou lookest on there is no more weakness, no more pain, no more weariness, no discomfiture, no sorrow, and no torment. Sickness and old age, hunger and thirst, for him are done with to whom thou givest thyself in love. Were such a one even dead, and didst thou clasp him with thy lovely arms, then would he come back again to life (iv, 14.61 ff.)." Even the women gaze only at her ; the trees seem to stand bowing before her ; no man can see her without being held by love (iv, 9). So that it is no wonder if Kīcaka says to her : " Who in the whole world must not fall under the sway of love, when he beholds the glorious moon of thy countenance, endowed with peerless splendour, along with the moonbeams of the smile in thine eyes and lashes,[1] and decked with heaven's beams, ravishing by its heavenly sweetness ? Thy two so glorious breasts, fit for a string of pearls, these well-shaped, splendid, plump, rounded breasts, set close to one another with no gap between, like unto lotus-buds, O thou with the lovely brows, thou with the sweet smile, goad me like the love god's own goads. So soon as I see that waist of thine, sweetly ringed by folds, bent by the breast's weight, and within the compass of the fingers, O thou slim one, and thy lovely secret parts, rising

---

[1] Sounds somewhat strange. Is perhaps īkshaṇalakshmāṇāṃ " having the eyes as moon-spots ", one of the many Prakrit forms in the Epic, to be read ? The text means literally : " in its smile (through its smile) like unto moonshine." A somewhat smoother reading would be smitaṃ. In the following half-çloka vṛitaṃ instead of vṛittaṃ is probably right, though " round, with heavenly beams " would also do.

like a river-island, I am carried away by a love-sickness beyond cure. Quench thou, O lovely-hipped, the glowing fire of my love with the rain of self-surrender, and the cloud of union in delight " (iv, 14.18 ff.).

An inventory or list of woman's charms like that just touched on, is given in v, 116.2 ff. Here the fair one is vaulted in six places, that is to say, according to the commentary, at the back of the hands, the top of the feet, the breasts ; or : at the breasts, the buttocks, and the eyes [1] ; she has seven things fine and delicate : skin, hair, fingers, toes, and the joints of fingers and toes ; three things deep : voice, character (sattva), navel ; five things red : palm of the hand, corner of the eye, palate, tongue, lips.[2] Then, too, she has like all goodly women other special bodily marks as well betokening good luck. When all are combined, it shows that she will bear many children, even a world-ruler. With words like those of Kīcaka, Rāvaṇa speaks to Sītā : " Of the right size, pointed, smooth, and white are thy teeth ; thine eyes are wide and great, unblemished, and with red corners and black pupils ; thy secret parts are spread wide and firmly swell ; thy thighs are as elephant's trunks ; thy two breasts have a fair, firm fullness, and are round, close-set to one another, bold, firm-swelling, with lifted nipples, graceful, smooth, and like unto wine-palm fruits " (Ram., iii, 46.18 ff. ; cp. his words to the state assembly in vi, 12.12 ff.). Still more eloquent does this woman-worshipper, and the poet himself become, when he sees the Apsaras Rambhā on her way by night to the tryst (Rām., vii, 26.14 ff.) : " Just at this time, Rāvaṇa saw the most splendid of all Apsarases, Rambhā with the full-moon face, decked with heavenly adornment, he saw her going along through the midst of the army. With heaven's sandal-wood

---

[1] Nīl. gives further a third possibility ; but this must be ruled out, for the woman's belly must for Indians be slim, not high-arched.

[2] As to " catalogues " of womanly beauty cp., say, Agnipur., 244 ; much better Garuḍapur., 65 ; R. Schmidt in WZKM, Bd. 23, p. 183 ff. ; *Ind. Erotik*, 614–632 ; *Zschr. d. Ver. f. Volksk.*, Bd. 18, p. 436 ; Max Bauer, *Das Geschlechtsleben i. d. deutsch. Vergangenheit*, pp. 305–315 ; here also especially Brantôme, *Œuvr. compl.*, éd. du Panthéon lit., ii, 301 ff.

her limbs were annointed, her hair was decked with mandāra-flowers, with heaven's flowers was Rambhā adorned—a feftival of heaven.[1] The eye and the heart were ravished by her moft intimate parts, swelling plumply, adorned with a girdle—that moft splendid gift on the altar of love's pleasure. With her moift beauty-marks, laid on (forehead and cheeks) with the juice of flowers from the six seasons of the year,[2] she shone, like another goddess of happiness and beauty, in loveliness, splendour, brightness, and glory. All wrapped she was in a dark garment, like the water-laden cloud, her face like unto the moon, her glorious brows like two bows of the bowman, her thighs like elephant's trunks, her hands tender as young shoots. Rāvaṇa rose, under the spell of love's arrows took her by the hand as she walked, and spoke to the shy one, as he smiled : ' Whither away, thou with the lovely hips ? What happiness art thou seeking of thine own accord ? For whom is the sun now rising under which he will enjoy thee ? Who will take his fill of the lotus-scented sap of thy mouth, tafting like neĉtar ? To whose breaft will these swelling, shining, close-set breafts of thine, like unto golden goblets, grant their touch ? Who will now mount thy broad secret parts, like unto a golden wheel, and decked with a gold band, and which are embodied heaven ? ' " Cp., too, the description of Rāvaṇa's harem in v, 9, 10.30 ff.[3]

[1] Or : made ready for a feftival of heaven.

[2] On these viçeshaka see my note in Daçakum., p. 239.

[3] The nose which we treat so scurvily, especially in poetry, among the Hindus and their poets comes better into its own. The lovely nose of women is here often spoken of, and the high-bridged nose is looked on as an attraĉtion in the woman (unnasā, tuṅganasā). In men a big organ of smell is a great diftinĉtion. In the MBh. Yudhishṭhira often parades his huge, long, hanging, handsome nose. So in i, 188.22 ; iii, 270.7 ; iv, 71.13 ; xv, 25.5. Cārudatta, the ideal man in the Mṛicchakaṭikā, has a very high-arched nose (ed. Stenzler, p. 144, l. 21). Bāṇa in his Harshacarita says in praise of Skandagupta's nose that it was as long as the pedigree of his king (transl. by Cowell and Thomas, p. 191). The big nose with the tip turned down is the mark of the hero and of the king (Mārk.-Pur., viii, 196). The importance of the bold organ of smell as a measure of capability in love (Krauss, *Die Anmut d. weibl. Körpers*, p. 230 ; Storfer, *Marias jungfräuliche*

As already suggefted, the figure, build, and beauty of woman have a great importance for her deftiny, quite apart from conquefts over the hearts of men. Çrī or Lakshmī is at the same time the goddess of beauty and also of happiness. Therefore in her wretchedness Sītā says : " The body-marks as a result of which the unlucky women are doomed to widowhood, them I do not see on myself. My hair is fine, smooth, and black ; my brows do not run together [1] ; my legs are

Mutterschaft, p. 68, n. 2) does not anyhow enter here. But in Agnipur. 236.43 f., it probably is among the marks of the hero in love and in war. The Aryan settlers in India in all probability were especially diftinguished as noble from the aboriginal population of India by this charaĉteriftic also. A flat nose on the other hand is a mark of ugliness (Zachariae, *Zeitschr. d. Ver. f. Volksk.*, Bd. 22, p. 132).

[1] That in a woman eye-brows which meet bring ill-luck is a universally spread belief. Thiselton-Dyer, *The Folklore of Women*, Chicago, 1906, p. 59, cp. 218. These are the brows which a witch has, the barren woman, the werwolf, the person with the evil eye, and the person who through his demoniac power sends the nightmare, or torments others himself as a nightmare. Crooke, *Pop. Rel.*, ii, p. 263, and the references there ; E. H. Meyer, *Mythologie d. Germanen*, 85 ; 133 ; 139. Cp. Th. Zachariae, *Kleine Schriften*, 361, note 2 ; 394 below ; Andree, *Ethnol. Parallel.*, i, 44 ; 63 ; E. Mogk, " Mythologie " in Paul's *Grundriss*, i, p. 1022 ; Krauss, *D. Anmut d. weibl. Körpers*, 110 (but the Persians and Arabs look on them as a beauty). A man muft not wed a maiden whose eye-brows meet. Agnipur., 244.5 f. ; Wilson's Vishṇupur., ed. Hall, Bd. iii, p. 105. In both places and in Garuḍapur., 65.116 (correĉted from Bṛihatsaṃh., 70.19) a warning is also given againft the girl that has dimples in her cheeks when she laughs (Schmidt, *Erotik*, 627, 628, 629, 631). In the man, however, here also it is otherwise : The peculiar marks of the hero are that he is tall, has a nose like a parrot's beak, ftraight-looking eyes overshadowed by brows that run together, and a disposition that is easily aroused, and is inclined to anger and ftrife. Agnipur., ccxxxvi, 43 (Dutt, p. 845). So too among the Buddhifts such brows show great diftinĉtion, and a brilliant future. See Schiefner, *Bull. der St. Petersb. Ak.*, Bd. 23, cols. 24, 33 ; Bd. 24, col. 449 ; Bd. 20, col. 383 ; Divyāvadāna, ed. Cowell and Neil, pp. 2, 58, 525, and elsewhere ; Chavannes, *Cinq cents contes*, ii, 389.

In Vishṇupur., Bd. iii, p. 105 also the warning is given, when marrying to avoid a maiden with teeth that ftand wide apart. Cp.

rounded and not hairy ; my teeth are close-set ; my temples, eyes, hands, feet, ankles, and thighs are well-proportioned, and have a fitting fulness.   My fingers have gradually rounded nails, they are smooth and well-proportioned.   My breasts show no gap between, swell up plumply, and have the nipples set deep ; my navel is well sunk and (at the edges) raised up ; my side and my breast are hard and well-filled.   My colour is like the precious stone,[1] and the hairs on my body are soft. I stand firm on my twelve (the ten toes and the two soles). So am I called a woman with lucky bodily shapes " (vi, 48.7 ff.). Cp. K, iv, 20.32 ff.

Garuḍapur., 65.118 f. (from Bṛihats., 70.21).   On the lucky meaning of such teeth see Thiselton-Dyer, *Folklore of Women*, p. 220.

[1] Maṇi. MBh., vi, 106.61 forms a commentary.   There the, as is well known, very dark Kṛishṇa is called maṇicyāma, " black as the maṇi " ; and Nīl. says there that maṇi = indranīla (sapphire).   See also v, 94.52 ; xii, 45.14.

XVIII

The Woman of Energy

A SOFT, swelling fulness of the limbs .is thus looked on as a matter of course in the pattern woman. It corresponds to the softness and fulness of her feelings, of the life of her soul. But we should be much mistaken, if we thought that the women who are actually shown us in action and speech by the Indian poets are all made after this pattern, or act always in harmony with it. No, the Epic particularly, in spite of much that is cast in a fixed mould, has in it a very long series of varying kinds of womanly figures. In this the Mahābh. especially stands out. But in the Rāmāyaṇa also we have two so utterly different representatives of .the sex as Sītā and Kaikeyī. Hard and ruthless is Kaikeyī, the spoiled favourite of the king and of fortune, when once her fear and her ambition have been aroused, as is described in cantos ii, 9–39, in numerous passages. Even the gentle Sītā is quite capable of blazing anger and harsh words. How hot she is against Lakshmaṇa, when he, faithful to Rāma's bidding, wishes to stay by her, and not to go off to his brother who seems to be calling for help ; she even hints, certainly not without womanly vanity, that Lakshmaṇa wants her husband to die that he may himself get her for his wife (iii, 278.25–29 ; Rām., iii, 45).[1] As a true Kshattriyā she is, too, so soon as she has seen the wondrous phantom gazelle when picking flowers, ruthlessly determined to acquire at least its skin, if Rāma cannot take it alive. She wants to sit on it, far too much. " Such a headstrong whim is held, indeed, to be a dreadful thing and unbecoming to women.

[1] This passage thus seems to pre-suppose the widow's marriage with her brother-in-law as a matter of course ; and here the younger brother would take the elder brother's wife, which is opposed to the passage already discussed on Tārā's and Sugrīva's relationship, but which is otherwise natural enough.

But the wonderful beauty of this creature fills me with
astonishment " (Rām., iii, 43.19.–21).[1]

Strong-willed women are found, above all in the Mahābh.,
in great numbers. Indeed Eastern literature in general shows
us, as has been already pointed out, the woman as being resolute,
full of fire, passionate in comparison with the often so slack and
sinewless man.[2] This characteristic comes out first of all in
love. The fire of the senses is here also on the Indian doctrine
far stronger in the woman, and it is not for nothing that the
tender, timid sex so often takes the leadership in the Indian
love tales, especially when it is a case of the fair one bringing
about the tryst for the delights of sexual union that they
desire as soon as possible, of keeping it successfully hidden,
and of finding a safe way out when it is discovered.[3] This
characteristic is further shared by the tales of the other parts
of the East, which for the most part come from India, or are
inspired by it, and, most certainly not without a connection
here, by the medieval, especially the French love tales.[4]
The woman is active, the man often quite passive ; he not only
just lets himself be made happy by his beloved, but, in India,

[1] So, too, the queen in Chavannes, *Cinq cents contes*, ii, 273 ff.,
wants to have a cushion made of the skin of the wonderful golden
stag ; and another lady clothing and ornament from the skin and horns
of the nine-coloured stag-king Bodhisatta (ibid., i, 220 ff.).

[2] Indian literature has not a single complete hero in our meaning of
the word, not one man corresponding wholly with the ideal of a
man ; for even Karṇa is not without a stain, perhaps in greatest part,
if not altogether, as a result of later distortions. On the other hand
not a few wonderful and complete women stand out, especially in the
Epic.

[3] Mucho sabe la zorra, pero mas la donna enamorada (The fox
knows a lot, but the woman in love knows more).

[4] It is from France that those usually even high-born, and very
high-born maidens, who often throw themselves, and at once, into the
stranger hero's arms, or who are anyhow utterly wretched if he does
not prove them his manhood in the most evident way within a very
few hours after they have first known him—it is from France that
these maidens then came into the literature of the German Middle
Ages ; for the older writings of the Germans, found before the courtly
culture, represent the woman in love in quite another light.

be also visited in the night. Juliet with her Romeo on the balcony is indeed to be found, but such things are by no means the cuſtom of the land—not Leander, but Hero swims to the tryſt in the Indian version of the well-known tale.[1] Even in the newer Russian literature—the lateſt of all I know too little about—the same Eaſtern ſtrength and firmness of will in the woman is to be seen alongside the wavering, useless weakness of the man. So it is above all in Turgeniev, and in Pushkin and others. Now as the Mahābh. has much more unspoiled naturalness and undiſtorted reality, as it is far truer to life than the Rāmāyaṇa, which is much more ſtrongly under prieſtly influences in its very foundations, so too the woman, as she is represented here in the narrative, is probably drawn far truer to the aĉtual conditions of earlier times than in the companion Epic.[2] Then the piĉtures drawn of women in the

[1] The young girl swims with the help of a baked pot or jar to her lover; an unbaked one is foiſted on her, and she drowns. J. C. Oman, *The Myſtics, Ascetics, and Saints of India*, Lond., 1903, p. 266 ff.; Huth, *Zschr. f. vergleich. Literaturgesch.*, N.F., Bd. 4, p. 189; cp. *Stuttg. Lit. Ver.*, Bd. 208, pp. 127, 131; Hagen, *Gesamtab.*, i, p. cxxviii f., and note. The jar or pot for crossing over is also mentioned in MBh., xiii, 34.18; Rām., ii, 89.20. Cp. Hertel, ZDMG, Bd. 65, p. 439.

[2] The Epic, above all the MBh., owed its birth originally to the Kshattriya environment, or at leaſt mainly so, and to the bardic poetry, which above all painted the warrior nobility. This muſt not be forgotten where the queſtion arises as to the influence and ſtanding of the woman. The Rājputs in particular, who at leaſt in part, are descendants of the Kshattriyas, may be brought in here as elucidation. Indeed their Bhāt or bards of to-day are etymologically the old Bharatas. And juſt as the old bard and his highly honoured position was kept up in Rājputāna and among the Marathas, so, too, the Johur cuſtom ('Tod, *Rajaſthan*, i, 284 f.; 331; 347 f.; 674 f.; ii, 66) and the like among them will be found to link them with the olden time and the bardic poetry, unfortunately dreadfully mutilated in the Epic. In a burning like this of masses of women we may, indeed, see but barbaric ways and inſtinĉts. But such things as this remind us of the old Germans. Anyhow, in this there is to be seen a higher value set on woman and her purity. Thus a Rājput had to kill his daughter with his own hand, if she had been found in the arms of a young man. Dubois-Beauchamp [3], p. 37. Especially does Tod, not very critically

minded, it is true, set before our eyes in his *Rajasthan* the tende and manly respect which the Rājputs show towards woman (i, 74, 295), and the truly noble romantic feelings they are capable of. Here belongs the custom of the " Gift of the Bracelet " : a lady in distress sends her bracelet to a knight often quite unknown to her ; he becomes thereby her " bracelet brother ", who hastens into the fray for her sake, looks after her interests, and never sees her, though he is in a near relation to her (*Rajastan*, i, 332, 614). Tod rightly points out that the European knight, or *cavaliere servente* of the Middle Ages is far less high-minded (see for this J. J. Meyer, *Isoldes Gottesurteil*, pp. 1–74). Akin to this is the fine relation between the sister and brother by election among the South Slavs (Krauss, *Sitte u. Brauch*, etc., p. 638 ff.). Mention may also be made of the rape of the Rājput princess, who calls on Rāj Sing for help, and promises him her hand (*Rajasthan*, p. 401). Now in the veins of at least a part of these very Rājputs there flows the purest Aryan blood. Fuller, *Studies*, etc., p. 47 ; Crooke, *The North-Western Provinces*, pp. 62 ; 201. And although Crooke in a later study : " Rājputs and Mahrattas," *Journ. Roy. Anthrop. Inst.*, vol. xl, p. 39 ff. shows that many originally Scythian, and especially Hunnish elements have been taken into the Rājputs, he still supports the view there expressed in *Tribes and Castes of Bengal*, ii, 184, that the higher classes can claim to be sprung from the Kshattriyas. The Agāriah of to-day in Bengal also claim to be sprung from the Kshattriyas, and among them likewise the women have an honoured standing. See *Ztschr. f. Ethnol.*, Bd. 6, p. 377 f. (according to Dalton). Mention should be made, too, of the ruthless revenge which the Gurkha in Nepal, who claims at least to be descended from the Rājputs, takes on the offender who dares touch his wife. Wright, *Hist. of Nepal*, p. 32. Clear traces of a higher value being set on the woman have often shown themselves to us in the narrative parts of the Epic, and elsewhere. Like the Rājputs, the heroes of the Epic feel themselves most deeply dishonoured if another man touches their wives, or even only their kinsmen's (e.g. iii, 243.5 ; 244.17–18 ; 248.8). And undoubtedly the glories of the old lyric poetry, whose gold still gleams out here and there from under all kinds of rubbish and dirt, have in this respect likewise had to suffer heavily from loss and distortion. Ideal men and women, and ideal conditions we must not, indeed, think of restoring in our dreams even there. But in spite of all, the woman of the warrior nobility stands proud, strong, and honoured wherever Brahman hands and later influences have not smirched her. It would, of course, be a hopeless undertaking to try to carry through in the present MBh.— and that is all we have—a clear-cut separation between old and new, between what belongs to the epic poetry of the warriors, and what

Mahābhārata have, too, very often an immediate and natural power of conviction which has an irresistible effect on the unprejudiced reader. Lastly it is highly instructive, often comic beyond words, to see how the revisers of this Epic not seldom tried to patch up, and in the most unskilful, nay, craziest way, the stark contradiction between what is actually said of the woman, and the ideal, or anyhow the ideal which was held later. Draupadī in particular has cost them much toil. This personage, who in the original poem was evidently highly natural, with strong feelings and will, and blessed with a clear understanding, will not let herself be put at all as she is priestly botchery. The Kshattriyas were, of course, Hindus too, and the Brahman certainly from early times had won an influence on the life and poetry of the noble class too, here more, there less. Moreover in Brahmanic literature there often can be found a higher view of woman; and the not seldom lofty moral doctrine which in Brahmanic circles along with all kinds of irritating trash was partly built up in independence, partly, however, taken over from outside, in very many aspects was to woman's advantage also. In the old Upanishad there is found instruction how to beget a learned daughter; and in the same place Yājñavalkya initiates his wife, who longs after instruction, into the deepest secrets of philosophy. Here Gārgī takes part, a woman, in a philosophical congress, and of a truth is not dumb. How unspeakably ridiculous such a thing would have seemed to men like Plato or Aristotle, or to a Council of Fathers of the Church, which would rather take up the question whether women had souls at all ! In the Brāhmaṇa literature the women speculate and argue with the men just as Draupadī does in the Epic. Of course, very much of this in the Brāhmaṇa may go back to the Kshattriya influence, which elsewhere, too, comes out so clearly.

Cp. further my note in Daçakum., p. 41, and Bhavabhūti's dictum, parallels for which are to be found elsewhere : " Excellence it is that yields the reason for respect in the case of the excellent, and not either sex or age " (Uttarārāmac., iv, 11). The thought : " Woman is the word, man the meaning " is directly uttered in the wedding ritual (see Winternitz, pp. 51–52. Cp. Vishṇupur., Bd. iii, p. 118). Particularly skilful and deep play is made with this thought in MBh., xiv, 21.13–26. Cp., too, Tennyson : " Till at the last she set herself to man Like perfect music unto noble words " (" The Princess," vii, towards the end). In short various currents, various social classes, various places and times are spoken of in the Epic. No universally valid picture can be given from it.

440

should into the Brahmanic strait-jacket; she is a spiritual daughter of the warrior nobility, in the beginning, judging from all appearances, like so much in the Mahābhārata, a pure creation of the Kshattriya poetry, and now plays very nasty tricks over and over again on the Brahmanic moral censors. Her kinsman Dhṛitarāshtra probably knew her, who was, indeed, born from the fire, very well ; he says : " The daughter of Yājñasena is wholly and utterly the strength of fire " (iii, 239.9 ; cp. ii, 81.13). We have already been told how in the section on Kīcaka she expresses herself with very scant ceremony indeed about her Guru Yudhishthira. When she lets strong words escape her even before him and the gambling company, he reprimands her and tells her she must not weep like an actress (before others' eyes), and he speaks of the wife's duty (iv, 16.40 ff.).

Among the most lively and striking passages of the great Epic is the dice-game. Yudhishthira has staked all his means, even his four brothers and himself, and has lost, and then last of all Draupadī also. Duryodhana spoke :

" Go, fetch Draupadī, O Prātikāmin :
Thou needst no longer fear the Pāṇḍavas,
Only Vidura is filled with fear, and does dispute ;
And he, indeed, ne'er wished our highest good."

Thus addressed, the Sūta swiftly went,
Prātikāmin went at the king's word ;
Even as a dog goes into the lions' abode,
So drew he nigh unto the Pāṇḍavas' wife.

Prātikāmin spoke :

" Yudhishthira is mad with the fumes of play,
Thee, O Draupadī, Duryodhana has won.
Go into the house of Dhṛitarāshtra ;
I lead thee to the toil, Yājñasenī."

Draupadī spoke :

" But how speakest thou thus, Prātikāmin !
When, then, does a king's son play for his wife !
By the intoxication of the game the prince is blinded.
Had he no stake besides me ? " [1]

[1] Probably, however, matto is to be taken as in çl. 4. Then :
Blinded is the prince, drunk with the fumes of play. Had he, then,

Prātikāmin spoke :

"Ajātaçatru went on playing
Until no other ſtake was left him.
Then did the king firſt give for it his brothers,
Himself also, then thee, O king's daughter."

Draupadī spoke :

" Go unto the gamblers, ask there,
(Ask) Thou in the hall, thou Sūta's son :
' Didſt thou firſt gamble thyself away,
Or me, Yudhishṭhira ? '

When thou haſt found this out, come
And lead me away, O Sūta's son ;
For when I know what the king wishes,
Then do I go, filled with sorrow."

To the hall he haſtened and spoke
There these words of Draupadī ;
He spoke these words unto Pāṇḍu's son,
Who was ſtanding amidſt the princes :

" Waſt thou the lord, when thou didſt me play away ? " [1]
Thus speaks tǫ thee Draupadī.
" Didſt thou firſt play thyself
Away, or me, Yudhishṭhira ? "

But senseless ſtood Yudhishṭhira,
Like one bereft of life,[2]
Answered not one word
To the Sūta, good or evil.

Duryodhana spoke :

" Let the princess herself come hither,
And put this queſtion ;
And all here shall hear
What she, then he, speaks."

no other ſtake for the dice ?   Hi in this reading ſtands in a curious
position. It is true that in the Epic it not seldom opens the pāda.

[1] Liter. : as whose lord didſt thou play me away ?

[2] Gatasattva lifeless, dead, annihilated ; probably also : robbed of the
senses (wanting in Böhtlingk). It is often found in the Epic (e.g. i,
226.9 ; ii, 65.42 ; 69.20 ; iii, 39.63 ; 52.48 ; 68.30 ; 161.5, 20 ;
162.36 ; 206.5 ; 272.22 ; iv, 13.36 ; vi, 107.40 ; 110.23 ; viii,
3.6 ; 19.35 ; ix, 1.40 ; 10.41 ; xiii, 71.8 ; xiv, 77.22).

The Woman of Energy

Faithful to Duryodhana's bidding,
He to the king's house went away ;
The Sūta spoke to Draupadī,
As though reeling with anxious fear :

Prātikāmin spoke :

" The lords there of the hall [1] do call thee,
Danger and doubt has crept o'er the Kauravas :
His own happiness, truly, he heeds not, the poor fool
That would take thee to the hall, princess."

Draupadī spoke :

" The Maker, of a truth, ordained he two :
Or young, or old,[2] good and evil befalls us.
Yet one law as the highest to the world he gave ;
If we follow it, it brings us peace.

This law must not glide by the Kurus—
Go, ask the lords that which I say of the Right.
The noble ones, they with the law in their souls, the wise ones,
Must give me the decision. I will follow."

When he her words had heard, the Sūta went
To the hall, then told of her speech.
They lowered their faces, and to silence fell :
Well they knew the stubbornness of Duryodhana.[3]

The king Duryodhana looked on their faces,
And joyfully unto the Sūta said :
" Bring her hither, O Prātikāmin ;
The Kurus shall themselves speak before her."

The Sūta said, obedient to his power,
Fearful of the anger of the king's daughter,
His pride disowning, to the lords of the hall said he
Once more : " What then shall I tell Krishṇā ? "

---

[1] Since the sabhā (hall) here also, as with King Virāṭa, serves both as gaming-house and as court of justice, the "lords of the hall" (sabhya, sabhāsada, cp. sabhāstāra = akshātivapāka) are here also both judicial assessors and gaming-fellows of the ruler. Indeed, the words in question have even the meaning of master or owner of a gaming-house. Cp. iv, 1.24 ; 16.32 ff., 43 ; 70.4, 18, 28.

[2] Or : Or stupid, or clever.

[3] I leave out here five çlokas inserted between the trishṭubhs as being foolish interpolations.

Duryodhana spoke unto his brother Duḥçāsana :

" Duḥçāsana, this dull Sūta's son,
My coward, is fearful of the wolf's belly Bhīma,
Do thou thyself lay hold of Yājñaseṇī and bring her.
What could the foes do to thee, the slaves ! "

When he heard his brother's words, the king's son
Arose with anger-reddened eyes ;
He went into the house of the great chariot-fighters
And spoke to Draupadī, the king's child :

" Come, Kṛishṇā, come ! Thou art won in play,
Leave thy shame aside, come unto Duryodhana.
Yield thyself up to the Kurus, thou with the lotus eye.
Thou art become their own by right. Come to the hall."

Then ſtood she up with deeply troubled soul,
And with her hand wiped her pale face ;
In torment and diſtress to the wives she ran
Of the old king, the bull of the Kurus.

Loud at her bellowed Duḥçāsana in anger,
Haſtening he ran to the prince's wife,
And took her by her long hair,
That flowed down black in heavy waves.

The hair that at the great sacrifice of the king
Was moiſtened by the prayer-consecrated water of the closing bath,
It the son of Dhṛitarāshṭra boldly touched,
Bringing shame on the hero soul of the Pāṇḍavas.[1]

To the hall Duḥçāsana brings Kṛishṇā,
Dragging her by the long hair, and he shakes her about
As the wind does the poor weak young tree,
As though she so rich in protecting lords had none.

Dragged along, her slender body
Bent and swaying, she whispers low : " I am not well ;
My covering, thou fool, is but one wrapping ;
Do not bring me to the hall, base one ! "

---

[1] To be laid hold of by the hair is looked on as particularly
ignominious, and the offence of thus dishonouring a woman as dreadful
beyond all comparison. See e.g. vii, 195.8 f., 19 f. ; 196.42 ; K, xii,
14.84. Cp. also viii, 83.20 f. [From Melanesia for the tabu head or
hair of a woman of the class of chiefs cp. G. C. Wheeler, *Mono-Alu
Folklore*, p. 23 (Translator).]

The Woman of Energy

Loud cries for help and rescue Yājñasenī:
" Come, Kṛishṇa! Jishṇu! Come, O Hari! Nara!"
Then said he to her, in a wild grip
Holding dark Kṛishṇā by her dark hair:

" For me be thou unwell always, Yājñasenī!
For me thou mayſt have one garment on or none!
Thou haſt been won in play, thou art become a slave;
To the slave a garment is given as one likes."

With loosened hair her clothing half slipped down,
Shaken wildly to and fro by Duḥçāsana,
Filled with shame, glowing with hot rage,
Then low to him Kṛishṇā these words did speak:

" Those in the hall are maſters of the doctrine,
Rich in works, and all like unto Indra.
They abide in honour and worship, all to me
Are worthy of honour; so before them can I not come.

Unutterably base man of varlet ways,
Take not my garb away, drag me no more! [1]
The king's sons will make thee pay for it,[2]
Even though the gods with Indra, too, were to help thee.

To the law clings the noble son of the law.[3]
The law is subtle and hard to know;
I would not that even through the word a whit of blame
Or lack of virtue should on my husband fall.

Yet this is evil, that thou in my sickness
Doſt drag me into the midſt of the Kuru heroes,
And none here raises one word of blame;
They all muſt be of thy mind.

Oh, shame! Gone is the law and cuſtom of the Bhāratas,
Gone are the ways of those learned in the lore of warriors;
The Kurus all with calmness in the hall see
The bounds overſtepped of Kuru law.

Ah! Droṇa, Bhīshma, these have no character,
Nor even Vidura, the high-minded one;
So here the oldeſt and firſt among the Kurus
Heed not the king's dread wrong."

[1] Hardly: deſtroy me not (from kṛi). Mā vikārshīḥ is probably
from kṛish. Cp. the already discussed apākarshuḥ, iii, 128.2.
[2] More literally: will not forgive it thee.
[3] Yudhishṭhira.

With these piteous words the slender one
Looked sideways at her angry husbands ;
With side glances the sons of Pāṇḍu she did
Set afire, she round whose body anger welled.

Loss of the kingdom and their treasures
And moſt glorious jewels was not for them
So painful as Ḳrishṇā's sideway look
She sent towards them in shame and anger.

Barely became Duḥçāsana aware that Ḳrishṇā
At her wretched [1] husbands was gazing,
Than he wildly shook her, who was wholly senseless,
And to her shouted " Slave ! " and loudly laughed.

And Karṇa to the word applause did give
In utmoſt joy, and he loudly laughed ;
The prince, too, of the Gandhāras, son of Subala,
Praised Duḥçāsana high with joyous praise.

Yet but for these twain and Duryodhana
To all the lords of the hall that were there
Came sorrow without measure, when they saw how
Ḳrishṇā was dragged around the hall.

Bhīshma now said he could not answer Draupadī's queſtion, for it was about a very fine point of law. On the one hand, he said, a man who was no longer his own maſter, a slave, could not play away another's property.[2] On the other hand the wife was always under the dominion of her husband. Çakuni [3] was without a rival in the dice-game, Yudhishṭhira had wished to play with him, and his wish had been granted by Çakuni. Yudhishṭhira had owned himself beaten, " won in the game," and did not look on it as any trickery. Draupadī made answer : " The king, who has had little pract̄ice in gaming, was challenged [4] by skilled, base, evil-minded, and malicious lovers of gambling in the hall. How can it be that his wish was granted him ! And how,[5] then, could he make

[1] Or : pitiable (kṛipaṇa).

[2] Juſt because he cannot have any property of his own.

[3] Yudhishṭhira's opponent, Duryodhana's fellow-conspirator and uncle on his mother's side, king of Gandhāra.

[4] He therefore, as we were told, as a Kshattriya had to accept.

[5] Probably kasmāt is to be read inſtead of yasmāt, although if needs muſt be, the latter is also possible.

a stake again, after he had unwittingly been won (as a slave) at play by the villains in union ? Let the free Kurus here in the hall decide." Duḥçāsana hurls abuse at her once more ; then Bhīma breaks out, and utters the bitter reproaches against his eldest brother which have already been spoken of. He wants to burn his two arms in the fire, so as to take insulting vengeance on Yudhishṭhira. Arjuna reminds him that unconditional obedience must be given to the eldest brother, and that a Kshattriya loses his honour, if he refuses after being challenged to play. But now Vikarṇa, a younger brother of Duryodhana, stands up, upbraids the assembly for not giving the law its due, and declares that as Yudhishṭhira has already played away his own person, Draupadī who was staked afterwards cannot be held to be lost in gambling ; moreover she is the property of all five brothers. Loud applause followed his words. But from Karṇa's mouth harshly come the angry words : " Yudhishṭhira staked all he had, and lost it. Draupadī is part of this. Furthermore the gods have appointed but one husband for the woman ; one that has more, like Draupadī, is a wicked woman, and cannot lay claim to any consideration or honour. Duḥçāsana, take the clothing of the Pāṇḍavas and of Draupadī ! " He that was now spoken to tears off her only garment from the wretched woman's body, but by a miracle from Kṛishṇa, whom she had called on in her need, a new one keeps on ever wrapping her limbs, until at length a great heap of garments torn off her by Duḥçāsana lies in the hall.[1] Loud reproaches on Duḥçāsana are then raised, and

---

[1] This miracle is probably, though not certainly, of a later date. But certain it is that Kṛishṇa as the worker of the miracle and the Kṛishṇa cult belong to a later time. Originally Draupadī probably had to stand there naked. Secondary, of course, too, is the statement that the sun has never before looked on the face of the noble woman who is now thus exposed to the eyes of the men. The expression, indeed, is often found. and along with other things has even penetrated into very old parts of the Epic. That the Kshattriya women in old days knew nothing of being veiled and secluded is quite clear. But the view of many Indians that it first came into the land through the Mohammedan conquest is refuted at every turn by Indian literature. But the watch over women was made much more rigorous after the coming

447

heartfelt praise for Draupadī. Bhīma swears he will drink Duḥçāsana's blood in battle. Vidura comes forward for Draupadī, and demands of the gathering that it should deal out juſtice. But Karṇa calls out to Duḥçāsana to bring the slave-woman into the house. Filled with shame, and weeping, Draupadī then once more turns to the circle of great men and princes and complains of the evil done : " Sun and wind before were not allowed to see me ; now in the midſt of the hall I am gazed on among the men, and the Pāṇḍavas allow it. That was never heard of, that an honourable woman should be dragged into the public hall. Where is the Kings' law ? The old eternal law is gone. Decide ye whether I was won in the game, whether I am a slave or not, and I will aĉt accordingly." Bhīshma sorrowfully holds : He that has the power has the right.[1] While she is bitterly weeping and wailing, Duryodhana declares with the proud smile of the maſter that Yudhishṭhira and his brothers muſt decide. Yudhishṭhira keeps silent, Bhīma bluſters and says that if his ſtrong arms were not bound by all kinds of considerations,

of the Moslems.—Anyhow the present seĉtion is among the oldeſt of the Bharata poem, but is often touched up or wholly recaſt.

[1] The saying : " Might is right," as in other Indian literature, is here emphatically made, and in many forms. Often the pāda is repeated : balaṃ dharmo 'nuvartate, " right follows might " (so e.g. i, 136.19 ; Rām., vi, 83.26) ; " above right (virtue) I set might " (xii, 134.6). Who has might and ſtrength is the free lord over right ; this is governed by might, as smoke by the wind. None, indeed, has seen the fruit of right or wrong ; ſtrive after might on earth, all obey the nod of him that has the might " (xii, 134 ; see the whole chapter). Especially for or among the Kshattriyas power and right coincide (ii, 23.28, and elsewhere Heaven knows how often, in the moſt Machiavellian tones). I have already touched on that in a note. But here in Bhīshma's words we have not his honeſt opinion. Hopkins miſtakes the meaning of the whole. Bhīshma says : " And that which here in the world the man, who has the might, looks on as the right, is called the higheſt right, when the queſtion arises of the right (or : where the queſtion arises of the limits of the right)." Perhaps, even, we should take dharmo 'dharmavelāyāṃ == " when wrong prevails ". But also without the apoſtrophe that is the true meaning of the words.

his foes would pay bitterly for their ill-deeds againſt Draupadī.
Karṇa is triumphant. "Three kinds of persons, it is well
known, cannot hold anything—the slave, the child, and the
(ever) dependent woman. Thou, O fair one, art the wife of
a slave without right to hold property,[1] and haſt loſt thy maſter ;
so is it with all the slave possessed. Take thy place in the
king's following, and be one of it ; that is thy portion, the reſt
will then be allotted thee. But thy lords, O king's daughter,
are all the sons of Dhritarāshṭra, not the sons of Pṛithā. Choose
thyself quickly another husband, O fair one, from whom thou
shalt not fall into slavery through the dice." Bhīma again
gives vent to his anger : " I am not angered againſt the Sūta's
son, O king ; he has therewith rightly set forth the law of the
slave. But would my foes so speak to me,[2] if thou hadſt not
diced for this woman ? " Again Duryodhana calls on Yudhishṭhira to give an explanation himself ; he keeps silence, as though
ſtupefied, and Duryodhana bares his left thigh and shows it
to Draupadī, as a scornful token that she is no longer of any
account, a woman worthy of respeét ; for it is on the left thigh
that the sweetheart is put to sit. Bhīma again flares out,
and makes the solemn vow to shatter Duryodhana's thigh.
But for all the words that are being bandied, she that is hurt
to her innermoſt being is ſtanding alone with her pride and
her shame until ill-boding beast-like voices are heard. Then
Dhritarāshṭra becomes afraid, upbraids Duryodhana, and
grants Draupadī three favours. She chooses two only : first,
that Yudhishṭhira shall be free, so that his and her son need
not hear himself called a slave's child ; and secondly, that the
other brothers shall be freed from slavery. Herewith Karṇa
finds a new opportunity to hurt the Pāṇḍavas and Draupadī : it
is by a woman that they have had to let themselves be saved !
Againſt this Bhīma is aroused in violent and useless sorrow,
and to Arjuna he says : " Three are the lights that mankind

[1] Karṇa rightly says that as wife of a slave she is *eo ipso* a slave
(MBh., viii, 73.86). See Meyer, Kauṭilya, 289.44 ff.; addit., 290.31.
[2] Mām sounds somewhat ſtrange ; tām (= " to her ") would seem
more natural. But it is quite right. Cp. v, 90.82 ; 137.22 ; vii,
40.4.

449

has : offspring, pious works, and knowledge [1] ; and when man is an unclean dead body, forsaken in the wilderness by all, then these three show their profit. For us now the light has been destroyed, by strangers having profanely touched our wife. How indeed could offspring come from a woman that has been touched ? " Arjuna brings out one or two wise sayings, and Bhīma has a fresh outburst of rage. But Draupadī has once more been stabbed, and deeply, in the breast, and though they can now all go away free, yet Yudhishthira lets himself be brought to dicing again, and once more loses all, whereupon Draupadī has to leave her children and go off with her five husbands into the celebrated thirteen years' banishment (ii, 67 ff. ; cp. v, 90.44, 47).[2]

There in the lonely forest she does her best to bring the listless Yudhishthira, always chattering of virtue and forbearance, to action. She describes to him how evil the foes are, she boldly attacks the very Godhead : " Not as a mother, or a father, O king, does the Maker act towards beings. As though in anger he acts by them like anyone else here on earth " (iii, 30.38). But man shall be up and doing, not fall a victim

[1] Or probably better, as I translated before : " Offspring, action, and knowledge." The conclusion, indeed, shows that religious works are at least included. How could this be thought of otherwise, indeed, in an Indian, who even " sins religiously " ? The forefathers' offerings made by the sons are of help, of course, in the world of the dead, through pious works men come into the heaven of the gods, the glories of which, it is true, pass away, and knowledge, philosophical knowledge, sets free from the Saṃsāra.

[2] This second dice-game (anudyūta) is of course a very stupid later distortion. In a more primitive form of the Epic, or of the Epic ballad poetry the Pāṇḍavas were, indeed, freed from slavery, perhaps, too, on Draupadī's prayer, but on the condition of going off into banishment, and so they went away into the forest owing to the first game. Thus Draupadī herself relates the matter (v, 82.28), and she must know about it better than the offenders against the poem who came later. Again and again the sharper sight can see the dreadful ravages done on the holy place ; often we can with certainty conclude to an older and better form, but only too often there is nothing left but painful anger at the bungling profanation of the old poetry of the Kauravas and of other Epic ballad treasures.

to doubt and brooding hair-splitting—this the fiery Draupadī argues in magnificent phrases. "It is armoured in deeds that we muſt go through life, he that is bent on aſtion is prized ; he is a fool who speaks of blind necessity and lays his hands in his lap. To him that lies there a sluggard, comes only evil, but the aſtive man has happiness. Now we are in the depths of wretchedness ; it would undoubtedly not be so, if thou didſt aſt energetically. And if success does not come after all, yet a man has tried his ſtrength, and finds a proud self-reliance and honour in this." [1] "The husbandman breaks up the ground with the plough and sows the seed, then quietly waits ; the rain muſt do its share there. If the rain does not favour him, yet no blame falls on the husbandman in this matter : ' I have done all that another man would do.' Therefore we muſt aſt with zeal and wariness ; let manly energy point the way, even though a mountain or a river have to be put out of the way, to say nothing whatever of a mortal man. He that earneſtly ſtrives does his duty towards others and himself. Let a man assert himself, and then fortune smiles on him. The patient man muſt bear with any and every mortification. Grief sheer weighs my heart down, when I think of all the former magnificence, and look on the wretched plight of us all to-day. Thou art a calm witness of it all, doſt seem to be utterly incapable of anger, and wouldſt be called a warrior ! Fiery ſtrength, a soaring will, an ever-lively feeling of honour—these are what the warrior muſt show, wherever needful " (iii, 27, 28 ; cp. e.g. iii, 32). [2] For her

---

[1] Whether abhimāna (32.45) comes from mā or from man would probably be very hard to decide. My rendering is meant to meet both possibilities.

[2] From the mouth of women and of men we are always hearing in the MBh. the praise of amarsha, " not brooking," the passion that flares up angrily and avenges an insult. Noble, good and glorious is anger, a magnificent thing is discontent—the never-reſting ſtriving for something always higher. It is only a poor wretch that puts up with everything ; content, fear, pity, virtuousness kill happiness, and greatness is not won by him who has such things for his own. Anger and impatience is the ſtrength of heroes. Cp. espec. Kauṭilya, 501.3 ff., 23 ff. ; addit., 501.37 ; Çicupālavadha, ii, 46 ; Kirātārj., xi, 57 ff.,

friend Kṛishṇa she clothes her anger and sorrow with eloquent words, paints to him all the shame that was done her in the gambling-hall, how, while her husbands were ſtill alive, the sons of Dhṛitarāshṭra had wanted to make use of her as a slave, even for the quenching of their luſt. She, the noble daughter of a king, and born in wondrous wise, the daughter-in-law of a great prince, she, the friend of Kṛishṇa, the wife of five such heroes, had to put up with all this ! Shame ! she cries on her husbands, and their much-praised greatness. " When a man wards his wife, then he has warded himself ; for from her his own self is born (anew). But how should a husband that muſt be warded by the wife be born from my body ? They take the shame put on me and my ill-treatment calmly, and I glow with anger againſt our evil foes, who are weaker than we." With her hand she covers her face, and with her tears moiſtens her firm-ſtanding, swelling, well-shapen breaſts. Kṛishṇa consoles her and promises that all this shall have its punishment ; but she looks sideways at Arjuna to see whether he also gives his assurance (iii, 12.61 ff.). She then accompanies the whole course of events with her flaming zeal and the full weight of her determined aĉtivity, presses and drives on with every means ; her thirſt for revenge can only be quenched by blood. As we so often find with the women of the Epic, she takes part in the men's discussions ; even where it is a case of deciding on war or peace she has her say like the moſt important of the heroes and great men ; and her words are not a whit less of weight. So in v, 82 (cp. also e.g. x, 16.26 ff.). Once more there has been much talk of what muſt be done. The queſtion now is about sending Kṛishṇa as an envoy to the cousins and foes. In what wise is he to make his appearance

espec. 65 and 70 ; Ṛigveda, x, 83 and 84. But Kauṭilya, 501.11 ff. agrees with Herman Melville when he says : " Hate is woe " (*Moby Dick*, ch. cxix). See also MBh., iii, 29 ; and so on *ad infinitum* in Old India. Tegnér's splendid song of praise to " Oro " (Unreſt) comes into the mind, when we read such verses as : " Discontent is the root of happiness, therefore I love it ; if a man ſtrives after rising, that, O king, is the higheſt wisdom in life." Cp. i, 180.3 ; ii, 50.17 ff.; 49.13, 14 ; 55.11 ; v, 160.61, 92 ; etc.; but especially the utterances of Vidulā (v, 133 ff.) to be shortly given.

there, and speak ? Even Bhīma, the man of fierce anger, drips moſt wonderfully with the milk and honey of gentleness and conciliatoriness. At laſt Draupadī, " eaten with sorrow," speaks, and in deep disguſt at Bhīma's being so friendly disposed, with tear-ſtained eyes, she reminds Kṛishṇa that their adversaries would come to no agreement earlier, even when this was deeply humiliating for the Pāṇḍavas. If Duryodhana would not give his cousins back their kingdom, then there could be no talk of peace. What was to the profit and credit of the Pāṇḍavas, of him, and of the whole eſtate of warrior nobles was this only : a crushing punishment for the irreconcilable ones. He that was a victim to greed muſt be chaſtened by the Kshattriya. Then she tells at short length again of the insult done to her in spite of her high rank, in all essentials as in her earlier conversation with Kṛishṇa.[1] " ' I was gripped by the hair, tortured and brought into the hall, while Pāṇḍu's sons looked on, and thou waſt ſtill alive. I ſtood in the midſt of the hall as a slave of the evil ones, and the Pāṇḍavas looked on without flaming forth or ſtirring a limb. If thou wouldſt please me, if thou wouldſt show me compassion, then muſt every drop of rage be poured out undiminished on the sons of Dhṛitarāshṭra.' Thus having spoken, she of the black eyes and lovely hips with her left hand grasped the loosely bound coil of her hair, curling at the ends, and glorious to see, deep-black, ſteeped in every perfume, endowed with every mark of good luck, shining like a great snake ; and so the lotus-eyed one went up with the proud ſtep of the elephant to him of the lotus eyes, and with tear-filled eyes the dark one spoke to him, the dark one : ' Of this hair, dragged upwards by Duḥçāsana's hand shalt thou, O lotus-eyed one, think on every occasion, if thou wouldſt make peace with the foes. If Bhīma or Arjuna, those miserable wretches, have a wish for peace, O Kṛishṇa, then will my old father fight beside his sons, the great chariot-fighters. And my five sons with the ſtrength of heroes will fight with Abhimanyu at their head againſt

---

[1] It is remarkable that she says : " I will say what I have already once said." Such a fear as this of repetitions, and such a memory the Epic does not show anywhere else. Cp. iii, 12.61 ff.

the Kurus. But if I do not see Duḥçāsana's black arm lying hewn off and covered with the duſt, how is my heart to find reſt ? Thirteen years have gone by me in hoping and waiting, while I have been foſtering my anger within me like a burning fire. My heart wounded by the arrows of Bhīma's speech, is burſting asunder, for this ſtrong-armed one now looks only to pious virtue '. When Kṛishṇā of the long eyes had spoken these words in a voice choked with tears, she fell to weeping, trembling and sobbing loud. The lovely one with the long swelling hips moiſtened her close-set breaſts, as the water flowed from her eyes like molten fire." Kṛishṇa comforts her and makes aloud to her the holy promise that, as she now weeps, so will one day the wives of their foes weep, all of whose kindred will then have been slain, and dogs and jackals will eat the bodies of Dhṛitarāshtra's sons. "The Himālaya mountains may move from their place, the earth be shattered into a hundred fragments, the sky with its ſtars fall down—my word cannot ſtay unfulfilled " (cp. iii, 12.139 ff. ; 51.36 ff. ; 235.4 ff.).

It has been fulfilled—Draupadī has seen all that insulted her lying on the ground, and given her ears their fill of the weeping and wailing of the wives of them that once had exulted in viƈtory over her. And Duryodhana himself acknowledges how much she has contributed to this end. Before the laſt day of battle, when his cause is already in great straits, Kṛipa begs him to make peace. But Duryodhana says it is too late, the Pāṇḍavas could not be held back from the fight, as they are thinking of the shameful treatment of Draupadī. "From the day when Draupadī was tormented, and to my deſtruƈtion brought to sorrow, she has slept ever on the bare ground, until hate shall have had its due. Dreadful is the penitential mortification that Kṛishṇā has undergone that her husband's cause may win ; and Vāsudeva's siſter (Subhadrā) dropping self-regard and pride, serves her continuously, obedient as a slave. Thus all is in higheſt tension, and can nowise come to reſt (nirvāti). . . . But this is not the time to play a manless part, but to fight " (ix, 5.17 ff. ; cp. v, 139.13, 18). But heavily muſt Draupadī pay for this happiness, too, and for the new royal splendour, moreover much lessened through the battles of extermination. Her father and brothers perish.

But the moſt dreadful blow for her is the death of her five sons, who are surprised in their sleep and slaughtered by Açvatthāman in the night, following the ending of the many days' conteſt of the nations. Yudhishṭhira at the awful fate of these youths has nothing more to show than his usual swoon, and then after coming back to himself his ſtill more usual loud and tearful cries of woe. Draupadī on the other hand, soon recovers from her great sorrow, utters scornful words for her husband, and goes on to say : " But I am burnt up with sorrow. If the son of Droṇa, the evil-doer, together with his following is not to-day bereft of his life by thee in ſtout fight in the battle, then shall I sit on in this place, and ſtarve to death. Hear ye that, sons of Pāṇḍu ! " Yudhishṭhira seeks to quiet her by saying that her sons and kinsmen have loſt their lives honourably in battle, so that there is no reason for her to mourn. Moreover, the slayer has taken refuge in the foreſt faſtness. But she will not be put off : " I have heard that Droṇa's son bears a jewel on his head, that was born with him. Only if the daſtard is slain, and I see this jewel brought hither, and faſtened to thy head, O king, will I live.[1] That is my resolve." She then entruſts Bhīma—whom she a long time ago put to trial as a rescuer in need, and whom she now, therefore, praises and spurs on—with carrying out the revenge (x, 10.24 ff.).[2]

When then at long laſt the kingdom is in Yudhishṭhira's hands, he begins a long lament, is tortured by remorse, and

[1] This of course is a wonderful ſtone of the kind often found in the tales : whoever wears it is proof againſt all fear and danger ; hunger and want, sickness and weapons have to leave him unscathed, even gods, demons, and spirits have no hold on him. See in my Daçakum., p. 166 ; K. Fleck's *Flore und Blancheflur*, 2884 ff. ; 6713 ff. ; Hagen's *Gesamtab.*, i, 463. With this piece of the MBh. cp. Bhāgavatapurāṇa, i, 7.14 ff. (Arjuna brings A. before Draupadī, and cuts the jewel out of his head).

[2] Probably after Sītā's celebrated example, Draupadī, when she is alone once in the foreſt of banishment, is carried off, and by King Jayadratha. But the Pāṇḍavas very quickly follow him, he lets go his fair booty, and flees. Yudhishṭhira advises Bhīma and Arjuna, who follow up the pursuit of the insolent fellow, to spare his life. This arouses the utmoſt fury in the injured Draupadī, and she hotly demands his death (iii, 271.43 ff.).

wants to go off into the penitential forest. Draupadī then shows him that by this he is doing ill by his brothers, who have shared all pains with him, and should now have their reward. " He that hath lost his manhood cannot rule the earth, he cannot enjoy riches, in his house the sons can as little dwell, as fishes in the mud. Without punishment inflicted no king is possible. To bear love towards all beings, to make gifts, to study, to practise asceticism—this is the virtue of the Brahman, not of the ruler. To hinder the wicked, to help the good, and not to flee in the fight—this is the highest virtue of the ruler. Through thy blindness the fight now has been for nought. If the oldest and highest is crazy (unmatta), then all that follow him are crazy too. Were thy brothers not crazy, then they would put thee and the wrong thinkers in prison, and rule the earth themselves. He that thus goes astray should be treated with fumigations, salves, sneezing remedies, and medicines by a physician.[1] I am most contemptible among all women in the world, I who even so, robbed of my sons,[2] still wish to live. If they were still alive and doing, then I should not now be uttering my words to the winds. But thou art leaving the whole earth to itself, and thyself rushing into unhappiness " (xii, 14).[3]

All this suffering and more, too, she has to bear,[4] for though she is a soul of fire, and a wonder of beauty, yet, like so many of her kind, she is unhappy in her marriage, and this through her own fault—the only man that is worthy of her, Karṇa who is made for her, she scornfully rejects in a supercilious blindness, and clings to a Brahman beggar.[5] One husband was what

[1] As one out of his mind.

[2] I read vinākritā (cp. 27.22). But K., too, has vinikritā : " mortified through my sons (through their cruel death)," an unnatural way of expression.

[3] Read kurushe in çl. 37.

[4] While living in the wilderness she is once even carried off by a Rākshasa, but quickly and once for all set free by Bhīma through the monster's death—a weak copy of the Rāmāyaṇa motive.

[5] What may the original lyrical poetry or the saga have had instead of the later priestly nonsense of Draupadī's choice of a husband ? Karṇa and Draupadī—Siegfried (he, too, according to the

she wanted, as every noble woman, and to give all her life and being up to him : five was what she got, and, oh ! greatest sorrow of all, none can be called a proper man—Yudhishthira is a poor creature, Arjuna a virtuous puppet of Brahman favour, the two twins hover like shadows through the poem ; it is only through the veins of the kindly, but not altogether polished or quick-witted Berserker Bhīma that red blood flows (cp. v, 90.46 ; K, iv, 22.115).

And yet they all five have divine fathers, and what is still better, an excellent and truly human mother. Kuntī also is an heroic woman, who not only nobly and steadfastly bears all the misery that comes upon her through her foes and her own sons, but who also, like Draupadī, strives to urge on her sons, above all their head, and to work them up to deeds. When Krishna, as a messenger of the Pāṇḍavas comes to Hāstinapura to treat with the foe, she is overwhelmed with sorrow and with joy ; now she sees someone that has come from her beloved sons and the daughter-in-law just as well beloved, and can give her news of the far ones. But alas ! they are in misery, and the poor mother herself has not seen her dear ones for the last thirteen years or more; and she has to bear a heavy burden, quite alone as she is among hostile men and forces. With a voice choked with tears, and a " parched mouth " she makes searching inquiries after them all, is filled with the tenderest anxiety as to how they are faring in the wilds, and bewails her own lot : in reality, she says, she is dead, and dead for her are her children. But then the Kshattriyā comes out in her. She charges Krishna to tell her sons : " Do not act wrongly, so that your great duty may not suffer harm. Shame on the woman who lives, like me, in dependence on strangers ! Let not time go by. Do not act so basely, else will I turn my back

Edda a foundling), and Brunhild (whose flickering flames likewise mark her as a fire-being)—may in it perhaps have been bound together by more intimate relations before the Fire Maid came to her Gunther. Useless dreams ! *Ignoramus et semper ignorabimus.* It is, indeed, possible, nay very probable that even in the older Pāṇḍava saga, probably under strong priestly influences from the first, the brothers, disguised as members of the Brahman caste, wooed the princess of Pañcāla.

on you for ever. The warrior muſt give up even his life, if the time demands it. That was not yet a sorrow, that the kingdom was taken from you, and that ye were beaten in the gaming and banished. But what greater sorrow could there be than that that tall, that dark woman came to the hall in but one garment, and heard the rough words ? In her sickness she with the lovely hips, ever joyfully submissive to Kshattriya duty, found no protecting lord, she Krishṇā, that indeed has protecting lords " (v, 90 ; cp. 137 and xv, 17.9 ff.). Krishṇa's mission does not bring peace but the ſtill greater hatred that he himself wishes for, and when he goes away again, Kuntī gives him a long message for her sons. Stormy, hot utterances on manliness, heroism, ſtrength of will, and mighty deeds ſtream from her lips. Fire darts from her words (v, 132. 5–137, particularly finely in 133). It is true that the moſt magnificent and far the longeſt part of her speech does not give her own words directly, but Vidulā's. The son of this woman, truly queenly not only by position, but in her soul, too, has been brought by his foes into a wretched plight, and yields himself to it, sluggish and inactive. Then his mother rouses him ; and her caſt of mind and her words are among the moſt elevating and moſt powerful things, not only in the Mahābhārata, which is rich in such passages, but probably, too, in all that the world's literature knows of martially virile inspired dithyrambs. Here we give a few ſtrophes only, which, indeed, come out very feebly in the bald and as far as possible literal prose rendering. Kuntī says among other things : " Say, O Keçava, to King Yudhishṭhira, the soul of duty : ' Let thy great duty not be harmed, O son ; do not act wrongly. O king, thou art a simple learned man without insight ; thy mind, spoiled by babbling and prating, looks only on the right and on pious virtue. Up ! Up ! Look but on the right and virtue as thou waſt made by God : from (Brahma's) arms the warrior was made, and he lives by the heroic ſtrength of his arms. Fight in accordance with the law and duty of the warrior, make not thy forbears to sink. Let not thy virtuous merit disappear, and go not with thy brothers towards an evil fate after death. There was once the very great Vidulā, gifted with glowing anger, born in a noble family, shining, joyfully devoted to the law of the warrior, self-checked, far-seeing, famed in the king's assemblies, one whose words were hearkened to,[1] who had learned much, and was of royal blood. She did upbraid her son, who had been conquered by the king of the Indus territory (Sind), and lay there with a sad and pitiable heart : " From me thou art not sprung, nor from thy father. Whence then art thou come ? Without the glow of anger, one that does not count, a man with a eunuch's organs, thou goest along without hope, so long as thou livest. Ho ! thou man of no account, raise thyself, lie not there thus overcome, a joy unto all thy foes, a sorrow for thy kindred, without the conscious pride of self. Easily filled is a wretched small river, easily filled the folded fore-paws of a mouse, easily satisfied a man of no account ; he avows himself satisfied with the very least.[2] Break out the tooth of the snake even, and so sink swiftly into death, or rush into danger, and show a hero's strength in life. Wheel this way and that, as the fearless falcon in the air, and spy out the foeman's weakness, either raising the battle call, or hovering silently. Wherefore dost thou lie thus like a dead man ! Why like one whom the thunderbolt has struck down ! Up, thou worthless man ! Rise and sleep not, overcome by thine adversary. Go not under as a pitiable wretch ; make thyself renowned through thine own deeds. Stand not in the middle, stand not behind ; lie not deep below as a thunderstruck weakling. Blaze up, if it is only for a moment, like the brand of tinduka-wood ; smoke not like a flameless fire of husks, thinking only of how to live. To blaze up for a moment, that is magnificent, but not to smoke a long time.[3] O may in no king's family a patient gentle ass be born. If a man has done all that men can, if in the race he has swept along to the utmost limit of his strength, then he has paid his debt to duty, and need not upbraid himself. Whether he reach the goal

[1] Or : " famed, one whose words were hearkened to in the session of the rulers."

[2] Cp. *Hindu Tales*, p. 305, ll. 9 and 10.

[3] Cp. xii, 140.19 (translated in note 60 on p. 249 of my book, *Isoldes Gottesurteil*, where through the mistake of the printer Mahābh. xiii, is given).

or no, the wise man does not grieve ; he haſtens to the immediate deed [1] ; he has no yearning for the good things of life. Unfold thy hero's courage in the light, or go the way which for all is sure, letting thy duty walk before thee [2] ; for wherefore art thou really alive ? Lift up thy race, which because of thee and of itself has sunk deep. He whose deeds and life are not so great and wonderful that men speak of them does but add to the heap, and is neither man nor woman. If a man's renown for open-handedness, asceticism, truth, for art and science, or for acquiring worldly goods does not rise high, then he is only his mother's excrement. He that outshines men in learning, or in asceticism, in pomp and power or in heroic ſtrength, he is a man—through deeds. May no woman bear a son that is without angry, impatient passion (amarsha), without energy, without manly courage, and that does but give joy to his foes—that is a curse bearing the name of son. Be not smoke, but a mighty rising flame ; be ſtout in the attack, and slay the foemen. Be flame on thy adversaries' heads, even if it be but for an hour, even but for a moment. A man is a man only when [3] he is filled with angry passion, when he bears with nothing patiently ; the patient man without anger is neither man nor woman. Content and pity deſtroys fortune and greatness, so, too, these two : want of energy and fear ; he that does not ſtrive, does not win greatness. Turn thy heart to iron, and then once more seek thine own. It is from being fit for the highest things that man is called man.[4] He bears the name in vain who lives on earth like a woman. When all beings live on a man as on a tree with ripe fruit, then his life has an end and meaning. The man who through his own ſtrength, and full of deeds, brings his life into the heights,[5] wins fame in this world, and

[1] Ānantaryam ārabhate. Cp. Rām., vi, 41.59 ; MBh., vii, 32.3. In all three passages, indeed, " unbroken series (absence of intervals) would also be possible, that is : " he is unbrokenly aĉtive."

[2] Less likely : Wherefore art thou alive, who haſt only virtue before thine eyes ?

[3] Literally : in so far as . . .

[4] Purushaḥ, thus, it would seem, = puru + √ sah (çl. 35).

[5] Literally somewhat as follows : brings his life forwards and upwards (abhyujjīvati). On the other hand in xii, 141.63 clearly : to support life.

THE WOMAN OF ENERGY

a shining lot in the world beyond. If a man is a warrior, and, wishing only to live, shows not, to the beſt of his power, fiery ſtrength in bold deeds, then he is deemed a thief. We are they with whom others find refuge and suſtenance, and we hearken to no one ; if I have to live in dependence on another, then I will leave life behind me. Be thou our shore in the shoreless, our ship where there is no ship, give us dead ones life again. I know the heart of the Kshattriya man as it ever and always is, as it has been proclaimed by fore-fathers and their forefathers, by descendants and the descendants of descendants,[1] made to be everlaſting and deathless by Prajāpati. Only upwards shall he ſtrive, never muſt he bow himself, for in upward ſtriving is manhood ; he may break in irreparable misfortune,[2] but never on earth bow before any man.[3] For fighting is the noble man made, and for victory. Whether he conquers or is overcome,[4] he goes into Indra's world. And even in Indra's holy house in heaven there is not that happiness the warrior feels who has trodden

---

[1] Pūrvaiḥ pūrvataraiḥ proktaṃ paraiḥ paratarair api.

[2] Aparvaṇi. Literally : where there is no joint, where one cannot bend and slip out. Here the explanation of the schol. is wrong. But he is right in giving in v, 127.19 the paraphrase apraſtāve "where there is no favourable opportunity". Parvan also means : "appointed time", and according to Wilson's dictionary then even "opportunity". Perhaps aparvan goes with it (that is = "not an opportunity ").

[3] Of course here, too, a "hornless ox" of Brahmanic race has been eager to hold its court in the shrine—the following ſtrophe is then smuggled in : "Like a rutting elephant let the man of great self go about the world, but before the Brahmans and the law let him always bow, O Sañjaya." Very remarkable, too, is the relationship with the çloka which after the same utterance in v, 127.20 has been dragged into Duryodhana's splendid speech. But it is left uncertain whether our "elephant" (mātaṅga) begot the Muni Mātaṅga, or the other way round ; but probably the firſt is the case. Mātaṅgavacana might even barbarously perhaps mean "The elephant's word". Then the mutual relation would be clear. The third repetition (xii, 133.9 ff.) also brings our utterance about the hero into relation with the beaſts of the foreſt ; he can be broken, indeed, but never bent. Here the clumsy botchery is not found.

[4] Or perhaps better : "slain," of course, when he fights.

461

his foes beneath him. He gives up his own life, or he cuts down the foe ; there is no other way to bring him peace. The foolish man wants little that is unpleasing here on earth. He that in the world has little that is pleasing has certainly little that is unpleasing. But if a man has nothing pleasing (no great love, no fair happiness for which he strives), then he never wins dazzling greatness, and inevitably loses himself in nothingness, like the Ganges in the sea.[1] With all energy to raise himself, to watch, and to be ever exerting himself in deeds that lead to success—this is the whole duty of man ; he must never waver, he must only think : It will be. To such a one good fortune comes as the sun comes to the east." ' " The son reproaches his mother with having a heart of black iron ; what advantage is it to her, he asks, if her only son is dead ! But she will not give in ; and in the end he pulls himself together, and does what she wants.

[1] I read ihāprajñaḥ. If prajñaḥ is kept, then we must probably translate : " the (soberly) understanding man," that is, who has no uplifting of the soul. Cp. there vi, 26.11 ; xii, 237.3–10. Only he that loves little, and seeks little has little sorrow. " He to whom sorrow from love never came, to him, too, joy from love never came " (Gottfried's *Tristan*, 204 f.). " For he that lives more lives than one More deaths from one must die." O. Wilde, *Ballad of Reading Gaol*, end of iii. And : Whoso will climb high must leave much behind. Therefore does xiv, 50.18–30 set forth : The means of transport and food for the journey must be chosen aright, if a man will reach the most glorious end ; he must not cling to old opinions, nor to his Guru, etc. Let a man drive in the cart where the cart is possible, but otherwise let him press on stoutly afoot. Then : " It is only the great that are hit by happiness and unhappiness, but not other men," as the Jaina tale Agaladatta, translated by me in the Kāvyasaṃgraha, exclaims. Cp. Maila Talvio, *Silmä yössä*, p. 255 : Surullaja kärsimykselle kelpaa ainoastaan kaikkein jalain ihmisaines ; my *Hindu Tales*, p. 275 ; my *Isoldes Gottesurteil*, pp. 59 ; 249 ; and the mighty verses in MBh., v, 90.96–97 ; v, 8.53 ; xii, 25.28 ; 174.33 ff. : Great men love the peaks, the greatest sorrow, and more than human joy ; indeed, it is just these that are their only pleasure ; that which lies between is villagers' happiness. Indeed, only the wholly wise are truly happy, as are, too, the wholly stupid, but the crowd, which stands between them, is ever tormented.

THE WOMAN OF ENERGY

Also Kuntī's fiery words seem not to have died out to no purpose. When she wishes to go off into the forest with Dhṛitarāshṭra, Yudhishṭhira says to her : " Formerly thou didst spur us on through the words of Vidulā, and we have listened to thy views, slain the foe, and won the kingdom ; do not, then, leave us " (xv, 16.20–21). And she gives a short description of the dishonouring events we already know of, goes into a longer account of all that befell Draupadī in the gaming-hall, reminds her sons how unworthy of themselves their wretched inaction was, and how sore their plight, and declares that it is for this, not that she may herself enjoy royal splendour, that she goaded them on with Vidulā's speeches, tried to arouse their heroic strength (xv, 17).[1]

In the same way Kālī or Durgā, the wife of Çiva, which Çiva, as an upstart god, has not been bidden to the horse-sacrifice of Daksha, shows that, as a true woman, she is more concerned in outward honour, and above all in the honour of her beloved, than he is himself. At first he does not think any more evil, but she fires him on to taking revenge and disturbing the sacrifice (xii, 283 ff.).

---

[1] The later legends and history of the Rājputs tell of very many sisters to these Kshattriya women Draupadī, Kuntī, and Vidulā. Read there particularly Tod, *Rajasthan*, i, 65 (the heroic mother of the weak son) ; 656 (with what anger the Princess of Udipur welcomes her brave, but beaten, husband) ; 657 ff. (how the Princess of Kanauj chooses Pṛithvīrāja of Delhi at the Svayaṃvara, takes part in the battle that arises out of it, afterwards arouses her husband against the Moslems, and then, when he has fallen, dies) ; 661 ff. (Korumdevī, who is fired with love for Sadu of Pugal, although she is already betrothed to a rajah, weds her beloved, looks on at the fight that breaks out as a result, and heroically inflicts death on herself) ; 709 (the Amazon) ; ii, 507 ; 513–515 (the fiercely heroic mother).

XIX

Position, Rank, and Importance of Woman

THUS the share taken in events by the woman of the Epic is very important, whether it is by urging on and arousing, the more usual case, or by appeasing, and seeking to reconciliate. Thus Dhanaṃjaya, when Dhṛitarāshṭra wishes to question him alone on important matters, says that Vyāsa and Gāndhārī, the queen, muſt be there too, for " I should never care to say anything to thee in secret, for resentment might lay hold of thee. But those two can [1] persuade thee from resentment, O princess ; for they are well versed in the law, ready, and quick at decision ". And so it is done (v, 67.6, 7). In v, 129.1 ff. all try in vain to induce Duryodhana to be reconciled to the Pāṇḍavas ; he goes off in a rage, and Kṛishṇa's advice is to bind the ſtubborn man and his fellows. Then Gāndhārī is called ; she orders Duryodhana to appear before her, and she harangues him violently—though fruitlessly in this case—as has already been mentioned. In v, 148.28-36 she uses the same angry and energetic words towards him, here, too, in a deliberative gathering of the great ones of the kingdom, where she has her seat and vote with the men. Cp. also ii, 75, where she even advises the harsheſt and not at all motherly measures to be taken with him. When Yudhish-ṭhira has won the kingdom in the bloody battles, he firſt satisfies politeness by " announcing " or offering it to Dhṛitarāshṭra, Gāndhārī, and Vidura (xii, 45.11). He waits, too, on Gāndhārī before any of the others, and on Dhṛitarāshṭra only after her, when, being invited to Hāſtinapura, he appears there (ii, 58.27 ff.).[2] See also iii, 9.1-3 ; 254.28, 34 ; v, 114.4 f. ; vi, 49.8-12 ; 88.47 ; 89.6 ff. ; xi, 11.1 ff. ; xiv, 52.25 ff.

---

[1] Or : shall.

[2] The royal ladies, too, are among the few persons named as being visited by Arjuna and Kṛishṇa, before these two go away to Dvāravatī (xiv, 52.25 ff.). Cp. ii, 45.56 ff.

POSITION, RANK, AND IMPORTANCE

With Satyavatī's approval Bhīshma appoints Vicitravīrya as king (v, 173.6) ; with her consent he sets out to bring him his wives (i, 102.4). As soon as he has brought them to Hāstinapura, he tells his "mother" of all (v, 173.22 ff.) ; it is with her approval that the wedding takes place (i, 102.60 ; v, 174.4 ; cp. 176.49). So also he asks leave of her when he wishes to leave Ambā to her beloved (v, 175.1 ; 176.52) ; it is her, too, that he first tells of his coming fight with Paraçurāma, and she gives him her blessing (v, 178.72 f.) ; in the same way he tells her of the result of the battle (v, 186.12). After Citrāṅgada's death he carries on the government, together with her (i, 102.1 ; cp. 102.72, 73). As we have seen, she also takes care that an heir to the throne is begotten (i, 103 ff. ; cp. 110.3). When Yudhishthira starts on his journey to heaven, he leaves the care of the kings he has established to Subhadrā, the wife of Arjuna and grandmother of the heir to the kingdom (xvii, 1.6 ff.).

Thus do these Kshattriya women stand with the men in the most important matters.[1] It is even held that where there are no sons, maidens shall be dedicated as rulers (xii, 33.45). It is true that even the Strīrājya, or empire of the Amazons, has a king ; he comes to the Svayaṃvara at Rājapura (xii, 4.7) ; and we are assured that where a woman takes the reins everything comes to grief (v, 38.43). That the "regiment of women" did often really oppress the land may be clearly seen also from ii, 5.76. Thus a most significant saying of an Asiatic despotic ruler, who offers to give everything to her that enjoys his favour, is that of Daçaratha, when Kaikeyī at the news of Rāma's coming dedication as prince asks her old lover for a "favour" (iii, 227.22 ff. ; cp.Rām., ii, 10.27 ff.): "'Tis well. I will grant thee the gift of wishing. Take what thou wouldst have. Who that should not be killed is now to be killed ? Or who that is doomed to death shall be set free ? Whose belongings am I to give thee ? Or from whom shall they be taken away by me ? Which poor man is now to be made rich ? And which wealthy man is

---

[1] Cp. Tod, Rajasthan, i, 643, as to the wife : " The Rajput consults her in every transaction " (probably to be taken with a pinch of salt).

to be left with nothing? I am the king of kings on earth and the shield of the four castes. Do but say at once what thou needest."

And in other ways also the women do not sit aloof from the world and its joys, but experience all kinds of things beside the men. While the Pāṇḍavas and the Brahmans are sitting there in earnest discussion, Draupadī and Satyabhāmā come in, merrily jesting and laughing, and sit down with them. Satyabhāmā playfully asks Draupadī by what means she keeps such splendid heroes as the five brothers under her heel (iii, 233.1 ff.). When the Pāṇḍavas' army goes forth to Kurukshetra to the fight, Draupadī accompanies the troops as far as Upaplavya, and then comes home again with her women (v, 151.60). And as several of the highest ladies strike up a wailing for the dead on the battle field during the days of the fight, Draupadī among them, it is evident that they often come on a visit to the camp. The wives (kalatra) are taken right into the field, and on the march to the battle-field they are in the army's centre (v, 151.58 ; 196.26 f.).[1] And these are not only the life-mates of ordinary warriors,

[1] Cp. xii, 100.43. But it is uncertain in this passage whether the army is meant to be marching out to the battlefield, or attacking. Judging by the somewhat loose formation, indeed, one would be inclined to think rather of the last-named alternative. " In front let the army of the men be, of those armed with sword and shield, behind let the army of carts be, and in the middle the womenfolk." Or, since the carts and the women always go together at other times : " Behind and in the middle let the army of carts and the womenfolk be " ? The carts (çakaṭā) are according to Nīl. on v, 196.26 bhāṇḍavanti anāṃsi " the waggons carrying the ' outfit '." By this is first of all meant all kinds of army implements (cp. e.g. v, 196.10), and then probably also table-ware, provisions, etc. In our passage, where āpaṇa is wanting, the carts may partly also contain traders' goods. These are anyhow also near the women. Cp. Kauṭilya, 565.7 ff. ; but also 515.3–4 ; 516.21 ff. These passages, it is true, show that probably also in the Epic by kalatra are meant, above all, the wives of the soldiers. Cp. Kauṭ., 515.25 ff.—Droṇa's wife, Tārkshī, looks on in the battle between the Kauravas and the Pāṇḍavas, and is there wounded by an arrow and dies. Mārk.-Pur., ii, 34 ff.

but the royal wives, too, accompanied by their guards (xi, 29.65 ff. ; 30.3 ; 62.4 ff. ; x, 8.24 ff.).

Duryodhana goes off hunting and cattle-branding with his brothers and friends ; it is a glorious journey through the forest and country ; thousands of women go with them, as also townsmen with their wives (iii, 239 f.). So also King Sumitra and Pāṇḍu both take their wives when they go hunting (xii, 126.9 ; i, 114). We have already spoken of the picnics in the open air, and the lively share taken in them by the women-folk. A festival often mentioned is that already spoken of, the festival of Indra's banner (Indradhvaja). We have heard, too, of the festival in honour of the mountain Raivataka. It is splendidly bedecked for this, and food is brought out in plenty. " Palaces " are built there, and " wishing-trees " (kalpavriksha) planted. Music rings out, songs resound, there is dancing, the *jeunesse dorée* drives about in chariots gleaming with gold, there are swarms of townsmen and their wives, and the princely personages show themselves with harems of thousands, and sumptuous trains of music ; Krishṇa's elder brother here too sets his usual example, copied by very many, and reels about drunk (i, 218.9 ; 219).

It is a pleasure-seeking, merry-making world that opens before our eyes in the Epic. Feast-days, particularly religious occasions, were found there in plenty ; all kinds of shows and entertainments, as also extraordinary and fittingly welcomed events broke the monotony of life ; and the flock of women, high and low, threw themselves into the waves of pleasure, merry, greedy to see and hear, and, so far as possible, taking an active part. There they showed themselves in all their finery, and, of course, sought to be seen. How often we are told—in the Epic and the other literature—that on such occasions the streets were watered, the city was decorated with flowers, wreaths, garlands, bright cloths, flags, and so forth, while sham-fighters, dancers, mimes, and the like showed off their arts, and all the people jostled one another, and gave themselves up to merry-making. And when something really startling happened, or was displayed before the eyes of the crowd or of the smaller select circle, then, in the Epic world, clothing was waved in joyful applause, just as it is so often painted for us in the Jātaka.[1] If anything special was going on below in the street, then from the houses, and from everywhere that gave a good opportunity for seeing, a thousand women's eyes looked down.

Men, women, and children come out from Hāstinapura to give a festal welcome to the Pāṇḍavas' envoy, Krishṇa (v, 86.17), and at his entry " the very great houses, too, (are) covered with women, and seem to totter under the burden " (v, 89.9). Not a soul has stayed at home, man or woman, child or greybeard, and the guest's horses cannot drive on for the throng (çl. 7). As he then drives in most splendid array to the royal assembly hall, women stand thickly crowded on balconies (vedikā, v, 94.26). Hundreds and thousands of women are at the windows, when Arjuna on his gold-hubbed chariot drives into the city of Dvārakā (i, 218.18). After the festival of the dead, Yudhishthira has dwelt a month long outside the city. He now comes back, and the houses on the main street almost give way under the crowd of women-onlookers singing the praises of him and his brothers (xii, 38.3 ff.). Especially when a battle has been won, and the conqueror comes back in triumph are the women again to the fore. So does King Virāṭa's son come back to the festally decked city, and youths and harlots, together with the young princess and her girl-friends, in choicest garb and ornaments come to meet him ; and the whole people and lovely women in magnificent ornaments, as also the army, and all kinds of loudly sounding musical instruments make up his escort (iv, 68.22 ff.). So, too, the public women and the young girls appear as the welcoming escort of the victor in iv, 34.17,18, and elsewhere, as has already been described. The Kshattriyas and the women, but anyhow only those of the better kind, of higher rank, especially the noblewomen, are there driv in in chariots, too. So it is when the five sons of Pāṇḍu are

---

[1] Cp. e.g. my Daçakum., pp. 51, 52 ; Kalpasūtra, i, 100 ; Aupa-pātikas., ed. Leumann, § 1 ; Bhāgavatapur., i, 11.14 ff.; iv, 9.53 ff., and for the celukkhepana, Lalitavistara, ed. Lefmann, p. 145 ; MBh., i, 188.2, 23 ; 190.1 ; ii, 70.7 ; vi, 43.30 ; 121.28 ; vii, 19.19 ; 21.13 ; 109.32 ; 114.96 ; viii, 23.2 ; 86.9 ; 91.58 ; 61.4 ; Rām., v, 57.26.

brought by the Rishis to Hāſtinapura, and the whole people
ſtreams out at their coming (i, 126.13). And when these
princes and their cousins have then passed through the inſtruction,
a splendid school feſtival is held, where they give proofs of their
skill in arms. A mighty ſtand is put up for the king and the
women. Broad, high-towering ſtaging and coſtly compart-
ments [1] the countrymen had to build. When the day had
come, the king with his great men came into the "heaven-
like ſtand, made of gold, adorned with jewels, hung with a
net of pearls. And Gāndhārī, the excelling one, and Kuntī
and all the king's wives with their serving-women and their
following joyfully climbed onto the ſtages, as the wives of
the gods onto Meru. The four caſtes with the Brahmans
and the Kshattriyas at their head came quickly there out of the
city, full of the yearning to see the princes' skill at arms.
Through the loud-resounding musical inſtruments, and the
joyously eager excitement among the people this gathering
was like unto the high-billowing sea " (i, 134.8 ff.). Amidſt
the crash of music the warrior school-display then takes its
course (135.6). The crowd billows and sinks in a mad
confusion, thundering shouts and loud applause rise from
the crowd of onlookers, when Arjuna, armed and in golden
armour, shows himself to their admiring eyes (135.8 ff.).
The moſt lively and ſtrained attention follows what is happening
on the ſtage. The wondrous son of the sun, Karṇa,
unexpectedly rises and shines as a hoſtile ſtar againſt the no
less aſtonished light of the bowman's art, and threatens to
obscure it ; " rent in twain was the theatre, and two parties
formed among the women " (136.27).

Then there were the great sacrifices of the kings and others,
and the many private feſtal occasions, as, for inſtance, the
feeding of Brahmans (often set on foot by women), whither
all kinds of people ſtreamed and made merry, and ate and
drank their glorious fill ; and women gueſts came to them,
too, and made themselves as drunk as the men (i, 148.5 ff.).
Further, women held puṇyaka, for inſtance, that is to say,
celebrations to ensure their husband's love and to get a son ;

[1] Çibikā. Perhaps less likely : balconies (or platforms). The
P.W. throws no light.

469

at these the Brahmans served, and liked to appear in rich ornaments (i, 3.96).

And there was very much else also to see. So (according to ii, 23) there took place a mighty wreſtling and boxing match between Bhīma and King Jarāsandha, and the women came thither, too, to delight their eyes and hearts at it (çl. 22). The ladies cannot have been over-delicate, for when we read of the hellish din which the warlike music of the Epic makes with its many inſtruments, to say nothing of the noise of the fight and the horrors of such exhibitions, we cannot but wholeheartedly wonder at the nerves of the weaker sex, that comes here with the crowd to the men's conteſt. The women take a great delight in heroes and heroic deeds. Whenever Arjuna shows himself in his panoply, the daughters of Brahmans and Kshattriyas, and Vaiçya maidens run up from their play to gaze on him—juſt as it is with us (v, 30.8). King Virāṭa makes the ſtrong Bhīma give real gladiatorial displays before the beauties of his harem : boxing displays, trying his ſtrength with wild lions, tigers, buffaloes, bears, and boars, and slaughtering them before the eyes of the ladies (iv, 8.10 ; 13.4 ; 19.5, 6 ; 71.5). They are also, it is true, entertained with milder arts. Eunuchs are appointed in the women's apartments to delight the women and the prince himself with tales and the reſt. So Arjuna disguises himself as a eunuch, and enters into the service of King Virāṭa. He is skilled in singing, all kinds of dances, and the various musical inſtruments, and has other accomplishments. By the ruler's orders he is examined by women as to his sex, and declared to belong to the third—how that can be is left, indeed, in the dark—and then taken into the girls' dwelling, where he inſtruĉts the young princess and her girl friends in dancing, singing, and music (iv, 2.25 ff. 11.8 ff. ; and often in what follows after ; cp. vii, 64.11).[1]

Also when the heroes travel to visit kinsfolk or friends, they take their wives with them, at leaſt at times. So the Pāṇḍavas, when they go to the dice-game, at Hāſtinapura, as also Kṛishṇa, who with Satyabhāmā makes a visit to the

---

[1] According to iv, 45.12–15 he was then no eunuch ; while iii, 46.59 and K, 3.49 make him become really sexless for this one year owing to the curse of Urvaçī.

banished Pāṇḍavas in the Kāmyaka foreſt (iii, 183). No less so Subhadrā is allowed to accompany Arjuna, though it is true this is on a visit to her own home Dvāravatī (xiv, 52.55 ; 61.41). The womenfolk then naturally greet one another moſt lovingly, although the seemingly so gentle ladies may often have the same feelings at heart as Dhṛitarāshṭra's daughters-in-law, of whom we read : " When they saw the peerless loveliness, as it were, blazing up, of Draupadī, they were not in an altogether happy frame of mind " (ii, 58.33). So, too, they made one another the richeſt gifts, especially on great feſtal occasions, as at the horse-sacrifice (xiv, 88.1 ff.). But in general people did not hold much with wives travelling. A saying declares : " A blot (shameful ſtain) for the earth is the Bāhlīka, for the man the lie, for the good woman curiosity, and for wives travelling " (v, 39.80).[1]

It is now clear from what we have shown up till now that women of the " higher circles ", especially those belonging to the warrior nobility, with whom the Epic is naturally moſt concerned, enjoyed no small measure of freedom. But the harem, too, is in the Epic an inſtitution taken for granted, for the reason firſt of all that those of high ſtanding often had many wives.

Polygamy is right for the man, but not for the woman : " Polygamy, O fair one, is no wrong for the men, but it is so probably for the women " (xiv, 80.14). Here as elsewhere it is also quite immaterial whether the husband is ſtill alive or is dead ; for the woman one man is appointed, none along with him, none after him. So does the Brahman woman exhort her husband in i, 158.35, 36 to send her as sacrifice to the man-eating monſter, for he can then take another wife. " And no blame is laid on the men that marry many wives, but very great blame is laid on women, if they offend their firſt husband (through a new marriage)." For : " This friendship the Maker has made an everlaſting, deathless one " (xiv, 80.15). The indissolubility of this bond of friendship is therefore only a one-sided one. Still the man, too, has certain duties in his polygynic marriage. This is what the

[1] Vipravāsamalāḥ ſtriyaḥ, which here probably hardly means : When the husband goes off on a journey, the women enjoy themselves elsewhere.

471

old legend says : Daksha had twenty-seven daughters, the conſtellations. He married them to Soma, the moon. They were all without compare for beauty ; but Rohiṇī outshone even her siſters. Therefore the moon loved only her, and partook of love's joys with her alone. Then the others went in anger to their father and told him that their husband kept always with Rohiṇī ; therefore they wished to live with their father, and take refuge in asceticism. Daksha admonished the sinner : " Behave in the same way towards all thy wives that a great guilt may not come on thee." To his daughters he spoke : " Now he will treat you all the same, since I have so bidden him. Go back to him." But the evil man went on doing as before. The poor rejeéted ones came with new complaints to their father. He warned Soma : " Behave in like wise towards all thy wives that I may not curse thee." But the ſtubborn man gave no heed to his words ; the daughters once more took their anger and grief before their father, and begged him to see to it that the moon god should also give them his love. Then Daksha grew angry and sent a decline on the offender. Sacrifices and everything possible the moon, ever decreasing, undertook, but nothing helped. As a result the plants and herbs also vanished away, whose growth and ſtrength, indeed, depends on the orb of night, the lord of plants ; and as these laſt grew dry and sapless, and had no new growth, all creatures suffered and died of hunger. The gods asked the moon what was the reason of his decline, and when he had told them, they begged Daksha to put a ſtop to the deſtruétion of the world. He spoke : " The moon muſt always treat his wives exaétly alike, and bathe himself in Prabhāsa, the holy pilgrimage-place of Sarasvatī. Then he will set himself free from the curse ; he will henceforth for a half month wane, and for a half month wax again " (ix, 35.45 ff. ; cp. xii, 342.57). Thus that curse that fell on him for his partiality is to-day ſtill at work (xii, 342.57, 58).[1]

---

[1] Kāmasūtra, ed. Durgaprasad [2], p. 253 demands : " But if a man has gathered many wives, then let him be the same (to all))." According to Osman Bey, *Die Frauen i. d. Türkei* (Berl., 1886), p. 15, Mohammed also had required the man to love and treat his wives all alike. But the Prophet was far too experienced in matters of women to make

POSITION, RANK, AND IMPORTANCE

But that one wife should be preferred is so natural, that we often hear of it elsewhere, too, in the Epic ; and there the lot of the wife passed over is often a most touching one. So in Kauçalyā's case : beside his favourite wife Kaikeyī she is as nothing to her lord and husband Daçaratha, in spite of all her charms ; she then comforts herself with the thought that her son Rāma will bring her happiness and joy, but when he is to be consecrated as heir to the throne, her rival at the last moment snatches this stay away from her also : Rāma has to leave his mother, go into fourteen years' banishment, and hand over the kingdom to Bharata. " Like the slender shaft of the çāla-tree that is felled by the axe in the forest, the queen suddenly fell to the ground." She makes her plaint before her son : " The barren woman has one anguish of soul, but no other. ' Neither happiness nor joy have I ever had of my husband's manhood ; may I see them in my son,' so, my Rāma, I lived in hope. I shall have to hear many unlovely words from my fellow-wives that stand below me, words that stab the heart, I that am the highest, too. What could there be more painful for the wife than my grief and endless wail ! Even when thou wast still here, I was the hurt rejected wife ; how much the more will it be so when thou art gone ! Death for me is a certainty. Never held in love or honour by my husband, I was oppressed by Kaikeyī's waiting-women, although I am equal to her, nay better. Seventeen years are gone since thou wast born, and I have been longing for my care to pass. That it still lives, this I, who am so harshly treated, cannot long bear, nor the slights from my rivals, if I am no more to behold thy moon-like countenance. By fasting and magic

such a demand. In the 4th sura of the Koran we find : " It cannot be that you should feel the same love towards all your wives, even if you wish to. But you must do your best not to show an open dislike for any of your wives " (p. 70 in Ullmann's German transl., Bielefeld and Leipzig, 1881). And the poor man with many wives often honestly tries to do this, as can be seen, for instance, from p. 76 in Osman Bey. On the waning moon Crooke, *Popul. Relig.*, i, 10–13. Soma, the moon, is also a giver of rain, and a god of fruitfulness. L. v. Schroeder, *Reden u. Aufsätze*, 409, 413 ; Meyer, Kauṭilya, index under " Mond " ; H. Winckler, *Die babylonische Geisteskultur* [2], p. 63.

and much hardship I, unhappy one, have in vain reared thee. For me there is assuredly no dying, and in the house of death there is no room for me, so that the god of death will not yet snatch me away, as the lion does violently a whimpering gazelle. My heart, it is evident, is ſtrong, made of iron, since it breaks not—before the appointed time there is assuredly no dying " (Rām., ii, 20.32 ff.). So also Devayānī and her son in the Rāmāyaṇa (vii, 58.7 ff.) arouse the deepeſt pity. King Yayāti has two wives : Devayānī and Çarmishṭhā ; he loves the latter, but not Devayānī. And in the same way all his tenderness goes to the favoured woman's son ; but Yadu, the child of the shunned wife is the father's ſtep-child. Then speaks Yadu to his mother : " Born in the race of Bhṛigu's son, of the god of unhindered deeds, thou beareſt with sorrow that goes to the heart, and with contempt that is hard to bear. We too will go together into the fire. The king may go on taking his delight for long with the daughter of the Daitya. Or if thou canſt bear it, then grant me leave. Do thou submit to it, I shall not ; I am going to die, that is sure." When Devayānī heard these words from her weeping, deep-tortured son, she went in hot anger to her father, told him of her contemptible position, and threatened to kill herself, if he did not bring a change about. In his anger the holy man laid the curse on the evil-doer of falling a victim to old age now in his very youth.[1]

But even without such injuſtice from the husband enmity between his various wives appears in the Epic as normal and quite a matter of course.[2] Needless was the ethical teacher's sermon there : " For wives, besides intrigues with other men there is nothing to do them hurt in the world beyond, and besides hatred againſt the fellow-wife nothing to do them hurt in this world " (i, 233.26). Already the two daughters

---

[1] Cp. Vishṇupur. (Wilson), vol. i, p. 159 ff. (aṃça, i, adhyāya, xi, the legend of Dhruva); for Yayāti, Wilson, Seleᒼ Works, ed. Hall, vol. iii, pp. 36–37. Schack, Stimmen vom Ganges, p. 189 ff., has given a poetical rendering of the tale of Dhruva after the Bhāgavatapur.

[2] Sapatnī means the fellow-wife, literally : the woman enemy. Cp. what Lane, Arabian Society in the Middle Ages, p. 245, says of the Arabic ḍarrah.

of Prajāpati, the maker of the world—Kadrū and Vinatā—
wives of one man, quarrelled with one another, and the one
as the result of a wager became the slave of the other (i, 20 ff.).
The holy man Mandapāla in the form of a bird weds a hen-
bird Jaritā. When she has laid four eggs, he leaves her, and
goes off with another hen-bird, Lapitā. In the Khāṇḍava
foreſt, where they dwell, the great fire now breaks out ;
he then wants to go off and see after his offspring. But Lapitā
is very angry, and sulks : " Thou only wanteſt to go to my foe,
and doſt not love me any more as thou didſt once." And
when he then comes to the fledglings and their mother, they
do not deign to give him one friendly look or word ; only
Jaritā throws at him : " Go away, do, to thy Lapitā ! "
(i, 229 ff., especially 233.7 ff., 24 ff.).—When Kuntī has
got three sons, her fellow-wife Mādrī says to Pāṇḍu that she
would also like to have children, but cannot in her jealous anger
againſt her rival (saṃrambha) ask her herself ; so he muſt
be the one to make of her the requeſt to help her fellow to have
offspring. This, she says, will be well for him also. Kuntī
teaches Mādrī how to go about it, and this obliging aćt is called
a very hard thing (sudushkara). But she that is thus favoured
gets at one swoop two sons from the Açvins, and then Kuntī
is filled with moral indignation at the bad woman who has
deceived her, she says, and filled with the fear that the hated
one will become too powerful by having more children, and
do her harm ; therefore she refuses to get her any more sons
(i, 124). That the fiery Draupadī does not look on with
particularly kindly eyes, when her darling Arjuna brings home
a new wife, Subhadrā, may be at once guessed. She flings the
words at him : " Go, then, I pray, to where the daughter of
Sātvata dwells. However tightly bound a bundle is, if it is
tied up once more, then the firſt faſtening becomes loose."
Arjuna tries over and over again to reconcile and console her,
and then sends his wondrous lovely new wife, clad in red silk
and as a shepherdess, thus to show her lowly ſtanding, into his
women's apartment. Kuntī kisses the new-comer. The
latter bows respećtfully before her rival, and says : " I am thy
servant." Then the deeply hurt lady makes the beſt of
a bad thing, and clasps Subhadrā to her. " Now were the

475

hearts of the Pāṇḍavas, the great chariot-fighters, joyfully ſtirred, and Kuntī filled with the utmoſt joy " (i, 221.15 ff.). Cp. also xiv, 88.

As so often in the Indian writings, the loss, by a wife, of her ſtanding to a new rival shows itself as one of the greateſt sorrows on this earth already so full of sorrows. " The sorrow of him that loses his all, and of him whose son is slain ; the sorrow of the wife that is robbed of her husband, and of him whom the king has laid hold of ; the sorrow of the childless woman, and of him that already feels the tiger's breath on him [1] ; the sorrow of the wife when her husband takes another besides, and of him that is convicted by witnesses—these sorrows are alike " (ii, 68.81 ff.). So also in v, 35.31, 32, among those who spend dreadful nights is found the adhivinnā ſtrī, the wife who is put in the background through a new wife being taken (This çloka is = Nārada, i, 203. Cp. Meyer, *Altind. Rechtsschriften,* 109–11 ; Kauṭilya, index under " Überheiratung "). No wonder if she then often left her husband's house in anger, as we may conclude from Manu, ix, 83.[2]

[1] Vyāghrāghrāta. So far as I remember, āghrā is found in this peculiar usage only with the tiger. According to the lexicographers and the commentators (e.g. Mālatīmādhava, v, 29) it means " to catch hold of " (gṛih). But I think that it has, at leaſt originally, the meaning " to follow the scent of, to follow after ". So we read in MBh., vii, 128.9 : " Thy followers in the battle ran away, like gazelles scented (tracked) by the tiger." It cannot mean " caught hold of " there.

[2] True jealousy is foreign to the primitive woman, at leaſt as a rule. The wife of the proud owner of many wives is often as proud of this mark of the power and influence of her lord as is the wife of the rich upſtart of his money-bags, and with not less reason. Indeed, the wife is often even angered, if her skinflint husband does not find her a new help for the household. Envy, indeed, is inseparable from woman, and Jean Paul therefore holds that all women should really go to hell, since there they could have so splendid a chance of showing their faireſt and ſtrongeſt virtue—sympathy, whereas in heaven at the sight of all the glories, particularly of their siſters, envy would almoſt kill them (in *Quintus Fixlein,* firſt edit. of the collected works, vol. 4, p. 118 f.). The husband with many wives has therefore even among savages his troubles at home, because each of his wives is always watching him to see whether the other is not getting something she her-

self has not, and so forth. Here Mark Twain has seen the truth very clearly in the delightful 15th chapter, vol. i, of *Roughing It*. Cp. e.g. Hertel, *Indische Märchen*, p. 131 f. When culture becomes higher, envy does not grow less, and true jealousy is found more and more; and in spite of all the men and women defenders who have come forward among us on behalf of the Oriental harem, and in spite of the apparent exaggeration in many cases of what has been written of the unhappiness of women in the harem, it still remains true that we see there picture after picture of hatred and darkness. Here we give only one or two examples from Old India. " What is the greatest sorrow of the woman ? " the king of Benares asks his wife. She answers : " Anger at her rival " (Jāt., No. 489). Cp. e.g. Shib Chunder Bose, *The Hindoos as They Are*, 38 ff.; 229 ff.; espec. 40; Bulloram Mullick, *Home Life in Bengal* (1885), pp. 26–28 ; Chavannes, *Cinq cents contes*, ii, 120. If a woman cannot have her revenge in this life, then she will probably at her own wish become a Yakkhinī after death, and eat the hated woman's children away (Jāt., Nos. 510, 513 ; cp. vol. v, p. 39 f.). " Of enmities, that between a head wife and a secondary one is the worst " (Schiefner, *Bull. d. St. Petersburger Akad.*, Bd. 24, col. 503 ; cp. Bd. 23, col. 558). One or two drastic happenings in a household of this kind are given in the passage from the Petavatthu which I have given in note 2 to p. 305 of the Daçakum. Here the fifty daughters of Māndhātar in the tale of the holy man Saubhari are worthy of remark ; it is told by the Purāṇas as an example of life in the house constantly increasing the wishes. These princesses are all married to this Ṛishi, who uses his wonderful powers among other things to split himself up into fifty husbands full of love, and each of the wives complains now to her father of one thing only : that the husband is always with her only, and neglects the other forty-nine. So Wilson's Vishṇupur., vol. iii, p. 273 ff. See also my *Hindu Tales*, p. 60, note 1. But a still greater self-denial is shown by the faithful wife of a Brahman in Mārkaṇḍeyapur., xvi, 14 ff. : She has a leper husband, and treats him most lovingly in spite of all his hideousness and spiteful outbursts of anger. He now wants her to introduce him to a beautiful hetæra, and she cheerfully sets about doing so. She acts therefore according to the commandment : " Let the wife show every kindness to the woman with whom her husband is in love " (MBh., K, xiii, 250.13); and according to the ideal put forward in Kāmasūtra, ed. Durgaprasad ², pp. 242–246 and 250 (the two last sūtras). A picture such as this of deep yearning is painted in glowing colours by the great English painter and poet, William Blake : " She shall begin to give her maidens to her husband, delighting in his delight ; And

All the splendour of the court must then usually have but little lightened the pain in the soul even of the ruler's wife, perhaps sometimes have strengthened it still more, even when she saw herself still outwardly honourably treated as before by her husband. This harem life, anyhow, is luxurious enough, as the Epic paints it for us in glowing colours. So, for instance, that of Rāvana (Rām., v, 9 ff.). Even the captive Sītā is housed in a fairy-like açoka-grove, which ravishes the senses with endless scented lotus-ponds, all kinds of trees, birds, and beasts, splendid palaces, and a thousand other glories (Rām., v, 15.1–15 ; 18.6–9). The dwelling of the favourite Kaikeyī is thus described in Rām., ii, 10.11 ff. : Parrots, peacocks, plovers, and swans were to be seen there ; musical instruments resounded ; hunch-backed and dwarf women ran here and there ; arbours of climbing plants, and painted houses met

then, and then alone begins the happy female joy." "Milton," p. 32, ll. 17 ff. Cp. the dithyrambs : "I cry : Love ! Love !" etc. in his "Vision of the Daughters of Albion ", p. 7 (both in Ellis's edit.). See there especially the verses : "But silken nets and traps of adamant will Oothon [the wife] spread And catch for thee girls of mild silver, or of furious gold . . . Oothon shall view his dear delight, nor e'er will jealous cloud Come in the heaven of generous love, nor selfish blightings bring." The pair of women rivals in the Mṛicchakaṭikā is well known, who outbid one another in "nobility of mind " ; and in Kālidāsa's Mālavikā and Agnimitra the thoughtful queen ; as also, at the end, the praise of the wife who even finds new ladies for her lord's heart, because, she says, the river carries hundreds of streamlets with it to the sea. See, too, my Daçakumāracaritam, p. 305. But despite these and other like cases there is found, so far as I know, in India no historically vouched for example of the kind told us of his own wife by an Arab historian, according to Lane, *Arabian Soc. in the Middle Ages*, p. 246 : She bought handsome girls for her husband, and hoped to be rewarded in heaven for her friendliness towards her husband. Cp. the Turkish examples in Osman Bey, 136 ff. ; 143 ff. ; as also the Chinese wife whose husband falls in love with another woman, and who uses every means for him to get her (Dunlop-Liebrecht, 523b). There are other such cases. He that knows will understand them too. Of the Thongas in South Africa we are even told : "So indifferent are the women to their husband's morals that they will play the go-between for them in their overtures to other girls." Hartland, *Primit. Patern.*, ii, 207.

the eye ; campaka-trees and açoka-trees spread their leaves and flowers; handsome seats of gold, silver, and ivory invited one to reſt ; cakes and the moſt various dishes and beverages enticed the palate ; and all was decked out as the gods' own heaven. The soft luxury, the pomp and splendour of the palaces, the mighty army of servants and hangers-on, the debauchery in eating and drinking, the beſtowal of gifts on the Brahmans and supplicants, and their feeding ; the sacrificial feſtivals, and so on—in short, the whole Eaſtern court of the rulers is very often touched on or drawn by the Epic. It is, however, true that the later a certain piece seems to be, the more the poet also intoxicates himself with this overflowing luxury ; while where older conditions are reflected there often can be seen an extraordinary simplicity in the life of the Kshattriyas.

Needless to say, there is no wish to find these soft delights lacking in war and in the armed camp. Yudhishṭhira's morning goes on, as it is described in vii, 82, quite as at court : the court singers and congratulators sing and recite, other singers are heard, the dancers dance, all kinds of musical inſtruments resound. Thus the prince awakes,[1] then goes into his bathing apartment ; there, having put on his thin bath-robe, and seated himself on a splendid seat, he has sandal-water, consecrated with prayers, poured over him from gold vessels by a hundred and eight white-clad bath-servants, is rubbed with ointment (kashāya = sarvaushadhyādikalksa), and sprinkled with scented water ; he carries out his sacrifices, beſtows gifts on the flocks of Brahmans in his usual crazed way, and so forth. All this after so many days of murderous fighting.— And the Kauravas take counsel comfortably ſtretched out like the deathless gods on the moſt splendid couches spread

---

[1] When the Pāṇḍavas come on a visit to their cousins to play dice, they are sung to sleep by women (ii, 58.36). The king is, indeed, always to go to bed and to rise to the sound of music. Kauṭilya, transl., 47.14 ff. ; MBh., i, 218.14 ; ii, 5.86 ; v, 94.6 ff. ; Yājñav., i, 330. His person is so precious and so exposed to danger ; but music drives away magical evil ; indeed, the knowledge of music leads to redemption. Yājñav., iii, 115 f.

with coftly rugs (viii, 10.7). Even at the time of the final blood-bath carried out by Açvatthāman he finds Dhrishṭa-dyumna lying on a "great linen-white bed, spread with coftly rugs, decked with the moft splendid wreaths, perfumed with incense and sweet-smelling powder " (x, 8.12 ff.). Cp. ix, 29.70–72. The women could accompany their husbands into the camp. So, too, Draupadī took many women and serving-girls with her into banishment in the penitential foreft (iv, 4.4, and elsewhere), a description due, of course, to later revisers, and one that does not tally at all with many other ftatements in the Epic. (Cp. e.g. Dubois-Beauchamp [3], p. 678 f.)

For the guarding of the women's apartments there are the often-mentioned " wardens " : old men and eunuchs ; and the need and duty of a ftrict watch on the harem and women in general is often emphasized ; for the woman has an insatiable sexual appetite—on this something will be said later—and she can never be trufted. On the other hand the Epic is always declaring that all watching over women is useless. Indeed, he who watches over them not only beats the air with his fift, but goes to hell (v, 37.1–6). Bhīshma speaks (xiii, 40.13 ff.) : " Love of scandal and the luft of sex did the Maker give to women. The man can in no wise preserve them—even were he the All-Maker, and how much less earthly men. Whether it be by words or blows or bonds or pain of various kinds—women cannot be preserved by anything ; for they are always unbridled. And yet I was once told of the following case, how in times gone by, the safe-keeping of his teacher's wife was really brought about by Vipula. There was a moft excellent Rishi, famous under the name of Devaçarman. His wife was called Ruci, and in beauty had not her like on earth. Gods, Gandharvas, and Dānavas were intoxicated by her beauty, but particularly Indra, the slayer of Vṛitra. Now the great Muni Devaçarman knew the ways of women, and looked after his wife to the beft of his powers ; and he knew full well that Indra, breaker of ftrongholds, gives free play to his lufts with other men's wives. Therefore did he keep watch on his wife with a ftrong hand. Now one day the Rishi wished to make a sacrifice (for someone), and thought

480

within himself : ' How could my wife be safely kept ? ' When
he had thought out in his mind a way of keeping her, the
great penitent called his beloved disciple Vipula, the child of
Bhṛigu, and spoke unto him : ' I am going away to make
a sacrifice, and since the ruler of the gods is ever following
Ruci, do thou watch over her with all thy strength. Thou
muſt ever be watchful againſt Indra, the ſtormer of ſtrongholds.
For he takes on the moſt manifold shapes, O beſt of the
Bhṛigus.' Thus by him addressed, Vipula answered, ' Yes '
—he, rich in penance, with bridled senses, ever given to ſtrict
asceticism, comparable to fire and the sun in brightness, with
knowledge of virtue, a speaker of truth. And he in turn, asked
the departing teacher : ' What forms, then, has Çakra, if he
comes, O Muni ? Of what kind is his appearance
and his power ? Do thou tell me that.' Then did he
blessed with grace make known Çakra's juggling trickery
to the high-souled Vipula according to the truth. Devaçarman
spoke : ' Many-sided is the trickery of the holy and auguſt
Indra. He takes on this being, and that, many kinds of being,
always and again. He wears a tiara, he carries the thunderbolt,
a bow, he wears a diadem ; he wears ear-rings, and then looks
at one moment like a Caṇḍāla. Then he appears again with
bushy hair on the top of his head, with plaits, in bark clothing,
at one time as a man with a mighty body, at another as a thin
wearer of bark clothing. Also he takes on light, and dark-
blue, and black colouring. He appears as one ugly and one
handsome, as a youth and as an old man, as a Brahman and as a
Kshattriya, as a Vaiçya and as a Çūdra. . . . Another time he
takes on the shape of parrots, crows, swans, kokilas, lions, tigers,
and elephants. And he wears the outward semblance of a god,
of a Daitya, or of kings. As one well-fed, as one crazed,[1]
as a bird, as one misshapen, as a four-legged beaſt—in many
shapes does the fool further show himself. He also takes on
the outward likeness of flies, gnats, and so on. None can
take hold of him, not even the All-Maker by whom this

---

[1] Or : as one possessed, as one with the falling sickness (vāyubhag-
nāṅga). Cp. my Daçakum., p. 241 ; Jolly, *Medizin*, pp. 118, 119;
Ward, *View of the Hindoos* [5], p. xxii ; Kathākoça, p. 157 ; Petav.,
ii, 6.1 ; and many other passages.

world was made. And then again Çakra is hidden, and he is seen only with the eyes of (supernatural) knowledge. Further the king of the gods also changes himself into wind. Thus is the chaſtiser of Pāka ever going into changes.[1] Therefore, O Vipula, look thou after this slender one so that the evil-minded Indra may not slobber over Ruci, like a dog over the offering laid there for an appointed[2] holy ceremony.' When the Muni had so enlightened him, that moſt excellent Devaçarman then went to carry out the sacrifice. When Vipula had heard these words of his teacher, he took thought, and kept the ſtricteſt watch againſt the moſt mighty king of the gods. 'What can I do now to preserve my teacher's wife? For this ruler of the deathless ones is rich in magical lore, and it is hard to lay hold of the skilful one. The chaſtiser of Pāka cannot be kept away by shutting up the hermitage or the leaf hut ; for his power of making many changes is too great. Even in the shape of the wind Çakra might sully my teacher's wife. Therefore I will go into this Ruci, and now ſtay in her. As a man,[3] however, I cannot preserve her. For one hears that the holy chaſtiser of Pāka has many shapes. I will protect her through the power of yoga from him. I will make my way into her, limb by limb,[4] to keep her. If my teacher now comes back to find his wife something left over from what has been enjoyed (ucchiſthā), the great penitent with the godlike knowledge will undoubtedly curse me in his wrath. . . . But if I were to be successful (in keeping her really pure) then I should have performed a miracle. Through yoga the penetrating into the body of my teacher's wife is possible. Thus will I abide in her with a collected and heedful mind, not clinging like a shifting drop of water on the lotus leaf. For me who am free of the caſt of passion that will be no sin.

[1] Already Rigveda, iii, 53.8 says that Indra takes on many shapes through his māyā.
[2] Or : that has been ſtarted (upahita).
[3] Or : through manly address (paurusheṇa).
[4] Or after all better : " Into her limbs I will penetrate with my limbs," that is, according to what is shown by what comes after : with the spiritual, ruling power in each limb I will sink myself in the corresponding limb of Ruci.

For as the wanderer on the road goes into an empty rest-house, so will I make the body of my teacher's wife my lodging (cp. xii, 320.172, 188). Thus shall I dwell in her body with collected mind.' Learn now, O lord of the earth, how this child of Bhṛigu practised the greatest care after he had thus looked from every side at what is right and at the Vedas of the Vedas, had looked on his teacher's and his own bountiful asceticism, and had thus in his mind resolved on taking her into his care. As his teacher's wife and he sat there, the great penitent Vipula enticed her of the faultless limbs into correspondence with his purpose.[1] With his eyes, with their bridles, Vipula linked the bridle of her eyes, with her organ his organ, and with her mouth his mouth, and so penetrated into her body as wind into space.[2] Without stirring, the Muni abode there, hidden, like a shadow. Then Vipula dwelt in the body of his teacher's wife, strengthening and wholly filling it, and heedfully thinking always of the care of her ; and she noticed him not at all.[3] All the time, so long as the teacher of this high-minded one had not completed the sacrifice and came not home, he watched over her.[4] Then came one day the ruler of the gods, thinking : ' This is a good opportunity ' ; he came in celestial embodiment and

[1] That is, he drew all her attention in a certain direction, enticed her away, according to K (75.57) by telling tales (kathārthaiḥ instead of yathārthe).

[2] That is, he permeated her with his mind, so that the guiding activity (" the bridle ") which goes forth to every limb no longer came in her case from her own mind, but from his : her eyes were governed by the power of his mind which was directed to the control of his own eyes ; in the same way her sexual parts and her mouth were under the government of the corresponding activities of his mind. " Bridle " is better than " beam " for the reason that raçmiṃ raçmibhiḥ stands on the same footing with lakshaṇaṃ lakshaṇena, etc. Cp. xii, 320.17, where the translation should be the same.

[3] Cp. how in the same way the begging nun Sulabhā through yoga goes into the body of King Janaka (xii, 320) ; or how Vidura by the power of yoga goes into Yudhishṭhira (xv, 26.25 ff.).

[4] Or perhaps rather : " He waited for the time when the teacher of this gloriously-natured man should come home after completing the sacrifice " ?

shape to this hermitage. When the king [1] had taken on an incomparable, enticing beauty, and become a moſt glorious sight to see, he came into the penitential grove. He saw Vipula's body sitting there without ſtirring, with ſtaring eyes, as though he were only in a picture, and saw Ruci with the splendid corners of the eyes, the swelling hips and breaſts, the great eyes like a lotus leaf, and the face that was as the full moon. When she saw him she was minded to rise up quickly and greet him, amazed at his beauty, and wished apparently to say : 'Who art thou ? ' But as she would have risen, she was hindered by Vipula ; held back, O ruler of men, she could not move. To her spoke the ruler of the gods with very fair and soft words : 'Know, O brightly smiling one, that I am the king of the gods, that I am come hither for thy sake, tortured by the love that has sprung from my longing for thee. Therefore, do thou receive me,[2] O thou with the lovely brows, before the favourable time goes by.' The Muni Vipula heard Çakra, the head herdsman of the gods, thus speaking, saw him, as he abode in the body of his teacher's wife. And the faultless one could not rise to meet him, and could not speak, being withheld by Vipula. But the child of Bhṛigu underſtood the mien of his teacher's wife, and the moſt mighty one held her back by force through his yoga. And he bound all her senses with yoga bonds. But when Çacī's husband ſtill saw no change in her, he spoke shamefacedly to her that was bewildered through the power of yoga : 'Come ! come ! ' Then she would have answered him. But Vipula twiſted the words of his teacher's wife— 'Ho ! what is thy purpose in coming hither ? ' sped the words, adorned with rightful speech,[3] from her moonlike face. But she ſtood shamefaced there, when she had spoken these words under the ſtress of another. And Indra ſtood there, and was filled with confusion ; and when he saw her unnatural condition, the thousand-eyed king of the gods gazed at it with his divinely searching look. Then he saw that the Muni was

---

[1] This sounds ſtrange, and probably we should have janādhipa (inſtead of -paḥ) : When he, O king, etc.

[2] Read samprāpnuhi inſtead of samprāptaṃ hi.

[3] Saṃskārabhūshaṇā ; she thus probably spoke Sanskrit.

within her body, like the reflection in the looking-glass, having gone into the body of his teacher's wife. When the breaker of strongholds saw this man, endowed with terrible asceticism, he trembled in deep fear, filled with dread of his curse. But the great penitent Vipula left the body of his teacher's wife, went into his own body, and spoke unto the quaking Çakra : 'Thou fool with unquelled senses, evil-natured Indra, not for long will gods and men hold thee in honour. Hast thou, then, forgotten, Çakra, is it not in thy memory, that Gautama made thee to run, with women's parts drawn all about thee as tokens ? [1] I know what a childishly stupid mind thou hast, what an ignoble soul, what a shifting nature. This woman here is being watched over by me, O blind one ; go thy way, thou evil one. For to-day I will not burn thee with my fiery strength, thou with the unseeing soul ; but it is out of pity for thee, O Vāsava, that I wish not to burn thee. And if my most terrible, wise teacher were to see thee, thou evil-minded one, he would burn thee now with an eye blazing with wrath.[2] But do not do thus again, Çakra ; thou must reverence the Brahmans, else comest thou together with thy sons and ministers to destruction, annihilated by the might of the Brahmans.' "—The shame-stricken Indra vanished without saying a word ; and when the teacher came back, Vipula told him of what the king of the gods had done. Devaçarman praised and rewarded the faithful man, and " together with his wife, he lived without fear of Indra in the unpeopled forest " (xiii, 40, 41). It is true Vipula had kept silence about a part of the matter, which was afterwards brought to his consciousness as a blameworthy thing ; he then avowed all the details to his teacher, and all was well. The account ends thus : " But Vipula alone was successful in ever preserving a woman ; no other in the three worlds has it in his power to safeguard a woman " (43.27).[3]

[1] Thus the tale at least on this point is exactly as in Somadeva, not as in the Rāmāyaṇa. See also MBh., xiii, 34.27 f. ; K, xiii, 215.10 ff.

[2] Instead of tvaṃ, tvāṃ at least must be read. K. has gurur me.

[3] Manu, ix, 5–13, and Bṛihaspati, xxiv, 4 well show that what best safeguards is work and occupation.

But the woman can well look after herself, and good women do so also, as the Epic in agreement with the rest of the literature often declares, and proves it in beautiful tales. On the other hand it is the man's duty, stressed over and over again, to shelter the woman, to cherish and care for her, and whoever does not or cannot do it, comes to shame in this world, and to hell in the other (e.g. iv, 21.40–43 ; xiv, 90.45 ff.). Especially must she be well provided with food and drink. Only then has the man's life any worth (v, 39.83). " Let not a man resort with empty hands to the king, a Brahman, or a woman " (vii, 174.43), refers, however, probably to other ladies than his own wife. A gentle loving treatment of the woman is repeatedly enjoined ; he that is a hero towards her falls from the stalk like ripe fruit (v, 36.61).[1] " Towards women a man shall be without jealousy, but shall ward his wife, and to her be generous and kindly-spoken, uttering tender, sweet words, but not be under her thumb (vaçaga). Women are called the worshipful, most glorious, holy lights of the house, the goddesses of happiness and beauty in the home ; therefore they must most particularly be sheltered " (v, 38.10, 11). He that upbraids his wife over-severely goes to hell (v, 37.5). To this place of torment he, too, goes who eats before, or without, his wife (xiii, 23.71 ; cf. 23.82) ; and the precept that the wife, and the children and servants also must be first satisfied is often found in the Mahābhārata, as we have already been told, but has, anyhow in the actual life of Epic India, indeed, no foundation ; for a good wife here does as for instance Draupadī, and as the Hindu wife still does to-day.

---

[1] Indian literature is rich in beautiful sayings on the loving treatment of the woman. Reference may be made here to Mahānirvāṇatantra, viii, 33–47. In the same work (ix, 64) it is laid down : If a man utters ill words to his wife he shall fast for a day ; if he hits her, three ; if so that she bleeds, seven days. According to Yājñav., ii, 232 he must pay a 50 paṇa fine who strikes his brother or his wife (he that destroys the fruit in a slave-woman's womb, one hundred, çl. 236). " Women must on no account be chastised." Jahn, Saurapurāṇa, p. 115. The man must quietly take their abusive words, and never dispute with them. MBh., xii, 243.14 ff. Cp. Parāçara, xii, 56 f. ; Mahānirvāṇatantra, xi, 64.

486

Draupadī, too, only eats after the servants even (e.g. ii, 52.48 ; iii, 233.24). On the other hand, it was always repugnant to the Indian's feelings that the husband should let himself be supported by his wife ; a word for husband is, indeed, bhartar (the nourisher, protector), and for wife bhāryā (she that is to be nourished, or protected). He that lives on his wife comes, after death, into dreadful worlds (vii, 73.33). In xiii, 130.38, 39 he is on the same level with the Brahman-murderer, the cow-slayer, him who visits another's wife, and the unbeliever ; he goes like them to hell ; has to nourish himself there on matter and blood ; and is roasted like a fish (cp. e.g. xiii, 93.125 ; 94.22 ; xiv, 90.46, 47).[1] So they also are among the most shameful beings, heavily punished in the other world, who stand under the rule of their servants, wives, children, and of such as depend on them (āçrita), and let themselves be ordered about by them (saṃdiçyamāna, vii, 73.33).[2] The incapable man that does not give his wife fitting care goes to hell (xiv, 90.48 f.). It is a dreadful thing for Bhīma that Draupadī begs him and his brothers out of slavery (ii, 72.1 ff. ; cp. v, 160.112 f.=161.30 f.).

Still oftener is stress laid on the sinfulness of killing a woman. The maxim : avadhyā (na hantavyā) strī, " the woman must not be slain," is often found (e.g. i, 158.31 ; 217.4 ; iii, 206.46 ; v, 36.66 ; vii, 143.67 ; xii, 135.13, 14 ; Rām., ii, 78.21 ; vi, 81.28).[3] He who kills a woman stands on a

---

[1] These passages, indeed, in the first place, anyhow, are aimed at the horrible practice, not confined, in Old India anyhow, to actors and suchlike, of a man living on his wife's vice. This crime is equal to killing a Kshattriya, Vaiçya, or Çūdra, or a cow, and leads to torture for a world-era in the twenty-one hells, and then to births as a water-beast. Vishṇusmṛiti, xxxvii, 25 ; xliii, 26 ; xliv, 5. One so without honour cannot be a witness. Nārada, i, 183. Food from such as allow their wife to have a lover, or live with him under one roof must not be accepted by the twice-born man. Yājñav., i, 164 ; Vishṇu, li, 16 ; Manu, iv, 216, 217 ; Gautama, xvii, 18 (cp. with xv, 17) ; Vasishṭha, xiv, 6, 11. Indeed, he that takes money from his wife's lover, and so shuts his eyes, must pay eightfold as a fine. Kauṭilya, 360.4–6 ; Yājñav., ii, 301.

[2] See also Manu, iv, 217.

[3] Cp. e.g. ii, 41.13 ; xii, 73.16.

level with the slayer of a Brahman, or of a cow, with the ungrateful man, with him that desecrates his teacher's marriage-bed, and with the man who does not honour the guest (xiii, 126.26 ff.). The murder of a woman, together with unfaithfulness towards a friend, ingratitude, and the slaying of the teacher, makes up a set of four crimes for which there is no atoning (nishkriti) (xii, 108.32 ; cp. xvii, 3.16). Cp. Manu, xi, 191 ; Yājñav., iii, 299 ; Vishṇu, liv, 32 ; also MBh., v, 36.66. Dreadful, therefore, after death is also the punishment for such a hideous deed : " The fool that has taken a woman's life will have to go through many tortures in Yama's realm, and twenty incarnations (saṃsāra) ; then in an existence he is born a worm. When he has been a worm for twenty years he comes into the world as a human being " (xiii, 111.117, 118).[1] To crown all, to kill an ātreyī, that is, a

---

[1] The slayer of a woman arouses horror even in the criminal (Rām., vi, 81.22). He has to look forward, like the child-slayer, to the existence of a worm, as we find e.g. in Mārk.-Pur., xv, 19 ; and according to Agnipur., 203.7, the woman- and the child-murderer is tortured in the hell Raurava during the time of existence of fourteen successive Indras. Nārada, i, 225, casts these two into the worlds of worst torment together with the murderer of a Brahman, the ungrateful man, and the false witness. The killing of one's own wife is, according to Manu, xi, 89, to be atoned for in the same way as that most awful of all crimes, the murder of a Brahman. In the atonement laid down the slaying of a Brāhmaṇī is in Vasishṭha, xx, 37 ff., the same as that of a Kshattriya man, of a Kshattriyā woman the same as of a Vaiçya man ; for a Çūdrā woman the Brahman-murderer's dreadful vow of mortification (which for him lasts twelve years) must be carried out for a year. On the other hand Baudhāyana, i, 10, 19.2–3 (= i, 10.23) makes Çūdra-killing and woman-killing in general equal to one another (ten cows and a bull are the money-penance here ; no vow is here expressly mentioned). Āpast., i, 9, 24.5 seems to demand for all castes except the priestly one, as atonement for the murder of the woman, the same gifts of cattle as for that of the man. So, too, perhaps, Gautama, xxii, 17 (but evam will probably refer to the foregoing Sūtra, and demand the one year's purification for Brahman-murder besides ten cows and a bull. Baudh. would seem to point to this). Cp. Meyer, Altind. Rechtsschr., 56–60. He that kills a chaste woman (apradushṭā) must according to Yājñav., iii, 268 f., like the

woman that has bathed after her menstruation, is looked on as an unspeakably awful deed ; it is twice as bad as killing a Brahman (xii, 165.55).[1] And where a woman is beaten

slayer of a Çūdra man, undertake for six months the purificatory vow of the Brahman-murderer. But if she has led a bad life (durvṛittā), then he need only give for a Brāhmaṇī a leather bag, for a Kshattriyā woman a bow, for a Vaiçyā woman a he-goat, and for a Çūdrā woman a sheep, and thereby he is cleansed. Manu, xi, 139, sets the same value on the unchaste woman. Cp. Gautama, xxii, 26. In Manu's law book the killing of a woman, as that of a Kshattriya, Vaiçya or Çūdra man, leads to loss of caste, and he that is guilty of it must still be strictly shunned even when he has cleansed himself according to precept (xi, 191 ; so too Yājñav., iii, 299 ; Vishṇu, liv, 32). There, too, the king is strictly enjoined to have the woman-murderers executed also, like slayers of Brahmans and children, and other evil-doers (ix, 232); and so, too, in Vishṇu, v, 9–11. This offence appears as the type of the most dreadful sin in Mahānirvāṇatantra, iii, 153 also. Indeed, in the case of strange women (parastrīshu), as in that of men of a higher caste than one's own, twice as heavy a fine must be paid as in the case of men of equal caste, if they are spit on, kicked with the heel, or have filth thrown over them. Yājñav., ii, 213 f. ; Kauṭilya, 306.20–22 ; cp. Kauṭ., 305.6–7 and addition to it (in the case of certain verbal insults double the fine).

[1] All the law writings put this crime, as regards the atonement laid down for it, on the same level as Brahman-murder. So Baudh., ii, 1, 1.12 (= ii, 1.11 ; milder in i, 10, 19.5 = i, 10.27) ; Gautama, xxii, 12 ; Manu, xi, 88 ; Āpast., i, 9, 24.9 (in every case the ātreyī) ; Vishṇu, xxxvi, 1 ; l, 1–9 (here further the twelve years' dreadful penance explicitly described ; in both passages, however, atrigotrā instead of ātreyī through a false interpretation). In Vasishṭha, xx, 34 this direction is restricted to the Brāhmaṇī, and the commentators fill in this word in the other law books also. But probably this is wrong. Vasishṭha explains the ātreyī as a woman that has bathed after her courses, and therefore, when her husband lies with her, gets a child (35–36). Nīlakaṇṭha explains (but wrongly) in the passage from the Mahābhārata the ātreyī as a woman with child. On the view which here lies as a foundation it would, indeed, come to the same thing. In the prescription quoted from Vishṇu, it is also said of the woman who is just menstruating (rajasvalā), and her that is with child, that her murder is the same as Brahman-murder, and to be atoned for like it. Among the Old Germans also for a woman with child a higher wergild had to be paid (Rullkoetter, *The Legal Protection of Women among the*

the house is stained, and sacrifice there is useless; for the gods and the shades will not accept anything there (xiii, 127.6 f.). In general, he who is cruel and in any way evil (nṛiçaṃsa and tyaktadharma) towards women is branded as a disgraceful and criminal man (xiii, 93.122; 94.29). The ravishing of a woman [1] is forbidden to his band, indeed, even by the robber leader (xii, 135.13); true, he is a very pious one. If the king watches over the land, women can walk in the streets without being attacked, unaccompanied by a man and wearing all their finery; here probably what is thought of in the first place is the robbing of the weak (xii, 68.32). And no woman with womanly virtues shall be lied to or deceived, says king Janaka to Sulabhā (xii, 320.72–74). Want of uprightness towards a woman brings, he says, destruction, as it does when towards a more mighty ruler, or a spiritually powerful Brahman.

Ancient Germans, p. 33 f., 36); among them, too, the value in law of the woman depended largely on her capability of bearing more children. And, as among them the pregnant woman enjoyed peculiar privileges (Grimm, *Rechtsaltertümer,* 1899, Bd. i, 564 ff.), so according to Smṛiti she need pay no ferry-money nor toll; so also according to Kauṭilya (see 199.10–12 and addit. thereto).

[1] Or to carry her off against her will (na ca grāhyā balāt striyaḥ). According to Bṛihaspati, xxiii, 10, 15 the man who rapes a woman shall have all his property taken, his member and scrotum cut off, and then be led round on an ass; if the ravisher is from a lower caste, then the woman must be killed. On the other hand Parāçara, x, 21–22 on the whole teaches that, when a woman has been enjoyed by force or by intimidation, she becomes clean again through certain fixed vows of mortification and by her monthly flow. For the ravisher of a maid Manu, viii, 364 demands death; Nārada, xii, 71, and Yājñav., ii, 288 do so only when it is the case of a maid from the highest or Brahmanic caste; the first-named also ordains the confiscation of all his property. In the case of other girls the cost is according to Yājñav. the hand, according to Nārada two fingers. This last-mentioned punishment is also in Manu, viii, 367. Besides these there are milder prescriptions. So in Manu, viii, 378 the Brahman who forces even a warded (guptā) Brāhmaṇī to his will gets off with a thousand paṇa fine, a very handsome sum, it is true, for a priest's offspring. Cp. also Kauṭilya, 357.18–20; 364.15; and addit., 364.45.—The South Slav severity against the ravisher and deflowerer has also good effects (Krauss, *Sitte u. Brauch,* 204–213).

490

Men, it is true, have at all times and in all lands given their approval to a saying that is often heard, but expressed in somewhat varying forms (i, 82.16 ; viii, 69.33, 62 ; xii, 34.25 ; 165.30 ; cp. iii, 209.3-4 ; xiii, 23.60), and which declares that this is a lesser sin, and does not do harm, indeed, is neither a lie nor wrong-doing at all—an untruth where women are concerned, or during (or rather for) the pleasures of love, at the wedding, in jeſt, in personal danger to life, and when all one's property is to be taken away (or where deſtruction threatens all one's kinsfolk, or where the higheſt advantage of a Brahman is at ſtake, or where that of the teacher is at ſtake, or in general, to save another's life).[1] The finer feelings, however, even in such cases shrunk from an injury to truth. King Çibi Auçīnara says in a solemn affirmation with magical power : " As truly as I have never uttered an untruth towards children or women, nor in jeſt, nor in attacks and fights,[2] nor in my own diſtress, nor when disaſter came on me—so truly shalt thou raise thyself into the air " (v, 122.9).[3] And

---

[1] " In marrying, in the game of love, in jeſt and in sorrow a lie is allowable." Gautama, xiii, 29 (and thus " some "). Vasishṭha, xvi, 36, has inſtead of the laſt two cases : when loss of life or of one's whole property is threatened, or the higheſt weal of a Brahman comes into queſtion. A false oath is no sin either, where a beloved woman, a marriage, fodder for a cow, or firewood is concerned, or for the purpose of obliging a Brahman, Manu, viii, 112. Cp. also Manu, viii, 104 f. ; Yājñav., ii, 83 ; Gautama, xiii, 24 f. ; Bṛihaspati, vii, 34 ; MBh., xii, 109.14-20.

[2] Probably this would hardly be " agreements " (saṅgareshu). Inſtead of vaihāryeshu (in jeſt) K has vaivāhyeshu (in wedding matters). I read tathāpad—inſtead of the always possible tathā tad.

[3] Even for the sake of mother or father a man shall not speak an untruth (xiii, 107.50). " They that neither for their own sakes, nor for the sake of others, nor in play, nor to make a jeſt say that which is not, come into heaven. They that neither to save their life, nor for the sake of a holy end, nor of their own free will speak untruth come into heaven " (xiii, 144.19 f.). And in xiii, 115.71 we meet the beautiful inſtruction : " Speak the truth and not falsehood ; truth is the eternal good (the eternal law, etc.) ; Hariçcandra walks in heaven in moonlike glory because of his truthfulness." This does not harmonize with ii, 12.10 ff., according to which this celebrated king won such great

according to xii, 23.64 the deceiver of women must go to hell. Nay, he that hates women is a very low fellow, as, too, is he who behaves ill, when an arrangement is made for the joys of love (v, 43.19 ; 45.4).[1] And one must yield (" give glory in heaven through his Rājasūya sacrifice, and the open-handedness he there showed towards the Brahmans (like xii, 20.14), but it coincides with the so lofty version of the legend still current to-day in India, as it is given by Rāmakrishna in his *Life in an Indian Village*, p. 164 ff. Here Hariçcandra, in spite of the more than human sorrow that thereby comes on him, acts unwaveringly after his maxim : " It is written that to kill a thousand cows is as sinful as to kill one child ; to kill a thousand children is as sinful as taking the life of a weak and helpless woman ; and to kill a thousand women is as heinous as the crime of slaying a Brahmin ; but to tell a lie is worse than killing a thousand Brahmins " (p. 173). Cp. also my Daçakum., p. 75, note, and for the tale itself there discussed, Chavannes, " Fables et contes de l'Inde" (*Actes du XIV. Congr. intern. des Orientalistes*), No. xxi = *Cinq cents contes*, etc., No. cxvii ; ZDMG, 46, p. 605 f. ; Rosen, *Tuti-Nameh*, p. 248 ff. ; *Decameron*, x, 5 ; Fr. v. d. Leyen, *Indische Märchen*, p. 151 ff. ; Chauvin, viii, 123–4. On the other hand we find in MBh., xiii, 23.60 that one may lie only on behalf of a person of standing (the teacher ? gurvartham), and to save oneself ; but that falsehood otherwise leads to hell. Further concessions are made in xii, 109.17–20, where he that for the sake of the truth does not lie in the cases there given is even called a beggar of virtue or worshipper of the letter, and a low fellow. Krishna the cunning one even teaches that one may lie without scruple for the sake of one's own life, and that untruth is older than truth (vii, 190.47), which is in utter contradiction to other Indian sayings and the glorious Jātaka, No. 422 (Chavannes, *Cinq cents contes*, No. 490) ; while what is told immediately after of Yudhishthira's chariot (MBh., vii, 190.56) makes a parallel to that Jātaka. The same hero and god further sets forth that truth even thrusts a man into hell, if it hurts others, and supports this by a tale of robbers (viii, 69.46 ff.). And in this he does not stand alone in India. Cp. further the discussions in xii, 109; 110.11. To be sly with women is even a noble thing according to a saying of Cānakya (Kressler, *Stimmen ind. Lebensklugheit*, p. 177). Moreover in vii, 190.47 the rendering is possible, though not very likely, as follows : Better than the truth is (in this case) untrue speech.

[1] Sambhogasamvidvishama. Or: who is so base as to talk of pleasures of love (or blabs about them) ? But only so if we follow the scholiast's reckoning. But it is not a very good guide, and his interpretation of

the road ") to a woman, as to a cow, a Brahman, the king, an old man, him that is bearing a burden, him that is driving in a cart (cakradhara), a blind man, and a deaf man (iii, 133.1 ; xiii, 162.38).[1]   Thus woman muſt be treated friendly, but she muſt not be truſted, nor muſt secrets be told her (e.g. ii, 5.83 ; cp. Rām., ii, 100.49).[2]   Therefore let a man be careful not to certain expressions is a wrong one.   The set of seven " base ", " evil-natured " ones in this verse is probably rightly as follows : (1) saṃbhogasaṃvid, he whose mind (consciousness) has nothing else in it but the pleasures of sex ; (2) vishama, the dishoneſt man ? he who torments, ill-treats mankind ? (3) atimānin, the haughty man (over-concieted) ; (4) dattānutāpin, he that rues it, when he has given something (or according to 45.4 : who boaſts, when he has given) ; (5) kṛipaṇa balīyaṃs (in 45.4 kṛipaṇo 'durbalaç is to be read), the ſtrong man who proves a wretched fool ; (6) vargapraçaṃsin (or bahupra-çaṃsin), he that praises with the crowd (with the many ; hardly : praises the crowd, the many, although this would come essentially to the same thing) ; (7) vanitāsudveshṭar (or vanitādvish), the woman-hater.

[1] One shall " give the road " to the aged, the sick, children, carriers of burdens, women, people driving in a cart, a bride going to her husband's house (Vasishṭha, xiii, 57 ff.) ; to an old man, a king, one with a burden, a Snātaka, a woman, a sick man, a bridegroom, and to a man in a cart (cakrin, as often elsewhere), say Yājñav., i, 117 and Vishṇu, lxiii, 51. So, too, Gautama, vi, 24 f. (Cp. K, i, 192.13–14, where anyhow bhāri muſt be read inſtead of bhīru). All three also lay down the rule that if a Snātaka and a king meet one another, then the king muſt give way, all being as in Manu, ii, 138 f.   Inſtead of the old man we have here the man who is in the tenth decennium of his life.   Āpaſt. has Brāhmaṇa inſtead of Snātaka (ii, 5, 11.5–7).   Cp. Çukranīti, iii, 279 ff.   Mārk.-Pur., xxxiv, 39–41, gives the Brahman, the king, him that is tortured with pain, him that is superior in art or knowledge (vidyādhika), the woman with child, the younger man dragging a load, the dumb, blind, or deaf man, the drunken man, and the crazy man, the man-mad woman (puṃçcalī), the enemy, the child, and him that has been caſt out of his caſte.   Cp. Agnipur., p. 596.   Āpaſt., ii, 5, 11.5 ff. gives carts, carriers of loads, the sick, women and such weaker persons, and a man of higher caſte.   Then he goes on : " For his own good everyone muſt give way to boors (açishṭa), those caſt out of their caſte, the drunk, and the mad."

[2] From " but " on this is of course a thought that comes up over and over again.   Later we shall say a few words about it.

deliberate with woman ; here she belongs to the company of fools, madmen, and so forth (iii, 150.44). A man may ask women, but only if he wants to hear not the salutary but the pleasing (ii, 64.15). They are no good for matters of business, and here bring danger (v, 38.42 f.). But that in reality the women of the Epic even in the most important matters at any rate have their say, urge on, arouse, and so on we have already seen ; as also this, that they read the men a lesson, when they are wanting in any way. Cp. here also Rām., ii, 48 ; 82.25, 26. Moreover where there is a close and intimate relation between the husband and the wife, where the two are one heart and one soul, and their love but grows, as we are particularly told of Rāma and Sītā (e.g. Rām., i, 77.25–28)—how could a far-reaching share but be taken in all as a matter of course by the woman ? And when in Old India she did not get what she wanted, then she naturally had there, too, her very efficacious means, above all her tears. Women of rank, or at least of princely rank, had their sulking-room (krodhāgāra), and understood this art very well indeed. A splendid example of this is Kaikeyī (Rām., ii, 9 and 10). With eyebrows furrowed in anger she rushes into her " room of wrath ", flings her wreaths and all her finery on the ground, ties her hair in a plait as a sign of sorrow, throws herself on the bare ground, and declares to her serving-maid she means to die there, if her wish is not fulfilled. Anxious and sorrow-stricken, the woman door-keeper tells the king, who has come there, that the gracious lady is very wrathful, and is in her sulking-room. The poor husband and lover strokes her as she lies on the ground, coaxes her, promises heaven and earth. For a long time she will not look at him, nor speak to him, only weeps and sighs, and at last comes out with what she wants. Daçaratha, indeed, has not pondered on the reminder in Mahābh., ii, 64.11 : " If a bad woman is treated too well, she turns her back on you." [1]

---

[1] Just as Kaikeyī, the queen in the Buddhistic tale in Chavannes hurries off to her *maison d'affliction*, and keeps stubbornly silent (*Cinq cents contes et apologues extraits du Tripiṭaka chinois*, ii, 273 ff.).

With this chapter compare especially the addition in the " Appendix ".

XX

THE WORTH AND NATURE OF WOMAN

BUT it is not the good women who are referred to in such words as these. Their praises are sung by the Epic in fiery tones. " Honour women " we hear again and again. "Women must always be honoured and cherished, and where women are honoured the gods are gladdened. And where they are not honoured all religious deeds are barren. A family goes to ruin where the women are sad. Houses on which the woman's curse rests are as though destroyed by an evil spell, they are without light, and thrive not, for they are forsaken by good fortune. When Manu wished to go to heaven, he entrusted men with women, as their weak, easily led away, in truth victorious friends.[1] But if they have to live in jealousy, in a yearning after regard, and in anger, then they are unwise friends. But women deserve regard ; give them your regard, O men. For of a truth it is from women that the good (dharma), and all the pleasures of love come. They shall always have at their disposal service, homage, and worship from you.[2] Look ! bound up with women is the raising of offspring, the care of the child, and the wealth of joys on the earthly pilgrimage. . . .[3] As goddesses of happiness

[1] Or : victorious through truth ; where perhaps the thought is above all of the truth (truthfulness, honesty, the right behaviour and nature) of the man towards the woman, or perhaps of the upright, noble mutual relation between husband and wife.

[2] Or : " It is on women that the good rests ; all the joys of love, service, homage, and worship ye shall zealously give unto them " (with āyatta cp. also vii, 135.1 ; ix, 23.91). If this verse is set close to what follows, it could also mean : " All your joys of love, service and worship (of the gods ? of husband and wife ?) must depend on them." The imperative sounds odd here.

[3] Lokayātrā. Even the pseudo-Ignatius holds that women must be respected and loved, because the man without them cannot beget. *Zschr. d. Ver. f. Volksk.*, xii, 351.

495

and beauty, women, indeed, are always to be held in honour by him that would thrive ; if watched over, and held in check woman becomes the goddess of happiness and beauty " (xiii, 46.5 ff.).[1] The Rāmāyaṇa tells us that at first all beings were alike in stature, sex, speech, etc. Then the Maker made a distinction, took the best from all beings, and from this shaped the woman-wonder Ahalyā (vii, 30.17 ff.).[2] The man may take a treasure of a wife out of a bad or lowly famiy, too ; for : " a woman, a pearl, and water cannot be spoiled (hurt) (are adūshya, xii, 165.32).[3]

Sharply opposed to such passages as these are others which paint the woman as the sum and essence of all that is evil. We have already met with a good many very strong utterances on the subject of the wickedness of women. Here we will give further only something out of the very abundant stock of harsh sayings against the fair sex. They are, as is well known, very much in the mouth of the Indian in general.

Yudhishthira spoke : " I would fain hear of women's character, O best of the Bharatas, for women are the root of evils ; for they are held to be light-minded." Bhīshma now, as so often, tells an old legend. The divine wise man Nārada would like to be thoroughly instructed on the character of woman, and therefore betakes himself to the proper source, a woman, for she, indeed, best knows her sex.[4] She whom he asks,

---

[1] Cp. Manu, iii, 55–62 ; ix, 25–29. Rabindranath Tagore writes : It is impossible for a woman in a European family to attain to the varied perfections which a woman can in a Hindu home. Our women make our homes smile with sweetness, tenderness, and love. . . We are quite happy with our household goddesses, and they themselves never told of their ' miserable condition '. Basanta Koomar Roy, *Rabindranath Tagore* (New York, 1915), pp. 123, 125.

[2] Cp. what the MBh. relates of the creation of Lopamudrā (iii, 96.19, 20), and Tilottamā (i, 211.12 ff.), as also Kirātārj., vi, 42.

[3] Cp. Muir, *Metrical Translations*, pp. 277–278.

[4] The most biting judgments on women are well known to come from woman's mouth. The saying of Lady Mary Wortley Montagu is among the wittiest : " It goes far toward reconciling me to being a woman when I reflect that I am thus in no immediate danger of ever marrying one." The disdainful Indian pronouncements

496

Pañcacūḍā, the lovely, but like all her heavenly siſters very profligate Apsaras, at firſt will not do as he wishes : " As a woman, I cannot rebuke women. Thou knoweſt full well what women are like." He will not be put off, however, and she begins : " Women that are of good family, beautiful, and well married do not ſtay within the moral bounds ; this is the failing in women, O Nārada. Of a truth there is nought worse than women ; for women are the root of evils ; that thou, too, knoweſt. If women have found husbands who are acknowledged as rich and are worthy of them, and ever ready to do their will, even so they cannot abide them, so soon as they get another opportunity. But this is the evil nature of us women, that we, putting shame behind us, throw ourselves into the arms of bad men.[1] For he that runs after women, comes near them, and courts them a little—it is he whom they wish for. Women know no moral bars, and if they ſtay faithful to their law of morality and their husband, this is only because men do not woo them,[2] or because they are afraid of their serving-women. For them there is not a man they would not go to ; they do not let themselves be decided by any age ; be a man ugly or handsome, ' He is a man,' they think to themselves, and enjoy him.[3] It is neither from fear, nor from pity, nor from any regard to what is profitable, nor for the sake of the bonds of kinship or family that women keep true to their husband. Seemly women envy those fair ones who are in glorious youth, and wandering about free in sex,

on women can point to a whole army of kindred souls throughout the world. Cp. with this and the next chapter, for inſtance, Fr. S. Krauss, *Sitte u. Brauch d. Südslaven*, the ſection on " Das Weib ; Rosegger, *Volksleben in Steiermark*[10], p. 394 f. ; Elsie Clews Parsons, *The Old-Fashioned Woman*, pp. 203 ff. The view of the Arabs ſtrikes one as thoroughly Indian : Woman is the source of all evil on earth, and God only made this monſter that the man should learn to turn from earthly things (*Anthropos*, iii, 65).

[1] Or : worse (than our husbands) ; or : very bad.

[2] Ovid's thought : " Caſta eſt quem nemo rogat " we often find in Old India very emphatically uttered. Cp. e.g. Hitopadeça; ed. Max Müller, i, ſtrophe 115 ; 118 ; Garuḍapur., 114.9–10.

[3] Cp. e.g. Manu. ix, 14.

and wearing costly ornaments and garb.[1] And those women who are ever held in high esteem, watched over, and loved, they, too, fasten on to hunchbacks, the blind, simpletons, dwarfs, and cripples, O divine Rishi, and on to other defective and little-prized men—for women, there is no man in this world they would not go to, O great Muni. And when they cannot come to a man at all, then they even fall on one another [2] ; for they are not true to their husband. Their nature flutters this way and that, it is hard to serve them ; in their meaning hard to grasp as the (sparkling, witty) words of the clever man here on earth—thus women are. The fire has never too many logs, the great sea never too many rivers, death never too many beings of all kinds, and lovely-eyed woman has never too many men. This and other things (of this kind), O divine Rishi, is the secret of all women. So soon as a woman sees a handsome man, her vulva becomes moist. Even if their own husband grants all their wishes, even if he does what is dear to their heart, and shelters them, yet women cannot bear him. Not the richest enjoyment of their wishes, not ornaments, nor protection and home do they hold in so high esteem as favour and satisfaction in the pleasure of love. The god of death, the wind, death, the underworld, the ever-burning entrance to hell, the knife-edge, poison, snake, and fire—women are all these in one. Ever since the five elements have been, and the worlds have been made by the Maker, ever since men and women were made,—ever since then these faults have been in women, O Nārada." Yudhishthira spoke : " Men here in the world cling ever to women, ridden by a frenzied delusion brought about by the gods, and women in the same way to men ; that lies before our eyes, and the world is a witness to it. And now a torturing uncertainty goes through my heart. Whence is it that men have the

---

[1] This is exactly the opinion of Kshemendra in the 3rd tale of his Kalāvilāsa (see my transl. of the Samayamātrikā, p. xlv).

[2] Nīl. says : They put on an artificial penis, and so come to coition, and this is known to all—when the husband is away, that is. Cp. e.g. R. Schmidt, *Liebe u. Ehe in Indien*, p. 254 ; Brantôme, ii, p. 278 (often in the gallant France of his time).

inclination towards them, and under what conditions [1] do women take fire and grow cold again ? And how can the fair under these circumstances be watched over by a man ? Tell me, pray, of this. For while they are themselves going to love, they deceive men here, and no man gets free of them that has fallen into their hands. As cows fall on new grass, so they are ever doing to a new man. The arts of deception (māyā) that Çambara, the arts of deception that Namuci, that Bali and Kumbhīnasi wielded, these all women understand. They laugh with them that laugh, and weep with them that weep, and him that is unfriendly they catch with friendly speech, all through the hand of fate. Untruth they call truth, and so truth they call untruth. Mainly for the mind of woman, I think, were the political books of doctrine drawn up by Brihaspati and the other most excellent men.[2] If women are held in honour by men, their heart is false towards them, and if they are repulsed, their heart is false. And yet we have been told that these creatures are virtuous. What man could watch over them ? . . ." Bhīshma gives this recital of woman's wickedness his strongest assent, and tells an old legend : In times gone by men were so virtuous that they became gods of their own accord. Then a great fear came over the gods. They went in their distress to the father of the world, and he now made the witch-like women, so that they should mislead the men ; for in the beginning there were only good women

---

[1] Less likely : towards which men (keshu). But the first half of this çloka perhaps better : " How can men arouse lasting inclination in them ? "

[2] This is the linguistically most natural interpretation of : strīnām buddhyarthanishkarshād arthaçastrāni . . . kritāni. But women's artfulness is inborn in them, they have no need to poke their noses into books. This is also directly stated by Hitopadeça, ed. Müller, i, strophe 120. Thus perhaps it is rather : mainly because of the mind of women (that their tricks may be known) ? The real meaning would best be given by : " It is by drawing on the wealth of women's mind (liter. : taking out, or : It is mainly according to the practices [things] of women's mind) that Brihaspati and the other most excellent ones drew up the books of doctrine of the things (practices) of worldly life." Also the preceding çloka seems to make this rendering a necessary one. Cp. Hindu Tales, p. 286 f.

499

on earth. The bad ones, the evil magical beings, came into being through this creation, and Brahma gave them as their inheritance these roaming wishes, a bed, a seat, ornament, base nature, an evil tongue, and lust.[1] Then Bhīshma tells him the old legend of Vipula and his teacher's wife, and makes the very reasonable conclusion : " Both things can be seen in them : good and bad. The good women, the so glorious ones, are deemed the mothers of the world, and it is they who keep our earth in being with its forests and groves." The wicked and evil-bringing ones, however, can be known by marks. They love no man, not even him with whom they unite,[2] and are evil witches. Them a man must shun (xiii, 38–43).

The accusations here made are often found again in the Epic, but perhaps none so often as that of the ever hungering greed of sex in the woman, and of her polyandric passion (i, 202.8 ; xii, 33.45 ; xiv, 90.13 f.). Cp. v, 40.7 (" the fire cannot get enough wood, the great sea enough rivers," etc., as above) ; 39.82 : " In love a man cannot overcome a woman "[3] ; xii, 33.45 : " The band of women is the seat of appetite." [4]

[1] Cp. Manu, ix, 17. How bad women arose is also told in the legend of Peter and the two heads that were changed by mistake. See Bolte, Ztschr. d. Ver. f. Volksk., xi, 254 ff.

[2] It is, however, in general laid down of woman that she never really loves. See Samayamātrikā, p. xlv ; Sūtrakritānga, i, 4, chap. 1, v, 24. If one wished to give parallels only from Indian literature for the badness, especially the lustfulness, of women, it would make a whole book. A small collection will be found e.g. in Hitopadeça, ed. Max Müller, i, strophe 109–120.

[3] In full somewhat as follows : through sleeping sleep is not checkmated, through love not women, through wood not fire, through drinking not spirituous liquor (all of them always keep their old strength and insatiableness, one is never done with them). The saying (with a slight variant) is also in Garudapur., 109.34.

[4] Or : of love (kāmāçayo hi strīvargaḥ). The Bible is in agreement: Three things cannot be sated, and the fourth does not say : " It is enough." Hell, the locked womb of women, earth—it can never have water enough, and fire says not : " It is enough." Solomon's Proverbs, 30.15–16 ; that is, almost word for word the celebrated Indian saying, for Luther's :" hell " is the kingdom of the dead.

So that in fact Gaya Āmūrtarayasa must have been a pattern king, for he sated the gods with soma, the Brahmans with possessions, and the women with bestowals of love (kāmais, xii, 29.116). This satisfying of "excellent women" is also expressly enjoined on the horse-sacrificer (xiv, 90.13, 14), where, of course, we need not have in our minds a direct activity of the "father of the land ", but the well-known Indian doctrine that a good king brings about the right conditions throughout his kingdom through his actions and the magic of his being. So a proverb declares : " Food is valued when it has been digested, the wife when her youth is gone, the hero when he has won the battle, the ascetic when he has reached the other shore " (v, 35.69) ; and v, 34.40 advises, like many other peoples, the woman being ill-clad as a measure of precaution. But both are suggestions of optimists. Woman is ever the very embodiment of sensuality (xii, 213.9), and as such the cause of Saṃsāra (xii, 213.7). Instability, however, is a matter of course in the woman (v, 36.58 ; is found again almost word for word in Rām., vi, 16.9). The wise Agastya thus enlightens Rāma : " This is the nature of women since the creation : if it goes well with the man, then they cling to him ; if it goes ill with him, then they forsake him. The restlessness of lightning, the knife's sharpness, and the swiftness of the Garuda and the wind are imitated by women " (Rām., iii, 13.5–6). Woman does not really love at all ; not him that attacks her hotly (Mahābh., ii, 5.45 ; cp. Rām., ii, 100.28), not the gentle man (Rām., v, 22.2) ; of the poor man she wants to know nothing whatever (MBh., vii, 29.42 ; viii, 9.19 ; v, 33.56). What she wants of the man is expressed in the saying : " Thieves live on the careless man, physicians on the sick, the fair on their lovers, the sacrificial priest on the sacrificers, the king on litigants, and the clever always on the stupid " (v, 33.85). Therefore, of course, women cannot and must not be trusted (i, 233.31 ; v, 37.57 ;

The often-repeated çloka is also found in K, i, 128.8–11, where among other things there is added : If women see even son or brother in secret their vulva grows moist, which is in harmony with a view very often uttered in India (see e.g. Vetālapañcav., ed. Uhle, iii, strophe 9–10; Garudapur., 109.36–37).

501

39.74–75 ; etc.). The verse : " The Brahman knows the Brahman, the husband knows the wife, the ruler knows the minister, and the king the king " is, then, probably to be taken pessimistically : the Brahman, the wife, the king, etc., may blind another, but the Brahman's fellow, the wife's life-mate, the king's colleague, etc. know better (v, 38.28). For that no man can ever see into the real being and the thousandfold deception of woman can be read in Indian literature till we are wearied. We have just heard an emphatic support by the Epic from the lips of the Apsaras Pañcacūḍā. But what man does understand is that they are his misfortune. " The fool and the wise man, too, in the world are led astray by women with their power, are led under the sway of love and hate (wrath krodha).[1] Woman's very nature involves the destruction of men. The men of understanding do not cling over-much to the fair " (xiii, 48.37, 38). They belong, indeed, to those four things of the world, but especially of nobles and princes, which are often referred to also in the Epic : wine, dice, hunting, and women (e.g. iii, 13.7 ; ii, 68.20),[2] and among these four was shared the dreadful monster made by Cyavana, Mada or intoxication (drunkenness, lust, pride, etc.), as is often stated elsewhere, and several times in the Epic (iii, 124.18 ff. ; xiii, 156.16 ff. ; cp. xiv, 9.31 ff.). But we are taught in xii, 140.26 that they are to be enjoyed warily (yuktyā), but that to cling to them brings destruction. In women, especially the lovely ones, there abides even something of that most dreadful of horrors : of Brahman-murder (v,

---

[1] = Manu, ii, 214. Women's love is the intoxicating draught of the three worlds ; but while wine only clouds when it is drunk, woman robs the understanding, if she is but looked on ; and so she has infatuated the highest of the gods and wise men. Agnipur., 372.12–14. Woman is the fire, man the butter, which is bound to melt from the fire, if it comes near it. Bhāgavatapur., vii, 12.9. Therefore a man shall not be alone even with mother, sister, or daughter ; for the senses are all too strong. Manu, ii, 215 ; Bhāgavatapur., ix, 19.17. This is still the view to-day in India (Dubois-Beauchamp [3], p. 131). And so on indefinitely, all bearing witness to the weakness—of the man.

[2] A glowing and convincing speech in praise of the four and of the great merits of devotion to them is given in Daçakum., 340 ff.

13.18–20), according to the usual account a fourth part (xii, 282.43 ff. ; 342.53 ; Rām., vii, 86.11 ff.). Nay, according to the last-named passage, comely young women stand there fully equal even to actual Brahman-murderers and all their stealthy ways.

Love and hate live side by side in one house—"anger was made to be a help-fellow of love by the Lord God, the ruler of the gods " (xiii, 40.10)—and not only is woman, as the seat of lust, the cause of enmity in the world, and, indeed, as the Indians often declare, of the worst enmity, that which never dies,[1] but the tender sex itself is inclined to anger and hate. So they are fond of quarrelling ; and what a wonderful model king must Rāma have been, when under his rule women did not have disputes, much less the men ! (xii, 29.56). Moreover curiosity is woman's defect (xii, 328.20). And when the urge to learn something is awakened in the woman, then she is lost to every consideration, then her wish must be fulfilled without more ado, whatever the cost. The Rāmāyaṇa on this has an old tale (here, it is true, twisted) ; it is told by Sumantra, King Daçaratha's chariot-driver, to Kaikeyī of her mother, that she may give up her stubbornness (ii, 35.18 ff.) : " One that could bestow supernatural favour, granted thy father an incomparable gift according to his wish, and through it the high herdsman of the earth understood the voices of all beings. Thus, too, he knew what the beasts were saying. Now thy father, the bright-shining one, once as he lay abed, understood what a jṛimbha-bird was uttering by its call. Then he laughed heartily.[2] At this thy mother, who longed greatly for the noose of the god of death, was angered, and she spoke : ' I wish to know why thou didst laugh, my dear king.' And the herdsman of men said to the queen : ' If I explain

---

[1] E.g. Çiçupālav., ii, 38 ; Mahāvīracar., ed. Ratnam Ayar, Ranga-chariar and Parab, 1892, p. 129; in Schiefner's " Erzählung von der Hetäre Āmrapālī," St. Petersb. Ak., Bd. 24, col. 475 ff. ; Bose, The Hindoos as They Are, p. 43. Cp. Rām., iv, 17.31 (where rūpam means : woman's beauty). Crooke, The North-Western Provinces of India (1897), p. 142.
[2] Or : again and again.

to thee why I laughed, then I muſt at once die ; of that is no doubt.' Thy mother, the queen, again spoke to thy father Kekaya : ' Explain it me, whether thou go on living or not. Thou shalt not laugh at me.' Thus addressed by his beloved, Kekaya, ruler of the earth, related this thing according to the truth to that beſtower of favours. Then answered this beſtower of favours, the holy man (sādhu), unto the king : ' Whether she die or perish, do not tell her, O lord of the earth.' When the prince had heard these words from the man whose heart had come into joyful freedom, he quickly put thy mother away, and lived now amid joys, like Kubeia." [1]

While now this fair one feels no pity even for her husband, and is quite ready to give him up to death, juſt because her curiosity demands satisfaction, and while many another woman in the Épic feels none for other reasons, yet we are told a few times, too, of the woman's pity. In the account of what happened after Yudhishthira's disaſtrous dice-game we find : " When the wives of Dhṛitarāshṭra's sons learned of all this, how Draupadī went to the gaming-house and was there dragged about,[2] they all wept loud and blamed the Kurus greatly.

[1] This tale, here very ill told, is often found. See Jātaka, No. 386 ; Chavannes, Aes du XIV. Congr. intern. des orientaliſtes (1905), Cinqu. sect., p. 125 (No. xviii) = No. cxii in his Cinq cents contes, and cp. Rosen, Tutinameh, ii, 236 ff. ; Kuhn, Barlaam u. Josaphat, p. 81 ; Jacobs, Barlaam u. Josaphat, cxxiii ; Benfey, Orient u. Occident, ii, 133 ; Archiv f. slav. Philologie, vii, 318, 515 ; Schreck, Finnische Märchen, 44 ff.; Zeitschr. d. Ver. f. Volksk., Bd. 19, p. 298 ; Hertel, Das Pañcatantra, p. 284 f. These Finnish, Serbian, Tartar, and Georgian versions all have the cock as the pasha of hens ruling his regiment of wives, the cock whose superiority to the husband is so admired by Reinmar von Zweter in his well-known poem. He is seen in the same light in Chauvin, v, 180 (from the 1001 Nights). There is a monograph on the tale : A. Aarne, Der tiersprachenkundige Mann und seine neugierige Frau, No. 15 of the " F.F. Communications " ed. for the Folklore Fellows by J. Bolte, K. Krohn, A. Olrik, C. W. von Sydow.

[2] Parikarshaṇam ca Kṛishṇāyā dyūtamaṇḍale. See as to dyūta-maṇḍala Lüders, " Das Würfelspiel in alten Indien " (Abh. d. Götting. Ges. d. Wiss., N.F., Bd. ix, p. 10 f.) ; Meyer, Kauṭilya, addit., 310.40.

And long they sat with saddened minds, leaning their lotus-faces on their hands " (ii, 79.32 f.). And yet they were not very fond of her, for the readily understood reason that the " dark one " put them all in the shade through her wonderful beauty. So, too, Dhṛitarāshṭra says later (ii, 81.19, 20) : " All the wives of the Bharatas together with Gāndhārī wept there terribly, when they saw Kṛishṇā in the hall, the dutiful lawful wife, her that was glorious in loveliness and the bloom of youth. Together with the children (or : the people) they stand, and ever mourn for her." [1] Maṇdodarī excuses herself by the body of her husband, Rāvaṇa : " I ought not to bewail thee that art fallen as a hero, but since I am a woman my heart is in the bonds of pity " (Rām., vi, 111.74).[2] It is Sītā who shows most beautifully this above all (at least so it is said) womanly virtue (Rām., vi, 113.27 ff.) : Hanumant comes to her in captivity, and tells her of Rāma's victory and the death of Rāvaṇa. Then he wants to kill the cruel monsters of women that have so tortured and mishandled Sītā. But she will not allow it ; these poor slave-women, she says, had only acted on the bidding of their lord. " This old strophe with its message of virtue did the bear recite before the tiger. Hearken unto it, thou that flyest through the air : The good man lets not the evil, that other men of evil ways do unto him, reach him at all, but he must live up to the duty he has taken on himself.[3] The good have a noble way of life as their ornament. Whether a man be good or bad, or even worthy

---

[1] But here the *esprit de corps* of the sex is perhaps also, and indeed above all, at work.

[2] Or has kāruṇya here the meaning : mournful bearing, to give oneself up to sorrow ?

[3] He does not take this evil to himself (ādatte), does not let it come into his soul ; it can, indeed, never touch his innermost self. And then he never makes such action his own, he does not requite evil with evil. Perhaps the interpretation should be according to Sītā's foregoing words—that man enjoys only the fruit of his own work, and the genit. taken in the meaning of an ablat. : Evil does not come to one man from another, the evil-doer. The duty, the law of the good is naturally love and pity.

505

of death—the noble man must have pity ; there is none that does not offend." [1]

But it is not only of that pity which is so often exalted by the Indian as the beginning and end of all ethics that the woman is capable, nay, especially capable, but of redemption, too ; just as the despised Çūdra (and Vaiçya), who is often set alongside of her, she can enter into the Godhead for all eternity (xii, 240.34 ; 250.23 ; vi, 33.32 ; xiv, 19.61). Women, indeed, come before us quite often as teachers of men, even of the holy men, and it is the begging nun Sulabhā that teaches the famous King Janaka, him filled with the deepest wisdom (xii, 320). Since no husband who was her equal could be found for her, she was initiated into the utmost bounds of knowledge, and became a lonely ascetic (çl. 183).

---

[1] The commentator gives a short indication of the contents of this old tale of the bear, the tiger, and the thankless, base man, and this note together with the translated verses are the foundation of my poem : " The Bear's Revenge " (*Asanka*, etc., p. 61 ff.). Cp. Benfey, *Pantschat.*, i, p. 208 ff.

Sitā reminds us of Gudrun : she bears with just as much strength, faithfulness, and nobleness captivity and mishandling ; and like Gudrun towards the old she-devil Gerlind, she lets pitying kindness prevail towards the women-monsters after the splendid victory of her side. But such comparisons were probably made long ago.

XXI

Woman is a Chattel

AS our old, splendid Freidank says, in woman the greateſt and the lovelieſt and the baseſt and the uglieſt are found side by side ; no man can be so good as the woman, but then, too, none so bad as she.[1] In somewhat these words the views as a whole of the Old Indian Epic, too, might be summed up. But no matter how high or how low the various sayings, discussions, and tales set women, and no matter how important a meaning women may have had in the life and the business of life of the Indian world of those days—the fundamental view, even as yet seldom outlived, in the hiſtory of human development throughout the world, is not found lacking in the Old Indian Epic either : Woman is a Chattel (e.g. iv, 68.32 ; 72.26).[2] As the booty of war woman has an attraćtion, indeed, in all times and ages.[3] Therefore xii, 131.8 advises :

[1] Cp. Wirnt von Grafenberg, *Wigalois*, 5393 f.; Thiselton-Dyer, *Folklore of Women*, p. 3.

[2] Here the Kaffirs, for inſtance, are quite logical. Among them the son inherits also his father's widows ; his mother he does not touch, but may sell her. Usually he lets children be produced for him by her " as everyone's wife ". Poſt, *Einleit. i. d. Studium d. ethnol. Juris-prudenz*, p. 38. So, too, the wives of the dead father fall to the son, and he takes them to wife, among the Batamba in Eaſt Africa (*Anthropos*, vi, 378) ; among the old Persians, Egyptians, and Israelites (Ed. Meyer, *Gesch. d. Altertums*, i, 1 [3], p. 28) ; among the pre-Mohammedan Arabs (Welhausen, *Gött. Nachr.*, 1893, p. 455) ; etc. The woman is currency, indeed, in many places in the world ; vasu, thing, valuable objećt, she is called times beyond reckoning in the Epic also. The Rājput's wergild is land or a daughter to wife (Tod, *Rajaſthan*, i, 194).

[3] Cp. the already named passages, Richter, v, 30 ; Manu, vii, 96 ; as also Tod, *Rajaſthan*, i, 74 : " I possess numerous inscriptions (on ſtone and brass), which record as the firſt token of vićtory the captive wives of the foeman."

" Let the king who is sore pressed by the foe yield up his harem. For why should he have pity for the possessions of his foe ? " The wives of him that is conquered fall as a matter of course to the conqueror. Treasures and maidens the famous hero Arjuna brings home with him from his victorious campaign (iii, 80.27). King Virāṭa speaks : " I give well-decked maids, and various possessions, and what the heart yearns after in the fight " (iv, 34.5). Beautiful women as gifts to some man are found time and again in the Epic. Truly we have here in moſt cases probably slave-girls, as indeed is often expressly ſtated. But it is always remarkable that withal the beſtowal of bondmen as human wares is relatively seldom to be found. There was, indeed, no so precious a thing, with which to bring honour and joy to a man, as enchanting maidens in the bloom of youth ; and the men of the prieſtly caſte above all, even the penitents and holy men, know how to value such treasures, and weary not in proclaiming the meritoriousness of this kind of open-handedness. Karṇa shouts out in the battle that to him who shows him Arjuna he will give a hundred cows that will conſtantly yield a brass pail of milk, a hundred fine villages, as also a chariot harnessed with white, black-maned, she-mules ; and if he be not satisfied therewith, then he will give him a golden chariot with six elephants, and also a hundred decked, dark women with a golden breaſt-ornament round the neck, and skilled in song and the playing of musical inſtruments (viii, 38.4 ff.). When Drupada marries his daughter to the Pāṇḍavas, he makes over to them along with other wedding-gifts a hundred slave-girls in the firſt bloom of youth, and dight in handsome clothes, ornaments, and wreaths (i, 198.16) ; and so, too, Kṛishṇa sends them on this occasion fair-decked waiting-maids from various places, who have the gifts of beauty, youth, and skill. At the wedding of Abhimanyu to Uttarā, Kṛishṇa also beſtows on the Pāṇḍavas women, jewels, clothing, etc. (iv, 72.26), and on Arjuna, as already mentioned, at his wedding with Subhadrā, a thousand girls to be made use of at drinking and bathing feſtivals (i, 221.49–50). Dhṛitarāshṭra wishes to give Kṛishṇa a hundred lovely slave-girls that have not yet borne children (v, 86.8). As messenger's fee, Bharata, among other things, gives Hanumant, who brings him the news of Rāma's home-coming, sixteen well conducted, ear-ring-decked girls to wife, golden-hued women with lovely noses and thighs, with moon-sweet faces, favoured with every kind of ornament, and with birth from noble families (Rām., vi, 125.43 ff.). Also beautiful women or girls are brought as tribute to the rulers ; so to Yudhishthira a hundred thousand slave-girls wearing cotton garb, dark, slender, long-haired, decked with gold (ii, 51.8, 9 ; cp. 52.11, 29) ; at his horse-sacrifice, among the treasures brought him by the other rulers are women, too (xiv, 85.18) ; and on his side he treats the rulers with the like delicate attention (89.32). So, too, on other sacrificial occasions they always make up a part of the more or less rich flood of treasures poured out by the holder of the sacrifice. Yudhishthira at his kingly sacrifice bestowed hundreds of thousands of young beauties (ii, 33.52), and Çaçabindu a huge number at his horse-sacrifice (vii, 65.6)—on the priests and Brahmans, of course. Lovely women are always being mentioned as the dakshiṇā, or sacrificial fee. King Bhagīratha so gives thousands and thousands of gold-decked maidens, each standing on a chariot drawn by four horses (xii, 29.65 f. = vii, 60.1, 2). Cp. xii, 29.32, 133; vii, 57.5–7; etc. Thus, too, lovely maidens, splendid women, and slave-girls are particularly advised as gifts to the Brahmans at the çrāddha or festivals of the dead, and are bestowed even by the hundred thousand (xv, 14.4 ; 39.20 ; xvii, 1.14 ; xviii, 6.12–13). It is, however, to the Brahmans that such sweet things must in general be dealt out most plentifully, and the king that does not do so is an accursed ruler (rājakali, xii, 12.30 f.). King Sagara makes over to the Brahmans a palace all of gold, filled with lotus-eyed women and with beds (xii, 29.133). King Vainya gives a thousand lovely slave-girls to Atri, who has sung his praises (iii, 185.34). So the holy Cyavana lets women be bestowed on him (xiii, 63.39 ff.). They are the natural gift for Brahmans (iii, 315.2, 6). Cp. iii, 233.43 ; iv, 18.21 ; xiii, 102.11 ; 103.10–12 ; etc. Even a young widow is made over to the pious Çabara ; he keeps her as his wife (xii, 168.33 ; 171.5 ; 173.16 ff.). A penance is given in xiii, 136.6–7, for when a Brahman has let a woman be bestowed on himself : he is to murmur a prayer, and hold bare iron in his hand.[1] Judging by the context, however, a woman is meant whom he has received from a bestower who is unclean for him. Whoever shows his piety through open-handedness of this kind is naturally magnificently rewarded with lavish joys in heaven (with Apsarases, etc.). So e.g. xiii, 145.2 ff. And the man must make the woman helpful in every way to his own profit *here on earth*. Where he himself is concerned, let him without hesitation sacrifice daughter and wife, like everything else ; this is often advised in the Mahābh., too, a teaching with which on the other hand, we find, of course, associated its opposite, often and powerfully glorified in maxim and tale. From the accounts we have had set before us we have seen over and over again how a princess is put by her father into the arms of any Brahman that comes, though, it is true, he is very holy, because the father is afraid of the Brahman's curse, and so on. This must have seemed the more natural in the case of Sukanyā : The Brahman Cyavana, mortifying himself strictly, kept in one place like a tree-stump. The ants built a hill around him, and completely covered him. Then Sukanyā, the only daughter of King Çaryāti, came that way ; together with her girl-friends she went wandering this way and that in play. With wanton hand she broke off the boughs from the trees, laden with glorious flowers. She went off from her play-fellows, and came to the spot where the holy man was doing penance. When he saw the wonderfully fair, magnificently decked young girl, he was filled with joy, and spoke unto her. But she did not hear his weakened voice, and saw in the ant-hill only his glowing eyes, which looked like two fire-flies. Full of curiosity, she thrust a thorn into these things she could not understand. The already very hot-tempered chastener of his senses took his revenge by bringing a stoppage of urine and of the bowels on the king's army. In vain the ruler tried in his need to find out who had injured the old penitent ; it was on him he threw the responsibility for the mysterious disaster. When the good daughter saw her father thus troubled, she told him of what had befallen her. At once Çaryāti hastened to the

[1] This is well known to be very efficacious against all kinds of evil.

ant-hill ; but Cyavana inveighed againſt the maiden, who, he said, was blinded by his beauty, and finally let it be under-ſtood that he would only grant forgiveness, if he was given her as his wife. The king at once gave her to him, and the king's daughter, once so full of youthful high spirits, clad in wretched garb served the old and ugly Yogi as a loving, obedient, ungrudging wife, and quickly won his utmoſt content (iii, 122).

It is, firſt of all, highly meritorious to give of one's free will one's own daughter, above all if it is a queſtion of honouring or gladdening a Brahman, a penitent, or a holy man. It has been already seen in the discussion of the different kinds of marriage that under the " Brahmanic " form of marriage the father gives the daughter for nothing ; and this method has been put at the head and diſtinguished with its name by the prieſthood, of course not on moral, but on very selfish grounds. The quite gratuitous marriage of a princess with a Brahman, a holy man, or a penitent is found, too, in many of the tales in the Epic ; and in the Brahmanic view a very great honour is done to a ruler when the pious man accepts such a gift. That the proud nobility, however, in reality often even looked down with contempt on the begging pack of Brahmans, is put on record by the Mahābh. in various places, as already indicated ; and we are told of King Duryodhana : " The prince would not give his daughter to the Brahman, for he said : ' He is poor, and is not equal to me in caſte ' " (asavarṇa, xiii, 2.22). It is no wonder that a whole set of pious kings of the fabled earlieſt times have their praises trumpeted as having thought otherwise and given their daughters to the Brahmans, and as a reward gone into the worlds of the bleſt together with all their kinsfolk. So xii, 234 ; xiii, 137.[1] Such a shining contraſt to rulers of Duryo-dhana's kind is the pious King Yayāti, who at once assigns his daughter Mādhavī to the Brahman Gālava, so that the Brahman, like a kind of better maſter of hetæræ, can even hand her over to one ruler after another, and so through her acquire his wonderful ſteeds (v, 106.19 ff.).

---

[1] Such pattern kings also give sons to the members of the prieſtly caſte. But there is less demand for them.

Juſt as high, nay, ſtill higher, ſtands the giving up of the wife. Thus King Mitrasaha gives his beloved wife to the Rishi Vasishṭha, and thus comes together with her into heaven (xii, 234.32 ; xiii, 137.18) ; on Yuvanāçva Vṛishādarbhi beſtows, besides " his beloved wives ", all his jewels, and a moſt delightful dwelling, and is then, of course, rewarded in the same way (xii, 234.25).[1]

Women for the temporary use of the gueſt, or as a definitive gift to him, have been already alluded to (allusion to Kṛishṇa in v, 85.13, 14 ; 86.8). Yudhishṭhira keeps hundreds of thousands of young girls (dāsī), wearing shell bracelets and moſt splendid ornaments, sprinkled with sandal, skilled in the sixty-four arts, and in dancing and singing songs, that they may hospitably wait on the Brahmans (snātaka), miniſters, and kings, and he then ſtakes this valuable property at the game (ii, 61.8 ff.). To give fitting pleasure to the newcomer, even with a man's own daughter or wife, is, as is well known, a thing that is demanded by good manners, and therefore by morality, in very many places in the world.[2] But beyond any doubt this " virtue " has nowhere found a greater glorification than in the Mahābh. For here we find the following tale of the man that overcame death (xiii, 2.34 ff.). Agni who as a Brahman sought the hand of Sudarçanā, the king's daughter, and was given her after some difficulties, had by her a splendid son, Sudarçana, who in very childhood " took for his own the whole of the moſt high and everlaſting word of God '. Now

---

[1] Cp. Oman, *The Great Indian Epics*, p. 205 (a later Rajah gives a Brahman one of his own wives).

[2] See e.g. McLennan, *Primit. Marriage*, p. 96, n.; Grosse, *Die Formen d. Familie*, p. 112; Müller-Lyer, *Phasen d. Liebe* (1913), pp. 2 ff.; Weſtermarck, *Human Marriage*[3], pp. 72–75; Hertz, *Giftmädchen*, 120–21; Finck, *Prim. Love*, 78, 429, 478, 638 f. and elsewhere; Hartland, *Prim. Patern.*, ch. vii; Ploss-Bartels [4], i, p. 402, 430; Dargun, *Mutterrecht u. Raubehe*, 43; Schweiger-Lerchenfeld, *Die Frauen d. Orients*, 234; Weinhold, *Die deutschen Frauen*, etc., ii, 199 f.; Feiſt, *Kultur, Herkunft u. Ausbreitung d. Indogermanen*, 283 f.; Chriſtian Schulz, *Aus Hagenbecks Jagdgründen* (Dresden, 1922), p. 110 f.; Günther, *Weib u. Sittlichkeit*, 29; Schmidt, *Liebe u. Ehe*, p. 543 f. In India, to do honour to the gueſt, the daughter is also given as wife. Wilson's Vishṇupur., iv, p. 79, etc.

there was a prince, by name Oghavant, the grandfather of
Nṛiga. He had a girl Oghavatī and a son Ogharatha. This
daughter Oghavatī, her with the godlike ſtature, Oghavant
gave of his own will to this wise Sudarçana to wife. In union
with this Oghavatī Sudarçana dwelt in Kurukshetra, devoting
himself gladly to a life as father of the house. ' As father
of the house I will overcome Death,' [1] this vow was undertaken by him so rich in insight, him that blazed with flames.
To Oghavatī spoke the son of fire : ' Unto a gueſt thou muſt
nowise do anything that might displease him. Whatever
it be whereby a gueſt would be gladdened, be it even the giving
of thyself—thou muſt never harbour hesitation or scruple.
This pious rule (vrata) is ever aſtir in my heart. For him
that dwells in the house, O thou of the lovely hips, there is
nothing higher than the gueſt. If my word is to thee as a
guiding thread, thou of the lovely thighs, thou shining one,
then do thou keep this speech of mine ever faſt in thine heart
with mind firm-set. Whether I happen to have gone away,
or to be here, O sweet one, O blameless one, thou muſt not
disregard the gueſt, if I have to decide for thee.' To him
spoke Oghavatī, her hands folded humbly on her forehead :
' For me there is nought that I would not do without queſtion
at thy bidding.' But since Death now wished to overcome
Sudarçana in his house, he, ever following, went after him into it,
and sought a bare spot on him. When the son of fire had now
gone out to fetch firewood, there spoke as a gueſt to Oghavatī a
glorious Brahman : ' I would have thee, O thou of the lovely
face, show me hospitality to-day, if indeed the law laid down
for the eſtate of father of the house is unto thee a guiding
rule.' Thus addressed by the Brahman, the glorious daughter
of the king welcomed him according to the precept made
known in the Veda. When Oghavatī had given him a seat
and water for the feet, she spoke to the Brahman : ' What is
thy business ? What shall I give thee ? ' To the lovely
daughter of the king then spoke the Brahman : ' It is with
thee I have business, O lovely one. Do thou carry it out
without hesitation or thought. If unto thee the law laid down

[1] This is otherwise done through knowledge, through asceticism,
or through holy living.

513

for the estate of father of the house is a rule of conduct, then show me an act of love, O princess, by giving thyself to me.' The royal maiden offered him anything else he might wish, but the Brahman wanted nothing of her but that she should give herself. The princess, however, bethought herself from the very first of the words of her husband, and filled with shame said ' Yes ' to the Brahman bull. ·Then laughed the Brahman Rishi, and he and she sat themselves down,[1] she remembering her husband's bidding, who as he strove was ever mindful of his headship of the household. Then the son of fire came there with the firewood, on whom followed always, as on a kinsman, Death in dreadful shape. When he begotten by the fire god had come into the hermitage he called out repeatedly to Oghavatī : ' Whither art thou gone ? ' But she made no answer, because she had been touched by the Brahman with his hands, and was a faithful wife. She thought to herself : ' I am only what another man has left over,' and was ashamed before her husband ; the good woman kept silent, and spoke no word in answer. Then spoke Sudarçana again to her[2] : ' Where is the good one ? Where has she gone ? What is there dearer to me than she ? Why does she not come to meet me smiling to-day as before, the faithful wife, the truthful one, ever joyfully given to perfect honesty ? ' But the Brahman in the hut made answer to Sudarçana : ' Know, O son of fire, that I am come as a guest, and am a Brahman. This wife of thine, O best one, offered me every kind of honour for guests, but I wished for her for myself. In this wise did the lovely-faced one come to me. Whatever else is fitting here, do thou do it.' But Death followed him, with an iron pick in his hand, and thought : ' If he is untrue now to his pledge, I shall slay him.' But Sudarçana, who in thought, deed, eye, and speech had put aside jealousy, had put aside anger, smilingly spoke these words :

---

[1] According to B. : they went in, into the house. K. has upaviveça (instead of atha viveça). The expression also means " to have connection ", but evidently not here.

[2] Tāṃ provāca. Probably not : "about her." Taken figuratively, the usual " to her ", it is true, could be used here, too.

'Luck to thee in the pleasures of love,[1] O firﬅ among Brahmans ! For to me this now is the greateﬅ joy. The firﬅ law of the father of the house is, indeed, to honour the gueﬅ that is come. The wise say there is no higher law and merit than this, that the gueﬅ go his way having been honourably entertained by him that dwells in the house.[2] I, indeed, have taken this vow : My life and my wife, and whatever else I have I muﬅ give my gueﬅs. And that this word which I have spoken will brook no doubt—in witness to this truth, O Brahman, I touch my own body. The earth, the wind, the ether, water, fire as fifth, the mind (buddhi), the soul (ātman), the heart (manas), time (kāla), and space (diças) —these ten conﬅituents, indeed, dwelling in the bodies of those that carry bodies, are ever beholding the good and the evil deed, O beﬅ among those faithful to the law. So true as the words are true which I have now spoken, so truly shall the gods shield me or burn me.'[3] Thereupon there was heard again and again from every direction a loud sound in all the quarters of the world : 'That is true,' and 'That is not a lie'. But thereupon that Brahman came out of the hut, filling heaven and earth with his form, as though the wind had arisen.[4] Making the three worlds to ring with the tone of recitation true to art, he spoke unto this man that knew virtue, addressing him firﬅ by name : ' I am the god of righteousness and virtue, come here, if so I may say, to put thee, O guiltless one, to the teﬅ ; and having come to know thy uprightness, I feel towards thee the higheﬅ glad approval. Thou haﬅ overcome Death, who

[1] That is, suratam used like susnātam, etc. Or according to the usual meaning: Let the pleasures of love be thine, that is, set about them!
[2] If a gueﬅ goes away disappointed or unsatisfied, he leaves his evil deed behind him there, and takes with him inﬅead the good works of the maﬅer of the house. This is the teaching of the MBh., and e.g. Vishṇupur., vol. iii, 94, 123 ; Mārk.-Pur., xxix, 31, 32 ; Çivapurāṇa, xlii, 23 ; Vishṇusmṛiti, lxvii, 33, and Jolly's note thereon in SBE, vii, p. 215. Cp. Manu, iii, 100, and especially my *Altind. Rechtsschriften*, p. 334 f.
[3] Of course, according as these words are true or not true.
[4] Or : set itself up (udyata). The wind does indeed fill the whole world.

goes in after thee here ; he was ever looking for a weak spot in thee, and now has been beaten by thee through thy staunchness. And none in the three worlds, O best of men, has the power even to look on this faithful woman, thy good wife. Whatever this woman that none can stain, sheltered through thy virtues and her virtues as a faithful wife, may say, so it is, and not otherwise.'" Then he further praises the moral greatness of the two, and says that Oghavatī, who has rid herself of all failings and vices through her obedience to her husband, and wields yoga, shall with one half be left to Sudarçana, but with the other half she shall become the river of her name that wipes away sin. Together with her he shall come into the worlds of bliss, from which none ever come back again into the Saṃsāra. The conclusion is made up of a fresh song of praise for hospitality, as being better than a hundred sacrifices ; and assurance is given that a man shall come unto holy and blessed worlds, if he relate this " tale—bringing fame, long life, and all happiness—of the man who as father of a house overcame Death ".[1]

[1] The tale belongs to the great cycle, well represented especially in the MBh., of the temptation of the good man, which I hope to treat separately some time. One or two knights of the same kind as this overcomer of Death may here be mentioned. In Yule's *Marco Polo* [3], vol. 1, p. 210, we find it said of the dwellers in Kambul in China : " If a foreigner comes to the house of one of these people to lodge, the host is delighted, and desires his wife to put herself entirely at the guest's disposal, whilst he himself gets out of the way, and comes back no more until the stranger shall have taken his departure." And the Venetian reports of the province of Caindu : " When they fall in with any stranger in want of a lodging they are all eager to take him in. And as soon as he has taken up his quarters the master of the house goes forth, telling him to consider everything at his disposal, and after saying so he proceeds to his vineyards or his fields, and comes back no more till the stranger has departed." The guest then has his pleasure of the women in the house that please him, and hangs his hat, or some other mark, on the door, that the master may know how long to stay away (ii, 54). Both peoples saw in this custom, handed down from of old, the necessary condition for the gods being well-disposed to them. On the other hand the purest good-fellowship is what seems to inspire the Namaqua Hottentots : " If a husband has been out hunting and on his return finds his place occupied, he sits down at the

WOMAN IS A CHATTEL

The splendid, bold flight of the unbending, pitilessly logical zeal of the dreamer for some one virtue or for virtue in general, the intoxicated ethical enthusiasm that so often carries the Hindu irresistibly away, is also brought out strongly by this legend. And needful, dreadfully needful, it is evident, was an incitement like this to the not at all so very hospitable Old Indian people.[1] This tendencious sermon, of course, does not refer to real conditions ; it did not occur to the Old Indian actually to practise this kind of " piety ". And as the Brahman who here appears as guest is any guest in the fullest meaning,[2] what we have, at any rate in the first place, is a show feat of priestly pride. It was quite in the same way that the often very bold, and bodily and morally louse-ridden travelling community of little poets and singers, the band of the unhoused, used to sing the praises in the Middle Ages of that incomparable " warm charity ", so pleasing to God, that they so ardently yearned for from kind-hearted ladies (cp. Hagen's *Gesamtabenteuer*, ii, 248 ff. ; Meyer, *Isoldes Gottesurteil*, 42–45, and the notes there ; *Altind. Rechtsschr.*, 340 ; 398 f.). To be taken somewhat more in earnest is what Sanatsujāta says about the six marks of true friendship (v, 45.12 ff.). Among these is the giving to a friend of son and wife.[3] A pattern friend of this

door of his hut, and the paramour handing him out a bit of tobacco, the injured man contentedly smokes it till the other chooses to retire " (Hartland, ii, 212 after Sir James Edward Alexander, *An Expedition of Discovery into the Interior of Africa*, 1838, vol. i, 196). He thinks, indeed, as does that Bushman : " What are women otherwise for ? " (Alexander, ii, 21).

[1] Cp. my transl. of the Kuṭṭanīmatam, v, 217 ff. (p. 32 ff.).
[2] So e.g. in MBh., iii, 200.61 ; xiii, 35.1. We find it expressly stated in Āpastamba, ii, 3, 6.3–6 ; Vasishṭha, xi, 13, that guest and Brahman are one and the same thing, as, too, in several other places. See my *Altind. Rechtsschriften*, pp. 334, 337.
[3] As is well known, a custom also, like the lending and exchanging of a wife, in olden and later times in the most differing places in the world. The most famous case is Cato, who gave up his Marcella to his friend Hortensius ; and according to Strabo this was here also in accordance with good and old tradition (Lippert, *Kulturgesch.*, ii, 18). But in India it is often declared that the wife must not be given to any man (e.g. Bṛihaspati, xv, 2).

kind would be Krishna, who is ready to give even his wives and sons to his dear friend Arjuna (x, 12.28 ; cp. v, 65.9). Karna even wants to bestow his sons and wives on him that shall show him in the battle where Arjuna is to be found (viii, 38.20). It is true that he may not have been left untouched by the customs of his kingdom ; anyhow, it was said of Angaland that in it the sale of one's own wife and own children, together with the exposure of the sick, was a native custom, and, indeed, this is brought before us as a heavy shame (viii, 45.40. Cp. i, 104.40 ?).

But *property* is what the woman is ; he that takes away from another his married darling takes away his property (vasu) ; he is freed from this sin if for a year he undertakes the mortification appointed for Brahman-murder (xii, 35.25 ; cp. 35.24). The owner can naturally do what he likes with his own, and this principle is, indeed, still applied to the woman also, in all its meaning, among many peoples and tribes. It is found juridically in the India of the Epic also. But nobler views on woman, a high position for the woman in esteem and her activities, which was really to be found, in the upper classes of the population at least, and a finer, purer ethic were alive. Here the already discussed Dyūtaparvan is instructive. Yudhishthira in the dice-game, having lost all his other possessions, first stakes his brothers, with an unwilling regret, it is true, beginning with the youngest, then himself, and finally, on his opponent's challenge, his wife—and her with the utmost, most matter of fact cold-bloodedness in the world ; indeed, he goes on in a long speech to praise her charms and gifts, as a slave-dealer might praise the beauty and accomplishments of his stock of women. The assembly of men has up to now calmly looked on ; there is no sound or gesture of disapproval. But so soon as the "wretched excrescence" Yudhishthira thus yields up Draupadī, it is: "Shame, shame ! "; the voices of the old men were raised from the hall (sabhya). The gathering in the hall was deeply moved ; sorrow and pain came over the princes ; the sweat broke forth from Bhīshma, Drona, Kripa, and the others. Vidura held his head in his hands, and was as one forsaken by life ; with bowed face he sat there in anxious, gloomy thoughts, and breathed heavily like a snake. But Dhritarāshṭra kept on asking in joyful excitement : " ' How ? Won ? How ? Won ? ' and gave no heed to his mien. Karṇa with Duḥçāsana and his other (brothers) rejoiced immoderately. But from the eyes of the other men in the hall the water gushed " (ii, 65.40 ff.). When Draupadī is then actually played away, and Duryodhana wishes to treat her as a slave, Vidura prophesies its fall to the Kuru race. Then follow the events in the hall so insulting to Draupadī, and she never raises any question as to her having fallen according to law and custom to the winner in the game, if only it is certain that Yudhishthira before putting her to the hazard of fortune has not lost his own freedom, and with it every right of property. She makes appeal to the noble and dignified lords, and begs them to decide whether she is really a slave or not. And now the thoughts of those present struggle and wrestle with this complicated question of law, seeking a solution. Where a good heart speaks, as in Bhīma, there is room but for one thing : a holy wrath at such a crime ; and even one of the sons of Dhritarāshṭra, Vikarṇa, presses his hands together in anger, pain, and despair, because the assembly, mainly out of fear of Duryodhana, sits there dumb, while according to Vikarṇa's loudly uttered consciousness of the law Yudhishthira was absolutely without the power to gamble away the noble princess, since from the first he had only a part-ownership in her, and then as bondman had lost all rights in her. A storm of applause follows his words. But then the scales again turn in Duryodhana's favour ; all the good ones utter loud cries of blame that the Kauravas would not settle Draupadī's case. But in the hall they are swayed this way and that, for and against the poor proud woman. Duryodhana then leaves the decision with the five brothers, especially Yudhishthira ; this way out of it is hailed by many with loud shouts of applause, and much waving of shawls, while others utter loud cries of pain. They all look intently at the brothers, especially the eldest one. The latter wraps himself in his silent wretchedness, Bhīma gives vent to his rage, the worthless Arjuna, who is also here, needless to say, dreadfully correct,[1]

[1] The only word for him, we think, would be that flabby, weak expression so dear to the mollusc-like mind : " faultless."

thinks : "The king was a free maſter when he ſtaked us. But what he was maſter of, when he had gambled himself away, this is the queſtion that the Kurus here muſt decide together." Then the evil-boding signs resound, and Dhṛitarāshṭra lets mildness have the upper hand. The difficulty around which everything turns in the long discussion is only this : Was Yudhishṭhira ſtill lord of anything (īça) when he offered Draupadī ? We know he was not so. But for the knowledge of law in those days the queſtion was a knotty one. For Bhīshma, the truly noble teacher of law in the Mahābh., acknowledges the matter to be too subtle for him : Yudhish-ṭhira, indeed, has already become a slave, he says, and thus without any possessions whatever, but on the other hand the wife ſtands always under the husband's sway. But what the bungling interpreter of the law has to leave doubtful, holds no darkness for the eye of the unspoiled mind, nor for the noble heart. " A dice-game (atidyūta, ii, 71.17) carried beyond the bounds of what is right was played here, since ye are disputing about a woman in the gaming-hall ; happiness and well-being will be utterly deſtroyed for you, O Kurus, for ye are plotting evil deeds "—shouts Vidura, and this is the feeling not only of the honourable Bhīma, but of almoſt all those there, as also of the people and the women. According to Dhṛitarāshṭra's own account the Brahmans also were " angered when Draupadī was dragged about " (ii, 81.22 ; see the whole matter in ii, 65 ff.). Now as the woman is herself property, she, of course, in principle cannot own anything. What she acquires belongs to her owner (her father or her husband).[1] The wife is here the same as the slave and the child (i, 82.22 ; ii, 71.1 ; v, 33.64). But that the woman could own private property beſtowed on her or inherited, this we have already seen.

In the same way the ſtandpoint of ownership was taken, where the wife offended in the case of the wife's adultery. The law literature deals but little with this ; is it, indeed, not a public matter, but one above all for the husband's decision. But in this also his powers are limited partly through prescrip-tions of the law, partly through the prevailing moral attitude,

[1] On the other hand, according to Mahānirvāṇatantra, xii, 25, 111, as already mentioned, what a woman acquires herself is her property.

as we have already often seen in the Epic. What is common to the whole of Indian literature is the casting off of the wife as a punishment for unfaithfulness. This punishment inflicted by the husband does not put any stain on him, and on the other hand cleanses the wife (xii, 34.30). Nīlakaṇṭha says on this point, in agreement with the law writings, that the punishment and atonement lies in the sinning woman being upbraided, having only food and clothing, not being allowed near him by her husband, and being debarred from sexual intercourse.[1]

[1] " Public punishments for adulteresses are only spoken of in general for particularly glaring cases ; they are then to suffer a more severe death penalty (M., 8, 371 ; Vi., 5, 18 ; etc.) ; in ordinary cases it was only the jurisdiction of the injured husband or his family that came into action." Jolly, *Recht u. Sitte*, p. 128. Yājñav., i, 70, 72, ordains : Let him (the husband) leave the unfaithful wife to dwell robbed of her dignity, dirty, living only on a mouthful, despised, and sleeping on the ground ; but if she has got with child by the stranger, then it is laid down she shall be cast off. Manu, xi, 177 f., is not so severe. In Nārada (xii, 91–92) we find : Where she is unfaithful to her husband, there is, for the woman, shaving the head, sleeping on the bare ground, bad food, and bad clothing (or : bad housing, kuvāsas), and for work the removal of garbage and rubbish. Vasishṭha ordains : If the woman has really committed adultery she shall for one year wear a garment smeared with melted butter, and sleep on a mat of (holy) kuça-grass, or in a pit with (purifying) cows' dung. At the end of the year the husband shall make a sacrifice in fire, reciting 108 times the Gāyātrī, and the formula : " Water is light, water is the deathless," and she at the same time shall bathe in water. Then she is cleansed once more. But she must be cast off, if she gives herself to the Guru, or to her husband's disciple, or to a man of lower caste ; and if she at the time of her ṛitu has carnal intercourse with another man, then she loses all religious and social rights (xxi, 8–10). According to Baudh., ii, 2, 3.48, the adulteress must do kṛicchra. And so on. But if the faithless wife has atoned for her sin, then she must be treated just as before her misdeed. Āpast., ii, 10, 27.1. A stirring picture of the delights and the woes of adultery is given in Kuṭṭanīm., strophes 789–838. Here the casting out from the family, the censure by people, danger to life, the journey to hell, and other pains are given as the lot of the wife forgetful of virtue. The cutting off of the nose, riding an ass, and so on is well enough known out of Indian literature. The adulteress

walks abroad as one unclean, the house she goes into is defiled, and the Brahman may take no food from her (Parāçara, x, 32–34; Āpast., i, 7, 19.16). As we have already been told, in losing her virtue she has also lost her womanhood and rights as a woman : if anyone kills her, he is practically left unpunished. But besides this there are, it is true, milder views enough. According to an old verse quoted by Manu, viii, 317, and Vasishṭha, xix, 44, the adulteress is not guilty in any way, but the guilt falls on her lord and master, who should have made the mistake impossible. The same view, it would seem, is found also among the Maori ; for among them the kinsfolk of a woman take a bitter revenge on the husband for a sexual offence on her part. Hartland, i, 279 ; cp. ii, 33. And among the Baganda he has to pay them a heavy fine, for he should have looked after her. Her offence becomes known through her dying in child-bed. Hartland, i, 276 (cp. here e.g. also *Zeitschr. f. Ethnol.*, v, p. 262). And in other cases too the general rule with mankind, which spares, and often even exalts, the man sinner in things of sex, but crushes the woman, is often reversed. See e.g. *Anthropos*, iv, 315 ; Hartland, ii, 220 ; Wright, *Hist. of Nepal*, p. 33 (among the Mewār in Nepal). The forbearance with which the adulterous wife is treated might be called something quite without example when set against the often very great severity shown towards the man sinner, such as we find in the Old Indian law literature, in the Purāṇas and elsewhere. Of this we have already often been told (pp. 206; 220; 227; 249 f.; 312; etc.). Here we will only give some further matter in short form from MBh., K, xiii, 58 f., and Agnipur., 165.6 f., 19 ff. Since the woman is not sullied by any sexual intercourse, or, anyhow, the uncleanness is always carried away by her monthly flow, the husband must not cast off the unfaithful wife. The woman's vulva is there for the member of all. But on the husband falls a very heavy guilt. Only when the wife becomes pregnant by a man of lower caste may the husband, according to MBh., K, cast her off, while the Agnipur. even then lays down : he shall wait till the " thorn " or " sorrow-bringing foreign body " (çalya) has come out of her through birth, and she has menstruated again ; then she is " clean " again for him. Between the ṛitu times (tīrthāntare) her vulva is quite free to all, says MBh., K, repeatedly (cp. p. 121 in the present work). See also Meyer, *Altind. Rechtsschr.*, 22 f.; 73 ; 141 ; 167 ; 342.

Among the old Germans also the wife was the man's property. According to Tacitus, *Germania* 19, the punishment of the adulteress was left in the hands of the husband and the clan. As is well-known, it was very severe. This standpoint made itself still so strongly felt in later times that, according to Gregory of Tours, a man named Eulalius, who complained to King Gunthram that his wife had left

WOMAN IS A CHATTEL

We muſt, indeed, hold xii, 35.30 to be very mild : " To wives, however, on whom the suspicion lies that they are bad the man of underſtanding shall not go. They are cleansed by the monthly flow like a vessel by ashes." Like the whole literature in many passages, so the Epic throughout shows a kindly and tender, or a cynical and cheerful forbearance towards women's miſtakes [1] ; indeed, we have already seen several cases of this. But this does not spring from any contempt of woman's chaſtity, praised, too, as it is in the higheſt terms by the Epic. For it is of infinite value for the continuance of the

him and was living with another man was only laughed at. Rull-koetter, *Legal Protection*, p. 77.

As among the old Germans (Grimm, *Deutsche Rechtsaltertümer*, ed. Heusler and Hübner, Bd. i, p. 563), among the old Israelites (*Ztschr. d. Ver. f. Volksk.*, Bd., 11, p. 249), and among other peoples, the woman in Old India is a chattel, or anyhow a ward, in this also, that she cannot bear witness, and this because of her lack of truthfulness (Nārada, i, 190 f. ; cp. Krauss, *Sitte u. Brauch d. Südslawen*, 514), or because of the unſteadiness of her mind (Manu, viii, 77). Still, this is true only as a general principle, and here a responsible personality is not denied to her so much as it is elsewhere. The Old Indian law, reminding us of the English jury : he that is equal in rank shall be witness for his equal, is applied also to her : Where women are concerned (ſtrīshu), women may and shall appear before the court as witnesses. Manu, viii, 68 ; Vasishṭha, xvi, 30. But does she who is on trial fare very well thus ? Cp. Daçakum., p. 59, note 2.

[1] The cynical, it is true, preponderates : women cannot help it, " every woman is at heart a rake," as Pope holds ; so that we muſt be indulgent (Jāt., Nos. 120, 220, 224). They are like the well, the bathing-place, the ſtreet—all have access to her (Jāt., No. 195 ; Divyāvad., p. 257, lines 12–20 ; Rājatar., iii, 514, and the whole tale from 496 on). So that we muſt not on account of them think of losing a man who is clever, or useful or dear to us, and has broken through our fence ; beautiful women can easily be replaced by others, but a wise man, a good counsellor, a friend is seldom to be found (Jāt., No. 224 ; Çukasapt., text. simpl., No. 57). Cp. MBh., xii, 168.22. King Pradyota sees from clear evidence that women cannot be kept from going wrong, and he therefore gives his whole harem leave to go roving about by night for adventures until a drum is beaten, then they muſt all come back to the palace (Lacôte, *Gunādhya et la Bṛihatkathā*, Paris, 1908, p. 242 ff.).

world, that is, the keeping up of the caftes (vi, 25.41).[1] Then morality in general is above all in the hands of the gentler sex : " Moft important of all is the way of life of womenfolk ; what way the woman takes, that is the way always which prevails in mankind " (xiii, 146.10).[2] Food from a woman that runs after men the twice-born man muft not eat ; for it is mūtra (urine, xiii, 135.14).[3] But Utathya is fully contented merely with having back again his wife that has been carried off and so long enjoyed by Varuna ; so likewise Gautama takes to himself again Ahalyā who has been defiled by Indra, though indeed only after a long penance. In the old legends and tales, however, the husband who has been really, or to outward seeming, injured by his wife's unfaithfulness often orders her without more ado to be killed. So Paraçurāma's father, and at firft Cirakārin's. When Svāhā burning with love has taken on the shapes of the wives of the firft six out of the seven Rishis and has thus received Agni's embraces, the six seeming cuckolds caft off their wives, but afterwards learn that the poor wretches are only victims of a clever trick, and are quite innocent ; yet they do not take them back again (iii, 226.8 ff. But cp. 230.1 ff.). The explanation of their action is given by Nīlakantha in a very characteriftic way : " Through fear of the talk of people like Rāma " (for çl. 17).

[1] Cp. Manu, viii, 353.
[2] Strījanasya gatih parā. Gaur yām gacchati, suçroni, lokeshv eshā gatih sadā. The dictionaries do not give this meaning for *go*, but refer to " mother " given by Indian lexicographers. The meaning in that case would come to the same thing exactly. Nīl. has another meaning for the passage. With this thought compare : " Les hommes font les lois, les femmes font les mœurs." Comte de Ségur in *Les Femmes, leur condition*, etc.
[3] According to xii, 36.28 the harlot's food robs him who receives it of his manly powers, juft as does that of the henpecked husband, and that of the wretched man who tolerates his wife's lover. But it is well known that even the truly good and holy men of India gave little heed to this the deareft treasure of man, for Buddha and others gladly accepted charitable gifts from hetæræ. Cp. Manu, iv, 211 ; Yājñ., i, 215 ; Āpaftamba, i, 6, 19.15 ; etc. While it is also impressed on the Snātaka, that is on the Brahman before all, that food from a king takes away his ftrength (tejas) (Manu, iv, 218) !

WOMAN IS A CHATTEL

When this hero has overcome and slain Rāvaṇa, and dedicated Vibhīshaṇa in Laṅkā as king, the Rākshasa miniſter Avindhya brings Sītā to him, who with weeping eyes, pining, in black, filthy garb, her hair plaited in the fashion of mourners,[1] gazes on him. But he speaks and says : " Go, princess of Videha, I have reſtored [2] thee ; that which was to be done I have done. I have slain that spirit of the night, for I thought : ' After having won me for a husband, thou shalt not enter into old age in the house of the Rākshasas. How could ever one like me, one that knows the decision of things of law, keep even for a moment a woman that had fallen into the hands of another ? Be thy way of life pure or not, I cannot have thee any more for the joys of love, since thou art like unto a sacrificial offering polluted by a dog.' Then did the young woman, the queen, when she heard these awful words, reeling in anguish, fall suddenly to the ground, like a banana-tree that is hewn down. And the redness brought to her countenance by joy vanished in an inſtant again, like breath on a looking-glass. When all the monkeys had now heard these words of Rāma, they ſtood like Lakshmaṇa, too, without ſtirring, almoſt robbed of life." Sītā now takes a solemn oath : " In beings dwells the ever moving wind ; may he take life away from me, if I have done any evil. Let fire, water, ether, earth, and wind take my life, if I have done any evil. As truly as I, O hero, have thought of none other even in my sleep, so truly be thou, the one ordained for me by the gods, be thou my husband." The gods bear loud witness to the innocence of the noble woman (MBh., iii, 291.6 ff.). It is not so unfeeling as in the very compressed account of the Mahābh.[3] that Rāma comes before us in the beautiful description in the Rāmāyaṇa (vi, 112.22 to 118). Hanumant speaks to Rāma : " Let the princess of Mithilā be pleased to see the queen that is afire with pain, her that is the cause of these deeds, the fruit that is their reward." Rāma's

---

[1] Jaṭilā.

[2] Or : freed (muktā tvaṃ).

[3] But I cannot hold it to be so secondary and unimportant as it has been represented. It often shows a freshness and ſtrength wanting in the Rāmāyaṇa ; and that it flowed from this latter seems to me highly problematic.

eyes fill with tears, he falls to thinking, sighs deeply, looks on the ground, and then gives orders for her to be brought, and to be brought "with her head bathed", and in moſt splendid array. She would but haſten to him at once, as she is, but muſt obey, and is then carried there in a litter. Anger, joy, and gloom fill Rāma as she approaches. Vibhīshaṇa has all the people driven back by men in chamberlain's jackets, and with cane ſtaves and drums in their hands. But Rāma upbraids him for thus harassing the folk : "Neither house nor garb, neither wall nor hiding-place, nor such royal honour, but virtue is a woman's covering. In misfortune, in pain and diſtress, in the fight, at the choosing of a husband, at a sacrifice, and at a wedding— in any of these to look on a (ſtrange) woman is not held to be sinful. Sītā is to leave the litter, and come hither on foot." Lakshmaṇa and the monkeys are very disconcerted, and Sītā draws nigh to her husband, almoſt ready to hide away in her own limbs for shame, and gazing, full of admiration, joy, and love, into Rāma's face. But he says : "The insult is atoned for, I have shown my manhood, and fulfilled my promise, and am now once more my own lord : our undertaking was crowned with success." The eyes of the poor woman open wide, and fill with tears at these remarkable words of welcome. Seeing his heart's beloved thus ſtanding before him, and with his heart in dissension [1] through fear of what the people say, he goes on : "That which a man has to do to wash away an insult I have done in my yearning after honour, but not for thy sake. But the sight of thee is to me as little pleasing as is a light to one with sick eyes, since thou ſtandeſt before me with the caſt of suspicion as to thy good way of life. Therefore go—I give thee leave—wherever thou wilt. Here are the ten quarters of the heavens, my dear one ; I have nothing more to do with thee. For what man born in a good family and of any worth would take back a wife again out of friendly yearning, a wife that has dwelt in the house of another man ? Rāvaṇa's bosom has hurt and soiled thee, his eyes aflame with sin have gazed on thee ; how could I take thee back again, who can point to high descent ? Turn thy purpose to Lakshmaṇa or Bharata, Çatrughna, Sugrīva, or Vibhīshaṇa, the Rākshasa,

[1] Or : torn (babhūva dvidhā 115.11).

or to whomever it please thee thyself.[1] For Rāvaṇa, who saw thee in such heavenly beauty and charm, assuredly did not leave thee long alone in his house." Weeping, she that is thus accused almoſt sinks into her own limbs for shame, and with noble dignity she remonſtrates with him : "What meaneſt thou by uttering such dreadful and unworthy words to me, like some base man to a base woman ? Because of the ways of some women [2] thou doſt doubt the whole sex. That which was in my own power, my heart, dwelt but in thee ; but what power had I over my limbs, that were in the power of another ? Together with thee I grew up, and together with thee I have lived ; if thou haſt not thus learned to know me, and put me to the teſt, then I am loſt for ever. But thou followeſt the way of thine anger, and holdeſt the faſt before thee, juſt as a man of no account, that I am a woman. To thee it is nothing that in my childhood thou haſt pressed my hand (at the wedding), and on my loving devotion and all my good life thou turneſt thy back." Then she begs Lakshmaṇa to set up the pyre, which for her, for her that is caſt off, is the only refuge. Wrathfully Lakshmaṇa looks on his brother, but he ſtands there only with downcaſt eyes, looking like the god of death. With folded hands the glorious one makes oath : "So truly as my heart never forsook Rāma, so truly shall the witness to the world, the fire god, shield me from all. So truly as the child of Raghu deems me, who am pure-living, to be ſtained,[3] so truly shall the witness to the world, the fire god shield me from all." Then before the eyes of the gods, of men, and of all beings she leaps into the glowing fire, and a loud wail rises all around. She is kept unharmed, and to Rāma, who ſtands there in gloomy thought and with ſtreaming eyes, the gods come down, enlighten him as to his own real and everlaſting nature, and out of the flames rises the god of fire in bodily form, brings him his beaming wife, and solemnly

---

[1] Any comment on these unspeakably base, but charaſteriſtic words is probably needless. But we muſt not forget that the whole thing is a ſtate matter.

[2] Or : common (low) women (pṛithakſtrī 116.7) ?

[3] Or perhaps : So truly as Rāma (in his heart) knows me, the sullied one, to be of a pure life (dushṭadūshita) ?

bears witness to her spotless purity, and heroic rejection of the amorous Rākshasa. Rāma says that he had thus to act so that his beloved, whose unwavering faith he had never doubted, might be cleared before the whole world also, and no shame come upon himself.

If here, too, the much-sung hero comes before us at first as very weak, nay, base, beside that gracious pearl among women, Sītā, yet this is not the view of the Epic and of the Indian in general, in spite of Lakshmana's and the monkeys' disapproving attitude ; and one can always forgive him, and even look with sympathetic interest on the struggle in his soul, perhaps even find greatness in his action, setting on one side, of course, a certain brutality which has perhaps been smuggled in by a later hand.[1] For often a ruler cannot, and must not act like an ordinary mortal, and the Indian especially sees, indeed, in the king's actions and example a curse or a blessing on his whole land. And it needs more than ordinary strength of soul to show oneself as inhuman as Rāma, and to practise such heavy self-denial. It would be a most clumsy and superficial reading of the case to choose to see in it only cowardice. But it is only repugnance that is aroused in us by the casting off of Sītā for the second time. The people now find fault with Rāma for having taken his wife to his bosom again, and it is put to him that this example will loosen morals. He therefore has Sītā taken in a chariot to Vālmīki's hermitage by Lakshmana, whose heart is almost broken at this, without her having any idea of what is before her. At length with downcast countenance and weeping eyes he discloses to her that Rāma, because of what the people are saying, must give her up, though his heart is torn, and has ordered her to be brought away. In Vālmīki's penitential grove all will be well with her. In spite of her dreadful sorrow and this awful news she gives only

---

[1] The matter is in doubt. The Rāmāyana often seems to show traces of natural, uncultured conditions—Vālin's widow falls to the conqueror, the slain man's brother ; Sītā points out that as a widow she would belong to Lakshmana. So that there may be here, too, some remains of an original barbarism : the woman cast off by the ruler may be taken by another man under him ; she is always good enough for that. Cp. Meyer, *Isoldes Gottesurteil*, Anmerk., No. 4.

loving, kindly words to her brother-in-law as a laﬅ greeting for her husband : " It is for suffering that I have assuredly been born. How shall I live without him, and to whom shall I here pour out my grief ? And what grounds shall I give in the hermitage for the high-minded Rāma having caﬅ me off ? Here in the waters of Gaṅgā I would leave my life behind, but then would the race of my husband die out. Thou knoweﬅ, O Rāma, that I am pure, devoted to thee in deepeﬅ love, and ever thinking of thy welfare. The happiness and well-being of thy subjeƈts is thy duty and thy glory ; be thou towards them as towards brothers." Deeply sorrowing, Lakshmaṇa comes back over the river, and keeps looking across to her, as she ﬅands in utter loneliness on the other side, and as he drives away on his chariot, racked with grief. What is left now to her forsaken by all ? She weeps and weeps ever. The children of the hermitage see her, and run to carry the news to Vālmīki of the wonderfully beautiful ﬅranger lady, who is overcome with sorrow. The holy man comes, tries to comfort her, and entruﬅs her to the women in the penitential foreﬅ. There she brings forth her two sons ; from there she comes once more many years later before Rāma's eyes ; he himself, to whom her sons and his have been brought, and in whom the former feelings have probably been roused again, calls her to him for purification before the whole people, and Vālmīki takes her there. The Ṛishi moﬅ solemnly swears to her spotlessness. Rāma would now be satisfied, but all the gods have come there, to be witnesses of Sītā's oath ; and she takes it, but otherwise than her lord has looked for : " So truly as in my heart I think of none but Rāma, so truly shall the goddess Earth grant me a cleft. So truly as in thought, word, and deed I honour Rāma, so truly shall the goddess Earth grant me a cleft." Then before her as she thus proteﬅs and prays there rises out of the earth a magnificent throne, reﬅing on the heads of snake spirits, and on the throne is seated the goddess Earth, the mother of the noble lady of a thousand sorrows, and she takes her daughter into her open arms, bidding her a joyful welcome. Down sink the throne, the goddess, and her much-tried child—the fragrant, shyly folded flower, to which so short a happiness in the sun, and but too much icy frost had been granted, has gone home again to whence she came (Rām., vii, 43–49 ; 95 ff.). Well may Sītā, the spirit of the field-furrow,[1] thus have vanished from the midst of mankind, and from her husband in tales of old, a sister in this to so many fays and spirit-women of legend who are only allowed to abide with their beloved one on earth for a time. But this part of the Rāmāyana does not belong, at least in its present shape, to the original poem, and in the Mahābh., too, the second casting off is not found.

Rāma might now at first wildly show his sorrow and wrath— his lot was not an undeserved one. And in other ways, too, he seems to us to be too much the Indian ideal king and far too forgetful of the tender and true lover, as which he is so often painted for us. Long has Sītā been suffering in bondage, and he has very often given loud utterance to his yearning to see his wife once more ; but now that the bold robber has been slain and his town taken, he that gave himself out to be so heavily stricken by the sorrow of separation, with the utmost calmness first of all has Rāvana burned, then Vibhīshana dedicated as king, and then at last sends Hanumant to Sītā with tidings of his welfare, and of the end of the evil monster (Rām., vi, 112.22 ff.).[2] He also shares in a thought that often comes up not in India alone : " In all places a wife can be found, in all places kinsmen by marriage, but I do not see the place where one's own brother could be found " (Rām., vi, 101.14 ; cp. 87.13–17 ; MBh., xiii, 4.30–35).[3] In like wise does

[1] She, of course, came forth from the field-furrow, like the Etruscan Tago (Crooke, *Popul. Relig.*, ii, 287).—A weakened Buddhist version is to be found in the curious treatment of the Rāmāyana material in Chavannes, *Cinq cents contes*, i, 177.

[2] It is only after Arjuna has told of all his own adventures to Krishna, who has come on a visit into the forest of Kāmyaka, that he asks after wife and child, after Subhadrā and Abhimanyu, whom he has not seen for many a long year (iii, 183.14).

[3] Cp. Jātaka, No. 67 : A woman whose husband, son, and brother have been condemned to death, is allowed to beg one off ; she chooses her brother ; for although she declares : ' Without water the river is bare, without a king the kingdom, without a husband the woman, though she have ten brothers,' yet she holds : ' The son I have in my womb, a man runs towards me on the road, but a brother I can

the Mahābh. speak : " Knowledge, valour, active skill, power, and strength of character—these are called the inborn (in man) friends (mitrāni sahajāni) ; with them it is that the wise live their lives. Dwelling and metal, field, wife, and comrades (suhṛid)—these are called the added (by chance, unessential, upahita) ones ; these a man finds anywhere " (xii, 139.85–86). A too violent love for one's wife is in general blameworthy. Sugrīva urges Rāma to have done with his sorrow and despair : " I, too, have known the great misfortune of learning of my wife being carried off, and I do not thus mourn, nor lose my staunchness. I do not grieve after her, and yet I am but a poor ape. How much the less shouldst thou do so, that art high-minded, well-schooled, and of a firm character ! " (Rām., iv, 7.5 ff.). The woman is, indeed, an object of the senses (indriyārtha), an instrument of pleasure, to use the Indian's expression ; she merely is one among the needs of life, such as a seat, a bed, a vehicle, a house, corn, etc. (cp. xiii, 145.4 ff.). It

nowhere find again.' The wife, indeed, of Intaphernes does the same in Herodotus. Cp. Antigone, 909–912 : Reinhold Klotz, *Antritts-vorlesung*, 15th April, 1850 (Leipzig, 1853) ; Finck, 764 and note ; Lippert, *Kulturgesch.*, ii, 55 ; Schweiger-Lerchenfeld, *Frauen d. Orients*, 358 f. ; etc. " In a folk-song the choice is left a girl whether she will save her brother, or save her beloved from certain death. She decides for the brother : ' For,' said she, ' I can find a lover at once, I only need walk once through the village ; but I can never get a brother again.' " Fr. S. Krauss, *Sitte u. Brauch d. Südslaven*, p. 166. Cp. *Ztschr. d. Ver. f. Volksk.*, Bd. 16, p. 459 (South Arabian form). And in Swinburne's " Atalanta in Calydon " Atalanta exclaims : " For all things else men may renew, Yea, son for son the gods may give and take, But never a brother or sister any more " ; and she kills her own son, who has slain her brothers (ed. Stoddard, p. 33). So, too, Edward III of Sicily mourned his father's death more than his son's, for : Jactura filiorum facilis est, cum cotidie multiplicentur ; parentum vero mors irremediabilis est, quia nequeant restaurari (Schultz, *Das höfische Leben*, ii, 472, note 5). So, too, K., i, 173.20 : Parents easily get other and good children again, but these latter never get parents again. Cp. B., i, 230.13. And Dietrich in Konrad of Würzburg's *Engelhard* resolves to kill his two children, and to heal his leper friend with their blood, since a man, he says, can always get children again, but not a friend (6184 ff.).

is therefore not only foolish, but utterly unworthy of the man to set up a long wail, when an article of necessity such as this is lost to him.[1]   Moreover—and this is the worst of it—he shows by attachment like this that he is far too deeply entangled in sensuality.[2]   And finally : For the sake of the wife the

[1] So, too, Kālidāsa is quite in agreement with the second casting off of Sītā. He says of her in Raghuv., xiv, 35 : "And when he had decided that the blame could not be turned aside by any other way, he yearned to wipe it out by renouncing his wife. For to those rich in renown renown is more than their own body, not to say than an object of sensual enjoyment."   In the 73rd strophe, it is true, the seer Vālmīki utters his angry rebuke on Rāma because of this "sin-stained behaviour".—Cp. my translation of the Kuṭṭanīm., pp. 103–104, note. The South Slavs, like other peoples, also lay stress on a man being able easily to get a wife for himself again. Krauss, *Sitte und Brauch,* etc., p. 304.

[2] It is from this that we find an explanation, at least in part, of why in Indian literature the man often seems so much colder in love than the woman. Were he more fiery, he would be less exemplary. It is especially the Jātaka that is always showing how harmful, foolish, and evil it is to depend not only on any woman, but even on the wife. Pictures of the fondest, tenderest love in the man, pictures of a love that even in danger and death thinks only of the wife, are set before us, but all this is meant to be by way of a warning. A fish was playing in the water with his mate. Fishermen caught him, threw him on the hot sand, and put up a spit to roast their catch in a fire. But the fish only kept on wailing : "Not the spit nor the fire does torment me, but the thought that my dearest one believes I have left her for another." Bodhisatta, who was then a house-priest of the king in Benares, and who understood the sounds of all creatures, came by : he saw that the creature in its passion must go to hell, and set it free (Jāt., 34 and 216). In Benares a festival was being held. A poor man washed his coarse garment, and set it out in a thousand pleasing folds that it might serve him for the day of joy. But his wife said : " I want a safflower gown (cp. Kuṭṭanīmatam, 675), and, hanging on to thy neck, to enjoy myself at the festival in it."   " Whence can I, a poor man, get it ? " "Then go with another woman." At last he resolved on her persuasion to get one by night from the king's house of safflower garments. But the watchmen heard the fence crack as he pressed it down, caught the thief, and he was impaled. But from his lips parched in torment the cry that came in his agony was : " It is not the stake that tortures

man heaps up evil deeds, which he then muſt atone for alone in this world and the other ; through their attachment to wife, child, and family men sink down in the slimy sea of sorrow (xii, 174.25 f. ; 329.30 ; cp. 175.17).

me, but this, that the tawny one cannot enjoy the feſtival in a red robe." A crow flew by, he entruſted a tender message to it for his beloved, and sent her word where various things for her were to be found. At length death set him free from his torment on earth, but took him to a worse, to hell (Nos. 147, 297). Cp. also Jāt., No. 207, and in my *Hindu Tales*, p. 77 ff.

XXII

THE POWER OF WOMAN

ALTHOUGH in the Old Indian Epic, as everywhere in the world, there may be the widest differences of opinion as to the worth and the nature of woman, on one thing, anyhow, we find an absolute agreement throughout the world, and in the view held by the two mighty poems : the Power of Woman. War and peace depend on her. What the Rāmāyaṇa hinges on is the rape of Sītā ; the adventures and battles of the poem all turn in the end about her. In the same way we are told in the Mahābh. that the great war broke out mainly on account of Draupadī and the wrong done to her (e.g. 11, 81.13 ff. ; v, 78.17 ; ix, 5.17–21).[1] At her very birth a voice " without a body " proclaims from the fiery altar : " Because of her great danger will arise for the children of Kuru " (i, 167.48, 49). It is true that the roots of that dire quarrel lay far deeper, as the poem shows in so many places ; and reference also might be made especially to v, 31.12 ff., where Yudhishṭhira, at least, is ready even to forget the insult done to his wife, if only his share of the kingdom is given him. But woman for the Indian, too, is looked on as the usual source of enmity, and of the worst, as has been already pointed out ; and according to xii, 139.42 hate arises on earth from the following five : woman, court pomp, words, rivalry, affront.[2] Woman also goads on to the fight and to courage through her mere presence. The man can never let her see him playing a small part, even at the cost of folly and destruction. So i, 170.68 ; iii, 11.55 ; 59.8 ; 249.6, 7 ; iv, 35.22 ; Rām.,

[1] Besides later passages there were some others belonging here : iii, 49.2, 9, 13 ; 51.9 ; 141.4 ; iv, 20.12 ; 50.14 ; v, 29.36 ff. ; 59.22 ; 79.17 ; 81.2 f. ; 90.80 f.

[2] Somewhat altered in the expression by Bhavabhūti, Mahāvīracar., 3rd strophe of Act 4 (p. 129 in the edit. quoted).

THE POWER OF WOMAN

iv, 14.18, 19.[1] The company of women is vīru pāna for the man, heady drink before fight and danger (iv, 11.38). Any man, even the moſt ordinary, praises and puffs himself up in the presence of women (xii, 284.27). But as a peace-maker, too, who parts the fighters and makes them ready for reconciliation, she wields her power over men (xiv, 78.22 ff. ; 84. 19 ff.), juſt as she does as a go-between who softens the angry man, and prevents the fight ; for her very presence disarms the ſtrong sex (Rām., iv, 33.28 ff., especially 33.36, 37).

But wherein lies woman's mighty power ? We have already heard many answers to this. Here we give only a few more of them. Women's tears have their well-known effect in India also.[2] No wonder then, that in the Epic also tales are told of their magic powers of quite cosmic ſtrength. Pulomā was firſt promised to the Rākshasa Puloman, but then was given by her father to Bhṛigu. Once when the husband has gone to bathe, the giant comes into the holy man's hermitage, is overcome by love, and carries off the wondrous fair one, who as a result has a miscarriage. The sight of the child burns the monſter to ashes. The faithful wife's tears are turned into the river Vadhūsarā (i, 5.13 ff.). The hot tears of the loving wife, whose husband in the very moment of the love embrace was devoured by the Rākshasa-possessed King Kalmāshapāda, turn to a mighty fire that burns the land

[1] Especially inſtructive is the Mārk.-Pur., cxxii, 13 ff. : Prince Avīkshita at the Svayaṃvara carries off many of the kings' daughters, whose choice does not fall on him. So also one day the daughter of Viçāla. Firſt he overcomes all the assembled kings, but on a new attack by vaſtly greater numbers, who fight unfairly, he is overborne and bound, all before the maiden's own eyes. His heroic mother, as being a true Kshattriyā, praises him for his deed, and prevails on her husband to make war. The young warrior is set free, but in spite of the maiden's love that has been kindled by his manliness, and in spite of the prayers of her father and his he takes his ſtand that " A man that has been overcome and insulted before a woman's eyes can never show his face before her again, how much less wed her " (see espec. cxxiv, 26–30; cxxv, 31) ; and he forswears all intercourse with women.

[2] " Pitiful, and yet full of ſtrength to break down the wrath of the wrathful, tears are called the woman's weapon in the fight." Çiçupālav., xi, 35.

535

up (i, 182.16, 17). The tears of a lovely woman blossom into golden lotuses on the Ganges, as they drop one after another into its flood (i, 197.9 ff.).[1] The moſt enticing of spells lies in the smile of a lovely face, in a sweet voice,[2] speech, or tone, in the tender, loving play of features, in the glance of the eyes, and in all the many charms of the woman that carry the man away. The Epic reflects the susceptibility to them, above all in the frequent embellishing epithets. Excellencies of mind, and virtuous conduct in the woman likewise confer the sceptre on her, as can be seen at once from very much that has gone before. A wise saying has it : " To harm is the ſtrength of evil men, the ſtrength of kings is the power to punish, but obedience is the ſtrength of women, tolerant patience the ſtrength of the virtuous " (v, 34.75). As so often elsewhere, the same teaching as to the humility of woman is also set forth in the fascinating, though undoubtedly not so very old, section iii, 233, 234 ; and this shows at the same time how the means that were so frequent already in Vedic and in all later India, and were especially used by women, to ensure the man's love and devotion, flourish greatly in the Epic world, too. Kṛishṇa is on a visit to the Pāṇḍavas, accompanied by his wife Satyabhāmā. She sits with Draupadī in long conversation on things that have happened among the Kurus and the Yadus. Then Satyabhāmā asks her friend : " What doſt thou do, then, so to rule the Pāṇḍavas, those heroes like unto the wardens of the world, and men of exceeding great ſtrength ?[3] And how is it that they are at thy call and are not angered, O lovely one ? For ever and always subject to thee are the sons of Pāṇḍu, O thou so sweet to look upon, and gaze on thy countenance

---

[1] Cp. e.g. also *Folk-Tales of Kashmir*, p. 443 ; *Folk-Tales of Bengal*, p. 102.

[2] Cp. Jātaka, Nos. 159 ; 267 ; Vasishṭha, xxviii, 6 ; Baudh., ii, 4, 5 ; Yājñav., i, 71 (in the laſt three passages : Gandharva has given women their sweet voice). Thus Eugene Field, too, sings : " For it's everywhere known That the feminine tone Gets away with all masculine gender " (" The Doll's Wooing " in *Poems of Childhood*).

[3] Or : bound to one another (faſt holding together). Cp. susaṃhata ſtraitly united in v, 125.25 ; saṃhata more or less = aṇyonyasya hitaishin in vii, 112.44.

all of them. Tell me this, and speak truly. Is it the praƈtising of vows of mortification, or faﬅing and other asceticism, or bathing arts ; is it magic spells and herbs ; is it the power of secret knowledge, or the power of roots ; is it prayers, sacrifices, or remedies ? Let me learn of it, princess of the Pañcālas, the means which brings renown and wedded happiness, that Krishṇa, too, may be under my sway." Draupadī spoke : " Thou askeﬅ me after that which evil women do. . . . So soon as the husband learned that his wife found her welfare in magic spells and roots, he would be filled with fear of her, as of a snake in the house. Moﬅ dreadful sicknesses sent by foes (they bring on their husbands) ; for they who wish to kill them give them poison through the magic of roots. What the husband touches with his tongue or his skin, on that they sprinkle a fine powder, and so quickly kill him ; of that is no doubt. Thus have women made their husbands dropsical, lepers, old men, without manhood, weak-minded, blind, and deaf.[1] I leave thought of self behind me, and no less conﬅantly desire and anger, and ever serve the Pāṇḍavas with earneﬅ zeal, and their wives also. I keep my inclinations in the background, and shut my own self into my self, obedient, without pride, heedful of my husband's thoughts, fearful and watchful leﬅ I speak unlovely words,

[1] Essentially the same in found in Kshemendra, Daçāvatāracar., viii, 509–513. Cp. Thurﬅon, *Omens and Superﬅitions*, p. 239. So among " woman's duties " there is also especially given : mūlakriyāsv anabhiratiḥ to take no pleasure in magic by roots. Vishṇu, xxv, 7. How often, then, may the hurt Indian fair one along with other magic (especially well represented in the Atharvaveda) have made use, too, of that so often recorded in Weﬅern lands, making a figure of the hated woman, ﬅudding it with needles, arrows, nails, etc., and by this means, and through the recital of witches' words, hoping to bring her into the same plight and kill her. See e.g. Agnipur. (Dutt), 167.42–44 ; 306.4 ff. ; Kauṭilya, 618.1–5, 27 ff. ; 657.17–20 ; Thurﬅon, *Omens and Superﬅit.*, etc., p. 246 ff. ; Dubois-Beauchamp [3], p. 389 f. ; Crooke, *Pop. Rel.*, ii, 278 f. ; *Geﬅa Romanorum*, No. 102 ; Pauli, " Schimpf u. Ernﬅ," *Stuttg. Lit. Ver.*, Bd. 85, pp. 156 and 500 ; Fr. v. d. Leyen, " Zur Entﬅehung d. Märchens," *Herrigs Archiv*, Bd. 114, p. 10.

537

show myself unlovely, caſt unlovely looks, be unlovely as I sit, be unlovely as I walk, show an unlovely play of features. Before my husband has eaten I do not eat ; before he has bathed I do not bathe ; before he has taken his seat I do not take mine ; and this is my way with the servants, too. Laughing but at a jeſt, conſtant ſtanding by the door, ſtaying long in the privy, or in the groves by the house—these I avoid. I never have a wish for anything unless my husband is there. If my husband goes a journey on some business of the family, then I give up flowers, salve, and rouge, and give myself over to vows of mortification. And what my husband does not drink, and what my husband does not do, and what my husband does not eat— I avoid all these." She then goes on to tell how her husband is her god, how she never offends her mother-in-law in any way, how she superintends all the hundred thousand splendid, skilful slave-women, and all the huge wide-ſtretched charity of Yudhishṭhira, all those employed by him down to the herdsmen and bird-keepers, as also his revenues and expenditure to the moſt minute details. She is the firſt to rise in the house, the laſt to lie down.[1] " This is the great magic spell which I know, to win the husband's regard. What is pleasing is never won through what is pleasing,[2] but it is through discomfort that the good wife wins happiness and joy. So soon as thou heareſt thy husband coming at the door, ſtand up and set thyself in the middle of the room ; and when thou seeſt he has come in, be swift to wait respeċtfully on him with a seat and water for the feet. If a slave-girl has been sent away, thou muſt rise up thyself and do all. If thy husband says anything before thee, then keep it to thyself, even when it is no secret ; some rival might bring it up before Vāsudeva, and he thereby grow cold towards thee. Do good to his friends,[3] keep away from his foes. Keep the company of good and noble women, and shun all others. Show thyself (before thy husband)

---

[1] Cp. ii, 65.37, where Yudhishṭhira gives her the same charaċter.
[2] Cp. Rām., iii, 9.31.
[3] This calls for self-denial ; for Gottfried of Strassburg is probably not altogether wrong :
Of women it is said that
they bear hatred towards their husband's friends (*Triſtan*, 13991 f.)

in fair garlands, splendid adornment, sweet perfumes. Thus wilt thou win good name and wedded bliss, and destroy thy foes."

It is, of course, above all through her beauty that woman carries the day : "The might of the king is his station as ruler, the might of the theologian is holy knowledge ; beauty, youth, and charm is the incomparable might of women." He whose own good lies near to his heart, let him draw nigh with frankness to those that are mighty through these powers, for here the want of it leads to destruction (xii, 320.73 f.).[1]

This "incomparable might" of the woman shows itself still powerful and effective where everything else fails, overcomes the wildest and strongest of men. There once lived two giants, the enormously strong Daitya brothers Sunda and Upasunda. "Always theirs was but one sorrow and one joy. They ate not one without the other, they spoke not one without the other ; lovingly they spoke to one another, lovingly did they deal with one another, one only was their character and life, they were but one being split into two." In the burning ambition to make all the three worlds to serve them they practised such dread asceticism that the Vindhya mountains began to smoke, and then they won from Brahma the favours they yearned after, and this one especially, that no one

---

[1] Even the unbending tree is filled with delight and life by woman's splendour : "Even the trees bloom through the secret of beauty of form," we find in Karpūramañjarī, ii, 49[1]. According to the poetical convention of the Indians the kurabaka, indeed, covers itself with blossoms, when a lovely woman clasps it, the tilaka, when she looks on it, the açoka, when it is touched by her foot, the mango, when her hand touches it, the priyala, when it hears her song, the keçava or the bakula, when sprinkled with intoxicant from her mouth. Raghuv., ix, 33 ; xix, 12 ; Gauḍavaha, 1087 ; Weber, *Ind. Studien*, xviii, 325 ; Karpūramañj., p. 62 ff. ; Pārvatīpariṇ., iii, 6 ; etc. Indians often give a list of the charms through which woman puts a man in fetters. According to Buddha's saying (Schiefner, *Bull. d. St. Petersburger Akad.*, Bd. 23, "Indische Erzählungen," No. xliii) this happens in eight ways : through dance, song, play, aughter, weeping, look, touch and question. Cp. also Lalitavistara, ed. Lefmann, p. 320 ; Kalpasūtra, ed. Jacobi, i, 221.

539

could harm them unless it were themselves. No arrow now harmed them, no stone hurt them, they felt no weapon, even the curses of holy men fell away from them powerless. They now wielded a reign of terror over the whole of creation, drove the gods out of paradise, brought death and wrong on the Brahmans, turned all into a wilderness of woe. The gods naturally called for help, and at Brahma's bidding Viçvakarman now had to make a woman glorious beyond words. The sculptor brought together what was most worth beholding out of all that was most lovely in the world, and thus shaped a maiden in whom there was not one small part anywhere but held fast the ravished eye—Tilottamā. Brahma sent her off to sow strife between the inseparable brothers. They were taking their delight with women and other pleasures in a great forest on Vindhya. " Then went Tilottamā slowly to the place where the two Asuras were, plucking flowers and blossoms in the forest, and wearing a bewitching [1] garb, consisting of but one red garment. The two, who had drunk most excellent drink, saw with intoxicated red eyes this woman with the lovely hips, and were at once violently excited." Each one now wanted her, and so they fell to strife, grasped hold of their clubs, and beat one another to death (i, 209–212).

Even one that has grown up in the forest, and has no knowledge what kind of being a woman is, falls helplessly before the charms of the fair, as the old tale of Rishyaçriṅga tells us. His father's name was Vibhāṇḍaka, the Kāçyapa ; his (V.'s) staring eyes were yellowish brown ; he was thickly covered with hair down to the tips of his nails ; he dwelt in the forest as a Veda-learned ascetic of pious life, and mystic powers of sinking deep in thought. Rishyaçriṅga's mother was an antelope, that had drunk the seed of his father which had escaped at the sight of the fascinating fay Urvaçī, and thus had conceived in her womb. He himself is said to have had a horn on his forehead. He had grown up [2] in the lonely forest, and had never seen any man but his father, to say nothing of a woman. But mighty was the magic strength of his chaste youth, and through it,

---

[1] So according to Nīl. But perhaps it is : sā ākshiptam " (lightly) thrown around "

[2] Read : abhyavardhata (iii, 110.38).

when there was a dreadful drought in the land of Aṅga under King Lomapāda, he forced the rain god Indra to send down the heavenly moiſture. The king's own daughter, the lovely and youthful Çāntā, came out to him in the penitential grove to fire him with love, and entice him into her father's kingdom, that through his presence the rain so long in vain yearned for might fall ; and she was given to wife to the wonderful, wonder-working youth from the foreſt and served him with the trueſt love. The later ſtory-telling art made a harlot inſtead of the princess carry out the conqueſt of this seemingly invulnerable youth, and so it reads in the Mahābh. also (iii, 110.22 to 113), although even only a few verses before this tale, the Mahābh. itself gives Çāntā as his seducer.

Lomapāda, the king of the Aṅgas, and Daçaratha's friend, had offended againſt a Brahman by promising him something and then not giving it.[1] Then the Brahmans turned away from him, and because of this offence againſt his house-prieſt it ſtopped raining in his land, and great want prevailed in it. He called on the Brahmans, "who had the power of making rain," and asked how the rain god could be brought to beſtow his gift. An old Muni said that the king muſt firſt atone for his offence againſt the wrathful Brahmans, and then have the foreſt man Ṛishyaçṛiṅga sent for, who was upright, and wholly without knowledge of women ; so soon as he came into his kingdom,[2] it would rain. After consulting with his miniſters the ruler bade hetæræ, washed with every kind of water, to come before him, and charged them to seduce the pious youth. They grew pale, and said the undertaking was an impossible one ; for they feared the holy man's curse. An old woman, however, promised to carry everything out, had a mighty, moſt splendid raft built, had it planted with trees

---

[1] K. reads tena kāmaḥ kṛito mithyā brāhmaṇebhya iti çrutiḥ (111.20). The Bomb. text has essentially the same meaning. As is seen from what follows, this Brahman was his house prieſt. Awful indeed is the punishment that the Brahmans hold out againſt the monſter that promises a member of their caſte something, and does not keep his word.

[2] Or more literally and perhaps better : "came down into his kingdom." He dwells up in the mountain foreſt.

covered with flowers and fruits, with bushes and creepers, and on this raft and penitential grove, together with a small following of lovely priestesses of love,[1] made her way to the neighbourhood of Vibhāṇḍaka's hermitage. When she had learned from her spies that the father was away, she sent her clever and moreover well-tutored daughter to the young man of holiness. The daughter asked him in the most penitent-like terms, whether the pious life in the hermitage was taking a prosperous course. He welcomed the " tall lord, shining like a light " most respectfully, begged him to be seated on the kuça-grass cushion spread with black antelope skin, and to accept water for the feet, fruit, and roots. Then he asked where was the stranger's hermitage-forest, and what was his penitential vow. The hetæra spoke : " My hermitage lies three yojanas beyond this mountain. There is the pious law of my life ; respectful greeting is nothing to me, and water for the feet I do not touch." His fruits she refused, but gave him delicious baked wares that he found surpassing good, sweet-smelling wreaths, and bright coloured garments, as, too, the most excellent drinks. She played before him with her ball, bent coquettishly this way and that like a fruit-covered tendril, and kept on putting her arms around him, setting limb fast against limb. She pulled down the flower-laden boughs of the trees, and broke them off ; she feigned bashfulness, and lured and led on, intoxicated, the youthful penitent. When she saw how Rishyaçriṅga had become deeply roused, she kept on pressing his body to hers, and then she went away, looking back again and again, pretending she must now make the sacrifice by fire. " When she had gone, Rishyaçriṅga was drunk with love, his thoughts far away ; his heart winged its way to her only, and in his loneliness he sighed deep out of his tortured soul. Soon after his father appeared, with his yellow-brown eyes, wrapped in hair down to the tips of his nails, rich in holy learning, equipped with pious ways and mystic depths. He saw his son sitting there alone in deep thought, with his senses in a whirl, sighing mournfully, and ever and anon lifting up

[1] So according to 110.58, 113.8. In truth this troop of girls seems to us somewhat needless, for it is only the old woman's daughter who infatuates the youth. Do they go, indeed, as mascots ? Or as a reserve ?

his eyes ; and he spoke to the sad youth : ' Art thou not,
then, making the firewood ready, my dear one ? And haſt
thou made the sacrifice by fire to-day ? Haſt thou well
washed the sacrificial ladles, and put the cow, that yields the
sacrificial milk, with her calf ? It would seem, indeed, that
thou art not as before. Thou art sunk in melancholy thoughts,
and diſtraught ; wherefore to-day art thou saddened beyond
all measure ? I ask thee : Who came hither to-day ? ' "
Ṛishyaçṛiṅga spoke :

> " There hither came a chaſte youth wearing tresses,
> Truly not small, not too tall, of good underſtanding,
> Golden his colour, long the lotus eye,
> Self-shining like one of the gods,[1]
>
> Of perfeɕt shape, beaming like the sun,
> His eyes soft and black, his skin bright-gleaming.
> Blue-black and shining his long tresses,
> Bound in a golden braid, and sweetly scented.
>
> On his neck something, shaped like the runnel,[2]
> Gleams, like lightning in the sky ;
> Two globes he has beneath the neck,
> That have no hair, and ravish high the heart.
>
> Thin is his body by the navel,
> And his hips over-great in girth ;
> From his baſt garb the girdle gleams forth,
> Of gold made, juſt as mine.
>
> Another thing, wonderful to behold,
> Shines on his feet, and sounds ;
> The hands, too, are twined about by two skeins,
> Sharp-tinkling, like unto my rose-wreath.
>
> And when he moves, these gleam
> Like in the pond the joy-drunken swans.
> His baſt garment is a wonder to behold.
> Ah ! mine here is not so fair and splendid.
>
> His face is a wondrous sight to behold.
> And what he says refreshes, as it were, the soul ;
> His voice rings like the cock-koïl's,
> My heart quaked within me, as I liſtened to it.

[1] K. reads sutaḥ surāṇāṃ, as Lüders conjeɕtured. But it may be
a later refinement. " Wearing tresses " = an ascetic.
[2] Which especially is made round the young trees to water them.

543

As in the time of the spring moon sweet scents
Are wafted [1] from the forest, when 'tis stirred by the wind's
    breath,
So from him are wafted the purest of sweet scents,
When the wind fans him, father dear.

And his tresses hang down well tied,
Parted in two, curling on the forehead ;
His ears are decked with fair things,
They seem as many-coloured cakravāka-birds.

One thing more : With his right hand he held
A round fruit of many colours ;
So soon as the wondrous-shaped thing reached
The ground it flew up high again.

And as he hit it, he moved in a circle
And waved like the wind-stirred tree.
I gazed on him as on a son of the gods,
And, O father, utmost joy and delight was mine.

He took me by the tresses, lowered
His mouth to me, set mouth to mouth ; thus
A sound he did make, ever clasping me anew ;
This brought me shuddering blissful delight.

He heeds not water for his feet,
Nor these my offered fruits.
He said unto me : ' This my vow demands.'
And other fruits he gave me.

With those fruits cannot be compared
The fruits which until now I've tasted.
The peel, too, is not like those,
The flesh is not as the flesh of those fruits.

And wondrous-good water to drink
He gave me, who is so nobly made ;
The utmost bliss, when I had drunk it,
Filled me, the earth to totter seemed.

And those are his many-coloured, scented garlands,
Fair-woven, O father, with strips of ribbon ;
He strewed them here around, and with asceticism
Shining, he then went to his own abode.

---

[1] The Jātaka reads vāyati = Skrt. vāti, and according to that bhāti
is perhaps to be changed to vātī.   But it is hardly absolutely necessary.

THE POWER OF WOMAN

His going has bereft me of my senses,
My body burns about me as with the glow of fire.
Ah ! my longing is but to him speedily to go,
And that he for ever with us here do dwell.

To him I go, my father dear.
And what kind of chaste life may his be ?
I will do with him the same penance
As he does, he, the man of noble ways.

To do it thus is the call of my heart's wish.
My soul doth burn, when I see him not."

Vibhāṇḍaka spoke :

" My son, devils here in the forest roam
In that same shape which is a wonder to behold,
Beyond compare in strength, sweet and lovely ;
Their thought is always to hinder our penance.

Most fairly formed, they entice us to destruction,
My dear one, by ways manifold ;
Of happiness and heaven these frightful beings
Deprive us holy Munis in the forests.

With them let the Muni have nought to do
That with self in check strives after heaven's worlds ;
They rejoice, the evil ones, when they hindrance
Bring to penitents. Ne'er let the penitent gaze on them.

Wicked and forbidden are the mazing drinks ;
They are drunk by evil folk only.
And these scented, brightly coloured wreaths
Are not for Munis, the tradition tells us."

He now set out to hunt for these devils or Rākshasas, but sought
in vain for three days long, and then came back. But when
he had again gone forth to fetch fruit, the bestower of love
came once more, and he called to her : " Let us go quickly
to thy place before my father comes back." She brought him
onto the raft, and on this to the land of the Aṅgas. " So
soon as the king had led the only son of Vibhāṇḍaka into
his women's apartments, he suddenly saw the rain god rain,
and the world fill itself with water." [1] He gave him his
daughter Çāntā ; then on the road from his capital to the

---

[1] Read pravṛishtaṃ (instead of pravishṭaṃ).

545

penitential grove of Vibhāṇḍaka, mighty in his wrath, everywhere he established tilled fields and herdsmen's stations with much cattle, and gave orders to the men there that, if the holy man came to look for his son, they were to entertain him most handsomely, and tell him that all this cattle and the fields belonged to Rishyaçṛiṅga. When the penitent came back, and could not find his son, he hastened, " bursting with anger, and suspecting that it had been contrived by the king, to Campā to burn up the king together with his city and kingdom." But as he was received everywhere with such kindness and humbleness, and was told that all the splendour had been given to his son, he blessed the union of Rishyaçṛiṅga with Çāntā, and only made the condition that his child should after the birth of a son come again to the forest. Thus, too, it was done, and Çāntā joyfully followed her husband.[1]

[1] Besides all the forms that H. Lüders sets forth in his studies on the Rishyaçṛiṅga tale in the *Göttinger Nachr.* of 1897 and 1901, from India here belongs first of all the very interesting variation of the Rishyaçṛiṅga tale (mentioned, moreover, also by Lüders) in Hemacandra's Pariçishṭaparvan, translated by Hertel, p. 29 ff. Cp. his *Nachweise*, 223, 224; Chavannes, *Cinq cents contes*, No. 453; Pālijātaka, Nos. 191, 523, 526; Oesterley's Baital Pacchisi, pp. 16–18; Tawney's Kathākoça, 179–183; Daçakum., p. 205 ff. and 4 together with the citations there; Winternitz, WZKM, xxiii, p. 119 ff.; id., *Gesch. d. ind. Lit.*, i, 344 f.; Jacobs, *Barlaam and Josaphat*, cxxx; Kuhn, *Abhandlungen d. Bayr. Akad.*, Bd. 20, pp. 80, 81; Dunlop-Liebrecht, 230, 462 f.; Liebrecht, *Zur Volkskunde*, pp. 112, 441; Liebrecht, *Übersetzung d. Barlaam u. Josaphat*, 220; Chauvin, iii, 104, 105; Boccaccio, "Prologue to the 4th Day"; Landau, *Die Quellen d. Dekameron* [2], 171, 223 ff.; Zambrini, *Libro di novelle antiche*, No. xxii; René Basset, *Contes pop. d'Afrique*, p. 127 f.; Sercambi, *Novelle*, ed. Régnier, p. 122 ff.; Hagen's *Gesamtabenteuer*, ii, 41 ff.; i, p. lxxxiii, note 2; "Die Komödie des Hans Sachs" in *Kürschners Nationallit.*, "Hans Sachs' Werke," ii, 268 ff.; *Bibliothek d. Stuttgarter Liter. Vereins*, Bd. 28, p. 148 ff.; Pfeiffer's *Germania*, Bd. 17, pp. 306 ff.; Cardonne, *Mélanges de Littérature Orientale* (à la Haye, MDCCLXXXIII, p. 10 ff.); and so on. That Daṇḍin in his tale should have re-modelled the Rishyaçṛiṅga legend, as is assumed by Lüders and after him Hertel, I still hold to be a mistaken idea, although my views on Daṇḍin's originality have greatly changed since my Daçakum. was published. I now credit him here, too, with little of

his own, with still less, indeed, than does Lüders for this part. I hope some day to be able to undertake a second edition of this book so long out of print, and will therefore only briefly set forth my present views. The following tales are found in India from early times :

(I) A youth grows up in utter innocence ; in particular he knows nothing about women. But so soon as he sees the first female being he feels himself powerfully drawn to her. In spite of his father (or : his teacher) warning him that such beings are fiends leading on to perdition, he gives himself to a sweet demon of this kind.

(II) As the king has the supernatural power of making the rain fall in his kingdom at the proper time, the Brahmans naturally had to credit themselves with the same magic power. It is, indeed, the primitive inheritance of the shaman, and in India, too, may have fallen to the ruler in a secondary way only. Cp. MBh., iii, 110.44 ; i, 78.40 ; K, iii, 130 ; Nirukta, ii, 10. The Brahman as a rain-maker is treated by Oldenberg, *Relig. d. Veda*, 420 ff. As an altogether extraordinary heroic deed of Vasishṭha, the devarāj, it is told that during a drought he bestowed life on all beings (xii, 234.27 ; xiii, 137.13). But here the rain-making is not expressly mentioned. Cp. Rām., ii, 117.9. So now we have had the tale of this Brahmanic counterpart to the king, Ṛishyaçṛiṅga, rich in asceticism and wholly chaste, whose mere presence brought the rain down in streams, and who during the drought in Aṅga-land made a brilliant show of his wonderful powers. Perhaps use was now made of the merry tale of the innocent youth, already to hand. That this delightful and suggestive tale in its original form gave us the blunt humour of the Jātakagāthās is not at all certain, although the Jātaka does indeed show that such a form already arose at an early time. In the MBh. (as to all seeming in the Padmapur. and the Rām. also) Ṛishy. keeps his body chaste until he comes into Aṅga-land, as is needful for the Brahmanic account, while Lüders's account would lead us to suppose otherwise. For quite needlessly the MBh. (110.24) also expressly says that he brought rain through the power of his asceticism. Any man that lives in unbroken chastity can do this. Āpastamba, ii, 9, 23.7. In his sexual purity, therefore, there lies magic power ; this is a widespread belief, indeed, in the world, and still alive to-day even among cultured European mankind. In an older form this may well have been the leading thought, and the partisan purpose of glorifying the priests have been wholly lacking.

(III) A wise man, perhaps an ascetic, fills the world with his renown. A lovely woman, probably from the beginning an hetæra, undertakes to seduce him. She is successful, brings him triumphantly into the city, and doubtless rides on his back in the way that is already very old (cp. Hiuen Thsang, and Jāt., No. 191). Here belongs the well-known history of Aristoteles and Phyllis, which is so beautifully told in the " Lais d'Aristote " of Henri d' Andeli (*Œuvres*, ed. A. Héron, Paris, 1891, p. 1 ff.). Cp. there p. xxviii ff.; Hagen's *Gesamt-ab.*, i, p. 17 ff., lxxv ff.; F. v. d. Leyen in *Herrigs Archiv*, Bd. 116, p. 298 ff.; Cardonne, *Mélanges*, p. 10 ff. (English transl., i, 14 ff.); Benfey's *Panschat.*, i, 46 ff.; ii, 306; Lacôte, *Guṇāḍhya et la Brihat-kathā*, p. 241; etc. (A whole set of references are already given in the first paragraph of this note. A great number of forms I have undoubtedly not seen, and so not mentioned them). Borgeld, *Aristo-teles en Phyllis*, Groningen, 1912, I do not know.

In Daṇḍin's version there are elements from the Ṛishyaçṛiṅga tale, and that of the wise man through whom the power of woman is so strikingly shown. Both tales are actually fused into one already in the remarkable Buddhistic story in Chavannes, *Cinq cents contes*, iii, 233 ff. (cp. ii, 282 ff.), which I only came to know after writing this note. The subject of the tale (of the wise man) is much like that of the merry tale of the innocent youth, and both, indeed, may possibly have grown out of one root. But, seeing the great number of tales of the seduction of ascetics, so narrow and one-sided a derivation would be highly risky. In the same way the rain-wizard Ṛishyaçṛiṅga in India might possibly be the original hero of the tale of the untutored forest man who is at once carried away by the woman.

I must further stress the point that Lüders in his criticism is beside the mark. My translation is enough to show that the account in the MBh. is not at all such a contradictory jumble as this learned man believes. Moreover Lüders, to all seeming, has not seen the delightful humour running through the MBh. version. The shaggy forest-bear in Vibhāṇḍaka, and his simple holiness is deliberately stressed. What a contrast on the one hand with the young man's tender love woes, and on the other with the harlot's cunning! She herself, therefore, probably has to thank above all a calculated artistry for the part she plays, which originally belonged to Çāntā; and for the later Hindu, too, the thing could thus be made far more piquant. The humour now becomes irresistible in the contrast between the real character and life of the delightful new-comer, and the innocent youth's idea of him. It is capital there, too, how the virtuous and simple hermit goes looking for the devil in the forest for three days, and then through this very thing loses his son to him. This account thus shows a refined art; whether also a lower age at the same time is a question in itself. One of the lists, so beloved in India, of holy men who are led away by women is given in Buddhacaritam, iv, 16–20. In it Ṛishyaçṛiṅga is also given, and Çāntā as his conqueror.

APPENDIX

ADDITIONS AND CORRECTIONS

P. 8, n. 3. At Draupadi's choosing of her husband her mother had no joy whatever, for her only thought was: "What kind of husband will she get?" K., i, 200.20.

P. 11, n. 1. Since the maiden, particularly the virgin (kumārī), is a lucky object, she is also called in for divining by dice, but not as the "substitute of the faithful wife", as Lüders holds ("Das Würfelspiel im alten Indien," *Abhandlungen d. königl. Gesellsch. d. Wissenschaften zu Göttingen, phil.-hist. Klasse*, Bd. ix, p. 9). He is mistaken also when in the same place he believes that Nala is determined to play, because Damayantī is looking on, and thus by her presence ensures him success. It is rather in the first place the inciting presence of woman, especially the beloved one. See p. 534. But it is to be noted that the magical help of the wife, especially the chaste wife, has a powerful influence on the man's luck. Cp. Meyer, *Isoldes Gottesurteil*, note 104; Elsie Clews Parsons, *The Old-Fashioned Woman*, 1913, p. 61 ff.

P. 13, l. 31. Devayānī says: "Why art thou taking my clothes, my disciple?" She is, or has been, teaching Çarmishthā, as teachers' daughters in India often have women-disciples.

P. 15, l. 17 from end. According to K., Çukra becomes anxious at Devayānī staying away too long, and he sends the nurse off after her. The nurse finds the poor girl in tears and quite worn out under a tree, and makes her tell her what has happened (72.29–34).

P. 18, l. 10. The reading in K., mahākavim, is smoother: "Vrishaparvan spoke to the great wise man."

P. 19, l. 8 from end. Devayānī says: "Thy semblance is like a king's, and yet thou speakest the speech of the Brahmans." In his mouth, then, this speech is something unusual. Devayānī's ill-humoured words are made easier to understand in K.: There in several çlokas he praises the wonderful loveliness of Çarmishthā, and declares that D.'s

549

charms are not to be compared with those of her slave-girl (75.14–17). Here çl. 24 betrays to us that Yayāti's secret reason in rejecting D. is that he wants Ç. for his wife.

P. 29, l. 14 from end. K. reads probably better " gehe suvihitaḥ ", well quartered (provided, treated) in thy house.

P. 32, ll. 18 ff. It is probably safer to keep to the usual meaning of kare grihītvā : " How could I then, who am now so alarmed, make a headlong marriage, and perform the giving of myself away, which lies not with me, out of my own full powers ? "

P. 34, n. 2. P. 33, l. 9 must be: " be a maid again (wieder)." "Still (noch) " is what I put in when reading the proofs (when the primary text was not by me) for an original " again " (punar), since I thought the reading was kanyaiva tvaṃ bhavishyasi, as immediately follows (" thou wilt be a maid "). For this expression is the usual one, and it is often hard to decide whether it means " to be still a maid unharmed " or " to become a maid again ". That these two conceptions were not distinguished is shown e.g. by the following passages : Satyavatī bore Vyāsa as a virgin (kanyaiva, i, 60.2). So, too, K., i, 114.32 makes Parāçara say to her : Garbham utsrijya māmakam . . . kanyaiva tvaṃ bhavishyasi (cp. B., i, 105.13). But in the next çloka we find : Kanyātvaṃ ca dadau prītaḥ punar, etc. And to Mādhavī the Brahman says : Kanyaiva tvaṃ bhavishyasi (v, 116.11), and then we are told of her kumārī kāmato bhūtvā (116.21), and kanyā bhūtvā (118.1), which can hardly mean anything but : " having become a maid again." Kuntī herself says : punar eva tu kanyābhavam (xv, 30.16).

P. 34, n. 1. As to sādhayāmas (sādhayishyāmi, etc.) with prasthita following with the same meaning cp. i, 3.126 ; iii, 206.47 with 207.5 ; 294.32 with 294.33 ; see e.g. also xiii, 85.27.

P. 40, l. 11. " On the other shore." So according to K. B.(64.114) has : " on both shores," and this is found also in the interpolation in K., 114.7.

P. 47, l. 15. As Svāhā takes the shapes of women desired by Agni, so does Anna Perenna take that of Nerio beloved by Mars, and she, too, has success.

P. 47, l. 36. According to 99.19 f. a mortal who drinks the milk of the wonderful cow lives for 10,000 years with no loss of youthful power.

APPENDIX

P. 48, bottom. Pratīpa's son is, of course, the re-embodiment of that same Mahābhisha. K. here not only describes in a dozen çlokas what a paragon of a ruler Çāntanu was, but also sets before our eyes in pleasing colours that are almoſt modern a picture of how Gaṅgā, who has juſt bathed, and is combing her loosened hair with her fingers, shows off the wealth of her wanton charms, and makes all kinds of voluptuous movements (103.31 ff.). Cp. how Hiḍimbā entices Bhīmasena (K., i, 164.24–32); also B., v, 9.9 ff., and who knows how many other passages.

P. 50, l. 4. " She so delighted the king that he found the utmoſt delight," sounds ſtrange, of course. Perhaps sā is to be read inſtead of saḥ : " As she with her . . . gave pleasure to the king, so she herself found pleasure " (98.10). K. has yathā rajyeta sa prabhuḥ (204.16).

P. 61, l. 14. Bhīshma after the Indian cuſtom calls Bālhīka his father. He was his father's brother (e.g.: i, 94.61–62; v, 149.15 ff.). Some lines below (" Therewith is judgment, too," etc.) we could also have : " For the greedy, the evil-minded, the decision may lie therein (in buying and selling)," etc.

P. 73, l. 36 would be literally : Because of the want of foundation in the nature (of women). But perhaps far better would be : " Because, indeed, the attributes (of the wooer) give no grounds." As the scholiaſt reminds us, in love women give no heed to heroism, learning, etc.

P. 75, l. 4. Baladeva probably wants to make all the Kauravas pay at once for Arjuna's crime.

P. 76, n., l. 30. K., i, 238 ff. relates : Arjuna hears through Gada of the lovely and moſt excellent Subhadrā, falls in love, and goes as a Yati with three ſtaves, a water-pitcher, a wreath of roses, etc. to her home, to see the fair one with his own eyes, and to sound Vāsudeva's feelings in the matter. During the rainy season (or : a rain) he ſtays in a hollow tree, and thinks of Vāsudeva. V. is lying with Satyabhāmā in bed, through his divine knowledge is aware of all, and laughs. S. wants to know the reason, and Kṛishṇa enlightens her. He goes to the Yogi Arjuna, and comes with him to the mountain Raivataka. It is now essentially the same as in B., 218.3 ff. But next morning Kṛishṇa dismisses A. who is ſtill disguised as a Yati. A. sits down on a ſtone outside the city in the foreſt, and thinks sorrowfully of Subhadrā. The Yādavas with Baladeva at their head see the holy man on their way back from the festival of Raivataka, and do him reverence. A conversation takes place; they welcome him as a stranger in the place (deçātithi), and bid him to stay during the four rainy months. Kṛishṇa also comes up now; the guest is entrusted to him by Baladeva. It is Baladeva who first advises that the penitent be housed in the maidens' abode; but the cunning Kṛishṇa rejects this idea in the first moment, as being dangerous with so handsome and excellent a Yati. But he then quickly agrees to it. Subhadrā has already heard of Arjuna through Kṛishṇa and others, and has long been in love with him on hearsay. The rest is then as in the note. But not only Kṛishṇa, but the other kinsfolk, too, purposely give Arjuna free play with Subhadrā during that thirty-four days' island festival. They have long known, indeed, about the matter. For Devakī, Rukminī, and other women have been let into the secret, and have helped. Nay, even Subhadrā's father himself, and the whole council of state have long ago discussed the matter, and resolved on a splendid wedding. The carrying off is therefore here no more than a romantic pretence. It is with the woman's own consent that the carrying off is often brought about in Old India, too, and then it is thus a seduction. So iii, 224.1–4. And Rukminī indeed was agreed that Kṛishṇa should carry her off, although she was already betrothed to Çiçupāla. It is several times pointed out in the Epic that it is wrong to carry off an unwilling woman. Even the splendid Svayaṃvara sometimes appears only as a means whereby the girl may get him whom she secretly loves. So with Damayantī. Ambā, the daughter of the king of Kāçi has secretly betrothed herself to the king·of the Çālvas, and this marriage is also after her father's will (otherwise on p. 381). Together with her younger sisters she holds a choosing of a husband, but with the arrangement that she shall choose the Çālva (i, 103.61 f.). This plan is upset by Bhīshma. And Drupada, too, at the Svayaṃvara of his daughter is bent on thus getting Arjuna as a son-in-law (i, 185.8 ff.). It is true that possibly this is a later falsification, in spite of i, 193.12–20, where the same underlying thought may well be. Cp. 195.8 ff. But love marriages without some such embroidering seem, therefore, among the nobles not to have been quite "seemly". Arjuna's fight for Subhadrā is found also in B. According to iii, 80.28 he had first overcome all the Yādavas before he took his beloved with him; and iv, 49.6 even says that on this occasion he challenged Kṛishṇa to fight.

P.78, l.6. Çiçupāla carried off this girl not for himself, but for another man. She was the daughter of the ruler of Viçālā, and according to K., ii, 68.21 had been chosen for his bride by Kṛishṇa's father. This explains Kṛishṇa's moral wrath, who even charges Çiçupāla with having

APPENDIX

tried to win Rukminī by a trick. Yet she was Çiçupāla's betrothed! His horror, indeed, is not only towards the robber Krishṇa, but likewise towards the shameless man that takes a woman who is no longer looked on as a maid (ii, 45.17–19). Cp. p. 44.

P. 82, l. 6 from end. In iv, 14.18 also aṃçu has the meaning "moonbeam". Cp. the more usual haṃsenduvarṇa.

P. 84, n. 1. In chapters i, 187–194 all that is written in çlokas belongs to a later version of the material, and all such passages are interpolations, often very clumsy withal, alike whether these verses were already to hand, or whether they were composed *ad hoc*. If all the çlokas are discarded, then we have a good account in the trishṭubhs, complete in all essentials. Çlokas 191.11–16 alone seem hard to dispense with. There probably trishṭubhs of like content originally stood.

P. 86, note. I have made a mistake—the nobody announces himself. K. in an interpolated passage (203.18–20) makes Dṛishṭadyumna expressly proclaim: " Brahmans or Kshattriyas, Vaiçyas or even Çūdras—whoever strings the most excellent bow, to him shall my sister be given." In fact it was felt that in the foolish account such an assurance was very needful. The trishṭubh passage in B., i, 193.23 f. is more important. But probably as elsewhere, so here also Yudh. does not shrink before distortion, where personal aims are at stake.

P. 93, n. With Stone-breaker Hans's saying cp. the fine essay of L. von Schroeder, *Reden u. Aufsätze*, p. 185 ff.

P. 103, ll. 19 ff. It is true that in K. (i, 107.86, 88, cp. 107.101) the fisherman expressly calls the succession to the throne the çulka of Satyavatī, as does Bhīshma in B., 103.14. How greatly the purchase price stood, or anyhow had once stood in the foreground is probably shown also by the usual word vīryaçulkā, and e.g. by i, 190.4: The mighty bow with which Arjuna wins Draupadī is called çulkāvāpta "wrested as the purchase price ", and in harmony therewith Draupadi herself is called pradishṭaçulkā (i, 193.23 f.). In note 3, p. 103, it should be remarked: In spite of the agreement with Citrāṅgadā's father, Arjuna looks on the son thus begotten as also the Pāṇḍavas' (i, 217.33).

P. 105, l. 20. The children of the first wife, it would therefore seem, cannot offer up the ancestral sacrifices.

553

P. 111, mid. K. inserts between the adhyāyas corresponding to B., 196–7 two others (212–13). They tell the tale of Indrasenā (Mahendrasenā) Nālāyanī (Nārāyanī, B., iv, 21.10 ff.), whom L. v. Schroeder has awakened again to so full a life (*Mysterium u. Mimus im Rigveda*, p. 346 ff.) : Indrasenā is the wife of the old penitent Maudgalya. This holy man not only has a spiteful and covetous disposition, but is also a leper, nothing but skin and bones, full of wrinkles, bald-headed, and " reeking with a smell that is very different from a perfume ". But the young wife serves him with the greatest faithfulness. One day the leper's thumb falls off, and right into her food. She calmly picks out this nasty addition, and goes on eating. This so pleases him that he tells her he is not really so bad or so old. He tells her to choose herself a favour. She answers : " Do me the pleasure of dividing thyself into five." He does so, and now leads a life of delight by her side, climbing with her in his various shapes into the sun, to the heavenly Gaṅgā, into the moon, to the gods, and so on, turning into a tree which she winds round as a creeper, and doing other things of this kind. Thus for her with the five-fold husband did years go by like a moment. Then the holy man turned away from the delights of the senses, and left her. The sorrowing woman fell senseless to earth, and made lament that she was not yet sated with joys. Because of her unseemly words he laid the curse on her of becoming in her future life Drupada's daughter, and having five husbands. Then she practised the sternest penance. The rejoicing Çiva came ; and now follows the well-known and here very needless tale of the words five times spoken : " Give me a husband." As Çiva keeps to his decision, she utters the wish that in her union with each of the five she may at least keep her maidenhead.

P. 124, l. 12. Or: "looked on him as one that gave the lie to the firmly laid down order " (frustrated, destroyed, harmed vitathamaryāda, i, 104.27 ; cp. bhinnamaryāda in the following çl.).

P. 126. Perhaps also xii, 207.40 speaks of the introduction of marriage. The passage might be translated : In the Dvāpara Age it was that the usage of copulation arose among creatures ; then in the Kali Age mankind came to pairing (dvandvam āpedire). Cp. e.g., xii, 301.37, which has dvandvānāṃ viprayoga, where Nīl. is undoubtedly right in saying : dvandvānāṃ dampatinām. Thus : while in the Dvāpara there was simply sexual union, it was only in our evil age that mankind took to marriage.

[From Melanesia for a time when the true sexual act was not yet

APPENDIX

known cp. the tale and notes in G. C. Wheeler, *Mono-Alu Folklore*, pp. 42–3, 242–3 (Translator).]

P. 130, l. 32. " Here the philosopher has the word " : It is significant that K., i, 128 after Pāṇḍu's words that "hetæriſtic" conditions are a favour towards women puts in several çlokas describing the insatiable sexual greed of woman (8–11). According to Nīl., MBh., ii, 27.16 speaks of seven peoples in the Himālaya who had no marriage, but woman and man came together and then parted juſt like cattle.

P. 131, note 5. With Kshemendra Yudhishṭhira is in agreement in iii, 189.31–32.

P. 132, n. 2. According to MBh., v, 109.9–10 King Raivata on coming back home finds his wives and miniſters dead, and his kingdom in other hands ; so he goes off into the foreſt to lead a pious life.

P. 149, n. 1. Here mention may be made also of MBh., i, 229.5 ff.: Mandapāla lived wholly chaſte, and was great in holy knowledge and asceticism. But after his death he found himself ill rewarded in the other world. He then asked why, and was given the answer : Man has to wipe away on earth a three-fold guilt by sacrifices, by chaſtity and Veda ſtudy, by offspring (read sutaiḥ for çrutaiḥ). Thou art rich in asceticism, and one that makes sacrifice, but thou haſt no children. Hand thy blood on, and thou shalt enjoy glorious worlds.

P. 160, l. 17. Kalmāshapāda's subſtitution in marriage by Vasishṭha, his Purohita (i, 177.38–39), is to be found in i, 177.32 ff. The curse is the same as in Pāṇḍu's case.

P. 163, middle. That Pāṇḍu is to beget sons by his Yoga power is perhaps not altogether certain. Kunti's expressions (121.3–5), and her recital seem to invite him to aĉtual union. Tapoyogabalān- vitaḥ would then mean : Since thou art endowed with the might of the penitent's Yoga, thou wilt be able to do it in spite of the curse. Manasā, it is true, can be so explained only at the coſt of some violence. By means of thy mind, that is, because thou haſt such a great manas, perfeĉted furthermore through asceticism ? Or : if thou only wilt (through thy wish) ?

P. 163, n. 1. "Go of his own will into heaven" is venturesome. What indeed seems to be meant is only the journey to the brahmaloka, which is spoken of in B., i, 120, and K., 125, or Pāṇḍu's resolve to win heaven through penance (120.2 = K., 125.2).

P. 164, near end. As to Kuntī's fear of moral ſtain cp. in the interpolated adhy. in K., i, 213, çl. 20–21 : In " misfortune " and when authorized, there is for the woman according to the holy tradition one other besides the husband ; but to a third man she muſt not go, otherwise she muſt atone for it. If there is a fourth the woman loses her caſte, and if a fifth then she becomes a vardhakī (is the reading bandhakī ? Or is it from vardh to cut ? Cp. chinnikā in Milindap., p. 122 ; Jāt., ii, 114, line 3 ; chinnāla " a loose fellow " (chinna + suff. āla) ; Uttarajjh., xxvii, 7 ; Deçīnāmam., 3.27 ; ZDMG, 58, p. 372 ; Charpentier in ZDMG, Bd. 70, p. 243. Skt. chinnā, according to the lexicographers " loose woman ").

P. 165, ll. 6–8. These words are said by Dhṛitarāshṭra to Vidura (i, 127.4). Duryodhana, be it said, reckons the Pāṇḍavas among those who are not of particularly good blood (i, 137.11–16).

P. 168, n. 1. Dārāṃç ca kuru dharmeṇa of course only means: Take thyself a wife, as the holy law bids. There is probably no suggeſtion of a marriage with Vicitravīrya's widows. Satyavatī makes two requeſts of him: (1) Raise up offspring for thy brother; (2) Found a household, and have thyself consecrated king (for a king muſt come to the land). Probably it is a case of either the firſt or the second of these. For inſtead of caiva in 103.11 a better reading probably would be vaiva ; c and v indeed are always being confused. Nīl., it muſt be said, even takes caiva = eva vā. But his caiva, too, is probably a miſtake in copying. Bhīshma answers: " I have taken an oath not to have offspring, and that I keep to." Now she throws herself with all her ſtrength onto the firſt part only of her words (i, 103, 21 f.). She wished probably to tell herself that the sons begotten in Niyoga were held to be not Bhīshma's but Vicitravīrya's children. Bhīshma takes his oath literally : That also will not do ; but I recommend thee a better subſtitute : a Brahman. Satyavatī then seems to have become reconciled with his ſtrait view also (105.34–35).—The Khaças are according to MBh., i, 175.37 ff. Mlecchas, juſt as the Kirātas, Çabaras, etc.

P. 172, l. 8. Therefore the man who sows seed in another's field is one among the seventeen arch-fools who beat the air with their fiſt (v, 37.1 ff.) ; while Brahma declares : Yasya bījaṃ phalam tasya (xiii, 85.120).

Appendix

P. 173, l. 23, and earlier. Cp. the statements on p. 314 on the *Jus primae noctis*.

P. 191, n. 1. The Rishi Bharadvāja burns himself in the fire that is devouring the body of his only son (iii, 137.14).

P. 212, n. 2. Further iii, 270.18–19; iv, 19.37–40; K., iv, 4.14. Subhadrā is just as loving to Draupadī's sons (iii, 183.27, 235.10 ff.).

P. 223. Furthermore L. v. Schroeder in *Mysterium und Mimus* has shown that already in primitive Aryan belief the departed souls are likewise fructifying spirits, just as their leader is likewise the god of procreative life (and of the storm; Rudra in India, Wotan among the Germans; etc.).

P. 225. If the menstruating woman comes into contact with the sacrificial fire, then as atonement a fixed offering must be made to a form of Agni (iii, 221.27).

[P. 231, n. 1. For the flatus in Melanesia cp. G. C. Wheeler, *Mono-Alu Folklore* (London, 1926), pp. 42, 244. (Translator).]

P. 232, middle. For Agastya and Lopamudrā cp. Sieg, *Sagenstoffe des Rigveda*, i, 120 ff.; Schroeder, *Myst. und Mimus*, 156 ff.

P. 232, l. 22. Like Phyllis with Aristoteles, the fair one while picking flowers makes her way herself into the king's neighbourhood. He has himself carried home together with her in a comfortable litter (çibikā avaghoṭitā), and then gives himself up so earnestly to the joys of love with her that he no longer admits anyone to himself (K. says more clearly : ramamāno na kāṃçcid apaçyat, 15). The first minister naturally wants to put an end to this. He asks the women who wait on the couple : " What is the matter here ? (kim atra prayojanam. According to Nīl. : " What is there to be done here ? " This seems not to fit so well). They answer : " We notice the strange thing that no water is brought." The minister, cleverly guessing, now has the pond made so that the king, too, believes there is no water whatever in it (cp. how Duryodhana is tricked in ii, 47.3 ff.). The prince's request to his wife is therefore jestingly meant. Cp. Hertel, *Indische Märchen*, pp. 33; 369.

P. 236. The tale of Pāṇḍu's and Mādrī's death is found in i, 125. Cp. 95.58–68.

SEXUAL LIFE IN ANCIENT INDIA

[P. 242. For sexual perversion in Melanesia cp. G. C. Wheeler, *Mono-Alu Folklore*, pp. 44–5, 196–7, 42–3, 242. (Translator).]

[P. 251, nn., l. 9 from end. For adultery through speech only in Melanesia cp. G. C. Wheeler, "The poele . . . among the Mono people," *Anthropophyteia*, x, p. 313. (Translator).]

P. 271, l. 10. For reasons of State-craft and his personal dislike for Duryodhana Kṛishṇa, indeed, does not make any use of these rest-houses (v, 85.18).

P. 310, n. 1. To the translation : " Mine house and my women's apartment . . . allotting all to thee (putting at thy disposal), I have come at all speed "—to this translation the foregoing çloka also points. The use of uddiçya, it is true, is not then the usual one.

P. 314, n. A noteworthy case of the *Jus primae noctis* from Old India is to be found in Chavannes, *Cinq cents contes et apologues*, iii, 95 : The people of a newly founded kingdom induce a strong man, who has done them a great benefit, to be the first to lie with every newly wedded woman among them. They wish thus to get fine children, and, secondly, to show him their gratitude. Later a wife makes them see they are all women, and they are revolted with the custom.

P. 316, l. 22. "Chambermaids are unprotected in the world, they are slave-girls, O Bhārata." So according to B. K., iv, 4.31 is probably more right with : sairandhryo rakshitā strīṇāṃ bhujishyāḥ santi, Bh. = "Chambermaids are the protected servants of women." They have a higher standing than other strolling women, as both texts hint in what follows (K., ekapatnyaḥ striyaç caitā iti lokasya niçcayaḥ).

P. 324, n. 1. These kalpavṛiksha also were probably a kind of maypole like the Indradhvaja ; and the festival in honour of the mountain Raivata also may have been a fertility festival, or anyhow one held at the same time as the other.

P. 325, n. 2. The kind of merrymaking that went along with the sacrificial festivals of Vedic times has been described by Schroeder in his great work *Mysterium u. Mimus im Rigveda* in various places.

P. 334, n. 1. The transl. given in this note for v, 33.55 is probably the right one. K. even reads : mūrkhāḥ pūjitapūjakāḥ (çl. 62).

P. 346, n. 1. The saying that the service of the husband is for the woman the only religious means to favour (nāsti strīṇāṃ) is found also in xiii, 46.13 ; K., iv, 20.47 ; and probably elsewhere in the Epic.

558

APPENDIX

As religious duties falling especially to the house-wife, iii, 233.34 f.
names : bhikhshā (to give to beggars), bali, çrāddha, sthālīpāka (on
the Parvan days), mānyānāṃ mānasatkāra, as also the niyama.

P. 351, n.2. Arjuna first stays three years (according to K., however,
only three months) with Citrāṅgadā, then visits the tīrtha in the south,
comes back to her for a short while, and hands over the son begotten
with her as a çulka to her father. As he has neither house nor home,
he leaves her with her father, but arranges for her to come to Indraprastha, when the thirteen years shall be over (215.27; 217.23 ff.).

P. 356, l. 15 from end. "Indra had slain Vṛitra, and thereby
burdened himself with the guilt of Brahman-murder. He therefore
crept away at the edge of the world into the water " (according to xii,
342.42 ff. into the lake Mānasa). This is in agreement with v, 13.12–13,
but should perhaps rather be as follows : " Indra had maliciously slain
Vṛitra, and moreover through slaying the pious demon Triçiras—in
the MBh. a Veda-learned brandy-hero—had burdened himself with the
guilt of ' Brahman-murder.' " The reminder may here be made that
Apollo, too, appears as a murderer, and like Indra has to flee and make
atonement, because he has killed the python. Schroeder, *Mysterium
und Mimus*, p. 213, after Aug. Mommsen, *Delphika* (Lpzg., 1876),
p. 296 f. Odin also has to flee from his kingdom into banishment;
another comes to his throne, and takes his rule for himself, until the
god captures his place once more. W. Golther, *Mythologie der
Germanen*, p. 304 ; E. H. Meyer, *Mythologie der Germanen*, p. 377.
His wife is not faithful to him (Golther, 433). The name itself of
Triçiras (" the three-headed one ") seems to point to an original snake
spirit. Vṛitra is a dragon.

P. 370, at top. K., i, 98.32 lays it down: The children (or: the sons
putrās) are like the father in their bodily characters, while those of the
soul arise through their contact with the outward world (through
intercourse, the world around) (teshām çīlaguṇācārās tatsamparkāc
chubhāçubhāt. Tatsamparka is probably hardly that fortunate or
unfortunate mingling of the parents for the purpose of begetting).
K., i, 99.39–40 on the other hand gives besides some bodily ones a
whole set of mental characters.

P. 374. Birth from the mother's side is, of course, quite well known.
So already in the Veda Indra comes into the world after having too
long tarried in his mother's womb. See Sieg, *Sagenstoffe des Rigveda*,
i, 79 ff. ; Pischel, *Vedische Studien*, ii, 42 ff.

559

SEXUAL LIFE IN ANCIENT INDIA

P. 390, laſt l. of text. Moreover, others know about it, too, for in v, 50.34 Saṃjaya gives a short account of the whole thing before the ſtate assembly, and evidently as being well-known, too.

P. 391, laſt l. text. Perhaps this is the place for a more detailed account of the demons that are especially dangerous to children according to iii, 230.16 ff. The six Kṛittikā (Pleiades), Skanda's nurses, in various shapes torment and eat children, but also proteĉt them, if they are given worship; a horrible demon sprung from Skanda's body is called Skandāpasmāra, and would seem to cause convulsions in children; Pūtanā (Çītapūtanā) carries off the fruit of the womb; Diti, the mother of the foes of the gods, as also all the youthful male and female beings born from Skanda's body, and the husbands of these latter (Kumāra and Kumārī, cp. 228.1 ff.) have a taſte for children's flesh. On Surabhi, the firſt mother of cows, rides the foremother of birds and Garuḍa's mother, Vinatā, and together with her eats children. In the very womb Saramā, the firſt of bitches, ſteals the tender forms; the mother of trees also, who dwells in the tree Karañja, and is worshipped there to get children, is dangerous to them, but becomes very friendly if she is shown fitting honour. All these graha, who all like flesh and honey (cf. p. 240, note 1), ſtay for ten days in the lying-in room. The mother of the Gandharvas, and the mother of the Apsarases carry away the fœtus. The daughter of the "red sea" (cp. iii, 226.28; 231.11), who is worshipped in the kadamba-tree, and takes the same high place for women as does Rudra for men, is also one of the demons who show their maliciousness towards pregnant women and children; but also she beſtows well-being, if service is rendered to her, as do all the other male and female beings that surround Skanda (cp. 228.1–9). For making these favourable or to ward them away praçamana (appeasing rites), snāna (bathing), dhūpana (incense), añjana (annointing), upahāra (dedicatory gifts) are used. Then they beſtow powers of life and manhood. People, be it said, are children up to the sixteenth year. In 231.16, too, we are told of man-eating female genii of growth, called Vṛiddhikā, who have their birth-place and probably abode in trees, and muſt be worshipped by those who wish for offspring. These spirit-beings are therefore nearly all clearly marked out as being demons of plant life and of fruitfulness. The Indian "Mars", Skanda, usually the son of the procreative godheads Çiva and Pārvatī, is himself a phallic being. One of his faces, and indeed that which his "mothers" like beſt, is that of a ram, his weapon is the spear, known as a phallic symbol; his mothers and his often half-animal following are likewise spirits that have a conneĉtion with growth and procreation. This following according to iii, 231.11–12 arises from trees. He is lord of the bhūta, the ghosts of the dead that grant the blessing of children, and also do harm to them (xii, 122.34). His names also may point to the phallus : Skanda, " the springer ", taken from the spurting seed ; Kumāra, "the boy" (as our old German story-tellers call the man's member) ; Guha, " the hidden one ". Indeed, Çiva, who is of the same nature as he, is called Praskanda, Bindu, and Visarga as a discharge of the seed (xiii, 17.63). The following also, among other things, seems to point in the same direction : Skanda's wife is called Shashṭhī and Sinīvalī, both being godheads of fruitfulness and birth (iii, 229.50 ff. ; 232.6) ; he is kanyābhartar (husband of girls ?), and has everything in red (clothing, banner, etc., 229.2, 32; 231.19,93); his creature and plaything is the sexually lusty cock, which often is found as a symbol of fertility (225.24–25 ; 226.14–15 ; 229.33 ; 232.16). On Skanda much that is important is furthermore given in ix, 44–46. But I am thinking of bringing out a separate work, " Die Kindlifresser ". Here, therefore, I give only a few suggestions.

The Yakshas, already marked as genii of plant life and fruitfulness through the fact of their abiding in trees and water, likewise eat children, at any rate the female ones do, as we are shown especially in Buddhistic literature. The Rākshasī Jarā is painted on walls as youthful and surrounded by children, and is worshipped with flowers, incense, perfumes and food. If this is done, then well-being holds sway in the house ; otherwise it fares ill (ii, 18.1 ff.). In Magadha a festival was held for her (çl. 10). Now the souls of the dead in Indo-Germanic belief further the growth of plants and fruitfulness ; and in India the Pretas, like the Rākshasas, dwell in trees (e.g. K., i, 163.28), and from trees there comes, indeed, in India, as is well-known, the blessing of children. Cp. my notes on pp. 158 and 223.

The Rākshasas likewise are among the ghostly figures of the dead, and like the Yakshas, with whom in Buddhistic literature especially they are near akin, among the genii of fruitfulness. Also the Gandharvas, so important for women's life and for conception, really represent, according to Schroeder's account, the souls of the departed (*Die Wurzeln der Sage vom heil. Gral*, p. 84, and passages there quoted). Cp. in J. J. Meyer, *Über das Wesen d. altind. Rechtsschriften u. ihr Verhältnis zu einander u. zu Kautilya* (Leipz., 1927), the passages given under " gandharva ". But in view of the original singular this is probably hardly the older belief. Anyhow, the Gandharvas (or : the Gandharva) are indeed found as the possessors of woman before marriage, and undoubtedly causing fruitfulness, just like the moon (Soma), the " lord of plants " or god of growth (and houser of the blessed), and like the fire god—this last probably here as life-bringing warmth, as a form of Kāma or the genius of Love, hardly as Agni of the hearth and warden of the ṛita, which binds the daughter to the father's house. Cp. my notes on pp. 227 and 312.

We have therefore no lack of kindly supernatural powers, although in certain circumstances they are also highly dangerous. It is no wonder then that the ideal Indian wife lets only an interval of one year come between the different children (i, 221.86 ; K., i, 134.1 ff. ; etc.).

P. 404, n. Majjh., i, 190, speaks with emphatic and quite unmistakable words : Seyyathā pi āvuso suṇisā sasuraṃ disvā saṃvijjati, saṃvegaṃ āpajjati, evam-eva, etc., " just as the daughter-in-law, when she sees her father-in-law, is disconcerted, is abashed, so, etc." This comparison is also found elsewhere in the Majjh. I have only just seen the short communications on Indian examples by M. Winternitz and B. Liebich, WZKM, xxvi, 237 ff. ; xxvii, 474 ff.

P. 405. Draupadī, as queen, did not pound her own sandalsalve (udvartana), but probably Kuntī's (iv, 20.23).

P. 431. So, too, to Iseult one who likewise is not in love with her says : " As this day raises daylight from the dead Might not this face the life of a dead man ? " Swinburne, " Tristram of Lyonesse," *Poems*, Lond., 1904, p. 20.—In K. several verses have been interpolated which explain v, 116.2 ff., and give further happiness-bringing charms of woman. We find : the two hips, the forehead, the thighs, and the nose—these six arched (unnata, 116.3). On the other hand strophe 7 states : chest, neighbourhood of the girdle (kaksha, that is, probably, hips, pubic region, and buttocks), nails, nose, shoulders, and the region between them (or : loins ? aṃsatrika)—these are the six unnata. According to str. 6 these must be long : jaws, eyes, arms, thighs, nose.

P. 444. " Coward " and " dull " is my translation for alpacetas, of small insight ? of little courage ? (ii, 67.25 ; cp. v, 105.28 ; vii, 72.50).

P. 445, 1st strophe : (" Loud cries "). The text is in disorder. The second half of 67.33 must be put before the first at least. But what is still more likely is that for vikroçati Yajñasenī we must read : vikroça hi (vikroçahi ? vikroça tu ?), Yajñasenī (or : vikroçatu Yajñasenī). Cp. viii, 86.18. The passage in other ways, too, will thus be far better : " Then spoke he to Kṛishṇā, hotly holding her fast by her ravishing black locks : ' Cry to Kṛishṇa, Jishṇu, Hari, Nara, That he may save thee, Yajñasenī.' " The second half of the trishṭubh in the text has probably been thoughtlessly transplanted here from 68.46. Duḥçāsana uvāca must now naturally be struck out. K., indeed, has not got this at all (89.45–46).

APPENDIX

P. 446, n. 4. Yudh. has over and above this taken the special vow never to refuse when he is challenged to play (ii, 58.16; 59.18; 76.4, 20).

P. 450, n. 1. The " three lights " are after all, it would seem, only the well-known trinity: sacrifice, offspring, and Veda study (cp. p. 150, note). Also K., i, 107.73.

P. 471, middle. Here we give a few more details throwing light on the life and standing of woman in the Epic. v, 59 = K., 47.17 ff. relates: Samjaya is led to Krishna and Arjuna in the women's part of the dwelling. There the two heroes are sitting, splendidly adorned and bewreathed, drunk with sweet intoxicating drink, both on a great golden seat, adorned with precious stones, and bespread with many kinds of rugs; Krishna is using the lap of his wife Satyabhāmā as a pillow, and his feet are lying on the lap of his friend Arjuna. (So K. According to B., Arjuna's feet are resting on Draupadī's and Satyabhāmā's lap.) The envoy Samjaya now brings forward his most weighty business of state. This voluptuous Eastern picture, however, probably comes from a later time. In any case this section does not belong to the older body of the poem. Adhy. 49–61, which arouse suspicion at once from the much too woeful and effeminate words of Dhritarāshtra, have been put in at some time or other. If we reject this whole set of çlokas, and go at once from the trishtubhs in 48 to the trishtubhs 62.1 ff., then we get a smoothly running recital. Another proof is the unskilful tacking on in the last çl. of 61 : Dhritarāshtra is made out to have spoken earlier, but it was Duryodhana ! v, 67.1 ff. is more pleasing : Gāndhārī at Samjaya's request is called into the sabhā, when the decision is to be taken as to war or peace with the Pāndavas. Then too in ii, 58.26 ff.: Yudhishthira and his friends have come to Hāstinapura to dice. First of all they greet Gāndhārī, and only then King Dhritarāshtra, her husband. They are welcomed by all the Kauravas, and called upon in their temporary abode, and this with Draupadī and the other women there. The daughters-in-law of Dhritarāshtra also come, and are vexed at Krishnā's loveliness. The heroes first converse with the ladies, then they enjoy themselves with bodily exercises. If this description so far reminds us of knighthood's days, on the other hand we are told that it is an honour for the woman if a stranger asks of her, who asks no questions, her name, family, husband, etc. (iii, 265.4–5). But how often this honour is done to the fair in Old India is shown countless times in the Epic. Thus King Jayadratha, who is on the way to the Çalvas to find a bride there, sees Draupadī in the forest, is quite lost, now wants her only, and without further ado sends a king from among his followers to find out more about her. As a woman dwelling there alone she should really not have spoken to this messenger, but she does so, first, because no one else is there to speak with him, and secondly, because the messenger is not unknown to her. She therefore invites them all to enjoy Yudhishthira's hospitality (iii, 266). But Jayadratha carries her off, her that is already wedded. Since we find an offence of this kind now and then only appearing as such if the woman is unwilling (or does not love the man carrying her off, akāmā, ii, 45.10; cp. note 1, p. 490), so this, just like the commandment which holds for the maiden-lifter, to leave her alone who loves elsewhere, is an indication that the woman's inclination had something to say. A maiden taken in the fight must be left alone a full year before she is asked (as to marriage, doubtless). xii, 96.5. But intimacies before marriage are looked on as shameful (iv, 72 : esp. 4–7). In the marrying of a child, particularly a daughter, the mother in Indian literature as a whole has an important, not seldom the first, voice; and the men in the Epic take counsel, as so often on other important things, so especially on this, with the wife.

The relation, too, between sister and brother comes to us in a bright and beautiful light. Subhadrā is married to Arjuna in Indraprastha. Her brother (really her half-brother) Krishna comes there on a visit, and, when he leaves again, directly he has taken leave of the high personages Yudhishthira and Kuntī he goes to his sister. "When Hrishīkeça had come to the sweet Subhadrā of the sweet speech the holy and august one, shedding tears for love of her, spoke to her deep, true, wholesome words, that flowed easily and pleasantly, fitting and without compare." She entrusts him with greetings and messages to her own people, and again and again shows him her honour. When he has taken his leave of her, he at once goes to Draupadī, just as in the Epic he is ever showing the most friendly marks of attention to this lady (ii, 2.4–7 ; cp., too, 24.54 f.). Then when the Pāṇḍavas go off into banishment, he comes and takes Subhadrā and her son home with him for the thirteen years, as Dhrishtaketu takes his sister, Nakula's wife, from Cedi. Draupadī herself, indeed, shares the fortunes of her lords and masters. But her children are brought by her brother into his own city ; from there they go later, it is true, to Dvārakā (iii, 22.47–50 ; 183.14, 24 ff. ; 235.10 ff. ; iv, 72.21 f.). The natural abode of the woman that has no children (and no husband) is with her brother (v, 33.70). Such things are, indeed, good Indo-European customs.

P. 474, l. 12 ff. fr. end. The same wise man, indeed, seems to be of opinion that jealousy is the natural way of woman, just as intrigue is.

APPENDIX

He goes on to say : Even the pattern of a good wife, Arundhatī, did angrily suspect her noble, faithful husband, Vasishṭha, one who was wholly pure, and thought only of what was for her good and dear to her ; therefore she now twinkles down as though with but one eye, the other being shut like that of one taking aim, smoky-red, ugly, and only slightly to be seen (nimittam iva paçyati ; nimitta probably here means : (1) target in shooting; (2) mark, proof, of the husband's wrong-doing, for which she keeps a sharp look-out. MBh., i, 233.27 ff.). Arundhatī is the small, weak ſtar Alcor, Vasishṭha one of the seven Ṛishis that make up the Great Bear.

[P. 476, n. 2. For jealousy between wives in Melanesia cp. G. C. Wheeler, *Mono-Alu Folklore*, pp. 26–7, 189–92 (Translator).]

P. 547, n., (II). I have already in my Daçakumāracaritam, pp. 4–5, given it as my opinion that in an earlier version, which can be inferred from the MBh., the love which is kindled by the royal maiden Çāntā in the wholly innocent and truthful youth, brings down the longed-for moiſture. A new, and not only surprising but also convincing light is thrown on the matter by the newer treatment of the Rishyaçṛiṅga legend by Schroeder (*Myſterium u. Mimus im Rigveda*, p. 292 ff. ; *Wurzeln d. Sage vom hl. Gral*, 76 ff. ; *Reden u. Aufsätze*, 410, 413). All these writings, I am sorry to say, I did not read till I was going through the proofs of the laſt sheets. Schroeder sees here a " generation rite "—the sexual union of the two in itself brings about rain. This undoubtedly exposes the root of the matter. Quite rightly the Buddhiſtic versions make the rain to fall so soon as the youthful penitent has carried out the copulation. Other, more polished versions have probably put love in the place of the procreative magic : the MBh. seems to show traces of this. Here also the absolute purity of body and soul is necessary for the miracle, and it is, indeed, several times given in the MBh. as the very reason (cp. besides iii, 110.24, espec. 110.47–48, also i, 2.168).

My translation on p. 542, ll. 15–16, is not the moſt obvious one. This would be : " There respectful greeting is no right of mine." This is also how the passage is underſtood, indeed, by the following çloka (iii, 12), an interpolated one, however. In spite of all the unsuspecting simplicity of heart in the youth, however, the hetæra could not help being afraid of betraying herself. Or is his ſtupidity to be ſtressed ? That would be too clumsy. Ṛishyaçṛiṅga, indeed, has asked pressingly about the newcomer's particular form of ascetic piety (vrata). The fair one would say : So much in earneſt do I take my self-denial that I decline the honourable show of politeness which other penitents are glad to accept. Rishyaçriṅga underſtands her, indeed, far better than the foolish interpolator (112.13).

In German we have, besides the fine version of the old tale in J. V. Widmann's *Buddha* (Song 9), the pleasing version by Isolde Kurz : " Die Büsser " (*Gedichte* ², p. 168 ff.). The tale of the woman on horseback has been given a fresh life by Rudolf Baumbach.

[P. 371, l. 16. From Melanesia for Cæsarean birth cp. G. C. Wheeler, *Mono-Alu Folklore*, pp. 54–5, 178–80 (Translator).]

INDEX

Preliminary remark.—It was my wish to present in this book as many as possible rather long and undivided pieces, but, at the same time, not to repeat more often than seemed absolutely necessary, certain statements, which, quite naturally in another connection, were again important, perhaps much more important. The Index should, therefore, not only serve to retrace passages, but also to collect together again the details of a particular subject. Here I will give just *one* example, right from the beginning of the book. On games and amusements of girls, page 9 gives only a very scanty account. If one reads on, however, then one receives, particularly from those sections of the Epic that have been translated, very much further information, and, finally, one has, after all, some of the main lines of the picture. If one wishes to read these together, one should refer to the Index, under Girl : games and amusements.—Add. means addition (to be looked up in the Appendix).

567

Bard, *see* Sūta
Bathing: naked, 262; men
waited on by women at the
bath, 134, 323, 508
Beans: forbidden, *see* Onion
Bear-worship, 395
Beauty: how a beautiful woman
was made, 149, 540; des-
cription of feminine beauty,
278, 335, 542; beautiful
woman shines, 280, 285 (cf.
J. J. Meyer, *Isoldes Gottesurteil*, notes, No. 159, and in
addition especially Arnold,
*Ztschr. d. Vereins f. Volks-
kunde*, Bd. 12, pp. 166 f.);
attracts too strongly to the
surata, 311; beauty of the
body and of the soul con-
nected, 430; ideal of beauty,
430; " catalogue of beauty,"
432; is woman's strength,
539; brings dead things into
life, 539, cf. 431
Begetting: other than natural, 33,
155, 241, 262 (cf. 370);
what is necessary for it, 60;
is the highest duty, 147; how
it happens, 182, 359; how to
accomplish it, 243; is a
matter of divine service, 367;
how does one beget boys, and
girls? 367; kinds of be-
getting, 370; with dead, 416.
Cf. Birth, Children, Pregnancy, Surata, Unfruitfulness
Begetting by proxy: by Dīrghatamas, 160; by Brahmans,
159, 169, 219; by Vasishtha,
161, 167, 234; by a disciple,
162; by gods, 162; in
general in India, 169; among
various peoples, 171 note;

sons of the wife by another
man, 174
Bhagadaivata, 288
Bhīma: how strong already as a
new-born infant, 164; his
wildness as a boy, 211; story
of his love-affair with Hidimbā, 291; kills the Rākshasa
Hidimba, 291; fetches the
golden flower for his beloved,
298; his chivalry towards
Draupadī, 298; his high-
spirited strength, 299; rebukes Yudhishthira, 302, 447;
kills Kīcaka, 304; shows himself gentle, 453
Bhīshma: his birth, 47; abducts
girls, 69, 381; has to raise up
children to his brother, 165;
his self-denying love for his
father, 194, cf. 165
Birth: other than natural, 25, 80,
87, 155, 262, 373, add. to
374; immediately after conception, 41, 295, 371; how
it comes about, 366; the
child at the same time loses
recollection of its earlier
existence, 367; renders the
father unclean too, 397
Birth-mark: the new-born child's
golden birth-mark, 192
Blood of the slain: drinking the,
303, 448; blood gives life to
departed spirits, 223
Body: its character and attributes
disclose the woman's worth
and ability, 41, 143, 431,
434; constituents are constantly changing, 93, 364; a
holy city and its gates,
248; lower half unclean,
249

Saṃsāra, a particular incarnation,
specially a low one, 247, 488
Samucchraya, 14, 363
Saṃvaraṇa and Tapatī, 278
Sandal : pounded by maidservants,
308 ; by the daughter-in-law
for the mother-in-law, 405
add.
Satyavatī : has a fish-like odour, 40
(since sprung from a fish),
224 ; manages a ferry, 40 ;
as a girl gives birth to
Vyāsa, 39 ; nevertheless remains a virgin, 40, cf. add. to
34 ; her glorious perfume,
40 ; Çāntanu's love for her,
278 ; her share in the government, 465, cf. 165
Saugandhika, (a kind of) lotus-
flower, 299 (cf. ii, 3, 31 ;
10, 7 ; iii, 43, 1 ; 65, 2 ;
168, 50 ; iv, 31, 14)
Sāvitrī : pearl of Indian womanhood, 427, cf. 340 ; her
" self-choice," 78, 89
Scholar : is only a parrot, 458
(cf. e.g. ii, 55, 1-2 ; iii, 35,
19 ; xii, 10, 1)
Sea : drunk up or dried up by
penitent, 232, 319 ; why
salt, 349
Seed : who has it muſt have the
" field," 63, 408 ; " seed
or field " ? see Field ; sent
by bird-poſt, 223 ; seed-
forming foods, 238 ; emission
of semen at the sight of the
beautiful woman, 261 ; how
the seed forms, 359, 361 ;
penance on involuntary
emission of semen, 256
Self : one's own self is all that
matters, 92, 96, 510 (cf.

Individualism) ; the son one's
self, see Son
" Self-choice," see Svayaṃvara
Self-culture : consiſts in self-
discipline, 93 (e.g. v, 69, 17)
Sense-organs : what they owe their
origin to, 366
Sensuality : powerful in Old India,
316
Sex of the child : determination of
(on begetting and in the
womb), 367
Shashṭhī, 392
Shell : signifies good fortune, 141 ;
= vulva, 128
Sight : the divine, 30, 484
Sītā : in an earlier exiſtence
Vedavatī, 23 ; sprung from
the furrow, 87, 530 ; married
to Rāma, 88 ; her grief when
she believes Rāma dead, 422 ;
how she behaves when Rāma
is banished, 423 ; as Rāvaṇa's
captive, 424; an ideal woman,
427 ; her beauty, 432 ; her
harshness, 436 ; her com-
passionate nature, 505 ; suspected of unfaithfulness and
purified in the ordeal by fire,
525 ; second repudiation and
disappearance into the earth,
528
Slaying of woman penalized, 488
Slowness : where good, 208 (cf.
202)
Smelling at the head, 183
Snake fairy, 51
Sodomy, 242
Son : how necessary, 7, 22, 58,
146 ; is one's own self, 22,
151, 184, 203, 341, 452 ; the
higheſt earthly happiness, 151,
183 ; the Veda, 203, cf. 150 ;

killed almoſt without punishment if a bad woman, 274, 489, 522; is holy, 341; has the higheſt dignity, 344, 486, 495; is like a warrior, 345, 390, 393; is source of the Saṃsāra and incarnation of the material and sensuous, 365, 500, cf. 7; a bad magical nature, 366, 499; has more pleasure in the surata and greater passion for love, 379, cf. 229; her refuge father and husband, 384; of a weak nature, 377, 387 (cf. 436); the spoil of war, 409, 507; in sorrow, 419; talkative, 428; ſtrong-willed and passionate, 436; is the word, man the meaning, 440; very important that she should be untouched, 450, cf. 20, add. to 78, 307, 382, 386, 439, 524; muſt not travel, 471, cf. 346; muſt be given presents, 486; is goddess of happiness and light of the house, 486, 495 (cf. 343); may not be killed, 487, cf., however, 274, 488, 522; not slain, 488; of no value for counsel and business, 494; makes possible the continuance of the world, 495, 500; cannot be spoiled, 496, cf. 227; root of all evil, 497; only chaſte when nothing else is possible, 497; prevents the over-population of heaven, 499, cf. 365; fickle, deceptive, and inscrutable, 501 (cf. 131); cause of enmity, 502, 534; of man's destruction, 502, 532; compassion-

ate, 504; capable of salvation, 506; inherits, see Division of inheritance; a chattel, 507; a Rākshasa, 545; as witness before a tribunal, 523; woman makes morality, 524; when she may be looked on freely by all, 526; her presence spurs man on, 534, cf. add. to 11; establishes peace, 535; copies women, 524; is objeſt of the senses, 531, cf. 523 notes, line 8 from bottom; man muſt not lose friend on account of wife, 523 note 1. Cf. Ideal woman, Love, Position, Rājputs, Warrior, Woman of energy

Woman of energy: generally, 436; in love, 437; Draupadī, 440; Kuntī, 457; Vidulā, 458

Woman-hater, see Hatred

Woman-murder, 487

Woman's property, 9, 65, 142, 143, 508

Womb: dwelling there gruesome, 370

Wonder-child, 113, 371 (such wonder-children of the Epic are also Parāçara, i, 177, [12]; Aurva, i, 179, [4]; his son Vyāsa, i, 60, [2]; Vyāsa's son Çuka, xii, 324, [22 ff.]; the son of Agastya and Lopamudrā, iii, 99, [24 ff.])

Yakshiṇī: eats children, 477

Yāna, 267 (cf. also iii, 69, [21], [23]; 299, [10]; i, 126, [13]; 194, [3])

Yautuka, see Woman's property

INDEX